The Systems of Nostradamus

The Systems of Nostradamus

Instructions for Making Sense of *The Prophecies*

Robert Tippett

Copyright © 2011
All rights reserved. Printed in the United States of America. No part of this publication may be reproduced, stored in a retrieval system, or transmitted, in any form or by any means electronic, mechanical, photocopying, recording, or otherwise, without the prior written permission of the author.
ISBN 978-0-9801166-2-5
Published by Katrina Pearls, LLC

Table of Contents

Guiding Gospel 9

Foreword 10

Part 1 - Non-Systemic Observations 17

Chapter 1 - The Obvious is Telling 19

Chapter 2 - Observing the Title of *The Prophecies* 22

Chapter 3 - Observing the Preface to *The Prophecies* 25

Chapter 4 - The Obvious Use of Latin in the Preface 34

Chapter 5 - The Biblical References of the Latin in the Preface ...44

Chapter 6 - The Central Theme Stated in the Preface 65

Chapter 7 - Observing the Obvious Oddities in the Quatrains 69

Chapter 8 - Observing the Oddities in the Letter of Explanation to *The Prophecies* 88

Chapter 9 - Reviewing the Observable 96

Part 2 - The Systemic Properties of The Prophecies 99

Chapter 10 - We Make Sense of Words through the System Known as Syntax 101

Chapter 11 - An Elementary Refresher 108

Chapter 12 - The Issue of the Holy Spirit 120

Chapter 13 - Analogies for the Systems of Nostradamus 129

Chapter 14 - Some Observations on Translations 135

Chapter 15 - My Experience with Translation 141

Chapter 16 - The Importance of Definition 146

Chapter 17 - Reminder: No Syntax Allowed 150

Chapter 18 - Poetic License 154

Part 3 - The Systems for Meaning 157

Chapter 19 - The System of Language 159

Chapter 20 - The System of Word Creation 168

Chapter 21 - The System of Word Selection 176

Chapter 22 - The System of Order 193

Chapter 23 - The System of Punctuation 208

Primary Punctuation Marks
Commas 213

Colons 221

Periods	227
The Rest of the Punctuation Marks	
Semi-colons	235
Question Marks	235
Parentheses	236
Exclamation Points, Apostrophes, and Hyphens	237

Chapter 24 - The System of Capitalization 240

Chapter 25 - The System of Symbols 256

Ampersands	257
Ampersands with Punctuation	292
Accent Marks	294
Numerals: Arabic and Roman	296
Greek Alphabet Letters and Glyphs	303

Chapter 26 - The System of Symmetry 306

Chapter 27 - The System of Figurative Language 312

Chapter 28 - The System of Astrology 328

Planets	333
Signs	339
Synthesis of Planets in Signs	351
Aspects	355

Houses	361
Elements	367
Qualities	368
Hemispheres	370
Moon's Nodes	372
Retrograde Motion	373
Synthesis of Nostradamus through Delineation	374
Astronomical Astrology	376
Chapter 29 - The System of Years and Degrees	380
Chapter 30 -- Summing Everything Up	394
Appendix	407
Concluding Scripture	409

Guiding Gospel

So when it was evening on that day, the first day of the week, and when the doors were shut where the disciples were, for fear of the Jews, Jesus came and stood in their midst and said to them, "Peace be with you."

And when He had said this, He showed them both His hands and His side. The disciples then rejoiced when they saw the Lord. So Jesus said to them again, "Peace be with you; as the Father has sent Me, I also send you."

And when He had said this, He breathed on them and said to them, "Receive the Holy Spirit." "If you forgive the sins of any, their sins have been forgiven them; if you retain the sins of any, they have been retained."

Jesus said to him, "Because you have seen Me, have you believed? Blessed are they who did not see, and yet believed."

Therefore many other signs Jesus also performed in the presence of the disciples, which are not written in this book; but these have been written so that you may believe that Jesus is the Christ, the Son of God; and that believing you may have life in His name.

John 20:19-23; 29-31
New American Standard Bible Version

Foreword

I knew about Nostradamus and his prophecies long before I began to understand what he wrote. I began to understand what he wrote without any burning desire to do so. As I began to understand, I saw that everything had meaning, and everything was explainable, because everything followed some set of rules. Simply because the rules are not what everyone naturally expects them to be, something understandable became unintelligible. I began to understand without knowing the rules, or systems at play in *The Prophecies*, because it was important I understand them by trial and error first. Not that I have everything figured out now, but I know what everyone needs to know, so everyone can see what is there to understand.

I have been allowed to know what I know, so you can know what I know, and so you do not have to go through the trial and error route. Surely, there is a learning curve to everything new, but this book will make a subject, once thought of as impossible to understand, quite inspirational in the way meaning begins to flow from what seemed so lifeless. Therefore, let me spend a few moments on precisely who can benefit from learning about the "systems of Nostradamus." Simply put, anyone who wants to understand will understand. However, this does not mean that everyone can understand.

Many people seem to have the impression that understanding Nostradamus requires some great degree of intellectual acumen. The reality is it is quite the opposite, although having a functional brain does play a role in any learning endeavor. If having a high I.Q. were required to understand Nostradamus, he would have been solved shortly after the first publication in 1555. As for myself, I had tried to solve Nostradamus (half-heartedly, using my knowledge of astrology mostly) for twenty-five years and knew little more than what I knew when I first learned of Nostradamus. Simply because Nostradamus wrote in French, I would surely be eliminated from every being able to figure out such a puzzling figure's work. As good an act as I put on, I really am not smart enough to understand Nostradamus. The fact that I am (as of now) the only one who does understand Nostradamus correctly shows that intelligence is not the key towards understanding. The good thing about that is that if I can understand Nostradamus, so can you. Just keep in mind, anyone who wants to understand will understand.

In imagine that the people who often pat themselves on the back, for being the brightest lights in the intellectual sky, will probably scoff at the nonsense that they see me offering. I doubt they would even pick up this book, much less actually read it. Their minds have them convinced that there simply is no real solution to Nostradamus. Their reasoning will stem from their assumption that no one is able to see the future. They counter all claims of validity with comparisons to known acts of past charlatans. This group of peoples likes to classify themselves as science-minded. This group has its mind made up, keeping it from being receptive to understanding; but this group is not completely against belief in Nostradamus.

There is a subset of this scientific styled group, one that leans in the other direction. It includes those who have investigated Nostradamus at great lengths, and have found strong reason to believe he was an amazing man, with amazing talents. These people also will have their minds filled with preconceptions; but instead of disbelief, they will believe that Nostradamus was indeed able to see the future. They still have not found out how he did it, but armed with some well-versed ideas about the meaning of selected bits of written material, opinions that have circulated for quite some time, they are strongly convinced that belief means there is a way to discover how everyone can see the future. Unfortunately, those people reject anyone who says belief in Nostradamus has to be based on the rules of logic, which they do always not follow.

Everything about this book is defended logically. Logic is the supposed ally of disbelievers, simply because it is so rare finding people arguing a subject logically. Logic destroys the argument of those who believe in Nostradamus, because they believe fore illogical reasons. However, those who disbelieve simply because an illogical argument fails to convince a non-believer to believe, they have stayed so far away from having to actually use logic that they dare not enter into a truly logical debate, unprepared, lest they be embarrassed as easily as an illogical believer. It is safer simply saying they believe Nostradamus was a charlatan, because he was a magician (a fallacy) , and they will reject this book and walk off in a huff, learning nothing new.

Still, those will not be the only groups in danger of not being able to understand. There will be another class of people who will not want to understand what this book offers. These will come from the ranks of those who hear the name Nostradamus and automatically cross themselves, or curse his name under their breath, due to some upbringing that associates the name Nostradamus with fear of evil. There are those who actually act as if they have encountered Satan himself, simply by having someone tell them anything positive about that name. Many of these people will call themselves Christians, but they will not act Christian towards anyone trying to promote belief in that 16th century seer. They will see Nostradamus as a false prophet, without knowing anything about his life, or works; and they will reject any and all understanding this book has to offer.

As a subset of this ultra religious group, there are the anti-religious, or those who call themselves members of some cultish form of religion. These are the people who have spent the most money over the past decades, attempting to find out the secret methods and formulas used by people "like" Nostradamus.

They buy books to learn the arts of prediction, to try to see the future themselves. These people might buy this book. Unfortunately, once they realize there are no methods of witchcraft to be found here, only basic systems of language, they will lose interest. Many of this "metaphysical type" people, after they see that the power Nostradamus actually had, as far as being able to see the future, came from a belief in Jesus Christ …. Well, they probably will want to have nothing to do with this book, so they will not truly want to understand.

This leaves a section of people who could really want to understand Nostradamus. For the most part, these people will not know much about Nostradamus. They will have mostly blank-slate minds about the subject. Therefore, they will not come to the subject with a heavy load of preconceptions. While they will approach with caution, they will be led by an inner calling. This is the same call that Nostradamus experienced. You see, belief in Nostradamus requires the acceptance of the premise that Nostradamus was a prophet of Jesus Christ. Logically, they accept this because that is what Nostradamus stated to be the case. Emotionally, those who truly want to understand Nostradamus will want to understand a message from God, through Christ, told to Nostradamus.

Those who will truly want to understand will understand because a higher mind will guide their understanding. They will intellectually realize that such a claim as divine prophecy requires serious examination, from an open mind. They will realize that anyone claiming to hold a prophecy from God must be tested for validity, because to ignore a true prophecy from God will be like signing a death warrant for some group of humanity. They will realize the worst that could happen is they would expose a false prophet justly. The only thing that can possibly defeat a logic-based belief in Nostradamus is logically proving one quatrain to be false. That is where the systems come into play.

This brings me to my analogy of who will have the very best results understanding Nostradamus, based on what I will reveal in this book. They will be people similar to me. As such, they will be like Chauncey Gardeners.

This is the name given to an innocent simpleton, who was nothing more than Chance the gardener. Chance the gardener is the main character in the novella written by Jerzy Kosinski, entitled *Being There*. This literary work became a driving force in actor Peter Sellers' life, who read Kosinski in 1971, and strongly identified with the Chance character. Sellers strove for years to have the book turned into a film, so he could play the role. Sellers finally succeeded in having the fiction made into the award-winning movie of the same name, in 1979.

If you have not seen the movie, I recommend it. Just know that the character, Chance, is incapable of caring for himself, due to his mind being slow. He had not been exposed to the outside world, before the age of 40-something, due (presumably) to his being the illegitimate son of a wealthy man. Chance was never told he had a last name, due to the unwillingness of "the old man" to share this with his son. The father's only responsibility to his offspring was to keep him alive and comfortable, but out of the public eye.

We do not get to know Chance's father. The book begins by exposing the reader to an adult Chance, who has been held captive in the wealthy man's inner city estate. As Chance's home is developed, we find that his regular routines were tending to the garden in the hot house, and watching television. Chance has no awareness of the outside world, although he has seen many sights on the tube. Still, Chance has gained no real knowledge from television, because he has what could be called "attention deficit disorder." He is simply pacified by the images he sees on the television, constantly roaming the channels with a push-button remote control. We learn how television affects Chance, when he happily explains, "I like to watch."

The character's story really begins with the death of his father and the liquidation of the estate. Chance has never fed himself, as the maid has always prepared and served him his meals, but this woman leaves when she is no longer receiving a check, due to the death of her employer. Chance is then faced with reality when he is found still in the house by a realtor showing the property to prospective buyers. This is when Chance is thrown out into a world that he clearly does not fit into, and has never been prepared for. However, instead of being torn to pieces, Chance just naively wanders into (a play on the character's name – he chances upon) the most opportune of circumstances, literally and figuratively by accident.

Chance is involved in traffic accident, as a pedestrian, with the car driven by a chauffeur for the wife of someone like a Rockefeller. To avoid an ugly lawsuit, Chance is taken to the wife's palatial estate, to be monitored by the physician on staff there. This is when he becomes known as Chauncey Gardener, again by accident. Chance does not assume this identity, because Chance has no capability of being purposefully deceitful. He does not realize others have assumed his last name is Gardener. He simply is a gardener. When Chance speaks, he speaks in the most simplistic statements; but his words are heard as if he were speaking profoundly, through metaphor. The wealthy man and his wife befriend Chance, enjoying the refreshing honesty he provides them (albeit nothing more than simpleton statements of gardening lessons learned). Eventually, Chance gives advice to the President of the United States, who is a political friend of the wealthy man who has befriended Chance.

The reason I identify with Chance the gardener is that Chance has no hidden agenda. He has nothing to hide. He is pure honesty. He is the bliss of ignorance. He is the blank-slate mind. Chance could never have survived outside that home he had been raised in, had it not been for the grace of God. Chance is the type of person who is most easily led by God; and once led, he does not know enough even to attempt to try to take credit for getting where he got to be. Chance is said by Kosinski to be a simpleton; but he is really the example of someone purely led by faith. Chance is simply *being there*, wherever "there" may be.

Therefore, when I say that those most likely to find out how to understand Nostradamus will be those like Chauncey Gardener, I say that as a complement. People of that nature will discover what I mean when I say, "Anyone who wants to understand Nostradamus can understand Nostradamus." One can find out just how little intellect counts in understanding, beyond being able to comprehend the written word. The written word is nothing more than just that. If you want to understand, then just like Chance the gardener you will have to find yourself simply *being there*. Just like Chance the gardener, you cannot figure out where *there* is. You will just know you are *there*.

The key to being like Chance is to keep an open mind. An open mind attracts thoughts like whispers. What the mind wants to see as one thing suddenly becomes something else too. The one thing is what no one understands. However, it is the something else that becomes awe-inspiring.

The systems of Nostradamus give one an intellectual edge, an advantage in only one sense. That is like a mountain climber's tools, where rope is looped through devises securely fastened to the rock, and to the climber's harness. That system is what keeps a climber from falling too far, should one lose one's grasp on a difficult reach and hold. Still, a system of ropes, carabineers, harnesses, and such, does nothing productive if one does not attempt to climb a mountain. The climbing requires faith that a system will lead to a successful climb. It is an advantage that one depends on, as one initially climbs into areas unsecured. When one wants to climb a mountain, one will reach the top. The tools that assist in that endeavor are available to those wanting to reach new heights.

As one goes through the individual systems of this book, familiarity helps one at times when reaching higher is most difficult. While "learning the ropes" one can see the systems as too difficult to grasp, or too many to learn. The systems can seem like a rope that has wrapped all around the climber, making the freedom of movement too restricted to take another step forward. That is when one is depending too much on the intellect.

The classic scene from the original movie *Star Wars*, where the Jedi pilots were assigned the task of destroying the Death Star, the pilots were intellectually trained in how to fly their warcraft, and fire lasers and bombs. They wanted to accomplish their mission, but none could do it only through intellect, when the Death Star was only vulnerable in one weak spot. That was when the words of the spirit Obi-Wan Kenobi whispered in Luke Skywalker's mind, "Use the force Luke."

That is how one has to approach the quatrains and letters of *The Prophecies*. Knowing these systems allows one to see what is clearly there, but see it differently than how everyone else sees what is there. Still, with so much written, one often has to stop thinking, in order to progress. One has to rest the mind, and allow oneself to be open to receiving the essence of the meaning. This is where one truly wants to understand. This desire acts as a prayer for assistance, which results in soft, reassuring whispers of thought, which does not tell the answer, but instead leads one to find the answer. Those whispers are always there to the seeker, like rope and harnesses to a climber. However, only the Chancy Gardeners of the world have their intellectual volume turned down enough to hear them, loud enough to heed them.

PART 1
NON-SYSTEMIC OBSERVATIONS

Chapter 1

The Obvious is Telling

When I first learned of Nostradamus, I went to a bookstore to buy a book about his prophecies. Upon opening that book, I found it intimidating. I found the only thing I could understand was what the author explained the meaning of a poem to be. Many of the four-lined verses were explained as nothing more than guesses. Some quatrains were not explained at all, and in the mid-1970s there were quite a few that only were explained as (paraphrasing), "This has not happened yet.", or "Too nonspecific to figure out."

When I looked at the actual poetry, I found it in two columns. One column displayed the French text; and the other column was the English translation of the French. Since I did not read French at that time, I only focused my attention at the English versions. Those left me scratching my head mostly, trying to see how the author's explanation came from those poetic words. Still, I was intrigued.

I knew I was entirely dependent on someone telling me what Nostradamus meant in his writings. For one thing, most of the interpretations were about some queen and her lover, or some other figures from antiquity, and their intrigues, all of whom I knew very little about. Beyond that, I did not want to learn more than a little about them.

For instance, one quatrain told of Nostradamus seeing William and Mary in England (historically they ruled together, between 1689 and 1694). Yawn. Why? What would be the important reason for Nostradamus seeing such boring, mundane glimpses of the future?

I was much more interested in those few quatrains that were said to be specifically about World War II, and generally about the Twentieth Century. In 1975, when I bought that book, those quatrains were, relatively speaking, about current events. Still, I was most interested in what Nostradamus said was going to happen in the future.

As stated, I bought my first Nostradamus book in the mid-Seventies. I did not buy another one until very late in 2001 (around November that year). A lot of the future, in 1975, had already turned into the past by then; and over those twenty-five years, or so, of book ownership, I had occasionally pulled that book out to see if I could solve anything. Maybe I did it once or twice a year, in the beginning, but as time went on, some dust settled on that book between readings. In all those times of checking, I never did solve anything.

On occasion, I would scribble some notes in the margin; trying to remind myself of what I thought I might possibility be here or there. Overall, in hindsight, my notes were best erased, as I never solved anything.

All that changed, for me, after September 11, 2001. I began to see the true meaning of Nostradamus' words. It all happened slowly at first, but then much faster as time went by. By slowly, I mean I suddenly knew I was onto something big; but that was because I understood almost intuitively. Because I was not understanding through intellectual acumen, it became en evolving process over years, becoming more and more aware of what it was I understood, and how. Once I realized how I was seeing what I was seeing, there was a faster progression in my learning curve. Everything that I have come to know about understanding Nostradamus' writings, all those directly associated with *The Prophecies*, have evolved over the past eight plus years, with me still seeing things I had not seen before.

Perhaps it would make sense if I used an analogy. I will use the analogy of one of those old black & white murder mystery movies from the 1930s and 40s, the kind typically set in an old castle. In those old movies, people disappeared suddenly, even when there was a crowd of people in a room. The reason was those old castles all were built with secret passageways and revolving walls. It all was a great mystery, until someone would accidentally lean on the secret revolving wall trigger, making the wall revolve. Then it became easier to solve the mystery. Well, Nostradamus has secret passageways and secret ways to make what seems impossible to understand open into a very readable series of stories. One just has to learn where to look.

Of course, if one had seen some of those old movies before hand, and then went to an old castle, one might immediately start looking for signs that there were some secrets built-into the rooms. Without something to spur our minds to think that way, we would constantly walk by the secret triggers, and never once open a doorway to a secret chamber. Even if we owned an old castle, without someone telling us what to find and where to look, we would never think of looking for something so hidden. All discoveries would be accidental. Still, to the observant eye, there will always be signs that something more is there. One simply has to learn to look for those signs.

Once I began to pick up speed with my awareness of Nostradamus' meaning, I was able to see the signs that tell us more is there. What I had been introduced to, originally, was a copy of what Nostradamus had written, presented by an author who had seen a publication that was more relative to the times of Nostradamus. That reproduction became a somewhat skewed perspective of the original. It took me a number of years to realize how I could see what the author had seen. When you realize there is more to see in the original, it becomes like a crime scene, where everything must remain unchanged, in its pristine condition.

When one truly sees what has always been there to see, one begins to see oddities as clues. The oddities are as simple as a seemingly misspelled word, which becomes "correctly" spelled in a reproduction; but the oddities are essential to observe. They hold the key to understanding. Unfortunately, most of these clues have been treated like wrapping paper on a present, not realizing the paper holds a clue to where the real present is, because the box under the wrapping is empty. If one simply rips off the wrapping, and then quickly discards it, the gift will never materialize. In order for one to understand there is much more than just individual quatrains in *The Prophecies*, one has to understand the "wrapping paper." Therein are the first signs, even though the whole appearance seems as mundane as any gift. The "trick" is to recognize the observable as a key to uncovering the true meaning of that which is hidden.

Chapter 2

Observing the Title of *The Prophecies*

There are several observations that have to be understood before one can begin to fathom that there are coherent systems at play in the text of Nostradamus' quatrains. These coherent systems are like the secret passageways – there, but unseen. However, it is these visible elements, which come from seeing the presentation of *The Prophecies* exactly as they have been seen for centuries, which lead us to find the secret triggers. Because they are so visible and mundane, they cannot be seen as part of the hidden, underlying systems for understanding. They are, in essence, the system that keeps one from understanding, simply by looking so normal and unimportant.

When one is dissecting a book of words, one finds there are several standard parts. Certainly, we all know the adage, "You can't judge a book by its cover." The cover is the initial part of a book; and while one cannot judge it by the cover alone, the cover gives a potential reader some good information. This is because on the cover one finds the title of the book, along with the name of the author, with other information about who published it, et cetera.

A well-designed cover can lure someone to open the book, but within all books should find an introduction, a body, and a conclusion. Those parts are outlined in a table of contents, and indexes can be available, with all providing quick glance ideas about what purpose the book has for being written. Those initial attractions play a role in one actually reading a book; and once reading begins, one should expect to find continuity in the storyline, as well as a story that compels the reader to continue reading. People most easily read books that contain language suitable for the reader's ability to comprehend the text. Some people enjoy large print type, and double spacing, with a certain number of pages. All of these are the mundane visible parts of all books, which can be seen while standing in a bookstore looking at books.

In order to best approach these elements of Nostradamus' book, a close inspection of each of the elements must be done. Otherwise, something can be mistaken as something else, seen as unimportant, or completely misunderstood. With *The Prophecies*, one has to look at everything closely, just like we would look at two side-by-side pictures, where one is the complete version of the picture, with the other changed so that it is missing five parts of the whole. One has to inspect Nostradamus' book thoroughly for visible signs, ones that can easily blend in as nothing more than background clutter, which are in reality clues for understanding.

This is because *The Prophecies*, as they have existed since publication, is a puzzle that requires clues to solve.

As an author who has self-published books, I understand that nothing goes into a book without planning and thought. The cover design is developed because a certain feeling is sought to be evoked, simply from the color or image on the cover. Everything is placed in the lap of the author for approval, if not left completely up to the author to design and develop. This means there is purpose to everything, whether or not the reader is able to understand that thought immediately. Certainly, a picture on the cover of a book can give some idea about the contents, but the one most important cover element is the title. The title is clearly the thought of the author, as an appropriate summation of that work created by the author.

The title is always a clue to the nature and focus the book holds, even if the title seems at first to be enigmatic. This can become a puzzle in fiction novels, where often the title is not understood until one has read a significant portion of the text, when one then finds the title comes from the text, becoming vividly clear after one attaches the contextual meaning. This is less of a problem with non-fiction books, where authors usually make the title a clear indication of what non-fiction matter is being analyzed. If the work is a biography, then that word often appears in the title, along with the name of the person of whom the biography is written. In many non-fiction works, the shorter the title the better.

Nostradamus wrote a non-fiction book and got right to the core of his focus in his title. *Les Propheties* is an accurate title.[1] The book is a collection of prophecies, written in French. When one opens this book, one finds a great many 4-line poems, called quatrains, separated into groups of one hundred. Because of the title, the reader supposes the book is about the future. However, does the title, *Les Propheties (The Prophecies)* really state what we have perceived it to be?

The title has led us to read the work as a book of many prophecies. We get that from the plural tense of the word, "prophecy," which has been applied in the title. However, that title has been misleading, in the sense that few (in modern times, at least) have ever ventured to see the true meaning of the word "prophecy." If the title were understood by the truth of definition, to be a book of divine utterances, not to be confused as a book of humanly motivated predictions, one would realize that the title, *The Prophecies*, states the contents to be a series of divine inspirations, all coming from God.

The title is then both accurately naming the book, but after one begins looking for holy prophecies within, it is then that one begins to lessen the importance of the title, because the introduction is difficult to understand, the body lacks continuity, and there is no ending to be found. Add to this confusion the fact that Nostradamus had produced yearly books that contained astrological predictions, entitled "*Presages*", and a lesser definition gets applied to the word "*prophecy*." The rejection of the divine source comes because that

---

1   Some mistakenly refer to the title of Nostradamus' work as "The Centuries". This is not and has never been the title. It is instead a description of *The Prophecies*, as it is subdivided into ten parts, each labeled as a "Centurie".

which is between the covers does not meet human expectations of what divine inspiration should look like.

Consider the book that most "Christians" accept to be from a divine source. If questioned, as to the name of that prophetic book, a large percentage of Christians would respond with, "The Bible." The correct answer would be, "The Holy Bible." That is because the word, "bible", simply means a collection of books. Thus, *The Holy Bible* is a collection of prophetic books, each being named within, as the "Book of Genesis", and the "Book of Amos", and so on. All of the books of *The Holy Bible* originally existed as an individual book, as someone's divinely inspired account of God or Jesus. The order of the compilation that is *The Holy Bible* is not fixed, as some Christians argue over what is holy enough to be in *The Holy Bible*, and what is not. Still, all of the books within any of the versions of *The Holy Bible* can be expected to be divinely inspired, because the title says everything within is *Holy*.

Realizing that, it makes one wonder if the contents of *The Holy Bible* would still be recognized as *Holy*, if all of the individual books were scrambled in order, such that the "Book of Genesis" followed the "Book of Psalms", with both following the "Book of the Revelations of John". All of those books are stand-alone in their prophetic abilities, regardless of where they appear in the text of a collection of similarly inspired books. However, it makes it easier for the reader to follow, when there is some attention paid to chronology. The recognized order of the books within *The Holy Bible* is not what makes it *Holy*, but it sure helps simple human beings recognize it as such.

It is in this way that one has to look at *The Prophecies*. By definition, the book could be called *The Holy Prophecies*, but the designation of *Holy* is manmade. The designation is based on understanding the contents, knowing the author, and proving the contents as truly prophetic. That, to this point, has been impossible, not because it cannot be done, but because of divine intervention. The systems of this book will make it become clear that Nostradamus named his work *The Prophecies* because it is indeed a true prophecy. It just needs some order to make it recognizable as such.

Chapter 3

Observing the Preface to *The Prophecies*

While it is correct to see each quatrain as a stand-alone prophecy, as each quatrain does have specific information relative to one specific set of related events, to see that as the intended goal misses the overall point of *The Prophecies*. When one sees each of the quatrains as if in a vacuum of time, due to their presentation as individual poems, having no obvious relationship to the poems surrounding them, it promotes a theme of randomness. Such a theme acts to lessen belief that the quatrains are truly prophetic, as the title suggests, due to the assumption that divinely inspired utterances would display evidence of chronology and lucidity, which is obviously lacking in the published versions of *The Prophecies*. This had led to assumption, even the alteration of the definition of the main word of the title, such that "prophecies" can be meant as "predictions."

Purely based on the randomness of presentation, another assumption has been that the order of presentation is directly related to the order that Nostradamus saw each prophecy, prompting him to write a poem about what he saw. Since it would seem highly unlikely that a deity would convey an important message for all to know in such random form, it has become easier to imagine Nostradamus as the lone source. Despite the fact that the title clearly states divine origin, this line of thought – predictions rather than prophecies – has prevailed since the original publication. Over time, those who could not find enough external evidence to support a judgment of sanctity on Nostradamus' work have seen the title as purposefully misleading. This, in turn, has been reason for some to cast the title of "charlatan" on the author.

In the days that Nostradamus published *The Prophecies*, there were none who would call him by that title. A big reason why people read the title, *The Prophecies*, and interpreted "Nostradamus' New Predictions" was his reputation at that time. Nostradamus wrote this famous work after he had become highly successful writing yearly predictions, which were based on astrological calculations. His popularity came from yearly publications, which came with titles like *Almanach*, which explained projected planetary movements, or *Prognostication*, which included predictive quatrains foretelling the coming months of the year, or *Presages*, which were monthly predictions, with or without the poetry.

Nostradamus had achieved critical success, to the level of what today would be called superstardom, due to his predictions having been seen as highly accurate. Many people, of all levels of status, read them; and everyone understood they were reading predictions prepared by Nostradamus, based on his astrological knowledge. Because of this history of publications under different titles,[2] the switch to a title stating *Prophecies* was seen as simply Nostradamus recognizing the accuracy of his predictions. The public had already bestowed upon Nostradamus the title of "prophet." Thus, from the pen of a prophet come prophecies, even if they may be secretly calculated, without an actually divine being visibly present.

This assumption that *The Prophecies* is only an argument of semantics, such that the title alone is not reason enough to believe the source to be divine, therefore does have some merit to it. By reading "prophecy" as defined to mean prediction, it recognizes the human element as the source, which allows for some degree of error to be made. If the title were to be officially recognized as a true Prophecy, the Roman Catholic Church would be the one bestowing that honor and designation.

The Church had the power to make life difficult for Nostradamus, had they actually believed Nostradamus was connected to God when he wrote his poems. They would have demanded a very clear explanation of the meaning of his poetic verses. However, the Church knew full well of Nostradamus and his uncanny abilities with astrology, and the popularity of his publications. Nostradamus came along during a favorable period, where the Church sought to learn astrology for their own use. Nostradamus was employed to teach the intricacies of this art to people connected with the Vatican. Due to this relationship, in the Vatican's mind they read Predictions, even though the title stated *Prophecies*.

The Church did not harass Nostradamus about the meaning of his book, but the king of France did find reason to demand some explanation. This led to Nostradamus writing a letter to the king, which was for the purpose of providing Henri II with his response to that demand. From that document comes more reason people have believed the word "*Prophecies*" meant, "Predictions." This clue comes from a statement made by Nostradamus in his explanation of *The Prophecies*.

Nostradamus produced the first edition of his book in 1555. That first publication included four parts (each called *Centuries*), with the first three parts containing 100 quatrains, and the fourth only 53.[3] In 1557, he published what is considered to be his complete first edition, which had six *Centuries*, with a seventh called a *Centurie*, but only containing 42 quatrains. Both of these publications from Lyon, France, included a letter addressed to Nostradamus' son, Caesar, at the beginning, before the appearance of *Centurie Premiere*, and the first quatrains.

Caesar was not much more than an infant by March 1, 1555, when Nostradamus penned that epistle. That document was headed as "Preface", in the original document's title, with the 1557 and 1568 Lyon

---

[2] For instance, in January 1554 a publication was released for "the year 1555", which advertised in the title, "PROGNOSTICATION nouvelle, & prediction portenteuse, pour Lan M.D.LV." That translates to state, "PROGNOSTICATION new, & prediction marvelous, for The year 1555". The word "prognostication" is defined as, "To predict according to present indications or signs." It is synonymous with "predict."

[3] There are 1555 editions from Vienna, Austria and Lyon, France (Albi-Bonhomme) surviving, which both show "*Fin*" immediately following the 53rd quatrain, in Centurie IV.

editions going so far as to head each subsequent page of that letter (9 more pages) as such, in all-capital letters ("PREFACE"). By definition, a "preface" is, "an introduction to a book, written by the author, which generally explains relevant details about what will be found within the book." While that is the identification of the purpose of the letter, because the title also states, "*Ad Caesarum Nostradamum filium*" ("*To Caesar Nostradamus my son*"), and immediately addresses him, with repeated references to "*my son*" in the text, the document is written off as nothing more than a father-son chat. Because the letter is difficult to grasp the meaning of, particularly in how it does not directly state, "this book is about what I see in the future, during these future years," the contents of the author's preface are quickly forgotten by the time one begins attempting to read the poems. There was no easily discernable coherency between the Preface and the quatrains, which would the reader to know clearly what to expect from the poetry.

By 1558, when Nostradamus published a second (and final for his lifetime) edition of *The Prophecies*, with ten parts (nine with 100 poems, and the seventh still with 42), there was nothing in the newly added 300 quatrains that made the Preface (which appeared unedited) make any more sense than it had originally. The confusion of quatrains that made little sense and a preface that seemingly added nothing towards understanding anything, led to Henri II demanding Nostradamus make an appearance before the king. Nostradamus was to come to Paris fully prepared to explain the book he had spent several years writing, at the king's expense. Nostradamus, understanding that the king could also make his life miserable, should he appear and talk the same nonsense he had published, decided instead to write a letter to his king. The letter was for the expressed purpose of explaining the unexplainable.

In that letter, Nostradamus explained quite enigmatically what *The Prophecies* were all about, in great detail. The letter ended up being much longer than the Preface, taking 21 pages of text in the 1568 Lyon edition (compared to 10 for the preface). The result was a letter that made Nostradamus appear as if he had gone stark, raving mad. Although there have been many since who have completely discounted the letter's value, due to a great difficulty in finding significant meaning, as an explanation for the book, small segments have been used to explain how Nostradamus was able to see the future (through mystical means). Likewise, primarily from the preface, people like to refer to that document as where Nostradamus explained how far into the future he saw.

Logically, it is difficult to trash a piece of evidence, as not being the author's explanation of his own book, while then cherry picking small morsels as evidence that the author did explain his own book. For instance, in the letter to Henry II, Nostradamus wrote, "*The whole concurred with & presaged the one condition tripod of copper (or bronze)*". This is my literal translation; but most see what Nostradamus wrote as saying, "All the predictions are a result of one method of divining, which includes a tripod made of brass." As you can see, what Nostradamus wrote is not what most people actually read. They convert words that are strangely placed together, into sentences that make sense to them. This one segment of words, in a very long letter, has been used as evidence that the word in the title, "*Prophecies*", means "Predictions."

The reference to *"presaged the one condition tripod of copper"* has been read as if it meant that Nostradamus stared into a bowl of water, suspended on a brass tripod. With this method of divination used, the "seer" somehow conjured up images in the water. Perhaps you have watched one of those programs on television about Nostradamus and seen this scene depicted. It gives the impression that Nostradamus practiced magic, making one recall the "Double, double, toil and trouble; fire burn, and cauldron bubble" chant witches make (according to Shakespeare, at least), while stirring a boiling cauldron with their broomsticks.

Of course, Nostradamus wrote nothing in either letter that would support a conclusion that he used any form of witchcraft, sorcery, or hocus-pocus. In fact, Nostradamus wrote in his Preface (and I translate literally, as close as literal can be to what is typically presented in translation), *"selves same the vanity of the more that detestable conjuring condemned in times past by the sacred scriptures"*. This states rather clearly states that Nostradamus saw witchcraft (*detestable conjuring*) as something *condemned* for doing nothing of worth (as a definition of *vanity*). This condemnation is stated in the *Holy Bible* (*sacred scriptures*), which means Nostradamus is stating he obeyed his religion by staying away from worthless practices, such as sorcery.

Still, evidence such as this is ignored; and even though Nostradamus clearly stated he was not using magic to foresee the future, those who claim to understand the meaning of Nostradamus' predictions lean heavily on this image of Nostradamus being able to use more than astrology to see deep into the future. The impression thus has been perpetuated, which nearly everyone who attempts to learn about Nostradamus and *The Prophecies* comes away thinking, that Nostradamus used some unrepeatable and unknown method to see the future. This fosters a belief that *The Prophecies* was a book of calculated predictions, and while not divine, additional hidden forces were at work. This view defends those quatrains that are said to be wrong, or only half-true, while allowing for a conclusion being drawn that something magical assisted Nostradamus to have enough truth result, validating believability. This is explained as his amazing ability to get some things so accurately that the accuracy defeats all odds of it being simply a guess.

When one loses sight of the divinity option, it appears quite reasonable that Nostradamus had no pinpoint control over what parts of the future he saw. This would account for the presentation of the quatrains in a random order, as individual glimpses into the future, with the power of seeing coming without control over the chronology of time. There are so many individual random glimpses that they all need to be counted out in groups of one hundred. Those divisions serve no purpose, other than to package 1,000 quatrains into 10 neat bundles. However, there is ample evidence that eliminates all suggestions that Nostradamus explained it was okay to lose sight of the work being totally divine.

While it is true the letters are difficult to understand, knowing there are systems to understand makes it easy to see how the evidence clearly states that Nostradamus offered a divine explanation. He went to great lengths explaining how astrology could play no role in predicting a very distant future, and he explained that only God knew what the future held. This means none of these individual prophecies can be completely independent of the others, because all are parts of a future worthy of divine revelation. This means there has to be some unseen ultimate purpose, which connects all the dots for better understanding.

There is further evidence to support this view, when one looks at what four-hundred fifty years of interpretations have solved. In my first exposure to a book of Nostradamus interpretations (back in the 1970s), roughly only thirty percent of the quatrains had the author feeling strongly enough about their meaning to write a full paragraph of interpretation. That estimation of mine means that seven out of every ten quatrains had little to no interpretation applied to them, with many simply listed with zero explanation. Even though a certain few quatrains are seen by most to make fairly strong statements about a particular event, many, many more seem to make absolutely no specific sense at all.

While I can imagine more recent publications on Nostradamus (post-2000 AD) could have serious interpretations on more than 30% of the total number of quatrains, this would simply be due to the times that we have entered. Not only have 35 years of time passed since the publication of that one book I owned, those past 35 years have been important times of global impact. I honestly do not see the number of fulfilled quatrains exceeding 25%, as of May 2010, after having read and sorted them all, according to the systems. That figure means that about 220 quatrains have already come true, as prophesied, with well over 700 still to come. In other words, most of Nostradamus' prophecies are still in our future.

If one watches a two-hour television presentation about the "hits of Nostradamus," one will find that, at best, ten to fifteen quatrains will be discussed. By "discussed," I mean an opinion will be presented, based on one possible translation. No more than those few will be publicized, because the weaker the interpretations become, the stronger the case against Nostradamus grows. When one realizes there are 948 quatrains to interpret, fifteen equates to almost 1.6% of the whole (.0158). The reason so few have been understood is explained in the Preface.

Nostradamus wrote in the Preface, a document designed to explain the author's intent, *"the whole written under figure cloudy (or nebulous)"*. He then added to this statement, *"more that* [the nebulosity] *of the whole prophetic."* This states that what you see is designed to be not what it appears to be. The poems are written in a *cloudy figure* of speech, so they seem difficult to grasp. It is difficult to see them as they really are. At the same time, these same words say *the whole* is *written* from a subservient position, *under* Jesus Christ, who appeared as his *figure* in life, while being undefined by limits and form (definition of *nebulous*) as a Spirit.

As such, *The Prophecies* are truly *prophetic*. Jesus Christ appeared to instruct Nostradamus in how to produce a Prophecy for the world. In the shape *The Prophecies* would take, as a published book with the nebulosity increased by dividing the quatrains into pieces and reordering them as randomness, the truth that matched the title could not be reached by simply reading the text. Understanding had then been *obscured* further by the limits created by a random presentation.

I do not want to give the impression that this is the only instruction that Nostradamus gave in his preface about the divinity of *The Prophecies*. There are many to choose from, in addition to those. He also wrote, "*that the whole is ruled & governed by the power of God inestimable*". The word "*inestimable*" means of immeasurable value. This says God is indefinable, such that God is *nebulous*, as the all-powerful God.

Nostradamus followed that statement with these words: "*Only divinity prophesy inspires prediction, & high spirit prophesizes the smallest part*". He then added, "*attributing the whole to be done by the virtue & inspiration divine*". You may note here that "*divine inspiration*" is the syntactical translation of the French; and this represents the definition of the word "*prophecy.*" While one is correct in seeing a *prophecy* as a *prediction*, as Nostradamus noted there, one cannot veer from the infallibility stated in a *prediction of divine inspiration*. This is completely opposite to a humanly calculated prediction, based on probabilities.

Nostradamus filled his letter of preface with many statements that reconfirm this instruction that *The Prophecies* is a divine work. He also further explained that he was instructed to present his prophecies in a manner that would make them impossible to interpret fully. He explained the reasoning for that as well. However, this is not the place to go through an in-depth analysis of the Preface. The importance at this point is to understand that there are visible instructions that state Nostradamus is not the sole author of his work. He is simply the chosen vehicle for a prophecy.

Before one can selectively choose any fraction of the quatrains for interpretation, as little as only one quatrain, one has to accept that the divine source makes everything written have meaning. That meaning is not a guess made by a man, but a prophetic vision supplied to Nostradamus, along with the words to write down, by the Spirit of Jesus Christ. Therefore, there is nothing that can be cast aside as meaningless. None of the poems can be discarded because they appear to be too general to make sense. Nothing can be seen as random and without purpose.

This means two things. First, anyone who has ventured a guess about the meaning of one of the quatrains has erred, if they have done so without referencing the claim of infallibility in *The Prophecies*, where *the whole is done by virtue*, meaning all is *perfection*. Everything that has been written so far, as explanation of the meaning of *The Prophecies*, is therefore fundamentally wrong, if not completely off base and wrong, if their explanation leaves any room for fallibility.

Second, every time one ventures a guess about the meaning of one of the quatrains, without referencing it as being out of context, as one of *the whole*, it is impossible to offer a valid conclusion without realizing that context. This means that the interpretation of one quatrain would need to refer to a quatrain that would contextually fall before that quatrain, and another to fall after it. In other words, all quatrains would need to be properly reordered first, so that all quatrains would then be seen in a larger context.

Consider this, which Nostradamus wrote in his Preface, as he was ending that letter. "*For the presage which itself made of the light exterior came infallibly in to judge part with that*". Without a deep interpretation at this time, realize that the word "*presage*" is defined as a "prophetic warning." This means the *light* of awareness to a prophecy is *exterior* to the one seeing the true meaning of a prophecy. This understanding is perfect, since this outside source has been enlightened *infallibly*.

Nostradamus then continued that line of thought by writing specifically about his prophecies, which he had been enlightened to see and write of, saying, "*Then through many times continuing the ominous overtakers, I will trample them, the Lord will say, & break them, & not show pity*" (Ezekiel 5:11). This is relative to the vision seen by Nostradamus, as he saw *many times* that which would come after his death, with those times *continuing* into the future. That is the primary focus of *The Prophecies*. The continuation of the times would include the continuation of those who would rule those times, who would cause "*sinister uproars*" (alternate translation of the French text, *sinistres tempestes*). Those *uproars* would lead to the *ominous* revolutions that would overthrow kings, leading to governments run by common men. Those *overtakers* would continue until completely corrupted.

It is at that point in time that Nostradamus was allowed to see, beginning with rebellions led by these overthrowers, one after another, *continuing* this pattern of stormy revolution until this time we live in now, where elections are no longer to be taken for granted as the will of the people. We are living in *ominous* times; and these who will have benefited from the *overtakers* of kings will be punished, as Isaiah prophesied. The ones who will attempt to destroy the world will be trampled upon and broken, with no pity shown to them.

At this point in his conclusion to the Preface, Nostradamus wrote, "*a thousand other adventures which will be coming by water & continual rains, like more to plain I have reduced by writing with them my other prophecies which are composed all to the great*". This is saying that even though so much time will pass between these *ominous overtakers*, and the times when their descendants will be *trampled and broken*, there will be *a thousand other* stories that will not be told in *The Prophecies*.

The holy Prophecy (*The Prophecies*) will not be like the *other prophecies* of Nostradamus. Those were written to be yearly predictions, which focused on the doings of the few who ruled over the many, as they were *the great* who all could easily recognize. While those of Nostradamus' times certainly experienced *rains* that caused distress to the greats and their subjects, *The Prophecies* would not focus on every flood that would come.

The key to telling the difference between one natural flood and one so significant that the Spirit of Jesus would come to show it as a sign the future held, *The Prophecies* would have to be read differently than the way one reads the Almanacs. Nostradamus told the reader that Jesus instructed him to write his revelation *more to plain*, rather than more to detail. This means they are not written like his other publications, which were vastly popular because everyone understood their wording. Therefore, the poems of *The Prophecies*, while similar in initial appearance, cannot be read like them.

This led Nostradamus to explain, "[The Prophecies were written] *in unrestricted speech, limiting the places, times, & the words assigned that the humans after arrived, will be seeing understanding the adventures* [of The Prophecies] *came to pass infallibly.*" This means the unusual style of writing, which has caused so many to change it to a more readable style (with syntax allowing the prophecies to be more like the Almanac predictions), has to remain exactly as written for true understanding to emerge. Because Nostradamus wrote a Prophecy, with *the words assigned* (or "*the terms prefixed*", alternate translation of *le terme prefix*), everything has to remain as it is. Only later, *after arrived* at this determination, can people begin *seeing* with *understanding*. At that time, those quatrains telling of past events will be understood to have *come to pass infallibly*. We can never forget that infallibility is impossible for human beings to achieve. Only God has that capability.

This conclusion of Nostradamus' Preface clearly states, in support of the other statements mentioned, and vice versa, that the quatrains are divinely inspired. Thus, it makes sense that all of the quatrains link together forming one long epic tale (told in poetic style), rather than a thousand random visions of a magical future. This realization allows one to establish context, which makes it possible to fathom all of the poems as infallibly prophetic.

Those most clearly worded quatrains, those seemingly freestanding quatrains of specificity, act then as the lead quatrains stating a central theme. Those quatrains that seem unintelligible are simply placed out of context, in a way that strips them of any specific meaning. When all are restored to their proper order, they each connect to those quatrains that ignite the missing element of understanding. That is when one can find those seemingly unintelligible quatrains making perfect contextual sense, adding depth to those surrounding them. Everything has purposeful meaning when stated as one long prophecy, where one quatrain is a prophecy in itself, but another adds minute details to those more obvious central themes, while also being fully prophetic. The result is a theme that is fully developed through many quatrains, rather than just one.

In other words, the ten to fifteen quatrains that are repeatedly presented in television programs are shown in a weakened state, by not explaining the quatrains that connect to those few. The individual quatrains appear as predictions when left to stand-alone; but when they are matched up to those quatrains that give supporting details, they have the strength of a true prophecy.

At that point, we can understand why Nostradamus wrote in his preface, "*to be able not to make a mistake, deceived, cheated*". This is a statement of infallibility and truth. No human is capable of infallibility. Human beings find it hard to admit to all the mistakes we make. Some purposefully make mistakes, which are designed to take advantage of others in a variety of ways. In this statement, Nostradamus was stating that he could not claim to be infallible, could not be misleading people into thinking he was a prophet, and he could not cheat people into believing he was the sole source of his words. Nostradamus stated how he was truly a vehicle for the infallible God, because he personally was as frail as all humanity. In that sense, God is the one who never makes mistakes, never deceives the righteous, nor cheats those worthy of just reward.

Of course, Nostradamus' prophetic epic tale is nowhere to be found within the pages of the original publications (and all since following). This causes the readers to see the non-linking quatrains exactly as they have appeared for over 450 years. Because of a lack of continuity, everyone has been content seeing *The Prophecies* as individual glimpses of the future. No one takes the time to realize that the original tale, in complete form, has been sliced into individual poems, and then purposefully reordered to appear as random visions. Publication in this style has ensured the document would begin, and remain, almost completely unintelligible.

We can count on this confused state being removed, due to Nostradamus promising that we, "*will be seeing understanding the adventures.*" That statement by itself means that after a number of the quatrains have come to pass (those telling of past *adventures*), we *will be seeing* those events played out in the quatrains. Since we do not have complete *understanding* now, at a time when people guess about the meaning of one quatrains, real *understanding* can only come from a reordering of the quatrains so those past *adventures* fully come to life, as having been prophesied *infallibly*. That means we have to reproduce an epic tale, written in poetic style. After enough of the past has been understood, that will become the foundation for building the whole story upon.

A visible document such as the preface should be the greatest source of information to confirm that we truly understand those past quatrains. Nostradamus could have prefaced his work by stating something to the effect of, "I had random visions, which I penned in the order that I saw them. In order to see these visions, I ingested some mushrooms, lit some candles, and looked into a bowl of water, which was suspended in a tripod." If Nostradamus had written those general instructions, everyone who has followed this basic belief would have the absolute best evidence for seeing *The Prophecies* as they have. Unfortunately, this is not the case, so we have to look at the Preface with new eyes.

Chapter 4

The Obvious Use of Latin in the Preface

Imagine if someone cut an epic poem (like Beowulf or Faust) into pieces, and placed the pieces back into some new random order. A few of the sections might allow one to get a good glimpse of the meaning; but taken out of context that way, no one would be able to figure out why such epics of poetic nonsense were ever written.

Could you understand the meaning in this, if it was presented as a stand-alone meaningful statement?

> *"I hope to give the good youth gold for his gallant thought. Be thou in haste, and bid them hither, clan of kinsmen, to come before me; and add this word, -- they are welcome guests to folk of the Danes."*[4]

These are all understandable words, as an acceptable English translation of a foreign epic poem. The poem is *Beowulf*, which has been made into movies lately, after some time as an accepted literary classic. However, this passage does little to convey the main theme of *Beowulf*, as a stand-alone segment from the whole. It is doubtful one could explain the meaning of this passage accurately, out of context. I imagine it would be impossible to capture the true meaning of *Beowulf* if the whole document was scrambled up and pieced back together in a confusing new order.

How about this passage from the epic poem *Faust*, by Johannes Wolfgang von Goethe?

> *"This life of earth, whatever my attire,*
> *Would pain me in its wonted fashion.*
> *Too old am I to play with passion;*
> *Too young, to be without desire.*
> *What from the world have I to gain?*
> *Thou shalt abstain—renounce—refrain!"*[5]

Again, regardless of how well we understand the words (another acceptable English translation), as a

---
[4] Orange Street Press Classics, *Beowulf*, Part VI, pp 31-32, http://www.scribd.com/doc/7359607/Beowulf
[5] The Project Gutenberg E-Books, http://www.gutenberg.org/files/14591/14591-h/14591-h.htm

stand-alone passage from an epic poem, of two parts, no one would be able to grasp Goethe's ultimate purpose for writing *Faust*, from this one quote. Most would not even realize it is a quote from the main character, again without knowing the context of a dialogue between Dr. Faust and Mephistopheles. While the quote has power to stand alone, as most adult human beings can identify with the character's obvious frustration with life's limitations, this quote by itself serves no ultimate purpose. Still, this is precisely what all past interpreters of Nostradamus have done, by cherry picking just a few quatrains over which to marvel.

I give the examples of *Beowulf* and *Faust* because they are epic poems. Nostradamus has not been recognized as having written an epic poem because he had his work published in a random format. Those two examples show how *The Prophecies* can be turned into a literary masterpiece simply by attempting to arrange the individual quatrains into one long tale. Scholastic recognition has come to those two classics because they tell a story full of meaning. A story brings value to the reader, because it allows one the ability to see a reflection of the challenges faced by fictitious characters, in real contemporary life. That is the purpose of Nostradamus' classic; but it is a purpose unrecognized.

Nostradamus' classic was focused on a real future, one where real human shortcomings were seen to play out with real human consequence. Rather than in a fictitious setting, where the frailties of the King of the Danes, and Doctor Faustus, created situations requiring superhuman efforts to escape, Nostradamus saw no such heroes or villains. His epic has a sad ending, one where no heroes come to save the day. Nostradamus' epic ends like the *Holy Bible* ends, in the Book of The Revelations. However, just as *Beowulf* and *Faust* carry the redeeming value of Salvation in their underlying themes, *The Prophecies* is designed to accomplish the same end, on a global scale. We could change the ending, if the warning is heeded and a positive moral change occurs in humanity, because that is the ultimate purpose of prophecy.

From this recognition of a real warning of an impending future, one has to realize that Nostradamus was not allowed to make *The Prophecies* a literary masterpiece telling of improbable, if not impossible events, none of which could ever materialize in the mid-16th Century. If published in the correct order, with the poems still shrouded in a nebulous writing style, *The Prophecies* would have been seen only as an epic tale with no clear meaning. Had it been published as such, it could be that the result today would be one only knows of the name Nostradamus from upper-level coursework, towards some Medieval French Literature degree, offered in limited colleges and universities around the world.

As I presented earlier, Nostradamus wrote, "*a thousand other adventures which will be coming*," meaning many events will occur in the time that will pass before the time of the future told of in *The Prophecies*. If thousands of events were to occur between the time of writing and the first abundance of *adventures* that will build to a tragic end, it is probable people would have given up on the prophecy aspect, focusing only on the scholastic aspects of importance.

Even *Beowulf* was seen as unimportant when it was first discovered in the late 19th Century. Translations were done, and some reports generated at that time, but the document was placed in storage for roughly 100 years, before being accidentally re-discovered in the early 20th Century. At that time, it created excitement and marvel, and became a very popular document of scholastic study. Such could have been the fate for *The Prophecies*, had Nostradamus left the verses in the correct order.

The scholastic approach would have caused other problems as well. As I mentioned earlier, Nostradamus did not face scrutiny from the Roman Catholic Church because *The Prophecies* appeared, on the surface, to be just like the Almanacs he produced. Those popular yearly forecasts were known to be the result of astrological calculations; and the Church knew Nostradamus as one of that period's best interpreters of astrological data. Had Nostradamus presented an orderly poetic tale, telling of events no one could understand, presumed to be based on astrological calculations, the Church would have begun to see their most favored seer as little more than a charlatan. In the prediction business, you are only as good as your accuracy rate; and astrology had been on the papal banned list before, just as it would be again, not too long after Nostradamus' death.

In fact, the Church's attitude towards such arts as astrology, and the Vatican's opinion on Nostradamus himself, waned after the publication of *The Prophecies*. The reason was the verbiage of the 1,000 quatrains (700 initially) was not as easy to discern as the simple riddles presented in yearly groups of ten to twenty quatrains. This gave the impression that Nostradamus was somehow tricking those in power, those who had supported his efforts in publishing. Even though Nostradamus continued the practice of publishing his almanacs and presages until his death (there was one published for the year 1567, the year after his death), the Church became wary of some sinister agenda possibly being in play.

It is probable that the missing quatrains of Centurie VII (roughly the last 55 are no longer available for interpretation) disappeared because of censorship by the Church. Since the initial publication was only seven parts, or Centuries, the Church could have viewed the book as a calculated set of predictions that followed a chronological order, even though they could not understand anything that was written. Rather than take the chance that some sinister ending was in the seventh "chapter," they could have simply axed the last half of that part, to prevent anyone from ever finding out the end and using that knowledge for their own personal good. Such an act as that would solely be based on the assumed accuracy of Nostradamus' predictions, which had been quite evident in his yearly verses.

As far as that uncanny accuracy Nostradamus displayed in his presages, he explained this in the Preface to *The Prophecies*. He stated his abilities with astrology came, *"from the good Angels have received the wit to foretelling."* By stating that an Angel told Nostradamus what to write in his predictions, he was saying he was intuitively led to certain conclusions, based on what he saw in the charts he prepared, from which he would contemplate in order to read into the future. Nostradamus was not stating that *Angels* were the source of his holy work (*The Prophecies*); because nothing had yet been made public announcing such divine guidance (the Preface accompanied the initial publication of *The Prophecies*). There is a difference between the two (prediction and prophecy) that has to be realized.

It is important to understand the word used by Nostradamus, which has been translated as *Angels*. The word written is "*Ange*," and this word not only carries the connotation of *angel*, but it was also commonly used to mean, "God's immediate messenger; our Genius; or the spirit (whether good or evil) that haunts and accompanies us."[6] Nostradamus made the distinction of good spirits accompanying him, as opposed to evil ones, by stating *good Angels* led him. This means Nostradamus' *Genius* (alternative translation of *Ange*, which means, "extraordinary intellect and creative power"[7]), particularly as relative to his reputation with astrology, was due to his being able to listen to his inner mind, where the voices of *good Angels* led his accuracy.

If you have ever seen the cartoons where someone has a little white angel on the right shoulder, with a little red devil on the left, with each telling the person what to do, the little white person with wings is a *good Angel*. That depiction is not standard because Nostradamus wrote about such winged creatures of influence. It is because we all hear a voice in our head that tells us what to do, and what not to do. Flip Wilson made a career out of saying, "The devil made me do it," because everyone saw the humor of falling to influences that are only in our minds.

It is up to our individual strength of character, as to whether or not we make decisions that will later be deemed good or bad (evil). Since Nostradamus was seen as an accurate predictor of events to come in the next year, the accuracy was seen as good. Still, he tried to find good predictions to make, which would be helpful to the people, thus good. As such, he was saying the inner whispers that led him to see how planetary patterns would play out were how he *received the wit of foretelling*.

It is also safe to assume that Nostradamus was a *good* person, since he was in touch with his *good Angels*. As a good person, he could also be expected to be an honest person and loyal to both his king and to the Church. Had Jesus Christ commanded Nostradamus to present *The Prophecies* is the right order, clearly pronouncing that Jesus was the source, but without any sense being possible from such a long tale, the Church would have been the power demanding an explanation. King Henry II would also have the power to make demands, as of Royal blood and responsible for the welfare of France (which he did), but in specific matters of announced contact with the Holy Spirit (ecstatic prophecy), the Church would have the ultimate investigative authority.

A summons to Rome would have taken Nostradamus well beyond the protections and safeties that existed in France. The pressure of the Church would have been more difficult for Nostradamus to handle, because it was one thing to be a great astrologer, but it was another thing indeed to be calling yourself a <u>Prophet, in a book</u> whose title indicated such, without any understanding found possible within that book.

6   Randle Cotgrave's 1611 French-English Dictionary
7   The Free Online Dictionary by Farlex

The Church would have demanded Nostradamus show his loyalty, and be most honest about the future he had seen. They would have demanded that Nostradamus fill them in, as the earthly institution that was dedicated to saving souls.

Since Nostradamus was forbidden from telling anyone about the future he had been allowed to witness (by the Spirit of Christ), such that beyond the cryptic letters he would write honestly stating the meaning, he was not free to make clarity known. Had he become a "captive" guest of Rome, such confusing explanation would not have been tolerated, meaning Nostradamus would have faced extreme persecution should he refused to cooperate fully. Therefore, Nostradamus could not leave a work entitled *The Prophecies* as one epic tale in need of full explanation.

On the other hand, as powerful as the king of France was, the queen, Catherine de Medici, tempered Henry's demands on Nostradamus for explanation. Catherine was enthralled with Nostradamus' astrological powers, and she had visited with Nostradamus for the purpose of gaining his predictions about the royal children's futures. Following the death of Henry II, Catherine de Medici would visit Nostradamus in Salon-de-Provence, bestowing upon him honors and titles, making France a safe place for his retirement. While *The Prophecies* was largely viewed as Nostradamus biting off more than he could chew, perhaps a mistake by an aging man, suspected of possibly suffering from the onset of senility, his other values would remain with him until his death. As long as he maintained a low profile in France, he would live out his days in southern France, free of persecution.

Fortunately, the Church was amid a period of time when popes were lenient towards the practice and study of astrology. They valued Nostradamus' abilities with this art as well as France's queen did. The Vatican wanted to learn to master the art of prediction for its own personal gains; and Nostradamus was one who they questioned for advice on how to create their own accurate predictions. Therefore, it was best that Nostradamus stay as far away from making it clearly known that a true Prophecy was his work.

Even though the truth was presented in title, Jesus foresaw a greater need to cloak the truth the verses hold. When Nostradamus had written verses in his *Prognostications*, they were known to be riddles, due to the use of symbolism. The verses of *The Prophecies* were made even more enigmatic, by the use of text that appeared to be in need of considerable editing, just to make the recognizable words fit together in a sensible syntactic state. To go beyond "bad writing style", by figuratively tossing all the individual poems up in the air, letting them fall on the ground, to then reassemble them in an illogical order, made the truth even more obscure. This secrecy was for many reasons, which Nostradamus explained in his letters; but one important reason was the foreseen need for the protection of Nostradamus from unnecessary persecution.

Still, Nostradamus never lied, even though he wrote that he was unable to explain clearly his work. As honest as Nostradamus was in the title, he continued his honesty in the words of the Preface, and later in the words of his letter to the king. I have presented some of the evidence where Nostradamus indicated that *The Prophecies* was indeed such. Still, Nostradamus offered another visible clue that the work was holy, while making this clue almost seem invisible. That clue was the use of Latin in his letters (and quatrains at times), which more often than not was a reference to a biblical verse. Simply by switching from French to Latin, and then back to French, Nostradamus was speaking the language of the Church to the people of France. This symbolized a level of reverence.

Earlier, I gave evidence that Nostradamus wrote (to the effect) "*only the divine prophesy inspiring prediction*," which stated the definition of the word "prophecy," while being an explanation for what Nostradamus wrote. His title, *The Prophecies*, was indeed meant to indicate divinely inspired predictions.

I repeat this here because that statement was written in Latin, with the whole segment being, "*Soli numine divino afflati praesagiunt & spiritu prophetico particularia.*" This is said to translate to mean, "Only those inspired by the divine Godhead can prophesy, and only those inspired by the spirit of prophecy can prophesy detailed events."[8] While this is not a biblical quote, the fact that it is written in Latin gives the statement a higher voice as the source. It acts not as Nostradamus' conclusion, but as a divine guidance embedded in the text to lead one to the truth required for understanding.

I also gave reference earlier to a quote from the fifth chapter of the Book of Ezekiel, where Nostradamus wrote, "*I will trample them, & break them, & not show pity*". This is not the verse verbatim, but similar language is found in the eleventh verse of that chapter from Ezekiel. In his Preface, Nostradamus wrote, "*Conteram ego & confringam, & non miserebor.*" Some of those words are found in Ezekiel's, "***ego quoque* confringam**: *et non parcet oculus meus,* ***et non miserebor***," which means, "***I will also break thee in pieces***, *and my eye shall not spare, and I* ***will not have any pity***."

The point here is that Nostradamus is not demonstrating an inability to memorize fully the Latin of the Holy Scriptures. More important is the fact that he switches to a holy voice, the same holy voice as led the writers of the *Holy Bible* to write. In doing this transition, Nostradamus is also bringing to mind a specific biblical verse, which would be recognizable to those dedicated to knowing the Latin Bible. That specificity of verse carries a deeper meaning by itself, from the context of the *Holy Bible's* book, which becomes attached to the context of the actual words written in the Preface.

Therefore, Nostradamus' use of Latin goes higher than the level of holiness represented by the Church. It goes directly to God, as coming from the instruction of Jesus Christ. Nostradamus became filled with the Holy Spirit of true Prophecy, while in this Presence. While Nostradamus the man actually penned everything, he was acting well beyond his abilities, to which he admitted in his explanations. It then becomes important to realize that Nostradamus spoke in this higher voice throughout the Preface, with each time signaling a heavenly instruction being sent to readers. This instruction is to realize

---

8   Translation by Peter Lemesurier, from *Prophecies On Line*, http://www.propheties.it/nostradamus/letters/cesar.htm

Nostradamus does not hold the ultimate authority of *The Prophecies*.

When one reads a translation of the Preface, sometimes these transitions between French and Latin get lost in the translation into English. Some of the more dedicated interpreters of Nostradamus, while way off in their interpretations, stay as true to the written word as they can. They usually somehow indicate when Nostradamus wrote in Latin, including bracketing a note that indicates Latin text being the root of part of the translation. This makes something become visible amidst a document all in one language, simply as making something stand out as a difference in presentation.

In the original publications of *The Prophecies* the Latin text was italicized. This acted to set that language apart from the standard French. While one can argue whether the author or the publishing house made the decision to differentiate the use of a second language in the text by this change in font, the fact remains an obvious difference is present on each page where Latin text is found. Therefore, the Latin is a sign of something that needs to be looked at more closely.

When I exposed where Nostradamus stated "*more to plain*," rather than "more to detail," and then added that his language was "*in unrestricted speech*," this was a reference to a style of writing that defied translation. Translation restricts the full possibility of meaning that one word possesses alone. This is because someone far removed from the author has later made a decision about which meaning was originally intended. This act of narrowing the meaning of words is based on the need for meaning matching interpretation.

Translation is like the uprooting of a living tree, cutting off all the branches from the trunk, and throwing the remains on a logging truck. One trailer of logs then represents an interpretive paraphrase of the author's work, where the translator has done all the necessary trimming to avoid confusion. When the author has written according to the limiting rules of syntax (as most all do), then a translator applying the use of a foreign language's syntax usually results in an accurate paraphrase. However, this accuracy is not beyond the scope of argument.

For instance, the *Holy Bible* is a document that has many varied translations. For many years, the King James Version was accepted as an accurate translation of the original languages into English. However, problems became apparent when some of the words were later discovered to be mistranslated. For example, in the story of the Exodus, where the Israelites were said to have crossed the Red Sea, modern scholars have found a mistranslation. The word misread as "Red" is more correctly read as "reed." The "parting of the waters" is then quite differently seen when the waters parted are in "the sea of reeds," rather than the much deeper Red Sea.

Part of the translation error comes from translating ancient Hebrew and Greek, which did not have vowel representation in their alphabets, as English does. Many words written in the ancient text can actually have multiple translations, depending on what vowels are inserted. This then is compounded when it is realized that Latin can act similarly to Greek and Hebrew, with Latin being its own form of limitation on the original written text. Simply put, it must be understood that translation limits the speech of an ancient text; and similarly, the translations of Nostradamus' Old French and Latin requires careful and complete analysis.

Nostradamus said that his language must be seen as *unrestricted*. Translation trims a word down to the detail of one specific usage, rather than leaving it to act *plain*, as containing all possible meanings one word can stand for. In addition, as far as natural French and Latin readers are concerned, syntax is another limitation on the way words are read. This restriction means that all French-speaking people should be able to understand the meaning of *The Prophecies* first, well before any translation to other languages could be attempted. Remember, syntax has to be applied originally, for translation to result properly. However, this obviously is not the case; and Nostradamus is stating such, by telling us his language was *more to plain*. The meaning of that is then, "less to syntax."

In the example that I have just recalled, Nostradamus wrote in both French and Latin. When he wrote, "*more to plain*," he used the French words "*plus à plain*". Later, in the same section, Nostradamus penned the words, "*in soluta oratione*", which I have translated as saying, "*in unrestricted speech.*" This is a literal translation of mine, as I see the word *soluta* being a form of the word "*solutus*," which means, "unbound, released; free, at large; **unrestrained**, profligate; lax, careless".[9] The word *oratione* is a form of the word "*oratio*," which means, "**speech**, oration; eloquence; prayer,"[10] as well as, "speaking; language, style," especially used to denote "a set speech; prose; an imperial message."[11] From this assortment of translation possibilities, I have chosen *in unrestricted speech*.

My translation, stating *in unrestricted speech*, is itself restricting. I have limited those three words from representing the other possibilities that those Latin words can carry as possible meanings. However, if you ask someone knowledgeable in Latin, as well as knowledgeable as a translator of Nostradamus, that person could become adamant in defense that *in soluta oratione* means, "in plain prose," and nothing more.

The reasoning behind such strong defense of a translation is that those three words, in that specific combination, represents an idiom, or a saying, one that is automatically interpreted by those knowing such ways with words. Translating them as an idiom is a way of stating that something is not profound. These people then imply that Nostradamus was stating his prophecies were written in an ordinary, everyday-style of speaking (the definition of "prose"), while using words just as *plain* as day to understand. While *in soluta oratione* may be a standard idiom in literature, yielding the understanding that those words

---

9   A Latin-English Dictionary Wordlist, http://users.erols.com/whitaker/dictpage.htm
10   Ibid
11   University of Notre Dame, Latin Dictionary and Grammar Aid, http://catholic.archives.nd.edu/cgi-bin/lookup.pl?stem=orati&ending=

carry the meaning, "in plain prose," there is nothing about *The Prophecies* that is clearly understood, with "prose" being a misnomer is there ever was one.

In reference to this appearance of *in soluta oratione*, let me present the full context of what Nostradamus wrote. As I have presented earlier, Nostradamus wrote, *"like more to plain I have reduced through writing with them my other prophecies which are composed all to the great,* **in unrestricted speech***, limiting the places, times, & the words assigned that the humans after arrived, will be seeing understanding the adventures came to pass infallibly."* All of those words were written in French, with the only exception being those three bolded words, which were written in Latin.

One has to notice that the use of three Latin words, italicized, in the middle of many French words is an obvious element of the Preface that stands out. Even if one could not read Nostradamus' book (for reasons of illiteracy or a lack of fluency in those languages), one could see clearly that the font is different. When one reads Nostradamus, one has to understand that difference is by design. When something is by design it has purpose; and this means there has to be a reason why Nostradamus wrote words in two languages.

First, one has to realize that in the mid-16th Century (regardless of the state of the Protestant movement, in particular the changes initiated by Martin Luther in Nostradamus' younger years) the language of the Roman Catholic Church was (and still is) Latin. As such, when Nostradamus shifted to Latin, he was giving the appearance of a level of piety, as a dedicated disciple of the Church. The appearance of Latin immediately gives a tone of holiness.

Second, once we realize Nostradamus has encountered the Spirit of Jesus Christ, and thus is writing the Preface to a true Prophecy, Latin acts to take a tone of holiness to an even higher level. Latin becomes, at least symbolically, the language of God, with Jesus adding the Latin while Nostradamus wrote the French. The Holy Spirit of Christ dictated the whole text to Nostradamus, but Latin becomes the beacon that must make one read very carefully, rather than try to whiz on by thinking we have everything syntactically understood.

When we realize this higher-level purpose of the Latin, it becomes easier to grasp how, in that series of statements that *in soluta oratione* appears, Nostradamus was explaining the difference in the manner of speech he used, between *The Prophecies* and his almanacs. When we see the Latin as from a higher authority, where no limits can be placed upon the meaning, we then realize that *in soluta oratione* has more than one application, with many possible meanings.

It becomes supporting detail for the presages in the almanacs being written "in plain prose," while also representing the *unrestrained* qualities that make *The Prophecies* a truly holy work. As such, the words filling the quatrains of *The Prophecies* are written *in unbound eloquence*, as befitting the Spirit of God as its source, and His inestimable glory. The words are thus also a form of *free prayer* presented to the reader, requiring a connection to God for understanding to come, from a work that has confused everyone for centuries. The reader has to see the Latin stand out in the text of the Preface, and realize how Jesus communicated everything to Nostradamus *in [an] unrestricted style of language*.

We should then take the time to go over all of the Latin uses in the Preface if we want to make a fuller connection to what is behind *The Prophecies*. Only by knowing what the voice of God has stated, particularly in the Bible references, can one begin to grasp the true meaning underlying this holy work created through Nostradamus. Just as *in soluta oratione* shows us how a little expands into a lot, we have to realize that all use of Latin acts the same way. When Nostradamus used Latin to elicit thoughts of comparisons to Biblical verses, it highlighted a need to not only recognize something holy was just alluded to, but the need to understand the full meaning of that biblical context referenced. In order to best understand the statements of the Preface as instructions in how to gain meaning from *The Prophecies*, in particular to find proof of a need to reorder the verses, we have to seek what God placed there for our guidance.

Chapter 5

The Biblical References of the Latin in the Preface

Nostradamus wrote this, in Latin, in his Letter of Preface: "*Nolite sanctum dare canibus, nec mittatism margaritas ante porcos ne conculcent pedibus & conversi dirumpant vos.*" This translates literally, yet similar to most accepted translations, as stating: *(All) be unwilling holy to give to dogs, nor cast out pearls before swine lest to trample under foot & to turn around and tear to pieces (or rend) you.*"

This Latin statement is similar to the quote from Matthew 7:6, but not quite exact. The Latin Vulgate states, "*nolite dare sanctum canibus neque mittatis margaritas vestras ante porcos ne forte conculcent eas pedibus suis et conversi disrumpant vos*." This yields the statement recognized from the King James Version, "*Give not that which is holy unto the dogs, neither cast ye your pearls before swine, lest they trample them under their feet, and turn again and rend you.*"[12]

Before we need to contemplate the meaning of Jesus' quote remembered by Matthew, it is important to see what Nostradamus wrote, in French, leading up to this Latin-Biblical passage. This becomes his explanation about why he quoted this verse from the Bible. As such, he wrote (literal translation), "*That he will be coming with to give judgment against those that through the centuries will come to pass will understand to be seen & marked: Considering also the decree of the Savior*".

"*That*" is a reference to the previous statement, which states, "[importantly] *faith could be finding whether evil agreeable with their affected hearing (auricular*[13])," where *auricular* also has a meaning relating to the upper chamber of the heart, with the accepted Old French use being as "little ear." Thus, "*that*" means the acceptance of evil into humanity's hearts (through the whispers to the minds) will be the reason a Prophecy of warning was issued to Nostradamus. This means that Jesus (*he*) *will be coming to give judgment*, which as we all know happens at the end of man's time on earth. That *judgment* will be *against those* who will have fallen victim to *that*, the acceptance of evil in their hearts.

---

12 Parallel Greek New Testament by John Hurt, http://greeknewtestament.com/B40C007.htm#V6
13 The Roman Catholic Church adheres to the principle of private repentance, which is referred to as Auricular Confession. This is the booth of confession, where one confesses to a priest secretly. Thus, "auricular" is defined as the "little ear." Still, in modern French the word translates as, "little finger."

This says that the story of *The Prophecies* is a prophecy of the time when Jesus will return in *judgment*. It then states that *those* who *that* (meaning "*that judgment*") will be *against* will be *centuries* after *The Prophecies* was written. This time will *come to pass*; and at that time understanding of what has been *seen* in the writings prophesying *that* future will become clear. More importantly, the understanding will be of how Nostradamus wrote an epic tale that explains of who is *marked* for *judgment*.

This means that *The Prophecies* holds some very important information; but *understanding* that information will have to wait *centuries* to become clear. The reason such a wait will be necessary to *come to pass* is then found in the quote from the *Savior*, who is Jesus Christ, remembered by Matthew, and known by Nostradamus. That biblical quote states that *The Prophecies* is a *holy* document, from the Spirit of Jesus Christ, and not from Nostradamus' mind. Such a *holy* document (as is the *Holy Bible*, whose pages all come from an equally *holy* source) is *not willingly to be given to dogs*. In this case, *dogs* would be those *marked* for *judgment*. Likewise, *those* would be the ones who would have *turned around and torn to pieces* Nostradamus' book of holy prophecy, had it been made easily understood long ago.

It is then important to note that Nostradamus wrote, in the French introduction to the Latin quote, "*Considering also the sentence of the true Savior*", where the word, *sentence*, also translates as *decree*, *judgment*, or *order*, from a court of authority. This word equally can be used as we typically use "sentence", as a structure in language. In that case, Nostradamus has just explained the strange style of *The Prophecies*, as it is "*the sentence of the true Savior.*" However, it must be seen as a word that denotes judgment. In this sense, this series of words is an instruction worth strong consideration ("*Considering*") that a *decree* by Christ follows that the *dogs* of the world will not *willingly be given* a *holy* prophecy. Therefore, Nostradamus has become bound by *decree* to present his *holy* document in *sentence*, which is *true*, but too difficult to understand to be of no assistance to *dogs*, as something they will find reason to *rend to pieces*.

When we look deeper into the meaning of Matthew 7:6, we find that this one verse is one of many, beginning in chapter five, where Jesus sat on the mount with his disciples, giving them a sermon. The Sermon on the Mount is the teaching of the disciples, which would become their source of guidance as ministers of the Gospel, following Jesus' death, resurrection, and ascension. Therefore, Jesus taught his followers not to waste time offering that that is sacred to those who have no appreciation for anything considered sacred.

In this instruction to the disciples, Mark remembered Jesus saying, "A prophet is not without honor except in his hometown and among his own relatives and in his own household." (Mark 6:4) Jesus then followed that statement with his commission to the disciples (apostles), giving them this limitation, "Any place that does not receive you or listen to you, as you go out from there, shake the dust off the soles of your feet for a testimony against them." (Mark 6:11)

Later, Mark recounted how Jesus told them on the Mount of Olives, across from the Temple, "But be on your guard; for they will deliver you to the courts, and you will be flogged in the synagogues, and you will stand before governors and kings for My sake, as a testimony to them. The gospel must first be preached to all the nations. When they arrest you and hand you over, do not worry beforehand about what you are to say, but say whatever is given you in that hour; for it is not you who speak, but it is the Holy Spirit. Brother will betray brother to death, and a father his child; and children will rise up against parents and have them put to death. You will be hated by all because of My name, but the one who endures to the end, he will be saved." (Mark 13:9-13)[14] This is repeating the instruction not to give that which is holy to the unholy, with the unholy being here identified as those one might expect to be holy, through association and relationship.

The Prophecies, as a holy document, could not be entrusted to a time that could not possibly understand its holiness. Thus, it was named as divine, but made unintelligible. Even though the royals and the Church were dedicated to connecting with God, in order to guide the masses, they too could be moved to rise up against something they could not explain. This means those who would have seemed to be the most trustworthy at that time, simply because they would not be capable of protecting its truth for centuries, could have destroyed Nostradamus' holy work inadvertently. God would have to be the protector, with the holy document enduring until its true time of need, when saving souls will be most important.

God's protection, through the direction of the Spirit of Jesus Christ, was to make the holy document appear non-threatening. While the title told the non-religious (the *dogs*) it was a divine document (*The Prophecies*), they remained sleeping dogs lying, not recognizing the title as saying anything more than, The Predictions Based on Astrology. They simply cannot sense the religious when it is inconspicuously under their noses, anymore than a dog can sense the differences in values between gold and coal.

The swine are those who certainly know such valuations; and they are those willing to trample and rend to make such nuggets of value their own. To them, the hint of divination in the title of Nostradamus' work leads them to sniff continually around rock-hard "oysters", trying to get at the potential "pearl" inside. However, the difficulties posed by the verses of *The Prophecies* having been written in a language thought to be prose, in a random format that hides the true contextual meaning, with all keeping them from seeing the source as holy, the swine have been forever faced with the prospect of finding those oysters of Nostradamus impossible to crack.

The truth, which is the pearls of true wisdom the quatrains hold, has been tightly locked away. Those coveting personal gain (the *swine* seeking to solve the mysteries of seeing the future) have stomped on the shells throughout 450 years of history. Because God was the protector, everything written by Nostradamus (save about 50 censured presages, which were most probably designed to be lost) has been

14   New American Standard Bible Version, http://www.biblegateway.com/passage/?search=Mark%20 13;&version=49;

saved. God has saved it because it is for our benefit now; and all the attention given to *The Prophecies* over the years has kept the spirit alive until now.

This use of a quote recited by Matthew, attributed to Jesus, answers the question, "Why can one not easily see the truth contained in *The Prophecies*, if they are indeed a warning from God?" The answer calls for evidence from Nostradamus that the truth can and will be seen, before the time of destruction is upon humankind. Since this Latin quote is just one of many biblical references, all of which add more detail to assist us in obtaining this answer, we have only to look to the next use of Latin in the Preface.

Shortly after Nostradamus wrote the Matthew verse in Latin, he wrote these words, also in Latin: "*Abscondisti haec à sapientibus, & prudentibus, id est potentibus & regibus, & enucleasti ea exiguis & tenuibus*". This Latin statement is said to be reminiscent of a biblical lesson in Luke 10:21, which says: "*Thou has hid these things from the wise and prudent and has revealed them unto babes*". In actuality, the Latin Vulgate of that full verse states, "*terrae quod **abscondisti haec a sapientibus et prudentibus et revelasti ea parvulis etiam**,*" making Nostradamus' statement remind us of that Luke quote, while adding details that differ from that scripture. The details added will be specific to the future he saw. The Latin Nostradamus stated says fully (literal translation), "*Hidden this from the wise, & prudent & rulers, & explained in detail to small extents & slight*".

This states precisely how Nostradamus presented *The Prophecies* in publication, including his letter of Preface, as well as the subsequent explanation letter to Henri II. Just as we read in Daniel 5:8, in reference to the writing on the wall, "Then all the king's wise men came in, but they could not read the inscription or make known its interpretation to the king", we see how the truth of the quatrains is *hidden from* the greatest thinkers surrounding the highest *rulers*. This includes the King of France and the Pope, and all those who are employed because of their intellectual acumen.

The statements made in the Preface (and later the letter to Henri) make *The Prophecies explained in detail to small extents*. In order to grasp the fuller meaning, one has to recognize the importance of a *small amount* (a definition of *slight*). This is a minimalist concept, where less is more; or, in other words, where what is seemingly *unimportant* (alternate translation of *tenuibus*) becomes profound. This then takes us to the passage from which yields the answer to our question, with Jesus saying, "*has revealed them unto babes.*"

The context of the verse in Luke (10:21) is after the successful initial travels of the seventy chosen disciples, sent out in pairs because of the Great Commission assigned to them by Jesus. They returned, reporting their happy news; but Jesus told them, "Behold, I have given you authority to tread on serpents and scorpions, and over all the power of the enemy, and nothing will injure you. Nevertheless do not rejoice in this, that the spirits are subject to you, but rejoice that your names are recorded in heaven. At that very time He rejoiced greatly in the Holy Spirit, and said, "I praise You, O Father, Lord of heaven and earth, that You have hidden these things from the wise and intelligent and have revealed them to infants. Yes, Father, for this way was well-pleasing in Your sight."[15]

I hope that you can see that *The Prophecies* has been sent out with authority, such that nothing could injure it. While there have been those who have rejoiced at the success of finding accuracy in one (or a scattered few) of the quatrains, the ultimate truth has been left unknown. That discovery waits until the time of the final revelation. Those who will ultimately be able to see the full glory that this holy document offers will not be great minded scholars, but *babes* or *infants* who simply place their faith in Jesus Christ, allowing for a connection to heaven, which will fill them with the Holy Spirit so they can see the power of prophecy. The answers to the full meaning of *The Prophecies* will come to those whose names are written in heaven; and they will be the disciples that will make the prophetic warning known to all (including the dogs and swine).

When we realize that this biblical reference is preceded by the statement written in French, "*the total written under figure nebulous, more that from the whole prophetic*", we see how the Latin details the nebulosity faced by both the *wise & prudent*. This statement gives us the obvious, as everyone knows the quatrains are like imagining shapes in a fog. The question that surrounds *The Prophecies* to this day is whether or not they are true Prophecies or calculated predictions. Certainly, a long line of *wise and prudent* scholars of Nostradamus have not been able to remove the clouds of uncertainty.

Nostradamus then buffered this French statement with another, stating, "*how many that*," before presenting us with the Latin words reminding us of the Luke quote. The *how many that* statement is not a question. It is a statement of the sheer number of *prophetic* verses that make up the *whole* of *The Prophecies*. While *all*, as one, is *prophetic*, the *whole* was originally 1,000 individual verses. If *everything* is *prophetic*, each one is a true prophecy. As such, *how many that* is stating that the number *that* will be seen *prophetic* depends on what remains *hidden from* typical applications of riddle solving *wisdoms*.

In fact, the Latin quote used by Luke, "*abscondisti haec à sapientibus*," not only can mean, *hidden from the wise*, but also morphs into a statement saying, "*concealed [within] this a wisdom*". Therefore, it states that *The Prophecies* is a sane work, full of rationale, discretely rationed, and found through sound judgment. All of this comes from the full scope of meaning found in the word *sapientis*. How much of *that* rationale will be found in the poems and letter(s) is perhaps not best left up to the *prudent*, as much as up to those who will be *aware* and *farseeing*, which are other acceptable translations of the word *prudentis*.

Earlier, I presented this segment of words as evidence that Nostradamus was confirming he had truly written a Prophecy. In that presentation, I mentioned that it was *written under [a] figure nebulous*, which I saw as a statement of Nostradamus encountering the Spirit of Jesus Christ. Therefore, *everything written*

---

15   New American Standard Bible, http://www.biblegateway.com/passage/?search=Luke%2010

The Biblical References from the Latin

comes from the mind of God. However, now I can open up other possibilities for this same statement.

The French word written by Nostradamus, *figure*, can also translate to state *figurative*. As such, *everything [was] written beneath [a] figurative cloud*, which means there is the allowance for symbolism, metaphor, and figures of speech, all of which create the atmosphere of nebulosity, as puzzles and riddles. This is a perfect match for the use of poetic verse, because with poetic verse comes poetic license. This was, in fact, the delight of Nostradamus' yearly almanacs, because the people loved being teased with having to solve something enigmatic.

While the yearly almanacs were fairly easy riddles and puzzles to solve, the quatrains of *The Prophecies* were beyond comprehension. Simply by name recognition, due to Nostradamus' popularity, copies of *The Prophecies* were bought and read by those of position and education. Certainly, the greatest minds of France and the Roman Catholic Church struggled to get *more from* those new riddles, finding *that* nebulosity impossible to wade through.

Still, in the Preface Nostradamus is making the statement that *more* is possible to be found *from the figurative and nebulous*, than what one finds when reading the words as a restricted form of prose. Once one realizes how to get *more from the nebulous*, one will begin to see more clearly the wholeness of the quatrains. A sense of wholeness leads invariably to the conclusion that there is method to the madness, with everything simply out of place. Once the quatrains have been revealed as in need of reordering into *the whole* form they originally took, *all*, individually and collectively, becomes *prophetic*.

This is a prediction that the prophecy will be known, which is why the Latin states, *"explained in detail to small extents & slights"*. In reference to why *The Prophecies* had to be kept from the *dogs* and *swine*, this says who will have the true meaning *explained* to them. Those who are far from the *rulers* of the world, who are *small* in their scope of power and control over others, and who have strong faith in Jesus and the one God, they will be the ones who will see the truth, in small amounts. Once their faith has allowed them to be filled with the Holy Spirit, they will see *the whole prophetic*.

Still, the same Latin segment yields the meaning that *The Prophecies* can be *explained in detail* by grasping what Nostradamus wrote, a little at a time. This discussion I offer now about one particular usage of Latin in the Preface. Just as all such uses I have already offered and others I will present later, this is only a *small extent* of the totality of what was written. However, when one is connected to heaven and able to understand, *detail* becomes the result, where others have seen little more than generalities.

Another *small extent of detail is explained* when one reads what Nostradamus follows his Latin statement, writing, *"to the Prophets by the medium of God immortal"*. Once again it becomes clear that Nostradamus is explaining *The Prophecies* has been given an apt title. When *the whole* has been truly revealed as *prophetic*, the distinction removes any possibility of them being the result of human calculation. Nostradamus has been inspired by the same source understood to have come *to* all *the Prophets*. As such, a *Prophet* acts as a middle man, or *medium*, receiving a message from *God*. The Spirit of Jesus Christ, as the one at the right hand of *God*, is the annointed Savior of humanity; and Jesus was with *God* at the beginning, as well as at the end (the Alpha and the Omega), being *immortal*.

Soon after Nostradamus penned this Latin quote, reminiscent of Luke 10:21, he wrote another statement in Latin. There, he wrote, "*Quia non est nostrum noscere tempora, nec momenta & c.*" This comes from the book telling of the Acts of the Apostles, in chapter one, verse seven. That verse reads in the Latin Vulgate, "*dixit autem eis* **non est** *vestrum* **nosse tempora** *vel* **momenta** *quae Pater posuit in sua potestate*," which is translated in the King James Version to state, "And he said unto them, **It is not** for you **to know the times** or **the seasons**, which the Father hath put in his own power."

This quote, again coming from Jesus, explains why nebulosity was important, while also supporting why clarity of holiness should not be given to *dogs* and *swine*. It clearly states that it is not up to human beings to figure out the future on their own. Only God knows the future; but God has not only the power to know, He has the power to let human beings share in that knowledge, at His discretion. Thus, Nostradamus was not producing a book of astrological calculations, because it was *not* for him *to know* such answers; but it also states that God chose Nostradamus as a messenger allowed such knowledge.

If you will take note, Nostradamus ended this string of Latin words with a single letter, followed by a period. There has been speculation that *c.* stands for etcetera, meaning the rest of the verse should be recalled, which implies Nostradamus reached a point of laziness and decided to abbreviate the conversation of Jesus Christ. The reality is that *c.* is a Latin abbreviation for *centum*, meaning "one hundred".

When one looks for the literal translation possibilities of *Quia non est nostrum noscere tempora, nec momenta*, it becomes possible to see a better meaning in the abbreviation that follows. Literally, Nostradamus wrote, "*because not is ours to get to know times, and not moments* (or *turning points in time*)," which becomes a way of saying history has always been known for repeating some of its moments, from time to time. A clock is circular because the hands of time always spiral towards the future. With this understanding, the abbreviation representing "hundreds" of moments and events will be mirrored in both the past and the future. Only God knows the minute details of those specific events to come that will be important enough to pass on to mankind beforehand.

Still, if we understand that the Spirit of Jesus knew an abbreviation would be misread as saying, "yada yada yada, and the rest of this verse," it becomes important to look into that statement attributed to Jesus in the Book of Acts, in order to get a greater understanding of Nostradamus' meaning in the Preface. This means the context of a statement stating why not to worry or fret over how one will recognize an important time in the future should give more insight.

This yields the answer of when and how that insight will arrive. In verse eight, Jesus stated the exception to this restriction on who has the power to know the times. He said, "but you will receive power when the Holy Spirit has come upon you" (Acts 1:8a)[16]. This is the same Holy Spirit that came upon the disciples at Pentecost, allowing them to speak languages they had never learned, and know explanations for things they had never deeply pondered. In other words, being able to know the future that God showed Nostradamus, through His Son Jesus, means the reader must be a disciple of Christ and chosen by God to receive the spirit.

Surrounding this Latin quote from the Book of Acts, Nostradamus led up to it by writing, "*As for us who concludes humans not able of nothing from our natural understanding, & leaning towards from craft* (or *deceit*) *to know of the hidden matters obstructions of God the creator*". Following his biblical quote, where Jesus told the disciples, "the Father has fixed [knowledge of future time] by His own authority," (Acts 1:7b)[17] Nostradamus continued to write, "*How much that also to present being able to happen & to be persons* (or *players*) *that God the creator has willed* (or *intended*) *to reveal through imaginations impressions*".

As one can easily see from this flow of thoughts, Nostradamus begins by saying human beings have natural limits, as far as seeing the future. We can have some abilities to predict the future with reason (use of one's mind), but most things that are out of the ordinary, that happen in our lives on occasion, these are beyond our abilities to see them coming. Therefore, when someone does go beyond *natural understanding* it is believed to be through the use of tools, or *crafts* such as astrology, or even through the *crafts* of computer-based modeling, which can yield very accurate weather predictions (and more). At those times, people assume "prophecy" means "calculated prediction." However, God keeps the future hidden from us to see who will live a good life as a blind believer, as well as to see who will take advantage of others that are blind.

How much of the future will be revealed by God to those worthy of heavenly assistance is not for us to know either. As far as *The Prophecies* is concerned, if the stories of events that make up the epic tale have nothing to do with someone's *present*, there is no need for that person to know of a future beyond their time. However, for those who will be *players* or actors in the playing out of this future, Nostradamus was shown that some will be led by God to get *impressions* in their minds, which will generate new and out of the box ideas of what the future should hold. This would include an inventive way to understand the riddles in Nostradamus' works.

A key element of having the future written of in *The Prophecies* is that it will become relevant to one's *present*. The future that was shown to Nostradamus in 1555 is now a part of the past. If the *present* has

---

16   American Standard Bible Version, http://www.biblegateway.com/passage/?book_id=51&chapter=1&version=49
17   American Standard Bible Version, http://www.biblegateway.com/passage/?book_id=51&chapter=1&version=49

become part of what was future, the past is related to the cause that has led to that *present*. When one is allowed to see clearly the mistakes of the past, the solutions to the problems of the *present* and future are suddenly within our grasps, as a *natural understanding* for what needs to be done. This follows the *natural* pattern in life, where people learn from past mistakes. It is from knowledge of the past that we become capable of overcoming similar scenarios that could end in repeated mistakes in the future.

This is the value of a warning, especially a warning from God. Nostradamus twice referred to *God the creator*, never to God the destroyer. The purpose of a prophetic warning is to elicit a response that is within the *natural* abilities of humanity. Nostradamus has also referred to Jesus as our Savior. As such, Jesus is the Spirit of God that communicated the Prophecy of John, and the Prophecy of Nostradamus. The *obstructions of God* will last only as long as a *present* danger for the end of the world has not yet arrived. Once the time does come, *God will reveal* the meaning of *The Prophecies* (and also *The Revelation of John*), through *imaginations* and *impressions* that will not have occurred prior. Thus, while it is *not* for us *to know the times* to come, the Holy Spirit will open the eyes of some when the time has arrived.

This issue of time causes Nostradamus to write later in the Preface, "*quia omnia sunt nuda & aperta & c.*" This is not a pure quote, but the key words are found in Hebrews 4:13, which states in the Latin Vulgate, "*et non est ulla creatura invisibilis in conspectu eius* **omnia** *autem* **nuda** *et* **aperta sunt** *oculis eius ad quem nobis sermo*".[18] That quote reads, "And there is no creature hidden from His sight, but **all** things **are open** and **laid bare** to the eyes of Him with whom we have to do."[19]

The element of time is then found in the French that leads up to this biblical reference. In those words Nostradamus stated, "*in presence of who the three times are comprised through eternity, a circular return* (or *revolution*) *holding in the cause past, present, & future*". This states the principle that the causes of the present and future are found in the past, as those are the *three times* that *comprise* all times. Further, the *revolution* of time means what has happened before will happen again, and again, and so on. Most importantly, it is the *future* Jesus spread out before Nostradamus, where *all causes were opened and laid bare* to see. We cannot possibly recognize that *future* until it has been allowed to become *comprised of the three times*, as one story with a *past, present,* and most importantly a *future*.

Once again, Nostradamus repeated the use of a *c.* at the end of his quote. This means that "hundreds" of times were exposed to him, appearing in the hundreds of quatrains. Still, when *c.* has an implied the meaning of "etcetera," urging one to read the full context of the Hebrews verse, we find chapter nine telling of the need for rest.

God has commanded the Sabbath be kept as a day of rest; but there will be some who will disobey this

---

18   Biblios.com, http://biblos.com/hebrews/4-13.htm
19   New American Standard Bible, http://www.biblegateway.com/passage/?book_id=65&chapter=4&version=49

law. Paul wrote in his letter, "Therefore let us be diligent to enter that rest, so that no one will fall". (Hebrews 4:11a)[20] God knows of all disobedience because He is, "able to judge the thoughts and intentions of the heart." (Hebrews 4:12b)[21] This context of the *past* is stating the signs of those *future* times in *The Prophecies*. Disobedience to God will rule the day.

Still, all is not lost. When we read to the end of chapter four, Paul offers that through Jesus, "we do not have a high priest who cannot sympathize with our weaknesses, but One who has been tempted in all things as we are, yet without sin." From confessing faith in Jesus, realizing the sins we too often fall prey to, Paul advised, "Therefore let us draw near with confidence to the throne of grace, so that we may receive mercy and find grace to help in time of need." Therefore, Nostradamus is telling the reader to realize every sin is exposed before God. To avoid our demise in that time of need, we have to seek higher help.

Part of that higher help comes to us from Nostradamus. God and Jesus Christ have foreseen a need for help in our times. Therefore, a Prophet was chosen to deliver *The Prophecies* that have the power to open our eyes to a real and *present* danger. From that basic awareness, positive changes can result. The most positive would be the complete avoidance of the End Times, and all the calamity that is said to bring. Of course, for such miracles to be in our future, people need to stop thinking Nostradamus was crafty with predictive tools, and start believing he was a chosen Prophet of the one true God.

At some theme amusement parks, there is an attraction to small children where someone operating a hand puppet makes the children believe that lifeless character knows all about them. The puppet appears to be telling them secret information, like their names and age, who their mommy is, and how their day has gone. In reality, one of the parents is standing by a separate booth, telling the person who is the voice of the puppet everything the puppet knows. This is then communicated to the child using closed-circuit televisions, cameras, and microphones that allow the "puppet" to see and talk. The child is thoroughly amazed by this.

Such tricks have the effect of initiating false beliefs that later turn into disbeliefs when the child grows up and realizes it has been fooled. Adults become wise to how easily tricks can be played on them, leading to belief no longer being something freely given. That lack of childlike faith is where the disobedience comes from, which we found noted in Paul's letter to the Hebrews. Without faith, there can be no rest; and no rest makes one disobedient to God. We have to have faith that Nostradamus was truly a Prophet of Jesus Christ.

Along this line of thought, where doubts have jaded modern man away from belief in either crafty predictors or Prophets, Nostradamus again wrote in his voice of Christ (Latin), stating, "*propheta dicitur*

---

20 New American Standard Bible Version, BibleGateway.com, http://www.biblegateway.com/passage/?book_id=65&chapter=4&version=49

21 Ibid

hodie, olim vocabatur videns". This is a near verbatim quote, from a portion of a verse found in the Hebrew book I Samuel. The verse, as completely stated in the Latin Vulgate, reads: "*olim in Israhel sic loquebatur unusquisque vadens consulere Deum venite et eamus ad videntem qui enim propheta dicitur hodie vocabatur olim videns*."[22] This translates to say, "Formerly in Israel, when a man went to inquire of God, he used to say, 'Come, and let us go to the seer'; for he who is called **a prophet now was formerly called a seer**."[23]

This quote found in I Samuel is read like an aside (some translations separate it in parentheses) in the narration of Saul going to find the prophet Samuel, because he needs help finding some lost donkeys. Once Saul finds Samuel, Samuel anoints Saul as the first King of Israel, much to Saul's surprise, telling Saul the donkeys have been found already. Samuel did this sacred act by instruction from God, who talked directly to Samuel. The part quoted by Nostradamus is a holy statement that confirms Nostradamus is related to Samuel. Both are true Prophets of God, meaning they were allowed to know the future, as spoken to them to know.

We get a better feel for this being a holy confirmation when we read the French text that leads up to the remembrance of verbiage in I Samuel. In those words, Nostradamus conveyed, "*For all that my son that I have implied the name of prophet, I not myself looks to attribute title of such high stateliness for the times present, because which **a prophet it is said today, was formerly called a seer***".

Here we see that Nostradamus explained the implication that the title of his work, *The Prophecies*, was a self-designation as a *prophet*. His further explanation that he did not seek to have such a lofty title placed upon him is a testament of his book not being by his own design. We get the feel that Nostradamus is reluctant to hold such a title; but the reality is the statement explains that he will not be seen truly as a *Prophet* until some time in the distant future, because nothing will be fulfilled in the *present*.

Still, the literal translation of the Latin, which is slightly different from the biblical quote, is a testament to the status Nostradamus enjoyed as an astrologer. His almanacs had been so highly accurate that the people had already taken to calling Nostradamus a prophet. While that meant *a prophet it is said today*, the understanding of what a prophet truly was had been lost. The easy interchange between prophet and predictor had already removed the *high stateliness of such title* as *prophet*.

As was the point in I Samuel, in reference to the early days of Saul's reign, ending Israel's direction by judges, there had already come a shift in the distinction of what to call someone directly connected to God. In the days of Moses, the Israelites were led by the one most holy, who talked directly with God in the tent of meeting. Moses' face would glow after these meetings, showing the people he had seen God. Moses was a *seer* who had seen God, in order to be shown an answer to a problem. However, in times after Moses, under Joshua and the judges, no high priests of the Tabernacle warranted being *called*

22   Biblios.com, http://biblos.com/1_samuel/9-9.htm
23   New American Standard Bible, http://bible.cc/1_samuel/9-9.htm

a seer. Thus, even Samuel, who God talked freely with, was seen as a step lower, being a mere *prophet*.

The important point to grasp in all of this is belief. This has been dwindling ever since God first made a covenant with Abraham. By the time Israel anointed its first king in Saul, there was already a level of disbelief, where high priests were crafty, more than directly linked to God. Israel would later split into two nations, as a further disintegration of belief. Israel and Judah would be lost because of the disobedience Paul wrote of to the Hebrews. Today we have only the belief that prophets existed long ago. This is because we have become almost completely lost. It is time to regain faith in God's ability to speak directly to man, at whatever time God chooses as necessary; and it is time to see Nostradamus' title being deemed worthy.

In reference to this time of importance, Nostradamus wrote a verbatim quote of part of Psalm 104, which states in the Latin Vulgate, "*non inclinabitur in saeculum saeculi.*" The whole of verse five states, "*Qui fundasti terram super stabilitatem suam:* **non inclinabitur in sæculum sæculi**", which says fully, "Who hast founded the earth upon its own bases: **it shall not be moved for ever and ever**."(Psalm 104:5)[24] As far as this quote relates to the true Prophecy in *The Prophecies*, and just like David wrote in this song about the power of God the creator of Earth, unlike God the Earth will not last *forever*.

In the French that leads Nostradamus up to this reminder of David's psalm, we see that he wrote, "*where the great God eternal will hold to make an absolute end of* (or *to accomplish*) *the circular return* (or *revolution*): *where the resemblances* (or *images*) *celestials will be coming back with themselves to provoke, & the moving higher who we give back* (or *return*) *the earth stable* (or *immovable*) *& constant*". This paints a picture of man's time on Earth having run full circle.

In the segment, "*where the resemblances celestials will be coming back with themselves to provoke,*" we have both a statement of Genesis and The Revelation. In Genesis, where it states, "Then God said, 'Let Us make man in Our image, according to Our likeness'" (Genesis 1:26a), this makes Man the *resemblances* of *celestials*, with the French word *celeste* also translating as, "divine." These *celestials* represent heavenly angels, which are seen when we read, "Then the angel whom I saw standing on the sea and on the land lifted up his right hand to heaven, and swore by Him who lives forever and ever, who created heaven and the things in it, and the earth and the things in it, and the sea and the things in it, that there will be delay no longer, but in the days of the voice of the seventh angel, when he is about to sound, then the mystery of God is finished, as He preached to His servants the prophets." (Revelation 10:5-7)[25] The *celestials will be coming back* at that time, *with* the seals having been broken, allowing *themselves to provoke* harm to humanity on earth.

---

24   Parallel Latin/English Psalter, Psalm 103 [Greek] (104 [Masoretic]), http://www.medievalist.net/psalm-stxt/ps103.htm

25   New American Standard Bible , BibleGateway.com, http://www.biblegateway.com/passage/?book_id=73&chapter=10&version=49

The segment that reads, *"we give back the earth stable,"* we can understand that Nostradamus is saying Man will be the cause of the instabilities that will bring about the return of *celestials*, whom mankind had acted *to provoke*. Still, with Man out of the picture, *the earth* becomes *stable & constant* again, which leads Nostradamus to speak for Jesus, *"it shall not be moved for ever and ever."* Nostradamus then followed that quote with more French, stating, *"out of brought that when his to mind will be finished."*

When Nostradamus wrote the word *that*, he was referring back to the Latin quote prior, referring to the *for ever and ever* part of the Psalms quote. It must be noted that the translation used, saying *saeculum saeculi* means "for ever and ever," is another of those limiting choices drawn from multiple possibilities. Various versions of the Bible translate those words to say, "age to age", or "forever and ever", or simply pared down to "never". The combination, *in saeculum*, is commonly used to state, "forever". However, the words *saeculum* and *saeculi* are different tenses of the same word, with one possible translation for both being, "worldliness". A slight variation (*saecularis*) brings about the meaning, "secular, of world not church, gentile". In fact, with no spelling changes both words can represent, "the world; time: past, present, and future (thus forever); and, heathenism".

As such, *that* of which Nostradamus referred to, *out of* which will be *brought* from the Earth, is *that* future form of humanity that will have ruined its time here. In that sense, *his* can then represent the collective being, man. As the opposite to *his* the Creator, we then see *his to mind* translating as *his to will* (acceptable alternative translation of *vouloir*), referring to man's gift of free *will*. The reason man will be removed from earth will be *his* complete addiction to *worldliness*, as well as a lust for the secular allowances that make it easier *to will* against serving God. When man no longer fears God enough to abide by God's *Will*, man is *finished*.

As harsh as this sounds, let us return to the quote I presented as evidence for the infallibility of *The Prophecies* only being possible if from God. There I showed Nostradamus quoting from Ezekiel, even if the quote was not verbatim. The Latin words written by Nostradamus were, "*Conteram ego & confringam, & non miserebor*", which literally translates to say, "*I will see destroyed* (or *crushed*) *& I will see broken to pieces, & not feeling pity.*" This is close enough to the context of Ezekiel, which says, "because thou hast defiled my sanctuary with all thy detestable things, and with all thine abominations, therefore **will I** also **diminish thee**; neither shall mine eye spare, **neither will I have** any **pity**." (KJV, Ezekiel 5:11)[26]

This means that Nostradamus was leading us to understand the nature of *The Prophecies*, as a parallel Prophecy to the one Ezekiel was sent to Israel with, after their defeat and exile in Babylon. In the verse that follows the one Nostradamus reminded us of, Ezekiel wrote, "A third part of thee shall die with the pestilence, and with famine shall they be consumed in the midst of thee: and a third part shall fall by the sword round about thee; and I will scatter a third part into all the winds, and I will draw out a sword after them." (Ezekiel 11:6)[27] This is the same story that is found in the quatrains, when they are placed in the

[26] Biblos.com, http://bible.cc/ezekiel/5-11.htm
[27] King James Bible Version, Biblos.com, http://bible.cc/ezekiel/5-12.htm

right order. It is also similar to the promise made in The Revelation, especially relative to the effects coming from the first three horsemen.

In other words, Nostradamus is saying that his story of the future matches The Revelation, and it matches Ezekiel. In fact, if you can find any place in the Bible that tells, through a Prophet, what God will see happen to those who have turned their backs on God, you can count on that equally being applicable to the tales of *The Prophecies*. It makes God as consistent as a mathematical law. If you put one with one, you will always come up with two. If you subtract one from one, you always come up with zero. No amount of wishing will change the results.

Nostradamus was shown the end of mankind, which will be brought on by mankind turning its back on God. This means the destruction, the crushing, and the breaking *into pieces* will be by the hand of man, not God. God will simply have *no pity* for a world filled with people who will have chosen selling souls, for temporary material gains, over a little self-sacrifice, for an eternity of bliss. Beside, it is not as if God did not give us prior warning. We have known of the end of the world coming since well before Nostradamus was born.

In reference to this self-destruction of humanity, Nostradamus made one more biblical quote to help us understand that our own actions will cause our punishment. Nostradamus wrote next in Latin, "*Visitabo in virga ferrea iniquitates eorum, & in verberibus percutiam eos*". This is very similar (almost verbatim) to the verse in Psalm 89 (Greek 88), which states, "**visitabo in virga iniquitates eorum, et in verberibus peccata eorum**", translated to say, "I will visit their inequities with a rod and their sins with stripes". (Psalm 89:33)[28] The usage of *stripes* has to be understood as meaning the marks left from a whipping, in this case from the aforementioned rod.

The meaning implied by the word *inequities* is captured from the verses in Psalm 89 that lead to this verse quoted by Nostradamus. David led up to this awakening of what *will* happen by writing, "If his children forsake my law and do not walk according to my rules, if they violate my statutes and do not keep my commandments," (Psalm 89:31-32)[29] then punishment will be justified. Other translations refer to both *inequities* and "transgressions," with others translating everything as "crimes". The point of this reminder of Psalm 89 is that judgment is based on actions, such that **if** something happens **then** a result will be fitting.

What has to be realized, as close as the quote is to what Nostradamus wrote, Nostradamus added one important word and changed the last two words to make different usage of the root words. What he wrote translates to literally state, "*I shall see often until a rod like iron injustices* (or *unevenesses*) *theirs, & beatings will be stricken until dawn*". This translation makes it more evident that God is only watching

---

28   English (Douay-Rheims), New Advent Bible, http://www.newadvent.org/bible/psa088.htm
29   English Standard Version, BibleGateway.com, http://www.biblegateway.com/passage/?search=Psalms%2089;&version=47;

mankind beat itself, rather than being the one inflicting it.

As close as Psalm 89:33 is to the quote from Nostradamus, the inclusion of the Latin word, *ferrea*, makes the beating come from a *rod of iron*. There are other biblical references to such a tool for punishment, including: "You shall break them with a rod of iron, You shall shatter them like earthenware." (Psalm 2:9); "and he shall rule them with a rod of iron, as the vessels of the potter are broken to shivers; as I also have received of my Father". (Revelation 2:27); and also, "From His mouth comes a sharp sword, so that with it He may strike down the nations, and He will rule them with a rod of iron; and He treads the wine press of the fierce wrath of God, the Almighty." (Revelation 19:15).

The one quote from The Revelation is reminiscent of when Isaiah wrote, "therefore this iniquity shall be to you like a breach in a high wall, bulging out, and about to collapse, whose breaking comes suddenly, in an instant; and its breaking is like that of a potter's vessel that is smashed so ruthlessly that among its fragments not a shard is found with which to take fire from the hearth, or to dip water out of the cistern." (Isaiah 30:13-14) While not stating as much, it could be assumed that a potter's pot would not be so broken without the use of a hard instrument. The point is Nostradamus inserted one word that took mankind's self-inflicted flogging to the harshest extreme, by the use of an *iron rod*, versus a wooden staff.

As such, there is somewhat of a paradox in the Latin word *"virga,"* which is used to denote *rod*." The Hebrew word, "שבט," is written as "bshbt," and it translates as "rod, stick." This same Hebrew word also represents the fifth Hebrew month of the year, "Shebat." The minor Jewish holiday that occurs on the 15th of Shebat is "B'Shebat" (bshbt); and this word (name) is then translated to say, "The New Year of the Trees." Thus, both the Latin word *virga* and the Hebrew word *bshbt* can also mean, "a green twig."

When one realizes this possibility in translation, the Psalm 89 quote then can state, "I will visit their inequities with a switch and their sins with stripes." This becomes a punishment typical of a father to a child, where the marks are the reddening of the skin from being whipped with a branch from a young tree (i.e. a switch). The use of a switch to teach a child what not to do, or to bring about the *dawn* of awareness they need to learn, is then the meaning behind the saying, "spare the rod spoil the child." Too often, we get caught up in the *rod* being seen as an unjust form of punishment, because a switch is far from our minds.

This makes David's quote in Psalm 89 become a metaphor for how God will bring the children of Israel back into their adherence to the covenant they had with God. David followed that verse telling of the result for violations of the commandments, by stating, "My covenant I will not violate, Nor will I alter the utterance of My lips." (Psalm 89:34)[30] This says God will do nothing more than teach his children the lesson of a Father, not whip them *until dawn with a rod of iron*.

---

30   New American Standard Bible Version, Biblos.com, http://bible.cc/psalms/89-34.htm

Nostradamus wrote that God would witness *often* the *injustices*, or the *unevenness* with which mankind would mimic such fatherly teachings. *Theirs* would not be with flimsy green twigs. Instead, the humanity of Nostradamus' future would be who was seen to administer justice with *a rod like iron*. It does not take much for the imagination to see the imbalance of powers that exist in the world today mirroring this unevenness. A current issue is over the rights of smaller nations to gain nuclear power capabilities, since the major powers wield this mighty sword as a great advantage. The *injustices* of this *uneven* ability of a few to administer the threat of punishment on those whose military arsenals compare as *green twigs* to *rods of iron*, is equally seen by the eyes of God.

In this sense, the prophecy of Nostradamus is that man's greatest power to administer justice will become the weapon that will turn the tables and beat everyone in the world. The powers of modern weapons have become that destructive in scope. For them to be unleashed there will certainly be a realization (or dawning) that *inequities* (or unfairness) will never be tolerated by God. If weapons of mass destruction are sought by the weak for equality's sake, God will not keep them from finding what they seek. Of course, this will mean God no longer protects any nation that abused power.

Man has forever tried to get an advantage over others, particularly by inventing new weapons. Such inventiveness has always had the initial effect of establishing an unfair advantage for one group, and making those without the advantage come under the domination of the one with the advantage. However, such imbalances are temporary. God knows who is disadvantaged; and it is those who can be led to find ways to even the playing field.

This becomes the meaning of, "*beatings will be stricken until dawn*." Mankind will never be able to keep one group in power over any other groups through the administration of severe *beatings*. Those who beat others with more than a green twig or switch *will* themselves *be stricken* equally as hard, in return. Justice will always prevail in the long run; but *until* this awareness comes to *dawn* on the leaders of the world, the world will always face the destructive powers that come from the minds of men willing to invent evil.

The return of Jesus, as is depicted in The Revelation, when the rule of *the rod of iron* will be administered over an earth gone badly wrong, will signal an end for the possibility for the dawning of awareness. The future shown to Nostradamus features the *dawn* of the End Times. Jesus is the light, and while Jesus brought the light of a new way to the people of the earth, that light will have flickered and dimmed before His return. This means Jesus will return to a world in darkness, unable to comprehend the instructions Jesus left during His first time on earth.

The simple message of Jesus was first to love God above all other gods, including the material idols that so many worship. The word, "worship," is defined as an addiction to something that cannot be ceased. The second instruction was for everyone to treat their neighbors as humanely as they themselves would wish to be treated by others. Obviously, when movie stars and athletes become idolized, and when genocidal war is somehow justified as something best not interfered with, and when all the world's problems are blamed on religion, neither of Christ's instructions will be seen as followed.

All such peaceful and loving natures of man will have been lost when the end is near. Therefore, Jesus will return as the *dawn* of a new day of enlightenment. However, this new *dawn* will be the realization that a time of punishment for past actions has come. Karmic debt will have to be paid then, because all lines of spiritual credit will have been shut down.

This is the meaning of the Latin quote made by Nostradamus. Leading up to this meaning, he wrote in French, *"that the mortal sword drawn near to us for assured by plague, war more horrible than in life of three men not had been, & hunger* (or *famine*), *such will fall on earth, & it will return often, because the planets agreeing with the accomplishment of a circular course: & presaged in saying"*. This talk of *sword drawn*, *plague*, *war*, and *famine*, confirms the *rod of iron* parallel in his Latin quote to those in The Revelation. Nostradamus is telling us of the Four Horsemen and their effect on the world. Both Prophecies had the same divine source.

Added to the Latin stating the future being about the most severe beating mankind could ever unleash upon itself, Nostradamus followed that quote by writing, *"because the mercy* (or *pity*) *of the lord not will be the dawning dispersed one time my son"*. This is explaining the Latin quote ending, such that the *beatings until dawn* will not cease due to *pity*, which makes it match the Ezekiel quote, which ended, "*I will not have any pity.*" This means there will be no tears shed for the loss of humankind. A sentence of death will be just, befitting the crime committed.

This lack of *mercy* in the tale's ending is the last use of Latin representing biblical parallels. The story the quatrains of Nostradamus tell is one of a great demise, which we find mirrored in the biblical Latin of the Preface. However, this is not the final use of Latin in the Preface.

In fact, it was shortly after the biblical quote telling of a whipping that Nostradamus wrote the Latin idiom *in solute oratione*, which I have discussed prior. That statement in Latin, amid segments of French, stated how *The Prophecies* had to be read, in order to understand this tale of horrific ending. Once it could be read *in unrestricted style of speech* the quatrains would all be found coming true *infallibly*.

Shortly after that instruction in Latin, Nostradamus wrote his final Latin statement in the Preface, representing the voice of Jesus Christ. As the Preface is ending, we read, "*sed quando submovenda erit ignorantia,*" which translates to say, "*but at the time when removal will be ignorance*". This certainly appears to be saying that *at the time when* life on earth will be finding its death sentence enacted upon itself, through the *removal* of mankind, the reason *will be ignorance* of God's Law. It *will be ignorance* of the ways taught by Jesus of Nazareth. However, there is another way to read these same Latin words, coming away with a different meaning.

Three of the words have alternate translations. First, the statement begins with the conjunction *but*, which is a word that states there is an exception to be considered. This exception is relative to the last French word written, before the Latin. That word is (in French) *intelligences*, which means the same as the English. Since this Latin statement ends with the word (in Latin) *ignorantia*, meaning ignorance, it becomes easy to get a feel that the *but* is pointing to two meanings for *ignorance*.

Second, the word *submovenda* does not cleanly translate as *removal*, since "to remove" comes from the word, "*removere*". We have the possibility of two words being combined, yielding a different meaning. While *movenda* has the meaning, "to move", as to arouse, to influence, and to affect, the *sub* prefix makes it closer to "submovere," which does mean, "to remove". However, the *sub-* prefix is not as common as the re-, meaning it could be possible to read the words as, "*close to influence,*" or "*underlying affect.*"

Finally, the word *ignorance* needs to be fully defined. This is clearly stating a state of ignoring; but the definition defines the intent of *ignorance*. Three is purposeful *ignorance*, such as one knows the speed limit is 55, but instead drives 75. Then there is unintentional *ignorance*, where someone does not know what a norm is, and acts against that norm without being informed. Thus, *ignorance* is displayed on two levels of *intelligence*.

When these other translation possibilities are considered, we find Nostradamus is also stating, "**but** one needs to have the proper intelligence, **when the** end **time**s are sensed prior to their arrival through **underlying influence** felt from signs of prophetic warning, this sense **will be** from a **understanding**". The alternative would read, "**but** if one fails to put good intelligence to use, **at the time when** the end has come for the **removal** of man from the earth, there **will be** no quarter given for those pleading **ignorance**."

In this sense, the conjunction acting as an exception means an alternative exists. There will be an underlying urge to move; and this urge will come from understanding. As multiple *intelligences* will be sought (due to the plural use presented), these will be multiple forms of prophecy, including the *Holy Bible*, *The Prophecies*, and others that have been publicized on television. Since before the dawn of the 21st Century, the new millennium, there has been interests in seeking out old knowledge and coming up with new ideas to meaning. These new awarenesses are because what had been seen, but not understood (*ignorance*), will then be found to be a revelation (*removal of ignorance*). In other words, the horror of this tale of the end of the world is not inevitable, once understanding *moves one* to avoid this end.

In Nostradamus' French that leads to this final Latin statement we see a train of thought emerging. In the text that follows *in soluta oratione*, Nostradamus wrote, "*the adventures* (or *chance* events) *come to pass infallibly, like (we) have observed* (or *noted*) *through the others, speeches more clearly* (or *plainly*), *notwithstanding that under thick clouds being comprised them understandings*".

This is saying that those events that have already come true, as having *come to pass infallibly*, will be those that will show us how to read the *unrestricted speech*. This language will become clear through fully understanding the quatrains telling of that part of the future shown to Nostradamus that is now past. Unwanted dangers on the horizon will then be visible from learning how to read Nostradamus' *unrestricted speech*. Those quatrains telling of a future still to come will be recognizable as possible, if not probable.

Once that *style of speech* is mastered, it makes all of the quatrains *more clearly* understandable, such that everything makes sense *plainly*. Just as *in soluta oratione* can mean "in plain prose", once the *unlimited language* is understood everything can be converted into an expanded prose (paraphrase) that can be *clearly* understood. Understanding comes from taking the full scope of meanings into account.

The word *ignorance* is then realized to mean, "the state of ignoring," where "to ignore" is defined as, "a refusal to pay attention to; disregard."[31] This definition means everything required to understand has always been in front of our faces for inspection, but the obvious has been disregarded. As such, The Prophecies have been in a state that leads the readers to refuse to pay close attention to all possibilities of translation, with no focus on the literal, minimalist, non-syntactical representations the written words have always conveyed.

The result has been 450 years of *ignorance*, which will be *removed when the time* for knowing has arrived. This *removal of ignorance* will be the key element for any chance of survival. If man decides to remove its *ignorance* and realize Nostradamus wrote a true Prophecy, which warns of a need to change, the future can be averted. However, if man decides to maintain its *ignorance* and keep on heading towards its end, the *removal* will be from self-destruction.

Nostradamus then followed his last Latin statement with these words, in French: *"the reckoning of* (or *case) will be more clarified (or enlightened)."* This is an assurance that God will not allow mankind to destroy itself without first giving it ample opportunity to change. This change would include a renewal of the covenants made with God through the instructions of Jesus Christ. A renewal of the covenants acts as a protection to humanity if the people of the world are sincere.

The use of *"reckoning of"* then states the purpose of a Prophecy. In Old French, the word *"cas"* meant: "case, cause, matter, thing; also, a crime, offense; fact; also, esteem, account, reckoning of".[32] Each translation possibility fits this End Times scenario. The *case* (or *matter, cause, thing*) of discussion is the *thick clouds* (or *nebulosity*) covering *The Prophecies*. Those *thick clouds* have to be *removed* so *understandings* come forth. The *crime* (or *offense*) being discussed is the *ignorance* of God, and the

---

31 Free Online Dictionary, http://www.thefreedictionary.com/ignore
32 Randle Cotgrave's 1611 French-English Dictionary, http://www.pbm.com/~lindahl/cotgrave/search/1621.html

The Biblical References from the Latin

instructions of Jesus Christ. The *reckoning of* importance (or the *esteem, account*) that *will be more clarified* is the karmic debt built up, with the bank of reincarnation no longer being open for business. The purpose of a book named *The Prophecies*, which has a Preface that tells the reader it is about the Day of Reckoning, is to warn so necessary changes may occur. *More will be* understood about this *reckoning of* no more credit in the eyes of God when one has become *enlightened*.

At this point, I believe a review of what we have just read about the Latin usage of Nostradamus is most important. We have looked at the title of Nostradamus' work and found it obviously stating *The Prophecies*, and not "The Calculated Predictions." By definition, we see how it is possible Nostradamus entitled his work as such because he was indeed divinely inspired. This has led us to the Preface, where instead of reading it all we simply observed that Nostradamus wrote in two languages, French and Latin.

Looking at the Latin, we found that eight of twelve uses were reminiscent of biblical quotes. From that observation, we got the feel of a second voice emerging from the letter, one speaking with the authority of Jesus Christ. This was observable through the three quotes attributed to Jesus of Nazareth, with another quote very close to the prophecy told to John of Patmos, by the Spirit of Jesus Christ. The use of Latin can be seen as a higher voice working through the pen of Nostradamus.

- The Latin first defined the title as it explained that *prophecy* could *only* come from *divine will inspiring* a prophet.

- Second, the Latin explained that Nostradamus' Prophecy was infallible, because it was *unable to err* or mislead.

- Third, the Latin explained that the quatrains told a story of a need for bad people to be *broken to pieces*, without any *pity* coming from God.

- Fourth, the Latin explained that this story would not become evident until people began to realize its unusual *language* was *unrestricted*, with limits in *speech* making it impossible to see *the whole* being *infallibly written*.

- We next found Nostradamus stating the strange writing style was to protect Nostradamus, the document itself, and a world that would never need to know of a future beyond their lifetimes. As such, the wording made a true Prophesy invisible to *dogs*, while enticing to *swine*. The invisibility would keep it from being destroyed, while the enticement would keep the world knowing the name Nostradamus.

- The sixth Latin quote told us that the writing style would keep the message of *The Prophecies* hidden from the most *wise* of the world. Thinking would not be the key to understanding.

However, certain parts of the quatrains would be *explained in detail to small extents*. This meant that each quatrain *explained* an event *in detail*, while the words used were *small*, but once *extended* they added great *detail*.

- The seventh Latin quote told us that the future *was not ours to get to know* until the time that God deems it necessary for revelation, due to the future having arrived.

- The eighth Latin quote told us that when that future time did arrive it would become *naked & open* because all three times would comprise *The Prophecies*, past, present, and future.

- The ninth Latin quote told us that Nostradamus was truly a Prophet of God, as a *seer*, who encountered the Holy Spirit.

- The tenth Latin quote told us that at the time when *the world* will turn *secular*, preferring *worldly* idols over God, man would be *finished*.

- The eleventh Latin quote told us that *a rod of iron* would be found *beating* everyone until a new day *dawns*.

- The twelfth Latin quote told us that the key to preventing this self-destruction would be from the *removal of ignorance*. This means if there is no more *ignorance* of God, then God will allow one to see the truth that has so long been ignored.

As we see, nothing spoken through the Latin voice, nor any of the French surrounding the Latin, yields any inkling of thought that *The Prophecies* were random glimpses of a future. Nothing states the prophecy would begin in 1556 and extend indefinitely into the future. We can firmly grasp that, just from these readings, the primary focus of the quatrains was to retell the horrific future told also in The Revelation of John. From that information, gleaned from a document designed to let the reader know the basic purpose of the main document, it becomes realistic to deduce the quatrains are in need of reordering.

Chapter 6

The Central Theme Stated in the Preface

To begin thinking about reordering the individual quatrains, so they present a consecutive flow of similar ideas telling a long tale of losing touch with God, we have to search the Preface a little closer for more clues that would help in this regard. So far, we already have discussed some key elements that are important to know.

First, we have read that it will be impossible to place any order to the poems before enough time has passed, so that the quatrains will be seen as telling of the *past, present,* and most importantly the *future*. That means reordering can only begin after enough time has passed so that the *past* is recognizable, with the *present* being a logical result of that *past*, and the *future* being identified as probable, because of the *past* and *present*. This means that all three segments of time are related by cause and effect.

Everything prophesied by Nostradamus was to happen in his future, but after 450 years of time, the *past* has become locked into a chronological order of recorded history. Those quatrains will become the ones easiest to recognize and reorder; and several of those quatrains that have been made famous by Nostradamus interpreters are ones that clearly identify past events. The most recent past event quatrains will be liable to have segments that allude to something still to come. In this way the quatrains dealing with *present* events will be connecting to those *past* events, as well as pointing to those still to come.

Second, in order to grasp fully the reading of the *present* and *past* one needs to realize the true meaning of those quatrains, to the fullest extent of each word's meaning. This comes from the realization that all *past* translations have been a result of seeing the text as prose, *restricting* the *speech* Nostradamus intended. By reexamining those quatrains, we can confirm or reject past interpretations, with confirmations yielding the *detail* necessary to specify one event over a similar historical event.

The third element needed for accurate reordering is a central theme, telling us what specifically to look for in history. Without such a limiting scope affixed to the purpose, the argument that Nostradamus' quatrains were so non-specific they could represent anything could hold merit. Without some clear parameters made to fit the quatrains, many events in history can be seen to fit one prophecy. This would be examples where history is said to repeat due to the *circular return* nature of time, and where *hundreds* of similar events (on a general level) could be mistakenly applied to one quatrain. All events told of in *The Prophecies* have to conform to a central theme.

That central theme comes clear when we read in the Preface where Nostradamus wrote, "*not so much only* (or *alone*) *of the time present, but also from the most great part to the future, of to put by writing, for that cause that the reigns* (or *kingdoms*) *sects & religions being changed ones such opposites, certainly in the respect* (or *comparison*) *to the present diametrically* (or *one over against another*), *that so I come with to report this that in them to come to pass will be, those of reign, sect, religion, & faith will be finding so bad agreeable to their judgment auricular* (or *confessional*), *that it will be coming to condemn this that through the centuries to come one will know to be seen & recognized*".

This longwinded statement (which actually is neither the beginning nor the end of one complete "sentence" in the Preface) certainly needs to be broken down slowly to digest a central theme statement. It says *The Prophecies* are *not so much* about the *time present*, meaning the mid-16th Century. Still, relatively speaking, there is one reference that *alone* will represent those times, while not specifically in Nostradamus' *present*. The focus of *the most part* (or *majority*) of his story will be *the most great* people who will come in the *future*. It will be those events surrounding those people who the stories tell *of*, which becomes the backbone of prophecies *put through writing*. Those events will be the root *cause for that* need to prophesy; and those being the root *cause* for those events of importance will be the three most important elements of 16th Century society: the kings of *kingdoms*, the *sects* of service to those kings, and the *religions* of the known world.

It is good to pause and understand the meaning and intended use of the word *sect*. It is very easy to blur the use of *sects* with the following use of *religions*, and come away with an impression that the *sects* Nostradamus referred to were some branch of the *religions* most prominent in those days. This would lead to imaginations of cultish groups, such at were made popular in Dan Brown's book, *The DaVinci Code*: i.e. the Knights Templar, and the Priory of Sion. We could easily see *sects* as *religions*, such that Protestant *religions* were *sects* of Christianity. While those images would not be wholly incorrect, they would be highly misleading, as limiting.

The word, "*sect*," is primarily defined as, "A group of people forming a distinct unit within a larger group by virtue of certain refinements or distinctions of belief or practice." When we stay away from any religious connotation to the word, we can see *sect* also means, "A faction united by common interests or beliefs." This means that Nostradamus himself was a member of several *sects*, simply due to him being one person of a larger group of people who shared common distinctions through their practices and common interests. Nostradamus was known as a doctor, an apothecary (what we now call a pharmacist), a published author, and certainly as an astrologer. He was not the sole person knowledgeable in those practices, thus he learned from others, with others seeking him out for his knowledge. This was Nostradamus' primary intention by placing *sects* between *reigns* and *religions*.

A *sect* was somewhat of an equal to *reigns* and *religions* in that it too represented a division of power, even though its power was bestowed to it from the other two, elite powers. Accordingly, its power of the *sects* was between those who wielded the greatest 16th Century power. Clearly, it was lower in rank to the overt importance of kings and popes; but the *sects* had tremendous influence on the masses.

Nostradamus was a person of the common ranks, one who represented the cream of that crop, so to speak. He was neither royalty nor clergy, during times when only a thin layer of commoners could afford to be more than another member of the local peasantry. Nostradamus would receive stipends for his work from both the King of France and the Cardinal of France, just as did others. A growing number of "specialists" also became influential, representing such *sects* as artists, thinkers, and educators, in many fields. This means the *sects* were those who were then budding into an ever-growing bourgeoisie, or middle class.

Once we grasp this intention of Nostradamus, we then find the theme of *The Prophecies* being an epic tale of the societal changes that will occur, whereby this 16th Century power structure is overturned. Nostradamus wrote of how these three prongs of power would be *changed ones*, such that the changes would make their ranking in power *diametrically opposite* to the way things were then, *in comparison to* Nostradamus' *present*. This means we need to realize an order to this power structure, so we can then reverse it.

Obviously, the king of a nation would have to be the highest individual of all. In the era that Nostradamus lived, and in France, the Roman Catholic Cardinals also carried considerable power, as extensions of the Pope in Rome. This would make then almost equals, since the Vatican could issue papal decrees upon the people, with the king advised to support such rulings. Perhaps, this power of the Church had waned in France by 1555, but it was far from subsiding in Spain, where the Spanish Inquisition still was enforced. There, the Church wielded its power greatly, particularly against Protestants, Jews, and Muslims, with Counter-Reformation Indexes, banning unapproved publications from public consumption, being its newest form of popular persecution.

This hierarchy would place the three: *reigns*, *sects*, and *religions*, in a V-shape, with the people making up the *sects* representing the lowest point, and with the *kings* point being slightly higher than the *religions* point. This means a complete opposite shape would be the result, flipping the shape over into an A-shape. Consequently, the *sects* would be at the apex, with the *religions* point being slightly higher than the *reigns* point. This is where the world stands today, *diametrically opposite* to the way it was in 1555.

The important elements that need to be known, when looking to past events to see order in the verses, are the events that *changed* this dynamic. One needs to look at history only to find evidence of this theme that raised the common man to the pinnacle of power, while placing those traditional powers at the feet of the *sects*. We need go no further than those known historic events that tell of *revolution* (a circular course of accomplishment) to see what events played a role in this reversal of power.

Nostradamus followed this statement of a future inversion with a statement that *faith* will have also suffered. This is not only religious *faith*, but also *faith* in the forms of *government* (an alternative translation for *reigns*) that will replace the *kingdoms*. Nostradamus prophesied that this future time will be when we *will be finding* things *so bad*, as far as religious *faith* is concerned, that government *evils* (an alternative translation for *mal [bad]*) will be condoned by *religions* as just (*agreeable to their judgment*). It *will be* this state that the world will have fallen into, when Jesus Christ *will be coming to condemn*.

This is stating that the central theme of the tales of *The Prophecies* is the end of humanity on Earth. Nostradamus stated this theme is not a new one, but a condemnation that has been prophesied for a very long time. It is a theme *that through the centuries* has been known to be expected, a time when *one* has been promised *to come* again. It is a theme found in the *Holy Bible*, most certainly, in the Book of The Revelation.

Chapter 7

Observing the Obvious Oddities in the Quatrains of *The Prophecies*

Once one has acquired the information Nostradamus meant for one to gain from the preface, one needs to look at the main presentation, which is the quatrains. Before any reading on the individual poems needs be done, there are several observations that stand out. These have to be considered as important, the same as everything about *The Prophecies* has to be realized as another clue towards unlocking the puzzle. A true Prophecy is infallible, thus everything prophesied has to be seen as by design and with purpose.

Three elements of the quatrains stand out through general observation and simple inspection. The first two stand out more readily than the third. The first is the most obvious, which is the separation of the quatrains into ten groups. Each group is headed by the title of the book, as *Propheties de M. Nostradamus*, with this heading followed by the group designation as a *"Centurie"*. Each of these pages acts as the introduction to another part of *The Prophecies*, with each *"Centurie"* identified by the appropriate sequence number, written out fully in French.[33] Certainly, a book divided into parts makes sense; but due to the random presentation of Nostradamus' verses, these divisions beg for more explanation.

The second is less obvious, but without too much search difficulty one finds that some of the words in the poems are written in all-capital letters. The preface had easily detectable font changes within the text, but no such usage of all-capitalized words.[34] These all-cap words are spread seemingly at random throughout the quatrains, with some verses having more than one all-capital letter word in them. With at least twenty-five of these words found[35], they leave an impression on the reader that some reason has led

---

33   The 1566 Lyon editions does not spell out the numerical sequence of the *Centuries*. Instead, it used Roman numerals (as *Centurie IV*, instead of *Centurie Quatre*). All editions headed each subsequent page of a *Centurie* by Roman numeral. A typical example finds the second set of 100 quatrains, in all editions between 1555 and 1568, with the exception of the 1566 Lyon edition, introduced as "*Propheties de M. Nostradamus Centurie Seconde*", with each following page headed "*Centurie II*"

34   There is one exception to this, which is found on the title page to the preface. The first two words are in all-capital letters (*TON TARD*, meaning *YOUR LATE*), with the first letter (T) in an offset, large, elaborate box. Some editions also show the fourth and fifth "words" also in all-caps, "*CAESAR NOSTRADAMUS*".

35   The first word of every *Centurie* is in all-cap letters, with the first letter in an offset large, elaborate box, accounting for ten of this number.

to these words being presented in this manner.

The third oddity is the hardest to find, because it is found in only one poem. This poem is actually not a quatrain, in the classic sense of the word. This one verse is also the only one written completely in Latin. It also is one of the quatrains with all-capital letter words.[36] In addition to all of these unique qualities, other oddities are visible surrounding this "quatrain." I will discuss all of this in more detail later.

All of these surface observation elements are immediately crying out for one to ask, "Why?" Unfortunately, the answer is not something that is obviously written in the Preface or the letter of explanation to King Henry II. This is why none of these obvious facts about *The Prophecies* has been discussed, or highlighted over the ages. However, from having looked at the observable in the Preface closely, I am prepared to venture some educated guesses about the intent behind these three observable oddities in the text of the main document.

I will address each in the order that I have presented them. This makes the first discussion focus on why the book is divided into parts, when parts imply sequential order (1 through 10). It is common knowledge that *The Prophecies* have been recognized for over 450 years as representing complete randomness. However, once one sees the need to reorder the quatrains into a new order, one that would result in an intelligible story of epic proportions, there would be a need for a division into parts.

With this realization, one needs to ask, "Why didn't Nostradamus call his divisions 'parts', instead of *Centuries*?" The answer has to be that such a title created an illusion to time, as "*Centurie*" seems to mean, to the English-speaking world, a hundred years. However, the French use the word, "*siècle*," when referring to one hundred years of time, and Nostradamus used that word in his quatrains, proving he fully realized how to distinguish time from measure. The word, *Centurie*, is actually rooted in the Latin word *Centuria* (with a French –*e* ending, replacing the –*a*) meaning, "a division of 100." That, in fact, is the core meaning for the use, as a divider in *The Prophecies*, denoting a group that measures 100 quatrains.[37]

This begs the question, why no one has put much thought into why Nostradamus divided randomness into groups. The assumption seems to have been that wading through random quatrains is like swimming across an ocean. Randomness is like water, in that if you threw handfuls of the ocean up into the air, the water would all land and become perfectly one again with the ocean. Order is not present in liquid and gas forms, just as it is not present in Nostradamus' work. Therefore, having an island chain like "*Centurie Premiere*" (*First One Hundred*) and "*Centurie Seconde*" (*Second One Hundred*) visible in the distance makes all the effort required, to stroke continuously through randomness, lend some sense of direction,

---

36 This actually depends on the edition observed. For instance, the 1557 Utrecht edition clearly shows all-caps in the first line, or heading. However, the 1568 Lyon edition shows this first line in a different typeset, with a larger font size, very similar to the presentation found in the preface, as a distinction between the Latin text and the French text.

37 One could even go so far as to see the individual quatrains as individual Roman soldiers, or "*centurions*".

with the purpose being to simply have a place to stop and rest, before swimming through another 100, on to the next island. Of course, when one thinks about this reasoning it really does not hold water.

The spelling out of the sequence number as *premeire* or *seconde*, rather than the French words *une* (one) or *deux* (two), has purpose. The word *first* is an ordinal number, while "one" is a cardinal number. The Latin root for the word *ordinal* is "*ordo-*," which means, "order." The term "cardinal number" is defined as, "a number denoting quantity but not order in a group"[38], which means order is the purpose of the *Centuries*, and not number. When order is the purpose, there are one hundred specific quatrains that belong *first*, with another specific one hundred that belong *second*, and so on. If Nostradamus was simply giving the reader a heading that communicated something like, "Here's another 100-group of randomness, which makes the fourth so far, I believe", he would have stated cardinal numbers, or used numerical figures. The use of roman numerals has been the preference of many who have reproduced translations of *The Prophecies*, because the randomness theory calls for a cardinal numbering system, not ordinal.

With the numbering of the groups seen to point to a specific order, *first*, *second*, *third*, etc., that specificity applies to what should follow in verse. The fact that we instead find randomness is a statement that supports the message found in the Preface, which is a need for reordering the quatrains. What we then have to assume by the use of the word *Centurie* is the reordered epic tale will be in ten parts, with each part told in one hundred quatrains. This is then a clue that the islands in the ocean are not mere resting points amid pointless exercise, but key elements in the timing of the epic tale.

We have already found that the Preface made a statement about time, such that *The Prophecies* would be cloaked in the clouds of obscurity and nebulosity until the time when enough of the story had passed, such that the work was viewed as representing the *three times*, *past*, *present*, and most importantly the *future*. This clue is then telling one that, minimally, *Centurie Premiere* is where one will find the *past* told. One could then assume that *Centurie Seconde* is where one will find quatrains telling of the *present*, if the order that Preface statement made (*three times*) is reflected directly on the *First three Centuries*. This would mean that, at the time of gaining understanding, the majority of *The Prophecies* would have yet been fulfilled, with the *future* being found in the last eight parts of the book.[39]

In any case, one would expect to find each division of the *future* also told in blocks of one hundred. This would be with the possible exception of the tenth part, or the "conclusion-epilogue" to *The Prophecies*. Since there no longer exist one thousand quatrains (if there indeed were one thousand to begin with), there would not be one hundred left to fill that final "century". One could also expect that the same rules

---

38   The Free Online Dictionary, by Farlex, http://www.thefreedictionary.com/cardinal+number
39   Based on my work with the individual quatrains, the first two centuries deal with that which can be considered past, with *Centurie First* approximately 80 quatrains telling the whole story in general terms first, as an "Introduction" to *The Prophecies*. The last 20 spots tell of pre-20th century history, with *Centurie Seconde* being the 20th century set-up, into the dawn of the 21st century.

found in literary masterpieces would apply, as to how one would end one part and begin another. There would have to be no overlap, making the end of one *Centurie* confusing, until one reads the beginning of the following division.

This means the challenge is to sort the quatrains not only in groups of one hundred, but also refine the reordering search so that a story within the overall story emerges. Just as *Centurie Premeire* would be a logical story of *past* events leading up to the *present*, there would be a watershed moment that would represent the doorway to a new set of adventures. As such, the reader would no longer be laboriously swimming in randomness, but instead would be visualizing history unfolding, with each part being the threshold, or portal, to a new focus in that historical timeline.

This does not necessarily have to adhere to a linear approach, once the linear of the *past* has led one through to the linear of the *present*. The *future* could take various forms, while being linear on parallel levels. An example would be history's view of the Second World War.

Due to so much detail coming from that war, it is impossible to report it in a purely linear fashion, without tremendous confusion being the result. In that instance, the stories of that war's campaigns are divided into the theaters of action, with each presented separately in linear time. Once, for instance, the early part of the European war is presented, say from 1939 to 1941, a shift of focus to the Pacific theater would not begin in 1941. It too could begin in 1939, or even before, representing an overlap in time between the two areas of focus. This style may well be how to approach the sorting of quatrains, so they fit snugly into groups of one hundred, with each group individually chronological, allowing for time overlaps between groups.

I hope this made some sense out of an element of entitling divisions of Nostradamus' book, as *Centuries*, which never has been given much thought. Now, let us move on and address the usage of all-capital letter words. This is another one of those observable parts of the quatrains, one that no one has been able to explain. Why would Nostradamus write all-capital letter words?

Most writers on the meaning of Nostradamus' works have taken these all-capital letter words and treated them as if they were as ordinary as all the rest of the words Nostradamus put into print. To their defense, there are some inconsistencies between the various existing publications of *The Prophecies*, which makes it seem some printers may have not followed the actual manuscript very closely. One edition's all-capital letter words are another edition's words in regular type. It depends on which edition one reads, as to whether or not the all-caps show up. Still, the most reputable followers of Nostradamus have come to agreement that Nostradamus did specify certain words to be fully capitalized, as they appear as such in multiple editions.

The question that has not been answered satisfactorily is, "Why?" There is nothing written in the Preface to *The Prophecies*, or in the letter of explanation to Henry II, which would shed some light on this matter. This means, as with my opinion on the divisions of the quatrains into ten parts, I am free to offer another opinion as to the meaning of all-capital letter words. Once again, I will base my opinion on the information gained from the observable in the Preface.

In today's computerized world, with chat rooms and text messaging, the use of all-capital letters has gained a reputation as meaning, "talking loudly." I have observed communications in chat rooms and seen someone ask another person, one typing in all-caps, "Why are you yelling?" Regular type indicates regular voice, while all-capital letters type indicates a higher level of voice, one where emphasis takes those words above and beyond the regular. In this sense, we have a clue found from the two voices found in the Preface, which were French = Nostradamus, and Latin = Jesus.

I do not want to make the assertion that all-capital letter words are as holy as the Latin uses in the Preface. Latin comes with the fact that it is the language of the Roman Catholic Church, and most of the Latin quotes in the Preface corresponded to similar biblical quotes in the Latin Bible. At this time, I will presume that all of the all-capital letter uses in the quatrains are French, although Latin may be necessary to solve some of the more enigmatic all-caps words. This is because French is one of the Romanic languages (a.k.a. Romance), meaning much of its root comes from Latin. However, I do believe the all-caps words represent a higher voice emanating from within the text of a quatrain, one emphasizing a higher level of importance being required for translation.

There is the possibility that all of the all-capital letter words could themselves be reordered into one or more statements, using only all-caps words. This is possible because the list of all-capital letter words includes nouns, verbs, articles, prepositions, and pronouns, everything necessary to make a complete statement. There could be one higher message found here; but I have not found this yet, if it is there. Of course, that does not mean one cannot be found.

Still, the important factor has to be that Nostradamus wrote words in all-capital letters. Since a word with one capital letter shows the importance of a proper noun, or the importance of beginning a new statement, a word written in all-capital letters has to be seen as having ultra importance. This could mean a variety of things.

First, an ultra importance could mean that the word used has multiple meanings that take it well beyond simple ordinary use. As such, all definitions for one word have to be explored, in order to find the one specific meaning of highest importance that could be the intent. An example of this would be found in one of the very first quatrains observed.

In the first line of the second quatrain in *Centurie Premiere*, Nostradamus wrote, "*The small staff in hand placed in the middle of the BRANCHES*." My translation of "*small staff*" is different than most people prefer, as they tend to choose another perfectly acceptable translation of the French word *verge*, which is "wand". This helps them develop the imagery of Nostradamus being a magician, because all magicians have magic "wands". However, other equally acceptable translations are "rod" and "stick", which would allow this quatrain to match the last biblical quote in the Preface, where a beating until dawn is said to occur with a *rod of iron*.

That imagery, of Nostradamus being a magician, leads to a translation of *BRANCHES* as the three legs of the tripod, the one mentioned in the Preface. They interpret a "*branche*" as being a "leg", which simply is not the case at all. The French word *branche* means, "the branch or bough of a tree; or the gill of a fish".[40] In that sense, a *rod in the middle of the fish gills* sounds more like Nostradamus was talking about fishing, rather than conjuring with a "wand". However, there is still another meaning in the French use of *branche*; and that meaning is, "a collateral degree or side of kindred; Lineage; or a branch or line of a Pedigree."[41] This, to me, is the reason the word appears in all-capital letters.

When one realizes the Preface has given clues that Jesus Christ is the source of *The Prophecies*, based on various factors, including the Scripture quotes of Jesus, one has to see why Jesus would return to tell a Prophet a Prophecy. That reason is Jesus is the Good Shepherd, who cares for the flock. As stated in Psalm 23, where we get a good idea about what a Good Shepherd carries around, we see, "thy *rod* and thy *staff* they comfort me." As such, *the rod in hand* means Jesus the Good Shepherd holds His *rod*, which is then grabbed by Nostradamus. *The rod* is *in* the *hand* of both Jesus and Nostradamus, at that point.

Once Nostradamus touches the *staff* of Christ, he is suddenly *placed in the middle of the LINEAGE* (or *BRANCHES*) that led to Jesus of Nazareth, and which will lead to the return of Christ our Savior. Certainly, this would be an explanation for why the word *BRANCHES* needed to be in all-capital letters. Just as chatroom etiquette would observe, Nostradamus is shouting out that he was not *placed in the middle of* just any old line of pedigree. He was at *the center of* (alternate translation of *milieu*) the *BRANCHES*, as one with Christ. He was showing a level of elation, which would be observable simply through the use of all-capital letters.

Before you shake your head too hard at the conclusion I have just drawn, let me fill you in on some further evidence that supports this claim. First, in line four of this example quatrain, Nostradamus wrote, "*Splendor divine. The most holy near sat down.*" This speaks volumes about the *rod*, as well as with whom Nostradamus was *placed*. Because Nostradamus repeated the word *divine* twice in this last line, spelled as *divine* (f) and *divin* (m), and the 1611 French to English dictionary translates that to mean, "divine, godly, heavenly, most holy; participating of the Godhead; belonging to, or coming from, God"[42],

---

40   Randal Cotgrave's 1611 French-English Dictionary, http://www.pbm.com/~lindahl/cotgrave/search/135r.html

41   Ibid.

42   Randle Cotgrave's 16111 French-English Dictionary, http://www.pbm.com/~lindahl/cotgrave/search/318r.html

it is illogical to associate "wands" and "*LEGS*" as some proven method required to God to come sit down with one. Logic leads one to see how the *BRANCHES* set the theme for the whole quatrain, such that the summation of that theme causes one to understand the *BRANCHES* are themselves *divine*.

Second, Nostradamus wrote in his letter to Henry II a rather detailed accounting of the time that elapsed between Adam and Jesus. I will explain more about this later, but what is relevant now is understanding that Nostradamus focused on the *LINEAGE* of the *Holy Bible*. This holy line included Adam, Noah, Abraham, Isaac, Jacob, Moses, and David, before he recounted the arrival of Jesus. Since that was a letter explaining the meaning of *The Prophecies*, of which this quatrain is one, it is logical to state that Nostradamus gave evidence that supports my conclusion. While Nostradamus did mention a "*tripod*" in this same letter of explanation, that has nothing to do with the French word "*branche*."

Certainly, since I have yet to present anything about the letter to Henry II, my point here is so much to defend my view on the meaning of *BRANCHES*, as much as I want to demonstrate how one has to approach an all-capital letter word. By giving logical evidence that backs my example, I have shown that one of Nostradamus' all-capital letter words has an elevated sense of meaning, well beyond what one would casually observe the word to mean, without any use of capitalization. Capitalization elevates the meaning of this quatrain, well beyond a wand being waved between a tripod's legs, transforming the quatrain into a statement of the presence of the LORD. I believe this is an example that is consistent with all of Nostradamus' use of all-capitalization; and I believe this is how one should approach interpreting them all. However, that is where determining "them all" comes into play.

As I mentioned prior, there can be disagreement over which words were intended by Nostradamus to be seen as all-capitalized words of importance, and which words were the result of printer discretion. For example, the first quatrain of each *Centurie* becomes a questionable presentation. In some early editions of *The Prophecies*, in particular the copies the predating the second edition (where three additional *Centuries* appeared, along with the letter to Henry II), the first letter of the first word is a special typeset, much larger, and offset from the rest of the type. It is like one side a child's building block, with a capital letter filling the middle, along with a background of foliage. This blocked-in capital first letter is then connected to regular type, where all-capital letters were used to form the first word. In later editions, however, this first letter is simply a much larger type, with some printers omitting the all-capitalization of the first word of those first quatrains in a new *Centurie*.

A perfect example of this is the first quatrain of *Centurie Premiere*, where the all-capitalized first word is *ESTANT*, which primarily translates as *BEING*. When one sees that the whole first line of the quatrain states, "*BEING seated with night secret study*," it makes me remember the ending of the last example quatrain, where line four said, "*The most holy near sat down*." This would make it seem that the all-capitalization of *BEING* is not a printer's statement of style, even though most interpreters have written this all-capital letter word off as such. It makes sense to see this *BEING* is the one who has the *LINEAGE* of importance, thus making it equally important, requiring all-capital letters of its own.

There is other evidence that supports all of these "first word of the first quatrain of a *Centurie*" appearances as intended by Nostradamus to be in all-caps. That evidence is the fact that all divisions (*Centuries*) do not have first words fitting this description. The one edition that seems to be truest to the all-capital letter word presentation is the Benoist Rigaud, Lyon Edition of 1568. In that edition, there is one *Centurie* not beginning with an all-capital letter word (*Centurie Sixsiesme – Century Six*), while all the others do. The first word (again, with the first letter capitalized in a large, separate, and offset box), shows as "*AUtour*," where the capital "U" is the first letter on the actual line the word is set on. Many other editions confirm this mixture of capital and lower case letters, only at the beginning of *Centurie Sixsiesme*.[43]

There is one other source of confusion. Besides trying to determine what all qualifies as an all-capital letter word, one also faces some difficulty determining what the accepted translation should be, relative to all-caps words. Sometimes Nostradamus used period marks along with his capital letters. The period marks result in some all-capital-letters usage appearing to be initials (*D.M.*, and *D. nebro*), with others appearing to be either one-word statements (*PAR.*, and *CAR.*, where both *par* and *car* are whole words, followed by a period mark) or abbreviations (*GRAN.*, *SEX.*, *SEXT.*, and *PAR.*, and *CAR.*, if abbreviations). Nostradamus wrote some all-capital-letter words that are not French, with Latin being the source of translation (*DUUMVIRAT*, *LEGIS CANTIO*), with some appearing to be new words formed from either Latin or Greek (*NORLARIS*, *HIERON*). At other times, a word of uncertain meaning is written in all-caps (*TAG*, *NERSAF*, and *POULA*). Still, other all-caps words seem to be misspellings, or words similar to known words (*RAYPOZ*, *MANSOL, and LONOLE*).

Certainly, I do not attempt to make the claim that I know all of the meanings and intentions of these most difficult elements of *The Prophecies*, but I do stand by my belief that an all-capital-letter presentation means one needs to search for a higher meaning than the norm. After I have presented the many "systems" of Nostradamus, which become the rules for translation and interpretation, all of these examples of all-capital-letters use will have a method by which the true meanings can surface. However, it would be premature at this point to delve into that analysis. At this point, just understand that the observable oddity of all-capitalized words has meaning that must be recognized.

The last of the observable oddities I initially mentioned, if you recall, pertained to a "quatrain" that is not truly a quatrain. All of *The Prophecies* were written in this consistent poetic style, with the exception of one. The word, "quatrain," is defined as a four-line poem, or stanza of a poem; and the root word stems from the Latin word *quattor*, which means, "four."[44] In other words, the one verse that appears with six lines stands out as the only non-quatrain in a sea of quatrains. That has to be seen as odd.

---

43 The 1555 Utrecht edition shows the first word of *Centurie Cinquesme* (*Centurie Fifth*) as *AVant*, but no other editions confirmed this. The 1650 Lyon edition shows the first word of *Centurie Sixsiesme* as *AU*, with a space leading to the second word, "*tour*".
44 The Free Dictionary by Farlex, http://www.thefreedictionary.com/quatrain

Nostradamus included one poem that has six lines of poetry, making it a sixtain instead of a quatrain. If that is not enough to set it apart, it is also the only poem, of over 940, which is totally written in Latin. We have already covered the higher voice Latin presents, when the Latin of the preface was discussed. I presented how Latin acted as the voice of Jesus and God. Without out consistency regulating hidden systems – if it works one place, it works in all places, or it is wrong – one could simply say Nostradamus simply liked to practice his Latin at strange points. However, the theory of Latin being a "higher voice" is confirmed in this sixtain, and when one realizes where this verse is found, the whole poem speaks without using words.[45]

> 114   CENTVRIE VI.
> XCVIII.
> Ruyné aux Volsques de peur si fort terribles,
> Leur grand cité teincte, faict pestilent:
> Piller Sol, Lune & violer leurs temples:
> Et les deux fleuues rougir de sang coulant.
> XCIX
> L'ennemy docte se tournera confus,
> Grand camp malade, & defaict par embusches:
> Monts Pyrenees & Poenus luy feront faict refus,
> Proche du fleuue descouurant antiques oruches.
>
> LEGIS CANTIO
> contra ineptos criticos.
>
> Quos legent hosce versus maturè
>   censunto,
> Profanum vulgus, & inscium ne
>   attrestato:
> Omnesq, Astrologi Blenni, Barbari
>   procul sunto,
> Qui aliter facit, is rite, sacer esto.

Obviously, this one sixtain (the one covering the bottom half of the page) is significantly different from the two quatrains that appear at the top of the same page. Several things jump out about this poem. First, the type size is much larger than that of the two quatrains shown (and all the other quatrains in all *Centuries*). That, and the fact there are six lines, sets it apart as very different. Next, there are two type styles used, one standard (first two lines), the other italics (the remaining four lines). Finally, if one closely inspects the three verses on this page, one sees the top two are numbered (in Roman numerals) as 98 and 99; but this one verse is not numbered at all. These differences all point to one logical conclusion.

All Nostradamus experts agree that this "quatrain" states a general warning to potential readers of Nostradamus' book of prophetic poetry. As such, it is not a prophetic vision, because it speaks as an after view of what has been completed. Some see it as a hex, or curse, telling potential readers to stay away,

---

45   Copy courtesy of Mario Gregorio, Prophecies Online, http://www.propheties.it/nostradamus/1557utrecht/1557utrecht114.jpg

and not attempt to read the contents. This means the oddity comes from this one passage not being in the very front, before any of the other quatrains, where it would serve as a foreword. However, this sixtain is found published as the last entry in *Centurie* VI.[46]

Upon further inspection of this sixtain, one sees that the use of standard typeset, along with italics, is following the pattern of the heading that leads into the preface. In addition, in the preface the Latin stood out as being standard type, amid a sea of italics. When one remembers that the Latin in the preface was Jesus speaking directly, while the italics in the preface were Nostradamus speaking for Jesus, the sixtain is all Jesus speaking again. Further, because Nostradamus presented his foreword, headed by all-capital letters, stating, "PREFACE," this sixtain is Jesus' preface, with an all-capital letter heading, stating, "COVENANT PSALM". Finally, by not being specifically identified as the one-hundredth poem in the sixth division of a hundred quatrains, this means *Centurie Sixth* is missing one quatrain. That missing quatrain could be explained as the quatrain numbered 101, in *Century Tenth*.

Clearly, this verse needs to be removed from its published position. It has to be reordered so that it becomes the first poem read, meaning it should be placed as the foreword, after the Preface, and immediately before the quatrains of *The Prophecies*. That simple observation goes a long way towards confirming the necessity of reordering the quatrains. If one must be moved, then everything can and should be moved. The realization of this one obvious oddity means it is okay to dump all the puzzle pieces on the table, begin sorting, and put together a puzzle that looks like it is explained to look.

This 6-lined verse (or quatrain with its own header) is not to be numbered, just as the Preface has no need to be numbered. This standout verse is not part of the stories that make up *The Prophecies*. It is in reality a precursor to the main event. The Preface is presented as a letter from Nostradamus to his son, Caesar, while being headed to be the essay introducing his book (defining a preface's purpose). A foreword is another form of introductory note about a literary work, typically written by someone other than the author.[47] In this case, the "other" who would be qualified to write such an introduction would be true source of *The Prophecies* (as well as the Preface), Jesus Christ. This acts to support the idea that Latin was the voice of Christ, even though Nostradamus actually physically penned everything.

As to this verse being removed from *Century Sixth*, and there no longer being 100 quatrains in that part, the missing quatrain brings up another obvious oddity. Due to Nostradamus' use of *"one thousand"* in the preface,[48] leads one to think of ten *Centuries*, each with a full one hundred quatrains. However, it is obvious that *Centurie Septiesme* (*Centurie Seventh*) falls well short of that number, with all editions, prior to 1600, presenting 42 quatrains in *Centurie Seventh*, immediately followed by the word "*FIN*",

---

46   The inset representation comes from the 1557 Utrecht edition. Other editions do not make this verse so pronounced; but all adjust the type and margins to denote a clear difference in this one poem.

47   Source: The Free Dictionary by Farlex, http://www.thefreedictionary.com/foreword

48   Approximately at the 80% point of the Preface, Nostradamus wrote, "*que encores que nous soyons au septiesme nombre de mille qui paracheve le tout*". This can cleanly translate to state, "*that for all that which we are in the seventh number of one thousand which (fully) achieved the whole sum*".

meaning "*END*".

If we assume that *Centurie Seventh* was a complete group of one hundred quatrains before it was first published in 1557, based on Nostradamus stating "*one thousand*", the excuse would point to censorship, and most probably by the Church. Assuming the original *Centurie Seventh* only had 100 quatrains, from which the "last" 58 were removed before giving approval to the publisher to print, that would point to the need for one extra quatrain needing to be added later.

There is such a quatrain. It is found at the end of *Century Tenth* (*Centurie Dixième*), with some editions numbering it as the one hundred first quatrain, with others showing it as "*added*" ("*adjousté*"), without a number. This "extra" quatrain does not appear in the 1568 Benoist Rigaud edition. It appears in the Lyon editions published after 1600,[49] which means it took over 30 years to find, with Nostradamus dying in 1566. This late addition has led many to write it off as a forgery, preferring to believe there are 100 quatrains in *Centurie Sixth*, even though one has six lines, and is not numbered.

Personally, I believe this found quatrain can be explained, in part, to printer oversight, due to the defining quality of "centurie" being seen as a maximum limit. No more than one hundred could be printed in a *Centurie*, although less than one hundred was perfectly fine. This negligence could have been corrected many years later, as the evidence indicates, or it could have been corrected sooner; but unfortunately, all possible editions containing the extra quatrain have since been lost. My belief is based on the wording of the extra quatrain; and I cannot go into that now because I have not yet presented the systems that make number 101 match the Nostradamus style. Therefore, at this point I can only express my opinion of belief.

As for the possibility that *Century Sixth* should only have 99 quatrains, it would make it harder to defend *Century Seventh*, as only contains 42 quatrains due to Church censorship. Since the Church found the same unintelligible nonsense everyone else was finding, keeping everyone from knowing exactly what anything stated, they could have simply decided to lop off the last fifty-eight quatrains, acting as the final editor for a work entitled *The Prophecies*. However, if there were not a 101st quatrain in part ten, an authentic one, there may be no need to make this accusation of the Church. In that case, Nostradamus would be confirming it was okay to reorder his quatrains in groups of less than one hundred, but no more than one hundred.

Both the 1566 Pierre Rigaud edition, and the 1568 Benoist Rigaud edition, list only 42 quatrains in *Century Seventh*. Immediately after the final word in number forty-two, the word *FIN* is typeset. These two publications were the first new editions of *The Prophecies*, which contain ten *Centuries*. The 1566 edition is important because it presents and "*EPITAPHE*", which announces that Nostradamus past away, on 2 July, 1566. This indicates the Lyon publisher was in contact with Nostradamus, prior to publishing

---

[49] The first edition available to examine, which has this extra quatrain in it, is the 1605 Lyon edition.

an updated version, which it announced about the three new *Centuries*, "*Which have not yet ever been Imprinted (quatrains).*" Still, with all announcements of a new edition, both the 1566 and 1568 editions were published with only 42 quatrains in the seventh part.[50]

The 1557 Utrecht edition supports the 1566 and 1568 Lyon editions, as far as showing only 42 quatrains in *Century Seventh,* followed by *FIN*. It included a note that followed, stating, "*Finished to print the 6th of the month of September, 1557.*" However, one of the 1557 Lyon editions, held today in the library of Budapest, Hungary, shows the same note, stated that the book was finished to print 30 November 1557. That edition, again, shows *FIN* after only 40 quatrains. The forty-first and forty-second appear in other 1557 editions.[51] This appears to shows that printers make mistakes, and by missing the last two had to adjust a "proof," to reach the final approved copy.

The point of this is that in 1557 Nostradamus was two years removed from publishing his original first edition, which only had four parts (1555). It would be 1566 before three more *Centuries* would be published as the third and final edition of *The Prophecies*. In 1557, however, *Centurie Seventh* represented "the end" of the story of the future, just as that conclusion ended in *Centurie Fourth*, in 1555. As such, one would not expect to necessarily have a full one hundred quatrains appear in the end of the new *Centurie Tenth*, in 1566. In 1557, the 53 quatrains in *Centurie Fourth* had ballooned to a full 100, with *Centurie Seventh* assuming the new "partial one hundred' status. One's future visions end when the future ends; and as unintelligible as everything was upon first release, randomness would have to be farthest thing in everyone's mind. After all, Nostradamus' almanacs were chronological, month-to-month. This means *Centurie Tenth* is as much of an oddity, as is *Centurie Seventh*.

All of this discussion now leads us back to the issue of reordering the quatrains, once the all-Latin foreword is placed in the front of *The Prophecies*, after the Preface. If one poem can be moved, they all can be moved. Still, reordering has to include the three additional *Centuries*, which each had a full one hundred quatrains (or 101 in part ten, if the extra is not a fake). With everything being free to be moved to a completely different place in the order, it does not matter if a quatrain comes from *Century Tenth*, to be relocated in *Century First*. As long as it properly fits the story being told, each has to move to where it belongs.

An oddity that points to this is the letter to Henry II. That letter is dated as written in 1558, the year after the seven-part 1557 edition was published. The three "new" *Centuries* are actually part of that explanation, which becomes clear when the systems are used to remove the enigma of this letter. However, one obvious piece of evidence comes from Nostradamus using the word, "*Pempotam*", a word of unknown

[50] It is interesting to note that the 1568 Lyon edition makes the same claim, as did the 1566 Lyon edition, that it included "*Centuries VIII. IX. X.*", as having had never before been in print. By the time the 1605 Lyon edition hit the presses, it was amended to say, "*Which had not been first Imprints: & are in the same edition from 1568.*"

[51] All editions were published in Lyon, France, but surviving copies are found today in places like Utrecht, The Netherlands, Vienna, Austria, and Budapest, Hungary.

meaning, near the end of his letter explaining *The Prophecies*. That word (or a close variation of it) appears in only two quatrains, the ones numbered VIII-97 and X-100. Both of those "new" quatrains, first publicly printed in 1566, were explained in 1558.

This means the logic that made *Century Seventh* come up short of one hundred quatrains (at 40 or 42) is invalid, when three additional parts see the future in full blocks of one hundred, with none of those being added to *Centurie Seventh* to make it reach its maximum capacity. If everything were random visions of the future, *Century Tenth* would be the likely one to come up short of a hundred. However, how can a future that was concluded in *Century Seventh* (which told of the end of the world) have three hundred more random visions make it to print, appearing separate from the future previously foretold?

The answer is obvious. The second edition additions were meant to be dovetailed into the first editions parts. The result would be ten *Centuries*, with the last being less than a full one hundred quatrains. The fullness of *Centuries* eight, nine, and ten is actually telling, as it confirms that reordering is required. The parts themselves must be reordered. With the grand total rising to 942 pieces to fill ten parts, it becomes pointless to have less than one hundred in *Century Seventh*.

Publishing various editions, each with more quatrains added, as if "new random visions" had been penned down, was the only hoax played by Nostradamus. It was a hoax instructed by Jesus, to cloak *The Prophecies*. All 942 quatrains (actually a few more also, which were not originally published) were written before the first edition went to the printer. If reordering is required, then there can be no other conclusion. This would mean that Nostradamus would know precisely where to cut his *Century Seventh* off, including the non-quatrain that filled up *Century Sixth*.

Nostradamus purposefully published 37 % of the whole first (352 quatrains arranged randomly), then he waited two years before raising that number to 68% (642 randomly placed quatrains). Much later, he would authorize the remaining 32% being put in print (942-948, again presented randomly), with some "lost" quatrains being added well after his death. By staging everything that way, it gave the impression of Nostradamus having random visions, and promoted doubt, where the issue of forgery arose. Yet, Nostradamus never once explained that random visions was what actually happened, and authenticity of everything would come once anything could be correctly analyzed. The one clue that opens ones eyes to all this stems from the one non-quatrain at the very end of *Century Sixth*.

Let me make a few last statements about the questionable 101st quatrain in *Century Tenth*, found the Lyon editions after 1600. Other quatrains had also been found by then, including some stragglers attributed to *Centurie Seventh*. There are even quatrains (partial) for a *Centurie XI* and *Centurie XII*, as well as presages and sixtain predictions, all published after Nostradamus' death. Some quatrains attributed to Nostradamus have been proven to be forgeries, but some are still worthy of consideration.

If the purpose was to confuse and make people think of randomness and censorship, the hoax of presenting *The Prophecies* in the manner that it was has worked wonderfully. Even though there are those who believe Nostradamus was a fraud, they do not see the hoax of randomness and censorship. They only see disbelief in astrology, as a means of accurately predicting the future; especially a future so distant that no human being could fathom the ways of life on earth then. These "experts" do not challenge the authenticity of a few found quatrains, because they do not believe the concept behind any of Nostradamus' quatrains.

With Jesus Christ as the source, and with Nostradamus acting as a true Prophet of God at His service, everything has purpose and design. All necessary quatrains will be found and added to the list of predictions attributed to Nostradamus, including the 101st in *Centurie Tenth*, and the 6 added to *Centurie Seventh*. If there is more to be added (such as has been promoted as the *Lost Book of Nostradamus*), that too will be predestined to be found. As such, several quatrains in Nostradamus' handwriting could have easily been written, then placed under the instruction of a devoted assistant or eldest son, to have them find a much later release for publication. The result would mean the whole of *The Prophecies* was written at one time, before any efforts to publish officially began.

Originally, there were 948 quatrains written, as one continuous epic tale in poetic style. It was then scrambled, creating a puzzle, which we now have to reorder so we can make sense of its full meaning. It is not beyond the realm of possibility that the one sixtain, the Preface, and even the letter of explanation to the king, were all penned and ready before the first efforts to publish. Everything was then scattered into an apparent random order, with the plan to have it published in multiple installments (with a few quatrains left over in a drawer for good measure), to confound everyone for *centuries*. However, the clues that would be left observable would finally be the key to return it all back into its original shape.

At this point, I would be remiss if I did not clarify this 5-line entry in *Century Sixth*, giving a literal English translation, showing that it is not a curse, and not harsh enough to be a warning. It actually tells you what can be expected to be found in *The Prophecies*. My translation is (following the format of the Utrecht edition):[52]

---

[52] This can be translated to say something quite different, although similar in tone.

> COVENANT PSALM
> against foolish critics.
> *Whom should read this verse*
> *prematurely to assess,*
> *Secular common people, & ignorant in*
> *order not to touch Destiny:*
> *All things as far as Astrologer*
> *Simpleton, Savage far off are,*
> *Whereby in different ways made, this duly,*
> *sacred be.*

The first two words are all-capital-letter words, written in Latin. This acts as a heading, rather than a simple line of verse; and it is of the highest voice. The first word, *LEGIS*, translates as, "law, statute, covenant, or agreement."[53] This comes from the root word, *lego*, which means, "bequeath, will, entrust," although *legi* is another form meaning, "read, gather, collect".[54] As such, the first word denotes a collection of readings, while also acting to state the laws governing *The Prophecies*.

I have chosen *COVENANT* as the primary translation because there is an obvious connection between the English versions of the *Holy Bible* and that one particular word. It is a word that conveys the higher voice we found in the Latin quotes of the Preface. Not only was it used biblically to show an agreement made between God and the Israelites (תירב [Berith]: meaning, "pact, treaty, alliance"[55]); it also was used to show a new testament between Jesus Christ and all humanity (διαθηκη [*diatheke*]: "a disposition, i.e., (specially) a contract (especially a devisory will) – covenant, testament"[56]). This makes the foreword instantly become an agreement between the reader and this higher source, about what that one can expect to read within.

The second word of this heading, *CANTIO*, translates best as *SONG*, but can also mean, "to sing" or "chant". The way songs were identified in the *Holy Bible* was as *PSALMS*. In either case, an all-capital-letter heading is stating loudly that *The Prophecies* (of which this is a foreword to) is the result of the New *COVENANT* of Jesus with humanity. The poetic style of the following quatrain connects it to all of the quatrains, making each a *SONG*, or chanted with music, just like the Psalms. This denotes an air of prayer to them. This makes the quatrain that follows the heading, as well as the quatrains within, rhythmic chants. This, then, is recognition that all that follows is in poetic style, with rhyming words.

---

53   Translation Experts Ltd., InterTran, http://www.tranexp.com:2000/Translate/result.shtml
54   A Latin-English Dictionary Wordlist, http://users.erols.com/whitaker/dictpage.htm
55   Milon.co.il, a Free Online English Hebrew Dictionary, http://www.milon.co.il/general/general.php?term=%D7%91%D7%A8%D7%99%D7%AA
56   Strong's Greek Dictionary, Biblos.com, http://strongsnumbers.com/greek/1242.htm

Following this all-caps heading we find a separate line in all lower-case words, which states, "*against foolish critics.*" The word *contra* clearly translates as *against*, but would best be defined as *contrary*. This means that the *SONG* of the foreword, just like the poems of *The Prophecies*, will be found to be "opposite in direction or purpose"[57], to what they initially appear to be. Those who will see them as something they are not are then designated to be fools. The *foolish* will then become frustrated with their inability to decipher Nostradamus' words (due to pushing on what should be pulled), causing their frustrations to become critical of the contents. The word *criticos* carries a meaning as a "literary critics," such that the *critics* of *The Prophecies* will also find fault with the poor grammar and spelling in the verses. They will complain these errors by the author make it difficult to say for Nostradamus what Nostradamus meant to say.

The first line of the foreword's lyrics says, "*Whom should read this verse prematurely to assess*". This is addressing the lower case part of the heading that stated this foreword *SONG* is *against foolish critics*, because fools will make interpretations about the poems too *prematurely to assess* properly their meanings. They will be unable to reach a *COVENANT* for understanding, as they can only read. These *fools* are then generally identified at the beginning of line two, as people not led by Jesus, said to be *wicked commoners* (alternate translation of *Profanum vulgus*), as Gentiles are *uninitiated* (alternate translation of *profanum*) into Christianity. This is then stating that one has to be led by God and Christ to understand (*to assess*), but only when the time is right (not *prematurely*).

In the second half of line two, where it states, "*ignorant in order not to touch Fate*," we have that word that popped up in the last Latin quote of the Preface, which stated, "*but when will remove what will be will be ignorance*". That statement meant understanding comes when *ignorance* of God ceases. *Ignorance* of God is seen when growing numbers of the *common people* have turned away from religion, becoming a *Secular* society.

Still, before time has matured enough for understanding, the presentation of the quatrains will keep *common people ignorant* of the true meanings. We then see the phrase, "*in order not*," which is a statement that *ignorance* comes because the quatrains are *not in* the proper *order*. This is done with the initial purpose of keeping people out of *touch* with the meaning of a future that is not theirs to live in and recognize. Therefore, the *ignorant* people will *not* be able to affect *Fate*, or be affected by having *Destiny* (alternate translation of *Fato*) revealed too soon.

In the third line, the foreword is simply saying that *Astrology* is only a *Small* part (alternate translation of *Blenni*, as a classification of *Small Fish*) of the whole; but *Simpleton Astrologers* will not be able to grasp what *Astrology* the quatrains do hold, even though only *Simple Astrology* will be found within the verses. The word *Astrologi* also meant *Astronomer*; and compared to present-day standards, of knowledge of outer space, an *Astronomer* of the 16th Century would now be considered a *Simpleton*. In those days, only

---

[57] The Free Dictionary by Farlex, http://www.thefreedictionary.com/contrary

seven orbs-planets were known,[58] due to the invention of the telescope still being over fifty years away. As such, all astrological references in *The Prophecies* can only be of *Simpleton* knowledge.

Most have translated *Blenni* as "Idiots," and while this is an accurate alternate translation, it is too limiting. The definition of "idiot" meets the requirement of *foolish*, but becomes too intellectually insulting to be the primary use, since one definition references an outdated system for measuring extreme mental handicaps.[59] Certainly, one of such physical restrictions (from brain imperfections) could never begin to grasp the meaning of *Astrology*, much less act as an *Astrologer*. Therefore, when *simpleton* is defined as, "A person who is felt to be deficient in judgment, good sense, or intelligence; a fool"[60], one can more readily see that an *Astrologer Simpleton* is one who thinks he or she knows *Astrology*, but really does not.

The word *Barbari* actually could translate as "Foreigner," but such use has to be recognized as meaning foreigners who were not led by Christianity. This in particular would be Arabs and Jews, who typically wore beards, which in Latin is a *barb*. Simply put, a *barbarian* was someone who was identifiable as uncultured, because wild heathen men were bearded. This cultural difference between clean-shaven holy Christians of Europe and the bearded clerics and rabbis of the East means a *barbari* (like a *barbarian*) identified uncivilized people, thus *savage* people.

The word *Savage* is then better able to connect to *Astrologers*, in a context of today's world, because of the adoption of that art by pagan people. Today astrology is largely rejected by Christian groups, while readily accepted by *Secular common people* (alternate translation of *Barbari procul sunto*). When the Vatican placed *Astrology* on the "bad list," only bad non-Christians continued to play with that "fire". The Vatican recognized the advanced astrological skills held by the Arabs and Jews; but when the religions held dear to those people became a threat to European theology, forced conversion became the Church's response (the Inquisitions).

This persecution also played a role in the Vatican's banishment of *Astrology* as a tool used by Roman Catholics. Due to this disconnect between God and Astrologers, these *Savage* people who practiced *Astrology* will be *far off* in their interpretations of *The Prophecies*. They practice an art simply, without truth guiding them, being foreign to the higher voice of God. Still, those knowing nothing about *Astrology* (as it is a foreign skill) will also be *far off* from understanding, *simply* from *ignorance* of the subject

The most profound statement of the foreword comes in line four, where it states, "*Whereby in different ways made, this duly, sacred be.*" It does not take a stretch of the imagination to see how the Latin phrase in the Preface, *in solute oratione*, which we found meant *in unrestricted language style*, is being restated

---

58   In astrology, a "planet" means an orb in the sky that moves, which included the Sun and Moon. The seven orbs were Sun, Moon, Mercury, Venus, Mars, Jupiter, and Saturn.
59   One Intelligence Quotient (I.Q.) scale used "Idiot" as its lowest class of mental deficiency, which was anyone below an I.Q. of 20.
60   The Free Dictionary by Farlex, http://www.thefreedictionary.com/simpleton

here as *in different ways made*. It then states that *The Prophecies* is *made* of words (*speech, language*) that must be read *in different ways*. They cannot be limited to the one way of reading that syntax (or *prose*) imposes.

The foreword poem then states that once *The Prophecies* have been *duly* read, meaning, "in a proper manner" (by a set of rules, just not the syntactical rules everyone is accustomed to) and, "at the expected time"[61] (when time has matured enough for people to understand), understanding will be the result. After that understanding has been reached, everyone connected to God and Christ will be able to see how Nostradamus' Prophecies are truly *sacred*. That, once again, supports the conclusions gained from the Preface: that the document is holy, coming from divine means.

The Latin word *rite* comes before the Latin word *sacer*, which has some translating the two as "sacred rite". This would be plausible, except it completely ignores the comma that separates the two words. The Latin word *rite* has a broader sense of meaning than does the English word, drawn from that Latin root. The Latin *rite* can mean an accompaniment of "proper ceremony", but it also means, "in due form, properly, fitly, rightly".[62] A translation as *"duly"* is universally accepted as correct for *rite*. It means the quatrains, *which* are *in different ways made*, are *duly made* so. They are *made* so because they are *sacred*, and when recognized as such the recognition will be *duly* deserved. The only ritual meaning that is acceptable (as a rite) is related to the systems that must be applied, for *duly* allowing a *sacred* document to be understood through *different* means.

I hope you can see the depth of meaning that comes from this foreword, which was placed at the very end of *Century Sixth*. It is clearly observable as out of place. Simply from that distinction, one finds that proper translation is necessary to yield the best interpretation. One cannot successfully force syntax on words not meant to be read syntactically. A foreword, just as a preface, needs to make sense so the book that follows also makes sense; and *The Prophecies* has made no sense through the use of applied syntax.

Perhaps, you have noticed that my interpretations have not been based on large gulps of words, but instead on individual words or short phrases. Nothing that I have stated is *against* the rules of language. In fact, everything I have presented is following the definition of the words, which allows the words to be free to set the parameters for contextual meaning. This is a rule of logic, which says the author is the ultimate source for the meaning of something written by the author. When that something has poetic license, allowing the written word to have hidden meaning, it is most logical to focus on what the author said the meaning to be. The foreword is such a statement by the author; and the author stated there are *different* rules by which to find true meaning. The use of Latin implies Jesus is the true author.

This instruction then takes us back to the all-capital-letter, Latin heading, which says in a *different way*,

---
61   The Free Dictionary by Farlex, http://www.thefreedictionary.com/duly
62   University of Notre Dame, Latin Word Lookup, http://catholic.archives.nd.edu/cgi-bin/lookup.pl?stem=rite&ending=

a higher voice, we must let the *READINGS SING* (alternate translation) to us. If we stop all *foolish* attempts at trying to force round pegs into square holes, by having faith, *The Prophecies* become *duly sacred*. We can then *CHANT* the quatrains as a way of reaching a higher level of soul awareness. With prayer for guidance, the meaning will come to us; and we will be amazed, in awe of the complexity and depth that comes from the *simple*, and understated. The quatrains, just as the foreword, can be seen to have both rhyme and reason.

This set of observable oddities in the first edition of *The Prophecies* (*Centuries First* through *Seventh*) makes it a logical deduction that Nostradamus was a true Prophet of God, and the quatrains are in need of reordering. We can also deduce that everything was written at one time, and then released in multiple installments. It made no difference if 300 parts of the story would be added every three years or so, because no one would make any serious attempt at reordering for quite some time. The problem, however, is now figuring out the correct order, once one has figured out everything is out of order; and this is where the letter to Henry II plays a vital role.

Chapter 8

Observing the Oddities in the Letter of Explanation to *The Prophecies*

In the 1566 - 1568 final edition of *The Prophecies*, the letter Nostradamus sent to the King of France first appeared for public view. Henry had demanded an audience with Nostradamus, for the expressed purpose of explaining the confusion that was the 1557 edition (which added to the confusion created in the 1555 edition). Instead of a personal appearance, Nostradamus wrote this letter as his explanation and sent it to Henry. Therefore, Nostradamus met the demands of the king, while also defying a serious royal request.

By having this letter published in 1566-1568, with it appearing as a buffer between the original seven parts and the new additional three *Centuries*, it acted as a new preface to a new book. All copies containing the letter have it presented immediately after another title page, announcing "*The Prophecies - of M. Michel Nostradamus – Centuries VIII. IX. X.*" The publisher appears simply to include this new book, along with a reprint of the first book. The result, which is how everyone presents *The Prophecies* to this day, is two parts together, making one book represent the completed prophecies of Nostradamus. The appearance of the letter to Henry II then seems to act something like a foreword to this second book, although it actually is the preservation of the author's own explanation of the meaning to everything, because the preface was not clear enough.

One needs to consider that observation of two books in one, by making a comparison to another famous book, where two parts make a whole. That comparison would be with the *Holy Bible*, known to have a longer Old Testament, which is then joined with a shorter New Testament. By Nostradamus having his book finalized to be presented in this odd format, it is making the statement that it must be compared to another holy work. As an author, who had had to deal with self-publishing (which I imagine is not too far from the way things used to be, long ago), every aspect of my books are based on my instruction, if not my actual doing. This makes me believe Nostradamus planned to have his book look, on the surface, as a *Holy Bible* looked on the surface.

As to the published letter to Henry, this gave the public the idea that Nostradamus had indeed gone mad. The preface was very strangely worded, so that it could be somewhat grasped, but as a private communication with Nostradamus' infant son; but the letter addressed to the king had no immediate sense of direction and purpose at all. It had moments of clarity, but was for the most part very long-winded, having very few physical period marks. It made rapid changes in focus, without warning. Nostradamus would begin referring to one topic, at one place, then suddenly be talking about another topic, to later come back to that first topic, with no logic in the transitions. The result was a document that was more confusing to understand than the document that it was written to explain.

The letter to Henry II was so enigmatic that few have put much effort into trying to make sense of it. In the *Millennium Edition* of Henry C. Roberts' book on *The Prophecies*, he had the letter to Henry footnoted, saying that his editor forced its presence in his book. Had it been up to him, he stated, the letter would have not been included due to it being nothing but nonsensical ramblings. Roberts did not attempt to decipher the letter's contents; and this has been a consistent approach by interpreters in the past. If one does not know what something says, then a good approach is to act as if it was never there.

I have owned one book on Nostradamus since 1976; but I did not learn of the Preface or the letter to Henry II until very late in 2001. Neither letter was deemed worthy of being included in that first book I owned. That author interpreted quatrains without caring what the author had stated the meaning of the quatrains to be, because no one could see any explanations by Nostradamus that assisted interpretation of the verses. I had to buy a book that had the word *Complete* in the title to find out about the Preface and letter to Henry.

When I first read Nostradamus' explanation, I had already begun to understand some of how to make sense of the quatrains. I skimmed through English translations of both letters, finding it too difficult to read normally, and come away with lucid instructions. I could, however, sense that what I had read did nothing to contradict what I was seeing, with small pieces seeming to verify that I was on the right track. At that time, I was so busily trying to write my own interpretations, and try to become published, in order to save the world, that I could not take the time to look at the letters more closely. I initially had no concept of just how important the letters were, even though I could see glimpses of evidence supporting my sudden ability to find meaning in the quatrains.

Part of this was my basic ignorance of every skill necessary to decipher a very old text written in a foreign language, one I had never learned. That ignorance had been compounded by the fact I did not know either of the letters existed. I began to translate and understand the Preface in late 2003; but it was not until August of 2005 that I began to look deeper into the letter to Henry II. That was when I first began to realize how important that letter is to solving the reordering problem; a problem I was able to see through nearly four years of figuring things out on my own. The Henry letter became the last major piece of the puzzle for me.

As far as the observable oddities that surface from this letter of explanation, nothing about it is as readily visible as the others oddities I have pointed out. One has to be looking more closely to catch the clues. Certainly, since the Preface is in letterform (worded as if written to Nostradamus' son, Caesar), there is a comparison-contrast analysis that can be made to the letter to Henry. While both have headings stating the overt intentions of the documents, and both are dated and signed at the end, the comparisons pretty much end there. It is the contrasts that most clearly highlight the oddities of the Henry letter.

The most obvious difference is in length. Both documents appear in the 1568 Lyon edition (by Benoist Rigaud), which allows us to make a comparison with both documents in the same font and style. The Preface is 10 full pages of text. However, the letter to Henry II is over twice as long, filling up 20 full pages, and ending a quarter-way down on the twenty-first page. Without even attempting to read any of the text of either document, this length difference is an obvious statement that the letter to the King of France contains significantly more information than does the letter designed to be "a preliminary essay introducing a book that explains its scope, intention, or background, written by the author."[63]

When one assumes that King Henry had read the accompanying Preface, along with the quatrains they introduced, and had his court "wise men" read everything as well, it makes sense that Nostradamus was summoned to explain himself further. Nostradamus could then be expected to have expounded on his Preface, only repeating what had already been stated if necessary. In other words, for Nostradamus to skip a personal appearance and not have to worry about being hunted down the rest of his life, the letter to Henry II would have to be full of explanatory details, thus fitting the doubled length. From that assumption, one should expect the letter to Henry to be a detailed explanation of the contents of *The Prophecies*, which are nothing but the quatrains. This is one very important assumption.

Such an assumption does require one to move beyond surface observations, to read the full contents of both letters. This is where one finds another comparison-contrast. Both letters employ the same "long-winded" style of writing, such that the use of a period mark is quite limited.[64] For instance, a 14-page copy of the Preface (in a 1555 Vienna edition) shows 22 period marks, while the 20 ¼-page letter to Henry II has 56 periods. That means the Preface averages 1.57 periods per page, with the letter to the king a whopping 2.77. Therefore, both documents are written similarly, such that one's ability to follow one train of thought is taxed to the maximum, before reaching the conclusion of one "sentence". It can then easily be observed that this is not a normal style of speech, which makes *in soluta oratione* (*in free prose*) be an accurate description of the letters. Unlike the quatrains themselves, the letters do make the appearance of being written in prose.

Beyond this comparison, there is a clear contrast in the apparent context each letter presents. The Preface,

---

63   The Free Dictionary by Farlex, definition of "preface", http://www.thefreedictionary.com/preface
64   A period mark was used after dates and numbers, which was not an attempt to denote the end of a statement. Those are not considered here as period marks.

while having less period marks per page, has an after effect of having followed some logical train of thought to a conclusion. While it is very confusing to follow all of the twists and turns, it seems like one has just read something that vaguely made sense. The letter to Henry, on the other hand, leaves no such impression.

An analogy could be made to a horse trail, where rented horses are available for city slickers to ride. Normal writing would be represented by a normal horse, which has walked the trail so often it needs no guidance. One just sits on the horse and rides along, as it follows a well-trod trail, from the stable, back to the stable. Since neither the Preface, nor the letter to Henry, are normal, there is nothing mundane about the trails one takes. As such, the rides each become a unique experience, and require more experience with riding, than just being a novice.

The Preface would be like riding a blind donkey, where the donkey knows the way back to the stable by scent, rather than sight. By following its nose, some wild shortcuts (or long cuts) would be taken, depending on which way the wind was blowing. The result would be some low branches to duck and an accumulation of burs on the pants legs; but a sense that the trail was always nearby would offer some sense of comfort. One would not be frozen with fear by the changes of course.

The Henry letter is not this tame. It is like renting a bucking bronco that soon leaves the trail, running off into the woods, where it then throws the rider. After the rider starts to walk back to the trail, the bronco returns to the rider and nicely lets the rider remount. Once back on the bronco, the wildness repeats, including circling back to cover the same parts of the trail, sometimes heading down the trail the wrong way, before bolting off into another wild direction. By the time the rider gets back to the stable, it is impossible to determine what just happened, and why the stable owner would have put a paying customer through such pain and agony.

This pain and agony is why Henry C. Roberts initially refused to include the letter to Henry in his work, *The Complete Prophecies of Nostradamus (Millennium Edition)*. Presumably, it is why so few interpreters of *The Prophecies* have bothered to mention either letter as their source of reasoning behind their interpretations. Since the author is the best source for meaning, especially when arguing something so antique, logic demands one first examine what the authors said the meaning is. Anything pronounced to be the meaning, by someone other than the author, requires such authoritative backing to be factual and true. Otherwise, everything is conjecture, usually based on biased opinion, and bears no truth that can be proven.

These letters written by Nostradamus are designed to provide all the evidence one needs to approach interpreting the quatrains, following the rules of critical thinking. The author has documented evidence that he explained the meaning of his work. To disregard those explanations simply because one does not understand them is *foolish*. It would be like writing a review for the local newspaper's Features section, about the joys of the local horse trail, when one never actually rode a horse on the trail, for fear of horses. To disregard instructions and explanations, to instead complain that the letters represent nonsense and insanity, but to then embark on the path of interpretations, without the author confirming those interpretations are accurate, makes one a *foolish literary critic.*

In reality, by remaining observant during the wild bronco ride of the letter to Henry II, one can begin to see some method to the madness. The method comes from recognizing the one time it comes out of the woods, and heads back down the trail where it had already been before. By this, I mean the letter tells the same story at two points in the letter, with those two points being separated by a trail of thought that has nothing to do with the story those two points tell. This is the "Rosetta Stone" for the Henry letter (so to speak), because it acts exactly like the one 6-line verse at the end of *Century Sixth*; and while nothing of this story (in two parts) is written in Latin, denoting a higher voice, the story told is biblical in theme.

The letter tells of the chronology between Adam and Jesus, with Noah, Abraham, and David being the first figures acting as time markers encountered. This first occurs on the fifth page of the document (1568 Lyon edition). Then, after nine full pages of text, relative to other context, there is a return to this biblical timing of the patriarchs spanning from Old to New Testaments. This second part begins near the end of the fourteenth page, extending onto the fifteenth. The return picks back up with Noah and Abraham, but then adds Isaac, Jacob, and Moses, before it substitutes Solomon (the son of David), and then finishes with Christ. These two sections of text should be read as one, meaning that at least one section is out of place and in need of reordering.

To give you an idea of what I am talking about, I will list the pertinent parts of the statements made by Nostradamus, while leaving out the details in between. I will list these side-by-side, in two columns, with the left column representing what was stated on page five, with the right hand column representing what was stated on pages 14-15.

<u>PAGE FIVE</u>	<u>PAGE FOURTEEN-FIFTEEN</u>
*that the first man **Adam** was before **Noah** around one thousand two hundred forty two years ...*	*And in the end here had six hundred years **Noah** will enter within the ark for to be saved from the flood ...*

THE OBVIOUS ODDITIES IN THE HENRY LETTER

PAGE FIVE (Cont.)	**PAGE FOURTEEN-FIFTEEN (Cont.)**
*After **Noah**, from him & to the universal flood, came **Abraham** around one thousand eighty years ...*	*And since the end of the flood to the birth of **Abraham**, will pass the number of the years of two hundred ninety five. And since the birth of **Abraham** until to the birth of Isaac, will be passing one hundred years. And since **Isaac** until with **Jacob**, sixty years ...*
*after came **Moses** around five hundred fifteen or sixteen years, & between the time of **David** and **Moses**, had been five hundred seventy years, there around.*	*And since the entrance of **Jacob** in Egypt until to the issue of them will be passing four hundred thirty years. And since the issue from Egypt until to the building of the temple made by **Solomon** in the fourth year of his reign, will be passing four hundred eighty or four score years.*
*Then after entered the times of **David**, & the times of our savior & redeemer **Jesus Christ**, born of the only virgin, had been ... one thousand three hundred fifty years:*	*And since the building of the temple until to **Jesus Christ** ... will be passing four hundred ninety years.*

As one can see from this side-by-side alignment, these two series of statements both are focused on the theme of accounting for the time that elapsed between Adam and Jesus. By not being shuffled together (dovetailed to match the people marking the passage of time), these two sudden shifts to biblical history make little sense to the reader. However, if they are seen to be in need of meshing as one, the letter to Henry II has just made the astounding statement that the quatrains of *The Prophecies* have to be reordered and matched together properly, just as this letter of explanation explains by demonstration. The letter to Henry makes no sense because it, like the book it explains, is not in a logical order for understanding.

Just like the discovery of the Rosetta Stone enabled Egyptologists to understand the meaning of Egyptian hieroglyphics, this reordering of two sections from Nostradamus' letter to the King of France allows studiers of *The Prophecies* to begin to see how to reorder the quatrains into an epic tale. The key is to reorder the letter so that it becomes an explanatory essay about an order of events told in the poetry. Once a chronological explanation is understood, the quatrains simply have to be matched together, to tell the same stories of the letter collectively, in greater detail. However, this tale of the history between Adam and Jesus would not be expected to be included in the quatrains, as they are *The Prophecies* of the future. More must be gleaned from this explanation of a biblical past, which will allow for better understanding the future.

If you recall the quatrain that I pointed out previously, as an example of the first quatrain including an all-capital-letter word, the line including that word stated, "*The small staff in hand placed in the middle of the BRANCHES.*" As I explained then, the all-caps word commonly translated as *BRANCHES* (from the French word of the same spelling) could equally translate to mean *LINEAGES*. That first line, from the second quatrain in *Centurie First*, matches the information detailed in the letter to Henry II, establishing the meaning as a theme telling of the *LINEAGE* between Adam and Jesus Christ. This acts to lend merit, as a letter of explanation about the future tale of *The Prophecies*, to the theme that the Spirit of Jesus Christ was the source.

In that sense, Jesus not only showed Nostradamus the future, but all time since Adam, but particularly that time which will lead up to the return of Christ, at the end of mankind. This gives additional meaning to the Preface's statement of the *three times, past, present,* and *future*. Nostradamus would have been shown God's plan for humanity, including the Son of God (the *past*), with Jesus' coming representing the new *COVENANT* that would govern the *future*.

The times of Nostradamus, being before the first event would initiate *The Prophecies* of the *future*, would act as the beginning of those *three times*. By the time when the quatrains would truly become understandable (now), the *past* and the *present*, with the *future* close enough to see as viable, if not probable. Everything becomes relative to the times of the *Holy Bible*, because those lessons of the *past* are about how one *present* time after another led to God sending a prophet to advise the proper path to take in the *future*, or face the setback prophesied. By Nostradamus having the *small staff in hand*, as the *rod* of true Prophet, he had joined the *BRANCHES* of holy guidance sent to humanity.

Further, since these references to biblical figures and patriarchs are only found in the letter to Henry II, it means this timeline of the *Holy Bible's past* is extraneous to the tale of *The Prophecies*. The definition of "prophecy", as a forewarning, restricts Nostradamus' book from having focus on the *past*, from his perspective in the mid-16th Century. Still, Nostradamus made note of Eusebius and Varro (two Christian historians and chronologists) in his timeline, indicating those two had not come to agreement on their calculations of the timeline of mankind.

This means Nostradamus was correcting their errors in the letter to Henry. The only explanation for Nostradamus having any knowledge of time, beyond what famous historians had stated to be reasoned judgments, could only be to prove he was not the source of anything related to the work bearing his name. Nostradamus, without divine guidance, would have no reason or ability to question how many years passed between Adam and Christ.

Even Nostradamus' knowledge of astrology would not explain this timeline correction. The art of astrology is based on fixed rates of motion for planets and luminaries, meaning forecasting the future is possible by calculating planetary positions that will be. The science of astronomy is based on these same fixed rates. Based on this, it would be possible to reverse the movement of planets and luminaries and relive past times. However, such hindsight is not worth the effort, beyond a normal lifespan of years, because predictive astrology (and thus explanatory astrology) is dependent on understanding the time, not guessing about an unknown that could have been.

The problem would have been the work necessary to calculate planetary movements over vast stretches of ancient times. The effort would have been too great for too little reward. Beyond calculating a few years, backward or forward, the 16th Century's lack of computers (to adjust for planets not moving in exact circles) would have made the error factors render useless charts. Accuracy would then have to be thrown out the window. There would be no purpose achieved by doing reverse astrology, especially when Nostradamus was talking about several thousands of years of astronomic history. Likewise, Nostradamus explained in his letters how useless it would be to try that into a distant future.

There simply is no point in explaining the biblical timeline other than to be explaining some of the other elements that went along with being in the presence of the divine. Understanding this basic concept allows one to see other sections of the letter in an entirely different light. The illumination helps one see the meaning that is within the letter written to Henry. Still, to understand that a complex letter needs to be reordered, so one can understand a divine explanation, is only the first step in a series of steps that have to follow. The second step is being able to read the letter properly; and that is where knowing the systems of understanding comes into play.

Chapter 9

Reviewing the Observable

Before one begins to learn how to read the "foreign language" that is *The Prophecies*, one has to agree on what has been expressed in the "ordinary language" we have observed. Keep in mind that the Old French text does not mean the letters and quatrains were written in the language understood by fluent readers of French (Old or otherwise). If that were the case, the French would have solved Nostradamus in 1555 and again in 1557 and 1568. The fact remains that the language of *The Prophecies* is just as foreign to natives of France as it is to anyone (myself particularly) with no formal training with French. Everything must be a translation; but, as we have glimpsed, some parts are easier to translate than others are.

We have seen that the title makes an instant statement about the contents of the book, where the translation defines the title. Nostradamus did not simply write "some predictions," he wrote *THE PROPHECIES*. By definition, this is an all-capital-letter statement of divine utterance from a Prophet. We have learned that Nostradamus did not write calculated predictions, because there is no error that will be found. Everything is infallible, which can only be possible in God. Anything seen as an error is a reflection on that one not being able to see the truth.

We have also learned that Nostradamus wrote in two voices in his preface. By definition, a preface is a document written by the author for the purpose of introducing the work to follow, through general explanation of what will be found in the text. One voice in this foreword was the French of Nostradamus, with a second voice being the Latin of the Roman Catholic Church. We could feel this second voice being higher, because it was the official language of Christianity. That feeling was confirmed by multiple Latin statements linking directly to biblical quotes, with many attributed to words spoken by Jesus of Nazareth. Therefore, we learned that Latin acted as the voice of Jesus Christ.

Many messages about *The Prophecies* came from those Latin statements, which let us learn some answers to age-old questions surrounding the verses. We learned who the true source is, even if Nostradamus is the human author. We learned why Nostradamus wrote documents that could not easily be understood. The wording was designed to protect those who could be harmed needlessly, if fear of a dreaded future was clearly known during times before that future would have impact. The wording also kept the powerful from using knowledge of the future for their personal gain, while preserving a holy document until that future arrived, when there would be the greatest need to understand the prophecies.

We learned what the prophecies told of, as the punishment mankind would bring upon itself, due to having fallen away from God. We learned that while nothing will make sense for a long time, enough would become clearly understood before it is too late, so we would know how a horrible future could be averted. We learned that the theme of the story revolves around a *diametrically opposite change*, which will flip-flop the order of *reigns, sects,* and *religions*. From this, we learn that randomness cannot make this story be known. There has to be order in the prophetic verses.

We also learned when this future would take place, such that the future would be during times of a *secular world*, one filled with *ignorance*. We learned that *The Prophecies* was written as a warning for humanity to change and stop ignoring God. It acts as a parallel to *The Revelation*, with both warnings being sent by Jesus Christ, to help save mankind from itself. We learned that the story told in the poems is one where a whipping with a *rod of iron* will bring about the *dawn* of how important *The Prophecies* are. We learned we could find out this message beforehand, or after the fact. The choice is ours.

We also learned from one Latin statement that *The Prophecies* were written in an *unrestrained style of speech*. This is most important to realize, because a lack of syntactical restriction is the key to the systems that will unlock understanding. One has to be free to read all definitions into the chosen words. In this way, a little becomes a wealth of detail.

We then learned that an all-capital-letter word is another clue, where higher meaning should be sought, for true understanding to be gained. We saw an example of how such a higher meaning could elevate us from the mundane to the holy. We learned how an all-capital-letter word is shouting out its importance, above and beyond that of an ordinary word. We learned how two quatrains, both with all-capital-letter words, fit together as one poem continuing another's thought, as a statement that all quatrains can be linked in this manner.

Next, we learned that one 6-line verse, written entirely in Latin, with two Latin words in all-caps, acted as a foreword to *The Prophecies*, additional to the preface. We saw how it was located within the text, meaning it had to be moved to the front of the book, because the words told potential readers what they could expect to find. Instead of telling the theme of *The Prophecies*, this one verse told what could be expected to be found by those not believing in God and Christ; and by being in all Latin, it is from the voice of Jesus.

From that discovery, we learned none of the quatrains could remain in their published positions. By the removal of one, so it could be moved to the front, all other quatrains are freed to follow suit. The publishing of three full parts, after *Century Seventh* was left with less than one hundred verses, means they most likely were already written as part of one epic story, before the initial publication date. Therefore, we learned all of those three hundred must be moved into their rightful place in the order of story.

Finally, with this knowledge revealed to us we learned that the letter explaining *The Prophecies* was itself written as a lucid whole, only to be published in a reordered manner, causing apparent randomness to make no sense. As a letter of explanation, we learned this confirmed that the quatrains must be reordered. When the letter to Henry II is reordered so that it makes sense, it will outline an overview of the stories detailed within the quatrains. We have thus learned that by knowing the chronology of this general tale our work reordering the quatrains can begin. However, we also learned that we must learn the systems within Nostradamus' writing style, so one can understand what was written, making reordering possible.

Without reading much more than a few words, of the sea of words that make up the letters and verses, we have read a lot. By simply looking more closely at a few of the oddities that stand out, we have seen that little really is as it first appears. If we had inspected these strange aspects and come away further confused, than we were at the start, we would have confirmed that Nostradamus wrote something of no real value. However, we have had the opposite occur. We have found solid directional guideposts, which are pointing us in the direction of complete understanding.

PART 2

THE SYSTEMIC PROPERTIES OF THE PROPHECIES

Chapter 10

We Make Sense of Words through the System Known as Syntax

Relatively speaking, to this point I have not presented more than a few of the many words written by Nostradamus, as evidence for the meaning behind the words. I have presented a part of the letter of Preface, focusing on the Latin text, with the French text surrounding that. I presented lines from two quatrains that contained all-capital-letter words; and I presented one 6-line verse that has to act as the foreword to his quatrains. This leaves the vast majority of what Nostradamus wrote, relative to *The Prophecies*, still to explore.

In what I have presented, I can see how a stumbling line such as, "*Hidden this from the wise, & prudent & rulers, & explained in detail to small extents & slight,*" seems more in need of restructuring in order to yield meaning, rather than having any immediate meaning. The line stating, "*All things as far as Astrologer Simpleton, Savage far off are,*" does little to arrouse one's mind to clear understanding. Nor does, "*The small staff in hand placed in the middle of the BRANCHES*" make a statement our minds can firmly grasp. The reality is that these are typical examples of the language contained within *The Prophecies*.

I am well aware that some, if not all of the presentations I have made so far, in the form of literal translations that bear the meaning, makes it difficult for the reader to follow my explanations with ease. While I have been able to make sense of what was written, most people on their own would never be able to draw the same conclusions I have drawn. The reason is not that I have played any tricks, since I logically explain how I draw my conclusions; but instead the reason is that most peoples' minds simply do not process such abstract thoughts quickly.

On the other hand, if I had translated the same three statements differently, less literal and more syntactical, they could have seemed to make more sense to the reader. To state that Nostradamus meant to say, in the examples presented so far, "You have hidden such things from the wise and prudent, while revealing them unto babes"; "Stay far away Astrologers, Idiots, and Barbarians"; and, "With the wand in hand waved in the middle of the tripod", such flows of words allow for visualization of what was written. By stating the Old French into a form of rearranged meaning, required to understand in English, everything would have seemed to make more sense. However, that sense would soon come a dead end, because Nostradamus did not state any of that. The adjacent lines of Old French text, when likewise "paraphrased" into English, would lead to the point of confusion. In that scenario, one could think I tricked one as well; but the real trick would have been convincing someone to believe my paraphrases had the same power as divine prophecy. That would be a lie.

When some people read a book, they expect to read it quickly. Quantity can have more appeal to some, more than quality. One can keep abreast on all the latest bestsellers with a learned ability to read fast, while still comprehending the true essence of meaning. Even if some of the details were skimmed over, more reading can be accomplished. This is often a necessary skill in college and business, where volumes of comprehended readings are expected.

Speed-reading is an art form, where certain elements of language are sought out for the mind to process quickly. Still, reading has been determined to be an automatic mental process, once reading has been mastered beyond one's elementary education. We master syntax, which is how we understand the written and spoken word. This is why translations must become paraphrased, rather than literal, because people want to understand what has been stated immediately, rather than be confused and questioning the meaning.

This means that reading becomes so automatic, it is like driving an automobile. Once driving has become mastered, conscious thought is no longer required. As such, an adult reader easily is able to follow long and even complex sentences, so they instantly grasp the intended meaning. This is not possible to a second grader (or an eight year old child), who has to read each word of something written, as a separate element that requires processing to understand. Likewise, a new driver often struggles to remember all of the lessons of driving, such that the "multitasking" required causes one to drive very slowly at first, or have accidents when driving faster than their mind can process everything.

All of this requires some system of standardization, just as a driver needs to learn the mechanics of how a car is made to operate, as well as the traffic laws that govern driving a vehicle. This is then synthesized through actual driving experience. The standardization that is required for learning language is syntax, where all the mechanics and rules are likewise synthesized. The word, "syntax," is defined as, "The study of the rules whereby words or other elements of sentence structure are combined to form grammatical sentences."[65]

For students in school, once they think they know how to "drive" their mental mastery of language, they learn some exceptions to those rules they practiced repetitively. By the time high school comes along, they meet poetry. The same rules do not totally apply to poetry, because sentence structure dissolves. A

---

65   The Free Dictionary by Farlex, http://www.thefreedictionary.com/syntax

word that usually is taken to mean one thing, can often mean something else.

This is what is meant by "poetic license." "Poetic license" is defined as, "The liberty taken by an artist or a writer in deviating from conventional form or fact to achieve a desired effect."[66] One does not speed-read poetry because that "desired effect" is then missed. The reason it is missed is the rules have changed, to rules our minds are no longer able to process subconsciously. It becomes a matter of realizing one is no longer on the familiar streets one is used to driving, requiring closer attention be paid, so one does not get lost.

One has to realize that Nostradamus wrote *The Prophecies* with poetic license. Every quatrain is an individual poem, because every one of them follows a rhyme scheme. In all of the four-line verses, the last words of lines one and three rhyme, as do those of lines two and four, using different rhymes. This is called an ABAB rhyme scheme; and it is very evident in the French text. The rhyme disappears in translation, which then seems to make the poetry turn into prose, but every one of prophecies is a poem. As such, all of the quatrains were written with poetic license governing them, meaning none of them can be read conventionally.

Past translators have largely disregarded this understanding of poetic license. They have created paraphrases that toss away the abstract nuisances poetry allows, transforming what was written into quickly understood statements that yield rather meaningless drivel. Still, this translation is due, to a large degree, on the French reading the poems with the automatic need to process poetry into prose.

I presented an explanation earlier, of how Nostradamus has been seen to state that he waved a wand between the legs of a tripod. This would seem to make sense, if one wanted to believe Nostradamus was a sorcerer conjuring up magical predictions. However, when the rules of a true Prophecy is known to be the governing factor for understanding all quatrains, just as poetic license governs understanding poems, it is wrong to jump to such quick solutions. To assume that magic explains *The Prophecies*, rather than divine inspiration, makes such a translation, as "waving a wand between the legs of a tripod," evidence of senseless talk (a definition of "drivel").

Some translators have even obliterated the line structure of the poems, blending all of the lines into some paraphrased series of implied sentences. The result is the removal of all evidence that a poem was written. This practice has resulted in large quantities of the individual prophecies being uninterpretable, senseless verses. These have been mostly swept away, as being unimportant or incorrect visions of the future, which is impossible from a truly divine source. Because most interpreters ignore this need to follow one basic rule, "divine poetic license", they are left focusing on only a few quatrains. Only the "mostly sensible" future quatrains, in the neighborhood of twenty-five or so, seem to be understandable.

---

66   The Free Dictionary by Farlex, http://www.thefreedictionary.com/poetic+license

This ability to see something right about *The Prophecies*, while reading them wrong, serves a purpose. A few quatrains being seen as remarkable, and beyond normal abilities, has kept the name of Nostradamus, and thus his remarkable work, in the public's consciousness for hundreds of years. If one does not realize how much of an accomplishment that is, try naming two other works of poetry from other 16th century writers. The typical human being of the 21st century could not name anyone at all; but they recognize the name Nostradamus.

Such recognition is based on incorrect interpretations, ones that have nothing to do with conveying the whole truth contained within *The Prophecies*. People hear Nostradamus and think magician, or con artist, or amazing astrologer, but none think he was a true prophet of God. This lack of proper recognition is due to none of the sensationalized quatrains coming with logical explanations, which back the interpreter's claims, as evidence that Nostradamus explained that as the intended meaning. While people know the name Nostradamus, they do not know that everything found amazing about the man has been based on a paraphrase, as a preconception by the translator, with Nostradamus acting more as a trade name, than as the author.

While some of the quatrains that have been sensationalized do brush against what appears to have been the intention of Nostradamus, by putting words in his mouth (or words on his quill pen) for him, the interpreters have interrupted Nostradamus, as though saying, "Here, let me tell you what the master prophet meant to say." This is putting the cart before the horse. It is the epitome of the idiom, "Haste makes waste." In the haste of past translators, they have wasted the vast majority of what was written, completely missing the point that all is prophetic. It is the *foolish* way to read *The Prophecies*.

If you remember the first line of the 6-line verse that acts as the foreword to *The Prophecies*, it was addressed as a caution to those who would be so bold as to do such interpretations. Line one, following the all-caps heading (or line two overall), stated, *"Whom should read this verse prematurely to assess."* While that statement certainly means that one cannot read meaning into what was written, before what was written has meaning, it also means one cannot read "overhastily, too rashly, or precipitately" (synonyms of "premature").[67] This means if you are reading at the right time, but reading too fast (speed-reading a poem), you will not be able to come away with any real understanding of what you read. One cannot properly *assess* the meaning by cutting corners.

In this day and age many people relate to the cliché that "time is money." It seems that doing things fast has become the norm; and simply by being different, this norm makes the merits of patience stand out. Patience is a virtue, at least as determined to be a Contrary Virtue (one of the Seven Heavenly Virtues), such that it is opposite the Vice (or Deadly Sin) called Wrath. Patience is defined as, "the ability to wait calmly for something to happen without complaining or giving up",[68] which is how one has to see *The Prophecies*.

67   The Free Dictionary by Farlex, http://www.thefreedictionary.com/prematurely
68   Collins Essential English Dictionary, 2nd Edition, 2006, Harper-Collins Publishers

The German philosopher, Friedrich Nietzsche, once wrote, "being able to wait is so hard that the greatest poets did not disdain to make the inability to wait the theme of their poetry," as if he himself had struggled to understand the poetry of Nostradamus.[69] Still, reading what other philosophers have said about this virtue makes it clearer how patience is the key to understanding *The Prophecies*.

The Roman statesman Cato the Elder (234 BC to 149 BC) wrote, "Patience is the greatest of all virtues." A "virtue" must be seen as a "moral excellence" or "goodness," which sets it apart from sin. Saint Augustine (354 AD to 430 AD) advanced this thought by surmising, "Patience is the companion of wisdom." This means that common sense and good judgment goes along with the ability to act morally. Both of those philosophers were making valid points, which would make judging a true Prophecy require patience.

Still, Isaac Newton (1642 to 1727) made the observation, "If I have ever made any valuable discoveries, it has been owing more to patient attention, than to any other talent." This says that trying to shape things to our preconceptions, as a sign of the impatience of ego, is not as powerful as simply letting something profound come to us naturally (like having an apple falling from a tree ignite awareness). Franz Kafka (1883 to 1924) said, "There are two cardinal sins from which all others spring: Impatience and Laziness." This clearly echoes the errors that are left in the wake of shortcutters. All of this makes the analogy correct, which states "good things come to those who wait."

Still, perhaps the most profound philosophy on patience is found coming from an old Dutch Proverb that says, "A handful of patience is worth more than a bushel of brains."[70] This is a perfect way to sum up how so many have come up with wrong conclusions about *The Prophecies*. There is way too much thinking going on, when there should be more praying, along with more faith that when the time is right the truth will be known.

What this means is there is no fast way to reordering the verses into the proper order. Given the assumption that we are now deep enough into the future (relative to the days of Nostradamus) to begin to find understanding from the quatrains, we cannot find meaning in all of the quatrains unless we know how to read them properly. Our normal way of understanding the written language will not allow us to read *The Prophecies* correctly. We have to approach everything written as *in soluta oratione*, in unrestricted style of speech. That then becomes the purpose of this book, and the remainder of this book's focus.

In this respect, one has to keep in mind that the title applied to Nostradamus' work is plural. It is a collection of *Prophecies*, such that each poem is by itself prophetic. By knowing the correct way to read Nostradamus for ultimate meaning, one will be able to see beyond the simplistic views that "to prophesy" means solely, "to foresee the future." It means, on a greater level, "to reveal the will or message of

---

69 *Human, All Too Human*, Nietzsche, 1878 (English 1984)
70 The Quotations Page, Patience Quotes, http://www.quotationspage.com/subjects/patience/

God."[71]

This means that all quatrains offer truth, more than anything else. A truth will always be true, no matter when the discovery of a truth takes place. This means that the 6-line verse that acts as a foreword to *The Prophecies* is stating a truth, which will be applicable at all times. This means the two quatrains that connected, with each containing examples of all-capital-letter words, state truths that tell of Nostradamus' experience with the Spirit of Jesus Christ. Even though that experience is not prophesied as a future event, it is a statement of truth that was true then, was true of past times of prophetic experience, and certainly would be true for all future encounters with God and Christ. Nostradamus was telling us how the message of God was revealed to him.

This means that the verses that tell of horrid future times (which are without a doubt obvious, from the terminology used in many quatrains) are true; but this does not mean everything stated is fixed and cannot be changed. Just as a mathematical truth can be stated A + B = C, such that this will always be the case, it does not mean a specific value (A) has to be added to another specific value (B), which would result in a known specific sum value (C.) We are living in specific times (A), but we have control over what will be specifically added (B), thus we control the outcome of our future (C). Nostradamus stated the truth of what will happen (C), should everything play out as foreseen.

It is for that reason that we should care least about what would happen, and focus on what has happened. The past is relative to the present and the future, and is the one variable that cannot be changed. The quatrains tell us what has happened already, which is recognizable in our history. While that is beyond our control, it tells us in what ways we have turned our backs on God. Through the realization that our past actions are driving our present actions, heading us towards horrendous future actions, we have to act now to change that future direction. This has to be understood as the purpose of true Prophecy.

One cannot become entrapped by some popular Christian views that the only measure of a true Prophet is whether or not what was prophesied came true perfectly (100%). While one certainly must hold that God is infallible, and as such a Prophet of God prophesying the future is 100% telling the truth, this does not mean the future cannot be changed.

Jesus, as remembered in the Book of Matthew, stated the perfect example of this. There, the Pharisees questioned Jesus, asking if he would give them a sign to let them know of the future. To this Jesus replied, "there shall no sign be given to it, but the sign of the prophet Jonas". (Matthew 12:39b) Jesus then continued to clarify this mention of Jonas (a.k.a. Jonah) by stating, "The men of Nineveh shall rise in judgment with this generation, and shall condemn it: because they repented at the preaching of Jonas." (Matthew 12:41a) In other words, Jonas presented the "men of Nineveh" a true Prophecy of God, which was 100% true; but because those men repented (changed) and condemned it (admitted their faults, thus

---

71   The Free Online Dictionary by Farlex, http://www.thefreedictionary.com/prophesy

having faith such a fate would befall them), they averted that future happening.

This means faith is the best understanding one has to have. One has to believe the bleak future one feels in *The Prophecies* will come true (100%), unless through faith one repents and condemns past actions. This means we have to have a clear understanding of what has been done, and why those actions were wrong in the eyes of God. Only from vividly seeing our past as having been prophesied, seen beforehand precisely as it turned out to be, can one truly have faith that *The Prophecies* are from Jesus Christ. Jesus told the Pharisees, "behold, a greater than Jonas is here," (Matthew 12:41b) meaning the sign of the "day of judgment" (from Matthew 12:36) will come from the greatest of all Prophets. We have to be moved to faith that Jesus sent Nostradamus as a messenger of God to save mankind, not to tease it.

With an ability to read the quatrains and clearly see the past open before our eyes, the future will begin to come into focus, although not be completely clear. What has yet to happen will still appear vague and strange, although understandable. That furthest away from the present will be least distinguished. This means that every quatrain has to be read accurately, simply to determine if it falls into the past, falls into the unknown future, or straddles the past and the foreseeable future. This means the first step that must be taken before any reordering of the verses, into stories with meaning, can take place is to learn how to read what was written. We cannot begin to do such a sort without this basic education.

I reference "basic education" because much of what needs to be learned about the operating systems of Nostradamus require nothing more than a refresher course on our most rudimentary education. The same rules we learned in grade school still apply, but they apply differently. Since it has been so long since we learned them, our minds now automatically process them without thought being required. This means we struggle with reading something that uses the same rules differently, because we have forgotten what our minds absorbed. Therefore, we have to relearn how to read, this time differently than the first time. In other words, we need to learn a new syntax.

Chapter 11

An Elementary Refresher

In its most basic definition, "language" is defined as, "Communication of thoughts and feelings through a system of arbitrary signals, such as voice sounds, gestures, or written symbols."[72] Since this arbitrariness is best understood within fixed parameters, "language" is also defined as, "Such a system [of communication signals, sounds, gestures, and symbols] including its rules for combining its components, such as words."[73] We have to begin to understand Nostradamus by realizing we cannot find definite meaning from language, without the rules of language being applicable.

From this basic understanding, it becomes important to re-grasp the fundamentals of grammar. The word, "grammar," is defined most basically as, "The study of how words and their component parts combine to form sentences."[74] This also covers "the system of inflections, syntax, and word formation of a language,"[75] which includes, "the system of rules implicit in a language, viewed as a mechanism for generating all sentences possible in that language."[76]

Since we have already discussed that the writings of Nostradamus were to be read *in soluta oratione*, or in a style of speech not restricted by the rules of syntax, this does not forego having the rules of language and grammar still apply. Their application would simply have to be in a different manner than is typical of the accepted syntactical manner. In this way, the definition of grammar that would fully apply is, "Writing or speech judged with regard to a normative or prescriptive set of rules setting forth the current standard of usage for pedagogical [teaching] or reference purposes."[77]

As such, normative means by a norm or standard; and "prescriptive," relative to linguistics, means, "Based on or establishing norms or rules indicating how a language should or should not be used rather than describing the ways in which a language is used." All of this means that Nostradamus wrote according to standard rules, but those rules were applied in a manner that indicated how they should not be used in everyday speech, such as prose would be considered. In other words, Nostradamus made up

72 The Free Dictionary by Farlex, http://www.thefreedictionary.com/language
73 Ibid.
74 The Free Dictionary by Farlex, http://www.thefreedictionary.com/grammar
75 Ibid.
76 The Free Dictionary by Farlex, http://www.thefreedictionary.com/grammar
77 Ibid.

a new language that only applied to *The Prophecies*; but it was a new language using standard rules of language differently.

This means that Nostradamus created a different standard of usage that causes the reader to have to relearn the rules of language. Since the rules of language are to a certain degree fixed, once all language rules are reviewed a different approach in the application of those rules can be seen in Nostradamus' style of writing. All of the rules he used have standard application, which means that in every instance where a rule would need application, it would need to be applied in the same manner at all times, without any excuse for waving the rules. This consistency would then allow for everything to be read with full meaning, simply by following the rules of grammar, specific to the grammar of Nostradamus.

It then becomes important to refresh our minds about the three major components of grammar. These consist of the parts of speech, punctuation, and composition. The parts of speech are the words, which are broken into the different types of words – nouns, pronouns, adjectives, adverbs, and verbs. The elements of punctuation are periods, commas, question marks, exclamation points, colons, and semi-colons. The composition is then the sections of writing, such as sentences, paragraphs, transitions, conjunctions, and clauses.

Since Nostradamus used all of the parts of speech, those usages must be understood to be following standard rules. As such, a noun can be expected to be a noun, rather than an adverb, simply because there are rules that determine a noun to be different from an adverb. While French differs from other languages, it still has a set use of endings as modifiers for words, as part of its rules to determine the use of a word. This use can be counted on as a standard way to determine such use. French can be expected to be French.

Nostradamus' use of punctuation has been an issue in the past, and to many it still is an issue today. Translators of his prophecies have questioned the published punctuation of the quatrains and its letters of explanation in the past, if omission and alteration can be seen as questioning. Most translators act as if the punctuation was the result of a lack of standards in the publishing industry in the mid-16th Century, if not a lack of education in grammar on Nostradamus' part. They see the inclusion of punctuation as something termed "printer's rights", where the typesetter was given free-reign to set all punctuation as he saw fit. In the minds of such translators, this lack of Nostradamus' control gives them the freedom to amend the punctuation to fit their own mastery of grammar and language, in their paraphrasing of the original text.

The argument for the reasoning, for these translators, would hold some merit, if it were not for the fact that the earliest publications of *The Prophecies* are not consistent with punctuation. This includes both the letter of Preface (all editions) and the letter to Henry II (post-1558 editions), as well as the quatrains. Collectively, there is no demonstration of consistency between the editions, with all originating in Lyon, which would act as evidence of such standardization. For instance, one edition shows a colon at the end of a line of a quatrain, while another would show a comma.

This inconsistency could make it seem that there were norms relative to punctuation, even causing some to go as far as to think Nostradamus used no punctuation at all. The differences could then be written off as a repeated use (if not misuse) of the printer, lacking the knowledge to correctly apply a punctuation component. However, that assumption is flawed, when one finds a seemingly incorrect use of a colon is verified by other editions showing the same strange placement.

This indicates designed usage of punctuation, where something's application is differently than one would expect, in standard grammar, but standard in Nostradamus' grammar. Naturally, French readers and translators would not expect a new standard of grammar rules, leading them to see *The Prophecies* as impossible to understand. That lack of understanding would automatically have them trying to make understanding appear by changing the punctuation to better suit their own standards of grammar.

This explains why translators would seek to discount the seeming lack of standards and rules; but it would be impossible to expect a typesetter to be the mind behind the perfect placements of punctuation, applicable to a new standard of rules only found in *The Prophecies*. The fact that the punctuation gives meaning to what was written, when a new standard is applied consistently to all punctuation presented in the text, is proof that Nostradamus is the source of that punctuation. The typesetter could have only been what one would logically expect a typesetter to be, namely a hired hand, simply duplicating a manuscript for print.

Therefore, one has to be prepared to see Nostradamus' use of punctuation as a new set of rules one has to see and comprehend. Punctuation cannot be expected to follow the rules that indicate how words combine to form sentences, as one's mind is trained to comprehend them as such. However, this does not mean that a period, a comma, a colon, etc. does not follow the rules that define each specific form of punctuation.

As confusing as this must seem to you now, imagine how confused a first grade reader is when learning to read for the first time. Sentences at that level are simple, with the only punctuation being a period at the end. The young student has to practice that, to learn a period means it is time to stop and comprehend what was just read. A simple sentence is a series of words, of different types, with each being a component that must be understood separately from the rest. The period mark tells the young student to synthesize those components.

The same can be said of adults learning a new language. When one struggles to grasp the meaning of individual words, several words are nearly impossible to absorb at once, as synthesizing the meaning takes longer to the untrained mind. A new learner reads each word separately, and processes each word separately, before reading the next word. Each new word makes the student repeat this process. Only after the individual words have been analyzed mentally can they be combined for greater meaning. With practice and familiarity, due to repetitiveness, this mental processing becomes faster.

For example, in my first grade *Dick and Jane* readers, I would read a simple sentence like, "See Spot run." I would have to process the word "see," and understand that was the present state of the verb that meant the use of eyes. I would have to process the name "Spot," and understand that Spot was the name of Dick and Jane's dog. I would then understand that I was seeing Spot. Then, I would have to process the action verb "run," and understand that this was the action of moving one's legs and feet rapidly, in order to cover ground fast. After all of the processing and understanding, I would know that what I just read meant that I was watching the dog named Spot running. Such is the way of elementary reading skills.

As such, one must be prepared to read Nostradamus with the same uncertainty of meaning. Until one learns the systems, and practices them repeatedly, the language of *The Prophecies* is foreign. One cannot simply bite off huge chunks of words and expect mentally to digest them for easy meaning, as though Nostradamus wrote in a standard form of prose. Nostradamus wrote in a foreign language, where it alienates the reader through its punctuation.

This feeling of alienation is strongly felt when one reaches one of Nostradamus' "complex sentences," in the letters. These are only "sentences" in the grammatical sense that one has been trained to see a sentence. Certainly, one sees something beginning with a capitalized word, leading to an eventual period, with commas, et al in between. However, Nostradamus placed about 2.5 periods per page of text, in his letters, on average. One can find around 60 words in one Nostradamus "sentence."

One cannot follow Nostradamus' "train of thought", by following standard rules. His components of composition do not march to the beat of standard grammar rules. The length of what would typically be defined as a "sentence" makes it impossible to comprehend the meaning as one central thought, with many related attachments. More than complexity comes from perhaps ten or twenty transition points, marked by internal punctuation (commas, colons, semi-colons) yielding more thoughts than a typical sentence "train" can bear, for understanding to result. This means the composition component of *The Prophecies* is clearly where new rules must be found to apply, such that true meaning can result.

The rules applicable to the composition component are the most difficult to comprehend. This is actually to be expected, especially since one is comparing Old French rules of language to modern rules of language, specifically in the area of composition. This means one is comparing apples to oranges, so to speak. This is particularly true of the rules of composition that have developed since the sixteenth century, particularly in reference to the construction of paragraphs, including paragraphs of transition and conjunction.

In the mid-1600s, the art form called the paragraph was not yet standardized. As such, a letter like Nostradamus' Preface, which was 14 pages (Lyon, 1555 edition) long, was presented in uninterrupted text (no indents to indicate more than one paragraph), and was not seen (by that one aspect) to be unusual. However, what would have been unusual (and what was found to be unusual about Nostradamus' letters) was to have something made public by an author that did not follow some form of logically grouped sentences.

This would be how a paragraph came into being, through the earliest efforts to differentiate between transitioning thoughts, by grouping related thoughts together, and by skipping a line before beginning a new group of sentences, relative to a separate line of thought. While 16th century authors might not have had a set rule for proper writing form, writers always had the purpose of making their sentences follow logically, in order. Without that order, there would be no way of convey the meaning, to make the point they sought to put into writing. In other words, while it was not a standard to mark changes in thought by indentures or blocks of text, it was standard to make these shifts known within one continuous block of text.

In Nostradamus' letters, there is evidence of sentences, through the presence of periods. There is evidence of transitions and conjunctions through the presence of the capitalized words, "And" and "But". At some points, one can get the feel of a paragraph developing, as the wording develops a line of thought by the use of clauses. However, nothing is according to the standard rules of grammar, making everything seem nonsensical and meaningless, when it is all put together as it is. The reason has to be that the standard rules of language do not work on Nostradamus' letters, most profoundly in the formation of sentences.

As I have mentioned previously, Nostradamus used period marks sparingly. The Preface averages little more than two period marks per page (based on the 10-page rendition in the 1568 Lyon edition), with the letter to Henry II having a slightly higher average. To compare how longwinded that is, count the period marks on this page and see if it exceeds ten. The reality is it will greatly exceed ten, and I have been called a longwinded writer. To give you one example of Nostradamus' writing, which would technically be labeled a "sentence", consider this sample from pages 2-3 of his Preface:

> *"Combien que de long temps par plusieurs foys j'aye predict long temps au-paravant ce que depuis est advenu & en particulieres regions, attribuant le tour estre faict par la vertu & inspiration divine & aultres felices & sinistres adventures de acceleree promptitude prenoncees, que despuis sont advenues par les climats du monde aiant voulu taire & delaise pour cause de l'iniure, & non tant seulement du temps present, mais aussi de la plus grande part du futur, de metre par escrit, pource que les regnes sectes &*

> *religions seront changes si opposites, voire au respect du present diametralement, que si je venoys a referer ce que a l'advenir sera, ceux de regne, secte, religion, & foy trouveroient si mal accordant a leur fantasie auriculaire, qu'il viendroent a damner ce que par les siecles advenir on congnoistra estre veu & apperceu : Consyderant aussi le sentence du vray Sauveur,* Nolite sanctum dare canibus, nec mittatis margaritas ante porcos ne conculent pedibus & conversi dirumpant vos."

You should be able to notice this is mostly written in Old French, which is shown here in italics. The ending is in Latin, and just as the 1568 Lyon edition shows, is in a standard type. As such, you could recall I have already translated the Latin from this "sentence" into English, along with some of the French leading up to the Latin. The point here is not to focus on the translation, because it would be impossible to understand simply, in any language, including French.

The point is to get a good look at what comes between a capitalized first word and the ending period mark. The "word count" function on my computer tells me there are 164 words in this "sentence". Regardless of the exact count, no sentence known to man, as long as man has been writing sentences, is ever supposed to be that long. Before the period mark ends this series of words, there are eight ampersands, 15 commas, and one colon. Among that punctuation are too many shifts of thought to follow.

Now, I could tell you the meaning that is contained in this "sentence", by telling you this is not a sentence at all, but rather multiple paragraphs, with many sentences making those paragraphs up. However, me telling you that would be no different than some other translator telling you Nostradamus meant to put a period in at places the printed text does not show. You could easily come away disbelieving what my opinion is, and rightfully so. Only the opinion of Nostradamus, as far as how to make sense of his "sentences", carries any weight of significance.

Nostradamus gave us instructions in his letters, which specifically mention his "sentences". The key is to search amid all these longwinded strings of words and pull out the pearls that tell us what we need to know in this regard. In fact, if you look closely at the example that I have given, you will find the word "*sentence*", which is spelled the same and has the same meaning in both French and English. Following the lone colon (rather than a period mark), a capitalized present participle verb leads a sting of words that state (in English), "*Considering also the **sentence** from the true Savior*". This is a statement that the whole sting of 164 words is not a sentence of Nostradamus, but "*the sentence from the true Savior*", who would be Jesus Christ. The use of the word "*true*" means nothing in the *sentence* will be found to be false.

What follows this statement, that Jesus spoke the *sentence* that Nostradamus wrote, is a sentence from the Book of Matthew (7:6), which was attributed to Jesus speaking to the disciples during the Sermon on the Mount. He said, "Give not that which is holy unto dogs, nor cast your pearls before swine, lest they trample them underfoot and turn and rend you." This means that the quote is a *sentence from the true Savior*, and the whole *sentence* in the Preface is a *sentence from the true Savior* as well. Keep in mind that I have already addressed the use of Latin as being the higher voice of Christ, which this Latin quote certainly is. What we see now is how the French of Nostradamus was from Jesus, as truth, in the manner Jesus stated His words to Nostradamus, such that nothing holy would be given to dogs or cast before swine in an understandable fashion.

Also, consider this statement from the Preface, which states, "*then to me follows meant to unfold explaining for the common people arriving through meanings difficult to understand & ones in a maze (or ones perplexed) sentences*".[78] As you can see, the word "*sentences*" appears again. This time it comes with the word "*perplexes*" actually preceding it, in the original French. The French word, "*perplexe*," is the feminine form of the past tense verb meaning, "perplexed", or "puzzled". This verb is pluralized, which means it accompanies the plural *sentences*, such that all *sentences* are *perplexed ones*. The usage of *perplexe* in Old French also carried the translation of, "intricate, entangled; in a maze, and at wits end"; and I have chosen to use *in a maze* because it gives more of an instant visualization of the puzzling state of *The Prophecies*.

Clearly, the *sentences* of Nostradamus are of this nature, with each *meant to unfold* into a clear form, which are *explaining* how to find their true meaning. This will only be possible by *common people arriving* at the time when Christ will allow understanding. Until then, no one will be able to get *through* the *meaning difficult to understand*, especially when the *sentences* are not in the proper order, being mixed like pieces of a puzzle. As perplexing as these long *sentences* most certainly will be, the time will come when they all will make perfect sense.

This statement gleaned from the Preface is the only other use of the word "*sentences*" in that document. However, I do not want you to think everything I offer is based on such limited evidence. I say this because Nostradamus also explained his *sentences* in his letter to Henry II.

At the top of page six of the letter to Henry, Nostradamus wrote, "*que par ænigmatique sentence, n'ayant qu'un seul sens, & unique intelligence, sans y avoir rien mis d'ambiguë n'amphibologique calculation*". This literally translates to state, "*that by enigmatic sentence, not having that one lone written meaning, & special understanding, without it to have anything laid to ambiguous not amphibological calculation*". This is some very powerful information to know and understand, before one approaches *The Prophecies* for interpretative purposes.

---

78 This is one translation, with each translated word chosen from the Randle Cotgrave 1611 French-English Dictionary. The French of Nostradamus for this translation is, "puis me suis voulu extendre declarant pour le commun advenement par obstruses & perplexes sentences …"

We are immediately told that Nostradamus wrote *that (The Prophecies) by enigmatic sentence*. Since the word *enigma* can be defined as, "A perplexing speech or text; a riddle"[79], we have just been retold what was stated in the Preface, about *perplexes sentences*, or (for all intent and purposes) *puzzling sentences*, or *sentences in a maze*. This confirms what Nostradamus stated over three years earlier, in the letter addressed to his son, Caesar (the Preface).

From this confirmation, Nostradamus next made the statement that the *sentences* of *The Prophecies* will be found *not having only one written meaning*.[80] This means that what was written has more than one meaning, or more than one way to understand what was written. In this regard, Nostradamus followed by stating the realization of this multiplicity of meaning requires a *"unique intelligence,"* or *special* talent for this type of *understanding*.

With this statement, where one needs to be able to see the *sentences* differently than one would normally see them, Nostradamus explained what the *sentences* would appear to be without this *special sense*. In that explanation Nostradamus wrote, *"without it to have anything laid to ambiguous."* This means that *without* the ability to read into what was written, which most people were bound to be blinded from, the quatrains could be said to contain *anything*. This is forecasting the quite common argument that came from the ambiguity, against belief in Nostradamus, where people argue his *sentences* are so vague that *anything* can be read into them. A synonymous word for "vague" could be "*ambiguous*", with *ambiguous* defined as, "open to more than one interpretation."[81]

By writing off the *sentences* as *ambiguous*, we see an example of this multiple meaning found in the French word "*rien.*" By itself, this word means, "*anything,*" but when combined in a *sentence* with a negative, such as *not*, it transforms to mean "*nothing.*" Since the next word is contracted with the word *not*, we can see how *without a special sense for understanding nothing is set* as the meaning. Everything is written off as too *ambiguous* to understand. However, this means *The Prophecies* are then deemed *not amphibological*, which means they are *not* "a word, phrase, or *sentence* that can be interpreted variously because of uncertainty of grammatical construction rather than ambiguity of the words used".[82] Further, once everything is written off, so that this multiplicity is *not* seen, one also fails to see that the multiplicity is by design. It is a *calculation, not* ambiguous stupidity.

This is indeed a very important statement. It reaffirms that Nostradamus is well aware of the *enigmatic* nature of his *sentences*. We see that they are by design, with meaning hidden within one's inability to

---

79   The Free Dictionary by Farlex, http://www.thefreedictionary.com/enigma
80   The word written by Nostradamus translated to state "*written meaning*" is "*sens.*" This is a valid translation, based on the RandaleCotgrave 1611 Dictionary, which lists acceptable usages to be, "sense, wit, understanding, judgment, reason, knowledge, opinion, thought; and also the sense, meaning and construction of a writing."
81   The Free Dictionary by Farlex, http://www.thefreedictionary.com/ambiguous
82   Definition of *amphibological* from the book –*Ologies & -isms*, Gale Group, 2008, from The Free Dictionary by Farlex, http://www.thefreedictionary.com/amphibology

read the purpose intended, because the words chosen are amphibological. Of course, the design is not by Nostradamus, because it would be humanly impossible for one to be so calculating. The design is divine; and Nostradamus offers plenty of statements that affirm this source, and reaffirm it, repeatedly.

Still, there is another statement made in the explanatory letter to Henry, where Nostradamus repeats his use of *enigmatic sentence*. In that statement, Nostradamus wrote in French, "*mais plustost sous obnubilee obscurité par une naturelle infusion approchant a la sentence d'un des mille*". The literal translation of this is, "*but most all under clouded hidden meaning in words by one natural infusion arriving almost in the sentence from one of the thousand.*"

This again identifies *enigmatic* or *perplexed sentences*, here by saying that *most all* are written *under a cloud*. This is a way of stating the *sentences* are clear as fog. The French word *obscurité* certainly can translate as *obscurity*, which does carry a meaning of being dimly lit or dark; but there is a meaning more specific to writing. In that sense, "*obscurity*" can be defined as, "The quality or condition of being imperfectly known or difficult to understand"[83]; and as such, Randle Cotgrave's 1611 French-English Dictionary lists one translation possibility for "*obscurité*" to be, "*hidden meaning in words.*" This *obscurity* is then another way of confirming the *amphibological calculation*.

Nostradamus then stated that this *hidden meaning in words* is *calculated by one*, which is a statement that another *one*, other than Nostradamus, is the creator of this stealth. Further, the *hidden meaning* is *natural*, meaning the *meaning* is *hidden* in the way it appears normal, while also meaning the *hidden meaning* becomes revealed through *natural* rules of language. However, for such understanding to occur, one has to experience an *infusion*, or has to be filled, as if through an in-pouring of understanding. IN that way, what was *hidden* becomes *naturally* exposed, without having to try hard to understand.

This concept is understood in Christianity as being filled with the Holy Spirit. This immersion is not commanded by the one being filled. Instead, God chooses the one to receive the Spirit; and that one has to be ready and willing to allow the Spirit full control. In other forms of religion, where holy men are considered mediums for the "great spirit", an *infusion* occurs after one has prepared for having a spirit inhabit their body temporarily. This can include preparations involving ingesting plants, meditations, or chants. However, Nostradamus makes it clear in his writing that he has been infused with the Holy Spirit. This means he was infused while writing his *sentences* and those who will later understand them will also be *naturally infused*.

Once this *infusion* comes about, the person reading *The Prophecies* will be *approaching* the quatrains *in a new light*. He or she will begin to see how the words of Nostradamus are *almost arriving at* a point, when suddenly *the sentence* structure leads to a shift of thought, which is designed to confuse. The acute sense of awareness leads one to focus on that part that *approaches* making sense, with the *natural infusion*

---

83   The Free Dictionary by Farlex, http://www.thefreedictionary.com/obscurity

leading one to make that segment, clause, phrase, or fragment become *the sentence*.

This is most recognizable in the quatrains themselves, although the letters give the term *sentence* a wilder (and wider) stretch of meaning, particularly because the letters allow for 164-word gatherings, before one reaches a period mark. Each of the quatrains (*one of the thousand*) follows a consistent format. For the most part, there is only one period mark per quatrain, with that coming at the very end of the fourth line. This gives the impression that the four lines all hook up as one lengthy *sentence*, which is then mirrored in the writing style of the letters. An example of how *one of the thousand* would be seen as *the sentence* is found in the quatrain representing *Century First*, number 3:

> *Quand la lictiere du tourbillon verse, / Et seront faces de leurs manteaux couvers, / La republique par gens nouveaux vexée, / Lors blancs & rouges jugeront a l'envers.*

Again, the point is not to translate this one quatrain. It is just one of many that follow the "one period mark at the end" format. Some quatrains have more than one period mark, with one having two question marks, which act to end a series of words, just as a period mark does. I only illustrate this format found in the quatrains so it can be understood how *the sentence from one of the thousand* is directly relative to the quatrains, and not the letters. Still, the letters follow the same rules, such that an *infusion* to understand the quatrains means the letters will also be understandable.

I hope that you can see when Nostradamus made multiple references to the language of *The Prophecies*, he was including his letters as well. That is why the preface did nothing to make the first two editions understandable, calling for the need to write the letter of explanation to Henry. The letter to Henry explained the need for reordering, by itself being disordered. As such, the disorder of the quatrains explains the letter, because they are all parts of the same whole. An explanation of how to read something applies to everything written. Nothing can be seen as longwinded *sentences*, because the minimal use of period marks says the *sentences* of *The Prophecies* cannot be governed by normal rules of grammar.

As we can see in the above example quatrain, when we string the lines together so they seem to grammatically flow, as segments separated by commas to one conclusion at the ending period mark, the illusion of one *sentence* is interrupted by the presence of capitalized words. The capitalized words of the example are all the first word of each line. Even though each line does not end with a period, the following line begins with its first word capitalized. Following the rules of grammar, a new *sentence* is denoted in this way.

Thus, we can begin to see that in a quatrain a comma does not act as a comma normally acts in *sentence* structure, while it does act normally as a comma does in general. By definition, a comma is "a punctuation mark used to indicate a separation of ideas or of elements within the structure of a *sentence*."[84] As such, the quatrain is called a *sentence* simply because it contains one period mark. The line ending commas then simply denote the separations of ideas or elements, which are within the structure of the quatrain. The capitalized first words that follow those separation marks indicate a *hidden* period mark at the end of each of the first three lines, regardless of what punctuation appears there. This would give greater insight into the *natural hidden meaning in writing* that Nostradamus explained could be found in his texts.

In this regard, Nostradamus wrote in his letter to Henry II this additional information. He wrote, "*advenir tout ainsi nommement comme il est escrit, n'y meslant rien de superflu*". This literally translates to state, "*to happen everything as it were particularly (or namely) like it is written, not in it mixing nothing (or anything) of superfluous*". When this states *not in it* (*The Prophecies* or letters) *mixing*, Nostradamus is telling us to keep the parts separate. They should *not* all be *mingled* as if everything written was simply a clause of one long *sentence*.

To do this would make *nothing* intelligible come from what was written, so that *anything* could be read into such combinations and bundlings. That would be *superfluous*, or more than what suffices for understanding (definition for *superfluous*). Therefore, by my only selecting the words that Nostradamus wrote that give these instructions, I have simply taken one slice of words that string together to yield lucidity, versus nebulosity. The surrounding *superfluous* text has purposefully been kept separate, as unnecessary to know in this specific instruction. Nostradamus is instructing one to do such separations (*not in it mingling*) to make sense of his *sentences*.

This is intended to be an instruction for how to read the quatrains, while also applying to the letters. As such, one can see, specifically in the letter of explanation sent to the King of France, no explanation was specifically demanded of the Preface itself. Nostradamus was called upon to explain his enigmatic verses, because his Preface did not appear to be explaining *The Prophecies*, as much as it appeared to be simply a personal letter to Nostradamus' son.

The letter sent to Henry II is thus explaining the need to view the *sentences* of the quatrains not as sentences, but as pieces that stand alone with meaning. Even while these complete parts are found grouped together in the appearance of being one definite string of thought, they are more than one complete thought. To be one overall thought would be what one would expect from a complex sentence that followed the syntactical rules of language, where words and punctuations are components that work as one. However, *The Prophecies* obviously could not be read according to those rules, which is evident in the demand for explanation.

Therefore, the ridiculously long *sentences* of the letter were themselves a way of explaining by demonstration, demonstrating the need to recognize the separate segments as independent thoughts. To

---

84   The Free Dictionary by Farlex, http://www.thefreedictionary.com/comma

confirm this, Nostradamus explained in words, *everything* is *as it were* meant to be by the definitions of the words, meaning *like it is written* as disassociated but related unpunctuated statements of thought, and *not in it* will the punctuation be intended for the purpose of *mixing anything* together as one long sentence. This demonstration and explanation are statements of a new set of rules being followed, by design.

Chapter 12

The Issue of the Holy Spirit

This issue of design requires more explanation. Earlier I mentioned how Nostradamus' use of the word *infusion* was an indication of one's need to be *filled in* (alternate translation of *infuse*) to the meaning of *The Prophecies*. In this regard, I stated how Christians could understand such an *infusion*, particularly in the context Nostradamus presented, "*by one natural infusion approaching*", which was to make sense of the "*obnubilee obscurité*" that covered the *thousand sentences*. Christians should be able to grasp this concept of receiving, as they profess belief in the Holy Spirit, which *infuses* one with divine presence and knowledge.

The best example of such an *infusion* is found in the Book of Acts, particularly where the disciples are together in a room at the beginning of the Passover period, soon after the Ascension of Jesus. We read, "And suddenly there came from heaven a sound as of the rushing of a mighty wind, and it **filled** all the house where they were sitting." (Acts 2:2)[85] Then, we read, "And they **were** all **filled** with the Holy Spirit, and began to speak with other tongues, as the Spirit gave them utterance." (Acts 2:4)[86]

In these two verses, the same root word is used to denote "*filled*". Both the Greek text and the Latin Vulgate uses the same root word, although each language has its own word that expresses the same meaning. The Greek root is *pleroo*, or *plhrow*, which means, "to make full, to fill up."[87] The Latin Vulgate uses the root *repleo*, which likewise means, "to make full, fill up, fill, to fill up again".[88]

Now, the Latin word *infundo* means, "to pour in or on", while having the forms *infusio* and *infusus*, meaning, "pouring in or flowing." This would be the source for the French verb *infuse*, from which Nostradamus wrote, "*infusion*." The English word, *infuse*, also comes from this Latin root, carrying the meaning, "to fill or cause to be filled with something,"[89] specifically something of emotion or quality.

---

85   American Standard Version
86   Ibid.
87   The New Testament Greek Lexicon, Strong's Number 4137, http://www.studylight.org/lex/grk/view.cgi?number=4137
88   The University of Notre Dame, Latin Word Lookup, http://catholic.archives.nd.edu/cgi-bin/lookup.pl?stem=reple&ending=
89   The Free Dictionary by Farlex, http://www.thefreedictionary.com/infuse

This means a humanly *infusion* brings forth a changed state in one. As such, understanding *The Prophecies* requires, minimally, being filled with an emotional desire to understand. Optimally, one would be filled with faith that *The Prophecies* are the work of the divine, through deep feelings that lead one to believe. These levels of belief open one spiritually, which makes it possible to being filled with the Holy Spirit and suddenly see what had been hidden.

In case some readers struggle with this concept of the Holy Spirit, thinking this is part of my own belief system and imagination reading into Nostradamus what I want to see read, let me offer some more proof that Nostradamus is the source of this direction that I have taken here. In the same section of the letter to Henry II where Nostradamus wrote, "*but most all under clouded hidden meaning in words by one natural infusion arriving almost in the sentence from one of the thousand*", Nostradamus explained this *infusion* just as I have. I believe this is saying an *infusion* with God; and Nostradamus supports this belief.

Soon after that segment of the letter, Nostradamus wrote another quote from the Bible, in a relatively verbatim duplication of the Latin Vulgate, directly quoting the prophet Joel. He wrote, "*Effundam spiritum meum super omnem carnem & prophetabunt filiji vestri & filiae vestrae.*" This comes from Joel 2:28b-c, which is commonly translated to state, "*I will pour out my spirit upon all flesh & your sons & daughters will prophesy*". In this Latin quote, we find the root word *effundo*, which means, "to pour out, to pour forth".

Since God is the source of the *pouring out*, the distinction, "*upon all flesh*", would be the receiving end of this pouring, and thus become the point of *infusion*, or *filling in*. The *pouring out / filling in* is then (God's) *spirit*, which is the Holy *Spirit*, such that this *infusion* allows an automatic ability to *prophesy*. An important aspect of this *infusion* is that Nostradamus was *infused* with the Holy *Spirit*, leading him to prophesy *The Prophecies*. However, since his prophecy was *most all under clouded* verse, with *hidden* (*obnubilee*) *meaning in words* (*obscurité*), which kept the prophesied meaning mostly unknown, another *infusion* is required for understanding to take place. This means Nostradamus is explaining, using *amphibology*, that the Holy *Spirit* gives prophecy and the Holy *Spirit* allows prophecy to be interpreted correctly.

The *sons & daughters* reference means those who have not reached a level of maturity to understand fully the workings of the world, as adults typically know. As such, the *spirit* allows the simple-minded (first graders perhaps?) to speak and understand. This is seen in the verse from Joel that is not stated here, where Joel also wrote, "your old men will dream dreams, your young men shall see visions". (Joel 2:28 d-e)[90] This implies the *sons & daughters* are not to be considered adults, but rather children. Children are seen as lacking mental capacities to speak on great levels of wisdom, which prophecy certainly would be recognized as containing. Thus, the only explanation for a child speaking on such profound levels would not be from an intellectual level, but a level of *infused* emotional being, which changes their state from

---

90   American Standard Version

simple child to oracle for the deity.

This level of maturity still is not limited to only children, per se. Earlier, I explained how one has to be like Chance the gardener, who was a simpleton, meaning his mind was as mature as a child's was. Another example would be like the Disciples of Christ, when they were filled with the Holy Spirit on the day of Pentecost. Throughout the Gospels, the disciples proved time and again how mentally dense they were, as they were simple men. The wise men, those knowledgeable of the Law, the pride of the Temple, were too blinded by their own intellectual conceit to see how Jesus was who he claimed to be. Jesus told them they could see, yet were blind, which meant they were not prepared to "receive the spirit." The quality of a childlike mind is its receptivity, such that the Disciples were like Chance the gardener.

It then must be understood that prophecy is not only speaking for God, but interpreting God's word too. Nostradamus was not himself *calculating* how to write a document that would make no sense until one was *infused by the spirit*. He was *infused* and pouring out *The Prophecies*. Those verses and letters will mean nothing until another *infusion* brings about the ability to understand. In that sense, another *pouring out of* God's *spirit* will allow understanding to come forth. This says the divine governs *The Prophecies* completely.

To show this divinity, Nostradamus used another Latin quote, which we have discussed as being the higher voice of Jesus Christ. He stated that the holy *spirit* would be how to understand *one from the thousand* quatrains. In addition to the Latin reflecting Christ, Peter quoted this same verse from Joel after the disciples spoke in tongues on the day of Pentecost. Being filled with the Holy *Spirit* was how simple men could suddenly speak as wise men. Peter knew what had happened, when it happened, because the Spirit of Jesus had prepared them for forty days, so they could receive the *spirit*.

Once again, I do not want you to feel misled by my interpretation of the one word, *spirit*, thinking that perhaps I am reading too much into too few words. Let me continue with what Nostradamus wrote in this one section of his letter. Following this Latin quote from Joel, Nostradamus returned to French, writing, "*Mais telle prophete procedoit de la broche de sainct Esprit, qui estoit la soveraine puissance eternelle, adjoinct avec la celeste a d'aucuns de ce nombre ont predit*". This translates literally to say, "*But such prophet will have proceeded from the mouth of the holy Spirit, which will have been the sovereign power immortal, adjoined with the divine in to some ones from this number had predicted*".

This confirms that Nostradamus clearly meant the *Holy Spirit* in his reference to *infusion*, by his reference to God *pouring out* (His) *spirit* to human *flesh*, and by his plainly stating no *prophet* can prophesy except *from the mouth of the holy Spirit*. The capitalization of *Esprit* certainly means a personified *Spirit*, as is the *Holy Spirit*, being equally personified with the Father and the Son, through the Holy Trinity.

If any further proof is needed, Nostradamus later wrote in the letter to Henry, "*le tout vient de Dieu*," which translates to state, *"the whole has come from God."* He also added another Latin statement, *"a Deo, a natura,"* which says, *"from God, by nature."* This matches the wording, *natural infusion*, such that there will be nothing unnatural about understanding The Prophecies. As a higher voice, the Latin reinforces the presence of the *Holy Spirit* (*from God*) infused with the *natural flesh* of humanity. No superhuman powers will be physically manifest. Only an enhancement of emotional qualities that are purely *natural* will result.

Certainly, with this explanation of mine, while proving my point with the words of Nostradamus, such that my point is Nostradamus' point and the *Spirit* of Christ's point, I realize it insinuates that I am *infused* with the *sainct Esprit* (*Holy Spirit*) simply because I am telling you what Nostradamus meant. Let me make myself clear on this matter so it does not seem that I am using some form of guile to lead you to come to this conclusion without me confessing to know the implications. I have been *infused* with understanding; and therefore I write this book so you too will be so *infused*.

Let me explain more. I have been allowed to see how to read Nostradamus, both his quatrains and his letters; and I have been allowed to understand the greatest bulk of what the epic tale presents. I say I have been allowed because at no time did I begin to understand Nostradamus simply by some concerted effort to solve what appeared to be the unsolvable. I was led to understanding by sudden thoughts that would fill my head; and I was not the creator of those thoughts. I simply followed the lead of those thoughts, which led to one eye-opening awareness after another.

This understanding was both instant and gradual, with each new revelation causing me to think I knew it all, only to have later new revelations that would make everything much clearer. For all I thought I knew, there was so much more there to be aware of that it becomes a life's work simply trying to verbalize it all. It has led me to understand how impossible it is to defeat what I have come to understand, through logical argument.

Everything I have been led to find has been so far beyond what my prior level of intellectual competence was, at least as far what one expected to understand Nostradamus would seem to require. I did not understand French (spoken or written, modern or old forms). While I had owned one book on Nostradamus, the topic was little more than a curiosity to me. I would never have attempted to challenge an "authority" opinion on Nostradamus, because I had nothing to gain by doing so. I wanted to think there was something special about someone like Nostradamus, as a man with special talents that allowed him to see the future, talents that none since had mastered. I was like everyone else who knew anything about Nostradamus, as far as not being able to make heads or tails of what he wrote. I was completely dependent on some translator-interpreter telling me what Nostradamus said and meant; and I was completely okay with that dependency, because I was not driven to know more.

Believe me when I tell you that the last thing I ever thought I would be dedicating my remaining life to would be explaining to anyone who would listen how to understand Nostradamus. I did not choose to do this. I was instead chosen. Still, I willingly accepted the role I was chosen to play, which has been to enter a quest to understand, and a challenge to teach what I understand.

Certain elements of my past seem to have qualified me, to some most ordinary degree, as some kind of explanation to the question, "Why me?" I wrote poetry in my youth, mostly between the ages of 18 and 25. I particularly enjoyed the use of *amphibology*, even though I had no clue such a word existed, until I read it written by Nostradamus and looked up the meaning. When I wrote poems, I never felt that I was truly the author. I felt like some ghost of a deceased poet-song writer, one who had not yet lost the desire to have words find a resting place on paper, was visiting me. Lord knows my English teachers did not see me as a master of language, or the art of writing.

I also seriously studied astrology, beginning in my early twenties; and like any serious study, it never leaves you once it has been ingrained in one's knowledge. I was led to learn astrology because I had questions that I wanted answered, and astrology seemed a good way to get answers. Still, the answers I found were always out of step with what others learning astrology sought. Others seemed more interested in answering the question, "How can I manipulate an advantage for myself?" I was more interested in answering questions like, "Why am I so messed up?" My answers had led me to a deeper understanding of astrology over the years, particularly up to the eve that I began to have a sudden awareness of the meaning of Nostradamus' words.[91] In some sense, because Nostradamus was such a renowned astrologer, I feel I was chosen because my understanding of astrology was on an elevated level of thought that gave all credit to God, as to the source of astrology on earth. Only later did I find Nostradamus made such a connection in his writing.

There is another reason why I would qualify to be chosen. I believed in God. I believed in Jesus Christ. While I had strong feelings against the organized religions of the world, seeing them filled more with hypocrisy than the Holy Spirit, I daily prayed to God and talked to Jesus as if he were my invisible brother. I did not see myself as being in any way holy. I knew I was addicted to the ways of the world, as much as anyone could be; and I quickly fell prey to lusts and desires, knowing certain tricks were customarily expected, just to be able to afford some comforts in life. Still, I felt a level of guilt and always repented my sins. I knew when things did not go my way it was my fault for being too addicted to things. This always kept me praying for forgiveness. I believe that this simple dependence on God had me on the list of possible *infusion* candidates. I was willing to be led by signs that God wanted me to follow His will.

The fact that I had a book of Nostradamus' quatrains, so that I knew something about Nostradamus, versus not knowing anything about the man or his writings at all, also might have placed some check by my name as a candidate for being filled. Like all who had found interest over a period of centuries, since

---

91   In the year 2000, I began to see deeper meaning to the "Traditional Astrological Rulerships" that are given basic lip service in the various "schools" of astrology. I wrote and spoke on this topic in the first half of 2001, which was well before I first had a Nostradamus revelation.

Nostradamus wrote *The Prophecies*, I had made a discovery that led me to explore what he had written. While history is filled with many who have tried to understand, only to come away with nothing but a sense that something is there, our more modern times have produced more avid disbelievers than wanton believers. I did not consider myself as either believer or disbeliever, as I knew too little to judge; but I was one who wanted a reason to believe to come, simply to prove the naysayers wrong.

Another possible qualification could be my interest in Greek mythology. My ears always perked up in school when elements of Greek mythology would pop up. For some reason, I enjoyed reading about how gods would assist humans, how gods would toy with humans, how gods would severely punish humans, and how gods would fight each other for having helped or harmed humans. To me, Greek mythology was a lot like Nostradamus. It seemed believable as metaphor, if not as a historical record of prehistoric times. I was willing to have some archeological find confirm everything about mythology, again just to have it be a slap in the face of those who think they know it all, those who downplay the importance of mythology. Nostradamus' references to mythological characters were an interest to me because of my interest in Greek mythology.

On a mundane level perhaps, the fact that I was unemployed at the time I first became aware of true meaning of Nostradamus' words made me simply "available." Because I had more free time on my hands, time that I could use to investigate the thoughts running through my mind, sealed the deal with God. I certainly was still looking for work at the same time I was feverishly trying to write my newfound explanation of what Nostradamus meant, which the whole world had so foolishly overlooked for 400-plus years. However, the more I began to write and explore, the less important employment seemed. When I finally did find gainful employment (an answer to my prayers), I was no longer able to compromise my inner beliefs, at the expense of innocent human beings, so that I could benefit financially. I felt the need to make telling people about the meaning of Nostradamus my new job, so I made the decision to do just that.

Other than those few historical tidbits of where my life had taken me up until the time I was able to understand Nostradamus, as qualifying factors, I cannot say why I was picked to serve this role I have willingly undertaken. I can only say that I know I have been chosen by a higher mind, because I know I could not understand Nostradamus one day, and then the next day I could. It serves me no good to know how to understand Nostradamus, because the only good comes from everyone understanding AND acting on that knowledge. I personally have no power to make anyone else understand Nostradamus, nor do I have the power to make anyone else believe Nostradamus was a Prophet of Jesus Christ. Each and every one of you has to open yourselves up to receiving the *infusion* with Christ, so each and every one of you can have your eyes and minds opened, along with your hearts, and understand for yourselves what I already understand. My only purpose is to open you up to receive this *Spirit*.

Therefore, I do not present you with the *Systems of Nostradamus* as a means to make myself wealthy. If that were the plan, I would simply be telling you the meaning, making you dependent on me for all that you know. That would have you coming back to buy everything I wrote, year after year, just to get the latest updates. However, I offer you a fixed set of guidelines, by which you can feel yourself through the quatrains and letters, coming away with your own meaning.

That I offer proof that Nostradamus explained these guidelines strengthens my position. A position that Nostradamus stated his meaning in his own explanations is the strongest position to have, because it is not my opinion. My opinion is based on the logic that requires an author explain that which is difficult to understand; and I explain this in order to give you logical reason to test those guidelines with all your might. Thus, I do not ask you to have faith in me, as other writers of opinion have done. I ask you to defeat my findings, if you want to defeat Nostradamus as a Prophet of Christ. I ask you to do this because I know it cannot be done. If you try to see for yourself, you can realize the reality of God.

If you are one calling yourself a Christian, you should be aware of how the apostles were filled with the Holy Spirit on the day of Pentecost. On that day, the twelve began to speak in tongues foreign to them, and they did so fluently. In other words, they were not in the middle of taking some "How to Speak All Languages" course when they were suddenly filled with that ability. Still, once they were filled with the Holy Spirit it remained with them, because they were believers in Jesus as the Christ.

From that initial filling of the Holy Spirit, the apostles began their ministries. They traveled around the Middle East and Mediterranean Europe in pairs, going to pockets of Jews, while welcoming Gentiles, spreading the Holy Spirit to other believers. Being filled with the Holy Spirit is a special blessing, which must be shared. Jesus spoke of this in his parable of the master who left talents of varying amounts with his slaves. Upon the master's return, the slaves who had spread the talents so that they grew in number were praised. The one who sat on his talent, and did not share it with anyone so that it could grow, was admonished. Therefore, I cannot simply sit on what I have been shown to understand. I must pass it on to others.

This is where faith and belief come in. I can tell someone all day long how to make sense of what Nostradamus wrote; but if that someone does not believe in God or Jesus, I might as well be spending my time telling a dog those instructions. Of course, the dog will not have a clue what I am talking about; but it would still wag its tail and lick me on the hand for spending time scratching its head while I made noises to it. This, in one way, makes light of why one should *give not that which is holy unto dogs*. It simply is impossible to *give* a *holy* message to one who cannot perceive holiness. As such, some will read my words and be just as confused as they were before.

This is not a request for anyone to have religious faith and/or belief, if one cannot grasp those concepts. It is a challenge to those who do claim faith and belief, to stand by your faith in God and Christ and prove me right or prove me wrong. I challenge those of you to seek this proof, because I tell you clearly that God and Christ have sent me to you with a message. If one truly believes in God and Christ, and has true faith, one will feel filled with the strength of God and Christ. That strength will enable one to find the truth in what I say. If I am wrong, any falseness in what I say will be exposed. There will be no gray area. It will be clear, one way, or the other. All truth must be spread for others to know, just as all falseness must also be shared as a warning against being misled. I have no fears that falseness will be found; and with God and Christ by one's side, there is nothing to fear from listing to what I say, and testing it for truth.

I tell you this because being able to understand Nostradamus requires more than simply knowing the systems. With basic belief in God and Christ, one can use the system to test what I say for truth. A willingness to receive God's word shows the level of belief that will allow God to open your mind's eye, and let Christ to fill your hearts. In this way, you can be *infused* with the Holy *Spirit* and see the clarity the systems bring to the quatrains and letters. Without that basic belief, one can look at the words Nostradamus wrote, and apply the systems, and come away even further confused than before.

Likewise, being *infused* with the meaning of *The Prophecies* is of little value if nothing is done to act on the understanding that brings. Jesus did not appear to Nostradamus simply to make Nostradamus feel special. If that were the case, Nostradamus would have written clearly about how cool it was to see the Spirit of Jesus in his room of study. Only as an aside would we realize his writing enigmatically, "oh by the way, Jesus *infused* me with a story of warning about a terrible end mankind will bring upon itself, should it do nothing to stop itself from going down that path past the point of no return." Nostradamus did nothing to exalt himself before others because the Holy Spirit worked through him.

While it is a special feeling, it is incomplete without the works that come with is. As such, I see a guiding verse of the Bible to be what Jesus said to the disciples on the eve of his being taken into custody, as related in the Book of John. Jesus said, as a determining factor to their having faith in Him, "Have faith that I am in the Father and that the Father is in me: at least, have faith in me because of what I do."[92] This means that the Father was in Jesus through being *infused* by the *Holy Spirit*. Jesus is telling those who doubt how one man can be God to have faith that only God could do what one man did. As such, actions speak louder than words.

Thus understanding the words of Nostradamus alone is not an indication to others that one is worthy of their faith, whereas acting based on those words can be. It means nothing if I understand *The Prophecies* and do nothing to share that knowledge. It means nothing if I understand the meaning and tell others I believe what I understand, but then demonstrate a lack of a sense of urgency relative to the urgency in the message. That would send a stronger message that I was selling fear for some hidden agenda, such as getting rich quick. I have to act in a way that will help begin to start a redirection, away from the end prophesied by Nostradamus, by knowing what that end will be.

---

92   Bible in Basic English, http://bible.cc/john/14-11.htm

I act because I believe it truly is Prophecy, from Jesus, from God. It serves no purpose if others do not share in this same belief that I have, do not find the same faith that I have found, do not feel the same need to act urgently as I feel. Only together, with all working towards the same purpose, can we avoid a horrid future. I believe we can steer the world to safety, if we all turn back to God. Regardless of what one's religion is, by facing God one is demonstrating a belief that God is the greatest power. Through such faith and belief, we can all become *infused* with the *Holy Spirit*, and be filled the strength of courage necessary to do what needs be done, through actions of peace, love, sharing, and caring. Otherwise, the end will come as prophesied.

Chapter 13

Analogies for the Systems of Nostradamus

Once everyone has come to terms with the realization that being *infused* with the *Holy Spirit* is the only way to understand fully how to read *The Prophecies*, everyone should see how my being *infused* first has no value, if what I have been *infused* to understand does not lead many others to also be *infused*. The mystery of Nostradamus' work has been looked at and pondered in the past, by some very bright individuals, much brighter than I could ever claim to be; and they have come away having not seen the truth that the verses hold. This means they did not look at it with eyes understanding how to see.

I will tell you right now that while I have seen the meaning of *The Prophecies*. Having seen that, I could not go right to a quatrain and fully tell you what that quatrain means. Certainly, a few that I have repetitively discussed, in writing, will be readily recognizable, and some of that meaning I will recall; but nowhere close to all of it. I have to readjust my eyes every time I look at one. The same goes for the words in the letters.

Since I know the systems, I can look away and return my eyes to seeing normally, like I am doing now, telling people about what I have learned from having viewed *The Prophecies* with "seeing eyes." By knowing the systems, and having had worked with them frequently, I have the ability to make my eyes begin to follow the systemic approach that allows the meaning to come forth. However, each time I look at the same quatrain, I see it in a slightly different way than I saw it before. This has nothing to do with a quatrain being so general it could mean anything. It means there is so much that can be read from one quatrain, looking at one only once means much could have been missed.

I have printed out quatrains that I felt needed to be shared, amazed at what they contained. Most all of them, I have shown to my wife. I let her look at them, along with some notes I might have added, which help me remember some information I researched about the quatrain's contents. My wife cannot see what I saw. Even when I tell her how each word's meaning reads according to a system, she struggles to grasp how what I say something means matches what was written. She always says that she can see what I mean, when I explain it, but she would never have seen that by herself. However, the more she sees, and the more she tries, the more she grasps.

It is not only my wife that had this difficulty. I have posted several quatrains online, breaking each down into what the meanings can be (certainly missing a lot of the additional meaning, due to length restraints), only to get responses that people cannot see how I came to conclude what I did, based on what was written. It is that difficult to see the truth come out. In the context of a blog, it is impractical to make sure someone understands what the instructions for how to see. I wish it were a course taught in colleges, where great depths of analysis could result. However, despite the difficulty, it is a difficulty that can only be overcome by faith, faith that there is meaning, which will be revealed to anyone who follow the systems and believe the source is Jesus Christ.

In this regard, I have found the best analogy I can make to show how this clarity comes out with faith, but remains hidden without it, is to compare it to something named the Magic Eye. Perhaps you have seen one in the Sunday Comics pages (Sunday because the Magic Eye is a color picture, not black and white), or in one of the Magic Eye books at the bookstore. The concept behind one is known as an "autostereogram" such that by focusing on a two-dimensional picture, a three-dimensional picture appears. This appearance comes from forcing the brain to, "overcome the normally automatic coordination between focusing (distinctness towards one point) and vergence (eye movement inward or outward to cover more than one central point of focus)."[93] Simply put, it requires an atypical way of seeing to see the intended purpose.

When one of these autostereograms is first seen, it appears to be a senseless repeating of some colorful images, or simply multicolor random dots. As a Magic Eye appears in the newspaper, the artwork is usually spread over a rectangle, measuring about 12 inches by 5 inches. The directions that are printed under the picture say to place your nose about 3 inches from the picture, until your eyes lose focus and then slowly move your head back away from the picture. If done right, a 3-D image appears from within this colorful collage. If one did not know that the picture had this purpose, and did not know how to make the 3-d image pop out, the hidden image would remain hidden until someone figured it out by accident.

This exercise is then similar to what makes the meaning of Nostradamus stand out. The Magic Eye works because underneath the appearance of a colorful collage is an image, like a negative on film. This black, gray, and white picture is then covered by the repeating colored images or random dots. When the eyes have had time to absorb the whole of the picture, the underlying image appears to make the covering color applications appear to separate, making the negative image appear as a colorful 3-D image. It is not really magic, because the hidden element is there by design, and meant ultimately to be seen. That which is hidden simply requires a lack of focus to bring it out.

Nostradamus' system can be seen similarly, on two levels. First, the wholeness of the overall message of *The Prophecies* is hidden in the random presentation of colorful quatrains, most of which seem utterly senseless. Here, our eyes are trained to expect the order to be correct, so we focus on the specificity of the individual pieces, while failing to see the whole picture. The second level takes place within the

---

93   Wikipedia article, http://en.wikipedia.org/wiki/Autostereogram

framework of an individual quatrain. On this level, the words are seen as if they follow the rules of language, because we see one quatrain acting as one sentence. We overlook how the individual words do not follow the rules so they join in coherent fashion. The focus is thus the opposite of how it should be, causing us to fail to immediately see the hidden truth.

The Magic Eye requires one to read the instructions to get the desired result. Equally, *The Prophecies* require one to be able to read the letters Nostradamus wrote, which act as the instructions for what will be found hidden in the quatrains. However, those instructions are also cloaked, meaning no one has really known what Nostradamus said about his enigmatic work. While many have come up with their own ideas about the meaning, and glimpses of truth have upheld some of those common beliefs, the whole truth has been kept hidden for over four hundred fifty years.

This book you are reading is the first and only book that I know of (other than other books I have written alluding to the topic of this book) that dispels all myth, folklore, and wild opinion, by letting the reader be the judge of what is hidden in every word Nostradamus wrote. I have given logical reasons why my opinions are supported by what Nostradamus wrote; thus being Nostradamus' instructions. This leads me to give you the systemic rules for gaining meaning from Nostradamus' texts. Once you have been armed with these tools, you are the master of the meaning hidden in the words. Just as I can lead you to a Magic Eye cartoon, I cannot make you see it. You have to make the image become real to you; and you have to realize the image is not coming from your imagination. It is coming by the design of a higher mind.

The systems of Nostradamus are both simple and complex. They follow a very logical pattern, if not a normal one. As such, once you have learned the systems and practiced their application, you will soon become well rehearsed in the language of Nostradamus. Simply because every quatrain has four lines, there will be a constant repetitiveness due to the applications requiring one to follow that pattern. You will not have to go through 900 quatrains to get this system down. You will be amazed how fast you can learn how to read Nostradamus, because the systems are simple enough for an adult to grasp. However, this simplicity is only the first step to total understanding.

This book will not attempt to present all 948 known quatrains, although I will choose examples that display the various systems. This book will not present what I believe to be a truer order of quatrains, nor will it fully explain both letters. This is too complex to cover in one book. I will follow this book with those "study aids". However, all that one must know now is that the complexity comes two ways.

The most obvious complexity is determining how to place the quatrains in the correct order. If one quatrain is not placed with others telling of the same topic, a lot of the totality of meaning within one quatrain can remain hidden. I will assist you with this complex problem by producing a book that lists all of the quatrains in a new order, one that will help sort the quatrains for seeing this fullness. In the mean time, I will leave it up to you to learn the systems on individual quatrain.

The other complexity comes with our ingrained ability to read fast, which is the brain acting quickly to limit word definition to the usefulness in a sentence. A good rule of thumb while reading a quatrain is to slow down and take each word one at a time. Each individual word must be understood for all of its meaning. As such, some words can be either noun or verb, present or past tense, depending on its use in a sentence. You have to stop thinking of anything written by Nostradamus being a normal sentence.

Each word can be a sentence, simply by understanding its definition; and each word can be multiple sentences, if it is a word that carries several uses. All usage must be considered before moving on to the next word, simply to get a 360-degree view of what could be the hidden meaning written into the words. All of this meaning must then be sewn into the fabric of the previous word, and likewise the following word. This is a complex way of reading; but the results are a delight to me, because of the depth of meaning that shines through. I feel aglow when the words suddenly shine a light of understanding into my mind, which once again proves the divine is at work.

As our eyes are typically adjusted to see normally, we expect to see everything within that norm of vision. This is how some newspapers and magazines present us with mind teasers; placing two almost identical pictures sided by side, asking us to pick out the five differences. These require some effort simply because our mind prefers to scan, rather than search for detail. A scanning eye sees both pictures as the same, not wanting to go through the trouble of closely inspecting both images for differences. One has to actually like to perform such tasks, and be willing to be keep trying to find something repeatedly missed.

Ask yourself, how many times have you seen someone after he or she got a haircut and you did not notice? I have shaved off full beards that I had worn for months, only to have people see me with my new cleanly shaved face and say, "You look different. Did you lose weight?" This demonstrates just how the *Holy Bible* can state, "They have eyes, but they cannot see." (Psalm 115:5)[94] Due to this natural blindness, we see the quatrains how Jesus and Nostradamus knew we would see them. The world would be blind to the message, until Jesus would make one born blind be able to see.

Viewing everything about *The Prophecies* as normal makes one blind to the truth. Normal scanning technique leaves everything appearing as little more than confused groupings of quatrains and words. Because the letters and verses were written in what is now an archaic form of French, the evolution to a new normal acts to create a cataract over the way we now see Nostradamus. The Old French-speaking people of France could not see the meaning when words were spelled the old ways, and when words bore the old meanings. The modern French have a more difficult time seeing the documents of Nostradamus in that old light, causing them to want to attach a new culture to the meaning that was never gained. The result is the French are just as blind to what Nostradamus himself wrote, even though they see everything through French eyes.

---

94   New American Standard Bible

Certainly, those who do not speak any form of French are at the mercy of those who translate Nostradamus for us. When the experts produce these translations for our benefit, they do so with normal eyes, such that they are expecting to see normal French in the Old French texts. When normal French is not there, they make it up. They translate abnormal French words into normal foreign language paraphrases, creating something that is only loosely associated with what Nostradamus wrote. Definitely, there is no divine source to what they paraphrase, leading the world to think propaganda, innuendo, and half-truths as being what Nostradamus called prophetic. It becomes an exercise in the blind leading the blind; and that perpetuates the inability to see what Nostradamus actually wrote.

If Nostradamus had written in plain French, there would be no problem with translation. An understandable paraphrase into a foreign language would be an accurate transformation of the truth, if the author had written in a plain form of writing. What makes sense in the native tongue will make sense in all subsequent tongues. The problem, however, lies in the fact that Nostradamus did not write in a standard form of French. He did not write in syntactical sentences. He did not use punctuation as a sane and mentally sound man of advanced education would. Therefore, if Nostradamus was not insane, it is insane to see what he wrote as being plain, normal French.

Nostradamus was French. Nostradamus wrote in Old French, with some Latin mixed in, and with some words, which nobody knows for certain what they mean, thrown in to spice things up. Nostradamus did not use punctuation normally. Nostradamus did not write words grammatically correct, nor did he always write words that properly connect grammatically. The only thing that can ever possibly yield what Nostradamus meant, due to so much not being normal French, is the original language of Nostradamus. Before any translation can ever be performed, one has to understand what Nostradamus wrote. It is, therefore, the only language that can be read, exactly as it was written (literally in French), to keep it undisturbed until meaning comes forth.

This becomes analogous to a crime scene. Just as a crime scene must remain as pristine as possible to solve a crime, based on evidence that can take many forms the untrained eye cannot see, a crime scene must be cordoned off (French for stringed, roped, or twined off) to keep the untrained eye away. One not trained to realize that everything present at the crime scene is telling a story about the crime could contaminate the scene by altering one or more aspects of that overall story. This means everything about *The Prophecies* must also be left alone. It must stay as it was written, because it is not a clear open and shut case as to its meaning. Everything must be seen as evidence, which then must be seen in microscopic detail.

This means *The Prophecies*, including the quatrains and letters, is a puzzle that must be reconstructed. Each quatrain is a piece of the puzzle. All pieces must be reordered to give the whole picture that is hidden in the randomness, just as the 1,000 pieces of a puzzle scattered in a box have to be interlocked with the other pieces to see the fullness of the one picture the pieces come from. Still, the pieces of Nostradamus' puzzle do not come with a clear picture of what can be expected to be found.

Nostradamus' "puzzle box top" is figuratively found in the two riddles that are the letters of instruction. While two quatrains may seem to piece together one way, one has to switch over to the riddles to see if the puzzle is correct, by solving a riddle that confirms that is the picture painted. In this sense, *The Prophecies* is the epitome of Winston Churchill's quote (in a speech about Russia), where he said the situation at hand was, "a riddle wrapped in mystery inside an enigma."

Once one is armed with the systems that unlock the riddle, remove the mystery, and erase the enigma, the truth can be told. This is how one must approach *The Prophecies* for understanding. There is a way to read it for meaning. That way has always been present; but it has not always been seen. The fact that embedded systems have existed for over four hundred fifty years, which have only now been seen, shows the systems could not possibly be manmade. It is the legendary sword in the stone, which has now easily been removed. It has been removed to become a tool for change, at a time when change is needed. May God and Christ give you the strength to pick up this tool and use it properly.

Chapter 14

Some Observations on Translations

I have stated previously, "Everything you think you know about Nostradamus is wrong." This means you do not know what Nostradamus wrote. I have made this statement repeatedly, only to have someone still ask me, "What does this quatrain mean, where it says …." They then go on to quote something they copied off the Internet, or pulled out of a book of popular paraphrases attributed to Nostradamus. The answer I always begin with is, "You have been misled by an erroneous translation. Nostradamus did not write that." Everything you think Nostradamus wrote (especially if you are not reading the French) is wrong.

The point in this is that even fluent readers of French cannot read Nostradamus correctly. The reason is they cannot translate without applying syntax, which is non-existent in anything related to Nostradamus' work surrounding *The Prophecies*. Therefore, all translations that exist now are mostly incorrect paraphrases. I say "most" because many lines in the quatrains are so "simple" they cannot be translated better than verbatim; those can then only be correct translations. However, these lines are always surrounded by other lines that are not so "simple", which leaves the correctly translated line in a puddle of paraphrase. The result is an impression of syntax that is not there, at least as you have been trained to understand syntax.

I have explained the point that Nostradamus did not use syntax in his writings surrounding *The Prophecies* previously. For that reason, I will not repeat my reasons or the examples I presented confirming my beliefs now. However, I will explain why translators, who for the most part feel called to translate Nostradamus and believe he had an ability to forecast the future accurately, stand firmly by syntactical translations. It is simply that there have been some in the past who have taken the literal approach in translation, and have been ridiculed for doing so.

The ridicule comes from the literal translations being so clearly without meaning (due to there being no syntax to structure the words for meaning) that opponents of Nostradamus have concluded his writings can mean anything. Again, natives fluent in French do not easily digest what Nostradamus wrote. Therefore, proponents of Nostradamus want to nail down one singular meaning, by a syntactically morphing a series of nonsensical words into sensible ones. The purpose is to show how Nostradamus did not write as nebulously as people thought he did.

Opponents of Nostradamus allow this exercise simply because they do not feel it is necessary to translate anything Nostradamus wrote. All they have to do is let foolish believers come to them with a translation. While this trick of added syntax has somewhat lessened that argument of non-specificity from Nostradamus opponents, it has not swayed anyone to belief. Belief does not come because an artificial application of syntax can only make sense of a handful of the quatrains; and there in lies the problem. The greatest portion of the quatrains cannot be magically turned into lucid, thus testable, predictions, simply by adding a few words or changing the marks. This is the greatest argument against Nostradamus: whatever few seem to be accurate, this is only due to chance, because over 85% of the quatrains have no apparent sensible meaning.

The reality is that the opponents simply oppose the premise that any human being can truly prophesize the future accurately, beyond predicting a repetition of history, based on calculations utilizing probability and chance. The proponents seek to make the quatrains seem as believable as possible (through understandable sentence structure). Therefore, when one truly amazing quatrain can be seen to have correctly predicted a past event, people will be attracted away from the argument against belief.

All the evidence I have presented makes the claim that Nostradamus is not the source; the source is divine from God, through the Spirit of Jesus Christ. Because the prophecies come from God, not man, all quatrains are prophetic. All are reason to believe, one at a time and collectively. One only has to know how to read the quatrains from that perspective. Therefore, neither opponent nor proponent arguments are addressing the real issue. Syntax can play no role in translation until the original French of *The Prophecies* has been understood to a perfect presentation by God, not by a man, and thus in no need of alteration.

Before you can comprehend the systems that were incorporated into the writings of *The Prophecies*, you must admit this premise. Whether or not you believe the premise, you have to admit that this is the claim made by Nostradamus. If Nostradamus made this claim, no one can defeat his claim by denying he made the claim. No one can prove that his work is not prophetic, from divine inspiration, as claimed by Nostradamus in the quatrains and letters, simply by ignoring those claims. One has to prove Nostradamus, right or wrong, by initially accepting his claim as true. Logic says that all false premises will lead to false conclusions. Therefore, accept the premise without bias, and let the chips fall where they may.

As you can see, the literal (which was never understood by the French wise men of Nostradamus' day) has to be understood before any interpretation can begin, no matter which end you seek to find. Because the preface made no sense from reading it, the wise men began looking at the quatrains that followed the preface, thinking they were wise enough to figure them out, without directions from the author. They found that to be impossible, such that the king demanded clear instructions.

One cannot sole the quatrains, collectively, without solving the letters of instruction. While a handful can make sense correctly, a bigger handful makes sense incorrectly, and the vast majority are left in the "makes no sense" group. The instructions to *The Prophecies* must be understood before anyone can run telling the world what Nostradamus meant. Logic tells us that has to happen, no matter what the topic of debate.

Imagine trying to put something together by not using the directions that come with that something. As a boy, I enjoyed putting together model airplanes and cars. While a model airplane might end up looking mostly like it was designed to look, if one tried to put it together without following the directions, the most probable result is some important parts would be left over when finished. That is something as simple as a model airplane, which most people have a mental image of what it should look like. If one had put together similar airplanes before, recognized the various parts, and had an idea where they had to go, less parts would probably be left over. However, imagine trying to put together the parts of real jumbo jetliner, if all the parts were just piled randomly in ten heaps, without having a blueprint that one could understand there would be little chance of success. This is how people have tried to put together *The Prophecies*.

Without good directions, people begin looking at parts they recognize and pretend they know how that part goes with this other part they recognize. This becomes an opinion without direction, which I call a paraphrase. To argue a paraphrase is only to argue an unfounded opinion. This is a pointless endeavor, whether the opinion is correct or not, unless one can back up a paraphrase with what Nostradamus confirmed in writing. The only way to prove that an opinion is correct is to find the author supporting that opinion. That can only come from Nostradamus having explained his work. That means one must understand the explanation first, before one can understand the work.

That is why I have begun this book as I have. I want you to see how my opinion is based on what Nostradamus wrote, which supports that opinion. It is the only logical approach to solving something mysterious, written four hundred fifty years ago. The fact that understanding Nostradamus' instructions has been difficult is what this book is here to alleviate. The systems allow for one to understand the instruction.

Since Nostradamus did not write syntactically (as evidenced by the Old French people not being able to understand Nostradamus' meaning), syntax has to be abandoned until after meaning has been established. A new system of writing has to be used that will replace syntax and allow meaning to come forth. By "system", I mean, "A group of interacting, interrelated, or interdependent elements forming a complex whole",[95] such that there will be specific guides for understanding, more than some special requirement

---

95   The Free Dictionary by Farlex, http://www.thefreedictionary.com/system

for intuitive insight. In this regard, "poetic license" allows us to seek such a new system, because poetry does not follow the same rules as prose. Without such a system being sought, particularly one intentionally ingrained as part of the text, no meaning will ever be found within the words that have maintained public interest for so long.

With all of this logic, and despite the attempts by translators to self-impose syntax on the words of Nostradamus, there are still places where everyone agrees that the literal translation is the only translation. For instance, in the quatrain that is found second (number 2) in the part known as *Centurie Tierce* (*Century Third*), we find Nostradamus wrote on line three of that quatrain, "*Corps, ame, esprit aiant toute puissance*". This line literally translates to state, "*Body, soul, spirit having all power,*" and this is also how others translate the words of this line.

The problem with this example does not come from a literal, word-for-word duplication of the text in translation. It comes from reading this string of words as a syntactical statement, as one sentence, where one could assume it means, "all three elements of a human being - body, soul, and spirit - have power." This assumption is misleading and limiting to the true meaning of the line individually, but especially to how this line relates in the context of the whole quatrain.

While this line ends with a comma, the need for syntax makes some show it ending with a period, to give this impression of one specific meaning in one complete statement. Still, some translate this line exactly as Nostradamus wrote it, but lines one, two, and four are altered to make one specific syntactical series of statements, which lessens the meaning of, "*Body, soul, spirit having all power*". All of the lines have to remain just as unchanged as line three for the whole quatrain to make perfect sense, as intended. Understanding the words written, as they were written, must come before any amending of the words can take place. Therefore, selective literal translation causes the loss of the full meaning, amid other syntactical translation.

The only solution is for each person seeking proof to do his or her own translations. This will prove someone else's translations to be correct or not, in one sense by checking the work of others. However, more importantly, if one is to start from scratch translating the Old French into another language, proof comes from seeing for oneself the lack of syntax. This proof has to be obtained by the person seeking the truth, because the written word has to be seen first as coming from the seemingly unintelligible. When a new system is learned, one is able to prove for oneself, how something can come from nothing, something valuable is actually there, by design. Everyone has to prove there is reason to believe.

If you do not believe in God, you still have to accept the premise that Nostradamus made a claim that God, as the Spirit of Christ, wrote *The Prophecies*. As such, a disbeliever in God only has to **PROVE** one quatrain is untrue. The only way one can **PROVE** such a point is to look at what was written in 1555, which has much later been claimed to be the truth, while relating that truth to a past event (not current or future).

In this endeavor, one has to be careful and not make the mistake of disproving an interpreter of Nostradamus, and thinking that disproves Nostradamus. One can only disprove Nostradamus by having a willingness to accept an argument for belief without bias, and then constructively determining if the conclusion drawn from that argument is true or false. As such, to find truth connected with quatrains said to be referencing the past, one has to evaluate the detailed specificity of a quatrain, in comparison to readily known history of one specific event, or series of events.

The words Nostradamus wrote have to detail specifically a past event, and this detail has to go well beyond the generalities that chance could explain. The only way to do any of this is to go directly from what Nostradamus wrote, with zero dependence on someone else translating what Nostradamus writings say. In other words, if you disbelieve Nostradamus was a true Prophet of God, is proves nothing by rejecting that premise. One still has to translate what Nostradamus wrote, literally, to make sure you see what was actually written. Then one has to realize how to understand that, without conventional rules applying. Only from that learned position, having developed an opinion based on facts, can one accurately conclude whether Nostradamus was right or wrong.

Likewise, if you believe in God, you also will have to accept the premise that Nostradamus made a claim that God, as the Spirit of Christ, wrote *The Prophecies*. You must realize that no Biblical Prophet of God ever spoke for God, without God telling the Prophet what to say first. While the *Holy Bible* is proof to a believer that God is real, Nostradamus has been covered with the stigma of having been rejected by the Roman Catholic Church, after his death. This rejection included his prophecies, but more because of his being known as an astrologer, during times when the Church rejected astrology as evil. You have to believe that Nostradamus explained astrology as not being the source of his Prophecy, in his quatrains and his letters. Therefore, the **PROOF** for God is found in the truth of the words of Nostradamus. If Nostradamus is found to be a true Prophet, he will only speak the whole truth, and nothing but the truth. This **PROOF**, once again, can only come determining logically that Nostradamus did not write the truth.

Once you see that the premise from which your conclusions will be drawn is true, your conclusions can also be true. If you believe Nostradamus was a Prophet of God, you will see how something humanly impossible has been achieved, with complete truth in every quatrain, even though none of them were seen to hold such wealth of truth. You can never begin with a false premise and conclude with the complete truth. You have to remove all possibility of doubt that someone else has played a trick on you and mistranslated a quatrain to fool you into belief in something false. You have to have ownership in the translation, to believe fully in your conclusion.

I do not want to give the impression that authors have made purposeful attempts to mislead others by their translations. While there have certainly been purposeful attempts to make Nostradamus appear to say what those translators want Nostradamus to have said, they usually promote belief in Nostradamus, while not actually trying to get you to believe in Nostradamus (Hitler for example, and Goebbles propaganda promoting such belief). Certainly, there have been outright liars posing as Nostradamus translators, completely making up a quatrain or two, to suit some specific need to sensationalize a current event, or just to make something up that will besmear Nostradamus' name. Just because of these few true charlatans, doubt is always in the air. This is removed by personally checking the right sources and doing your own translations.

I will be the first to admit that there is a tremendous amount of work involved in the translation of all 948 quatrains and two letters. Still, one cannot know what Nostradamus wrote by depending on what someone else said Nostradamus wrote. I have completed my own translations and I will make those available (in time) for all to see; and while I promise not to mislead anyone in the translations that I will present, one can only know for sure that I am not lying by doing the work oneself. I want everyone to realize the importance of self-translation, even if Old French is not a natural language to translate. Look at it as if Jesus wants to see if you are truly serious about knowing what Nostradamus wrote.

Because translation is such a huge task, I recommend that people find quatrains that appeal to them personally, through the promotion of translations by others. These can be found in books on Nostradamus, seen on television shows about Nostradamus, or from a search of "Nostradamus quatrains" on the Internet. I offer a selection that tells of the events of September 11, 2001 on my website (www.pearlsofnostradamus.com), and I have a group of Facebook named "Serious About Nostradamus", which provides individual quatrain interpretation, with instructions. I offer both the Old French (as it appeared in print) and my literal translation in English. Many others offer a similar combination of French and English. However, I highly recommend you compare multiple sources, once you find a few quatrains of interest. See if they all agree, in the French and the English translation. Then, it will be time to do your own translations.

Once one finds some of interest, focus on those few quatrains at first. One can accomplish two important tasks at the same time that way. First, one can see any errors that may have been presented, seeing if a correct representation of the Old French has been preserved, as well as an accurate translation coming from that. Second, one can practice using the systems one can learn from this book, and see how correct the promoted interpretation was or was not. The most important thing is to practice seeing for oneself what can be seen in one quatrain.

Chapter 15

My Experience with Translation

When I first began to understand the meaning of the quatrains of Nostradamus, I perceived that meaning solely from the translations of one author. For the most part, once I began to see meaning, my perceptions were nothing like those the author had perceived in the interpretations presented in that author's book. While that was enough to suffice at the beginning, I was invariably led to test the waters of translation. This was because it did not take me long to peek across the column of the page, from the English I was reading to the Old French text, and wonder how four French words had turned into seven English words. I soon found myself feeling around for how to translate a foreign word, because I felt I had no authority to do so.

Let me explain here that my first enlightenment to Nostradamus' meaning was only in reference to 200 of the 942 quatrains that author's book contained. I chose 200 simply because that was the final count of those quatrains I found that were either not explained by the author, explained by the author as still far in the future, or contained clear references to Muslims, Arabs, or the Middle East (whether or not the author had explained them). The only reason I did not select the other 742 quatrains was the author appeared to have more deeply explained those. I did not feel I was in any position to challenge those explanations. Still, in all of the 200 I eventually did choose, I was completely dependent on the translations made by the author, to have some clue as to what those meant.

I will readily admit that my earliest attempts at translation led me to some incorrect finds. Part of the reason was I was looking up Old French words in a modern French dictionary. While I was convinced that I was onto something, as far as retranslating certain key words, I was myself doing the same as the other authors on Nostradamus had been doing for centuries – making up things to suit my needs. The more I explored and questioned the translations of others, the more I was amazed by the clarity I found coming forth. The more I looked, the more that voice in the back of my mind was saying, "Stay on the path. You have to translate every word of every quatrain."

Before I began my quest to do a complete translation of all the quatrains, I communicated with a well-publicized author on Nostradamus about what I had perceived the quatrains to be saying. That author warned me that Old French was a tricky language to translate. This made me a little more hesitant to attempt my own complete translation of *The Prophecies*; but I could not deny what I was finding, as checks and rechecks confirmed my first simple translations to be what was actually written. What was actually written made much more sense than the paraphrases.

Certainly, the voice in my mind was a more powerful influence; and I soon after began the task of translation. Armed only with a Harper-Collins French Dictionary, which I purchased for this purpose, and my old college English dictionary, for etymology assistance with English that has similarly to a French root, I began a four month period where my only focus on Nostradamus was the translation of 948 quatrains (by then I had found out there were six more). The deeper I got into the translations, the more I realized I had made some mistakes previously, because of the trickiness of Old French, just as I had been warned. By the time I finished my first attempt at translating the quatrains, I knew the first third of them were in need of serious editing for corrections.

I quickly learned that Old French is only tricky if you do not know French, which I did not know. Still, this is like saying Old English is a tricky language, to someone who speaks English. Old French is, simply put, modern French with some extra letters that are no longer used (usually, accenting made them go away). It is about as difficult to figure out that the Old English word "*maketh*" means "makes". In Old French, the word "*faict*" (English "made") is now "*fait*" (English "made"). Simply by realizing changes of this nature, I was able to look up one difficult word several times (not all French changed), until I found something that seemed accurate. Usually, I was led to make correct translations, but occasionally I blundered, particularly due to my unfamiliarity with French verb endings and tense.

Those additional six quatrains I found came from another book that I had purchased by that time. I collected several others as well, which were all different views by authors on Nostradamus' verses. In one of those new books, I first became aware of the Preface, the letter to Henry II, and the various presages Nostradamus produced after he began *The Prophecies*. As I was feverishly translating only the quatrains (and sorting them into the new order that I had found, from the original 200), I attempted to read one author's translation of the Preface and letter to Henry. I could make little sense of the Henry letter, but the Preface seemed to be something I would need to spend more time on later. Once I was finished with my first-pass quatrain translations, I began to translate the Preface.

When I was finished with the Preface, I had found support for my theories, realizing there were indeed systems embedded in the style Nostradamus used, which made the verses consistently read for meaning. I had also made new discoveries about words I had struggled with earlier, finding solid proof how those words actually translated. I knew that all of the quatrains had to be double-checked, because I realized I had to make sure I had not used an incorrect translation in my work.

Again, as daunting as this task might have been initially, and may seem impossible for the reader to fathom now, the more I was led to find, the more amazed I was at what was newly appearing to me, making my understanding grow by leaps and bounds. I was enjoying the exercise of translation because it kept everything new and refreshing, as well as heart warming, despite the horrid nature of the words. My amazement came from the literal translation becoming so obviously the only way to read Nostradamus, because it allowed for so much more meaning to come out.

As exciting as it was to see something new exposed to me in the translation process, it was the horrid nature of the overall story told by *The Prophecies* that filled me with a sense of urgency to make public what I was finding. Knowing I needed more time to correct my translations, I felt a stronger need to interpret what I had already translated and ordered. As I interpreted, I double-checked my translations. Within a year, I produced a 740-page book that explained what I had found, including presenting the systems for understanding, as well as an in-depth interpretation of the Preface and some quatrains. However, even though over 400 of those pages were interpretations of quatrains, they numbered only 111, or under 12% of all 948.

In that process, I did not edit the text properly (inexperience as a writer). I stopped after 111 quatrains because there were so many left it felt like it would take a decade to finish. Writing 4,000 pages before publishing would be too late. I felt rushed and the results show a rushed book. My translations were amateurish in many places, laughably wrong in others, and incorrect educated guesses in others. I had written so fast that I made many errors of grammar, thinking faster than I could type, and writing as though the reader was sitting inside my head, looking out my eyes with me, and could read my mind. In short, the book was excessively long, necessarily repetitive to the point of maddening, and generally painful on the eyes to read (10 pt. font, single-spaced). With a glaring lack of editing acted as a built-in deterrent that would (and should) prevent anyone hoping to read it from actually doing so. Don't buy that book!

The value of that first experience is it taught me more of what I needed to learn. First, I needed to learn how to deal with publishing (and agents) in general, but more specifically the new self-publishing industry. So many authors wanting to get published, with too few opportunities in the New York mega-publisher market, had led to an increasingly popular print-on-demand possibility on the web. I had to learn how those companies act like vultures circling over a dying beast.

Secondly, it taught me not to think I knew when this future would begin, or end. It is enough that I know how to understand Nostradamus, so I can teach others. Beyond that, I have no need to tell the timing, and I have no sense of urgency to know the timing. The only time of importance is now. Now allows everyone to see the past, and project the future. The future is not up to me to prevent alone. Alone, I am prepared for any future, and have no fear of the future.

Finally, I learned that people buy short books, due to a short attention span. The prefer free, which makes the Internet an ideal place to set out freebies. The problem with freebies is people think free stuff is cheap, and worthless. I used to do translations in a coffee shop, with a sign up announcing I would do Tarot readings for anyone wanting one. The sign announced, "Free Readings for Fools – All Others $5". The reasoning was simple. If someone paid $5 they would actually listen to what was said. Otherwise, anything I would say would seem like useless chatter. I try to post things on my Internet sites, which are free, but I can only go so far with information, or people get bored and go somewhere else. All this means I learned I have to sell what I have to say in a way that people can afford it, and think there is some value to it. I learned I had to write shorter, easier to read books.

I learned those lessons over time, but the need for a short book brought other demands. My plan to continue interpreting the quatrains, in the order that I had rearranged them into, would mean another seven, or so, 400-page books. At four pages per quatrain, which was my first book average, it would take years to get to the end of the story. A friend with publishing industry experience told me that I needed to tell the whole story of Nostradamus in 250 pages, or less. If I took any more than that, no one would buy my book. Since I feel it is extremely important that I make the best efforts possible to get people to take notice of what I have to say, I considered this advice a sign to change directions.

By that time, I was ready to do my own translation of the letter to Henry II. I had only read other author's translations, and while the letter was difficult to follow, I could tell Nostradamus was actually explaining the stories that I had already seen the quatrains telling. I figured that a short book focusing only on interpreting the two letters explaining *The Prophecies* would be the shortest way to tell the whole story. While that would invariably lead to more questions – like, "How did you get that for that?" which would require answers – like, "You see, there are these systems …." I would just have to leave the explaining for later.

After I was about a third through translating the Henry letter, two new watershed moments occurred. First, I happened upon an online version of an Old French Dictionary. This is "Randle Cotgrave's 1611 French – English Dictionary", with 1611 being a mere forty-five years after the death of Nostradamus. This immediately made my translations easier, because not only had I found a positively correct source, but also because it gave me more than any modern French dictionary could. I suddenly had many new word options for translation; and I had words that were used in the late 16th, to early 17th centuries. This was a godsend, literally.

Second, it dawned on me that Nostradamus was explaining *The Prophecies* in his letter to Henry the exact same way he published his work. By that, I mean he scrambled the letter to Henry just like he scrambled the quatrains in *The Prophecies*. That meant to make the letter make sense one had to rearrange the pieces of the letter to match the order of the stories the quatrains told, and vice versa. In that way, both documents were evidence supporting each other. They told the same story, one generally and one specifically.

All I had to do was see how the systems would allow me to split the letter up into parts. There had to be consistency in how I made that determination for breaks. That would preserve the new language rules for reading Nostradamus, since none would be broken. The fact that the letter was not written in poetic style, while the quatrains were, meant there had to be a rule that would allow for splitting apart the letter, while keeping the poems intact. The systems once again proved themselves to me, as I was able to see where such breaks were designed to be made.

Once I saw the letter to Henry needed to be reorganized, I could not write a book until this restructuring was finished. My guide to the reordering was the reordering I had done with the quatrains. Since I had not written interpretations for roughly 750 of the 948 quatrains,[96] I had the majority of the quatrains simply sorted into general storyline "buckets". The statements in the letter to Henry II were giving me detail for what to expect when I do those translations, adding some clues for subplots within those buckets. In addition, the letter to Henry added detail that was completely outside the scope of the quatrains making up *The Prophecies*.

With all of this newfound information, the idea came to me that the only way simply to tell the meaning of Nostradamus' work was to rewrite the Preface and the Henri letter, and do it as if Nostradamus had written both letters with syntactical clarity. I would have to assume the voice of Nostradamus in order to do that. The whole book would become my paraphrased opinion of what Nostradamus conveyed in *The Prophecies*, with limited explanation.

Only one small problem was the result. I could not boldly publish me pretending to be Nostradamus, simply telling what Nostradamus meant in 250 pages. First, I had Nostradamus go for 300 pages. Then I added another 100 pages of background stuff, including some general explanations. Still, this book is the answer to the question, "How did you get that from that?"

I have recounted this history for only one purpose. That purpose is to let you know that I have put in seven years of trial and error learning for your benefit. I want every reader that wants to know the message that Jesus Christ sent to humanity, through Nostradamus, to be able to do so with the least amount of work necessary. I will help you find the Old French Dictionary website. I will help you find original copies of *The Prophecies* on another website. I will provide you with my personal website where you can correspond with me with questions and comments. However, I cannot see what Jesus gave Nostradamus through your eyes, for you. Only you can do that.

---

96   I did write interpretations for the original 200 quatrains that I found, which told a quickie version of the whole story. Because I had written those interpretations based on the translations of others, I was unable to publish anything that I had written (due to copyright difficulties). Still, I had a good idea what 200 quatrains told, before I translated and wrote in-depth interpretations for 111 quatrains.

Chapter 16

The Importance of Definition

All of us have learned many words over the years. So many words stored in our brains that we could listen to a conversation where a word is used that we do not understand, and still have a good sense of what is being said. We do not typically slow down a conversation by asking someone to stop conversing and define a word used. Normally, we depend on the context of the surrounding words, where we grasp the meanings of known words, and make assumptions as to the meaning of any words we do not recognize.

Often, we incorporate words we only have vague understanding of, correct or incorrect, into our own conversations. We are capable of this because our memory has stored the word, along with the context that surrounded its use. On occasion, we might actually look up a word in the dictionary, but not often. Because words are not looked up for the definition, we can only guess at that word's meaning; but still we use them, not really knowing what we say. If someone were to halt our conversation and ask us what we meant by using some word we used, but did not fully understand, we would experience some embarrassment. We would stumble to define a word we had never had defined to us.

There are many more words in a language than any individual will be able to adequately define. Mastery of a language comes from study and effort, in addition to the practice of using an extensive vocabulary. To be able to choose the one word that most meticulously defines the point meant to convey is something of an art form. Still, as intelligent as one appears, when displaying a mastery of language skills, it is not a sign of stupidity when one does not know the definitions of the words one uses in speech. It is a sign of laziness.

I have found the use of foreign language words in a conversation in English a way to show one's multilingual abilities. It gives the air of fluency so much that it seems to say, "I know so many words, the best choice for this conversation is a word best used by other peoples." When one does not know a foreign word, hearing one spoken makes them think they have just heard a word in their native language that they have not learned before. If the speaker does not appear to be from a position or class, where one could be afforded schooling in multiple languages, a foreign word used in conversation could sound like slang. Since slang cannot be looked up in a dictionary before it has become a standard form of use, one hearing a word thought to be slang will simply begin using it, without understanding why that particular word was created. Such a word can be incorporated into standard conversation without knowing the meaning of the word, or how to spell it.

For instance, my first wife would typically indicate a large number of something as "beaucoup". I did not know French, so my ears heard, "boo-coo", and I thought the word was Vietnamese, perhaps spelled, "bookoo". I thought this because the United States was involved in a war in that country at that time, and veterans were regularly coming home from their tours to South Vietnam, using some Vietnamese terms they had learned there. These became mixed in with English. It took me a while to realize the word "beaucoup" was French, and the Vietnamese often spoke French, due to Vietnam having been a French colony for a period. Before I learned that, I would use "boo-coo" in conversation, never knowing it was French, meaning, "a lot, many, or much". I simply made assumptions, based on the context of the conversation; and never once asked, "Excuse me, but you lost me at boo-coo. What language is that? What does it mean?"

When we are involved in a conversation that only uses words we have been taught in grade school, we still depend on the context to know the meaning of the individual words. As such, we might hear someone say, "Take the right branch, and hit the western connector." If the people involved in the conversation knew that "the right branch" was an exit ramp off a highway, with "the western connector" being another highway heading west, no misunderstanding would occur. However, for someone not familiar with why such a statement had been made, it is conceivable one could think an instruction had been given to use a tree limb (branch) and beat (hit) someone from the West (western). This means knowing the context specifies the definition.

The context becomes specified through syntax. The presence of syntax allows one generally to make the correct assumptions as to the specific meaning of a word used in speech. However, since Nostradamus does not write with the syntax of Old French applied, the reader no longer has the right to assume words with multiple uses can be limited to only one definition.

The context is still relative to the specific series of words written within the lines of one quatrain (and even continuation quatrains), but each word with more than one definition must be considered as if each definition could be relative to that context. Without a standard application of syntax, the context is meaningless without a substitute set of rules to be guided by. As such, every definition has to be considered.

An example would be the quatrain I presented previously, where the all-capital-letter word *"BRANCHES"* was written. Most interpreters have been so caught up in setting up a context of Nostradamus sitting before a tripod, which held some bowl of water, that they translate *"BRANCHES"* as the legs of that tripod. The word, "branch," can be defined as a limb or root of a plant (not a piece of furniture or structure); a division of an organization (as an office branch); a division within the circulatory or nervous systems of the human body (as a nerve branch); a division of a flow of water (as a river tributary branch); a subdivision of a language (such as the Indo-European branch); or an ancestral or relation division (as a family tree branch). Beyond that, the word can even be used as a verb, becoming the action of taking a "branch", as where one would veer off.

To make one specific usage become fixed as the only intended use, as when translators of Nostradamus have changed "*BRANCHES*" into "tripod legs", such a specific limitation demands evidence that context guided that choice for translation. Certainly, a tripod has three legs, where "legs" can be seen as branching for the torso, but there is nothing in the context of the quatrain that supports this choice. Nostradamus' line states, *"The small staff in hand set in the middle of the BRANCHES"*, which in no way indicates a tripod. In fact, nothing in the whole quatrain states a tripod is involved, nor is it made clear exactly what *BRANCHES* means. The limbs of a tree, several flows of water, or divisions of a bloodline, all could make sense in interpretation.

This is a perfect example of how ill prepared one is to see all of the variety of usage in one easily understood word. One could pick out a few of these defined uses of "branch," but without the assistance of a dictionary one would be more inclined to skip what we cannot remember, and pretend there are no other definitions. Rather than simply guess at the one meaning, we need assistance, being reminded of all possible meanings. This means to do interpretations of Nostradamus quatrains one will need a good dictionary, either a printed book or an online variety.

This multiple usage capabilities of one word, through multiple definitions, become even more pronounced when one realizes that one French word can equally translate to multiple English words, based on its multiple uses. As an example, I will use the French word, "*neuf*." This word can translate two ways, either as, "nine," or as a form of the word "*neuve*," meaning, "new." While the word "nine" is limited to the numerical definition, there can be many uses for "new". Once again, we cannot assume which meaning is the intended contextual usage to focus on. Both "nine" and "new" may be correct, with "new" possibly meaning, "recent", "unheard of before", "fresh", or "uncouth". All have the potential of being correct, each intended to play a role in expanding the meaning of the whole line, by using all possibilities.

Certainly, when one finds Nostradamus having written a word that is not commonly used, a dictionary is the only way to know what the word means. Many words of Old French still survive in modern French, but they have lost the old meaning, becoming adapted to modern terminology. Some Old French words will only show in modern dictionaries as an "archaic" usage. Still, since several Old French words are no longer used in modern French, an Old French dictionary is the most accurate source to use. They should always be used before going to a modern source.

In my use of an English dictionary, while doing my initial translations, I found the etymology tool very useful. Simply by knowing the root word's source and meaning, possibilities for definition open up.

Often, the root word will have a meaning that has been lost or modified through the years. For this reason, I highly recommend a dictionary be utilized that offers the etymology feature, especially when seeking word meaning in secondary sources.

Finally, there will be times when Nostradamus will appear to misspell a word. Keep in mind that Nostradamus is not the source. Nothing is misspelled without reason and purpose; but Old French words are not always spelled the same as modern French words. The point to realize at this point is not to jump too quickly into thinking a word that is very close to being one recognizable word (via search), only with an extra or missing letter, thus misspelled, is the meaning of what was written. I have typed in words and done searched, only to be prompted to look at a different word. By putting the word in quotation marks and searching, I have found many words are actually properly spelled words from Nostradamus' time. Exhaust all means if making what was written be what was written, before going to the next step, which is basically guessing.

Chapter 17

Reminder: No Syntax Allowed

I cannot state this too many times. You cannot read Nostradamus for true meaning by trying to make it conform to language, as you know it. I know that I have told you this before, but once one begins trying to look at the literal translations of a quatrain, there is a strong mental urge to read the way you have been trained to read. Reading is an automatic process that subconsciously takes over. You have to be aware of this.

Here is a simple experiment you can do to prove to yourself that your mind's training will automatically try to interfere with your conscious attempts to read Nostradamus differently. Take a piece of paper and five colored markers. Write out the color word in the same color marker, such that you would write "RED" with a red marker. Do this in a scrambled order, such that you have 50 words on one page, with 10 words representing each color word, all written in the same color marker. With that page done, do another page with the same order of 50 words, only this time write the color words in a color marker that does not match. For example, write "RED" in green, blue, brown, and/or orange, just not in red.

With the two pages prepared, take a stopwatch and time yourself "reading" the first page, where the color word matches the color marker used. Instead of actually reading the written word, time yourself to see how fast you can state the color of the marker used to write the color word. Once you have gone through the 50 on the first page, time yourself doing the same thing on the second page. You will find that your fastest time will come from reading the colors that match the word color. This is because even though you have an instruction to not read the word, to read only the color used to write the word, you mind continuously tries to read the written word. You will experience more hesitancy reading the colors on the page where the word color does not match the color marker used.

In this same way, you cannot read Nostradamus in groups of words. Instead, you have to look at an individual word, and then slowly connect that word to other words. Still, even with those instructions, your mind will not be able to stop trying to read phrases, or whole sentences. That will slow your ability to grasp the full meaning of what was written, because you mind will have already processed limited meaning from multiple word grouping. Your mind will automatically attempt to apply syntax subconsciously.

REMINDER: NO SYNTAX ALLOWED

Despite your mind's natural drive to do what it has been conditioned to process, you have to train it to read Nostradamus differently. After regular practice, you will no longer see the words of Nostradamus as normal language, but more like an unusual form of math. Each word will seem more like a number that becomes added to another word's number. To demonstrate what I am saying, let us use the line from the quatrain where the all-caps *BRANCHES* is written. That line states, "*The small staff in hand set in the middle of the BRANCHES*". However, one needs to state it more like a problem than a statement.

When one sees the French text of this line, one sees, "*La verge en main mise au milieu du BRANCHES.*" This needs to be written like this:

La ………verge………en ………main ………mise ………au ………milieu ………du ………BRANCHES

From this point, the translations need to become "drop-down menu selection," such that every possible translation is displayed. This would result in the following matrix:

The	rod	in	hand	set	in the	middle	of the	BRANCHES
There	small staff	into	quire of paper	put	at the	midst	from the	TREE BOUGH
Here	wand	at	public power	laid	to the	center of	with the	LINEAGE
Then	stick	on	authority	placed	with the	setting	to the	PEDIGREE
	switch	upon		planted	from the	environment		SIDE-(piece)
	twig			brought				
				thrust into				

Every word listed is an acceptable translation of the French words written by Nostradamus, with each translation being based on different contextual usage. This context is dependent on all of the words having been purposefully strung together to yield a single statement in support of that context. However, without the context known, as would be the case with the first line of a quatrain, it is ill advised to jump to a conclusion about the context. Again, one cannot fall prey to the trick of limiting, when one is reading Nostradamus for the true meaning.

When one looks at this line as a mathematical problem, each column of possible translations can be chosen to "fill in the blank" for that French word's position. Each choice would then be "added" to a translation choice for the next word. Only after all possible combinations of translation selections have been considered can the full scope of meaning begin to emerge. While all possible translations can add to the overall meaning of a string of words, some translations will have a stronger impact than others will. Some translation possibilities could be totally rejected. To grasp the full meaning of this one series of words written by Nostradamus, in one line of one quatrain, the following is now possible to interpret:

> *The small staff in hand thrust into in the setting of the (greatest [due to capitalization]) BLOODLINE,*

> *There. (a quill-like) wand on quire of paper placed (seeing the source of the writing that is) at the center of (all religions to the one God,) to the SIDE-offshoots (Christianity and Islam, as the Torah, and Old Testament books).*

> *(While I sit) Here (in Salon, France I see the) rod (that will come) upon (mankind due to quests for) public power (which will have) brought to the environment from the PEDIGREE (that man is god on Earth).*

My point now is not to explain how I got the above from nine words written by Nostradamus, although I can explain it in great depth. At this point, it is important for you to see how I have not limited any of the words written to only one translation. By doing so I have been able to supply additional text (with explainable reason) to make a string of words that make something seeming to make little sense blossom into some very detailed syntactical statements. While I have produced paraphrases, I have produced paraphrases that accept what was actually written; and I have reasoned those paraphrases based on the context of: a) the whole quatrain this line comes from; b) other quatrains that logically connect to this quatrain; and c) explanations stated by Nostradamus in his letters. In short, I paraphrase with proof, rather than pure conjecture.

You too can reach this point of understanding. All you have to do first is understand that syntax is only used after each word is fully understood. It is just like a child first learning to understand language. You have to learn the words first. You have to speak in one-word sentences, meaning you have to know what is being conveyed by one word being used. Only then can you begin to put the meaning of two words together for greater meaning to come forth. Syntax is then the final addition that acts to synthesize meaning for quick reading. However, there is nothing quick to be found at first.

You have to speak for Nostradamus as a parent speaks for his or her 1-year old child. The baby knows many words by that age, but typically only uses one at a time. The baby speaks in one-word statements, asking for something, demanding something, or telling something. The parent learns what the baby means by one word, but a stranger might hear the baby speak one word and not understand. When this lack of understanding happens, the stranger will look at the parent and ask, "What does the baby want?" The parent, understanding full well what the baby meant, then adds syntax to the baby's word for the stranger's benefit. The parent is capable of explaining what the baby meant by its use of one word. Still, no parent expects their baby to speak in full syntactical sentences, before they have learned the basics of verbal communication. Nostradamus, as the "voice" of Jesus and God, wrote as if "out of the mouth of babes".

Chapter 18

Poetic License

Due to the different way one has to read Nostradamus, one has to come to grips with what appear to be recognizable idioms, axioms, and sayings. They may exist, as we discussed with the idiom, "*in soluta oratione*"; but groups of words cannot be gulped up as one. No matter how quick your mind recognizes meanings, like "in plain prose" representing "*in soluta oratione*", this cannot be seen as the primary translation for interpretation. It can be read as an intentional misleading combination of words, one which may still have a secondary application for meaning, but such misleading was by design.

Also keep in mind the poetic nature of the quatrains. Poetry is not prose. Every quatrain has an ABAB rhyme scheme (in French), and it does not matter if translation makes the poetry seem to change to prose. It is impossible to call the quatrains of Nostradamus anything other than poetry; and with poetry comes poetic license. This means the poet does not have to abide by any rules other than the poet's. If you want to know what went through the poet's mind as a poem was written, it is up to the poet to let you know what that was. Some poets do not make it easy to understand their words, and they do this on purpose.

As a child of the 1960s (I mean I was not an adult during that decade), I grew up when The Beatles were the Fab Four with moptop hairdos. When John Lennon made his infamous comment about the group's popularity, comparing that to Jesus's popularity, I lost interest in buying their albums. Certainly, I heard their chart-topping songs on the radio (it was only AM radio, until 1972), and I liked their songs still; but by not buying the albums I did not hear the "deep cuts" the radio did not play. I also did not see the lyrics they began putting inside their album covers, especially like the lyrics for Sgt. Pepper's and Magical Mystery Tour.

By the time I had grown to adulthood (a whopping 18 years of age in 1971), I "rediscovered" The Beatles. The group had already disbanded. I bought every album they made between 1965 and 1970 and heard them all as though a new record had just come out. Not only was the sound new, but so were the lyrics. I especially found myself drawn to the lyrics of John Lennon. He had a way with words that I loved and tried to use in my own poetry. It was the way he would use words that seemingly had no meaning, until you sat and pondered them.

I particularly loved the way the words flowed in "A Day In the Life" (Sgt. Pepper's Lonely Hearts Club Band), "I Am the Walrus" (The Magical Mystery Tour), and "Glass Onion" (The Beatles [White Album]). Lyrics that sing, "I read the news today oh boy / Four thousand holes in Blackburn, Lancashire / And though the holes were rather small / They had to count them all / Now they know how many holes it takes to fill the Albert Hall." To me, an American, "A Day in the Life" sounded wonderful to my ear, but I did not know what the words meant.

The whimsical "I Am the Walrus" sang, "Expert texpert choking smokers, / Don't you think the joker laughs at you? (ho ho ho, he he he, ha ha ha) / See how they smile like pigs in a sty, see how they snide. / I'm crying". What is a textpert? Who is the joker? Smiling pigs sounds like, "Give not that which is holy unto swine"; but I know a "pig" was often a slang term for a police officer.

Then, "Glass Onion" had lyrics that sing, "Fixing a hole in the ocean / Trying to make a dove-tail joint-yeah / Looking through a glass onion". How does one "fix a hole" in water? Here is another reference to holes; is this related to the holes in "A Day in the Life"? None of these songs can perfectly be understood simply by knowing the lyrics. Interviews with John Lennon were necessary to clear up most of my questions. He wanted to generate questions, because if he was clearly understood by the general public, he would have felt like the writer of simple poems. John Lennon took pride in making people think when they heard one of his songs.

In this sense, The Beatles are similar to Nostradamus. You have to think to solve the meaning, but you cannot think like ordinary people think. As much as you can read the words or hear the lyrics, and as strongly as you can feel meaning coming forth, you can never be completely certain of the meaning without the author helping out by explaining what a song or poem meant when it was written. A good example of such confusion is found in another song by The Beatles, written by John Lennon, entitled "Lucy in the Sky with Daimonds" (Sgt. Pepper's Lonely Hearts Club Band).

The song "Lucy in the Sky with Diamonds" has lyrics that are surreal, like, "Follow her down to a bridge by a fountain, / Where rocking horse people eat marshmallow pies. / Everyone smiles as you drift past the flowers, / That grow so incredibly high." With such surreality, which by definition is something that has "an oddly dreamlike state",[97] many people made the assumption that John Lennon wrote this song while on drugs. When they saw the three capital letter words in the title began with L, S, and D, they then further assumed that the lyrics were about an acid trip.[98] This rumor grew and became an "urban legend", which means, "a story that appears mysteriously and spreads spontaneously in various forms and is usually false."[99]

---

97 The Free Dictionary by Farlex, http://www.thefreedictionary.com/surreality
98 L.S.D. stands for lysergic acid diethylamide, which is a hallucinogen of the psychedelic type, commonly called "acid".
99 Based on WordNet 3.0, Farlex clipart collection. © 2003-2008 Princeton University, Farlex Inc., http://www.thefreedictionary.com/urban+legend

John Lennon never denied that the imagery of the lyrics were based on experimenting with LSD, although none of The Beatles admitted using this drug publicly until after the release of the Sgt. Pepper's album. Lennon did deny, however, that the title was ever meant to be acrostic or a type of acronym. When asked he stated, and always maintained his position by repeatedly stating, that the name for the song came from his son, Julian, who brought home a finger painting from preschool one day. John asked Julian what the painting was about, and Julian told him it was a picture of "Lucy in the sky with diamonds." Lucy was one of Julian's classmates.[100] The picture has been preserved as proof of this story. Therefore, we can see how easy it is to jump to erroneous conclusions when attempting to interpret poetry. The only failsafe method is to have the author explain his or her work for the public.

Nostradamus explained in his Preface that he did not write "in plain prose." He explained he wrote amphibologically, or purposefully with double meaning, designed to confuse. The systems that I am about to present to you are part of this intentional, built-in set of rules, which becomes a special form of syntax only for understanding Nostradamus. Nostradamus confirms some, while others have to be realized by their repeated function throughout all the quatrains and letters. This consistency qualifies them as systems. Over the remaining chapters, I will give examples of how each part of the systems applies; and I will point out where Nostradamus gave supporting evidence for that system, as well as specific examples.

---

100   Snopes.com, Hidden Messages, http://www.snopes.com/music/hidden/lucysky.asp

Part 3

The Systems for Meaning

Chapter 19

The System of Language

Nostradamus was a man of letters, meaning on today's terms, he was a college graduate. He also lived in Europe, where the western countries of that continent take up little more territory than does the southern United States. Italy is comparable to the state of Florida. France is about the size of Alabama, Mississippi, Louisiana, Arkansas, Tennessee, and Kentucky. The area covered by Germany, Belgium, The Netherlands, Switzerland (and Lichtenstein), Austria, and the Czechs Republic is roughly comparable to that of Georgia, both Carolinas, with Virginia (maybe add in Maryland too). Spain and Portugal are slightly smaller than the state of Texas. Therefore, Nostradamus could have traveled to most, or all of these European countries, in his lifetime, because they are not that far away from each other.

There is evidence that Nostradamus did do some extensive traveling, especially to Italy. The Provence region of France, where Nostradamus was born and lived, was closer to the borders of Italy and the Swiss Federation, than they are today. While still close, in 1555 Lyon, France, where Nostradamus published his books, was a border city. The regions known as Besse, Bugey, and Burgundy were not part of France then, as they are today. Northwestern Italy was named Savoy, which was between the western Piedmont (Italy) and Geneva (Switzerland). Next to Piedmont, to the east, was the area known as Milan, with the northeastern mainland of Italy under the rule of Venice. In the peninsula of Italy were regions known as Florence, the Papal States, and Naples.

Hapsburg Spain controlled Milan and Naples, along with the islands of Sicily and Sardinia. France, especially under Francis I, and his son Henri II, warred with Spain over their control of Milan; but the Spanish during that period were able to prevail and force French concessions. This history, relative to the lifetime of Nostradamus, could mean that Nostradamus would not have been as free to travel in some areas as one might expect. Nevertheless, one could expect that a college education, combined with considerable travels, meant Nostradamus was multilingual.

Perhaps it is because of this history of Nostradamus that translators have stated Nostradamus wrote *The Prophecies* in many languages. One finds footnotes for these languages when one runs across a word they do not recognize while translating. Suddenly, Nostradamus is writing in Spanish, English, Greek, Hungarian, German, and a variety of other languages. This is not how I have experienced the words of

Nostradamus.

I do not see this need for "international" fluency being a requirement for translation. The broader the allowance for languages used in *The Prophecies*, the harder it is to nail down an unusual word to its true meaning. In my Internet searches for words, spelled exactly as Nostradamus spelled them in his publications, I have returned results (more than a few times) that confirmed the spelling to be a word, but in the Philippines, or Vietnam, or some other Asian-Pacific Rim place. Certainly, one has to establish limits in what can logically be expected to be a language known to Nostradamus, where the spellings is limited to those, when they do not meet the Old French – Latin standards.

In my opinion, Nostradamus wrote primarily in only one "foreign" language. We have already discussed this as being Latin. This is actually not a foreign language, but the language of the Roman Catholic Church, different from the different languages of Italy. Since France was a Roman Catholic nation, Latin would have been a native language for educated French people, like Nostradamus. Most versions of the *Holy Bible*, in France, were in Latin, although French translations began appearing around 1530. Therefore, Nostradamus would naturally be able to switch to Latin, when he would need to make a point that had a religious perspective. This ability would have been part of Nostradamus' normal fluency, which would have been planned for utilization in the call from Jesus Christ.

In this respect, Nostradamus primarily wrote in Latin in his Preface, with a few references made late in his letter of explanation to Henry. The language of the quatrains does not include italicized Latin, as the letters do. Thus, the quatrains are written basically in French, as are the letters. However, some exceptions can be expected, with logical explanations.

The most frequent exception that could be seen as a "foreign" language word is the use of a name from Greek literature. Nostradamus refers to *Deucalion, Selene, Myrmidon, Endymion*, and many other figures of Greek mythology. He refers to the ancient names of places, such as *Pannons, Cherronesse*, and *Ibere* as well. However, these words cannot be seen as purely foreign. They would have been understood in the 16th Century as known names from literature, used by educated men in common conversations. Simply by using one word from classical literature (primarily from Greek, but potentially from all languages of antiquity) the whole history behind that name or place becomes the meaning behind the usage.

There still is some evidence of Greek root usage by Nostradamus, which is commonly known prefixes that are not matched in Latin. One such example is "*anti-*", which is Greek, and incorporated into Latin words. The French also use this prefix, as French is based in Latin, but the root is still traced to a Greek origin. Nostradamus wrote the word, "*Antipolique*", which is not French, or Latin, but a word of possible "foreign" origin. In that case, it would be allowable to see "*Anti-*" as having possible meaning from Greek, in a combined form word.

THE SYSTEM OF LANGUAGE

I will state here that a rare case of Hebrew can play a role in translation, similar to the slightly more frequent Greek role. In these few cases, the word is one that is associated to the Old Testament text, coming from the Torah. Words of this nature would not be due to Nostradamus' travels, but from his home schooling, from his grandfather. Again, these cases are rare, but this allowance, like Greek, falls under an umbrella of antiquity, where Biblical scholars would be forced to know Hebrew. This then balances Greek, as it is the language of the New Testament.

As to Nostradamus writing in Spanish, which appears obvious in a few quatrains, the dialects of southwestern France (Occitan and Catalan) are very similar to Spanish and Portuguese in appearance, while technically being a version of French. An example would be in quatrain X-25, where Nostradamus wrote, "*el tago fara muestra*", which is not exactly Spanish, but seems so, just by the article "*el*".

The same can be said for some words appearing to be in German, as the dialect known as Arpetan can resemble that language. That is spoken in the region of France close to Switzerland. In the northern regions of France, some people speak dialects that are similar to Dutch, or English. These too would technically be versions of French, as recognized regional dialects. Nostradamus would not be expected to be unfamiliar with these. However, it must be realized that the overall percentage of such words in low, which means one should not quickly jump away from French or Latin to translate a word.

This means the heuristic rule to follow is Nostradamus wrote *The Prophecies* (including his letters of explanation) in French, with Latin being the only other primary language used. Latin denoted a purposeful switch in both his letters (Preface and Henry), where it acted to explain the divine source of everything written. Beyond that use of Latin, which was clearly displayed different from the French text by the printers, allowing everyone to know a language switch had occurred, Nostradamus did not write in any other standard languages. Any switch to something appearing "foreign," I believe those words are designed to mislead, more than to actually be that language. The possibility always remains that by looking to a foreign language, which was intentional by Nostradamus, making the search act secondarily, as an indication of a foreign place where that language is spoken. I prefer to stay away from French and Latin. This is my firm opinion, one I welcome scrutiny over it. My opinion is based on my having translated every word of *The Prophecies* multiple times, but if I can be corrected, it can only make the meaning more profound.

Let me make the point that the reason past translators have ventured upon some wild assumptions that Nostradamus was fluent in every language in Europe is because every word written by Nostradamus is not found in an Old French dictionary. They assume, "If it is not clean French, it is open season for any language to be the source." This is an erroneous assumption, because all words written in the works surrounding *The Prophecies* can be completely explainable as French or Latin based. In that regard, Italian and Spanish have that same relationship.

What helps one remain focused on only French and Latin is the fact that Nostradamus made up words. This should not be a shock to anyone. When one is speaking from a 16th Century perspective, writing poems about the 20th and 21st centuries required describing more than a few things that had not yet been invented. As such, the same language process used today for inventing a word to fit something new was used then.

For instance, before Alexander Graham Bell invented the telephone (or whoever invented it first) there was no word in anyone's vocabulary, in any language, that meant, "the thing one uses to speak (phonics) over a great distance (tele-), other than something used to amplify yelling." The word "telephone" was created, from Greek root words, to meet the need for a new word; and Nostradamus did the same thing at times.

One example, of the many, can be found in the eighty-fourth quatrain of Century Tenth. In line three of that quatrain is found a capitalized word, "*Recloing*." This is not a word in French, and it is not a word in Latin. It does appear to have a Latin prefix (*re-*) and an English ending (*-ing*), leaving a root for of *clo*. There are many words that begin "*clo*," in both Latin and French, which makes it uncertain which one would be the right one to choose. That is what translators have done, however. They have made such choices, incorrectly I might add.

The answer that I have found for this manufactured word comes from looking at the first three words of this line, "*Le Recloing ne*", and moving the space between "g" and "n" to between "o" and "i". The result is still three words, which now say, "*Le Reclo ingne*." This is then very close to "*Le Reclos ingens*", especially if "*ingne*" is rewritten as "*ingen*." This can then translate as a form of Latin, where "*reclusi ingens*" means, "*revealed enormous*," or "*opened vast*". As one word coined to fit one specific event, and if the word "*Reclos*" is seen as French, combining "*Re-éclos*," as "*R'éclos*", it becomes "*Re-open*", on a vast scale. The remainder, if as an "*-ing*" ending, is only used in English. Such an ending would be for secondary purposes only, creating an Anglo-Franco word, meaning "*Reopening*." On a secondary level, an "*-ing*" ending would be an indication of some place where English was spoken.

When the context of line two is seen to state, "*The late return will make displeased ones held ones*," a "*Reopening*" of a "*late return*" is very much like a "*Recount*" of a vote that "*The late return*" made "*displeased ones*" out of "*ones*" who first appeared to have "*held*" the vote. That then is in line with the main theme of line one, which states, "*so high not low*," which says one was once "*so high*," but "*not*" anymore. That one would be made "*low*", by "*The late return*". It all begins to make perfect sense, once one begins to look at all of the possibilities of how a word that is not a word could be a combined-form new word, created to fit one specific event.

As exciting as that possibility becomes (and I believe that cannot be discarded as playing a role in interpretation), a word like "*Recloing*" eliminates all need for seeing an "*-ing*" ending when the word is divided into "*Rec-loing*". The word "*loing*" is clean Old French, meaning, "long way off, much off, a distance away." The "*Rec*" is then seen as "*Re-ce*", or "*R'ce*", or *Re c'loing*". This manufactured word makes a statement in itself, saying, "Again this far away", or "Back this long way off".

In the context of the line, the quatrain says, "*Them Again this long way off not will do without debates*". The capitalization of *Recloing* then personifies it as a statement indicating someone or something, which would itself be *Again this one far off.* I believe this is the primary translation for interpretation, as it becomes solely French, with no magic involved. However, in the context of the whole quatrain, having "*Recloing*" act as a "*Recount*" relative to "*This one again*" being "*far off*", but in a "*debate*", adds to the interpretation being about the 2000 Presidential election in the United States.

As you can see from that example, the most obvious language choice for a Frenchman to create new words would be to take from French or Latin roots, with French specific endings. This is because French is a Romance Language, meaning it is primarily rooted in the language of Rome. Therefore, many words manufactured by Nostradamus will be found to take this route to understanding, simply because they are unrecognizable as words in the French language and make no sense otherwise. However, one first has to exhaust all possibilities that the word written by Nostradamus is French, including a regional dialect, before looking to Latin.

One example of how a word written by Nostradamus can easily be mistaken for what it is not is found in quatrain thirty-seven of Century Seventh. There one will find line four beginning with the unusual, "*Leryn*". This word has frequently been seen as a reference to the Lérins Islands, which are in the Mediterranean Sea, off the French Riviera coast. However, to make this word that, the missing "*s*" leaves it open for debate.

There is another alternative, which does not require adding missing letters. This is because there are two European cites named Lerin (in the singular as written), one in the Basque country of Spain, and another on the northern border of Greece, near Macedonia. However, both of these cities are landlocked; and the theme of this quatrain is of ships and a sea battle. It has been because of this obvious theme that translators have mde the word stretch to fit the Lérins Islands.

The answer is not found to be related to the Mediterranean Sea, although that could have secondary implications. This realization comes from the other quatrains that match the context of quatrain VII-37, which do not point towards Europe. This means the word is best seen as in a combined form. This could then make "*Leryn*" visible as either "*L'eryn*", or "*Le rin*". In the case of "*Le rin*" (where it is acceptable to see Nostradamus interchanging *y* as *i*), this would indicate "the Rhine", when West Frisian is the spelling. West Frisian is the language spoken in parts of The Netherlands, in particular where the Rhine River flows. However, this option does not seem to best suit the context.

This means the word might best being translated as, "*L'eryn*", becoming a statement of "*The eryn*". The word that then has to be sought in translation is thus "*eryn*". There is no such word in French (Old or modern), but in Latin we find the word "*erynge*," meaning, "sea holly", which is a flowering plant native to Iran and the Caucasus. Another possibility is the name, "Eryn," which is a form of "Eris," a Greek goddess of strife, related to Ares (the god of war). Eris is said to be related to "Enyo," the goddess of war, whom Homer did not differentiate form Eris in his writings. The point is of these possibilities is the context can be accommodated, while adding details that would enhance understanding the quatrain it appears in, much more than just one limiting place that has little known history that could add to its meaning.

There is another element that must be understood in this specific example. Where "*Leryn*" is being seen as Lérins Islands, one is seeing a place in the world. Nostradamus gave instructions in his Preface, where he wrote, "*limitant les lieux,*" which says, "*limiting the places*". He wrote this instruction in two places in the Preface, with one being only these three words between two commas. Before this, Nostradamus wrote, "*reiettant loing les phantastiques imaginations qui adviendront **limitant** la particularité **des lieux** par divine inspiration supernaturelle*". This translates (literally) to state, "*rejecting long those fantastic thoughts which will be coming **limiting** the particularity **of the places** through divine inspiration supernatural.*" In other words, if it looks like a place being named, you might best look a little harder, just to make sure.

In this example, it seems so close to being spelled correctly one is immediately tempted to go with what appears to be the obvious translation. Missing only the "s", with a "y" being always possible to be the Old French version of a modern "i", many have fallen for this lure, just as Nostradamus wrote that people would. The translators have *long* see Nostradamus as a special person with predictive talents, while *rejecting The Prophecies* as inspired by God and truly being prophetic. They have seen Nostradamus as someone *fantastic*, as if seeing images and visions that lead his *thought*, to a mental state or brainpower, to figure out that *which will be coming* naturally. Because they miss the prophecy part, they read Lérins Islands when they see "*Leryn*". Thus, in error, they are *limiting the particularity* the word truly holds; and the biggest place they do this is in *the places* they think Nostradamus is referring. Only *through divine inspiration*, which is how Nostradamus wrote, can one also interpret. This means one cannot look for the natural in the words, but the *supernatural*.

This does not meant that Nostradamus did not list places of the world in *The Prophecies*. He did, and he did often. It depends on the context of the quatrain and those surrounding it, which would call for some specificity of location. Thus, there is always the possibility that what looks like a place is a place; and just like *Leryn*, there is a possibility that a place will not appear to be correctly spelled.

One explanation for this is that pure French was not always spoken throughout all regions of France. France certainly had a number of regional dialects; and many translators often refer to Nostradamus using

Provençal French. Nostradamus was born in St. Remy, France, and he wrote *The Prophecies* while living in Salon-de-Provence, with both cities being in the region called Provence, in southeastern France. The language of this region is Occitan, of which Provençal is a dialect.

This southern French region had its own form of Romance Language, which Nostradamus used while writing. For this reason, some words written do not readily appear to be "correctly" spelled, as found in a French dictionary. Occitan was the language not only of Provence, but also of the regions known as Languedoc-Roussillon, Midi-Pyrenees, and Aquitaine. Languedoc used to be its own province, and the word actually means, "our [own] language".[101] Along with Occitan, Arpetan and Catalan were other unique dialects of southern France, found in the area from the Mediterranean coast, along the Pyrenees Mountains, to the Atlantic coast.

Nostradamus used spellings of French words that were specific to these languages, which will not be found spelled exactly the same in French dictionaries. In particular, he spelled the names of places in this region as the people living around those places typically spelled them. This would have been the way the locals of the time spelled them, in older or archaic times, and not necessarily the way they are spelled today. Just as Nostradamus wrote in Old French, his use of French dialects would have been consistent with the spellings of the day. Still, all languages and dialects used were Latin based and under French sovereignty.

Since Occitan, Arpetan, and Catalan are still functional regional languages, searches of known French words, ones similar to those written by Nostradamus, can lead to verification of his spellings being from these dialects. The Wikipedia source (Internet website) often has articles for topics posted in multiple languages, with a list of the available languages found on a menu bar on the lower left (headed: languages). When Occitan, Arpetan, and/or Catalan are an available option and clicked on, the article becomes one written in that dialect, with the specific topic word listed in its translated form. If this form is still not an exact match for a word written by Nostradamus, the etymology listing (usually in parenthesis at the beginning of the article) will show root-spelling possibilities. I have found many words, seemingly "misspelled", to be correctly spelled by Nostradamus as a regional dialect.

What has to be the overriding guide, as far as translating the words of Nostradamus is concerned (specifically referencing *The Prophecies*), is that they are from the Spirit of Jesus Christ, thus God. As such, they are of perfection. There can be absolutely nothing misspelled by accident. There will be words that are misspelled, as far as being able to find them in an Old French dictionary is concerned, but there is reason behind the misspelling. The reason is for the translator to determine through insight, in order to enhance the understanding of the meaning of the word.

One example of such a case is found in the quatrain published in Century Tenth, number 74, where the

---

101   Wikipedia article, Occitan language, http://en.wikipedia.org/wiki/Occitan

word, "*Hacatombe*" is used, as published in the 1568 Lyon (Rigaud) edition.[102] The correct French spelling is "*Hécatombe*," with the Latin word being the same spelling and with both translating to "Hecatomb" in English (meaning a sacrifice of animals or slaughter). The funny thing about this misspelling is few (if any, other than me) notice it. Everyone sees it as "Hecatombe," perhaps because Nostradamus correctly spelled this word in the sixteenth quatrain in Century Second.[103] The point I want to make at this time is there is reason for this misspelling, although the primary intention of translation is "Slaughter". The "*Ha-*" becomes read as an addendum to that translation.

In the portion of the Preface that I quoted earlier, which told of "*limiting the places*," Nostradamus was shown to have written, "*phantastiques*". The word of translation actually comes from the Old French word, "*fantastique*", which is how the word is spelled today. In this case, Nostradamus used the Latin-Greek root word, *phantasticus*, from *phantastikos*. This helps focus the definition to the "imagery" and the ability "to create mental images" aspects, perhaps beyond simply the word "*fantastic*". There are many words where Nostradamus makes such substitutions; but it is up to the one translating to figure out why. One must accept that nothing in the language of Nostradamus is coincidental.

Old French was written during a time when the language was different. For instance, there were no words beginning with the letter "J". Words that would later be recognized as beginning with "J", such as "justice" and "juex" (games), were instead written with an "I", as "iustice" and "ieux". The times of Nostradamus were already, seemingly, in a period when words written with a "y" were already "i" interchangeable. For example, the modern French verb "suivre" (to follow) was written "suyvre". A word like "tryane" (a part of a garment) was acceptably written either as "traine" or as "trayne".

As such, the element of phonics was in play, at a time when French was not as fixed as it is today. Thus, to spell a word in French with an "f", instead of the Latin use of "ph", becomes naturally reversible. At times, Nostradamus would replace a "-ch" ending with "-c", or a "th-" prefix with a "t", due to the silent "h". The basic French verb "*être*" was written "*estre*," but the silent "s" has since been replaced with an accent mark (circumflex accent) over the "e". All this means that if a word appears to be misspelled, because it cannot be found in a French or Latin dictionary, it is acceptable to make substitutions in phonic cases.

The point of this system is to understand one must always try to solve a difficult word with French first. Nostradamus was French, so he wrote in French. French is a language stemming from Latin, and Nostradamus knew Latin. It is obvious that Latin is a natural second language, and thus words not recognized as French need to be searched as if made into French, by the addition of a French ending on a Latin root. When French and obvious Latin are not the answer to a most difficult word, because it appears

---

102   The 1566 (Benoist Riguad) Lyon edition shows "Hecatombe".
103   The spelling in II – 16 is not in the upper case, being "hecatombe". Nostradamus spelled "heccatombe" (and extra 'c' misspelling) in quatrain V-18, and the printing in quatrain IX-84 shows a space as part of the spelling, as "he catombe".

to be misspelled, try to see it is a French regional dialect spelling of a word spelled similarly in French. Keep in mind that phonic exceptions can be made on occasion, if Greek is the source, and a word is correctly spell in French when a phonic replacement is made. With the rare possibility of Hebrew (when in Biblical context), all other languages must be considered last resort only.

Chapter 20

The System of Word Creation

I have already pointed out that it is a necessary element of language that words must be created simply to keep up with the times. These words often take the combined form, such that a prefix, root, and ending are sought within the word written. No changes to the written order of the letters are required, even though very slight variations may result after the parts have been determined.

We saw an example of this when we turned *Recloing* into *Re-c'loing*. The only changes required to make sense of what was written, keeping the letters in the exact order they were written in, with no letters added, was to spacing. The assumption of standard French abbreviations, such as "*c'*" becoming an abbreviated contraction, meaning "*ce*", is not beyond the scope of naturally viewing words of *The Prophecies*.

At many places in the quatrains, Nostradamus wrote a word that is missing the abbreviation apostrophe, although it is clearly understood the apostrophe is required. One example of this is the word "*lon*", which appears several time. This is found in the Old French dictionary under "L", as spelled "lon", but the dictionary shows it as meant to have an apostrophe, as "*l'on*". This means one is free to look at words beginning with "l", "s", "d", and others, as naturally requiring an apostrophe, due to common contraction of combined words.

Nostradamus created words that are nothing more than the merging of two or three words together like this, where only French and Latin elements are used. Due to space, hyphens, or apostrophes not being inserted in the word's typeset, between words, words that would easily be understood become clouded, and begin to appear as one word that is foreign. This is why one should always look to French as the first language to exhaust, with Latin second, before jumping to the conclusion that Nostradamus wrote in any number of languages.

Still, after all combined form possibilities have been thoroughly combed through, some words showing up in the verses (and letters) cannot produce such a "clean" combination result. Some words written by Nostradamus appear impossible to divide into roots and language attachments. When all attempts at keeping the letters in the position they were written in fail to produce anything of valuable meaning, before one searches dictionaries of other languages, one has to begin to look at a word as an anagram.

The System of Word Creation

By definition, an "anagram" is "again" (ana-) "letter" (-gram), such that the same letters used to write one word are used again to write another word. This is typically taking a known word and replacing it with another known word, such as, "Mary" is an anagram for "Army". Since both words are known, it becomes confusing when a statement intended to make sense with "Army" is instead using "Mary".

The confusion is by design, as a puzzle, and purposeful anagram use was all the rage during the Middle Ages. Of course, this was when Nostradamus wrote *The Prophecies*, and Nostradamus became very popular writing *Almanacs* and *Presages* that included poems utilizing such puzzles. However, his use of anagram in *The Prophecies* only played on this sense of delight, which people took from challenges to solve tricky words.

Nostradamus' use of manufactured words, which are not anagrams, makes his puzzle much more complex than simply solving anagrams. Most translators have seen the anagrams Nostradamus wrote as either misspelled words, or foreign. This is why they fail to recognize compressed words, or words presented unnaturally in combined form. If one was to fly off and begin seeing every confusing word written by Nostradamus as an anagram, especially with some of his longer creations, there would be too many possibilities to turn letters into. Therefore, some limitation is needed to determine is a word should be considered as an anagram.

There are two types of anagrams. One is the most simple, and the other is the most difficult. The most simple anagrams are the ones that appear to be misspelled, simply by the addition of one extra letter. A typical example ops such a simple anagram is the first word of the 100th quatrain in *Centurie Ninth*. The word written is "*Navalle*", which has an extra "*l*", as the French spelling is "*Navale*" (fem.), with the Latin equivalent being "*Navalis*." Translators have simply overlooked the double "*l*", and translated it as "Naval" or "Navy". In the system of word creation, "*Navalle*" becomes "*l'Navale*," meaning "*the Naval*".

Similarly, a word with an unexplained "*s*" in the middle can act as a simple anagram by the "*s*" being placed either at the beginning, as a contracted "*se*", or at the end, making the word plural. There are a considerable number of words like this, where the assumption seems to have been to see it as a difference between Old French and modern French. The change to the overall meaning of the quatrain is not amazing, but significant. This is one reason why an Old French source is needed to confirm how words were spelled.

Once the simple anagrams are identified, one comes upon the more difficult anagrams. In these cases, a more radical reconstruction of the original word is required. This means that more than one letter is moved to create a new word. An example of such a word is found as the last word of line one, in the quatrain known as X-77. That word is "*quyretres*", and this is not a word of any known language. I have found this can be rearranged to become "*requerits*", which is using the Catalan spelling (SW France dialect), in the past tense, of the French word "*requerir*", meaning, "required, called for, demanded." The "*s*" at the end is standard in the language of *The Prophecies*, such that it means "ones of", when attached to a past tense verb. This choice makes sense in the context of the line (a main theme line), as well as that of the overall quatrain. However, because the same word could be seen as, "*qui r'estre-s*" (translating as "who again to be ones"), nothing becomes set in stone, other than "*quyretres*" is not a word.

One caveat that I believe should be attempted first concerns seeking a solution where the first letter remains in place. This is more important in words that are capitalized, as Nostradamus selected one letter to denote the higher level of meaning that is attached to an upper case letter. If a capitalized word is not a known word, which is frequently the case, I believe the capitalized letter should remain capitalized, acting as a fixture, to which the remaining letters must reaffix. However, as demonstrated in the previous example, involving a difficult to solve anagram, this rule of thumb did not hole true.

One possible example of a capitalized word not keeping the actual letter capitalized in that state comes from seeing the word "*Rion*" as an anagram. This word appears as the third word of the main theme statement found in the 35th quatrain in *Centurie Sixth*. Some translators have seen this as a misprint for "Orion", or "Triones", both Latin names of constellations. The obvious problem with that is the lack of a capitalized "O" at the beginning. This means "*Rion*" is not what it seems, and has to be considered as an anagram. Unfortunately, due to this being only a four-letter word, the combinations possible, where "*R*" remains the first letter, yields no word that is definable. However, the letters make a perfect anagram for "*Noir*", which is French for "*Black, Dark, Sable, or Obscure.*" While the "*R*" cannot remain the capitalized letter, the capitalization means the word must retain that elevated importance.

A large part of the confusion that has kept *The Prophecies* such a mystery over the last 450 years is the fact that there are many obvious words that are not known words. Standard riddle-puzzle solving techniques must be used to solve these words. What one has to keep in mind is to always having an open mind. Since no readily known words in *The Prophecies* can be nailed down to only one definition,[104] an anagram must be seen likewise flexible. When one rearrangement seems to work perfectly, that does not mean another rearrangement cannot also work. This is one of the beauties of this masterpiece, as every time a new way to see something shines through, it makes the whole more understandable, and more divine in origin.

All this means seeing anagrams is necessary; but one cannot place the burden of a quatrain's meaning on one way to read an anagram. An anagram is best solved by reading the rest of the quatrain, so the rest is understood first, lending a guiding hand to how to solve the anagram. The first solution should always be to look at the simplest solution: Latin root; French dialect spelling; combined form; simple anagram; <u>complex anagram</u>, etc. The overall meaning will still be visible without the need of corrupting the whole,

[104] This applies to all words that have more than one common usage. If a word only has one translation, then it is impossible for it to have multiple definitions.

by trying to make something into something it is not supposed to be. This allows for someone else to see the true meaning quite easily, while most others struggle, when many minds are open and receptive to how to read the text.

Most of Nostradamus' anagrams will be as simple as switching one or two letters around, or as we saw with "*Rion*" becoming "*Noir*", simply a mirror image becomes the solution. Another example of how people see something that looks like they want it to look, although it is not anything known in that condition, and trying too hard to solve something simple. This example of this "over thinking" is how most ponder the well-publicized "third antichrist" of Nostradamus, *Mabus* (found in the first word of quatrain II-62). I have seen television programs talk about this, making sure they mention how the name can be stretched to be say Usam[a] bin, Am[erican]Bush, or (when still with us) Sabum [for Saddam Hussein].

The reason people want to see Nostradamus as having actually named an antichrist is lore has come up with the idea that he named all three. The first was Napoleon, and the second was Hitler. Supposedly, he named Napoleon "*NAY, PAU, LORON*" (quatrain VIII-01), and Hitler as "*Hister*" (quatrain II-24), which are thought to be the first two antichrists. That makes "*Mabus*" the name of the third antichrist, because Nostradamus wrote "*L'antechrist trios*" as the first words of a different quatrain (VIII-77). Interpretations like this have given Nostradamus a bad name, because all of this conjecture is completely unfounded, and wrong. There is logical explanation for everything that has been illogically seen to be coming from these quatrains.

There is reason to see *Mabus* as representative of a "name", as an anagram. That anagram is *Musab*, which is created by keeping the capital *M* in place, then simply switching the "*us*" at the end to before the "*ab*" in the middle. As of more recent Internet postings about the possible identity of *Mabus*, people have tossed about the name "Abu Musab al-Zarqawi", who was a Jordanian terrorist leader, killed in Iraq in 2006. While this is not as wildly off as is thinking *Hister* means Hitler, it is missing the point.

Musab is a very important name to Muslims, which is why someone like Abu Musab al-Zarqawi had that name. It is a common name, just as is Muhammad, where many Muslims have that name as their own, out of veneration of the famous Muhammad. Musab is in veneration to *Mus'ab* ibn 'Umair, the "first envoy of Islam", and companion to Muhammad. The meaning of this Islamic figure's history could act to name someone as the Antichrist, but that history needs to fit the context of the quatrain. Minimally, on a secondary level of interpretation, it identifies someone of importance (capitalization) who is Muslim. However, there is a more logical explanation of *Mabus*.

Simply by looking at *Mabus* and immediately seeing it as a name, we have applied syntax to that one word. Syntax is what keeps one from reading *The Prophecies* so they can be understood as they need to be. When one takes away that instant bias and follows the systems, the first step is to see if it is Latin or a combined form of French or Latin. When seen not Latin, it becomes quite quickly, "*M'abus*". The capitalized "*M*" is a standard abbreviated form of "*Monsieur*" or "*Maistre*", which today means, "Mister", or "Master", but in Old French could mean, "Governor, Commander, President, Principal, Teacher, Chief ruler, Instructor, Overseer, or Owner." The word "*abus*" is clean French, dating back to Old French, when it meant, "abuse, deceit, imposter, disappointment, fallacy, misspending, or disorderly employment." In short, *Mabus* is not a name, but a description of an important "*Master imposter*".

After seeing this solution, by having seen *Mabus* as *Musab* can direct one to look for an important Muslim *Master imposter*. This can assist the actual recognition of someone fitting that description in the international setting surrounding us now. It could keep us from seeing a *Master imposter*, or a *Commander misspending*, who was not Muslim. Again, one always needs to maintain an open mind when solving something that is not immediately clear. The simpler anagrams are the safest ones to count on, because the part of the limb closest to the tree trunk is the strongest to stand on.

At this point, I want to present one more example of a capitalized simple anagram. This one is found in the seventy-third quatrain of *Centurie First*. In the second line, the second word is written, "*Argel*". This follows the word the first word, *Tunys*, and a comma. Since *Tunys* is the same as *Tunis*, with "*y*" and "*i*" interchangeable in Old French, the focus leading to *Argel* is the Mediterranean coast of North Africa, where *Tunis* is located. *Argel* can then be seen as *Alger*, which is the French word for Algiers, Algeria. To reach this anagram conclusion, one only has to switch the *l* at the end, with the second letter *r*. Because *Tunis* and *Algiers* are close in proximity, relative to North Africa, the solution of this anagram is logically determined to make sense contextually.

I give this example because it shows an anagrams that becomes understandable as the name of a place. When Nostradamus wrote in the preface the instruction that he was "*limiting the places*", especially the "*peculiarity of the places*", one has to realize places are called by name. This means that "*limiting the places*" can manifest through finding a name in a quatrain that is the name of a place; but by interpreting that name as that place, the meaning then becomes *limiting*. It is especially *limiting* if a quatrain seems clearly headed toward describing one known event, only to veer wildly off that topic. Simply by appearing to name some place, which provides no assistance in solidifying the event seen as accurate, the name of a place becomes confusing.

The confusion stems from people having lost touch with how names originated in the first place, long ago. This means we have to understand how a place came to be named. If one has read some of the Old Testament books of the *Holy Bible*, one repeatedly comes upon an event happening; and due to that event having occurred at one place, that place was named for the event. For example, in Genesis 21:31 it states, "This is why that place is called Beersheba, because both of them swore an oath there." This means the name of a place usually has some history or etymology that relates the source of the name.

THE SYSTEM OF WORD CREATION

The same is found for people names too, such that in the *Holy Bible* we also read, "Afterward his brother came forth with his hand holding on to Esau's heel, so his name was called Jacob."[105] The forenames, or given names of people, typically have meaning (unless formed by Scrabble tiles), and biblical names (especially Hebrew) all have meaning. If you have ever prepared to name a baby, perhaps you have looked up the meaning of names you liked. My name, Robert, is said to be from Old German, meaning, "bright fame".[106] Most surnames, or last names, are relative to ancestral place of birth, or a trade that was passed down through the generations. My last name, Tippett, is said to also come from Germanic origins, from the personal name Theobold, meaning "bold people".[107] Still, a "tippet" is "a stole or scarf-like narrow piece of clothing, worn around the arms and above the elbow."[108] The point is that a name can be much more than a specific person, place, or thing. That is a limitation on meaning.

Knowing this, consider the example of the fiftieth quatrain in *Centurie Tenth*, where it appears Nostradamus named three places, *Meuse* (a department in the Lorraine region of France), Luxembourg (a duchy bordering France, near Meuse), and Lorraine (the region containing Meuse, which borders Luxembourg). All seems fine, except for two things. One, there is no history of significance that has taken place in this area, on a level of importance that would apply to the story line of Nostradamus. That would relegate this quatrain to some future event, if those names are indeed what they appear to be. Two, one publication of this quatrain (1568 Lyon edition) shows *Lucembourg*, not Luxembourg, and *Lorrain*, not Lorraine.[109]

The etymology of Luxembourg is said to come from the name Lucilinburhuc, which is today the place known as Luxembourg Castle.[110] The word, lucilinburhuc, meant "small castle".[111] The word *Lorrain* is actually the name of the language spoken by some people in northern France, in the area that was once known as the duchy of Lorraine, which included a piece of what is today Belgium. In other words, both words can be seen as correctly spelled, which appear to be something other than what is actually written.

The lack of an "e" on *Lorrain* gains more significance when the correctly spelled place, *Lorraine*, appears on line one of the fifty-first quatrain. The two words appear on the same page of the 1568 Lyon edition, with *Lorraine* appearing just below the one without an "e" at the end. At minimum, that is proof that Nostradamus knew how to spell Lorraine correctly, which would lean one more towards thinking the language of a region is the intention. However, this would be a purposeful misleading use of words, ones designed to appear as *limiting places*.

---

105   Genesis 25:26, Standard English Version.
106   http://www.thinkbabynames.com/meaning/1/Robert
107   http://www.houseofnames.com/xq/asp.fc/qx/tippett-family-crest.htm
108   http://en.wikipedia.org/wiki/Tippet
109   This is important to know, because some editions appear to make unauthorized changes to Nostradamus' text. I have found the 1568 Lyon edition to be (in my opinion) the closest to the original manuscript.
110   http://en.wikipedia.org/wiki/Luxembourg
111   http://en.wikipedia.org/wiki/Luxembourg_Castle

Without getting into a discussion over all of the additional details the other words of this quatrain add, which have led me to my conclusion, I will simply state that *Lucembourg* (or *Luxembourg*) and *Lorrain* are not the names of the specific places they seem to be. They are manufactured words, which were made to appear as the names of places, *limiting* one's scope to one relatively small point on the globe. They represent how a name is created for a place or thing

If one understands that this system is embedded in the writing style, it becomes possible to see *Lucembourg* as *Lucem bourg*, and *Lorrain* as *L'or rain*. With no letters switched, dropped, or changed, one has come to the meaning of the words created. *Lucem* is a form of the Latin word "luceo," meaning "shine, or light",[112] and *bourg* is a French word that means "fortress" or "town without walls (surrounding a castle)." *L'or*, in French means, "*The gold*," with "*rain*" also being an Old French word meaning "*bough or branch*". I believe these root word meanings are how one accurately interprets the *places* of this quatrain. Without this meaning known, this quatrain is uninterpretable, beyond taking the position that it can only be about some future event yet to occur, around the land between France and Luxembourg.

The place named *Meuse*, which is correctly spelled as the name of a French department and a river that runs from France, through Belgium and The Netherlands, to the North Sea, is already less limited. The ambiguity of being neither river nor department, since the surrounding verbiage does not make this clear, suddenly makes both of those possibilities seem very out of place when *Meuse* is no longer associating with Luxembourg and Lorraine.

Due to this newfound uncertainty, it is helpful to look to why the *Meuse* River got its name; and what is the meaning is behind the name? The etymology says *Meuse* comes from the Latin name, *Mosa*, which would itself be rooted in the Latin word "*Mos*". This word, *Mos*, means "will, inclination, custom, rule, manner, habit, or character". When the Romans named this river such, it marked the western border to the Holy Roman Empire (9th century). Therefore, the river could have been named to be representative of a natural boundary between two areas of dominion.

With this possibility recognized the first line of the quatrain that originally seemed to state, "The Meuse of the day land of Luxembourg" now says, "*The Character in the day land of Light fortress*". We are no longer limited to looking for something to happen in Luxembourg. We are now free to look for a *land* or nation that stands as a *fortress* that *Shines*. That *Light fortress* will also be a place that *in the day* of reference showed strong *Character*. This is so much more meaning to interpret than just getting a mental picture of a river in northwestern Europe. It is representative of the power that word creation brings to understanding *The Prophecies*.

The important thing to remember when reading the quatrains of *The Prophecies* is every line makes sense by itself, before it applies to the other lines. This mirrors how each quatrain makes sense by itself,

---

112   The Latin forms of *Lux, Lucis* also mean "light," as well as "hope and encouragement".

before it applies to the other quatrains. When this concept is grasped, one has to see each line as being in need of making a meaningful statement, through the series of words that make up the line of thought. To encounter a line that appears to have nothing but a series of names, be those names cities of Europe, mythological people, or planets in the solar system, the specificity of names brings little to the table, as far as why those names are placed together. As such, one has to look carefully for telltale signs of oddities, or etymology, which could change a name into a meaningful word, which becomes the inspiration for meaning. The correct meaning will then match the meaning found in the other lines, causing a powerful impact on total understanding of the line, the quatrain, and the role that plays as a connecting unit in a larger scope story.

One of the tools that make this happen is recognition of word creation. Nostradamus wrote so that God is speaking through words, in a way that requires a different way of reading to hear the message. The words are created according to a new syntax, while following the rules that all words created have followed, or the standard rules for solving word puzzles. When one realizes the words are a challenge to discern, as a mental teaser, solving their riddles actually becomes fun and rewarding.

The words were created, or manufactured, so that some effort would be required to figure them out. On a religious level, this equates with the argument of faith and works, as to which is more important. In that regard, as to understanding *The Prophecies*, the works of work analysis must be based on the faith that the words were created with meaning. Simply by believing in Nostradamus will not unlock all the mysteries of their words, nor will in-depth analysis, without true belief that anything exists to be revealed, yield more than glimpses of truth. The combination of faith and works brings God to one's aid, whispering hints to follow, leading to the true purpose behind the meaning. That is a delight that makes it all worthwhile.

Chapter 21

The System of Word Selection

Once one understands that there are no misspelled words, because everything written is from a perfect source, one has to progress to the logical conclusion that every word is the perfect word for its position in the text, perfectly written. The only changes allowed are to words that are not known words. To make those known, one has to separate the written letters into recognizable combined words, or to rearrange the letters into words that are known. In these cases, the written word has been pondered deeply, in order to allow the hidden to surface, and be seen. The eyes adjust so the underlying meaning can rise. Still, after pondering created words, "misspelled" names of places, and anagrams, one is left with many normal words to translate that, due to the absence of syntax, roll across the mind like a car driving on a road filled with potholes.

The most obvious of these potholes, to me, is the regular encounter one has with verbs written in the plural number. That should not be, and the syntactically trained mind rejects this plurality. By this, I mean the addition of an "s" at the end of a verb that typically has already been modified to represent the plural by tense ending.

This is absolutely not an element of inflection in French, even though French (unlike English) inflects the plural number on articles (*le* becomes *les*), prepositions (*de* becomes *des*), adjectives (*legier* becomes *legiers*) and nouns (*cheval* becomes *chevaux*). A verb is inflected by changing tense, such as to the past participle, and as determined to be a regular verb (*pincer* becomes *pincé*) or irregular verb (*dire* becomes *dit*). Some present participle verbs do require an "s" ending, for plural number agreement (*donné* becomes *donnés*); but a present tense inflection to the third person plural makes an "s" become unnecessary.

This addition of an "s" in unnecessary cases happens repeatedly in the wording of Nostradamus. One of the many examples of this modification can be found in the fifty-third quatrain in Century Fifth. In line one, Nostradamus wrote, "*La loy du Sol, & Venus contendens,*" where *contendens* is actually a contracted form of the plural inflection on the irregular verb *contendre*, in the third person plural, fully written as *contendent* (the absence of the last "t" is a common contraction). The line states, "*The law of the Sun, & Venus contendings*". It implies the plural, as "they contending". Adding an "s" is not proper French, as it implies, "they contendings".

That is not all. In line three of the same quatrain as above, we find the word "*entendens*" written. This is again the inflected third person plural form for the irregular verb *entendre*, meaning, "to understand". The present tense is not a comfortable fit in this use, making the past historic feel best applied. This means the implication is, "they understoods," which is impossible to fathom.

The whole of line three states, "*Neither the one, nor the other not being understoods,*" we can see there is a multiplicity, "*the one [and] the other*", but nothing indicating the application of plural number. This is a match to the multiplicity of "*Sun & Venus*", where nothing indicates the plural number, demanding the verb be in agreement. There is absolutely no need, nor is there any language rule in French that calls for an "s" to be added to the end of either of these verbs.

Naturally, past translators have seen this absurdity and moved right past it without giving it any consideration at all. The unnecessary "s" is immediately tossed; and the words are translated to become whatever words their preconceived minds desire. In this example, most have translated "contending" or "contention", and "understood". I call this the "heads buried in the sand" method of translation, because there is a method to this madness of unnecessary "s" endings.

The answer is to see the "s" as an addendum. It acts as such as its own word, but relative to the verb. It becomes "those" (the plural number) who act according to the verb chosen, or the "ones" (the plural number) known for such actions. In the example above, line one becomes stated meaningfully as, "*The law of the Sun, & Venus contending ones*". Line three then states, "*Neither the one, nor the other not being understood ones*". Nostradamus, in effect, has changed a verb into a noun by adding an "s" at the end. This plays a very important role in interpretation.

In addition to these verb-nouns, but to a lesser extent, is the presence of word combinations that do not match gender. This is most evident when the word "*la*" is spelled out, preceding a masculine noun. The word "*la*" is the feminine form of the article "the," whereas the word "*le*" is the masculine form, which should precede a masculine noun. We have just seen a line that stated, "*La loi*". The word *loi* (*law*) is a feminine noun in French, thus there is agreement with the feminine *La*.

One example where this agreement is not found is in the ninety-fourth quatrain in Century Sixth, where in line three it states, "*La poison taincte au succre par les fragues*". In this statement, it appears *La* is referencing *poison*, but *poison* is a masculine word. The only feminine word it could relate to, as a feminine gender *The*, is *taincte* (a phonetic form of *teincte*), the past participle of *teindre*, meaning, "to dye, stain, or tint", from its Latin root that means, "taint". That would mean the focus is *The tainted*, not *The poison*, if agreement is the intention. However, there is an easier solution that eliminates such difficulty looking for article-noun-verb gender agreement.

The answer is *La poison* is two separate words, unlike *L'poison*, which in the contracted form represents one word. Because the word is spelled out, it has to be read by itself. This is regardless of whether it is a gender match or not. Only when an article is abbreviated into the word it references can it be read as one with that main word. If Nostradamus spelled *L-a*, rather than *L'*, there was a purpose. I have found that purpose, specifically in reference to *la*, is to read it as if it were *là*, which translates to mean, *"there, here, or then."*

In the example stated above, the last word, *"fragues"*, is questionable, as to its translation. It appears to be from the Latin root *"fraga"*, as in the plural form. The Latin word *fraga* means "strawberry", which assumes *"fragues"* means "strawberries." Certainly, this meaning plays a role in interpretation, but there is another possibility, rooted to Latin, as is Italian. The word *"frague"* means, "slight, rotten, fragile, flimsy, brittle, and brash", in that language. When an "s" is added to this translation, as Italian, it is best shown as *"fragile ones"*. The use of *poison* is understood to be served on *strawberries*, but the *poison* is explained as having been put there by *rotten ones*. The use of Italian then acts to lead one to seeing this taking place in Italy.

Another option comes forth when one then finds the Spanish word *"fragües"* fits the word perfectly. This is the infinitive of *"fraguar"*, in the informative second-person singular; and means, "to forge, conceive of, or hatch." This option allows one to see how the line focuses on *"strawberries poisoned by brash ones who hatch"* a plan for murder. This then allows for a lean towards a Spanish influence. All is possible, from layers of depth emerging from one odd word, whose meaning is initially uncertain in French.

Through such analysis, a legitimate substitute translation can make this line read as, *"There poison tainted with the sugar by the breakable ones"*. The point of *strawberries* is important, when the word *"fragues"* is seen as based on a Latin root. However, the closest French root word if *"fragile,"* which is more in line with the Italian word *"fragues."* When ones sees the gender disagreement causing *"La"* need to be seen as "There, or Here," as an important (capitalized word) place where *poison* would be put on *strawberries*, as part of a plot by *fragile ones*, that place is better identified by the type of people *"There"*, than by the type of food used in a murder *"There"*. It is important to solve where *"There"* is, when the line is read as, *"There poison tainted with the sugar."*

The point of highlighting this lack of gender agreement is to show the importance of interpreting each word as selected with purpose. By viewing each one word as intentional, the irregularities, which arise from trying to make groups of words fit nicely into a preconceived syntax, disappear. *La* is still acceptably translated as *The*, but on a limited level. In the example used, the *La* beginning line three is limited as only being relative to *tainted*, when the oddity of gender is recognized. Recognition of the mismatched gender, created by combining *La* with *poison*, can cause one's syntactically trained mind to speed past that, as if it were a typo, with *"The poison"* instantly comprehended, incorrectly.

By seeing "*La*" as a purposefully chosen word, highlighted by its seeming incorrectness, one is drawn to seek importance (capitalization) through an interpretation directed towards place, as "*There*." This translation adjustment allows a strong suggestion to be made, which is to look at the place where "*poison*" exists, in all of those possibilities, relative to the whole context of this quatrain. Some specific place, *There*, then acts to connect this line to lines one, two, and four, where we find *A King* (main theme line), who *interdicts* (secondary theme line), with *bruised ones* (supporting line four). It allows one to see how this place is where "*The tainted*" are the "*poison*" "*There*." This flexibility allows each word to have its own gender, regardless of the gender of other independent words. All words can then individually express their full range of meaning, while also sharing a more intimate association with other words of the same gender, throughout a quatrain.

All words must be seen in this light, where independence and singularity yields multiplicity of meaning. As such, every use of *la* in *The Prophecies*, even when preceding a feminine noun, can mean both *the* and *there*, because alone all is possible. Likewise, the use of *le* can also have multiple meanings as in independent word, being *the*, *a*, *an*, *him*, or even *them* (if linking to a plural noun). By checking each possibility of meaning a word independently owns, seeing how each can fit into the stream of words communicated in that word's line, a greater meaning appears. Not only does the line have greater meaning, but greater meaning also spreads among all of the other words, in the same line, and the other lines of the verse, yielding a quatrain that is highly specific, rather than general.

Just keep in mind that the contracted form loses this flexibility. Had Nostradamus written, *L'poison*, instead of "*La poison*", the word "*Le*" would become the focus, linked with "*poison*." The article becomes one with the noun due to the contraction. Therefore, the article bears little weight, if any, in translation or interpretation. For instance, *l'France* literally translates as *the France*, but this spelling translates as *France*. The fact that Nostradamus used both the contracted form and separated words demonstrates there is a difference to notice; and in *The Prophecies*, differences are with purpose.

From this example, it is easy to see how small words bring greater meaning. The French prepositions, *à*, *de*, *en*, and *par* each have multiple usages, thus multiple translations. By itself, a preposition does little more than indicate direction; and because it is alone first, in the syntax of Nostradamus, it is free to be all directions. Once this full scope is recognized, any and all of those directions will link to the other words in the line.

For instance, in line three of the first quatrain in *Centurie Tenth*, Nostradamus wrote, "*le reste en chemise*". The preposition "*en*" can mean, "in, into, upon, on, or at," as the direction of this phrase. The word "*reste*" can mean, "rest, residue, remnant, remainder, or surplus." The word "*chemise*" means either "shirt" or "smock." By having "*en*" free to be all directions, we can read, "the rest into shirt", or "a residue on smock", or "the remnant in shirt". In the contest of the quatrain, everyone of those directions may play a role towards deeper understanding.

Unless a word, by definition, is limited to only one meaning, as is a number (the word "*cinq*" only means "five"), one can never restrict a word from potentially having all of its contextual meaning available for use. This puts the responsibility upon the reader to try and see how each possible usage would link to the surrounding verbiage. Because prepositions are so frequently used, a preposition like *de*, which can indicate "to, from, of, or with", when repeated multiple times in one quatrain, or in one line, can be found to run the gamut of it us. It becomes necessary to consider all directional flows, where one direction relates to one party, while the reverse direction indicates another party, before moving to a conclusion that involves two parties.

In this regard, the philosophical concept called Occam's Razor explains the language of Nostradamus. Basically, this says the less you say the more you mean. Simply by not limiting what one says with unnecessary words, like flowery adjectives and prepositions, what one actually does say becomes freer to have more meaning. One-word statements have nothing attached to them, which could limit the meaning, beyond the scope of a word's definition. This is the most efficient form of communication, as far as the conservation of space (print) and energy (talk) is concerned. However, a lot can be stated without extra words.

Nostradamus used this style, at the direction of Christ. He wrote only the words that best described a specific situation. He used all types of words doing this: main focus nouns, main action verbs, descriptive adjectives, directional prepositions, and modifying adverbs. Someone took the time to list alphabetically every word written by Nostradamus in *The Prophecies*[113], and it lists there are 602 uses of "*la/là.*"[114*] There are 375 uses of "*a/à*",[115*] and 916 uses of "*de*". Many other words show only one usage, which highlights just how important these small words are.

Still, no matter how frequent or how rare, every word used is vitally important towards telling an event's story: plot, characters, and scenes. Every word acts intentionally to direct the reader towards completely understanding the story told in the quatrain; and every quatrain acts with other quatrains to ensure there is no doubt about what specific events make up the greater, overall story. Everything written has reason and purpose, precisely as written. Therefore, there are no unnecessary words written into *The Prophecies*.

In the very top of the heading to the letter sent to King Henry II, Nostradamus wrote (in all-capital letters), "*A L'INVICTISSIME*". We have already discussed the importance all-capital-letter have, especially as a way of denoting a higher or heavenly focus. In addition, the root for the main word, *invictus*, is Latin;

---

113   List compiled by K. Lowey, prepared and saved to a new site by J. Flanagan, http://alumnus.caltech.edu/~jamesf/nindex/indextop.html
114   The noticeable difference in these spellings is a stress (acute) accent mark, in French called *accent aigu*. I will address this in more detail later.
115   Ibid.

and we have already discussed how Latin speaks as if directly from Jesus Christ. Still, the word has a French superlative ending (-*isme*, the English equivalent -ist), with French leading to the word, making the statement, "*FROM THE MOST-INVINCIBLE*". However, the standard translation says Nostradamus was addressing his king, "*TO THE MOST-INVINCIBLE*".

Before I address this all-caps line, let me continue with what Nostradamus wrote on the second line of the heading. Following a comma at the end of the all-cap line, he wrote, "*tres-puissant, tres-chrestien Henry.*" This states, "*most-powerful, most-Christian Henri*", which means that three "*mosts*" (superlatives) are used in the first two lines of the heading. Naturally, all interpreters have concluded that Nostradamus was being super-friendly to the king, presumably so the king would not get angry at Nostradamus for not showing up in person to explain his book. I imagine Henry saw this heading and thought the same thing; but then those people did not realize that Nostradamus did not write gratuitous superlatives. That would be (by definition of "gratuitous" "superlative") "unnecessary or unwarranted; unjustified"[116] use of "excessive or exaggerated"[117] language, which Nostradamus did not write.

Knowing what I have already explained, a simple check of a dictionary tells one "invincible" cannot possibly be used to address a human being. The word is defined as, "incapable of being overcome or defeated; unconquerable."[118] Even if Henry would have ruled France for a thousand years, mortality has a way of eventually overcoming, defeating, and conquering even the best of us mortal souls. For Nostradamus to add an "–ist" to invincible, making the word become "*THE MOST-INVINCIBLE*", is even more of an impossibility. That is then meaning, "Above all others unconquerable". The only possible, logical, believable, and necessary use of such a created word is for it to describe GOD. Since Henry was not that high up that food chain, Nostradamus could not have been writing a letter *TO GOD*. The letter was thus addressed, in the heading, as *WITH GOD (A L'INVICTISSIME)*.[119]

In line two of the letter to Henry, Nostradamus twice used the superlative *tres*, which my modern French dictionary states to mean, "very". It also indicates that when added before a past participle (past-tense verb) it can mean, "much". However, when I go to look up the word in an Old French dictionary, I find Randal Cotgrave writing the following about the little word *tres*:

> "A particle, or indeclinable word, never used but in composition, and then, for the most part, adding to that which it precedes the superlative energy. (Such as) thrice,[120] most, excellently, passing, or above all others, etc. In which sense being applicable to many Verbs, and to most Adjectives and Adverbs (which are in their original and due places expounded) I have purposefully omitted all, except four or five of them. (For reasons,)

---

116   The Free Dictionary by Farlex, http://www.thefreedictionary.com/gratuitous
117   The Free Dictionary by Farlex, http://www.thefreedictionary.com/superlative
118   The Free Dictionary by Farlex, http://www.thefreedictionary.com/invincible
119   The French article à means, "in, with, at, or to", depending on the context. However, the preposition "*de*" is more appropriate as indicating the direction "to."
120   Meaning "extremely, greatly".

it being an easier matter for simple Readers to find out the meaning of the rest by the application to them of these few, or by the general direction of this Rule, than for me to please the judicious, by stuffing up (through some warrant of example) much Paper with needless repetitions."[121]

The word that follows this "definition" in Cotgrave's dictionary is "*tresabonefcient*". This (without a hyphen) is said to translate as, "most wittingly, most earnestly, or in exceeding great earnest." The next word, "*tresacertes*", is described as, "thoroughly, in great earnest, as much, or as far as may be." A later word, "*tresarriere*," shows, "exceedingly backward, very far behind-hand." From these examples, one sees how "*tres*" was typically built-into the word, rather than separated. Still, it acted upon the word it fused with as raising the level of that word's meaning to is highest level or magnitude. Nostradamus' use of hyphenation has the same effect, but the hyphen separates the particle, "*tres*", so it is free to have the full scope of its superlativity surrounding it.

From this detail Cotgrave presented about the use of "*tres*," which was not something frequently done in his dictionary of 1611, he explained how the word only had use in printed communication ("*in composition*"). The use could be applied to just about any word, such that knowing the base word was what was important to understand. The addition of "*tres*" was then a way of recognizing an elevation to the word used, to a level that no other one word was known to express such excess. As a letter presented to King Henry II, the typical address would be, "Most Christian Majesty",[122] written as "*Tres Chrestein Majesté*."

The word "*puissant*" means, "powerful," such that "*tres-puissant*" means, "very powerful," "much powerful," or "*most powerful*". Certainly, a common description of *GOD* is one of being *all-powerful*, the Almighty, or omnipotent. In this regard, in the second letter by Paul to the Corinthians,[123] he stated, "κυριος παντοκρατωρ", or "*kurios pantokrator*", which in Greek means, "Lord Almighty." The word "*kurios*" is used much as is the word "*tres*," because its etymology has it rooted in a meaning of "supremacy," which a *Lord* holds.

Following an all-capital-letter, Latin-rooted, superlative word that states, *MOST-INVINCIBLE*, and knowing that Nostradamus used that style to indicate a higher voice, it is logical to see *tres-puissant* as a clarification, letting the reader have time to make this connection. It has the effect of stating the one *MOST-INVINCIBLE* is also the one *lord-almighty*. Still, because Nostradamus dropped to the lower-case, he has taken the highest level of God down to earthly status, as the *very-powerful*. The comma after *MOST-INVINCIBLE* shows a separation from God, leading to a natural sequence from God. That *very-*

---

[121] Randal Cotgrave's 1611 French-English Dictionary, with my adjustment in punctuation and modernized spelling of English words used. http://www.pbm.com/~lindahl/cotgrave/search/928l.html

[122] Wikipedia, the free dictionary, "Henry II of France" article. http://en.wikipedia.org/wiki/Henry_II_of_France

[123] 2 Corinthians 6:18 (International Standard Version), "I will be your Father, and you will be my sons and daughters," declares the Lord Almighty.", http://bible.cc/2_corinthians/6-18.htm

powerful form of God would be the one who would follow on earth, as Jesus, the Son of God. Jesus, although his actual years on earth were only 33, displayed a lasting earthly power, because his name (by 1555) had have lasted many hundreds of years, with no signs of weakening.

This is an important connection to make, from all-cap letters, to lower-case letters. Symbolically, Nostradamus has shown heavenly and earthly, simply by case. The use of superlatives, separated only by a comma, shows the ONE flows to the other, as FATHER to son. This association is there, but needs to be understood as Jesus, because Nostradamus explained Jesus repeatedly in the Preface.

From that understanding, one next finds more separation, but this time after a comma and an ampersand. Without translating the punctuation marks and symbols as words ("and and"), one sees what follows, which is another superlative word, but this time directly connected to the name *Henry*. This is another indication that *tres-puissant* is a trait of *GOD*, more than of Henri. That then supports the idea that makes *GOD* the one *WITH* whom the letter was written, and how the power *TO* be king originates (*A L'INVICTISSIME*). *GOD* is the power behind all kings.

This then leads to the *tres-chrestien Henry*, which is the normal address to the king. By one seeing the ampersand leading up to this standard address, it becomes an intentional misleading header, where all the superlatives are seen as towards Henry, because the ampersand is translated as "AND." Jesus instructed Nostradamus to use the precise words that would honor the true sources, while also recognizing the stature of Henry II, while being mistaken as Nostradamus "sucking up" to the king. However, much more is written, all of which has meaning relevant to the purpose of the letter, which is to explain *The Prophecies*.

Following the comma-ampersand combination, Nostradamus is actually making a statement of the bloodline to Henry, which gives him the right to become king in the first place. This is at the root of why *Tres Chretien Majesté* was the common address to Henry, as his royal reference style. The use of *tres-chrestien* means that the king was *most-Christian* personage in a nation of Christians. As the *most-Christian*, Henry is the closest to Christ.

Kings can only claim such a royal birthright because of the "Sang Real" (Blood Royal) that is within them. That is the theme of the book, *Holy Blood, Holy Grail*, and regardless of one's personal opinion of the worthiness of such a theme – Jesus had a child, which led to a line of European royalty – the statement that *Henry* is *most-Christian* means he is *above all others-Christian*. That scenario means a king from this bloodline would supersede the Pope in rank, when one defines *Christian* as a religion. However, this is where the use of the lower-case again becomes significant.

There is nothing about Old French that would naturally state the Christian religion in the lower case. A "Christian" is defined as one who follows Jesus, in recognition of his being the Christ, or promised

Messiah. Nostradamus even wrote in the letter to Henry, "*par le moindre d'eage sera la monarchie Chrestienne sousteneue*," ("*by the least of age will be there monarchy Christian sustained,*"), where he demonstrated the capitalization of the religion named after Jesus, as the Christ. The lower-case then denotes the more earthly form of Jesus, as the human who walked the earth as the promised one, with a relatively small following of Jews. The lower-case then states a bloodline to the man who would generate a religion. Henry was addressed as of that bloodline, which followed Jesus, who followed as the Son of God.

The point I want to make here, because I could go on and on explaining how Nostradamus began his letter of explanation by explaining his sources, is these superlatives are not written without deep meaning. Nostradamus did not write meaningless dribble, in hopes that he would be saved from punishment. Nostradamus wrote the truth at all times; but the whole truth is not always determined immediately. That truth is contained in the preciseness of the words chosen to pen onto paper.

This exercise in pointing out the use of seemingly meaningless verbiage, easily written off as Nostradamus buttering up his king, is to move you towards another similar example of overlooked wording. These examples of superlatives, where a prefix or ending has denoted a word as the greatest (-ist, most-), beyond a comparative (-er), are bumps in the translation process that cannot be missed; but they can be overcome and soon forgotten. What I am about to introduce you to is like a superlative, but is seen as nothing more than a simple adjective. Therefore, it does not feel like a bump in the process, so it is never noticed as important.

Even though you would read *The Prophecies* and afterwards not be able to recall one word's use, any more than any other word's use, there is one word that plays a significant role in understanding the stories Nostradamus told. That word has so much impact; it could be given its own systemic category. That word is "*great*." When Nostradamus wrote "*great*," it meant more than a mere descriptive adjective, easily replaced with a synonym, such as, "large, big, huge, vast, enormous, extensive, tremendous, immense, gigantic, important, extreme, excessive, famous, or outstanding." He used the word "*great*" with a very specific purpose.

I have already mentioned that someone has taken the time to list every word found in *The Prophecies* (quatrains only), and to count how many times Nostradamus used each word.[124] For words used a reasonable number of times (less than 150), the quatrain numbers were individually referenced. Those used more frequently than 150 times, primarily articles and prepositions, were simply listed as how many times those words appeared.

For instance, each use of the French word "*plus*" was referenced as being found stated 137 times, with

---

124   http://alumnus.caltech.edu/~jamesf/nindex/fh_index.html

nearly that many quatrains specifically identified (i.e.: I-4, I-5 [twice], I-15, I-36, I-44 [twice], etc.). According to that list, "*plus*" is the one word listed that specifically identifies the most individual quatrains in which it appears. For those words used more than 150 times by Nostradamus, the top five "most used words" are:

    1.) "*de*" (preposition meaning, "*to, from, of, with*") – 916 times

    2.) "*le*" (masculine article meaning, "*the, an, a, him*) – 702 times

    3.) "*la/là*" (feminine article or preposition meaning, "*the, there, here, then*") – 602 times

    4.) "*par*" (preposition meaning, "*by, by reason of, for, through, of, on*") – 595 times

    5.) "*a/à*" (preposition or verb meaning, "*at, to, with, in,* or *has*") – 375 times.

The plural form of *le*, "*les*" (article meaning, "*the, them*"), comes in a close sixth at 369 uses.

Behind that is the adjective "*grand*" (meaning, "*great, big, large, huge, mighty, substantial, high, lofty,* or *stately*"), which was written 357 times. This one spelling becomes the most used non-article/preposition. However, that spelling is in the masculine form, with another spelling, "*grād*", being an abbreviated form, also in the masculine, which was written an additional 5 times.[125] That addition jumps the total number of times "*grand*" was used to 362.

In the "top five" list, both "le" and "la" have a position. When both are seen as representing the same word, as the article "*the*", one masculine and one feminine, the total times "*the*" appears in *The Prophecies* jumps to 1,304 times. That takes over the number one position, but "*de*" has its own variations, as "*d'*" (contracted form of "*de*"), "*du*" (a contraction of "*de le*"), and "*des*" (the plural form of "*de*"), which raises its total uses (without being combined with "*the*") to 1,022 times.

This means, if all the variations of "*grand*" are likewise counted, its total would become much more significant. When one adds the total feminine form uses (*grande* – 62 times), with the plural form uses (*grands* – 36 times; *grandes* – 3 times; *grans* – 9 times), the meaning of "*great*" makes 472 appearances in *The Prophecies*. That total rises this adjective to the number four position, clearly becoming the most important word used that can act as a noun.

This has to be seen as a significant number of uses, regardless of the use of "*great*". For it to be seen as an adjective, one would expect an ordinarily use to be more limited in typical literature. That is unless one assumes that Nostradamus loves to toss about superlatives, which is the assumption made when Nostradamus addressed his letter to King Henry II. By seeing that many uses as an adjective, the quantity is a clear indication of the quatrains focusing only on the "biggest" and "most important" events of the future. However, the word "*great*" can be used as a noun, as an indication of one who stands above others in renown and praise. This is especially seen in the plural uses, as "*greats*."

---

125   This form would be due to a printer using standard abbreviation liberties, where the "*ā*" indicated an "*n*" followed, but was omitted, due to space limitations. This number is based on the specific edition of *The Prophecies* that was analyzed, and does not apply to all editions.

Nostradamus made 48 references to "*grands*", in one form or another, in the quatrains of *The Prophecies*. He made three more of these plural references in the letter to Henry. Because some can doubt the translation of *grands, grandes,* and *grans* as "*great ones*", as I see them meaning, many see this as an unimportant description of something more important – the focus seen as the reason for using the plural number.

Due to the fact that the French language correctly modifies articles and adjectives to match the number of a noun, typically by adding an "-s" ending, the French would read all of plural forms of "*grand*" as, "*great*", if there was agreement with other plural words. For instance, from the letter to Henry, Nostradamus wrote, "*adjoincte avec celeste a d'aucuns de ce nombre ont predit de grandes & esmerveillables adventures*". In syntactical French (with the Old pared off), this says, "*adjoined with celestial with of some of this number have foretold to great & marvelous adventures*". However, this is not what that series of words are informing one to know, when read like that.

If one wants to return to square one and believe one can understand Nostradamus by understanding the rules of French, one can join the ranks of French people who cannot understand Nostradamus. When one reads every word Nostradamus wrote individually, before connecting the thought that arises from one word, realizing all of each word's possible meanings, one has to read the plural form of all article or adjective as a noun or pronoun. For example, *les* becomes *them*; and thus, *grandes* becomes *great ones*.

In the example from the letter to Henry, Nostradamus told of being "*adjoined with (the) celestial*", which is being in-touch with Heaven, or the divine. While "*in*" that state, or "*with*" his "*celestial*" guide, he was shown the future, being taken "*to some*" (plural number) events important to write about. These events would be "*of this number*" in his published book, *The Prophecies*, which no one could understand. These visions "*have*" (plural number) within them stories that "*prophesy*", or "*predict*" the coming times "*of great ones*". Importantly, the times of this future will be "*miraculous ones*", or "*marvelous ones*", or "*wonderful ones*", when seen from Nostradamus' perspective. In this series of words, Nostradamus used words that can only be plural, but none that can be simply read as only plural to match number.

The mental acceptance of "*grands*" as being an indication of "*great*" (a singular noun, as "the great") "*ones*" (plural noun, as those making up "the great") is how one realizes Nostradamus referred to "*the ones*" of this "*marvelous*" time in a distant future, in over 472 uses in the quatrains. The stars (if one could call them that) of his tale of the end of the world are none other than the "*great ones*", those who rule the world. These come in all shapes and sizes, as nations, as empires, and as individuals at the helm of large entities.

Without grasping the specific purpose for Nostradamus choosing that one word to be used more than any other having the capability of being a noun, means no true level of meaning can be achieved by the reader. One simply is left with the impression that Nostradamus overused an adjective that described a noun in a superlative sense. We can get this sense from realizing the complete range the word *great* has in definition. Due to the primary use in conversation being a reference to the meaning, "very large in size,"[126] when we hear a statement like, "Go to the great big building downtown", our fast-paced mental approach to reading with syntax basically drops the *great*, and focuses wholly on *big*. The word *great* becomes, in our minds, unnecessary clutter to process.

When one looks up the Old French translation possibilities to English, Randal Cotgrave listed, "Great; big, large; huge, mighty; substantial; also, high, lofty, stately".[127] If one then looks up the word *great* in an English dictionary, it has such meanings through usage as, "outstanding in magnitude", "outstanding significance or importance", "superior in quality or character", "chief or principal", "grand; aristocratic", "eminent", and "powerful; influential".[128] Still, the primary usage is "very large in size". While we may say in English, "The great big building downtown," and the French could say, "La grosse grande construction en ville," in essence either has just stated, "The big big building downtown." Such use is redundant, thus superfluous, and unnecessary.

In English, the plural form is acceptable as a noun, and defined as, "*pl.* **greats** or **great** One that is great", as "a composer considered among the greats."[129] With that in mind, imagine a person, place, or thing that would justifiably (not superfluously) be described as, "Great; big, large; huge, mighty; substantial; also, high, lofty, stately". When one pauses to think deeply about this one particular word thusly, one can see how *great* is used to represent an individual entity, much more than being an unnecessary descriptive adjective. It takes on the power of the word's definition, becoming one of greatness.

When one gets the "big picture" of *The Prophecies*, as I have discussed, with the embedded systems making this possible to see, the work is a true Prophecy. It deals with the future as a warning from God for humanity, and presented to Nostradamus through the Spirit of Jesus Christ, so it would be written and preserved until time to understand. The future told was not close to the times of Nostradamus. The future told of in the quatrains of his book was very distant in time. In hindsight, one can see it was not shown to begin in earnest until the 20th century, and not to be revealed until the 21st century. Thus, when Nostradamus used the word *great* (in all forms), he used it to describe those elements of the common man's rise to power, who would become the *greats* of the world.

In 1555, when Nostradamus published the first edition of *The Prophecies*, Spain was one of the *great* powers in Europe. The islands that were separated from Europe, but significant players in European affairs, were each separate nations: England (*l'Angleterre*), Scotland (*l'Escosse*), and Ireland (*l'Irin*).[130] The English were the ones with the strongest desire to expand and control other nations, particularly

126   The Free Dictionary by Farlex, http://www.thefreedictionary.com/great
127   Randal Cotgrave's 1611 French – English Dictionary, http://www.pbm.com/~lindahl/cotgrave/search/499r.html
128   The Free Dictionary by Farlex, http://www.thefreedictionary.com/great
129   The Free Dictionary by Farlex, http://www.thefreedictionary.com/great
130   Wales had become incorporated with England in a series of legal acts, between 1535 and 1542.

those in and around their location. However, in 1555 the English were not world powers. Only after the death of Nostradamus (1566) did the English begin to grow and built themselves into a nation that was bigger, mightier, and loftier in international affairs.

The English began colonization in the New World in 1607 (Jamestown, Virginia), experienced its lone period as a republic (1642 – 1660), and after long warring against the Irish and Scottish, became *Great Britain* in 1707. This later became formally known as the United Kingdom of Great Britain (1801), or more simply the United Kingdom; but following this forced union forging the British Isles, the British began to develop as an Empire, with colonial possession around the globe, particularly in North America and India. From this history, one has to see the *greats* of Nostradamus' future being those nations that have supported over 300 years of British world dominance or importance; and this is greatness that has been passed on to its eldest heir, the United States of America.

This is the strongest element of Nostradamus' *greats*. Since he was very familiar with the English, as they shared a strong connection to France through the Celts and the peninsula of Brittany, Nostradamus knew them well. However, he did not know the names of the British descendants who would rise to *great* heights of power. Nostradamus could only name them as "*greats*", making that a descriptive name the fits perfectly.

With this seed of thought planted, let us look at a few of the many quatrains where one finds some form of *great* used. An excellent example is found in the sixty-fifth quatrain in *Centurie Ninth*. Nostradamus placed three different forms of "great" there, with one in line three, and two in line four. Those lines state, "*Les fruitz immeurs seront à grand esclandre / Grand vitupere, à l'un grande louange.*" Before one even begins to translate this, one can see that there are there is a lower-case masculine "*grand*", a capitalized masculine "*Grand*", and a lower-case feminine "*grande*". A literal translation thus becomes, "*The fruits immature ones will be at great slaughter / Great blame, with the one great praise.*"

Now, I have not presented all of the systems at this point, so there is no point in going into an in-depth interpretation, especially with the two theme statements absent. What is important, at this point, is to recognize that the same word (basically) is presented in a poem three times, over a span of seven words (when "*l'un*" is seen as contracted to act as one word). This is an example that says clearly, albeit indiscreetly, "*grand*" has three different uses.

Despite the fact that a writer of college-level talent would be schooled with enough writing skills to know repeating the same word three times is a sign of (minimally) a lack of imagination, there are some things to notice about these three presentations of "*grand(e)*". The first is there is only one use of "*grand*" in line three, while there are two in line four. Line three is more closely related to the main theme line, due to it being closer, and the main theme (line one) controls the focus of the whole quatrain. Line three places that focus on *"great slaughter"*.[131] The difference comes from seeing how a focus on one *"great"* becomes split into two separate *"greats"*.

Next, there is a lower-case *"grand"* of line three leading to a capitalized *"Grand"* in line four. This denotes a difference in importance, and due to them being so close together, *"Great"* becomes directly related to the *"slaughter"* of line three. The difference hints at the possibility of one *"great"* being cut to pieces, with the responsibility placed upon a very import *"Great"*, who is *"blamed"* for that *"slaughter."*

Finally, in the two *"greats"* together in line four, one is capitalized and in the masculine gender (*"Grand"*), while the other is in lower-case, of the feminine gender. Additionally, the two are separated by a comma, which means there is punctuation that denotes a difference through separation. The first use points to an important mistake (*"Great blame"*), which then leads to just the opposite (*"great praise"*).

Because all are in different relationships to one another, they must be identified individually. The only way to do this is to use different translations, even though the simple translation would repeat "great" three times. Add that redundancy to the mind's wanting to disregard a superlative adjective as meaningless, and so many uses of *"grand"* lead to a quatrain that seemingly makes no sense. The trained eye has to spot such multiple uses, and realize each use should steer clear of repetition in translation.

In the case of *"great"*, each can certainly qualify as being identified as *"great"*. That translation can apply in each placement. However, it would be no different than having an ice hockey team with three forwards each named Bob. All could certainly be called Bob correctly, but confusion comes when a play-by-play announcer says, "Bob skates in and passes to Bob, who drops it back to Bob, who passes it across to Bob, who shoots at the net, but the goalie blocks the shot, still its loose in front, and Bob scores!" It would be easier to follow if each was more easily identifiable.

Again, I could continue much further with the delineation of these uses of *"great"*, and then the rest of the quatrain; but that is not the point. The importance is to recognize that the use of this adjective must be seen as identifying a noun. The reason there are 472 uses of *"great"* in the quatrains is the word identifies the main characters in this story of the future, the one we are in the middle of now. When one looks carefully to the verbiage of the surround words, it becomes easy to determine which *"great"* is in the scene. Sometimes, there are two on the stage at the same time. However, that is where the differences become important to understand

Let me move on to another example where the word *"great"* appears in a quatrain. In the quatrain numbered seventy-eighth, in *Centurie Second*, Nostradamus wrote in the first line, "*Le grand Neptune du profond de la mer,*" which translates literally to state, "*The great Neptune to the deep of the sea*". One has to keep in mind that there are multiple possibilities that relate to the translations of *du*, *de*, and *la*, such

---

[131] This translation is the choice for example purposes. There are other translations possibilities, with all having merit.

that the translation I have stated above is not fixed. It just as aptly could state, "*The great Neptune from the deep to there sea.*" The initial focus has to be on "*The great Neptune*".

Once again, we encounter how easy it could be to skip past the obligatory descriptors and get right to interpreting *Neptune*. Everyone knows that *Neptune* was the name of the Roman god of water and the sea. Certainly, a god is *great*, so to state anything less than "*The great Neptune*" would be somewhat of a slight; but if *Neptune* is the ultimate meaning of this line, it would not have been necessary to describe *Neptune*. Nostradamus could have easily just written, "*Neptune of the deep to the sea.*" As one can see, that is a vague statement, which only develops an image of mythological *Neptune* in his normal domain. As the first line, that is too weak to develop into a meaningful main theme. Therefore, *The great*" has to play the role that brings specific meaning to this line.

As we discussed in the last example, the word "*great*" must always be seen as a noun. With that understood, it's being combined with an article means the article is pointing to "*The great*". The line begins by identifying the subject as "*The great*", such that it is not just any *great*, it is an important (capitalization) "*great*". When one sees this in that light, the following *Neptune* is no longer subject material. It becomes supporting information about "*The great*".

Simply by naming *Neptune* as a descriptor, one is able to see that "*The great*" in question is the one that controls the waters and seas like a god. Even though Nostradamus had no clue about the planet *Neptune*, the use of that name can still act be a timing element, based on the planet we know, which would make the use more believable than a mythological god. The timing would not be astrological, based on modern astrological symbolisms, since attached to that planet. Instead, it would assist as a means to determine a timing for "*The great*", based on when Neptune was discovered.

Such an indication would mean "*The great*" will be "*great*" in 1846, when a new planet would be found, and given the name of the Roman sea god. In 1846, the British Empire was the world's most formidable navy. It was an empire because it has established itself on the high seas. The British navy had reached around the globe, and established colonies from Africa, to the Pacific, to the Americas. Certainly, Great Britain was "*The great*" when *Neptune* was discovered. However, there is still another possibility, based on that timing.

In 1846, Britain was in a peaceful phase. Queen Victoria had taken the throne in 1837, and during her 64 years as Queen, there were no wars, thus no need to prove their greatness. However, in 1846 the United States of America began the Mexican-American War, by the use of its navy, which landed troops at Palo Alto and Resaca de la Palma (near the Texas-Mexico border today). That war was concluded in the U.S. favor in 1848.

In one sense, certainly secondary to the meaning of this example line, one can see how the United States of America made a step towards expansion, in the year that *Neptune* was discovered. In 1848 all the land that would eventually make up the 48 continental states of America had been ceded to the U.S. Afterwards, due to its increasing naval presence, the United States would become empirical, seeking foreign lands as holdings. Its progress in that direction can be traced to the time when *Neptune* was discovered.

That planet, once discovered, would later gain astrological meaning, relative to hindsight analysis of what was taking place in the world in the late 19th century. Still, while "modern" astrologers were trying to figure out the symbolisms of the first new planet added to astrology, since Uranus in the previous century (1781), there was an immediate need to determine a glyph to denote *Neptune's* presence on a chart. That glyph became the trident, his powerful staff.

This association between *Neptune* and his trident it the primary focus that must always be taken from the mention of *Neptune* in *The Prophecies* (there are five mentions in the quatrains, and one in the Henry letter). The names, Trident, Poseidon (the similar Greek god), and *Neptune* all have been used in naming naval and aerial crafts, with Poseidon and Trident the name of British and American submarine-launched ballistic missiles (SLBMs). When line one is seen to go on and explain, "*of the deep to the sea*", this is a main theme about mastery of the deeps, through submarine weaponry.

These all act as important possible character traits for "*The great*," because the word "*great*" is surrounded by "*Neptune*" and "*The*", both capitalized words, thus pointing towards higher importance. One becomes "*The great*" (an indication of singularity, above others) because one is "*great*" as "*Neptune*", who was "*great*" because he controlled the seas, and had a powerful trident. Nostradamus identifies the trident in three quatrains (two along with *Neptune*), which is further evidence of this being a characteristic of one who is "*The great*".

What must be realized is the words selected by Nostradamus carry everything that one needs to know, in order to be able to understand a quatrain's meaning. Nothing is chosen haphazardly, as every word has perfect reason for being where it has been placed. The philosophy that less means more has to be grasped. Once one adopts that view, it becomes clear to see how repetitiveness is a signal to look into a fixed number of words yielding multidimensional meanings, all based on the multiplicity of definition, through assumed contexts. A word that seems little more than a superlative adjective, quickly forgotten, becomes an identifier of key characters that must be distinguished from one another. It is imperative to realize there is no word in *The Prophecies* that is insignificant.

Chapter 22

The System of Order

With the concept in hand that no words in *The Prophecies* are frivolous and without purpose, it then becomes logical to believe that nothing can be out of place. Everything has order. Everything is where it is for a reason, and there are no rights given that allow one to alter that order. This is a most important concept that must be grasped, because it has nothing to do with the order of language, as one has been trained to understand syntactically.

There are several forms of linguistic topology, which deals with word order. Two basic types of languages are identified as Verb-Object (VO) and Object-Verb (OV). These are then further modified when the element of Subject is intermixed (VOS, OSV, SVO, etc.). Both English and French are Subject-Verb-Object (SVO) based, for the most part, so it is possible to do a literal translation of French and make some sense of it in English.

German is not so easily classified, as it depends more on clauses, where SVO is used in main clauses, with SOV and VSO being normal in subordinate clauses. As such, a literal translation of the German statement, "He knows, I every Sunday to church go," would naturally be altered to mean, "He knows, I go to church every Sunday." This is then an example of how order can vary from language to language; allowing translators the freedom to change what was literally stated, to what was meant to be stated.

From this freedom of translation, one can see how the line written by Nostradamus in the thirty-forth quatrain of Century Sixth, "*Du feu volant la machination*," can come out translated as "*The machine of flying fire*". The literal translation, "*From the fire flying the machination*", makes less sense, when one is seeking a comfortable syntax from which to understand. However, when one is reading Nostradamus, only the syntax of Nostradamus brings meaning out, with order part of that syntax. Only the literal translation can maintain the proper order.

In the example given, one's preconceptions of order mislead towards an incorrect translation, seeing words that are not written. For instance, the directional preposition half of "*du*" has been lost; and the word "*machination*" has been transformed into "*machine*", presumably to make that the cause of the "*fire*", through an ability to "*fly*". However, the word *machination* meant in Old French, the same as it means in today's English, "contriving; a subtle plot or conspiracy; shifting stratagem, circumventing trick",[132] or "A crafty scheme or cunning design for the accomplishment of a sinister end."[133]

The subject of this statement is *"fire"*, and the verb, *"flying"*, is relative to that subject, with the object of the subject being *"machination"*. This is then ordered like a subordinate clause would be, in German. Still, the language of Nostradamus cannot be categorized as to be expected to follow such traits. Each word makes it own, whole and complete statement, based on all sentences that can be constructed to define each word. Because of this freedom, the example line can be read like this, based on the order of the words written:

> Coming from a distance (*From a*) the burning of fuel or other material (*fire*) done or performed swiftly as if in the air and extremely mobile (*flying*) to into or towards that place (*there*) a crafty scheme or cunning design for the accomplishment of a sinister end (*machination*)

As this demonstrates, the order makes the definitions of the words flow into a tale of trickery, through some form of aerial bombardment. This shows how the order of Nostradamus' words is as important as the order of a fiction writer's sentences. One should be realize that sentence order is what tells the story, with word order only being important within the structure of a sentence. While a line of Nostradamus' poetry gives the appearance of being a sentence fragment that is the illusion that maintains its cloak of nebulosity and confusion.

There is no need to worry about word order topology when reading Nostradamus. Because each word is its own sentence, one just has to follow the order of words to the end of the story each quatrain tells. Seeing each word this way means each is free to have all the meanings applicable to that word. There is no need to worry about word order when there is only one word to consider.

From this perspective, the word order is where the word was placed when written by Nostradamus. When one realizes the placement is what makes the quatrain make sense, to change it would be like this paragraph being rearranged. Certainly, some changes could do little to alter the overall purpose, but others would make something sensible make no sense at all. Thus, order is everything, and everything has its specific order.

When I state that order is everything, I base that statement on the same principle that I presented previously. The reason behind seeing every word as being perfectly chosen, with no errors or triviality, because Jesus Christ is the source of *The Prophecies*, equally applies to where those words appear. If each word is the perfect word, each word's placement is equally perfect. In my examples used in the last section, I

---

132   Randal Cotgrave's 1611 French-English Dictionary, http://www.pbm.com/~lindahl/cotgrave/search/594r.html

133   The Free Dictionary by Farlex, http://www.thefreedictionary.com/machination

presented how logical and reasonable meaning can come from words having more than one translation, thus multiple meanings, while never once changing the order of the written words. Each word links to the words that surround it like a chain. This is the central idea behind the system that relies on method among the madness.

Obviously, I have already made the statement that the quatrains themselves are purposefully out of order. Due to their presentation as random individual poems, it is very difficult to see how one main theme can be developed, through the development of short stories and subplots. The difficulty comes from a lack of an overall order, which needs to be restored. The restoration of *The Prophecies* thus becomes like a puzzle that must be reordered in order to see the true meaning that it holds.

Earlier, I gave my reasons for seeing the need to reorder the quatrains. When I suddenly began to understand there was a connection between 200 quatrains, scattered throughout the ten Centuries, I saw them (the 200 total) as a separate story being told. I did not immediately understand the need to rearrange every quatrain. As time went on, I saw that need; and I realized through insights I experienced that the wholeness of order is where total understanding lies. I have had these thoughts confirmed over and over again, through the writings of Nostradamus.

Almost as an afterthought, I found where Nostradamus gave this instruction about order. In the letter of explanation sent to Henry II, Nostradamus wrote this segment of words: "*le tout selon **l'ordre** de la chaysne qui contient sa revelation*". This literally translates to state, "*the whole according unto **the order** of the chain which will be containing his revelation*". When one reads "*the whole*" here, specifically as an explanation for *The Prophecies*, it means "*all*" (alternative translation of *tout*) the quatrains. The word "*selon*" is translated to state "*according unto*", meaning "brought into harmony or agreement," but it can also mean, "*after the manner of*",[134] or "*in accordance with*".[135] This means that "*the whole*" of *The Prophecies* is one harmonious document, rather than the crazy mess everyone thought it to be. Everything links as a "*chain*".

At this point, Nostradamus stated "*the order*", identifying this as the key to the harmony. In other words, to make "*the whole in accordance with*" itself, as a meaningful Prophecy, "*the order*" must be restored. Then, he clarified this *order* by writing "*of the chain*", or "*to the chain*", which is clearly stating each quatrain is a link that must be connected into a string of links, in "*the chain*" form that originally ordered the work. After "*which*", the correct *order* of "*the whole will be containing his revelation*", "*which*" is necessary for "*whom*" (alternate translation of *qui*) "*will be comprehending*" (alternate translation for *contient*) "*its*" (alternate translation for *sa*) "*revealing*" (alternate translation for *revelation*) prophecies.

I do not mean to limit this segment from having other relevant meanings from other possible translations.

---

134   Randal Cotgrave's 1611 French-English Dictionary, http://www.pbm.com/~lindahl/cotgrave/search/8601.html

135   French Concise Dictionary, 3rd Edition, Harper Collins, Glasgow, GB, 2004, *selon*, p.390.

There certainly are other applications for *"the order of the chain"*. However, as far as the system of order is concerned, this one series of words, written as an explanation of the enigma surrounding *The Prophecies*, sums up how important order is. Still, the system of order goes well beyond simply reordering the verses so they tell an epic tale.

Order applies everywhere, such that order is all-important. A good place to begin to understand the importance of order is the dictionary. One finds that there are many possible uses for the word, both as a noun and as a verb. The most basic noun definition is, "A condition of logical or comprehensible arrangement among the separate elements of a group."[136] Certainly, this states that order is how one can make sense of *The Prophecies* (the group), when each element (a quatrain) is arranged in a logical order. Still, while each separate element is a link with logical order in a *chain*, each has its own internal need for order as well.

Each quatrain is a stand-alone prophecy. Thus, the name of the book is *The Prophecies*, in the plural. These units can be moved into a new order of overall presentation, without doing anything to alter the order of the lines within one unit of poetry. This license to reorder the whole does not allow one the freedom to change the order within the quatrain itself. Each individual prophecy has perfection in the order of its lines, and in the order of the words. This perfection comes from God; and thus, no human has the right to alter this order, without changing what was perfect into something quite flawed.

Each quatrain is an independent element in the chain of *The Prophecies*. Since each is written in poetic style, each quatrain is a 4-line poem. Each is a whole poem, by itself; and as such one needs to understand some rules that pertain to the parts of a poem. First, each poem has a speaker, which is correctly presumed to be Nostradamus, as long as it is also presumed that God is influencing the speaker. Second, a poem is addressing an audience, with the standard audience of a Prophecy being those in need of hearing a prophetic message. That would be you, the reader (and me, the writer). Third, a poem addresses a subject, the topic about which the individual poem is written. Fourth, a poem states a theme that is related to the subject; and last (as far as this lesson is concerned), a poem uses diction to represent the poet's specific choice of words that will address the subject.[137]

This rule of diction, as it applies to a poem, means that thought has gone into the deliberate placement of each word. Thus, each word is in the proper order. Each word is also carefully chosen to represent the subject of the quatrain. As such, each line has been carefully crafted to place words that present a theme and relate to that theme. All of the order that has come from the poet must then be maintained.

The order of the line is evident in the fact that each quatrain is a poem. By being a "quatrain," there are four lines of verse. There is order in the numbers, 1, 2, 3, and 4, which relate to each line. We see these

---

136   The Free Dictionary by Farlex, http://www.thefreedictionary.com/order
137   Gallaudet University English Works!, http://depts.gallaudet.edu/englishworks/literature/poetry.html#theme

four-lines make a poem because the lines contain an ABAB rhyme scheme. By this, line one ends with a word that rhymes with the word that ends line three. This would be the A rhyme. Likewise, lines two and four end in rhyming words that are different from the A rhyme, thus becoming the B rhyme. This order is important as the rhyming words identify each line as being in poetic relationship with another line.

The order of the line has meaning that is parallel to the number and rhyme scheme. The line numbered one carries the meaning of being "number one," or the main line from which all other lines follow. Line one's rhyming word is related to line three's rhyming word (A-A), which is therefore a relationship to odd numbered lines (1-3). Line two follows the "main" line, and is completely separate from line one, due to different rhyming words. As line two is the first of its rhyme, it becomes the "secondary main" line; and this line's rhyme is in relationship with line four. This makes both relate as even numbered lines (2-4) with rhyming words (B-B).

This is then relative to the subject and theme that each poem contains, based on the order of the lines. The rules are, and can always be found to be as follows: Line one is the "main theme" line. Line one states the primary statement (through the ordered statements of individual words) relative to one specific subject. The line one subject is the subject to which all other lines will be referencing. Line two is then relative to the subject of line one, but stating its own "secondary theme," which is a clarification of any possible generality stated in the main theme line. Line three, as related to line one in number and rhyme, is then read as directly adding supporting information (through the ordered statement of individual words) to the main theme. As it follows line two, it is relative as subsequent elements attaching to the secondary theme. Line four is then related to line two in number and rhyme, adding supporting information to the secondary theme, while following line three as subsequent elements that relate to the subject of line one.

The result of recognizing these rules of order is that they turn a seemingly vague and unintelligible series of ill-fitting, out of order words, into a very specific and detailed number of statements. This specificity becomes important when it is recognized that many general events appear as episodes where history repeats itself. However, history can never completely repeat itself, due to different times and different details making all historical events easily identifiable from one another.

While some repeat events in history appear as identical as human twins do to the casual observer, the minute details are where the differences are found, making each stand out separately. Individual characteristics that make twin babies easy for a parent to tell two apart are likewise how historians can clearly see Napoleon's defeat in Russia is different from Hitler's defeat there. The system of order allows for such distinction, because it differentiates through the specificity of order. No two events will have the exact same order of occurrences, although many events repeat similarly through the physics (or metaphysics) of natural order.

In this regard, I will demonstrate the mechanics of this system of order on a quatrain mentioned, in part, previously. The quatrain is the one containing the words, "*The great* Neptune", and it is commonly identified as the seventy-eighth quatrain in *Centurie Second*. There, Nostradamus wrote, in entirety:

Le grand Neptune du profond de **la mer**, (A)	The great Neptune to the deep of the sea,
De gent Punique & sang Gauloys **meslé**: (B)	Of people Punic & blood French mixed:
Les Isles à sang pour le tardif **ramer**, (A)	The Islands with lineage for the slow to row,
Plus luy nuira que l'occult **mal celé**. (B)	More it will hurt than the hidden evil secret.

As can be observed from the bold letters, the rhyme scheme established a relationship between lines, while also keeping each line intact, unable to be blended into another line, as has commonly be the case with translators. The English translation makes this relationship seem to disappear, as the rhymes of poetry have an appearance of prose. Still, as can be demonstrated in an in-depth analysis of each line, following the order of the words, and each line's in-depth relationship to the other lines, the order established by the rhyme scheme is shown to be all-important to understand.

Follow as I now analyze this one quatrain. Based on the same principles of order, every quatrain follows the same rules. The main theme must be developed from line one. A secondary theme will emerge in line two. Supporting details to the main theme will appear in line three, as well as clarifying information to the secondary theme. Finally, the supporting details to the secondary theme will be presented in line four, with subsequent information applicable to line three. All will be under the general heading of the main theme.

Line one is stating a main theme relative to "*The great*", and their "*profound*" control of the waters of the earth, including the "*depths of the sea*". In this breakdown of the main theme line, the presence of "*du*" (the contracted form for *de le*), followed by "*de la*" can translate to establish directional movement, "*to the deep*" "*from there sea*", or "*from a high*" "*to here sea*". It can equally establish a presence or surrounding, "*with them secret*" "*of the sea*". All are valid readings, such that all are meant to be read for total understanding, but the order must maintain "*profound*" before "*sea*".

Together, the wholeness of this line is highly indicative of submarine travel. It shows one of the major characters of *The Prophecies* ("*The great*") as the one known above all other to have mastery of the oceans and seas. This is stating a "*mighty*" (alternate translation of "*grand*") naval presence, with an ability to strike lightning quick. The words "*du profound*" could indicate the sinking of a surface ship, sending it "*to the depths*". The object of this theme seems to *the sea*, which is unidentified. The use of a separated "*la*" (meaning it can be read as *là*) places focus on "*there sea*", "*here sea*", or as the target of a mission, "*then sea*".

Line two is divided into two halves, surrounding an ampersand. There is focus on the capitalized word, "*Punic*", in the first half, and focus on the capitalized word, "*French*", in the second half. When the word

The System of Order

"*Punic*" is seen as relative to ancient Carthage, which is now Tunisia, we see focus on North Africa. This balances the focus "*of France*", which is in Europe, and identifies "*the sea*" of the main theme, as being the Mediterranean Sea. That is only *sea* that is in common with both Tunisia and France; but this identification is not the focus of the secondary theme.

A separate theme is developed, such that the "*people*" involved in the ancient "*Punic*" Wars, which were the Carthaginians and the Romans, are importantly joined (the ampersand) with people "*of France*". The focus of this joining is termed, "*mingled*", or "*intermeddled*". This later choice infers a level of interference, directly involving the "*French*", as a response to a rekindling of differences between North Africa and Italy. The word "*blood*", which is intended to show the relationship between the three entities (Tunisia, Italy, and France), in particular the "*French*" relationship to Italy and Tunisia, shows that there is both good and bad "*blood*" there, due to the "*mixing*" that has become ingrained in the histories of the three.

This secondary theme is related to the main theme. It identifies secondary characters that are separate from "*The great*", while having all been themselves "*great*", at some times past. The three countries indicated are all major players in the Mediterranean Sea theater, with significant coastlines along those waters, with all in relative proximity to the others. Each can then also be expected to play roles that "*mingle*", to the point of interference with the others, through naval exchanges. Thus, line two is a theme of the encounters between "lesser creatures" that tests the powers of a sea god.

Line three, as a line adding supporting details to the main theme, tells the reader that "*The great*" is specifically "*The Isles*", with "*Isles*" capitalized. Due to the Mediterranean Sea only being identified in line two, neither lines three or one are so restricted. The importance of a capitalized article, as "*THE*" one of most importance, links "*The great god of the seas (Neptune)*" to equally important "*Islands*". That distinction belongs to the United Kingdom of *Great* Britain (an *Island*) and Northern Ireland (another *Island*), which is commonly referred to as *The* British *Isles*.

Because line three follows line two, there is also a secondary meaning of significance, which comes from "*The Isles*", as relative to the Mediterranean Sea region. While it would be easy to see Greece as this focus, the "*islands*" of Greece are in the Aegean Sea, and not the Mediterranean. Since line one is not limited to any particular "*sea*", the Greek "*isles*" are still part of the mix. However, when line two is focusing on Italy and France, "*The Isles*" of the Mediterranean that claim those nationalities are Corsica, Sardinia, and Sicily. Tunisia is separated from the island of Sicily by the part of the Mediterranean called the Strait of Sicily.

Line three repeats the word "*sang*", which was used in line two. The focus is then about "*blood*", or "*kindred*" on these major "*Islands*" being in danger. The French word "*pour*" can simply mean "*for*", but it also can translate to state, "*in defense of*". In this scenario, the reason "*The great*" is called upon to show its naval might, is *"because"* (alternative translation of *"pour"*) *"Punic"* *"blood"* going *"for The Islands"* that are close. *"The great"* are called *"in defense of"* those of their own *"race"*.

The last three words of line three, *"le tardif ramer"*, is an indication of all parties involved, such that the separately written article *"le"* can be translated as the plural *"les"*, stating *"them slow to row"*. Rowing confirms the naval aspect of line one, and shows activity on the waters of the Mediterranean as being without a sense of urgency. *"The great"*, with its vast naval superiority, can be *"tardy"* or *"long in coming"* *"because"* there is a mismatch of strength. Those reaching *"The Isles"* of the Mediterranean could be on small rafts, or boats, which proceed *"slowly"*, perhaps in *"row boats"*, indicating a flood of refugees. Those who have flooded *"The Isles"* already, may be causing difficulties the Italian government cannot handle, having a hard time getting the refugees deported. There could even be a storm (caused by *Neptune*), which has sent some *"blood"* to the *"deep of the sea"*.

Line four begins with the capitalized word *"Plus"*, which means, *"More"*. This directly relates to those who are *"rowing"*, or sailing, such that the numbers will significantly increase. This then is related to the secondary theme, where the *"French"* are called upon to *"mingle"* with the Italians and Tunisians, where the *"More"* there are to deal with, the *"More French"* are requested. Then, line four uses the masculine pronoun, *lui*, which usually means "him", but without a person identified as such, *lui* translates as *"it"*, which is the *"French"* presence. The line states *"it will offend"*, or *"will annoy"*, or *"will hinder"* the removal of the unwanted refugees.

This brings out the series of words that say, *"that the hidden evil secret."* A word like "that" is always referencing back to what has previously been stated, such that "that" annoyance, or offence, is due to something being "hidden" within the "More". This which is *"hidden"*, or *"secret"*, or *"obscured"* is of an *"evil"* nature, designed to cause *"harm"*, or *"damage"*. The presence of *"The great"* could discover their *"secret"* too soon, which *"will hurt"* their chances (variation of *"nuira"*) to *"hurt"* their enemy.

This quatrain has been sloughed off as irrelevant, with most giving Nostradamus credit for seeing something that vaguely matched Mediterranean intrigue, in 1558. That was before the last version of *The Prophecies* was published, even though this quatrain was available for public consumption in 1555. The focus of *The Prophecies* was explained as happening well after Nostradamus' death. The focus is the 20th and 21st centuries. When realizing that, this quatrain is obviously one that has yet to occur, and is therefore a future quatrain.

I will tell you that this quatrain fits snugly into a rather long series which tells in great detail what this quatrain touches on in its four lines. The events of this example quatrain, just as that series it is part of, a step in that story within the whole, that subplot, will take place prior to the outbreak of the last war that will affect the world. That is a reference to the *"hidden secret"* that awaits the French, Italians, and British, as well as all of *"The Islands"* of the Mediterranean Sea. I have no doubt about what this quatrains says. However, my purpose for interpreting it is not to prove anything more than the systems that make understanding come forth.

I have demonstrated how the system of order guides interpretation. I have followed the order of the words and lines. No words were moved to satisfy some personal need for syntax or preconception. No lines were bled into other lines, from a need to make one sentence from the four. The words written have been shown to have multiple possible meanings, with each line acting to continue adding specificity to a main theme. A theme was stated, with subject matters relative to that theme added, in ways that identify the characters, places, order of events, and infers a tone of danger, with a lackadaisical attitude towards sensing that danger. All of this comes from realizing the order is everything.

When a spreadsheet is created that shows all of the possible word usage, it would look something like this:

The	great	Neptune	to the	deep	of	the	sea	,
Him	stately	God of the Sea	of them	profound	from	him		
		Trident	from the	height	to	a / an		
			with them		with	them		

Of	people	Punic	&	blood	French	mixed		:
To	nation	Punished-like	and	lineage	of France	put among		
From	race	Treacherous		royalty		huddled with		
With						meddled with		
						mingled		

The	Islands	with	lineage	for	the	slow	to row	,
	Great Britain	at	blood	because	him	tardy	to prop up with	
	Greece	to	kindred	considering	a / an	long in coming	limbs	
	Sicily, Sardinia, Corsica	from	race	in defense of	them	late		
			stock	In regard of				

More	it	will hurt	than	the secret	evil	hidden		.
Plus	him	will offend	that	the covert	hurt	concealed		
	he	will do damage	who	the concealed	harm	covered		
			what	the obscure	damage	kept secret		
			which	the supernatural	pain	disguised		
				the unknown	disease			

From a matrix like this, one is assisted in both the order and the translation possibilities. When at one's fingertips, it becomes easier to see greater details, which can be drawn, due to the multiplicity and the interrelationships. That depth of analysis allows one to find the specifics necessary to associate this quatrain (or any quatrain) to one historical event. There can be no ambiguity possible, and there can still be other possible translations added to the above.

This example quatrain logically be said to be without specific meaning. It can only mean what these words state, individually and in combination. When the order of the words is maintained as written, with the word choice recognized as selected with reason, based on the multiplicity of use, a very specific event is the result. If no historic even can be found to match, then the quatrain cannot be found wrong. It has to be set aside as a predicted future event.

This matrix makes for easy reference, allowing the reader to play with a combination of translation choices. In a future book that I will make public, I will provide such a matrix for every quatrain. I have already prepared these in my research quest. Hopefully, this demonstration makes it possible for the reader to see how such complexity, based on each definition a word can have, interpretation of one quatrains yields many paragraphs of information. What I have stated in the example quatrain is not representative of the full depth of interpretation that can result, especially when it is woven into the fabric of many other quatrains, and the details they present. A wealth of information can be gleaned from only four lines of poetry.

This system is of utmost importance. In order to be able to comprehend the verses written by Nostradamus, this system of internal order must become a natural way to read the written word. It is the syntax of God; and once one becomes comfortable with reading Nostradamus, one will be amazed at how much more comes from other divinely inspired documents written, in particular the books of the *Holy Bible*.

Once one has reached this state of understanding the purposeful order within each quatrain, the overall order becomes possible to rearrange. As I mentioned earlier, Nostradamus wrote quatrains that clearly tell of major earthquakes. When one is able to see the connections certain quatrains make to those yet to occur disasters, one is able to fit several of the quatrains together in an order that tells the story of those earthquakes. That story then falls within the overall story, which is a series of stories that relate to historical events, past, present, and future. This whole order is only visible after internal order has been respected, in both the quatrains and the letters.

Let me state that I understand how some will find this system difficult to grasp. It requires patience more than it requires any ability to read French. Dictionaries are a necessity for understanding, with enough to cover words in Old French, Latin, and English. I recognize that many people tend to shun taking the time to look up words in a dictionary, but to understand Nostradamus, one has to get beyond that phobia. With practice, this system can become quite enjoyable, particularly after the meaning of an very enigmatic quatrain suddenly becomes quite clear. That clarity can only come from applying the system of order to the words.

The greatest difficulty comes when confronted with quatrains that deal with the future, as the example I just presented does. It is much easier to decipher a quatrain that is telling about a known historical event, especially when that quatrain seems to be apparent without any systems being applied. However, such quatrains are limited.

Those few easy to understand quatrains are comparable to the pieces of a puzzle that form the outline of the picture contained in the puzzle. As such, the easiest quatrains are like the ones with a 90-degree angle cut, with the relatively easy ones being those with one straight edge. Quatrains of this nature act as the ones stating a main story theme, to which multiple quatrains will attach to add the details of that story. Mostly, the easiest stories are those that have already happened, with the details capable of being confirmed through historical documentation.

The greatest bulk of the quatrains are not this easy to discern, without the application of the system of order (and other systems). Many are more difficult to interpret because they are not as simply stated. Some will have manufactured words that cannot be looked up in a dictionary as one word. One has to do deeper searches for meaning, through etymological roots, or seeing if one word breaks into multiple French words, or anagram, as discussed in the last chapter. Some quatrains are so enigmatic that very little of the quatrain makes sense, particularly the main and secondary themes. It is at times of difficulty where knowing the system of order comes to the rescue.

I have come across quatrains in which the first two lines made no sense to me, even knowing the systems. Reading further in one of those quatrains, I found that one of the last two lines made some sense, and the other the only one that had any clarity at all. In those cases, I have reversed my interpretation process. I have begun with a line that I knew, and worked from there, following the relationships of the system of order.

The system tells one that lines three and four will offer the supporting details to the theme lines in one and two. If I see clarity in line three, I follow that up to the main theme line, then down to line four, and back up to line two. Through this bottom-up-inside-out approach, I have been able to bring the clarity out of the main and secondary themes, exposing the subject and all of its supporting detail. Without knowing this system, that approach would never have been taken, and the quatrain would be a piece of the puzzle still sitting outside the puzzle frame.

Let me give an example of this reverse approach. This quatrain is the one found ninety-sixth in *Centurie Fourth*.

La sœur aisnée de l'isle Britannique,	*The sister eldest to the island Britannic,*
Quinze ans devant le frere aura naissance :	*Fifteen years before the brother will have birth:*
Par son promis moyennant verrifique,	*By his promised working for shining fastened,*
Succedera au regne de balance.	*Will come to pass with the rule of balance.*

In this quatrain, the main theme appears to be about a woman from the "*British Isles*"; but it is vaguely stated as such, and needs clarification for who "*The sister*" would be. The secondary theme is equally vague, as it seems to indicate a "*brother*" to the "*sister*", who is "*fifteen years*" younger. This, again, is of little help towards solving this quatrain's puzzle.

In line three, we find supporting information relative to the "*sister*" in line one, but the possessive pronoun, "*his*", makes it appear to instead relate to the "*brother*" of line two. Further, line three has a strangely spelled word, "*verrifique*", which is one "*r*" too much to be Spanish for, "I checked". There is a lean towards simply translating it to state, "verified," but that word is spelled, "verifié". Therefore, "*verrifique*" is one of those manufactured words that require figuring out.

In Old French, the word "*verri*" was a word related to the word *verre*, which means, "glass". *Verri* meant, "*shining, or transparent like glass*". When we remove "*verri*" from "*verrifique*", we are left with "*fique*". In Old French, there was a verb, "*fiquer*", which was evolving "*ficher*", with both meaning, "*to fasten*".[138] The past participle of "*fiquer*" would be "*fiqué*", just as "*ficher*" changed to "*fiché*." This means that a manufactured word, "*verri-fiqué*," was coined to mean, "*shining fastened*". Further, "*fiche*" is known also to mean, "*fixed; thrust in; or decreed*".[139] As such, "*verri-fiqué*" becomes descriptive of one with a sparkle attached, by "*decree*".

While this exercise in solving a manufactured word is good practice (notice there were no great stretches of the imagination to come to the translation above, only one French word stuck to another French word), line three still does not do much to clarify the main theme of "*The sister eldest to the island Britannic*". This leaves us all the way down at line four, as our last hope to figure out what this quatrain is trying to say.

Line four states, "*Will come to pass with the rule of balance*", which places all of the emphasis on "*rule of the balance.*" This says someone in the secondary theme, "*the brother*", "*will come to rule*". This does not mean *rule Britannic*, which would be *rule* over the *British*, because *Britannic* is in line one. It states the place "*of rule*" is a place known for "*balance*". As Nostradamus was an astrologer, "*balance*" is representative of The Scales, which is the symbol for the zodiac sign Libra. Looking up the word "*balance*" on an Internet dictionary, I immediately found it stated, as capitalized "*Balance*", "See Libra.*"[140]

The United States of America has an astrological natal chart, just as a person can have, which is calculated from its "birth" data. We all know that the nation's birthday is July 4th (making it a Cancer Sun native), 1776, in Philadelphia, Pennsylvania. The only question is the birth time; but since businesses are best when incorporated with the Sun in the 10th house (due to a several reasons), a noon time will usually result in that placement. Such a time, with the aforementioned place and date, gives the USA an Ascendant that

---

138   http://www.pbm.com/~lindahl/cotgrave/search/445r.html
139   http://www.pbm.com/~lindahl/cotgrave/search/440r.html
140   The Free Dictionary by Farlex, http://www.thefreedictionary.com/Balance

is Libra. A Libra Ascendant means the USA likes to show a face to the world that is fair and *balanced*. Thus, our founding fathers created a system of *"rule"* that had checks and *"balances"* built in, so we would never turn into a tyrannical *rule*.

When one reads line four as stating, *"Will come to pass with the rule of America"*, one is now looking to see if an American President fits the information in the other three lines. This process is begun by seeing line four's information directly supporting the secondary theme in line two. That theme states, *"Fifteen years before the brother will have birth."* Here, it becomes important to remember that each word is read separately, before it is paired with another word. Therefore, *"Fifteen"* has significance by itself, as a number, before it is restricted to *"Fifteen years"*; but *"Fifteen year"* (not plural) is significant as one specific *"Fifteen"* of importance.

To save some time and space, I will let you know that the vast majority of Nostradamus' quatrains occur after the year 2000. The ones that lead up to that year tell of the history of change, relative to the *Reigns, Religions, and Sects*, as we discussed previously. The majority of those quatrains occur in the 20th century. In the 20th century, only one *"year"* was *"year Fifteen"*, and that was the *"year"* 1915. When one sees *"Fifteen"* as simply stating the *"year"* of a century, *"years before the brother"* can be any number greater than one added to 1915. For example, 1915 is *"years before"* 1917, while not 1916. This means one born in the *"year Fifteen"* of the 20th century will be born *"years before"* anyone born 1917, or later. This would mean a search of past American presidents would have to focus on the year of birth, somewhere between 1915 and 1930 (*"Fifteen years"* later).

American presidents born after 1915 and before 1931 (to date) are only three: George H. W. Bush (1924); James E. (Jimmy) Carter (1924); and John F. Kennedy (1917). Of these three, only George H. W. Bush and John Kennedy had a *"brother"* who was born *"years before"* them (Prescott Bush, Jr. – 1922; and, Joseph P. Kennedy, Jr. - 1915). This makes John F. Kennedy the most probable subject of this quatrain, simply because his *"eldest brother"* was born in the *"year Fifteen"*.

When one looks at the Kennedy family tree, John F. Kennedy is the second born, with his brother Joseph being the *"eldest"*. This means that the main theme of line one is actually stating, *"There ... sister ... eldest ... to the island ... British,"* which is actually recorded Kennedy family history.

John Kennedy's *"sister"*, born Kathleen Agnes Kennedy, spent time in London when her father was ambassador to the Court of St. James (1938-1940), attending college *"There"*. She returned during World War II (1943) and married William John Robert Cavendish, Marquess of Hartington, the heir to the 10th Duke of Devonshire. This made the *"sister"* Kathleen Cavendish, Marchioness of Hartington. The only Kennedy to attend the wedding (1944 - wartime) was *"eldest brother"* Joseph Kennedy, Jr. Joseph had been sent to England to be stationed *"There"*, in September 1943. Thus *"There"* both *"sister"* (first), and then *"eldest"*, who was her *"brother"* (second), went *"to"* where England takes up two-thirds of *"the island*" named Great Britain. The Romans used to refer to Great Britain as "*Britannia*".

Joseph P. Kennedy, Jr., as the "*eldest*" son of Joseph Kennedy, was groomed to enter politics. Line three, which adds the supporting details to the "*eldest*" in the main theme line, states, "*By his promised*," which certainly can mean "*promised By his*" father, especially when the word "*par*" can also translate as "*By reason of*". Joseph, Jr. was *working* towards being a military war hero, as those always garnered votes, as war heroes are known "*for*" the medals "*shining fastened*" to their uniforms. Unfortunately, Joe Kennedy was killed when his bomber exploded in midair, before he could parachute to safety. His body was never found; but he was posthumously awarded three medals: the Navy Cross, the Distinguished Flying Cross, and the Air Medal.

With Joseph P. Kennedy, Jr. no longer able to meet "*his promised*" obligation to his father, John F. Kennedy took on this responsibility, "*By reason of*" being the "*eldest*" surviving male Kennedy. This is seen in line two's secondary theme statement, where the word "*devant*" can also be the present participle form of the verb "*devoir*", meaning, "to have to" or "to owe". Additionally, the word "*naissance*" can also mean, "beginning, rising, or first appearance". This means the secondary theme can be stated as, "*Fifteen years owing the brother will have rising*". With Joe Kennedy's death occurring on August 12, 1944, it would be "*Fifteen years*", four and a half months later, when John F. Kennedy would announce his candidacy for President of the United States of America. He did that on January 2, 1960.[141]

After the 1960 presidential election, it would "*come to pass*" that John F. Kennedy would be "*in the*" office of the Presidency, the leader of the "*rule*" of government that celebrated its "*balance*" of powers. This is the line of the quatrain that made it possible to see the accuracy of this quatrain's dialog, which is quite specific and detailed. By working in reverse order, according to the relationships of lines and word order, what appeared to be vague and general turned into an amazing prophecy that fully came true. We were able to see this miracle by relying on the system of order.

One final aspect about the system of order should go without saying, but because Nostradamus authors have commonly made two errors interpreting some quatrains, I need to point them out. First, I have found ridiculous claims made that expresses the opinion that half of a quatrain is about one event in time, with the other half about a completely separate event, nowhere near the same time. Usually, these events are separated by hundreds of years. There are no quatrains that make such splits, into two topics, with two distant timeframes. While each line can present a series of events in linear time that can span several years (ex.: the JFK quatrain, in essence, spanned from 1915 to 1960), all events are relative to one central topic.

Second, I have read some interpretations that state something akin to, "Nostradamus got this one wrong." Nostradamus got nothing wrong because the Spirit of Jesus Christ was telling Nostradamus what he got.

---

[141] Wikipedia, the free encyclopedia, http://en.wikipedia.org/wiki/John_F._Kennedy

Obviously, the interpreter is always the one responsible for getting something wrong. In the previous example quatrain ("*The great Neptune*"), some have stated that Nostradamus was seeing the past, referring to some events that occurred well before Nostradamus was born. This primarily dealt with quatrains that saw Arabs and Muslims wreaking havoc on the high seas. Interpreters who have made those statements have attributed the verbiage to naval prowess that existed in the 11th-12th centuries. This is not the case at all. Nostradamus wrote every quatrain of a future that would not begin until after his death.

I state, "every quatrain," because Nostradamus did write about the biblical past in his letter to Henri II. These words, as we have discussed, demonstrate the need to rearrange that letter, putting it into a coherent order. That recount of the past did not extend beyond the time of Mohammed (est. 630 A.D.). Since the past is historical record, it is foolish to believe one would prophesy about something having already occurred. Therefore, telling of the past in the letter had a purpose relative to order; and all of the quatrains are relative to an ordered future.

Chapter 23

The System of Punctuation

This system is almost as important as is the system of order. The system of order establishes that everything is in its proper place, and for good reason. As such, one does not arbitrarily have permission to change the order of any words. The system of punctuation lets one know that the same importance applies to all punctuation marks found in the letters and the quatrains of *The Prophecies*. Since Nostradamus' work includes punctuation, which does not always follows the rules of sentence punctuation we know and love, it requires learning a new system that will make what was written sensible. Without such a system known, past translators have found it necessary to change what was published, as though Nostradamus' punctuation was irrelevant.

The biggest argument against maintaining the punctuation presented in Nostradamus' work is that it does not follow the rules of syntax, as we know those rules today. For instance, his use of colons, and the lack of periods in many places, does not make sense. Some argue that this misplacement of marks is not the fault of Nostradamus, per se. In the 16th century, punctuation was not uniformly used. Prior to the 18th century, punctuation was primarily used in oral communication, through the use of gestures and delivery emphasis (elocution). Thus, speech was punctuated in this manner; but people had not yet standardized how to transfer such punctuation to the written word.

As evidence, these scholars reference the ancient (classical) languages, particularly Greek, Latin, Hebrew, and Aramaic, as having used no punctuation at all. It was up to the reader to understand the pauses, breaks, emphases, and asides. Thus, it is from this understanding of the history of punctuation that researchers of Nostradamus' writings can assume that Nostradamus presented his publisher with documents absent of punctuation. This makes the punctuation present in the earliest copies of his book editions assumed to be the result of how a 16th century typesetter-publisher understood punctuation. Simply put, Nostradamus is not believed to be the author of the punctuation. When seen as once removed from the source, punctuation by "printer's rights" becomes an excuse to alter that punctuation, to make it meet today's syntactical standards, and of course, modern preconceptions of meaning.[142]

---

142   Printer's rights did exist, to the extent that hyphens were occasionally inserted to utilize a full line of type. By hyphenating a word at the end of a line, and completing the word at the beginning of the next line, space was conserved. The abbreviation of words was also their privilege. The hyphenation right was exclusively applied to the letters of Nostradamus, but not to the poetry.

Obviously, there are errors to this logic, beyond what I discussed earlier about a printer not being learned enough to understand punctuation, more than an educated writer. If punctuation was being inconsistently applied in 1555, it was at least understood that its application to written documents was necessary. Thus, punctuation had already been "invented" and was in use, however misused that use was. Those who wish to rewrite Nostradamus can only do so due to this presence of some form of punctuation. One cannot argue that a printer had rights to add punctuation, with a defense that no form of punctuation existed in the first place.

A caveat exists from this logic, where inconsistent use of punctuation is believed to be a reason to place a writer's responsibility onto a printer. True logic sees that Nostradamus' words have not been understood for over 450 years. Changing the punctuation has had no effect on this understanding. This means it is more logical to believe Nostradamus himself applied punctuation marks, which the printer simply copied, than to assume that Nostradamus wrote strange words, which were made stranger by a publisher compounding the strangeness through odd punctuation application. Further evidence is the consistent repetition, where seemingly misapplied punctuation repeats in later editions, such that the same "wrong punctuation" is found without correction. That indicates printers only copied; they did not edit manuscripts.

Without the actual original manuscript, written by the hand of Nostradamus, which would prove all differences of opinion over punctuation, the earliest copies of *The Prophecies* have to be the standard (1555, 1557, 1566, and 1568). If all words are accepted to have been faithfully reproduced by the printer, so too must the punctuation marks. One cannot pick and choose what one wants to believe was written by Nostradamus. Without clear observable proof to the contrary, it is logical to assume that Nostradamus marked his work in a way that best elocuted the speech he was presenting in the written word. We simply need to understand why odd punctuation was meshed with odd wording.

The biggest error one makes, which allows this argument over punctuation to seem valid, is the failure to recognize God as the source, and the punctuation then being as perfect as the chosen words. I would venture the guess that Nostradamus made it explicitly clear to his publisher in Lyon that his work was quite enigmatic, yet well thought out and edited. It makes sense to me that Nostradamus made demands that every letter and mark be reproduced exactly as written, including his own abbreviations of words.

The fact that there are clear differences between the earliest editions of *The Prophecies*, where words are not always the same, and punctuation is regularly found missing or different, is an argument for printer's rights. Those differences can be explained as someone at the publisher end changing what was written, either on purpose (a correction) or by mistake. Since Nostradamus could not (per instructions from Christ) explain openly that the Spirit of Jesus Christ was the true author, it would become Nostradamus' responsibility and right, as the paying customer, to reject any publisher's proof (first copy) that did not meet his approval, after careful inspection.

This makes the result be a book in mass print (relative to the times), which reflects the true intention of God's Prophecy. I see that book as the 1568 Lyon edition, which was published about two years after Nostradamus' death. I make that assertion based on extensive work with the various editions, and comparisons make the 1568 edition stand out as best representative of the totality of the systems. I have found some who believe the 1568 edition is a forgery, but I wholeheartedly reject that notion, simply because the 1568 edition is truest to form, and entirely consistent with the style of Nostradamus, and Old French. I see huge differences between the 1566 and 1568 editions, which seem to me to be due to Nostradamus making one last demand on the publisher, to take a little more time and ensure his legacy be copied "to the letter."

In regard of an explanation for this matter of questionable punctuation, as some specific instruction written by Nostradamus to guide us, one has to search the letters of instruction for words that carry meaning relative to some form of punctuation. The only such word that I could find is "*point*". The word "*point*" (Old French also spelled *poinct*[143]) translates as, "a point; a prick; a center; **a period, or full point**; a minute, instant, or moment in time",[144] to list its primary uses. As such, this is the only word that Nostradamus wrote in his letters, which is applicable as a reference to a particular form of punctuation (a *period*).

This is relevant, I believe, because the *period* is the one form of punctuation that is most agreed upon, as it appears in *The Prophecies*. For the most part, a *period* ends each quatrain, and each of the long-winded "sentences" in the letters. This word appears only twice in the letters, with both being in the Preface, meaning its rarity is not happenstance. As such, one has to view one possible translation as, "*period*", which means a full stop is reached in language, with a complete *point* made.

With that understood, consider that Nostradamus first wrote the word "*period*" following his Latin quote, from Psalm 104:5. That quote shows in the *Holy Bible* as, "*it shall not be moved for ever and ever*". After this, Nostradamus wrote, "*hors mis que son vouloir sera accomply, mais non point autrement*", which literally translates to state, "*without put that his meaning will be furnished, but not period otherwise*".

This can be read as a statement saying it was God's "*intention*" to write "*without*" the limitations of punctuation. This means, "*his meaning will be furnished without that put*" into the sentence structure. The "*exception*" (alternate translation of "*autrement*", which can translate as "*except that*") being the use of a "*period*", or "*point*", which did end a specific series of words, "*but not a period*" as one ends a sentence. A "*period*" is used "*otherwise*", as is all punctuation. Thus, "*period*" is somewhat of a misnomer, as a mark of punctuation. A mark of punctuation denotes a full stop, or a "*point*" made, no

---

143 The Old French spelling, *poincte* (feminine form) is shown to be translated more as a sharp end *point*.
144 Randal Cotgrave's 1611 French-English Dictionary, http://www.pbm.com/~lindahl/cotgrave/search/7391.html

matter what the mark is, including a "*period*" mark.

When seeing this statement in connection to the biblical quote from Psalm 104, the issue of punctuation is shown as, "*it shall not be moved for ever and ever*". By "*not being moved*", Nostradamus is stating the need to respect the marks shown. The marks shown are not internal marks, like those used in syntactical sentences. They mark "*periods*" of words, where a series of words make one "*point*". This is God's way of communicating to prophets, with all writing in the same manner, "*without that* (internal punctuation marks) *put*".

In other words, God spoke words, which the prophets heard and wrote down (or spoke, with others writing them down later). No punctuation was part of the Word spoken. However, there were break "*points*", such as the end of one verse, and the end of one chapter, and the end of one book, all of which acted like a "*period*". God "*furnished meaning*" through signs of transition, "*not*" through syntactical sentence structuring.

There is a good reason for this, as we have seen already, through working with interpreting some of the quatrains. Syntax limits how we read words, with limits being how we quickly make sense of the meaning of the words read. Part of that limiting comes from punctuation. This form of limitation gives important pauses and directions before other words are read; and how we read the words tells us how we understand the meaning the words convey.

For instance, let me give you an example that I received a long time ago on email. I was sent a series of words, which I was then instructed to punctuate. The unpunctuated words were, "Woman without her man would be lost". The email then informed me (after scrolling down for the correct punctuation answer) that males tend to punctuate those words as, "Woman, without her man, would be lost." Females, on the other hand, tended to see it differently, as, "Woman, without her, man would be lost." This example, where order is preserved, demonstrates how punctuation effects the meaning we receive from the written word, through limiting the possibilities the words could mean.

God does not speak in limited ways. In the above example, "*without*" punctuation "*placed*" among those words, all "*meanings will be supplied*" (alternate translation of "*accomply*"). Thus, God would have us read how man is lost without woman, and how woman is lost without man, such that man and woman are both lost without each other. That would be "*his purpose*" (alternate translation of "*vouloir*"), by "*not*" marking "*points*" of pause between words.

To apply this concept to the last quatrain example, presented in the system of order chapter, the first line of that quatrain shows how "*points*" are implied, even though not marked. The line states, "*La sœur aisnée de l'isle Britannique,*" which initially appears to state, "The eldest sister of the British Isles". We want to see that because our minds read automatically, such that a series of words without punctuation means to us one clause, phrase, or sentence. Thus, we automatically rearrange the words, causing us to see "*La sœur aisnée*" as "The eldest sister", and not as "*There, sister, eldest*". The lack of punctuation means punctuation can be anywhere, allowing God's "*purpose*" to *be* "*accomplished*" through that lack of restriction. However, the presence of a "*point*" of punctuation is "*not*" relative to what has been stated, as it works "*otherwise*".

That use of the word "*point*", in this example from the Preface, is not the only "*meaning*" that can be read as an instruction. There can be other "*meaning intended*" from this same instruction, which is more guidance for reading *The Prophecies*. That is the beauty of Nostradamus' writings, as a prophet of God. It is the amphibological way that Holy Scripture is written. The use of "*point*" can explain punctuation marks, while equally explaining "*for ever and ever*" as relative to the "*one moment in time*" (alternate translation for "*period*") his future story is about. Likewise, Nostradamus' second (and last) use of "*point*" in the Preface has this ability to have more than one "*intention*".

That second segment of words, where Nostradamus again used the word "*point*", also follows another Latin quote, this one being, "*Visitabo in virga ferrea iniquitates eorum, & in verberibus percutiam eos*". That comes from Psalm 89, which states, "I will visit their inequities with a rod and their sins with stripes"; but literally says, "*I shall see often until a rod like iron injustices* (or *unevenesses*) *theirs, & beatings will be stricken until dawn*". Following this, Nostradamus wrote, "*car la misericorde de Dieu ne sera point dispergée un temps*", which translates to state, "*because there mercy from God not will be point dispersed one time*".

Certainly, this use of the word "*point*" could be more difficult to comprehend as an explanation for the lack of punctuation. However, seeing the Holy Scripture (the Latin verse from Psalms) as an indication of the overall result of *The Prophecies*, Nostradamus can be seen saying, "*because*" of this punishment coming, "*there will be mercy*" through "*God*" giving a Prophecy. By "*not*" having "*dispersed*" the words, which means having "*not separated*" the words through "*points*" of punctuation, there "*will not be one point*" made in the words written. The more "*points*" made, the more an understanding of this coming punishment can elicit behavioral changes, allowing this future to be averted. Such would be the "*mercy of God*".

The *point* of all of this discussion about punctuation is *The Prophecies* are a result of this *mercy*. Thus, the letters and quatrains are perfect, meaning the punctuation is perfect as well. Still, the punctuation is not present to act as elocution to the words written. Such gesturing, delivery, and manner of style would limit one word's (or group of words') use to one specific meaning. "*God*" did "*not intend*" for only "*one point*" to be the result, as that would show "*God*" as limited, through words. This means there is no punctuation that plays a syntactical role that limits what *God* has said. The actual presence of punctuation means it plays another role altogether.

To understand these other roles, one has to understand the normal function each mark of punctuation denotes. Punctuation marks actually play the role of "traffic cops" in language, giving directions amid the traffic of word flow. Punctuation was designed for maintaining order in the written word, where chaos could prevail without it. Each mark thus carries a specific purpose that can be uniformly applied, depending on the contextual usage. A writer thus, as the source of the theme conveyed in words, directs the reader towards capturing that theme by best utilizing marks of direction.

Those marks become shorthand instructions that our minds instantly process, causing us to respond automatically without actually thinking about what a mark means. In a classroom setting, such as an upper-level college English course, where all of the intricacies of writing are taught and learned, the course instructor and students are all supposed to be on the same page, as to the correct use of punctuation. On the reader level, however, no one is present to question that knowledge. Therefore, one might be amazed at how little is remembered about the rules of grammar, the ones we learned in grade school, in particular those that pertain to punctuation use. That makes it necessary to review here the meanings of the various punctuation marks found in *The Prophecies*.

The Primary Punctuation Marks

Commas

The most frequent form of punctuation used in the quatrains and letters is the comma. This should come as no surprise because it is also the most frequently used mark of punctuation in English. Our eyes are trained to read sentences with multiple commas. We read commas so well we rarely slow down as we pass one, although the comma is typically known to represent a short pause. These short pauses come after introductory words, clauses (independent or dependent), and/or phrases. As such, the comma indicates a separation between groupings of words, or individual words.

The normal rules governing comma use do not apply to *The Prophecies*, or in the letters explaining that work, in the sense that the words in print are not grouped syntactically. Each word, as we have discussed, can be its own sentence, or multiple sentences, depending on the word and its definitions. Therefore, the most important aspect of a comma when reading Nostradamus is that it separates segments of words or single words. As such, by being a separator, a comma can be defined as a mark that is designed, "to set or keep apart; disunite; to sort; to differentiate or discriminate between; distinguish; to become divided into components or parts".[145] In short, a comma represents a separation from what preceded the comma, by time, space, or importance.

One of the most typical uses of a comma is it replaces the need to write the word, "and". For example, if

---

145   The Free Dictionary by Farlex, http://www.thefreedictionary.com/separate

I were to list the ingredients of a cake, I would not have to write "and" between each separate ingredient. I would simply mark a comma between them all, only writing 'and' to signify the last ingredient. In this use, while I am separating, I am also joining by implying 'and'. All of the ingredients are shown as being all into one, such that if I wrote, "Add the flour, milk, eggs, vanilla, salt, sugar, and butter into the pan and stir", there would be no difference in my meaning if someone altered my instruction, to say, "Mix the flour, butter, sugar, milk, eggs, salt, and vanilla together." Mixing like this cannot be done with Nostradamus' work, because a comma immediately separates, meaning each element separated is, "existing as an independent entity," or "withdrawn from others; solitary."[146]

Mixing would change the order of the words, or groups of words presented. That would break the rules of the system of order. Nostradamus' use of a comma certainly does act to join word groups together, but not before each group of words between marks of punctuation are seen as stand-alone segments. As such, a comma acts more like a mark that identifies a need for a new paragraph, which follows the train of thought established in the prior segment (its own paragraph), yet free to go in a separate direction.

This is a key instruction to understand, because the order of the words indicates the specificity necessary to establish the uniqueness of the event being detailed in a quatrain, or the instruction from one of the letters. Just as each word must maintain its position, regardless of the presence of punctuation, so must each segment of words, which appear between marks of punctuation. Each word or group of words following a comma is then a separate related sequence, usually later chronologically, but possibly an indication of an importance related to the prior segment.

To look at an example we have already discussed, where I presented the general theme of *The Prophecies* as having been stated in the Preface to be, "*pource que les regnes, sectes, & religions seront changes si opposites*". This literally translates to states, "*because that the reigns, sects, & religions will be changed ones so opposite ones*". This means the theme, which will be found developed after the rearrangement of the quatrains into their proper order, will be one where "*reigns, sects,*" and "*religions*" change from their order in the 16th century, to "*one opposite*". Still, there is much more that comes from this series of words, with comma separations, when one recognizes how seeing a comma effects how this is read.

This separation of "*reigns, sects,*" and "*religions*" means each of these words must first be understood individually. As such, the words that directly attach to "*reigns*", in French, "*pource que les*", are also in their own right individually read, while all are within a single grouping that included "*reigns*". The word "*pource*" translates as "*because,*" but can also mean, "*for that cause*" (from "*pour ce*"), which indicates that the beginning of this group is related to a "*cause that*" preceded it. Each use of the word, "*que,*" meaning, "*that,*" is always a direct reference to the subject presented previously, as referencing *that* subject with new details. Therefore, a comma is joining the following segments through such words *that* connect one to another, while the segment retains its individuality.

---

146   The Free Dictionary by Farlex, http://www.thefreedictionary.com/separate.

Prior to this group, Nostradamus wrote several segments that connect with commas. Each relate to "*that cause (because)*" about to be stated, most previously as "*cause*" for writing The Prophecies ("*de mettre par **escript**"*– "*to put through writing*"). Before that segment was the *cause that* would be found in the future ("*mais aussi de la plus grande part du **futur**" – "but also from the more great part of the future*"). Then, before that segment Nostradamus stated, "*delaissé pour **cause** de l'injure*", which translates to state, "*forsaken instead of cause of the abuse,*" or "*abandoned in respect of reason to the injury,*" or "*neglected in defense of case from the wrong*". Thus, "*because that*" is referencing the reason for Nostradamus "*writing*" The Prophecies, a book about the "*future*", as a warning to recognize "*wrong through neglect*" as the "*cause*" to avert.

The word "*les*" is a plural form of the article "*le*". Thus, as a plural form of *the*, it becomes *they* or *them*, as *the ones*. This then is clearly stating "*them*" of the "*reigns*", who will be the "*cause*". The "*cause*" is not just "*the reigns*" of France, but of every European nation where kings "*reign*". This will be those "*great*" rulers of the world, who had a "*part*" in setting up the "*future*", by "*neglecting*" their subjects, "*instead of*" seeing the "*case*" of the impoverished, who felt "*abused*". Obviously, the word "*reign*" means more than just "rule."

The word "*regne*" can translate as, "*A realm, or kingdom; a sovereign rule; dominion; government; or the continuance or manner of that government, as a reign.*" This was the way of *reigns* in Nostradamus' day. It was the way of *reigns* for hundreds of years. Thus, it is not only all current people of *reign*, but also all who will have ever *reigned*, as rulers over nations subservient to royal rule. Nostradamus used other words to denote the rule of elected officials, so "*les reigns*" means "*them born with a right to rule*". It is "*for that cause*" (the right to rule) "*that them of reigns*" would become "*part of the future cause*" for Nostradamus needing to "*write*" The Prophecies.

The same understanding of the three segments leading to that segment stating "*the reigns*" is then continued to the single word that follows another comma. From one separate period of time when the "*reign*" of "*those born to rule*" ends, it is followed by another separate period of time, this one where "*those*" trained in the arts of "*sects*" have usurped the "*reigns*". As I have already discussed my view on what a *sect* is, I will not repeat it here. Still, that view applies here, in all of its possibilities. The plural form indicates no one particular "*sect*" is the point. Rather, all forms of "*sects*" will follow the rule of kings and queens. This is not only the historical rebellions that replaced the rules of royalty; it signifies the Age of Reason, and the advent of the common man, where all are said to be created equal, as far as opportunity to own and possess things is concerned. All of this meaning comes by simply stating one word, "*sects*", between the separations of commas.

When we follow the comma that was placed after "*sects,*" we come to "*religions*", which are clearly separate in their "*reigns*" over people and nations. This segment began by this word, continues to state that "*religions will be changed ones so opposite ones*". As an independent train of thought, one has to see that the plural form is making the statement that all "*religions*" are to be considered, in regard to the "*future*" of The Prophecies. By Nostradamus' time, Henry VIII of England, and Martin Luther, had already begun the Reformation. This certainly represented "*changes*" to the "*reign*" of the Roman Catholic Church, putting "*them opposites*" concerning the "*reigns*" of nations run by kings seeking less religious interference. The "*future*" would bring more kings to be "*opposites*" of the power wielded by the Church, and its many branch "*religions*".

The real contention for "*religions*" is then seen to follow in time, after the "*reigns*" of the "*sects*" of philosophy, i.e.: forms of government, such as democracies, republics, and later, but in particular, governments banning freedoms to "*religions*" (Communism). All these forms of government will bring "*changes*" that will reduce the influence of "*religions*", through the laws created by the "*sects*". Democracy will declare a separation of Church and State. Communism will declare no Church allowed in State. All "*reigns*" of "*sects*" will be "*opposed ones*", as to the idea of giving "*religions*" any power over the people.

This is how a comma separates and conjoins, particularly in the letters. Each segment of words between commas must be identified for its own merits individually first. In this way, that identity will make sense, as one, and as one with the preceding segments. The use of a comma acts to set apart the important elements necessary for understanding the overall flow of thought that develops in the segments, over a chronological period.

The comma use in quatrains plays the same role as it does in the letters. It is a separator of time and sequence, and/or it denotes something of related importance. One regular placement for a comma is at the end of a line. When that happens, the comma is stating that the line just completed is separate from the following line, in either time or importance (or both). Since each line is independent of the other lines, as the system of order states, a comma at the end of a line is an indication that the following line is not a direct continuation of thought. A line ending with no punctuation indicates the next line is subsequent (following in order), while a separate series of consequence (a logical effect thereof). A comma can interrupt one line's flow of events, where the marked point of separation allows for a jump to events that are relative, but *non sequitur* (inferences that do not logically follow).

For example, in the quatrain introduced that gives history of the Kennedy family, the first line, "*There sister eldest to the island Britannic,*" tells of two children (*sister* and *eldest*) traveling to Great *Britain*. The two are listed in the chronological order of having gone "*there*" (*sister* – in 1938 & 1943; *eldest* – in 1943), but without a need to punctuate that order (as *sister, eldest*). The importance was two going to England, in particular the "*eldest*", with the lack of punctuation acting to support both going the same year, although separately. From this lack of punctuation, line one of this quatrain ends with a comma, separating that main theme statement from the secondary theme.

The main theme is then separated from the statement, "*Fifteen years before the brother will have birth*". While we have discussed the many meanings that come from the words that make up this line, one of the meanings of "*Fifteen*" is it represents the year the "*eldest*" was born. This is then a statement of time, which is prior to the "*eldest*" going "*to Britain*", not sequential. However, since the use of "*Fifteen*" also has chronological meaning, after the travels of two to England, "*Fifteen years*" will pass "*before the*" next oldest "*brother will have rise*" to national prominence, the comma indicates a separate (secondary) theme. Due to the comma separating this line, it is able to have a broader scope of meaning, while still adding supportive elements to the main theme.

A comma that is internal to a line, not at the end, is where most people want see a comma act like a standard syntactical unit of punctuation. They think Nostradamus meant to bundle words together, as a comma is often used when listing elements. If one looks through interpretive books on Nostradamus, one will see where the author has rearranged these bundled words, simply because a writer hates copying everything verbatim. Such uses of commas seem like a harmless place to put a writer's paraphrase on the words of another writer. However, these changes are made without placing the required amount of thought into each element separated.

The use of more than one internal comma is not as regularly found in the quatrains. It is most prevalent when Nostradamus has needed to state multiple cities, or astrological names. Most English-speaking people will not know much about European cities, and most everyone knows less about astrological planets and signs. Due to this lack of knowledge, the mind's tendency is to group multiple elements into one huge lump, as an "I don't know this" category, and move on. In the end, these people simply look for one geographical element or astrological catchphrase that may bring some sense of commonality of meaning.

By this, I mean if commas connect three French cities, even if none of the cities are recognized, one knows something about France is stated in those listings. One's mind then processes France into the meaning of the quatrain, rather than the specificity of individual French cities. Likewise, if commas list two planets and two zodiac signs, and nothing is known about astrology, one might recognize planets and star groups as possibly being indicators of seasonal changes on earth. Everything becomes overly generalized. The true meaning can only come out when each separated element is understood.

For example, in the quatrain numbered sixty-seven, in Century Tenth, the second and third lines read, "*Saturne, Caper, Jupiter, Mercure au bœuf, / Venus aussi, Cancer, Mars, en Nonnay,*".[147] This translates to state, "*Saturn, Capricorn, Jupiter, Mercury in bull, / Venus also, Cancer, Mars, in Nun,*". There are five total internal commas, with both lines also ending with commas. All of these names are capitalized, <u>personifying them</u>: 1.) With the names of Roman mythological deities, 2.) With specific astrological

---

[147] This is the appearance in the 1566 Lyon edition. The 1568 Lyon edition has removed most of the commas.

significance, and 3.) As representative of known astronomical phenomena. Due to this set of identifying traits and characteristics, each comma-separated element has the potential for bearing meaning relative to iconic meaning, metaphoric meaning, and physical meaning.

Dealing only within the realm of the physical here, these two lines list planets, along with signs of the zodiac. The planets are physically a part of our solar system, while the zodiac belt is how astronomers track where the planets travel. The sun's movement throughout each year follows a natural zodiac path (circular), which begins in Aries (Spring) and ends in Pisces (Ides of March-April). In this quatrain, the signs Taurus ("*bull*"), "*Cancer*", and Virgo ("*Nun*") are all stating a natural progression in this space around the sun, as seen from earth's perspective, with all planets traveling in the same direction around the sun.

Taurus is the second sign of the zodiac; "*Cancer*" is the fourth sign, and Virgo the sixth sign. This means two planets in Taurus ("*Mercury*", then "*also Venus*") would be together in that sign, with "*Mercury*" first in Taurus (end of line two, before the line's ending comma) by itself. Later (following the comma), "*Venus also*" enters Taurus. Later still (following another comma), these two planets relate to the sign of "*Cancer*", which would be an indication that "*Mercury*" and "*Venus also*" are conjunct now (within 5 degrees of separation). Then later still (another comma), those two planets move into close relationship with the planet "*Mars*". All three planets would be close together at this time, possibly at the end of the sign of Leo, because later once again (another comma) all would travel together "*into*" Virgo, and Leo is the sign between "*Cancer*" and Virgo.

Since "*Mercury*" and *Venus*" have orbits around the sun that are closer to the sun than the earth's orbit, they are called, "interior planets." The interior planets appear to move faster than the exterior planets, because their orbit path is shorter. Thus, "*Mercury*" and "*also Venus*" are faster moving planets (as they appear to move from Earth), than are "*Mars*", "*Jupiter*", or "*Saturn*". Also, due to an occasional apparent backwards movement all the planets make (again, as seen from earth), the faster planets could join together in three separate signs, over a period of months, with both catching up to and joining the slower moving "*Mars*" at the end of that run. While all the planets repeat their cycles, this progression is a rather specific statement, one that makes a specific statement of timing, relative to those times when those occurrences will take place in that precise order and combination.

The specificity of that timing statement is made even more specific when one realizes the second line begins with the movements of the slower moving planets, "*Saturn*" first (comma), moving into the sign of "*Capricorn*" by itself (another comma), before being joined by "*Jupiter*". "*Saturn*" and "*Jupiter*" in "*Capricorn*" together is an astronomical event that is even rarer than "*Mercury*", "*Venus*", and "*Mars*" being in Virgo at the same time. Put all of these together at the same time, and it points to a period between 1960 and 1962 (line one helps narrow this down more precisely). The order of everything presented, as emphasized by the comma placements, makes this a unique occurrence.

Another example, one denoting places, is found in the fifteenth quatrain in *Centurie Second*. In line four of that quatrain, Nostradamus wrote, "*Pise, Ast, Ferrare, Turin, terre interdicte*", which translates to read, "*Pisa, Asti, Ferrara, Turin, land interdicted.*" The four names listed are all cities in northern Italy, which could have little meaning otherwise. With the word "*interdicted*" having a Roman Catholic definition, this line could easily be written off as a predicted papal punishment for the people in those four places. However, each city is the capital of a province bearing the same name.

Because each name is separated by comma, each must be seen for the totality of that name's meaning. All the names listed are cities, but each city also represents the name of its own province. Those three provinces are located in three adjoining regions of northern Italy, with *Pisa* in the Tuscany region (west peninsula, Ligurian coast), *Ferrara* in the Emilia-Romagna region (east peninsula, Adriatic coast), and *Asti* and *Turin* in the Piedmont region (west mainland, Alpine border with France and Switzerland). *Pisa* and *Ferrara* are both at the mouths of significant rivers. *Pisa* was once a seaport, where the Arno River ran into the Ligurian Sea; and *Ferrara* is at the lagoons where the Po River empties into the Adriatic Sea.

Knowing all of this geographic information allows one to get a handle on how the "*land interdicted*" can be vastly greater than four cities, regardless of how big and important the cities are. The word "*interdicted*" also bears the definition, "To cut or destroy (a line of communication) by firepower so as to halt an enemy's advance."[148] This, as the line four supporting elements for the secondary theme of line two, as well as completing the theme begun in the main theme of line one, is a serious definition that would need other verbiage indicating possible destruction.

In support of this definition, particularly the mention of "firepower" that "*interdict*" carries, Nostradamus' spelling of "*Ast*", instead of *Asti*, becomes suspicious. The French spell *Asti* just as that (*Asti*); but the people of the Piedmont region, who speak their native dialect (Piedmontese), spell *Asti* as *Ast*. The caveat is that Old French used the word "*ast*" to mean something, "to be cast". Randal Cotgrave, in his 1611 French-English Dictionary, specified this meaning, exemplifying it as it was used in speech, "*Armes d'ast.*" That idiom meant, "Weapons to be *cast*, as darts." This means "*Ast*" very well could be confirming an "*interdiction*" by fire.

When "*Ast*" is seen as weapons "*launched*", or people "*cast*" inland, they would then be directed towards "*Pisa*", as this is the initial point of focus. Separately (comma), "*Ferrara*" would then become another center of focus, with both "*Pisa*" and "*Ferrara*" being associated with this "*Ast*", due to both names being directly connected to "*Ast*" by commas. As such, "*destruction*" would first begin in "*Pisa*", and then begin on its own later in "*Ferrara*". From those two points of entry, a path of "*destruction*" leads northwest, towards "*Turin*", which would take one through "*Asti*", from "*Pisa*". "*Turin*" would be a path that followed along the path of the Po River, from "*Ferrara*". This would mean the entire northwestern

---

148 The Free Dictionary by Farlex, http://www.thefreedictionary.com/interdict

quadrant of Italy would be *"interdicted"*, from paths of *"destruction"*.

Certainly, this idea of attack and *"destruction"* would need to be corroborated by the other lines, particularly the secondary theme in line two, to which line four offers direct support. In that line Nostradamus wrote (translated), *"Castor, Pollux in ship, star bearded"*, which appears to reference the Gemini twins, whose names were *"Caster"* and *"Pollux"*. While this might be a viable meaning, due to the mythology that says *Castor* and *Pollux* are protectors of seafarers, the comma means each must be understood separately, before they can unite as one.

The French word, *"castor"*, means *"beaver,"* and this is rooted in Latin. A *"Beaver"* is a semi-aquatic, large rodent, known for its engineering skills, particularly for building dams, canals, and lodges. This could be an indication of the aquatic landing abilities of an enemy, particularly in areas known for river outlets to seas. As for the mythological figure named *"Castor"*, he was known as an excellent horseman, which immediately brings to mind one of the Four Horsemen of the Apocalypse. Beyond that, a horseman in military terms is a cavalryman. Since advancement in mechanization took the horse out of combat duty at the beginning of World War II, the modern equestrian equivalents are mobile armored vehicles, equipped with cannons, which move in support of land troops. All of this meaning must be considered due to *"Castor"* being made to stand alone, due to a comma.

The Old French word, *"pollu"*, meant, *"Polluted, defiled, distained, corrupted, dishonored, and violated."* By the addition of an *"x"* at the end, this past participle verb becomes pluralized, as *"pollux"*. In situations like that, the verb becomes a noun, as the *"ones"* who act *"polluted"*, with the capitalization personifying this noun usage. This means these types of people who are *"in"* one particular *"ship"* near Italy are *"corrupted ones"*.

Once we have these together in a *"ship"*, we can return to *"Castor"* and *"Pollux"*, and see that *"Pollux"* was known as an excellent boxer. This would make the *"ship"* a fighting *"ship"*, as opposed to a luxury liner, because (comma separation) *"Pollux"* is *"in"* the *"ship"* itself. As the twins together, *"Castor"* and *"Pollux"* are also said to have brought about the creation of St. Elmo's fire, which is defined as discharges of electricity into the atmosphere, particularly from a *"ship's"* mast or spar. What would appear like discharging electricity to Nostradamus could well be some form of missiles being fired. That could connect to *"Ast"*, as being representative of some form of fire *"cast"*.

The words translated as *"star bearded"* are *"astre crinite"*. This is representative of the Latin idiom, *"stella crinita"*, which means, *"a comet."* Thus, a comet was known as a *"bearded star."* They were called this because of their appearance as a streaking point of light, followed by a long luminous tail, like the tail that would trail a running horse. In English, the word *"crinite"* is defined as, *"having a hairlike tail or train."*[149] This could then be referencing the appearance of something fired from the *"ship"*, which

---

149   The Free Dictionary by Farlex, http://www.thefreedictionary.com/Crinite

would have a trailing streak, similar to electrical sparks as seen in St. Elmo's fire.

With this directly relating to the elements found in line four, this *"bearded star"* would affect the places listed in Italy. It also would not be expected to be an Italian *"ship"*, because *"bearded"* is rooted in the word *"barb"*, meaning *"beard"*, thus the real reason we call barbarians barbarian. They have unkempt beards. Still, Barbarians play a major role in many quatrains, most of which have yet to occur. It should not be forgotten that men of religion in the Middle East (Jewish and Muslim) are respected for the beards they wear.

I hope that I have made it apparent how a comma must be viewed when reading Nostradamus for meaning. Just as all words are important and must be considered as stand-alone statements, simply by definition, a stand-alone word, or a segment of words between commas means each word and each group of words must be understood individually for their own merits. Only after all aspects have been considered can that word or segment fit as one into the other words or segments. A comma then serves the same function as one does in a syntactical sentence, but with Nostradamus, a few segments of words can mean multiple pages of sentences.

Colons

The second most frequent form of punctuation Nostradamus used is the colon. A colon acts similar to a period, representing a longer pause than a comma, but not a full stop. A colon is also followed by a capital letter. A colon comes at the end of an independent clause, with the mark used to indicate emphasis on what follows, unlike a semi-colon. Often, a colon is used before a list; and typically, one will appear before a lengthy quotation. There are other various uses for colons, including their use in times (5:15 PM), biblical references (Psalm 89:5), and before subtitles, etc. However, when Nostradamus used a colon it always was to indicate the joining together of two relative segments of words, where the following segment will act to clarify the previous segment, or to indicate the following segment will present an example of what was introduced in the prior segment.

I did not explain the disclaimer for my explanations of how punctuation acts as a guide to *The Prophecies*. I only stated the punctuation acts like signs along the highway, put there to keep one from getting lost, and to keep one within the rules. I used the metaphor of a traffic cop directing traffic. The traffic cop analogy works for a comma, because a traffic cop directs traffic at one specific location, where traffic is heavy and signs (like a signal light, or stop sign) make traffic worse. As such, a comma is local like that, whereas other marks of punctuation are road signs to exit the heavy traffic, and head in another direction. Thus, a comma works the same in the letters and the quatrains; but a colon cannot be said to be so consistently applied.

The reason is the letter to Henry II is not in the correct order. When one cannot trust that what follows, and what precedes, is correct, one cannot trust a colon as representative that what was stated before the colon will then be emphasized (by clarification or by example) by what follows. For instance, in the letter to Henry, Nostradamus wrote the following segments of words, connected by a colon:

> *"que par le cours du temps on cognoistra advenir: Car Dieu regardera la longue sterilité de la grand dame"*, which translates to literally state, *"that by the course of the times one will know to happen: Because God will behold the long sterility of the great lady"*.

When one knows the function of a Nostradamus colon, it is easy to see how *"the course of the times"* is confused by the specificity of it yielding *"sterility to the great lady"*. This is because these two segments of words are not in the proper order. As such, in the letter to Henry II, a colon acts as one of the markers where a break in order occurs. A colon acts to separate sections of segments, turning them into individual pieces of the puzzle the letter is. One has then to join the segment that needs clarification for *"the course of the times one will know to happen"*, with a relative happening found elsewhere stated (in the letter). Likewise, the statement, *"because God will behold the long sterility of the great lady"*, leads a new section of segments, which will follow this train of thought, also found elsewhere (in the letter).

This application is consistent in the letter of Preface, and in the quatrains, without the need to seek new order. The quatrains are pieces of a puzzle that cannot individually be altered, but their placement in the publications of *The Prophecies* is in an incorrect order. The end of a quatrain signals the need to find another that relates, according to clarification or example. As this is in essence the definition of a colon, the actual use of a colon, in the letter to Henry II, acts to explain this lack of order in the quatrains. Meanwhile, internal to a quatrain, and the Preface, the presence of a colon acts the same, except no reordering is required.

This restriction on the colon use is then globally applied, to represent another function served by a colon. It ends a paragraph, so to speak, where it acts like a period in that sense, but a period ends a chapter. The "pause" is not as pronounced. In this manner, a colon can be seen to apply to the letter of Preface and to the quatrains in the same consistent way. Whereas a series of words represent a series of sentences (based on multiple definitions), a comma represents the end of a paragraph of text. This means one word, separated by commas, is in itself a paragraph. Commas then denote a series of paragraphs in a section of relative paragraphs; but a colon ends this section, by beginning a new section relative to an emphasis on what has already been stated, but independently supported by its own paragraphs indicated by segments separated by commas.

In the Preface, Nostradamus began each of the Latin segments with a colon, a period, or a comma. Those begun by comma mostly followed with a colon, making biblical quotes reflect what was stated surrounding those quotes, one way, or the other. That would make his colon use appear conforming to syntactical use; but the same rules apply to the breakdown of each quoted word's meaning, as potentially being its own sentence. The best view of how a colon works in the Preface comes from the examples where it connects separate segments of French words.

For example, Nostradamus wrote the following text on the first page of his Preface (1557 Utrecht edition):

> "*mais tes moys Martiaulx incapables à recevoir dan ton débile entendement ce que je se ray contrainct apres me jours definer: ven*(t) *qu'il n'est possible te laisser par escript ce que seroit par l'injure du temps obliteré: car la parolle hereditaire de l'occulte prediction sera dans mon stomach intercluse: considerant aussi le adventures de l'humain definement estre incertaines*". This translates to state, "*but your selves Warriors incapable ones in to comprehend within your weak understanding this that I myself beam constrained after my days to waste: breath that he not is possible you to relinquish for written this that could be through the harm of the times obliterated: because the word belonging to inheritance from the obscured foretelling will be inside my stomach enclosed: considering also the chances of the human end time to be uncertain ones*".

This example shows a series of four segments of words, all joined by three colons. Without attempting to go into detail about the full meaning of these segments, the point of showing this example is to address how the colons are not used as one would normally find a colon used in text. However, the colons create a cascading effect to the flow of words.

The series goes from one basic theme about the difficulty "*understanding*" the obscure nature of *The Prophecies*, proceeding through stages explaining why. Nostradamus clarifies that "*writing*" clearly "*could*" do "*harm*", thus the obscurity protects against that possibility. He then clarifies this by stating that "*the word*" is set in the womb, to be passed through "*heredity*" to the future, to a time when the obscurity will be removed. Finally, Nostradamus states that the obscurity will prevent a self-fulfilling prophecy from being the result, for nothing about the future is fixed and inescapable. Thus, in the obscurity lies hope, and hope is the ultimate "*understanding*" that must be found.

Certainly, many words can be written that detail what I have encapsulated here. My translation is designed to lead one to see this use of colons more easily. Other possibilities of translation exist, which could slant the same segments toward other possibilities. One slant, particularly because these segments come early in the letter, is based on the verbiage of the Preface being apparently directed to Nostradamus' son, Caesar. The personal pronoun use ("*your*" twice, and "*you*" once) is seen as a father's letter to his infant son, who is far too young to "*comprehend*" the writing Nostradamus had just created. Some people refer to the Preface as "The Letter to Caesar", and that can skew how the words are read.

One has to come to the *"understanding"* that Caesar symbolizes the natural propensity of humankind to propagate. The future is for those yet unborn. Caesar was the first of six children Nostradamus would have with his second wife. Nostradamus would have twelve years to tell Caesar about *The Prophecies*, making a letter to a baby seem as a blind spot to a seer's knowledge of that future. However, a letter to Caesar is not the true reason for the personal addresses. The Preface is a letter designed to speak to the reader as if the reader were Nostradamus' child. Since the source is the Spirit of Jesus Christ, the language identifies all readers as God's children. This is an important element to consider when sorting through the multiple translation choices the wording of the Preface offers.

The colon use in both the Preface and the letter to Henry allows for *"comprehension"* and *"understanding"* to come from the unfolding of the *"constrained"* into the fullness each document contains. The colon use in the quatrains helps this to happen there too. It acts similar to a comma, as it appears regularly at the end of a line, letting the reader be advised to see the following line as relating through example or clarification. Whereas a comma at the end of a line marks a separation of time or importance being established, a colon marks the freedom to expand beyond those boundaries.

For example, in the quatrain telling about the *sister* and *eldest brother*, the second line ends with a colon, as such: *"Fifteen years before the brother will have birth: / By his promised working for shining fastened"*. The quatrain is leading us to the realization that John F. Kennedy will become the leader of the United States of America. The main theme in line one is that JFK was not originally planned to fulfill this role. His older *"brother"* was so *"promised"*. Thus, the secondary theme is primarily relative to the *"Fifteen years"* that would pass, from the time of Joseph Kennedy Jr.'s death (1944), until John Kennedy declared his candidacy for President (1960). At that time, the second oldest *"brother will have rise"*, to become the torchbearer for the Kennedy clan.

Recall that we came to this conclusion about the quatrain's meaning by working in reverse order, because of the system of order makes that possible. Therefore, we did not pay close attention to the wording of line three. Now, we see that a colon at the end of the secondary theme line is preparing us to see the information contained in line three as being an example of this *"rise"* to national prominence, and/or be a clarification of it.

Line three states, *"By his promised working for shining fastened"* (we discussed how the word *"verrifique"* could become *"shining fastened"*). Certainly, John F. Kennedy *"promised"* to take the place of his older *"brother"*, Joe, and enter the political arena. The question is, "Who did John Kennedy *promise*?" The answer is he *"promised"* his father, Joseph Kennedy, Sr. When one realizes that line three is providing the supporting detail for the main theme, in line one, we see that the *"sister"* (Kathleen) and *"eldest"* (Joe) are *"his"*, meaning the patriarch of the Kennedy clan. This is also clarifying that *"the brother"* in line two (John) is *"his"* too. This is a very important possessive pronoun to understand, especially when line three has been identified as clarifying John Kennedy's *"rise"*, or *"birth"* as a politician, ready to run for the highest office in the land.

What once was rumor has all but been confirmed, that Joseph Kennedy made some "*promises*" to certain unethical people, said to be significant criminal underworld bosses. Once they were swayed "*By his promise*", they then played a role "*working for*" bringing JFK the "*rule of balance*". According to what I have read, the Chicago political machine rounded up enough names of the deceased, to have them become registered voters, who cast votes for Kennedy. So many voted this way that the people "*promised*" favors (should victory result) were able to swing Illinois in favor of the Democratic candidate. That won the election for Kennedy. Thus, it was "*By his* (Joe Kennedy, Sr.'s) *promised*" protection of certain unethical figures, to allow them to operate their businesses with the government having a blind eye to those businesses, that organized crime and government began "*working for*" the same goal.

By the time the November elections were over, Kennedy was the "*shining fastened*" winner in Chicago, by a landslide margin. The margin of victory in that one major city was enough to win the majority of the vote for the entire state of Illinois, barely. At this point, we can consider the possibility that the word "*verrifique*" is a combination of French words, to see how they could apply to this scenario.

The two closest to the spelling, "*verrifique*", are "*véridique*" (truthful) and "*vérifier*" (to verify). As such, these similarities work on a secondary level, as purposefully intended to be read as such, when one sees how the mob lived up to its end of the bargain. They were "*truthful*" in their "*promised*" goal. Additionally, since Richard Nixon was convinced it would be political suicide to demand a recount, he reluctantly conceded the victory to Kennedy. All votes were then "*verified*" as the truth, and upheld as valid.

This element of "*truth telling*" (alternate Old French translation of "*veridique*") is only possible by recognizing the power of direction a colon yields. Without keying on that one mark, we could sufficiently check off this quatrain as one telling of John F. Kennedy's "*rise*" to power, with line three stating "*his promised*" dedication to his daddy's wish that his "*eldest*" son have the "*reign of balance*". By seeing the need to emphasize line three, as a line of clarifying information, we get to see the hidden nature of how common men (not born to royal right to rule) "*rise*" to great heights of power. Nostradamus' quatrains have a knack for letting things hidden become exposed.

Still, not all of the colon use in the quatrains comes at the end of a line. There are examples of a colon being present as internal punctuation within a line. In these cases, it plays the same roles, only to clarify the segment of the line preceding the colon. One example of such use is found in the eighty-sixth verse of *Centurie First*. Line four is where the internal colon placement is found, as Nostradamus wrote, "*Suite par fer: à foy fera oultrage.*" This literally translates to state, "*Pursuit by weapon: with confidence will cause outrage.*"

As a stand alone, independent line of thought, the main thought focuses on the act of following, particularly as a chase. The French word, "*suite*", is rooted in the Latin word, "*sequere*", meaning, "to follow", where the present participle form, "*sequita*" (Vulgar Latin), means, "the act of following."[150] Thus, Randal Cotgrave offered its meaning as, "A suit or pursuit," with the word "*suitte*" an alternate spelling. The word "*suitte*" translates as, "A chase, pursuit, prosecution of, suit against; also a sequel, issue, consequent, or consequence."[151] This means that line four begins by stating a reaction to something has generated the "*consequence*" of "*Pursuit*".

This "*Pursuit*" is "*by weapon*", which is synonymous with weapons. The actual word written is "*fer*", which literally means, "*iron*." In the singular, as this is, it was understood in Old French to also be representative of, "the head of a pike, lance, arrow, etc." In other words, it was the sharp metal at the end of a stick, which was used as a "*weapon*". With this realized to be the standard "*weapon*" of the 16th century, a modern equivalent would be rifles and tanks, or something of that nature. Thus, line four appears to be making a statement that "*Pursuit*" is "*through*" (alternate translation of "*par*") military personnel and equipment making advancements.

This is where line four introduces a colon. The word "*fer*" becomes clarified through the segment stating, "*with confidence will cause outrage*." Obviously, one is braver "*with*" a "*weapon*", while in "*Pursuit*" of someone dangerous, than without one. On the other hand, should the "*Pursuit*" be coming after one, "*by weapon*", "*confidence*" is not a sign of running away. With the options being to be shot or surrender, most would find surrender the option with the best outcome. In that case, "*through trust*" (alternate translation of "*foy*") surrender would save lives, a "*Chase by weapon*" would be brought to an end with a prisoner secured in "*iron*" chains. However, that conclusion is not upheld when we find the result being to "*cause outrage*".

The Old French word, "*oultrage*", can also be translated to state, "*excess, unreasonableness; injury, wrong, abuse, insult, much violence; extreme breach of duty of any kind*".[152] In English, the primary definition states, "An act of extreme violence or viciousness", while also meaning, "An act grossly offensive to decency," and "Resentful anger aroused by a violent or offensive act."[153] In this sense, a "*Pursuit by weapon*" is clarified by stating that no prisoners will be taken. A "*trust*" in the pursuer's "*loyalty*" (alternate translation of "*foy*") to standard military protocols related would end the "*Pursuit by*" surrender, to "*iron*" with surrender. However, with the "*weapon*" yielding the "*confidence*" that nothing "*will make*" the pursuer be prevented from "*causing*" an "*outrage*", the pursuer will then act out a massacre of "*extreme violence*", which "*will*" be "*made*" easier by the pursued one's surrender, from misplaced "*trust*".

150   The Free Dictionary by Farlex, http://www.thefreedictionary.com/suit
151   Randal Cotgrave's 1611 French-English Dictionary, http://www.pbm.com/~lindahl/cotgrave/search/888l.html
152   Randal Cotgrave's 1611 French-English Dictionary, http://www.pbm.com/~lindahl/cotgrave/search/682r.html
153   The Free Dictionary by Farlex, http://www.thefreedictionary.com/outrage

The colon is then emphasizing the nature of "*iron*". We have read in the Preface where Nostradamus wrote in Latin (literally translated), "*I shall see often until a rod like iron injustices theirs, & beatings will be stricken until dawn*". This near biblical quote is a statement of "*injustices*" always being righted by an equal and opposite "*injustice*". This is a "*Pursuit by iron*". It is clarified by stating, "*with assurance* (alternate translation of *foy*) *will commit* (alternate translation of *fera*) *outrage*", just as the "*injustices*" of "*their beatings by iron*" would be. This "*Pursuit*" is designed to inflict pain "*through*" retribution. This "*Pursuit*" is "*for*" (alternate translation of "*par*") a show of "*iron*", both in will and weaponry. This "*Pursuit*" is a form of righting an "*injustice*", a "*wrong*", with an equal "*injustice*", or "*wrong*".

This line is self-sufficient because the colon emphasizes, with clarity, what the first segment is stating. It has meaning that can be understood without any specifics leading to that concluding synopsis. It is a conclusion that mankind has faced time and again. Line four says that "the other cheek" does not get turned. The pendulum of "*injustice*" always swings one way, then the other. Someone is always in "*Pursuit*" of someone who has wronged that someone.

Still, for this line, as line four in a quatrain, the specifics are provided, which make this time of retribution stand out. The meaning in line four supports the secondary theme of line two, as it should, where line two mentions "*excesses*" (a parallel between "*excés*" and "*oultrage*"), having been previously "*made*" (repeated use of "*fera*"), and requiring "*courage*" (similar qualities in both, "*foy*" and "*courage*"). The main theme mentions "*vanquished*" (similar word to "*oultrage*"), which has supporting detail in line three that tells of "*horse*" (remember, "*horse*" in modern military terms means armored vehicle), being "*exposed*" along a "*river*". These key terms make this quatrain connect to the one where three Italian cities surrounded the word, "*Ast*". The attack seen in that quatrain is here described as the rod of "*iron*" bringing retribution.

This quatrain shows the use of a colon at the end of line two, which makes line three an example or clarification of the secondary theme. Then, in the supporting details for the secondary theme, after the clarification of line three, line four produces two segments separated by a colon. The colon plays a major role in having this quatrain make perfect sense. I hope that these examples demonstrate the important quality a colon brings to understanding.

Periods

The period is the mark of punctuation third most used by Nostradamus. A period is a mark that indicates a full stop, rather than a pause. As such, in print a period is followed by two blank spaces, indicating the longer pause. It indicates the completion of a declarative sentence, one typically stating an idea. A capital letter always follows a period. However, periods also are used to mark abbreviations, with Nostradamus using period marks to separate numbers from dates and degrees (ex.: "*17. d'Avril*", which means "*17ᵗʰ of April*"; and, "*48. degrez*", which means "*48 degrees*").[154]

I have already discussed the less than normal use of a period in the letters of instruction. In the Preface, these placements are not indications of longwinded "sentences", but signs showing when to end a series of thoughts (broken into segments of words by other marks of punctuation), and when to begin a new line of thought. While this same indication is also found in the letter to Henry II, it must be remembered that that letter must be reassembled.

In the letter to Henri II, a series ending with a period need not be seen as subsequent to a prior series ending with a period, or directly leading the next series of segments ending with a period. One only knows that period is connected to one segment of words preceding it, while not knowing what all preceded it, now what should follow it. The period follows the rules of period use, relative to *The Prophecies*. However, a period's total application can only be seen in the Henry letter after it has been put back together.

One sign that the letter to Henry is different than the letter of preface, comes from the period use. While the preface is only half as long, and has about half as many periods, there are spots in the Henry letter that appear as if Nostradamus suddenly realized proper syntax. Unlike in the preface, Nostradamus began to write relatively "normal sentences", after a long run of segments. In one instance, a string of over 50 words runs, from capitalized first word to ending period, marked in between by many commas. From that forest of "insanity", the reader wanders into this clearing, where relative complete thoughts make syntactical sense. Nostradamus wrote:

> "*Et depuis la fin du deluge jusques à la nativité d'Abraham, passa le nombre des ans de deux cens nonante cinq. Et depuis la nativité de Abraham jusques à la nativité d'Isaac passerent cent ans. Et depuis Isaac jusques à Jacob, soixante ans, des l'heure qu'il entra dans Egipte, jusques à l'issuë d'iceluy, passerent quatre cens trente ans. Et depuis l'issuë d'Egipte jusques à l'edification du Temple faicte par Salomon au quatrième an de son regne, passerent quatre cens octante ou quatre vingts ans. Et depuis l'edification du Temple jusques à Jesus Christ selon la supputation des hierographes, passerent quatre cens nonante ans.*"[155]

One does not need to read Old French (or French in general) to see there are five periods in this quote of roughly 100 words. Within this block of "sentences" are six commas, with one "sentence" having multiple commas (2). One "sentence" is not broken into segments at all. Every "sentence" begins with <u>a capitalized first</u> word, and ends with a period. However, each first word is "*Et*," which means, "*And*".

[154] This is still a common practice in German (*23. Juli* = 23ʳᵈ of July), which means it could have been a common practice throughout Europe in the 16ᵗʰ century, with Germany holding a remnant of that past use today. The French today mark numbers greater than three digits with period marks, instead of commas (ex.: 1.213.876 = 1,213,876), which would mean *23. Juli* would be akin to *23, July*, marking a separation between day and month.
[155] Source is the 1566 Lyon edition, verified by the 1568 Lyon edition, although slight differences appear in the 1568 Lyon edition (one *Temple* not capitalized, two comma placed before *passerent*).

This is a sign that this grouping of "sentences" is marking an unusual segment of the letter. Each "sentence" is representing the beginning (capitalized first word) and concluding segments, which would represent one complete series of thought, where a subject, object, and verb are indicated. In this case, the subjects are important biblical figures: *Abraham*, *Isaac*, *Jacob*, *Solomon*, and *Jesus Christ*, with Noah implied by the *"deluge"* (*"flood"*), and Moses implied as the leader of the *"l'issuë d'Egipte"* (*"them risen from Egypt"*). As complete thoughts, no other segments should be found about these subjects, unless they too are complete thoughts, with capitalized first words beginning a separate series on the subject, ending with a period.

It is not an accepted practice, in our understanding of proper rules of the English language, to begin a sentence with the word "*And*". Still, we can easily recognize the meaning of the word, "*and*," such that we know it to be a conjunction. The word is known to have the definition meaning, "Together with or along with; in addition to; as well as. Used to connect words, phrases, or clauses that have the same grammatical function in a construction."[156] As the capitalized first word of a "sentence," we can immediately assume that this "sentence" is connected to another "sentence" that did not fully state the completeness of one topic.

Because these "sentences" do seem to connect to each other, due to the topic matter being the biblical chronology of the patriarchs, the use of "*And*" appears to make sense. With each "sentence" being relative to the time after the Great Flood (*"deluge"*), until *Jesus Christ*, with the order of Noah, *Abraham*, *Isaac*, *Jacob*, Moses, *Solomon*, and *Jesus* being the correct chronological order, we can make this syntactical connection at this one point in the letter to Henry. In this oasis of clarity, it all seems to make sense. However, this clarity is an illusion, when we realize that this is not everything Nostradamus wrote on this topic (biblical chronology), nor those subjects (the patriarchs).

Considerably before this aforementioned "five-sentence" section of the letter to Henri II,[157] Nostradamus wrote the following "two sentences":[158]

> *"Après Noé, de luy & de l'universel deluge, vint Abraham environ mille huictante ans, lequel a été souverain Astrologue, selon aucuns, il inventa premier les lettres Chaldaïques: après vint Moyse environ cinq cens quinze ou seize ans, & entre le temps de David &, Moyse ont été cinq cens septante ans là environ. Puis après entre le temps de David, & le temps de nôtre Sauveur & Redempteur Jesus-Christ, né de l'unique Vierge, ont été (selon aucuns Cronographes) mille trios cens cinquante ans: pourra* <u>*objecter*</u> *quelqu'un ceste supputation n'étre veritable, pource qu'elle differe à celle*

---

156   The Free Dictionary by Farlex, http://www.thefreedictionary.com/and
157   The Preface in the 1566 Lyon edition shows these two sentences on page 114, with the previous five-sentence block found on pages 121-122. The 1568 Lyon edition shows on pages 135, and pages 144-145. Thus, they are clearly separated.
158   The 1568 Lyon edition has this beginning with a capital letter, following a colon, making this only one and a half "sentences".

d'Eusebe."

Again without the need to translate, one can see only two period marks appear in these roughly 100 words. Unlike the other section with five periods, there are seven commas and one colon between the capitalized "*Aprés*" and the first period. There are four additional commas and another colon before the second period. While that states there are several paragraphs of meaning in these "two sentences", the same biblical chronology exists as we found before, with the same characters listed: *Abraham* and *Jesus-Christ*. The references to *David* are practically synonymous with *Solomon*; and "*deluge*" is found in both sections, with *Noah, Moses,* and Mary ("*Virgin*") added.

All of this shows segments of words that relate to the subjects contained in seemingly complete sentences. Knowing how the period, as used by Nostradamus, indicates the end of string of paragraphs relative to one topic, these segments are out of place. Without a clear capitalized first word, or period ending segment attached to them, they are in need of these signal guides to make a complete thought. Therefore, when these segments of the first section are woven into the period ending segments of the second section, we have a string of segments together, all relative to the same subjects.

Consider these segments, which only refer to *Abraham*, being spliced together, such that they begin with a capitalized first word, and end with a period. No order of the words will change, relative to each segment being spliced. The segment that begins with a capitalized first word and ends with a period, as the "sentences" in the second section seemed to indicate, is simply divided at its internal punctuation point (a comma). When those are separated at the comma, the other segments, from the first section, are placed in between. With the first section's segments of words are shown in regular type, and the later section's segments of words shown in bold type, it is easy to see how this perfectly fits together, as two matching puzzle pieces.

> **Et depuis la fin du deluge jusques à la nativité d'Abraham,** de l'universel deluge, vint Abraham environ mille huictante ans, lequel a été souverain Astrologue, selon aucuns, il inventa premier les lettres Chaldaïques : **passa le nombre des ans de deux cens nonante cinq.**

This translates to state:

> **And since the end of the flood until to the birth of Abraham,** from the universal flood, had come Abraham around thousand eighty years, which has been excellent Astrologer, according unto some, he will invent first commands Chaldean: **will pass the number of the years to two hundred ninety five.**

As one can see, this "normal sentence" has expanded to give additional information, which occurred after "*the birth of Abraham*", but before he died at the age of "*two hundred ninety five*". One is able to realize that he was the "*first*" to produce "*documents*" (alternate translation of "*letters*") about "*Astrology*", because *Abraham* was the "*principal*" (alternate translation of "*souverain*"), or "*first Astrologer*", who "*invented*" what he wrote. Although "*he*" is probably a reference to God as the actual "*inventor* of *Astrology*", *Abraham* is said to have produced written teachings on "*Astrology*" before the Bible begins to account his life.

It is documented evidence that the earliest known "writings" on astrology were in cuneiform. We know this because the oldest known archeological records of astrology are such artifacts dated to the Sumerian Dynasty (2600 B.C.).[159] Chaldea "was a Hellenistic designation for a part of Babylonia, mainly around Sumerian Ur, which became an independent kingdom under the *Chaldees*."[160] The Bible first tells of *Abraham* at the age of seventy-five, where it states that *Abraham* was born in Ur of the Chaldees. God "*commands*" *Abraham* to move to Haran, which would signal the change from the end of the Sumerian Dynasty, around 2004 B.C.

The colon that is found following "*Chaldean*" is an indication that something follows, which will be a clarification or example of the "*first commands*" related to *Abraham* being a renowned "*Astrologer*". Since this can only connect to the segment ending with the period, stating, "*will pass the number of the years to two hundred ninety five*," we see the clarification as the life span of *Abraham*. As a clarifying element, we can understand that until his death, "*Abraham will pass the tally*" (alternate translation for "*nombre*"), meaning he will teach others the art of how to calculate planetary movements and interpret meaning into those movements.

This example is to show how the placement of a period is not an assurance that everything before or after it is related to the segment containing the period. This then becomes a most important realization about the letter to Henri, and *The Prophecies* in general. For me, it was my "Rosetta Stone" for understanding this enigmatic letter. The letter to Henri is a model of how the quatrains are, as both documents are puzzles in need of finding matching pieces to join with.

Every quatrain ends in a period,[161] which means the end of its grouping of lines (or segments) represent a separate unit (related paragraphs); but this unit is one of several units that join to tell a broader picture (sections of a chapter) of the same topic. The quatrains do not join to those quatrains surrounding them; neither do the sections marked by periods in the letter to Henry join consecutively. The period thus acts as a signal for a full stop. The stop in the quatrains is time to look for other quatrains of relative topic. The full stop in the letter to Henry is time to look for other segments in need of that period. The above

---

159   This date is representative of the second period of the Early Dynasty, known for Gilgamesh. The 3rd period of Ur, known for Abraham, is dated to be between 2047 and 1940 B.C. [see following reference]
160   Wikipedia, the free encyclopedia, http://en.wikipedia.org/wiki/Chaldea
161   This depends on the source for verification, as some later editions indicate otherwise. Those do not match the period placements of the 1557, 1566, and 1568 editions.

example offered a full stop on the subject of *Abraham*'s time and relevance, which connected loose segments in a completely different section of the letter to Henry.

In the various editions of *The Prophecies*, a period at the end of a "sentence" was not the only use. Periods are used to denote abbreviations of words. This is possibly the act of a printer, where making the most of the space on a line of typeset could explain some irregularities in the consistency of abbreviations. In these cases, it is left up to the reader to explore the possibility that Nostradamus meant a period mark, to be a designed indication of additional meaning. This feeling is justified, as there are some consistently applied, which make it appear Nostradamus was the author.

One such abbreviation appears as a shortening of the first word of the first line, in the ninety-fourth quatrain of Century Second. The word is written in all-capital letters, with an abbreviation period in the 1557 Utrecht edition, supported by the 1568 Lyon edition showing the same. The first line appears as, "*GRAN. Pau grand mal pour Gauloys recevra,*" which appears to state, "*GREAT Pau great evil for French will receive*". The 1566 Lyon edition seems to make this assumption, having the line shown as, "*Grand Pau grand mal pour Gauloys recevra*", which removes the period mark from consideration, while also failing to reproduce an all-capital-letter first word, which is a sign of inconsistency relative to earlier editions.

I believe the all-caps give "*GRAN.*" the most elevated meaning possible, which includes all meaning possible to an Old French word based on "*grand*" (i.e.: *grandeur, grandissime, grandement*, etc.), due to the period mark being an indication of abbreviation. Since the word "*grand*" is found stated as the third word, there certainly is a clear difference shown, between one abbreviated with capital letters, and one in all lower case. Further, since the abbreviation mark would be irrelevant if *GRAN* stood for *GRAND*, the period mark could actually represent a signal for a full stop, so that *GRAND* can be fully comprehended independently. That would be an indication of supreme importance needing to be contemplated, before beginning with the next word. That is possible because the second word is capitalized (proper noun name of a French city), allowing it to naturally follow a period.

There are other examples of a period mark clearly being used in abbreviation, which match this example given, as an abbreviated all-cap word (*SEX.*, *SEXT.*, *PAR.*, and *CAR.*). There are also examples where words with lower-case letters are abbreviated (*Satur.*), with some seeming to indicate initials (*D. nebro*, and *D.M.*).[162] In all of these cases, I believe it is important to see how the period can act to expand the meaning of what is abbreviated.

With this explained, there are some instances where multiple editions clearly support the presence of a period internal to a line, thus internal to a quatrain with an ending period. This means there are two periods within one quatrain, and there are quatrains that have multiple lines ending in periods. An example of a

---

[162] Some show Quatrain IX-30 as including P.U.O.L.A. as abbreviations. However, I see this simply as a manufactured word in all-caps, PUOLA.

quatrain showing two periods on one line is the second one found in *Centurie First*. There, the line of reference is the fourth, which states, "*Splendeur divine. Le divin pres s'assied.*" This translates to say, "*Splendor divine. The godly near himself sits down.*"

In this example, line three ends with a colon, making line four the clarification of the statements related in line three. Line three states, "*Un peur & voix tremissent par les manches:*" which reads, "*One fear & voice will be trembling through the sleeves*". Thus, the clarification does not go beyond the full stop the first following period denotes. The clarification of "*One*" and "*voice*" is, "*Splendor divine.*" The "*fear & trembling*" are the result of the "*Splendor*" of the presence of the "*divine*".

The words that follow that period are then a stand-alone series that explains this "*divine*" presence. The word "*pres*" can translate as if, "*touching,*" which would be an indication that the Spirit of Jesus Christ was conjoined with the body of Nostradamus, more than simply taking a seat nearby. The "*voice*" is "*divine*", which means hearing the "*voice*" is not through normal physical sensation, as heard by the ears. "*Voice*" is a vibration created by passing wind through vocal cords. However, a "*divine voice*" simply vibrates through Nostradamus' arms as he writes, causing his "*sleeves*" to "*tremble*". The second "sentence" then captures this state of "*divine*" possession, as a stand-alone topic, not unique to Nostradamus. It is a standard form of closeness with God, allowing prophets to differentiate "*divine*" instruction from normal ideas.

Another such quatrain is found with two periods within one line, is the twelfth listed in *Centurie Third*. Line four of that quatrain states, "*Prins mors noyés. Partir humain butin.*" This translates to state, "*Taken bitten overwhelmed with water. To divide belonging to a man booty.*" Both series of words begins with a capitalized first word, making each clearly divided into separate, self-contained statements. In Nostradamus' form of syntax, the periods indicate two paragraphs of thought, based on the verbiage contained in the two "sentences."

At this point, one knows that the system of order calls all information found in line four to be subsequent to line three, while stating support of the secondary theme of line two, and being a natural development of the main theme, found in line one. The whole quatrain states:

Par la tumeur de Heb. Po, Tag. Timbre & Rome,	*Through there swelling Ebro Po, Tagus Crested & Rome,*
Et par l'estang Leman & Arerin :	*And by the pond Geneva & Plowed one:*
Les deux grans chefs & cites de Garonne,	*They two great ones principal commanders & cities of Garonne,*
Prins mors noyés. Partir humain butin.	*Taken bitten ones overwhelmed by water. To divide human booty taken.*

As one can quickly see, line one contains a period mark used to abbreviate. While other possibilities arise, for the sake of brevity I will state the main appears to list a minimum of three rivers, with "*Timbre*" being seen by most as a misspelling of the Tiber River. Line two lists, in essence, Lake *Geneva*; then line three lists the name of a major French river, the "*Garonne*", which is where the major Atlantic port "*city*" of Bordeaux is located. Thus, water is present in all of the line that leads to line four's first series ending with a period, which states, "*Taken bitten overwhelmed by water.*"[163] In essence, this is the actual culmination of the quatrain, as the period indicates.

With a completely new series starting up after that period, itself ending with another period, in essence an epilogue is being added. This "afterword" then states that the "*spoil taken*" (alternate translation of "*butin*") are to be "*divided*", with the "*spoils*" relative, to and from, those "*belonging to man*" (alternative translation of "*humain*"). As a survivor of Hurricane Katrina, a flood that did great damage to personal property, including the loss of "*human*" life, which would appear to be the theme of this "*water*" quatrain, the fact is the result of water damage leaves little to be considered "*spoils*" or "*booty*". This epilogue is giving a clue that those "*biting*" the ones "*drowned*" are also "*human*".

As such, the first three lines are making statements about where defeat will be found, along known waterways in the nations the rivers and lakes are found: Spain, Italy, Switzerland, and France.[164] The second series of words, acting separately, states that, following a foreign victory in those lands, the property and possessions of those peoples will be "*parted, severed, or removed*" (all alternate translations of "*Partir*").

The point of these two examples is that while all quatrains end in a period, there are quatrains where multiple periods exist. In these instances, the function of an internal period must be seen as ending the flow of a quatrain, before beginning a new flow relative to the main theme. This will then lead to the complete ending of the quatrain. However, the complete ending of a quatrain is not necessarily the end of the topic represented by other quatrains that interlink. The flow continues to the next quatrain, particularly when multiple quatrains are telling of related events along the flow of one storyline.

---

163   When the word "*mors*" is translated as Latin, or as French, abbreviated from "*morts*", the line can (and does) state (and mean), "*Taken cause of death overwhelmed by water.*" The word "*noyés*" can state, "*drowned ones*", instead of "*overwhelmed by water*". Either way is an explanation of a "*cause of death*".

164   Due to the abbreviation of "*Heb.*", Greece could be added to this list, as "*Hebrus*" is the Latinized name for the Maritsa River, which flows through Thrace, into the Aegean Sea, sourced in Bulgaria.

The Rest of the Punctuation Marks

Semi-colons

I can find only one possible occasion where Nostradamus used a semi-colon. That was after the first word of line three in the one hundredth "quatrain" of Century Sixth, which is the quatrain that acts as a foreword to the quatrains. Line three is actually the fourth line in all, since the first line is the all-caps heading. Everything in this "quatrain" is in Latin, with that line stating, "*Omnesq; Astrologi Blenni, Barbari procul sunto*". However, the 1557 Utrecht edition shows a mark below the line of type, as more of an attachment to the "*q*", than as a mark of punctuation. Such a mark would have to be seen as an abbreviation mark, which would indicate the "*q*" should be read as "*qua*" or "*qui*".[165]

In order to see other editions showing this as a semi-colon, one must look at the rules governing that marks intended usage. A semi-colon acts like a colon, and is basically used to join two independent clauses together. Like a colon, a semi-colon represents a longer pause than a comma, but less than the full stop of a period. A semi-colon is used when two independent clauses are so closely related the two clauses are best read as one sentence; but due to comma use, semi-colons act as a breather.

As far as Nostradamus having possibly intended the use of a semi-colon in his foreword cinquain, one would have to see "*Omnesqui*" as meaning "*All ones who*" (*Omnes-qui*, as a manufactured word).[166] A semi-colon would then pause the understanding of this one word, while closely relating it to the two segments listing capitalized personifications of the "*who all*". Such a punctuation mark here would act to connect both "*Astrologi*" (*Astrologers*) and "*Blenni*" (*Simpletons*), as well as the following segment's "*Barbari*" (*Barbarians*). Without the use of a semi-colon, the "*All ones who*" would be restricted primarily to the "*Astrologi Blenni,*" with the "*Barbari*" separated by comma.

Question Marks

On four occasions in the quatrains, Nostradamus used a question mark. Two of these uses were in the same quatrain. There are no question marks to be found in the letters of instruction. Three of the four uses in the quatrains are preceded in the line by the use of the word "*quelles*" or "*quelle*". The plural indicates "*what ones*", "*which ones*", or "*whose*", and is thus asking the reader to answer this question. In the other usage, there is no word preceding the question mark that is as indicative of a question.

In that usage, which appears in the first line of the fifteenth quatrain in *Centurie Second,* Nostradamus wrote, "*Un peu devant monarque trucidé?* This can translate as, "*One few* (or *A little*) *before monarch*

---

165   The 1568 Lyon edition (the one I believe is truest to Nostradamus' manuscript) shows a mark above the "*q*", as an indication of abbreviation, with a semi-colon following.
166   The 1568 Lyon edition makes a space appear between "*Omnes*" and "*q';*", which would avert the need of a manufactured word, "*Onmesqui*".

slaughtered?" In this situation, one sees how a question mark stands as its own sign, signaling the purpose of questioning, rather than trying to make the preceding words transform from one declaration, into one question. It stands alone, following a series of words stated separately, such that it represents the definition of the word "question."

That is then defined to be, "Inquiry requiring a reply; open controversy, or an issue; Uncertainty; doubt."[167] The reader must see this as a main theme statement that says a *"monarch"* is *"destroyed"*, resulting in uncertainty as to "why" (a word of question). Typically, should a *"monarch"* be *"slaughtered"*, a large-scale investigation ensues (questions about who, where, what, etc.). However, imagine a situation where a *"monarch"* died of questionable cause, but the body was *"destroyed"*, through some post-mortem procedures being ordered *"before"* an autopsy could be performed. That situation would make it impossible to determine any certain answers, relative to questions about the true cause of death. The question mark makes that statement all by itself, by seeming oddly placed.

A question mark typically is used to denote a direct request (state a question), rather than a declaration. Some uses will indicate the author's uncertainty about something, but these are generally surrounded by parentheses (?). As far as the use of question marks in the quatrains is concerned, the questions are not an indication of the author's uncertainty. The use of a question mark is a sign to state the existence of doubt, while also being a question for the reader to answer. Certainly, one must ask why Nostradamus used that mark, to find that answer.

Parentheses

At one time in the quatrains, Nostradamus inserted parentheses around words. This was in the one numbered fifty-sixth, in *Centurie Fourth*. According to the 1568 Lyon edition of *The Prophecies*, their copy of the letter to Henry II indicates two other uses of parentheses, both coming in the sections referring to the biblical chronology. This use of parentheses in the Henry letter is not found in the 1566 Lyon edition. However, to be sure, one must be prepared to examine all possibilities.

The use of parentheses indicates an interruption or an aside, as a supplementary explanation. As such, the exclusion of the material contained within parentheses will not alter the meaning found within the sentence. In the case of the confirmed use in the quatrain, the line states, *"Le ciel (de Plancus la cite) nous presaige,"* which translates as, *"The sky (of Plancus the city) we presage"*. As an aside, which if removed, the line states, *"The sky we presage."* This is the main theme, as an aside is a departure, or digression relative to that theme.

The plural pronoun, *"we"*, means Nostradamus and the Spirit of Jesus Christ, which defines *"presage"* as prophetic prediction, requiring the presence of one divine. With this distinction made, the word *"ciel"*

---

167   The Free Dictionary by Farlex, http://www.thefreedictionary.com/question

is best translated as *"heaven"* or *"firmament"*, which is the territory of God, particularly from a 16th century perspective. As such, it is an indication of Nostradamus' abilities with astrology, which is the art of discerning heavenly movements. That is then both his predictions in other publications, as well as *The Prophecies*, where astrological terminology is used, but the pronoun *"we"* makes the statement Nostradamus' understanding is assisted.

The aside is then the separate focus of the prophecy this quatrain contains. The confusion comes when one tries to understand a digression like, *"city of Plancus"*. What does that mean? Who is *"Plancus"*, and where is his (?) *"city"*. Many people make the standard assumption that *"Plancus"* was a Roman senator, consul, and censor, who was fully named Lucius Munatius *Plancus*. He was associated with the founding of the *"city"* in Gaul, now known as Lyon, France. Still, the nationality *"of Plancus there city"* (perhaps not where here would be to *"Plancus"*) could be a reference to Rome, which most do not consider. Rome is the one *"city"* most connected to a religion based on belief of Jesus Christ as the Son of God. This series of words set off by parentheses must then be seen as necessary information for understanding the rest of the line (the connection Rome has to *"heaven"*), while being set aside to also represent the earthly limits placed upon the *"city of"* Rome, through the non-religious rule of senators, like *"Plancus"*. The rest of the quatrain could then tell of changes that will bring about the need to prophesy about the future of Rome.

I will tell you that this stretch of the imagination is not the main focus of the use of parentheses. It is denoting an aside relative to *"we"*, where Nostradamus is calling himself *"Plancus"*. His partner is unnamed, but known to be in *"heaven"*. The point of distraction (a constant point of distraction, frequently in *The Prophecies*) comes from the use of the word, *"cité"*. This word does in fact mean, *"city"*, but it is more used as a past participle (indicated by the accent make at the end) of the verb, *"citer"*, which means, "to cite, to summon to appear, to war to appear, to allege." As such, *"de Plancus la cité"* is saying, *"with [Nostradamus] there alleged"*. This makes seeing *"Plancus"* as a manufactured word, and not the name of an irrelevant ancient Roman, the thing to solve.

The answer comes from seeing it as a simple anagram. Simply by taking the *"c"* out of the middle, and placing it at the beginning, as a contracted *"c'Planus"* one sees Nostradamus calling himself, *"this Charlatan"*. The fact that *"Plancus"* was Roman becomes a clue to search Latin, where *"ce Planus"* means, *"this Vagabond,"* or *"this Charlatan."* As an aside, Nostradamus is seeing a future time, when his prophecies will be for so long unsolved; people will have resorted to calling him a *"Charlatan"*. The humor of such an aside is those people would call him that thinking it was only him predicting, rather than *"we prophesying"*. By seeing there was reason for using parentheses, one is able to come to the true meaning of this profound main theme statement.

Exclamation Points, Apostrophes, and Hyphens

There is one use of an exclamation point [a.k.a. exclamation mark] in Nostradamus' works, although some editions mistake (or purposefully alter) the question mark use as exclamations. That use is not consistently found marked as an exclamation point, but it is clearly shown as such in the fifth quatrain of *Centurie Third*, in the middle of the third line.[168] That line states, "*O quel cherté! mais deux grans debonnaires,*" which translates to read, "*Oh what dearth! more two great ones courteous ones*".

This showing as an exclamation point perfectly fits the use of "*O*", which is a word of exclamation, used as an interjection. Words of this nature are often shown as capable of standing alone, accompanied by the mark that indicates a sudden expression of emotion. Still, the use of the word "*quel*", a standard word of questioning ("*who, what*"), would turn the focus of the line into an implied question, without the presence of an exclamation point turning it into a statement of astonishment. It follows the word "*cherté*", which can mean, "dearness [expense, or high price to pay], dearth [famine, shortage of food], scarcity [a lack of something], or want of." The application of the mark of astonishment attaches to this level of shortage.

An exclamation point would act as a period, such that it would end a statement of exclamation. This would then naturally be followed by a capitalized word, indicating a new statement beginning. The fact that the word "*mais*" follows, in the lower-case, means the placement of an exclamation point was primarily to clarify the prior words, to show them making a statement, rather than a question. Since all of Nostradamus words are capable of acting as one-word statements, any word in the lower-case is simply a statement of a lack of excessive importance, as capitalization denotes. As such, this use mirrors the system of punctuation, as it acts more as a direction to the reader, how to read the words prior, while following the rules that would govern the use of an exclamation mark.

The only other punctuation use worthy of note is frequent use of an apostrophe, and the rare use of hyphens. I mention both of these together because both have a common use, which is the combination of words. As such, contractions like the ones found in *n'aura* and *l'autre* (to list just two) mean "*not will have*" and "*the other*", while "*Jesus-Christ*" means *Jesus of Nazareth, the promised Christ*. The importance of such combinations is these words are to be read as one in the translation-interpretation. This would make them read differently from fully spelled out words, like *ne aura*, *le autre*, or *Jesus Christ*.

The important thing to know is there are no mistakes when it comes to punctuation. The use of a hyphen makes a big difference, whenever a number is found hyphenated. There are three ways numbers will be found written: 1.) two numbers written consecutively and separately; 2.) two numbers written around an

---

[168] The 1568 Lyon edition shows an exclamation point, as well does the 1566 Lyon edition. The 1555 Bonhomme edition turns the mark into a letter that looks like an "*l*", merging it with the word that follows; however, the 1555 Vienna edition also shows a clear exclamation point. The mark is completely missing from the 1557 editions, found in Utrecht and Budapest.

ampersand; and 3.) two numbers joined with a hyphen. The mistake is to think the same two numbers result in the same one number. Only when the hyphen is used can two words be known to be joined as one, such that *"forty-eight"* is the equivalent of 48. The same cannot be said for any other forms involving the words "forty" and "eight".

Chapter 24

The System of Capitalization

I have already presented the importance of an all-capital-letters word. While relatively few in numbers, their presence gives immediate attention to the fact that every letter is capitalized. This indicates a significant difference from the other text, which can only lead to one assuming some heightened sense of importance is the reason. Simply from that recognition, and the knowledge that a "prophecy" has a divine source, one is able to see how these words have higher meaning, as coming from Christ directly.

In short, a word written in all-capital letters stands out, setting itself apart from the other words, as more important. This importance makes this type of word one part of the system of capitalization. Due to the limited use of all-caps words, those uses become a relatively small part of the whole system of capitalization. However, Nostradamus' use of all-capitalized words draws the necessary attention that makes one recognize there is importance of all of Nostradamus' use of capitalization.

The word, "capitalize," when one is discussing writing, means, "To write or print in capital letters", and "To begin a word with a capital letter."[169] In the English language, there are specific rules that apply, as far as when one should capitalize, such as the first word of a sentence. A sentence ends with a period or colon, usually, which is why a capitalized word most often follows those two marks of punctuation. An exemption is given specifically to poetry, where a new line in a poem is allowed to begin with a capitalized first word, regardless of the punctuation used in the line that preceded that capitalized word. However, if one is familiar with the poet E. E. Cummings, a poet is not forced, by rule, to use capitalization at all.

Nostradamus does begin every new line of every quatrain with a capitalized first word. This acts in conjunction with the system of punctuation, where a line ends with a mark that directs the reader how to proceed to the next line. The line, as part of the system of order, is its own entity, thus the end of a line acts as a period normally would, regardless of the presence of another form of punctuation (or lack thereof). Therefore, a new line, as its own entity, must begin with a capitalized first word.

The system of punctuation means that an explanatory or clarifying line follows a line ending with a colon. Such a line begins with a capitalized first word because it is a new and separate entity. The last line of a

---

169 The Free Dictionary by Farlex, http://www.thefreedictionary.com/capitalize

quatrain ends with a period, indicating finality in the series of events contained within that one quatrain. However, as the quatrains all interconnect, the first word of a new line is capitalized to denote a new and separate theme, which follows the previous quatrain's event theme (as long as the quatrains have been properly reordered), as a logical continuation of an overall topic theme.

The point is that these capitalized first words are not capitalized simply because they are the first word of a new line. Each word that begins a line in Nostradamus' quatrains is specifically chosen to be the first word because of the importance the word bears. This importance is particularly related to the last word of the previous line (or previous quatrain, if it is the first word of a new quatrain), as a connector of lines, while also acting as the lead word in a new and separate line. Thus, all first words of lines are words of great importance, which is indicated through the capitalization. One cannot read any capitalized word as not bearing this importance or the meaning of the whole quatrain can collapse.

Before I give examples of this importance, let me immediately state that many lines will be found that begin with words that seem insignificant. They will seem this way simply because they are not words typically known for bearing importance. By this I specifically mean articles (*A*, *An*, and *The* – *Un*, *On*, *Le*, and *La*), conjunctions (*But*, *And*, *Then*, *Or*, *So*, and *That* – *Mais*, *Et*, *Puis*, *Ou*, *Or*, *Si*, and *Que*), and prepositions (*Of*, *From*, *To*, *With*, *In*, *At*, *By*, etc. – *De*, *A*, *Par*, etc.). All of these words are found to be capitalized at the beginning of lines, for the specific purpose of denoting importance.

Articles show the singularity of importance that is found in the following (second) word. For example, a line beginning with the words, "*The great*" (written "*Le grand*"), is a statement of "**THE** *great*", or "*the* **Great**". Similarly, a line beginning "*Un Romain chef*", or "*A Roman chief*", is showing the importance of "*ONE*", which is important as not just some, or just any "*Roman chief*", but a significant "*One.*" It would carry this importance to the word *chief*, as *one* very important *Chief* of *Rome*. In the case of the feminine article, such as a line beginning with "*La*", both "*The*" and "*There*" can be read as an indication of importance, more than "*THE*", but as also "*THERE.*" Both individuality and place are significant, which then transfers to the following word(s).

Conjunctions are stating either the importance of connection to another line (or quatrain), either through the indication of a significant exception (But), the indication of a significant addition (And), the indication of a significant sequence (Then), or the indication of a significant option (Or). The use of subordinating conjunctions, in particular the use of *Que* (*That*), is always a direct reference back to something stated prior. The importance is then placed on "*THAT*" which was stated, beginning a new series of words to show how "*That*" is important in a new focus of thought.

The prepositions offer important physical direction, with the meaning of "*De*" being any and all of the word's normal uses: *To*, *From*, *Of*, and *With*. Likewise, the letter "*A*" can have the multiple uses: *At*, *With*, *To*, *In*, and *From*. The word "*Par*" can mean: *By*, *Through*, *Of*, *For*, and *On*. In particular, to the use of

241

De, after it is used as a capitalized first word, it will not be uncommon to find another *de* in that line, or find another *De* beginning another line. This is to show the way direction changes, such as *To – from*, more than to repeat the same direction.

One also has to add to this variety of use possibilities, when Nostradamus writes one of the preposition-article combinations that are common in French (*Du = To the, Au = In the,* plural – *Des* and *Aux*). In these singular words, two words are written, with each word read with the importance of capitalization. The result is the adding of an important "*THE*" to the important direction stated. In the case of the plural forms, instead of *THE* one reads *THEM* or *THEY*, as an indication of one important group.

There are many examples of combination first words, like "*L'oiseau*" (THE-bird, or the-**B**ird), "*L'an*" (*THE-year*, or *the-Year*), "*D'un*" (*OF-one*, or *of-One*), and "*Qu'on*" (*THAT-one*, or *that-One*). Because these are two words joined together, they act as one, with the greatest emphasis put on the noun that follows the abbreviated article or preposition. Still, because the contracted letter is the one capitalized, and because it represents the article or preposition, the contracted word retains importance. This is unlike a mid-line word, like "*l'France*", where the lower case contraction of the article is lost in translation (becoming simply *France*).

I have hyphenated the translations here to show how the two words share importance, rather than show them as separate words. This is not necessary when doing a translation of a quatrain or letter. Contractions do not translate equally between French and English, and adding a hyphen is an alteration that detracts from all instances where Nostradamus did use a hyphen. The hyphenated demonstration above is designed to show the close relationship between an article and preposition to a following noun. In all cases where a line begins with a capitalized article or preposition, the importance denoted must always be seen as transferring to the second word as I have indicated. As such, "*Le an*" bears the same meaning as "*L'an*", because the same words and the same meaning are stated in both styles. All this means that there is nothing insignificant about any capitalized first word.

With that stated, let us take a look at a couple of quatrains that have already been discussed, in other system applications. Since all quatrains have four capitalized first words, we need to see how this element of importance plays a role in understanding. In the quatrain telling of the rise of John Kennedy to President of the United States, we find this stated:

La sœur aisnée de l'isle Britannique,	*The sister eldest to the island Britannic,*
Quinze ans devant le frere aura naissance :	*Fifteen years before the brother will have birth:*
Par son promis moyennant verrifique,	*By his promised working for shining fastened,*
Succedera au regne de balance.	*Will come to pass with the rule of balance.*

In this quatrain we immediately see the first line beginning with the feminine article "*La*" ("*The*"), which when written "*Là*" means, "*There*". When line one is seen as making the important statement of "*THE sister*", or "*the Sister*", one can become confused when one tries to affix great importance to Kathleen Kennedy-Cavendish. This Kennedy "*sister*" is not the focus of the importance the capitalized "*La*" brings. That focus lies at the end of line one, where the capitalized word "*Britannic*" shows its importance. Thus, "*La*" is indicating an importance related to Great "*Britain*", such that the reference is to "*THE sister eldest to the isle*".

This means "*There*" is a relationship to "*Britain*", as an offspring. With nations usually referred to in the feminine (Germany under Hitler an exception), the United States is "*THE eldest*" of the "children" of Great "*Britain*" (with Canada and Australia younger "*sisters*"). Therefore, line one is making a statement about the importance of "*There*", which is the United States, which is confirmed by the details of an American family to "*There*", Great "*Britain*". The capitalization of the article-preposition (*La-Là*) elevates it to applying to "*sister*", "*eldest*", and "*Britannic*". It does not apply to "*l'isle*" simply because an article is attached in contraction, as one with that word.

The capitalization of the word "*Fifteen*" then shows the importance of this number, some of which we have already discussed. One level of importance applied to a specific year of birth, for the "*eldest*" offspring of Joseph Kennedy, Sr. (19*15*). Another importance was the time between the death of Joseph Kennedy, Jr. and the announcement that John Kennedy was running for the office of the President. That was the number of years spanning between his death, in August 1944, and the announcement of JFK, in January 1960 (*Fifteen years*, due to being less than a full sixteen). However, when we see line one ending with the importance of "*Britain*" stated, with line one a statement of the importance of the United States of America, "*the birth*" of America as the dominant power on earth took rise "*Fifteen years*" after the official end of World War II.

Those "*years*", between 1945 and 1960, were when America established its dominance in the world. This dominance was primarily led by it having been the first nation the development, test, and deploy the atomic bomb. Those "*Fifteen years*" were America's head start on the world. However, beginning in 1960 the Soviet Union (and Cuba) tested that domination, meaning for "*Fifteen years*" after the surrender of Japan, there followed a period of uncontested power for America, at which time the United States assumed its position of power from its parent nation, "*Britain*", as the "*eldest*" heir to an Empire.

Line three is then confirming this transfer of power, with the capitalization of the preposition "*Par*". The word can mean "*By*" or "*Through*", which is an important indication of time being finished. As the first word of line three, which relates in support of the main theme of line one (the system of order), Great "*Britain*" has dropped "*By*" the wayside, in those "*Fifteen years*" since the defeats of Germany and Japan. The world domination that "*Britain*" once enjoyed is now "*Through*". The anointing oil of this power transfer is then placed "*On*" the "*eldest*" heir, who is descended "*Of*" British lineage. It is an important time "*For*" America, as it stepped into the role as the world's greatest nation.

Line four then has the capitalized future tense verb, "*Succedera*", meaning an important "*Succession will*" occur. The word "*Succession*" carries the definition of regal rights to "*succeed*", which is an elevated meaning of the word, on kingly levels. This right to regal "*rule*" is of greater importance than the "*Coming to pass* (alternate translation) of another President, in a never-ending string of elected officials. While Kennedy did "*Succeed*" Eisenhower as President, of greater world importance is the United States had already risen to a height that Kennedy would enjoy. The world would place the name "Camelot" on his time in office, because Nostradamus' prophecy that America "*Will Come to pass*" Great "*Britain*" as the "*ruler of the balance*" of the Free World.

It is in this way, from understanding the effect of capitalized words on meaning, that this quatrain is further distinguished as a focus on the timing of the transfer of power from the United Kingdom (an empirical "*ruler*"), to its "*eldest*" heir. The specifics of this time of transfer symbolize the lusts for power held by Joseph Kennedy, Sr., specifically for his "*eldest*" son(s). The rise, and later fall, of John F. Kennedy is a real event that occurred in history, but it is also symbolic of greater changes that took place. This greater meaning comes forth through the system of meaning found through capitalization.

To demonstrate that this is not a fluke, I will go through the first word capitalization used in the quatrain that told of submarines. In that quatrain we read:

Le grand Neptune du profond de la mer,	*The great Neptune to the deep of the sea,*
De gent Punique & sang Gauloys meslé :	*Of people Punic & blood French mixed:*
Les Isles à sang pour le tardif ramer,	*The Islands with lineage for the slow to row,*
Plus luy nuira que l'occult mal celé.	*More it will hurt than the secret evil hidden.*

This quatrain begins with a combination that is repeated many times throughout the quatrains (no less than ten times [10%] in Century Ninth alone), which is "*Le grand*".[170] This is how one knows that the word "*great*" is not just a meaningless word. Line one is beginning by referencing "*THE great*", or "*the Great*", who are the most powerful nations on earth. There is no difference between "*Le grand*" and Nostradamus simply writing "*Grand*", as a capitalized word. The word "great" (English translation) is always to be read as a noun, indication one of the main players in *The Prophecies*. Therefore, line one begins by stating, (in "*Le grand*") "Here is another quatrain about the rulers of the Free World."

As we discussed earlier, "*the Great*" are "*great*" sailors, as Britain is the "*Lord of the sea*" (representing "*Neptune*"). The use of the contracted preposition-article, "*du*" (*to-from-the*), means this god can go both "*to*" and "*from the deep*", which indicates an ability to travel under water. We then see "*de*" used near the end of line one, to confirm that the "*deep*" is "*of the sea*".

---

170 This number reflects similar uses, or derivative, such as "*La grande*", "*Au grand*", and "*Un grand.*"

That "*de*" leads to the capitalized "*De*" beginning line two, which transfers to the word "*gent*", meaning "*people*". However, when "*De gent*" is seen as transforming into "*de Gent*", in particular side-by-side with the capitalized word "*Punic*" (which means "*Treacherous foe*", in one sense), we get a sense of opposite important traits. Line two is then beginning by stating "*THE great god of the sea*" has both "*Gentleman*" and "*Untrustworthy*" warrior in its character. As such, it has the power to change "*From Gentle*", "*To Treacherous*". This is a sign of a culture possessing a long history of civilization, having achieved greatness, which became secured by a strong willingness to strike down all threats. Its greatest capacity in that later regard is through naval superiority.

Line three then begins with the capitalized word "*Les*", the plural article, thus individually stating the importance "*They*" have, where "*They*" is not only transferred to the following capitalized word "*Isles*", but also to "*Them Of Gentle Treachery*", who are "*The Great Neptune*". With that importance established, we see that is descriptive of "*The Isles*", which would be "*The*" British "*Isles*", or Great Britain. Still, the capitalization of "*Isles*" applies to all islands (plural "*Les*"), as was discussed in the previous system breakdown. The capitalization elevated to a wider scope of application.

The last line begins with the capitalized word, "*More*". As a line offering supporting detail to the secondary theme of line two, "*More*" is then stating an important furthering of "*The Isles*" ability to change "*From Gent To Punic*", where "*Pun(ir)-ique*" is French, meaning one characterized by (*-ique* suffix) its ability "*To Punish, To Correct,* or *To Avenge*". In other words, the British will be called upon to act once "*More*", as if they ran an Empire through naval prowess. The line states, "*More it will hurt*", which is an indication of "*More Punishing*", having become a British signature way of civilizing the world. Still, the same importance falls upon reading "*More*" in the opposite extreme. This means some of that naval power will have been "*hurt*", requiring "*More*" numbers in reinforcement.

I did not choose these two examples to show a connection between the two. One quatrain is telling of an event timing to the post-World War II / Cold War-Kennedy era; and the other is telling of a still future event, one waiting to occur. They are linked only in the sense that America's rise to become the world's greatest nation, as the "*eldest*" heir to the British Empire, will involve it in the rapid disintegration world affairs, calling upon the old emperor to renew its "*Neptune*" act.

As I have shown how the Kennedy-United States quatrain represented the transfer of empirical power to the Americans from the British, the other quatrain is making the statement, through "*More*", that Great Britain will be called upon to carry a load that will be "*More*" than it will be prepared to bear. Great Britain will have lost its taste for "*Punic*" control, having retired to the life of country "*Gentleman*". It will play back-up roles, behind the United States, until that time when "*More*" will suddenly be required. At that time, it will not be prepared for "*the secret evil*" that will await its presence.

As these examples have shown, the presence of other capitalized words within the quatrain plays important roles, to which the capitalized first words connect. The two types play off each other, from being on the same level of importance (capitalization), while also acting to develop the specific details each line has to convey, as mundane shifts of directions (first words) enhanced by basic names, titles, and places (mid-line personified words).

The interpretations I have given here, through use of the system of capitalization, do nothing to deter from the previous interpretations. In fact, they add to those interpretations, but on a higher level. Kennedy becomes the specific leader of America, but America becomes the specific leader of the Free World. The United Kingdom was once the leader of the Free World, as its naval might allowed it to conquer an empire, where it introduced civilization (as the English knew it), and savagely enforced compliance in a politely subservient manner. It had retired from its "*Punic*" ways, and let the Americans run the family business, the one of establishing puppet leaders abroad. However, the time will come when "*More*" will be expected of "*Them*", all of which is a higher view of a mundane event that would have the British navy sailing towards the Mediterranean "*Isles*", which range from those of Spain, Italy, France, and Greece, as well as a few independent "*Isles*".

In these examples, each of the mid-line capitalized words are easily recognizable as proper nouns, or words commonly read as capitalized: *Britannic, Neptune, Punic* (as in *Punic* Wars), *French*, and *Isles*. Each word conveys a specific name applied to the generality of: European people, Roman god, Mediterranean wars, or island nations. This specificity instantly allows one to focus on something more concrete in meaning. These words are more easily seen as important because they have recognizable proper noun status. However, that ease of recognition is what keeps one from seeing the full importance Nostradamus' capitalizations bring.

In the quatrains, perhaps the most prominent use of mid-line capitalization comes from his naming of European cities, peoples, or countries. I gave an example of this when discussing the system of punctuation, where the use of commas comes into play. At that time, I presented that Nostradamus wrote, "*Pisa, Asti, Ferrara, Turin, land interdicted.*" The problem with these cities being normally capitalized is that we do not see importance, as much as we see a standard capitalization of a proper noun. We therefore only see a list of Italian cities leading to "*land interdicted.*" That keeps us from seeing the importance that is held in the specificity of those four cities. It keeps us from seeing the mistranslation of "*Ast*" as "*Asti*", which causes us to miss completely a word that is not a typically capitalized as a proper noun being capitalized ("*Dart, Weapon-to-be-cast*").

The first-word-capitalization presents this problem as well. We are so used to reading a sentence beginning with a capitalized first word that we think nothing of trying to convey the importance of personification onto an article, conjunction, preposition, adjective or adverb. We simply see a word like "*Le*" as "*le*", or "*More*" as "*more*", and move on from there. This is the problem we face when we read normally, expecting normal syntax always to be in place; but we cannot expect that when reading Nostradamus.

THE SYSTEM OF CAPITALIZATION

There is nothing that is meaningless, thus something out of the ordinary is extraordinary. Since most words are written normally, all-capital-letter words are extraordinary. Since most words are written in lower case alone, the use of a capital letter is extraordinary.

To give another example of a mid-line word that typically is not seen as personified, let me refer to the quatrain found listed sixty-first in Century Second. In that line, Nostradamus wrote, "*O sang Troien Mort au port de la flesche*", which translates to read, "*Oh blood Trojan Death at the port of the arrow*". After the first word "*Oh*", which implies an exclamation of deep emotions, we find two capitalized words together, "*Trojan Death*", where the only reason the word "*Death*" would be capitalized is if it were necessarily personified, as a known form of "*Death*", in this case, "*Trojan Death*". Unfortunately, there is no such known disease (with all apologies to computer programmers, who would argue a *Trojan* virus).

I have made it clear that every word written by Nostradamus has to stand on its own, understood individually, before it can be connected to another word that has to stand on its own merits first, as well. Thus, the word "*Trojan*" is a recognizable capitalized word, while "*Death*" would most normally be written in the lower case. I say normally because there is a personification of the word "*Death*", which is found in the Tarot.

The *Death* card is the thirteenth card of the Major Arcana (from Latin, "*arcanum*", meaning, "deep secrets; mysteries; specialized knowledge or detail), found in a deck of Tarot cards. A Major Arcana card is one of twenty-two cards (21 progressively number valued, with one valued at either 0 or 22) that represent a higher level of secret meaning being symbolically revealed, such as showing the timing of major life shifts, versus day-to-day goings on. This higher meaning is opposed to the meaning found in the minor arcana, which are four suits (Wands, Cups, Swords, and Pentacles) numbered like a deck of regular playing cards (Ace [1] through King [13]). The difference is the Tarot minor arcana have a Page representative (1 of each suit), such that the minor arcana totals 56 cards, versus a regular playing card count of 52.

Thus, "*Death*" is capitalized as a personified card of importance in Tarot. It bears the meaning of "*Change*", more than "*Death*", although "*Death*" certainly is a "*Change*", from life to no life. When poetic symbolism is understood, a lower case "*mort*" could just as easily mean a lower case adjustment, or "*change*"; but that would be minor arcana, bearing minor significance. A Major Arcana "*Death*" represents a major "*Change*", where "*Death*" would be strongly symbolic. It would represent the end of the way things had been.

Certainly, when one sees this line beginning with an emotional cry, both angrily (an indication of battling "*Change*") and grievingly (an indication of mourning "*Death*"), we see how that importance elevates "*blood*" (*OH blood*) to "*Blood*" ("*oh **Blood***"). This is another word that typically would not be personified, nor capitalized to represent a proper noun. This means we have to look to a higher meaning of "*Blood*", where "*Lineage*" certainly covers a greater scope, than does the "*blood*" lost from one or several random living creatures. This elevates "*Blood*" to a race of people, or a whole population of kindred. The lamentations of anger and grief are then more identifiable as on a grander scale.

As a stand-alone word, "*Blood*" can also be elevated to a religious connection, as the "*Blood*" of Christ. This one word has the elevated meaning from the Eucharistic sacrament, where Episcopalians read:

> "Likewise, after supper, he took the cup; and when he had given thanks, he gave it to them, saying, "Drink ye all of this; for this is my "*Blood*" of the New Testament, which is shed for you, and for many, for the remission of sins. Do this, as oft as ye shall drink it, in remembrance of me."[171]

This is then elevating "*Blood*" to the level of meaning that is synonymous with Christianity. It is then a lament about the loss, of a time no longer remembering this major sacrifice made by Jesus. It is stating a time when all will forget that "*Blood*" had been spilled on the cross, so that many could be forgiven their sins. From Nostradamus' perspective, as a devout Catholic, whose sacraments were very similar to those used by Episcopalians, it is a lament that no one is remembering Jesus through symbolic sipping of wine. This is a symbolic "*Death*" of religion. The cry, "*Oh*", is due to the vast amounts of "*blood*" Nostradamus was shown being spilled, because of this failure for remembrance.

This is confirmed by the capitalized word "*Trojan*". The word "*Trojan*" is defined as, "A native or inhabitant of ancient Troy", and "A person of courageous determination or energy."[172] Thus, the word bears the important meaning that is behind the history of Troy, while also making an important statement about courage and determination. In short, this means facing down fear, from a complete resolve to resist it overtaking one's self. It is, in essence, bunker mentality, which says, "As long as I have these walls of protection, I'll be okay." The "*Trojans*" were okay, until they were deceived into opening the gate of their defensive wall, to let in a wooden horse.

It is then this cry of pain coming from Nostradamus, caused by him seeing the collapse of the "*Bloodline*" of Christ (Christianity). To see it come by trickery, the same way Troy fell, will be emotional for him to watch. Christianity will be tricked into willfully welcoming something appearing as a gift, or offering, even celebrating it, although it will later become a poison. One that will be injected into the veins of that religious culture, causing its '*Death*'. Because the "*Trojan*" War signaled the end of Troy's days of power, due to the "*Trojan*" horse, there was, in essence, a "*Trojan Death*".

As such, a similar major "*Change*" will come upon Christianity, causing Christianity to "*Cease-to-live*" on the level it once had. The trickery that will begin the fall of Christianity is also a stratagem of war, <u>on a grander scale</u>. The two parallel powers in this long-fought war will be competing over who has the

---

171   From The Holy Eucharist: Rite I, from the Book of Common Prayer.
172   The Free Dictionary by Farlex, http://www.thefreedictionary.com/Trojan

control of the minds of the people, which had been balanced between Kings and the Church. Thus, the "*Death*" of Christianity will be when the walls of this protective balance will have been breeched.

This is the higher meaning associated with this line, due to it containing internal capitalized words. This does not mean that the mundane focus of the quatrain is the cause of the "*Death*" of Christianity. Just as the cause of Israel's collapse, and Judah's fall, to the Assyrians and Babylonians respectively, were not because of one event, one battle, or one war. The mundane says they were defeated by a stronger foe; but the higher reason is they had turned away from God. This higher focus covers a much wider scope of time.

The same line of thought can thus be applied to this mundane battle event, where "*blood*" will lead to "*Death*". The mundane meaning coming from the basic words of this line is that "*blood*" will flow, because of an attack on a "*port*" city. This line is stating the secondary theme for the quatrain, of "*blood*" spilling, which follows the main theme's indication that France is the site of bloodshed. Nostradamus did this through listing a French Department, and a French city not far from that department. Thus, the mundane meaning is war in France (one still awaiting in the future); but the higher meaning is France will have ceased to be of the "*Blood*" of Christ. France's Christian-poor "*Blood*" began after their revolution in 1789. The capitalization elevates the meaning to span over hundreds of years of history, relative to one specific focus – losing one's religion.

It is not necessary at this point to further interpret this quatrain, as it presently deals with a future event. The point here is only that there are many capitalized words internal to one or more lines, in many quatrains. It is vital that all of Nostradamus' capitalized words be given attention to this higher level meaning; but this brings up a problem that must be addressed. That problem is the consistency between the various editions of *The Prophecies*. Some of the mid-line capitalized words are not shown to match, as some appear in the lower-case in some of the print editions closest to the original manuscript. Because of these differences, interpreters of the quatrains have been all across the board on how they handle these words.

Understand that I am not talking about the greatest number of mid-line capitalized words, which are the names of places (remember Nostradamus warned about place names in his Preface), mythological names (like "*Trojan*"), titles of royalty (like "*King*" and "*Pontiff*"), and astrological names (like "*Mars*" and "*Cancer*"). I am talking about the words that are not typically written in the upper case, as proper nouns, like my example of "*Death*". There is ample proof and general consensus[173] that Nostradamus capitalized the word "*Mort*". However, despite the fact that there is some confusion about whether some words were

---

173 Nostradamus writers Leoni and Lemesurier each use the 1555 Lyon Bonhomme edition, which shows line two as, "*O sang Troien! Mars au de la port flesche*", which is the only edition to show "*Mars*". The 1557 Lyon du Rosne, the 1557 Utrecht du Rosne, the 1566 Lyon Pierre Rigaud, and the 1568 Lyon Benoist Riguad editions all show *Mort*, although the 1566 Lyon shows it in lower case (*mort*). Nostradamus writers Cheetham and Hogue both show "*Mort*" in their works.

capitalized by Nostradamus or not, there has been a consistent tendency by translators to ignore some words that have proven capitalization, while glorifying others, written in the lower-case, by anointing them with capitalization.

One example of the mutation of a capitalized word, to a lower case word, is found in the quatrain published as number seventeen in *Centurie First*. All of the sources at my disposal clearly show Nostradamus writing in the main theme line (line one), "*Par quarante ans l'Iris n'aparoistra,*" where *l'Iris* is written as a proper noun. That personification of the Greek goddess *Iris* is not carried over to the translations made available to non-French readers. Others translate it to state (similarly to the literal), "*For forty years the rainbow not will appear*". The word "*rainbow*", in the lower-case, has been consistently substituted for "*l'Iris*", in all cases that I have researched.

Naturally, there is reason for such unanimity in that translation. The goddess *Iris* was the goddess whose presence was known to mankind (the Greeks at least) through the rainbow. Therefore, "*l'Iris*" means "*the Rainbow*", but that does not make any sense in a translation, as far as capitalizing a common word like "rainbow". No one would understand what, "*For forty years Iris will not be seen*" meant. Who is Iris? It cannot be the Greek goddess *Iris*, because no one has seen her for almost two thousand years.

It is simpler to translate this unnecessary use of a capitalized name of a Greek goddess as "rainbow". That allows one to imagine that Nostradamus figured "*l'Iris*" was a shorter way to write "*l'arc au ciel* »", as Randal Cotgrave placed in his 1611 French-English Dictionary, as the idiom meaning, "the rainbow".[174] However, this is not why Nostradamus wrote "*l'Iris*", and it is not up to us to alter what was written when we cannot make sense of it. It is up to us to realize it must make sense, and we must protect it so it will make sense when we are ready to have our senses enlightened.

Consider what Wikipedia posts immediately in its article about *Iris* (mythology).

> "Iris (Ἶρις) is the personification of the rainbow and messenger of the gods. As the sun unites Earth and heaven, Iris links the gods to humanity. She travels with the speed of wind from one end of the world to the other, and into the depths of the sea and the underworld underworld."[175]

This is better information to know about the goddess *Iris*. She was not only "*the Rainbow*", but she was the messenger of the gods. When we start connecting the number "*forty*" with "*the Rainbow*", we start getting into a biblical lesson from the Book of Genesis. After God made it rain for "*forty*" days and "*forty*" nights, He made His first covenant with Noah, to never again ruin the world through flood. As a sign of this covenant, God sent "*the Rainbow*" (or "*Iris*", if you are Greek) as a messenger to remind

---

174 Randal Cotgrave's 1611 French-English Dictionary, http://www.pbm.com/~lindahl/cotgrave/search/061r.html

175 Wikipedia, the free encyclopedia, http://en.wikipedia.org/wiki/Iris_(mythology)

humanity of this promise. This is higher-level awareness stuff to know; and it is higher level because it deals with the grander scope of God connecting with mankind. It is letting us know that God's reminder of a covenant to protect humanity from destruction *"will not be seen"*. We miss knowing that when we alter a capitalized word and make it one in lower case.

There are several examples of how capitalized words (consensus approved) become mutated to the lower case, or altered into a lesser state, throughout the quatrains. One other case is found in the twenty-fifth quatrain of *Centurie First*, where Nostradamus wrote, *"Sera pasteur demy Dieu honoré"*. When one recognizes that Nostradamus wrote each word to be understood separately, before any combinations of meaning can take place, this literally translates to state, *"Will be pastor* (or *shepherd) half God honored"*. The capitalization of *"Dieu"*, or *"God"*, is making the important statement about the Christian view of *"God"*, because a *"pastor"* is a title for an official leader of an individual Christian church. The title is bestowed as a model for the Good *"Shepherd"*, who was Jesus. However, this meaning is not to be found in most translations.

Due to two words being together, as *"demi Dieu"* are, just about all authors on Nostradamus have mutated these two separate words to read, "demigod". This places *"God"* not only in the lower case, where lesser gods roam, it morphs two words into one, where *"God"* loses His meaning to man. The non-mythological definition of demigod is, "A person who is highly honored or revered."[176] While this definition works on the mundane interpretive level, it prevents a higher level meaning to emerge.

In Randal Cotgrave's 1611 French-English Dictionary, one finds *"demi-dieu"* listed, defined as, "A demigod [spelled as two words, "demy god"]; one that is partly God, and partly man."[177] This second definition is a statement of the mythological definition, where we find a demigod to be, "A male being, often the offspring of a god and a mortal, who has some but not all of the powers of a god."[178] This definition allows a "real" god to be involved with humanity, but due to the lower-case being used, it is an unproven god of myth, or less god than *"God" is*. Still, the Old French hyphenated to combine two words into one, while using the lower case spelling *"dieu"*. This is not what Nostradamus wrote.

In this quatrain, of which many have offered the opinion that it might be directly naming Louis Pasteur, due to Nostradamus using a word (lower case *pasteur*) that became a name (upper case Pasteur), the capitalization elevates the meaning. Regardless of the mundane possibilities of this line, one has to see how *Sera* (*Will be*) transfers its capitalization to *pasteur* (*shepherd*). This allows *Pasteur* to come forth, but Louie *Pasteur* is too specific to be anything more than a mundane interpretation.

As such, this is telling of a time in the future where there *"will be"* a *"Shepherd"*, who will care for

---

176   The Free Dictionary by Farlex, http://www.thefreedictionary.com/demigod
177   Randal Cotgrave's 1611 French-English Dictionary, http://www.pbm.com/~lindahl/cotgrave/search/281r.html
178   The Free Dictionary by Farlex, http://www.thefreedictionary.com/demigod

people on a great level, as did Jesus. It will not be Jesus, as Jesus was "*God*" incarnate as man, thus man wholly led by "*God*". This "*Shepherd will be*" only "*half*" what Jesus was, but the same "*God*" will lead that "*half*". The form "*God*" will take will be Jesus, much as Nostradamus was led to write *The Prophecies* by encountering the Spirit of Jesus. Once we see this higher meaning, it becomes easy to see that Nostradamus produced "*half*" of what is now the whole. A true Prophecy only "*half*" understood for centuries is now being understood. The "*pastor*" of writing, and the "*pastor*" of understanding, are two "*halves*" that make a whole, but all "*Will be*", through the "*Will*" of "*God*", through His Good "*Shepherd*".

As such, Louie *Pasteur* was not the true source of his breakthroughs in science, which helped mankind. That "*honor*" belongs to "*God*". Human beings can only take credit for having acting on "*God's behalf*", as Nostradamus explained he did. The Good "*Shepherd*" leads all who work for the betterment of humanity. Those who are "*honored*" on earth for their achievements, have "*honored God*", just as "*God honored*" them with the ability to produce amazing works. At times, the way humanity has repeatedly fallen into a false comfort through idol worship, especially today but also in the past, one who does miraculous deeds for humanity is bestowed "*honors*" as a demigod. The capitalization shows us where the true "*honor*" comes from, and where those "*honored*" must give "*God*" the "*glory*" (synonym of "*honor*").

These examples of places where Nostradamus capitalized "*Iris*" and "*God*", only to have the majority of people translate those higher-level names to lower case importance; one has to realize there is a difference between "*Iris*" and "rainbow", and between "*God*" and "god". They are, in each case, two different things; and there is specific meaning that is relative to each the lower case and the capitalized forms. This concept, commonly found, is required to discern Nostradamus' use of royal titles.

According to the list of Nostradamus' word usage, prepared by J. Flanagan, originally prepared by K. Lowey, the word "*roi*" ("king") appears fifteen times in the quatrains. The same word, spelled "*roy*", appears ninety-nine times. In the list of "Caveats" found on the "Introduction" page to this list's website, the first bullet point states, "Capitalization has been omitted; all entries are in lower case." This is an important disclaimer, because Nostradamus wrote both "*Roi*" and "*Roy*" ("*King*"), and "*roi*" and "*roy*" ("*king*"). He also wrote "*Roine*" ("*Queen*") and "*roine*" ("*queen*"), as well as (translated): "*Prince*" and "*prince*", "*Duke*" and "*duke*", "*Lord*" and "*lord*", and "*Lady*" and "*lady*" (and others). All of these differences in spelling (capitalized versus lower case) are done with a specific purpose intended.

When syntax is to be expected, one looks for the rules that govern the proper use of capitalization to be in place. In this regard, there are rules for when to capitalize and rules for when not to capitalize. In the area covering titles, the rule states, "Capitalize titles when they precede proper names, but not when they follow proper names or are used alone."[179]

Due to this general rule, when Nostradamus wrote "*The King*", some translators have corrected it to

---

[179]   Paradise Valley Community College, Online First-year English FAQs, Kathy McLain, MA, http://www.pvc.maricopa.edu/lsc/faq/eng/enggrawhen.htm#titles

state, "*The king*". Therefore, when Nostradamus wrote, "*the king*", the translation agrees with what was written. While this normally would be grammatically correct, *The Prophecies* were not written according to the normal rules of writing. Corrections of this sort make it difficult, if not impossible, for one to grasp the full meaning that Nostradamus conveyed. There is a difference.

In the times of Nostradamus, kings or emperors ruled throughout Europe. Kings were not elected to power, through a popular vote determined by the peasantry. They were born to rule, or elected through a consensus of related royalty. Because there was a special descendancy that was inherited through royal blood, all born of that blood were ranked in order of ascendancy to the throne (thus *roy*-alty). This royalty is believed to come from God, or in particular, Jesus Christ. This is the concept behind the book, *Holy Blood, Holy Grail*, where in Old French "*sang roial*" ("*blood royal*", also said to have been "*sang raél*"), which then changes to become "*sangrael*" (presumably "*san graél*", where "*sang*" mutates into an abbreviated form, "*san*", the root of "*sainct*"), meaning, "holy grail". Randal Cotgrave called that notion "foolish" (the Arthurian Holy Grail),[180] but the birthright to rule (divine right) was believed to be due to this "*holy blood*".

The Columbia Encyclopedia explains "Divine right" as, "a right based on the law of God and of nature. Authority is transmitted to a ruler from his ancestors, whom God himself appointed to rule."[181] Thus, a king was one chosen by God to rule. Such a designated ruler was listed by Nostradamus as a "*Roi / Roy*", where the capitalization elevated the title word to that higher-level distinction. Therefore, a lower case "*roi / roy*" is one who has powers equal to a king, but not divinely chosen.

In short, a "*roi*" is the equivalent of a president, a prime minister, or the highest elected official of a nation. With a limit on true "*Kings*" these days, unlike in Nostradamus' days, the capitalization becomes an important identifier of a specific character referenced in a quatrain. The same applies to all true royal figures, versus those having positions of power and wealth not predestined by God. Therefore, a "*Queen*" is married to a Royal King, or of royal blood, like "*Queen*" Elizabeth, while a "*queen*" is akin to a woman chancellor, like Germany's Angela Merkel.

In some cases, Nostradamus wrote words in the lower case, which are difficult not to translate into capitalized form. For instance, the French do not typically capitalize the months of the year, while English speaking nations do ("*mai*" = "*May*"). Nostradamus would write some months in lower case, while he capitalized others, thus making a capitalized month stand out as important. Still, in translations into English, particularly relative to the month of May, if Nostradamus wrote, "*mai*", it is confusing to translate this into "*may*," as English sees that word in the lower-case as an entirely different word, one

---

180   By the Old French listing of the word "*sangreal*", Cotgrave wrote, "Part of Christ's most precious blood wandering about the world invisible (to all but chaste eyes), and working many wonders, and wonderful cures; if we may credit the most foolish, and fabulous History of King Arthur."
181   The Columbia Encyclopedia, Columbia University Press, http://plus.aol.com/aol/reference/divineri/divine_right?flv=1

which bears no relation to the French word "*mai*." Therefore, "*mai*" has to be translated as "*May*".

Nostradamus also wrote several times of "*lac Leman*", which translates as "*Lake Leman*" (old name for Lake Geneva). He would name mountains by writing, "*monts Pyrenées*" or "*monts Apennines*", where it is standard to translate these as "*Pyrenees Mountains*" and "*Apennines Mountains*". Still, he would apparently name places by writing word combinations like "*saint Quintin*" and "*sainct Felix*". The likes of these have had translators bringing out their box of hyphens, creating *Saint-Quintin* and *Saint-Felix*.

The point is there is no importance to convey in a lake, a mountain, a month, or a title bestowed by the Roman Catholic Church. The type of place or person is generally stated by these words. A lake is a small body of water; a mountain is a large mass of rock; and a saint is someone who lived a holy life. Thus, those words are generally descriptive and better serving in the lower case. They are all mundane, particularly when compared to the specific capitalized name they precede.

Up until this point, my focus on capitalization has been on the quatrains. The same rules apply to both letters. Most of the capitalization in the Preface is focused on where the periods are found, with most capitalized first words being words like "*Because, Like, But, Which, And*", and other such wording that is connective and directional. The mid-line capitalization largely focuses on "*God, Angels, Lord, Divine*", and references to Jesus ("*Savior*"), although there are others ("*Martial-ones, Astrology, Vulcan*", and so on). Depending on the edition one chooses, an important difference is found in Nostradamus writing "*my Prophecies*" and "*the prophecy*".[182] This is an indication of a difference between his yearly periodicals, which contained presages and predictions (lower-case "*prophecy*") and *The Prophecies* (the book he was explaining in the Preface).

The letter to Henry II has many more uses of capitalized words, particularly mid-line capitalized names that can also be found in the quatrains. Since this letter is not in the correct order, the capitalization helps act as a sorting device. Through the capitalized names of biblical patriarchs, found in two different parts of the letter, it is possible to link those two parts together. Likewise, the matching of capitalized word use, like "*Aquilon*", "*Pyrenees*", and "*Antechrist*", between the individual quatrains and this letter, makes it possible to sort each into sections that become larger pieces of the puzzle. While the letter to Henry II is a "graduate level" piece of work to solve, as is solving the riddle of putting all 948 or so quatrains in the correct order, the principles of the system of capitalization remain consistently applied.

One must always look at how capitalization affects the meaning of the word written, regardless of where it appears, and no matter how incorrect it may seem to be. Some capitalized words can be subtle in their higher meaning. Regardless of the difficulties one may encounter, seeing the higher value of capitalization always leads towards a fuller understanding. Capitalization is also an important tool in differentiating one similar event from another.

---

[182] The 1568 Lyon edition shows this lower-case/upper-case difference.

If there is a difference of opinion, as to which publication to translate from, consider all options. If a capital letter added makes the line clearer, on a higher level, while maintaining the mundane level of one specific event, then that is probably correct. I prefer to use the 1568 Lyon edition as the standard-bearer of the true manuscript, but that distinction can only come through comparison. Some publications may be less true to the author's instructions, to "make sure you do not change a mark", especially if they were influenced by higher powers (King or Church) to make edits. Consistency among publications is the key for determining, with the highest probabilities, what Nostradamus intended.

Chapter 25

The System of Symbols

Let me begin this system with the most common definitions of the word, "symbol." A symbol can be "an arbitrary sign (written or printed) that has acquired a conventional significance," or it can be "something visible that by association or convention represents something else that is invisible."[183] With these definitions, it is easy to see that you are reading my thought (the invisible) on paper through the conventional use of symbols, known as letters of the alphabet, forming recognizable words (another invisible). In addition to those words being formed by symbols, I mark pauses in my thoughts with another use of symbols specifically called punctuation.

In a thesaurus, one can find a long list of words that are synonymous with "symbol," based on which definition is used. Among those synonymous with the first definition, where an arbitrary sign has achieved conventionality, are metaphor, image, number, symbolism, allegory, and emblem. As something visible representing the invisible, words like representation, mark, sign, token, figure, type, logo, and glyph are a few that are synonymous with "symbol."[184]

In that sense, all of Nostradamus' work could be classified as a system of symbols, but there needs to be more diversity than that, with classification based on the specific types of symbols he used. I have chosen to identify this class as the system of symbols, as a way to incorporate a class that I had seen as a division of the system of punctuation, as punctuation is certainly a set of symbols. Nostradamus repeats one symbol so often that it demands significant recognition, but it is not an accepted mark of punctuation. It has a specialized niche, as an abbreviation. Along with that one symbol, other scattered symbol uses also do not fall into the category of punctuation, which calls for a broader umbrella under which all these marks could fall. For that reason, I have decided to call this category the system of symbols, as a way to covers all uses of symbols not covered by marks of punctuation and not spelled with alphabetical letters.

The symbol I referred to that makes up the majority of this category is a symbol is that has 666 appearances in the quatrains. That figure comes from the research mentioned earlier, which does not take

---

183 Collins Essential Thesaurus, 2nd Edition, 2006, HarperCollins, from The Free Dictionary by Farlex, http://www.thefreedictionary.com/symbol
184 Ibid.

into consideration the uses in the letters. That symbol is the ampersand (&).[185] I have not mentioned this specific symbol yet, because it is not classified as punctuation. It is more like a shorthand symbol for the word, "and." The ampersand use is so widespread it becomes one of those clues that blend into the background, thus easily missed; but it means much more than three letters could spell. It plays a vital role in understanding *The Prophecies*.

In addition to the ampersand usage, there are other important symbols found in the documents Nostradamus produced, relative to his prophecies. I just used one in the last paragraph, when I listed the number of ampersand uses in the quatrains. A number is not a letter, but a written sign that conveys a conventional meaning. Just as an ampersand is a shorthand mark for the word "and," the numbers 666 make a quick way to state, "six hundred sixty-six." Likewise, there are glyphs that are used in astrology (♈, △, ☽), with some making their way into print in the quatrains (some editions). Marks of this nature act in the same shorthand manner. Other such marks covered in this system are Roman numerals, Greek letters (some editions), the use of accent marks, and a new discovery I have realized since my last explanatory book. That discovery identifies the unusual combinations uses of punctuation marks with ampersands (such as ",&"). All have importance that must be understood, with the ampersand holding an essential importance.

Ampersands

Nostradamus used ampersands frequently in the quatrains. As far as I could count (my eyes start to cross), I found 90 ampersands in the Preface, written in French and Latin.[186] That is an average of nine per page, with the Preface totaling 10 pages in the 1557 Utrecht edition. For the letter to Henry, I reviewed the 1566 Lyon edition of Pierre Riguad, which gave credit to Fr. Jean Valliet and his convent in Salon, for the imprint. In that edition there were 17 pages used to depict the letter, with at least 229 ampersands found. Again, these were found present in both the French and the Latin text,[187] averaging almost 13.5 ampersands per page. The grand total comes to at least 319 ampersands used in the letters.

These numbers are important, because their use is so common it makes it seem that Nostradamus wrote hurriedly, with not enough time to spell out the long French word for "*and*," which is "*et*." Thanks to J. Flanagan's efforts, we know that is not true, at least as far as the quatrains are concerned. Not only did he count 666 ampersands used, he also listed each of the 87 times Nostradamus wrote the word, "*et*."

I have audited this list and found two errors; one where the particular edition Flanagan gleaned his count from shows "*et*" following a comma, in line four of the quatrain found number thirty-nine in

---

185 Index of the Centuries of Nostradamus, prepared by J. Flanagan, originally prepared by K. Lowey, http://alumnus.caltech.edu/~jamesf/nindex/a_index.html
186 As found in the 1557 Utrecht edition. The Latin type is italicized in this edition.
187 The 1566 Lyon edition has the letter to Henri II, unlike the 1557 edition (it was written in 1558). This edition shows the letters in almost a script style; with the Latin a standard form of typeset.

Centurie First. No other edition shows anything other than the comma in that quatrain's fourth line. The other error is in his reference to the seventy-eighth quatrain listed in *Centurie Sixth*, where all editions I researched show an ampersand, with no presence of the word, "*et*". With those two exceptions tossed out, there are still 85 clear examples of Nostradamus writing that word out fully, without finding a need to symbolize it.

Another important find in this audit is that, with the exception noted, where "*et*" was in one edition, following a comma, every use of this word, "*and*", is capitalized in the quatrains, as the first word of a line. As we have discussed in the system of capitalization, such a conjunction shows importance as an addition to what has been stated prior. The power of the capitalization then flows into the word(s) following that capitalized first word, while being a strong link to the previous word. As such, the use of the word "*And*" in *The Prophecies* acts as the beginning of a new paragraph would in literature.

While a symbol has been defined as something visible that by association or convention represents something else that is invisible, this does not mean the visible is actually a mark. A conventional symbol used today, visibly to indicate the invisible, is the call for a paragraph break; by double-space either following a period or an indent on the following line, after a period. No physical mark is made to represent this; instead, the invisible (space) marks the invisible (new line of thought). As such, this symbol of space is conventionally understood to state, without thought, "**And** in addition to what was just stated, this naturally follows as a logically separate, yet sequential offering on the subject." By Nostradamus physically writing the word "*Et*", he is drawing importance to a conjunction that marks such a separation.

For example, let us look at one of the first listed uses of "*Et*" in the quatrains. This one comes as the first word of the fourth line, in the thirteenth quatrain listed in *Centurie First*. Beginning with line three, that quatrain states:

Secret mettront ennemis par la mine,	Secret will be putting enemies for there undermined,
***Et** ses vieux siens contre eux sedition.*	**And** its old of itself against them uproar.

Generally, line three is making a statement about the placement of "*Secret enemies*" somewhere. The capitalization of "*Secret*" means the personification of people who purposefully act in "*secret*". These are typically called spies, who are "*enemies*" of the places where they are sent to spy. This makes determining where important.

The combination of words together, "*la mine*", gives the appearance of "*mine*" being a feminine word, because "*la*" is the feminine form of "the." That would make "*la mine*" translate as, "*the mine*," which is certainly part of the interpretation in this quatrain, but not the primary focus. This translation does not allow for insight as to where *"the mine"* would be. This means one has to read *"la"* as a stand-alone word (*"là"*), which translates as, *"there"*. This is then stating the "where" that the *"secret enemies"* are being sent. Once this is known, a *"mine"* can become a *"secret"* place where *"enemies"* could store weapons, once *"there"*.

With that realization, we can then read *"mine"* as *"miné"*, turning a rather meaningless noun into the past participle of the verb *"miner"*, meaning, *"undermined"*. This translation allows one to see the purpose *"for"* sending *"Secret enemies there"*. They are not only *"there"* to spy on a foreign nation; they are *"there"* to plot to weaken the foundation and base of the nation they have infiltrated (the definition of *"undermine"*). As such, one word can have multiple ways to add valuable information in this quatrain.

I did not offer line one for this example, but line one uses the word *"exiles"*. This word translates the same in English, meaning peoples banished from their native land. With this in line one and the system of order stating that line three will offer supporting details line one, the *"exiles"* are *"enemies"*. As *"exiles"* are not in their native lands, they are the ones *"there"*, in the country or countries that will be *"undermined"*. Those of their native lands will have played an important role to plan the *"exiles"* ending up *"there"*, meaning the *"exiles"* will be acting as agents for their *"Secret"* recruiters.

One must understand the meaning coming from line three, to begin to understand the linking *"And"* that begins line four. The importance of this conjunction is that it generally marks additional comments about the *"Secret enemies"*, while directly stating an additional condition relative to the subversive acts of *"undermining"* a nation of people. Further, as the capitalized first word of line four, which is the line offering supporting details to the secondary theme of line two, the word *"And"* is stating a continuation of that theme. Line two states, *"Feront au roy grand conjuration:"* This translates to state, *"Will be making with the king great calling of the people together:"*

This theme revolves around a lower case *"king"* (elected official of the highest degree) of *"people"* in a *"great"* nation, which is certainly a Western nation, most probably the United States or *"Great"* Britain, although France and Italy are possible as well. There is something important that *"Will be making"* the *"king"* call upon his *"people"*. That something important is the issue of *"exiles"*.

This issue is more prominently known today as the debate over illegal immigration, or the hardships encountered by refugees in overcrowded camps, attempting to escape from war-torn lands. People of this nature suddenly appear in large numbers, and suddenly become a problem for a nation to absorb, particularly one known for being a haven to the world's oppressed. Therefore, *"And"* in the fourth line is following the colon (system of punctuation symbol of clarifying information to follow) that ended line two, making it clarify additional information about the *"conjuration"*, or *"calling of the people together"*. The word *"conjuration"* can also translate as *"conspiracy"*, or the casting of a magic spell (English *"conjuration"*).

The possessive pronoun in line four, "*ses*", assumes the power of capitalization from "*And*". This word represents the plural form of "*son*" (French possessive pronoun, "*his*"), acting then as "*One's*" or "*Its*". This is the important personification of the "*people*" being called upon by their "*king*" (or "*president*"), who is "*calling the people together*" because they are in an "*uproar*" over the increasing number of "*exiles*" in their land. These "*people*", also possess the "*king*" (or "*highest leader*"), having him as "*One's king*", or the "*People's king*". When "*And*" is seen as adding clarification to the secondary theme, we then see, "*Will be making with the king great calling of the people together*" and the "*People's old himself*". This is the "*king*" specifically referencing the "*old*", in some way related to the "*conjuration*".

The "*people*" identified in line four as "*old*", or "*aged*", can be an indication of older citizens, meaning "the elderly". That could imply that the attitude of the younger citizens is the one most held by the "*king*", "*president*", or "*prime minister*". Still, when we see "*And*" as clarifying which "*people*" would be "*called together*", the use of "*exiles*" is referencing the nations of the "*exiles*". This makes the "*old*" be those who have long before become citizens of the "*king's*" land. The word "*siens*" is then understood as the possessive pronoun identifying the "*king*", as "*his, his own,* or *belonging to himself*", meaning he will make a personal plea to the "*One's*" owning citizenship, who themselves will have similarly gone through the process of naturalization, to come forward and help the "*exiles*".

This means it is those of "*age*" and maturity (experienced) who begin to see their "*king*" as "*against them*", or acting "*contrary to*" the nature of the office of "*king*". To ask someone who is a naturalized citizen to assist in the welfare of illegal immigrants, simply because the financial burden is too great for the nation, means national security is being endangered. With the nation's highest-ranking leader calling for all to get along, his actions can be seen as if he is in with the "*enemies*" of state. This causes an "*uproar*" among "*them*", the "*People*" who are strongly attached to the "*old*" ways, who feel threatened by the presence of "*exiles*".

This then leads to the word "*And*", in line four, acting as an addition to the act of "*Secret undermining*", in line three. The "*One's old*" ways of guarding against "*Secret undermining*" will have been through strong immigration policies. Due to out of control conditions, making strong controls impossible to enforce, the "*enemies*" will be able to "*undermine And*" do it without resistance, because the "*One's old*" policies of accepting the world's abandoned is used "*against them*".

This example shows how one small capitalized word ("*Et*") acts to show an intended separation of space, as a new line represents a new paragraph of meaning. It shows how the word also indicates a connection (as a conjunction) to what preceded it, relative to order (three to four) and relationship (two to four). In other words, the spelled out word, "*And*", in the quatrains demonstrates a multiplicity of importance. Nostradamus did not write any lower case "and" words in the verses, which makes an audit of his use of the spelled out word in the letters important to note.

In the Preface (as best I could find), Nostradamus wrote out the word "*And*" three times, all capitalized, following a period mark. These were accompanied by the 90 uses of ampersands I previously mentioned. In the letter to Henry II, Nostradamus again only spelled out the capitalized form, "*Et*", following period marks, doing this (as best as I could count) twenty-four times. This was in addition to the use of 229 ampersands. This lack of the lower case spelling of "and" being present is an important sign for how to understand the ampersand symbol.

I have mentioned several times that there is nothing insignificant in anything relative to *The Prophecies*. I have mentioned several times that there is no normal syntax to be found, either in the quatrains or in the letters. Let me add now that when I was turning in essays in my college 101 English class, my teacher noticed my love for the word "and", which led him to teach me that a simple comma could eliminate much of what I felt was a need for writing that word. In short, Nostradamus had no need to write "and" at all, because he used commas more than any other symbol of punctuation. However, he did have a need to write "*And*", as a sign to separate by additional space, as a sign to make multiple connections within the whole. Therefore, an ampersand is not a symbol that simply means, "and", it is a sign that is synonymous with "*And*", complete with its multiplicity of purpose.

By making this statement, I mean that an ampersand is a signal to the reader that one must act as if a period was just encountered, causing the need for a full stop (long pause), and reflection on what has just been stated. This separation, as an ending point, is then followed by the need to recognize the symbolized form of "*Et*" is being expressed, where the symbol lends the power of capitalization (as if "*And*" were written) to the following word. As such, an ampersand generates the equivalence of capitalization, because the separation of segments begins a new line of thought. Finally, once that new line of thought is understood, the ampersand then acts to connect the words surrounding it (two linking segments), yielding the combined form as one additional thought. This means an ampersand first separates into the singular, second addresses importance to that singular through capitalization, and then third, conjoins two as one, allowing both sets surrounding the ampersand to act as if an important "*AND*" was then in effect between them.

This is like the use of the spelled out and capitalized "*Et*", but not exactly. There is a difference, which is the reason "*Et*" is spelled, rather than symbolized. Certainly, one would not expect to see a "sentence" begun with a symbol, but there is more to the spelling than that. The capitalized first word of a line stands for the direction that an entire line takes, with that direction relative to the other lines in the quatrain, particularly those preceding it. In many cases, the first word of a line will be that line's only capitalized word, thus the only word expressing as a higher sense (multiplicity of meaning, plus the ability to assume or pass on emphasis). Therefore, the first word conjunction influences, minimally, one other line, if not two or three. The ampersand, as a mid-line representation of a capitalized conjunction, only serves the information contained within its line.

To diagram this difference, it should be easier to comprehend the greater significance of a spelled out and capitalized "*Et*". Using the example of "*Et*" appearing as the first word of line four, it maps out as such:

Line one	"*And*" Line four,	as:	Additional information to the main theme.
Line two	"*And*" Line four,	as:	Direct supporting detail to the secondary theme.
Line three	"*And*" Line four,	as:	Sequential additional information to main theme supporting detail.
Line four	"*And*" Line four,	as:	Lead director for separate thought.

The number of lines a first word "*And*" connects to is then relative to its placement in the quatrain. A second line placement would combine it with the information relative to the main theme, while directing the secondary theme as an additional separate thought. In any case, "*Et*" has the power of connecting multiple lines. An ampersand is restricted to the line in which it appears. The diagram for the use of an ampersand in one line is then linear, with all being relative to that line, as:
"Prior sequence   &   following sequence".

- Marker for sequence leading to "&" to be read as having reached a full stop, denoting a self-contained thought has ended.
- Marker for sequence following "&" to be read as a separate self-contained thought (lower case).
- Marker causing first word following "&" to act as capitalized, denoting importance to that which follows.
- Marker to join word(s) before "&" with word(s) after "&", as "one *AND* another".

This profound symbol must be fully understood. Due to its prolific presence in the quatrains and letters, a wealth of meaning is lost when one simply sees an ampersand as a simple conjunction, as "one and another". Additionally, the simplicity of such a combination leads to mistranslation and misinterpretation.

In a religious course I have taken, I learned that a major characteristic of Hebrew poetry was parallelism. This characteristic is particularly evident in the poetic oracles of the prophets. These poems differ from English poetry due to a multiplicity of rhythmic stresses, which can be difficult to translate fully. In the instruction manual for that course, I read the following observation made, about Hebrew poetry:

> "Verses are made up of two or more statements that (a) repeat the same thought though in different words, (b) compare thoughts so as to bring out some inherent relationship between them, or (c) contrast them."[188]

---

188   Education for Ministry course, Sewanee, the University of the South, School of Theology, 2006, Parallel Guide 26, p434.

While this explanation of prophetic Hebrew poetry is not a precise match for the prophetic Christian poetry of a 16th century Frenchman, of Jewish descent (i.e. Nostradamus), it is the essence of multiplicity that comes from the same higher mind source (i.e. God). The ampersand causes the same words to be repeated with different words. As a word of conjunction, it establishes important inherent relationships otherwise missed; and it creates a comparison-contrast through the joining of two words together.

I offer this as a way for one to see, again, that the person Nostradamus is not to be expected to have planned such multiplicity of meaning in one symbol. None of the systems Nostradamus employed was his personally constructed devices, and none is purely unique to *The Prophecies*. Much of these systems can be applied to Biblical texts, with equally amazing results. I see the system relative to ampersand use as God's ways of making a simple mark expand minimal word use into a depth of meaning.

While explanations of this nature are well and good, a demonstration of this application of use is usually better than a description of this meaning. I will then interpret examples of how ampersands work, from both the quatrains and the letters. I will give examples of a quatrain using only one ampersand, then show one where two ampersands are found. I will also give an example of an ampersand use from each letter. Every example will show the same application as I have described. There are no examples where this meaning is not applied. Every ampersand can be depended on to act in the same way.

There is no need to bring in a new quatrain at this point to discuss ampersand applications. I have already presented several with ampersands, although the focus was not on that mark's meaning. Let me now take one's focus back to the example I used earlier, where I discussed some of the attributes of the fifty-third quatrain found in *Centurie First*. The first line of that quatrain contains an ampersand, and that is the only appearance of an ampersand in that quatrain. The line states, "*La loy du Sol, & Venus contendens,*" which translates to read, "*There law of the Sun, & Venus contending ones*".

With the ampersand producing a full stop, such that what leads to that full stop acts as its own statement, we see this unfolding different ways. First, "*La*" is written as a separate word, such that it can be read as "*There*". As a capitalized noun[189], "*There*" represents an important place to be referenced, which means one can expect "*There*" to be identified soon after. Second, when "*La*" is seen as a capitalized article ("*The*"), we see the transfer of capitalization power going to the following word, "*law*". Rather than "*The law*", we find "*the Law*", or "*THE Law*", making this an important "*Law*" governing "*There*". Since we have discussed the system of capitalization, such that a higher-level meaning comes to capitalized word, one can expect "*THE Law*" to be the "*Law*" of God, given to Moses. Thus, "*There*" is identified as a place where Mosaic "*Law*" is important.

Once one has made these realizations, we see that the remainder of the statement pertains to further identifying "*There*", the place obedient to Mosaic "*Law*". Here we find a preposition-article combination

---

189   The noun definition of "*there*" is, "That place or point.", as defined by The Free Dictionary by Farlex.

("*du*"), which is directional ("*to, from, of,* or *with*") in reference to "*the Sun*". This means "*the Sun*" has to be seen as representing something other than the physical sun, because that sun is too hot to live on, much less live to obey "*the Law*" of Moses. To make this task easier, I will inform you that Nostradamus often used "*the Sun*" as a metaphor for Jesus Christ (this will be explained in another system). Therefore, "*There*" is where "*the Law*" of Moses is relative "*to the Son*" of God. This identifies "*There*" as a place where Christianity reigns. This eliminates Israel, but identifies all nations where the majority populations deem themselves to be Christian; and this is primarily "the West", where "*the Sun*" figuratively sets.

Following the ampersand, one then addresses the separate line of thought that states, "*Venus contending ones*". Again, there are different ways to interpret this statement. First, "*Venus*" is not the planet we see in either the morning or evening sky. It too is a metaphor. For expediency sake, "*Venus*" is a reference to Islam, where pre-Islamic religion believed Allah had three daughters, one of which, Al-Uzza, is considered the "*Venus*" of Mecca. This means "*Islam*" will be "*contending*", such that those people in Muslim lands will be struggling, striving in opposition, or competing. As a separate statement, following an ampersand, the "*contending*" is only relative to "*Venus*", or "*Islam*".

Second, the word "*venu*" is the past participle of the irregular French verb, "*venir*", which means, "*to come*." Thus, there is the possibility that "*Venus*" is stating a major arrival of "*ones*" who "*came*" for the purpose of producing struggle, strife, and competition. One could then see how these two views produce the binocular vision of Muslims "*coming*" to others with a fight, rather than "*contending*" with those "*coming*" to them. Due to the word "*Venus*" already being capitalized, the power of capitalization moves to the following word, "*contendens*", meaning the greatest of all forms of contention is the result, which is war. The capitalization is raising this to the higher-level meaning, which is the history behind a Crusade, or a Holy War, only with the Muslims being the ones who will have "*come*".

When this information is obtained from the separate segments surrounding the ampersand, the line is read as one, as if stating, "*The law with the Sun, AND Venus contending ones*". In this view, there is a literal and a symbolic way to read these words. First, the literal separates "*Sun, AND Venus*" from the line, causing the subject-verb statement to be, "*The law with the contending ones*". This is a statement that each of the "*contending*" parties have "*laws*" on their side, which support their willingness to "*contend*". The "*Law*" is then the separate Holy "*Law*" for each "*the Sun*" (the Ten Commandments and New Testament) "*AND Venus*" (the Koran). This means a Holy War is best waged, with both sides seeing God as on one's side. The ampersand acts to show the importance of both sides "*contending*", while both see God's favor blessing the one and not the other.

Finally, "*the Sun, AND Venus contending*" is an astrological/astronomical statement of timing. When "*contend*" is seen as struggle, "*the Sun*" is seen as a star, and with "*Venus*" called a star (morning or evening - because it so brightly reflects the "*Sun's*" light), "*Venus contending ones*" becomes a time when "*the Sun*" is blocking "*Venus*" from view. This is an aspect known as a conjunction, as both orbs appear to be in the same area of Earth's sky. The *"Law"* of astronomy tells one that *"Venus"* is either behind *"the Sun"*, or in front of it, as viewed geocentrically (from the earth), but because of the bright glare of *"the Sun"* *"Venus"* cannot be seen. All planets are thus *"contending ones"*, when *"the Sun"* blocks their view.

Astrologically, the time of *"Venus"'* conjunction with *"the Sun"* is a time when the ego can override one's sense of peace and beauty. However, this aspect is not a very long-lasting one, certainly not long enough to maintain a Holy War. As far as a significant timing event is concerned, relative to a *"Sun-Venus"* conjunction, it becomes important to realize it is rare to see *"Venus"'* path take it directly in front of *"the Sun"* (as seen from earth's position in orbit). On these rare occasions, the silhouette of *"Venus"* can be seen as a black dot slowly moving across the yellow background of *"the Sun"*. However, this event can only be seen by using the same precautions one would use to view a solar eclipse.

This phenomena is not as frequent as one might imagine, occurring in pairs eight years apart, with long spans of 121.5 years before the first and 105.5 after the second, before it repeats again (a total span of 243 years). There was such a conjunction in 2004 (June 8, lasting 6 hours), with the last such time occurring in December 1882. The second such conjunction of the new millennium will be on June 6, 2012. Following that, the next pair will come in 2117 and 2125.[190]

I must warn anyone about attempts to nail down the timing of Nostradamus' astrological-astronomical clues in his works. All planetary patterns repeat. What will happen at one time will happen at many other times. The point of understanding Nostradamus is not to promote fear of the future, through forecasting such grocery store newspaper headlines as, "Nostradamus says war in 2012!" It is to prevent any possible war from happening, at all times. If it is theoretically possible a war could come in 2012, now is the time to act to cease *"coming contentions"*.

This example is typical of the way a line containing an ampersand, in a quatrain, expands that line's meaning tremendously. It takes a completely symbolic and mostly meaningless main theme line (the first line) when seen as, *"The law of the Sun, and Venus contending,"* and turns it into a multi-dimensional view of the conflict between two religious worlds. Before one begins to proceed to line two, a theme of holy war between east and west is understood. When this quatrain's main theme is compared to the information found in other quatrains, this one line is confirmed as conflict that arose because of the creation of Israel, on land previously known as Palestine.

For instance, the quatrain found listed ninety-seventh in *Centurie Third* has its first two lines stating, (translated) *"New law land new to occupy, / Near there Syria Judea, & Palestine"*. Without fully breaking this quatrain down here, this quatrain is clearly prophesying the recreation of the State of Israel, but not by war. It will be by *"law"*, in particular a *"new law"* never before used, which simply changed the deed of ownership from the Palestinians to the Jews. This *"law"* was enforced by those of *"the Sun"*, as the

---

190   Wikipedia, the free encyclopedia, http://en.wikipedia.org/wiki/Transit_of_Venus

most dominant Western-Christian nations, Great Britain and the United States. Therefore, this quatrain (III – 97) helps confirm all that I have stated about the main theme in the example quatrain (V – 53).

As one can see, when multiple quatrains are interconnected, as links in a chain or pieces in a puzzle, they each get stronger and clearer. The ampersand works in the same manner (microcosm-macrocosm), strengthening the meaning of a line, making that line clearer to understand. Still, there are quatrains that have multiple ampersands; and this acts to compound the meaning, especially when multiple lines have ampersands present.

I have stated that the research of K. Lowey showed 666 ampersands in the edition of *The Prophecies* he observed. That, in itself, means at least 277 quatrains had no ampersand usage whatsoever; but that number increases with each quatrain that has multiple uses. Most quatrains showing ampersand usage only have one ampersand. The above examples (V – 53 and III – 97) are quatrains where each only has one ampersand. Still, a sizable number of quatrain have two uses, including a few with both on the same line. A few have three ampersands present, one with all three on the same line; and at least one that I found (IX – 22) has four ampersands, where one line has none and one line has two. As the number of ampersands increase, so too does the amount of information that can be gained from a fixed (limited) number of words.

To present an example of a quatrain that has multiple ampersands present, I have chosen one with two ampersands. To make it interesting, I have chosen one with the same theme as the two previous examples. Not only will the increased meaning that two ampersands convey be shown, but also one should get a better feel for how all of the quatrains link together in a specific order, based on the themes they present in *The Prophecies*. The quatrain I offer then is the one found as the twenty-fourth in *Centurie Fifth*.

Le regne & loy soubz Venus eslevé,	*The reign & law under Venus elevated,*
Saturne aura sus Jupiter empire :	*Saturn will have upon Jupiter empire:*
La loy & regne par le Soleil levé,	*There law & reign for the Sun risen,*
Par Saturnins endurer le pire.	*By Saturnine ones to endure the worse.*

Before I begin to explain how these ampersands expand within the lines in which they appear, let me focus only on those two lines for a moment. We need to see clearly the parallels at work in this quatrain, remembering we just saw evidence of two quatrains talking about "*New law*" and "*The law of the Sun, & Venus contending ones*". The two lines with ampersands in the example above are as such:

"*Them reign **&** law under Venus elevated,*" is the main theme statement in line one.

"*There law **&** reign for the Sun risen,*" is the supporting details to the main theme, in line three.

One can clearly see that line three is a mirror image to line one. Surrounding the ampersands, *"reign & law"* is inversely reflected in *"law & reign"*. Because both lines are divided into two segments by the ampersands, the divided supporting details also become mirror images of the divided main theme. As such, we find:

- The supporting details for *"Them reign"* (first half of the main theme) is *"There law"* (first half of line three).
- The supporting details for *"law under Venus elevated"* (second half of the main theme) is *"reign for the Sun risen"* (second half of line three).
- The supporting details for *"The reign AND law under Venus elevated"* (the combined form of the main theme) is *"The law AND reign by the Sun risen"* (the combined form of line three).

Seeing this breakdown according to the system of symbols, concerning ampersand use, combined with the line relationships established by the system of order, one sees how expansive an ampersand acts. This is imperative to comprehend now, because when I get into the interpretation of the meaning of this quatrain it can become confusing and difficult to follow. It can become confusing when I interpret from a "whole view" method. I find it helpful to be able to look ahead, or behind in the quatrain, for assistance in understanding a segment that might be too difficult to fathom by itself. However, I will attempt to explain as well as I can each step taken, in breaking down this two-ampersand quatrain.

Let me also make it clear that the relationships I mapped out above can only be transferable to those quatrains with two ampersands, one in the first line, and one in the third line. That is an A1-A2 relationship, main theme to supporting details of the main theme. A quatrain with one ampersand in the first line, but a second ampersand in the fourth line, an A1-B2 relationship, would not have the same relationship patterns. The same can be said for any two-ampersand quatrain where lines one and three are not the pattern. With that disclaimer made, it is time to interpret quatrain V – 24.

Line one begins with the segment stating, *"Le regne,"* which becomes a complete statement, because of the presence of an ampersand following the word *"regne"*. This translates most phonetically similar in English as, *"The reign"*, but a better translation than *"reign"* is available. An alternate word makes a more important statement, as one sees when realizing the word *"regne"* can translate as, *"realm, kingdom; sovereign rule, dominion, or government"*, in addition to *"reign"*.[191]

This assortment of translations works much better, particularly when *"The kingdom"* is seen to transform into *"the Kingdom"*, or even better as *"THE Kingdom"*. When this is then read with the higher sense that capitalization brings, *"THE Kingdom"* is relative to God's *"kingdom"*, as in the Lord's Prayer, which

---

[191] Randal Cotgrave's 1611 French-English Dictionary, http://www.pbm.com/~lindahl/cotgrave/search/804l.html

states, "Thy *kingdom* come". However, knowing *The Prophecies* holds an overall warning for humanity, to prevent the need for Christ to return, when "*the **K**ingdom*" of God will mesh with earth, that is not the meaning of this quatrain's main theme.

The earthly "***K****ingdom*" of God is the Promised Land, where Moses led the children of Israel. Thus, the first half of the main theme statement is about "*The Dominion*", which becomes defined as the "territory or sphere of influence or control",[192] coming from the Latin word, *dominium*, meaning "property". This identifies that land given by God to the descendants of Abraham, Isaac, and Jacob. We are first being told about "*The Government*" of that land, which had ceased to exist well before Nostradamus' time, not to reappear until 1948. The two words, "*Le regne*", speaks loudly, telling all of the history of a land: the belief of a birthright for land ownership given by God; a land, since the Exile, being far from "*The Kingdom*" of David and Solomon; and a legal matter over ownership of that land.

Following the ampersand, one reads, "*loy soubz Venus eslevé,*" or "*law under Venus elevated*". This immediately brings the focus to the legal issues over land ownership, where "*law*" indicates how "*The Kingdom*" returned to its glory. Through the connection to the quatrain stating, "*Novel law land new to occupy*" (quatrain III – 97), one sees that the "*Novel law*" was the United Nations turning over Palestine to Jewish settlers, for the re*new*al of the "*land*" Israel. Nostradamus saw this takeover as an "*occupation*", meaning there was not a war for the "*land*", nor a surrender of the "*land*". The Jews would "*occupy*" Palestine and rename it Israel.

This is then where the ampersand acts as capitalizing "*loy*", as beginning a new statement, as the second half of the main theme. This makes it become the "*Law*", which is a higher "*Law*" than is "*law*". It was the "*law*" of man that gave Palestinian "*land*" to "*occupiers*", making it the "*new land*" Israel. It was the "*law*" of Palestine that was turned "*under*", making it "*beneath*" the "*law*" of the United Nations charter and the initial "*law*" of the "*Government*" of Israel. In the capitalized form, "*Law*", the issue of legality is then based on a belief that God deeds ownership.

This works two ways. First, "*Law*" is the Mosaic "*Law*", where Moses told the children of Israel, "If you follow my "*Law*" you will be My people forever." Second, however, "*Law*" is equally the Islamic "*Law*" that "*Governs*" all Arab "*lands*". This is the "*Law under Venus*", with "*Venus*" understood to be the daughter of Allah.

Once one moves beyond the element of "*Law*", one finds that "*Venus*" is "*beneath*", or "*under*" some legal obligation. This means Muslims, or Arabs (Palestinians) who are still in the "*land*" of their ancestors, are "*under*" the "*law*" of the new Israeli state, and seen as "*beneath*" the status of Jews, because citizenship in what was formerly Palestine could then only be enjoyed by Jews. Thus, Palestinians (Arabs) are to be "*underlings*", if they are to remain on what was once their "*land*", due to the return of Jewish "*rule*"

---

[192] The Free Dictionary by Farlex, http://www.thefreedictionary.com/dominion

The System of Symbols

having "*elevated*" their people from wanderers, to "*new land*" owners.

The issue that will lead to the prophetic state when "*Venus*" will be "*contending ones*" (from quatrain V – 53) is then found to be the timing of when "*Venus*" will itself be "*elevated*". In 1948, following a long war that involved the whole world (WWII), particularly after several nations in the Arab world favored the Nazis (due to their anti-Semitic views), the nations of the Middle East were weak in strength. The "*novel law*" of the United Nations, recreating a "*land*" that had historically existed, made a "*new*" Israel (quatrain III – 97), but that did not come without armed resistance.

A civil war broke out in Palestine in 1947, following the United Nations announcement for a Partition Plan for Palestine. The Arabs rejected this idea violently. The Arab nations supporting Palestine officially declared war in 1948, but with Israeli military leader Ben-Gurion having foreseen this coming, in 1946, arming Jewish fortifications through secret deals with the West, "*the Sun*", the Arabs capitulated in 1949. Wars were later fought in 1956 (the Sinai War), 1967 (the Six Day War), and between 1968 and 1970 (the War of Attrition), before the Palestinians began to regularly turn to terrorism as a means for "*elevating*" their plight for the whole world to view.

The time when "*Venus*" will truly become "*elevated*", as an influence against total Western support for Israel, will begin after the terrorism displayed on the public stage of the 1972 Munich Olympics. Israel will face yet another war in 1973 (the Yom Kippur War), followed immediately by an OPEC oil embargo, because of the United States support of Israel in the Yom Kippur War. This created the oil crisis of 1973, and "*elevated*" the power the Arabs held, through the West's growing dependency on oil.

This first effect, caused by an "*elevated Venus*", is still not the primary focus of this half of this quatrain's main theme, although it does signal the beginning of that rise in power. The main focus is that an issue has been "*raised*" (the artificial creation of the State of Israel), which will never be lowered, until Palestine is returned to the Arabs who had their land stolen, "*under*" the guise of "*law*". The success found in the 1973 oil embargo allowed the Muslim world to realize it will have to become "*elevated*" to the level of power held by the West. From a position of increased wealth, power could be purchased, in order to use the force of war to physically remove the "*occupiers*". Just as Ben-Gurion bought the weapons necessary to defeat the ill-equipped Arab nations, "*Venus*" would use oil money to become just so "*elevated*".

When the whole of line one is then read in the combined form, as "*The government AND law under Venus elevated,*" one see how Israel is a non-Muslim nation, amid nothing but Muslim nations. It has thus been injected "*under*" the skin of the Muslim world, as a satellite for the West. World War II proved the importance of oil in a modern, mechanized world, with the world's richest deposits of oil being "*beneath*" Arab "*land*". The West would not go to the lengths it went to, legalizing the theft of "*land*", supporting "*The government*" of Israel, had it not been for a weakening of "*The government AND law*" of Great Britain.

The British had been mandated (a League of Nations designation) protector of Palestine, after the Ottoman Empire surrendered its possessions as a settlement ending World War I. The Turkish "*dominion*" over Palestine, Syria, Jordan, Mesopotamia (Iraq), and Lebanon had gone "*under*". At that time, "*Venus*" fell "*under*" Western (French and British) "*government AND law*". However, both England and France were made "*beneath*" their past abilities to control their possessions, due to the costs of a world war. Great Britain recognized they would have to relinquish all of its holding to independence, thus "*Venus*" would be "*elevated*" to its own "*governments AND laws*".

Due to the power of the West being so dependant on oil, "*The law of the Sun*" (quatrain V – 53) would have to be maintained in the Middle East, through the mutual support of an Israeli "*land*" that would be nothing like the old Israel, but a "*new*" version designed to get "*beneath Venus*" and "*under*mine" their "*government AND law*". This would assure that the West would retain their post-World War II "*elevated*" position, as the world's most dominant nations.

As one can see, the ampersand expands the seemingly simple statement, "*The rule and law under Venus raised,*" from a meaningless statement about a metaphoric "*Venus*", to one of great depth, full of all the richness of the 20th century history in the Middle East. In case one has any doubt as to how this meaning can be brought forth, the parallel ampersand line, where the supporting details to the main theme are found, offers the support that makes it easier to understand.

Skipping over line two's secondary theme for now, it is best to see how line three acts in support to the main themes surrounding Israel, the West, and the Middle East. The first half of the third line also acts as a complete statement, due to the ampersand calling for a full stop. This leaves one with only "*La loy*", or "*The law*". These are the same first two words from the quatrain found fifty-third in *Centurie Fifth*, which states, "*The law of the Sun, & Venus contending ones*". When I went over the meaning of that line that includes an ampersand, I explained how "*the Law*" was also "*THE Law*", the higher sense "*Law*" of Moses. Thus, as the supporting details for the first half of the main theme, "*The Kingdom*" is verified as being the unified "*Kingdom*" of David.

The second half of line three then states, "*reign for the Sun risen*". This then becomes the supporting details for the second half of the main theme, "*law under Venus elevated*". The word translated as "*risen*" or "*raised*" ("*levé*") can also translate as "*advanced*", or "*grown up*". This is then supportive of the new power held by the United States, as the son of the British, particularly as the dominant power behind the formation of the United Nations in 1945. With Great Britain having had to relinquish its control over Middle Eastern affairs, the "*reign by the Sun*" (an important Christian nation) had "*advanced*". Thus, the "*rise*" of the United States is explaining the "*law*" that created Israel.

The United States swayed the "*law*" that placed a satellite to be "*under*" its "*rule*", as a subversive element "*beneath*" Muslim oil interests. American interests would be protected through an "*elevated*" presence, due to the "*elevated*" importance of Arab oil, which had "*elevated Venus*" to the most strategic hot spot on the planet. However, it would be America's obvious sabotage of Islamic "*Law*", the supplying of Israel with "*advanced*" military weaponry, and the "*elevation*" of puppet "*rules*" through "*under*handed" means, that would cause Muslims to have "*elevated*" hatred for the United States, as the Great Satan.

The combined form of line three then is seen to be, "*The law AND government through the Sun levied*". This is a statement of the costs of America's involvement in the Middle East. The alternate translation of "*levé*", as "*levied*", brings a meaning relative to, "declaring and waging war; the confiscation of property, especially in accordance with a legal judgment; and the money, property, and troops levied."[193] America would pass "*laws*" that would send yearly defense (military) assistance to Israel ($2.4 billion/year).[194] This would cause the Israeli "*government*" to act "*for the Sun*", or have America act "*through*" Israeli agents.

As the supporting details for the combined form main theme, "*The rule AND law under Venus elevated,*" it is evident that the control once afforded the British "*rule AND law*" in Middle Eastern affairs is passed on to "*the Son*", America. "*The Kingdom AND Law*" of a new Empire has been born. Just as Palestine was a strategic jewel for the Assyrians, Babylonians, Persians, Greeks, Romans, and Turks, where the religions of the people were never quelled, as long as subservience to domination resulted, the British and Americans became the latest in a long line of "*Rule AND Law*" over Arabs.

This element of empirical "*Rule AND Law*" is not something without its own support in this quatrain. The secondary theme of line two states, "*Saturn will have upon Jupiter empire*". Without getting deep into the symbolic meaning behind "*Saturn*" and "*Jupiter*", the last word, a colon follows "empire", making line three become a clarification of the use of that word. That makes the example of line three, due to the presence of an ampersand there, act on three levels of clarification. There is an "*empire*" through "*The Law*" (Judaism). There is an "*empire*" through the "*Rule by the risen Son*" (Christianity); and there is an "*empire*" through "*The Law AND Rule of the Sun advanced*" (the United States of America).

To state briefly the esoteric meaning of "*Saturn*" and "*Jupiter*", they represent opposing principles. "*Saturn*" is called the "Greater Malefic," because in the times of Nostradamus "*Saturn*" represented the harbinger of hard times. "*Jupiter*", on the other hand, is called the "Greater Benefic," which is due to it being representative of times of wealth, growth, and expansion. Thus, the secondary theme is stating there will be an "*Expansive, Wealthy empire*", which are terms that could be used to describe the wealth and growth of America. However, with "*Saturn*" seen to be "*upon Jupiter*", this is a statement of hardship caused to and by the "*empire*". This "*Saturn*" hardship is directly related to the "*Venus elevated*" aspect of the main theme in line one.

---

193   The Free Dictionary by Farlex, http://www.thefreedictionary.com/levied
194   American Free Press, Aug. 15, 2007, "US envoy signs 30-billion-dollar Israel arms package" article.

The fourth line, which offers the supporting details to the secondary theme of line two, then states, "*By Saturnine ones to endure the worse.*" The use of "*Saturnine*", which is a word derived from "*Saturn*", is generally known to mean, "Having or marked by a tendency to be bitter or sardonic." The word "sardonic" is then defined as meaning, "Scornfully or cynically mocking." As such, the capitalization identifies a people (rather than a small group), who have this quality about then, forced to "*endure the worse.*" This allows one to see the Palestinians being representative of such bitter and scornful people, for having had their land stolen, cast into a state of exile.

These are also Muslims, in the broader sense of the meaning, as their "*Law*" calls for more restrictions (with both "*Law*" and restriction being words attributed to "*Saturn's*" realm), than the good-natured "*Law*" of "*the Sun*". Their willingness to patiently resist, as a constant thorn in the side of this "*Expansive empire*" in their midst, will allow them the perfect nature to "*endure*" the taxes "*levied*" by foreign "*occupiers*". While there will be punishment to "*endure*" (another term attributed to "*Saturn*"), both sides will feel the pain, with both sides stubbornly "*enduring*". The question this quatrain leaves the reader is, "Who will "*endure the worse*"? To date, this appears to have been the Palestinians.

I hope that I have been able to demonstrate the compounded depth multiple ampersands bring to the quatrains. Without an ampersand, each line contains words that can have multiple applications, which is the most basic way to find depth of meaning from a limited number of words. However, the ampersand is like raising that number to another power, with each word still having its depth, only multiplied. This depth takes away all argument of vagueness, and reveals concrete meaning to what appears to be a simple poem.

Because a quatrain is a poem, it seems odd to think that an ampersand acts as an indent or paragraph break. In a quatrain, an ampersand always comes in the middle of a line. Even with my interpretation being broken into paragraphs of explanation, based on the transitions of thought coming from the words, punctuation, and symbols, it does not seem the poem itself is dictating those breaks. The poetic style and format seems fixed, with me being the one dividing it all up and explaining it. That is not the case, which will be more clearly demonstrated when I give an example of how an ampersand plays in the letters.

The letters are different, in the sense that the text appears to be extremely long-winded. Due to this, unlike the quatrains, the "sentences" of the letters are vastly in need of being broken down into digestible bits of information. The shortage of periods makes it seem as if Nostradamus rambled to wherever his mind took him, never once giving much consideration as to whether or not anyone could follow his train of thought. Other than one indent found, separating a small, last portion of the text, from the bulk of the letter to Henry II, Nostradamus wrote mostly long blocks of words, accompanied by unintelligible punctuation. This style, unlike the quatrains' poetic divisions, into neat segments of four lines, screams out for someone to do something to make it an easier task to comprehend.

That is where ampersands come into play. On a page from any of the oldest copies of *The Prophecies*, where the letters are present, the typeset used to denote an ampersand is quite noticeable. With periods being few and far between, the ampersand becomes visible as the separators of continuously flowing text. While that is the illusion, the reality is they do act to separate thoughts, emphasize that which follows, and conjoin thoughts together.

I will present two examples; each representing one of the places Nostradamus used ampersands in the letters. From the Preface, I have chosen a complete string of words, incorporating punctuation and ampersands, which begins with a capitalized first word and ends in a period. This is the only such example where a manageable number of words (39) appear as a relatively normal "sentence," complex as that number ordinarily would be. From the letter to Henry, I have also chosen an example that represents a mere segment of what flows between capitalized first word and period. Due to this letter being in need of reordering, one cannot look for capitalized first words and periods being together in the same section, much less the same "sentence." I demonstrated this previously, where the biblical references in the Henry letter proved this, by being disconnected. When these examples have been presented, ampersands will be shown to all work the same.

For the first example, Nostradamus wrote in his Preface the following series of words:

> "*Que possible fera retirer le front à quelques uns, en voyant si longue entension, & par soubz toute la concavité de la Lune aura lieu & intelligence: & ce entendant universellement par toute la terre les causes, mon filz.*"

This translates literally to state:

> "*That possible will cause to entertain the forehead to some ones, in seeing so extended perceptions, & for beneath all the concavity to the Moon will have place & intelligence: & this knowing universally by all the earth the causes, my son.*"

This, in this condition, makes little sense to most people initially, including myself. Certainly, it has been taken out of context. I make that statement because order is present in the Preface, which allows for context, although that context is difficult to keep a handle on. The words themselves seem to make some sense (due to me selecting translations that make that possible), but part of the reason it makes little sense is the overall writing. The Preface is written in the same manner as the quatrains, where there is a lack of syntax.

It may be easier for some to adjust to poetry being free of rules, but the Preface (and the Henry letter) is presented in block letter form, making it seem more like prose, and thus in need of syntax. As close to prose as this letter may seem, it is no different from the quatrains. Each word must be examined individually, before connecting it to other words. The mind's struggle adjusting to the words in the letters is due to it seeing a problem in the presentation style. To solve this problem, the answer is rather simple. One needs to transform the letter into a more poetic format, making the lack of syntax appear more consistent with the quatrains.

The way to make this transformation, while staying true to the written word's order and marks, is to write the letter as self-sufficient individual lines, just as a quatrain is self-sufficient individual lines. While the quatrains have some self-sufficient lines that contain no punctuation at all, that luxury is not afforded to the letters. In the letters, each self-sufficient line is segmented by marks on both ends, or a capitalized first word (following a period mark) leading to a mark: comma, colon, semi-colon, ampersand, or period. The ampersand then clearly shows its role as a separator-enhancer-joiner.

To demonstrate this segmenting into a more poetic style, the above translation of a small part of the Preface transforms as follows. Please notice that the only changes are those of presentation. All contents remain unchanged.

That possible will cause to entertain the forehead to some ones,
in seeing so extended perceptions,
& for beneath all the concavity to the Moon will have place
& intelligence:
& this knowing universally through all the earth the causes,
my son.

One will note that three "lines" of this section from the Preface begin with ampersands. This acts as a period, to show two segments of words as separate lines of thoughts, the line of thought before the ampersand, and the line of thought after it. It then acts to emphasize the line of thought following the ampersand, which is why the ampersands above are shown leading their lines. This yields the importance of capitalization onto the first word, as if the line began with "*Et*". Those first words then carry both the mundane meaning and higher sense values capitalization brings. Lastly, the ampersand acts to join both lines of thought surrounding the ampersand as one, as symbolizing the word "AND", with the two words surrounding the ampersand seen as conjoined by the word "and".

Because an ampersand is always in the middle of two lines of thought, any examples given would have to begin with a series of words that lead to an ampersand. This means that for one to see how the ampersands bring out its full effects, one has to understand the train of thought leading up to one. In the example I have chosen, there are two lines of thought leading to the first ampersand, with the first line of thought a completely independent series, which leads to the second line of thought. In order to keep the focus on the power of the ampersand, as a symbol designed to direct the reader to depth of meaning, I will briefly summarize the first independent line. This will establish, essentially, what the main theme statement is for the "sentence" segment.

Just as in a quatrain, where the first line states the main theme, similar themes are stated in the letters. A capitalized first word (following a period) introduces a series of words that present a topic, from which punctuation and ampersands mark the separate threads of thought connected to that topic. The first series of words in the example from the Preface act in this way. However, the "sentence" structure of the letter to Henry II is out of order.

In the letter to Henry II, the capitalized first words (following a period) show where topics are presented, but those topics are separated from their supporting detail statements. Instead, most have been combined with the supporting details written for other topics; and due to the length of some "sentences," more than one topic can be represented between a capitalized first word and the next period. The ampersand usage plays a role in determining where to divide these "sentences" into "missing pieces" that need the correct mate to which to attach.

I have chosen the shortest "sentence" in the Preface as the example, because it is short and includes ampersands. Since I have already explained the rarity of periods in that document, it should come as somewhat of a surprise that this example only breaks into six pieces. However, the seeming shortness of this example does not mean one can quickly explain the whole meaning.

It will be good to remember the matrix method I discussed previously. Each word written by Nostradamus was specifically chosen to serve the role of bringing with it more than one meaning. In the poetry of the quatrains, a meter seems present in the ABAB rhyme scheme. This is absent after the breakdown of the "sentences" into a series of lines. One string of words can be rather numerous, before a mark of some kind signals an end to that line of thought. The longer the string is, and the more numerous the word count, the more the complexity grows, from each word bearing multiple translation possibilities.

Consider the one line that I will sum up briefly, before beginning to breakdown the meaning of the line that follows, which leads to the first ampersand. With all of the possibilities of translation being given equal opportunity to express, I will be producing a summary from a staggering 2,280,960 potential word combinations. The math can be seen at the bottom of each row on the matrix that follows.

Que	possible	fera	retirer	le	front	à	quelques	uns
That	likely	will do	to retire to	the	the forehead	at	some ones	ones
Which	possible	will act	withdraw	him (m)	the brow	in	any ones	some
Whom	may be	will make	to take back	her (f)	the front of something	to	whosoever ones	
Who		will exploit will	to gather up to	them	the forepart of something	with	somewhat ones	
Then		perform will	recover to bring	it				
Unless		commit	back to					
Because		will work	shorten to					
Except		will cause	contract					
Partly		will form	to shrink					
		will forge will	to receive to					
		compose will	entertain					
		fashion						
9	3	12	11	5	4	4	4	2
9	27	324	3,564	17,820	71,280	285,120	1,140,480	2,280,960

Now, let me state that this calculation is much higher than the reality, although the potential is there. Several of the possible translations I see as unnecessary to apply, because they state the same meaning, only slightly differently. If I was to limit my interpretation of the first word to only one possibility, do likewise for the final two words, and then limited all the other words to just two possible choices, the result would still come to 64 combinations (1x2x2x2x2x2x2x1x1). However it is calculated, the result is considerably more ways to look at, *"Que possible fera retirer le front à quelques uns"* than simply, *"That possible will cause to entertain the forehead to some ones"*.

The matrix is a tool to assist one seeking to learn how to read Nostradamus. I do not use one personally, as it is time consuming to create such a work for each line of words from the letters, as arranged in the breakdown of a segment.[195] I base my interpretations on a word-by-word approach, understanding the definitions of each translation possibility, feeling how those connect to the next group of possibilities. While a matrix is useful, I utilize going back and forth between screens, on my computer.

From my viewing the relevant context (text leading to this segment), and definitions relative to the example's possible translations presented in the whole of the first line (nine French words – roughly 15 translated English words), I see the line making a statement that acts to explain *The Prophecies* as being from a divine source. This is then consistent to the theme of the Preface, which as the foreword is generally presenting *The Prophecies* as known (by Nostradamus) to be an uncommon work, from a holy source.

---

195 Segment is defined as: All words between a capitalized first word and an ending period. A line is then each series of words, ended by either comma, colon, semi-colon, ampersand, or period.

To summarize this first series of words generally, Nostradamus stated a foreseen inability for people to figure out *The Prophecies*. He predicts that groupthink will prevail, with most people attempting to build a "box" within which to place himself and his writings. This is particularly relative to a statement made just prior to the beginning of this segment, where it appears Nostradamus made a specific prediction about, "*the year 3797*". Thus, because "*That*" is seen "*possible*" to conceive, it "*will cause*" those fretting over the meaning of Nostradamus to think the eventual End Time to be well into the future. Nostradamus knew that his writing that number would have the effect of misleading, immediately causing him to explain that something else was the meaning of that information.

He explained "*That*" ("*the year 3797*") would "*entertain*" (translation of "*retirer*") most, while the actual time found to be relative to *The Prophecies* will "*shorten*" "*That*" projection considerably. When "*the forehead*", or the frontal lobe's conscious processing capabilities, is the only way one looks at Nostradamus, the result will be "*to receive*" (translation of "*retirer*") false conclusions. As such, one cannot think one's way to solving Nostradamus, as one would think to solve a numeric equation. Only with God's assistance, with "*him*" at "*the forepart*" of one's thoughts, "*some ones*" will become wise enough "*to retire*" (translation of "*retirer*") the "*3797*" idea.

I recommend playing with the possibilities that are listed in the matrix on your own. It is important to see how other combinations work for you, along this theme. Certainly, much more can be written, but that is not the primary focus now, for this line summarized above has no connection to an ampersand. The primary focus is to demonstrate how an ampersand's role expands the meaning of a fixed number of words.

It is important to know that line summarized, as the first line of a series of lines, is the "topic statement" line. The topic of this series is then that Nostradamus will be misinterpreted without God's help. The rest of the lines in the series can then be expected to support this topic. This is why I included the whole segment, rather than beginning in mid-segment. However, at this point it is best to make a disclaimer about summarizing.

A summarization is made by one person, one who has done the work necessary to understand what can then be reduce into a condensed version. While this works well in many areas of study, it becomes problematic with Nostradamus. It is problematic because I (so far) seem to be the only person who understands how to read *The Prophecies*. When I make summaries, as I just have, it can be difficult for some (if not most) to follow. This is why I have compared understanding Nostradamus to viewing a *Magic Eye* stereogram. I can tell people what can be seen in the picture, but until they see it for themselves, a summary does not have the same effect.

An ampersand does have basic functions, as I have explained. I have explained how they work in a quatrain, and I have stated that all ampersands work the same in the letters. Therefore, there is no reason to summarize how the three ampersands affect the meaning of this example segment from the Preface. The summary was made when I stated they all work the same.

From this point on, the explanation of ampersand usage will represent only a part of the whole interpretation of the rest of this series. In order to best bring out the function of an ampersand, the words leading up to and surrounding an ampersand must be analyzed deeper than a summary allows. At this stage of this book, a book designed to explain the systems that make understanding Nostradamus possible, some application is necessary.

This application may be difficult to follow completely at first, as one could very easily get lost. I will move slowly through the remainder of this "sentence" from the Preface, as the remainder of this series of lines surrounds the three ampersands. Nostradamus must be read slowly due to this need to grasp fully how each word relates to the words surrounding it. I will try to be as brief as possible, but that could add to the confusion. In that case, this section may need to be read more than once, with references made to the matrices I will include. At the end of this example's interpretation, I will then summarize the ampersand use, based on that interpretive work.

Once the segment's main topic has been revealed, we find that the first line ends with a comma. This is a directional punctuation mark, meaning this line of thought ends. Remembering that the system of punctuation tells one to see all marks of punctuation as a sign of transition, the presence of a comma here acts to end the first line with a period's full stop. The comma is then only a sign of how to proceed to the next line. It symbolizes a related thought will follow, as sequential, while free to go in any direction relative to the topic.

In the second line, Nostradamus wrote, "*en voyant si longue entension,*" which can translate as, "*in seeing so extended perceptions*". In this series, the word "*entension*" is translated as being a state (*-ion* ending) relative to the verb "*entendre*".[196] That translates as, "*to understand, conceive, apprehend, perceive, judge of;* also *to learn* or *hear*; *to have notice, get intelligence,* or *come by the knowledge of.*"[197] Therefore, as the act or process, result of such act or process, or the state or condition of "*entendre*", "*entension*" means "*understanding, conception, apprehension, perception, judgment, learning, recognition, education,* and/or *awareness*". All of this meaning comes despite the fact that "*entension*" is not a true word in French. It is a manufactured word, designed to show those states. Context will show that it is not a misspelled word, one reflecting a state of intent ("*intention*"), a state of lengthening ("*extention*", or "*extension*", or "*étension*"), or a state of strain ("*en tension*"). The word "*entension*" means a state of "*conception*",

196   The 1555 Bonhomme edition, the 1557 Budapest edition, as well as one 1566 Pierre Rigaud Lyon edition, all show the word *extension*, such that *longue extension* would mean "longer than long," or "*long extended longer.*" Another 1566 Pierre Rigaud Lyon edition shows, "*intension,*" which is not a word, just as *entension* is not a pure word. However, the 1557 Utrecht edition, and the 1568 Benoist Rigaud edition clearly show *entension*.
197   Randal Cotgrave's 1611 French-English Dictionary, http://www.pbm.com/~lindahl/cotgrave/search/3691.html

synonymous with that which produces *ideas*.

en	voyant	si	longue	entension
in into at on upon	seeing viewing perceiving beholding	so if yes	long tall slim extended out-stretched continual tedious wearisome much great large	understanding conception apprehension perception judgment learning recognition education awareness
5	4	3	11	9
5	20	60	660	5,940

The first word of the second line is the preposition "*en*", which acts as a direction to follow. This direction is relative to "*some ones*", which ended the first line. The word "*en*" then can translate as, "*in, into, at, on,* or *upon*", which applies to the human beings finding knowledge "*possible*". One is then directed to focus initially on an "*inner*" presence in line two, which as far as thought about *The Prophecies* is concerned is either a mental concept, as "*in the forehead*", or a spiritual concept, as "*in some one's*" heart and soul. The presence of God coming "*into some ones*" is then what allows "*some*" understanding of *The Prophecies*.

Both of these relate paths to understanding relate to how the eyes will be "*seeing*" the meaning coming from "*some*" individual quatrains ("*ones*"), or "*some*" information in the Preface (like "*the year 3797*"). In this sense, "*seeing*" is believing, with "*voyant*" meaning, "*viewing, seeing, perceiving,* or *beholding*". One's beliefs are based on how one "*sees*" what one "*sees*". The biological function of sight is then "*seen*" as an occipital lobe-controlled function (back of the head), where the meaning of what one "*sees*" is then processed by the "*forehead's*" frontal lobe.

This means that what "*some ones*" are "*seeing in*" their minds ("*foreheads*") is representative of what they think they see, more than being representative of what they actually see. In essence, "*in seeing*" is a statement in itself, of what will be "*perceived*" (alternate translation of "*voyant*") from *The Prophecies*. Perception is generally based on information gained from one or more of the direct (physical) senses (as opposed to the "sixth sense"), in this case "*seeing*", specifically that which is "*seen*" while reading. Reading is an automatic response trained into the brain, such that a written text sets off the automatic cerebral functions, which inserts syntax where none is present.

This is confirming the theory that what actually is meant in the written words of Nostradamus would be overruled by what is *"perceived"* to be meant. In that case, *"perceiving"* is not *"seeing"*, because this book is explaining how what was written does have greater meaning than what has historically been passed off as the meaning (if any meaning). This is then relevant to the use of the word "seer", especially since many have used this word to describe Nostradamus. This type of *"seeing"* goes beyond the normal physical senses. To be able to *"see"*, as Nostradamus was *"seeing"*, means God must be *"in one"*, and the Holy Spirit was *"in"* Nostradamus.

This then leads to Nostradamus writing, *"si longue,"* which can translate as, *"so long"*. Still, the word *"si"* can also translate as *"if"*, which then makes this become a statement of uncertainty. This matches the use of the word *"possible"* in the first series of words, as this states a less than 100% chance. This uncertainty is once again relative to the reference in the topic statement where *"That"* alluded *"the year 3797"*, as *"if"* Nostradamus wrote such clearly understood dates, particularly one that foretold the date his predictions would be finished. By now, I hope I have demonstrated that *"if"* something written by Nostradamus looks like it is easy to understand, it is more likely to be a trick to mislead.

The word *"longue"* can translate as any of its possibilities: *"long, out-stretched, extended, continual, great, large,* or *much"*, which generally states length as distance. When *"the year 3797"* is known to be a reference to time, *"so long"* is reference to the great distance in time until then (2,242 years after the year 1555). However, as these words are read as, *"if extended"*, this states the uncertainty of *"seeing"* that specific date as being *"in some ones"* of The Prophecies, *"to make That possible"*.

This is then a statement that whatever seems *"possible"* in the Preface must be found confirmed in the quatrains, *"if"* it is as it seems to be. The evidence will confirm each other, *"in some ones"*, where a quatrain will hold the same information as the letter. This is an indirect statement that the quatrains will specifically support (yield the supporting details) the generalities presented in the Preface (the main themes).

Nostradamus then concluded this series with the word *"entension"*, which means *"perceptions"*, or *"conceptions"*, as explained earlier, as coming from the root verb *"entendre"* (to understand). This is then the condition of *"understanding"* that comes *"into one"*, *"seeing"* the words Nostradamus wrote. When combined with *"si longue"* it means, *"so much to judge of"* or *"so long to conceive"*, or *"so much"" understanding"* is *"possible"*. Each is showing how the *"conceptions"* of *"some ones"* can grow over time. This also becomes how misunderstandings can become so widely spread. However, when *"perceptions"* are combined with the question, *"if"* so far *"extended"*, then *"some ones"* can be led to doubt that *"so much"* time is necessary to tell the tales The Prophecies tells.

The second series ends with a comma, indicating that line of thought has concluded, and is to be separated from some new line of thought that is subsequent, yet relative. Following the comma is where one encounters the first ampersand in this segment. The ampersand is now confirmed to act to separate, or to indent into a new paragraph. While each of the previous strings of words (in lines one and two) can (and do) generate paragraphs of explanation, the ampersand marks an emphasis placed on what follows. A more important shift in thought is signaled. The comma's presence with an ampersand (where "**, &**" symbolizes "**and AND**") then acts as a sign that what follows is a sequential line of though, relative to the thought just completed; but the ampersand acts to focus attention strongly on the direction its segment will take.

par	**soubz**	**toute**	**la**	**concavité**	**de**	**la**	**Lune**	**aura**	**lieu**
by through for by reason of of on	beneath under	all whole everything total	the there	concavity hollowness bowing	to from of with	the there	Moon Round Compass Half-moon	will have will hold will own will use	place rank calling degree credit esteem reckoning account degree
6	2	4	2	3	4	2	4	4	9
6	12	48	96	288	1,152	2,304	9,216	36,864	331,776

As such, we encounter a shift that is more difficult to comprehend, as one reads, "*for beneath all the concavity to the Moon will have place*". We have just come from a line questioning "*if the year 3797*" really meant "*That*", and "*if*" The Prophecies was so "*far-extended*"; but this string of words seems to be making a statement relative to lunar movement. When one is "*seeing*" something not making sense, one is trying to "*see so long*" a string of words (which this line is 10) and "*judge*" it as a syntactical sentence. This series needs the same individual word analysis that we have been doing, for it to make sense too.

The first word, "*par*", is another directional preposition beginning a line. As with "*en*", the first word always links back to the word before it, which is the last word of the previous line. The last word of line two was translated as "*perceptions*", which comes from translations related to "*understanding*". Thus, "*par*" is best translates as the directions the process of "*understanding*" takes, where "*perceptions*" are created. The word "*par*" is derived from the Latin word "*per*", which best translates as, "*through*", and is likewise a translation for "*par*". Thus, line three begins with a focus on "*perceptions*" that have come "*through*" to one. However, "*par*" can also translate as "*by, for,* or *by reason of*", which is how one comes "*by perceptions*", how our "*perceptions*" are "*for*" practical use, and particularly how one's "*perceptions*" come "*by reason of*" thought.

This is then connecting to the second word in this series, "*soubz*", which means "*under*" or "*beneath*".

When this word is teamed with one's "*perceptions*", which work "*for*" one, which becomes the means "*by*" which one almost automatically acts, and are how one rationalizes the things surrounding one, "*by reason*", we see how "*perceptions*" are not all conscious. For all one experiences in life, it is impossible to remember everything. The mind absorbs these experiences and the knowledge they bring, and stores it "*beneath*" our conscious awareness. Often, people react later in life based on forgotten fears from childhood, which are "*sub*conscious" fears. These people act out their fears "*through*" an uncontrollable and unseen stimulus that is "*beneath*" the surface.

Still, from the topic of this segment - mistaking the meaning of Nostradamus, particularly when one does not have God's assistance – "*perceptions*" of that meaning are varied, from person to person. How one comes "*by*" one's "*perceptions*" depends on how deep one has dug into this topic. Some can see Nostradamus as "*beneath*" any level of dignity, even to "*entertain*" the "*possibility*" that Nostradamus merits discussing. Some may have so little "*understanding*" of who Nostradamus was, what he wrote, and what the general opinion is about *The Prophecies* that those individuals feel "*under*" educated enough to offer an opinion. Some may see that the key to "*understanding*" Nostradamus is reading between the lines, getting "*beneath*" the literal, to the esoteric meaning.

This means "*all*" is relative to those who have an opinion, while also being relative to how much of "*the whole*" one is familiar. This encompasses "*all*" opinions, right and wrong. However, "*all*" is primarily a statement about *The Prophecies*, as the Preface is directing the reader to "*understand*". The "*understanding*" comes "*by*" realizing what is "*beneath*" the surface meaning of "*everything*". This is the parallel to the Magic Eye, where the surface is designed to hide the true purpose "*under*lying".

This topic of "*understanding*" *The Prophecies* is then being furthered by stating "*for beneath all*", which says the underlying meaning is where "*all*" answers are. While this meaning is not fully understood, only estimated "*through perceptions*", never close to being fully accurate, the meaning "*comes by the knowledge of*" (alternate translation for "*entension*") a feeling that something important is there. Enough of Nostradamus is clearly written to leave the "*perception*" that true meaning is "*for*" one to find, "*beneath*" it "*all*". This is then pointing out the underlying elements that become realized "*by*" systems, one of which I am going "*through*" now.

This hidden element is there, but appears not to be there when one looks at "*the whole*" (alternate translation of "*toute*") as one syntactical sentence. This then is leading us to realize that there is more "*there*" (translation of "*la*", as "*là*"), in "*the totality*" of *The Prophecies*, when "*all*" is taken into consideration. To realize "*the whole*", one must be able to see "*the concavity*" of what is written. This requires "*understanding*" the definition of "*concavity*".

The word "*concavity*" is defined as, "The state of being curved like the inner surface of a sphere," or a "*structure configured in such a curve*".[198] The French word also bears the ability to translate as "*hollowness*", which represents something sunken, as is a cave, or hole. From our perspective on earth, the heavens (or sky) appear to surround us, making us be within the "*hollowness*" created by the outer shell of sky and space. The earth is then "*under*" this "*concavity*". Thus, the heavens "*encompass*" the earth.

Likewise, one can then see how "*the whole*" of one word's meaning "*encompasses*" that one word. The context of that word's use is then the restrictions that limit one word's meaning. However, when syntax is not present, "*all*" meanings "*under the concavity*" of that word's definitions are viable. This is how one either finds "*all*" meaning "*beneath the concavity*" of The Prophecies.

When prophetic language is seen as "*under the concavity*" of Heaven, as from God, one word bears "*all*" of that word's meanings, but only one meaning can be "*perceived*" at a time. The other meanings are still relevant, but they become hidden "*under the concavity*" that is the shell forming the word. What gets "*through*" to us are the "*perceptions*" derived from the "*ones*". This is then explaining the multiplicity that is found by not limiting a word to one syntactical meaning.

At this point, this line has made several important points, leading to the only mid-line capitalized word found in this entire series of lines. One next finds the preposition-article combination, "*du*" ("*de le*"), telling the reader that the directions "*to, from, of,* or *with*" follow this "*concavity*". This connection leads to the capitalized proper noun, "*Lune*", commonly seen as representing "*Moon*". However, when viewed as "*Luné*", it becomes a reflection of "*concavity*" as, "*round, compass,* or *bowed* like a *half-Moon*."[199]

This reflection is important to see, as "*the Moon*" does not create a "*concavity*" over "*the whole*" earth. It is only part of the "*concavity*" of the heavens, as a changing luminary that is mostly visible in the night sky. Thus, a "*half-Moon*" is representative of the "*concavity*" of the earth, which blocks the "*concavity*" of the Sun's rays, making "*the Moon*" appear to change shape. This is an important concept to understand.

When "*the Moon*" is "*beneath all the concavity*" mentioned, it is always moving to find its "*place*" (translation of "*lieu*") in the Sun. In that way, "*for*" one to see the meaning "*beneath*" the writing style of Nostradamus, so that "*all*" his work "*will have*" its "*place*" in the public eye, "*the concavity*" of meaning is as fleeting as a phase "*of the Moon*". It is difficult to grasp without God's light, but God's light will wax and wane because of the physical (earthly) restrictions "*placed*" on humanity.

On must recognize that the capitalization of "*Moon*" means it has a higher-level meaning. The personification makes it readily known to be the earth's moon, as the lower-case word, "moon," is used to denote all planetary satellites. Still, there is a higher meaning than simply that name.

---

198   The Free Dictionary by Farlex, http://www.thefreedictionary.com/concavity

199   Randal Cotgrave's 1611 French-English Dictionary, http://www.pbm.com/~lindahl/cotgrave/search/5931.html

On one level, as seen in the direction, "*to the Moon*", or "*to there*", is an indication of timing. This timing is relative to the mistaken timing of "*the year 3797*". Thus, "*beneath all the concavity*" represents the meaning found in the quatrains, with "*to the Moon*" representing the timing of man's travels "*to the Moon*" (1958-1976, manned and unmanned, American and Soviet). This timing is when one "*will have a place there*". In short, the 20th and 21st centuries "*will have*" more importance in *The Prophecies*, than "*will have*" the 37th and 38th centuries.

The concept "*to the Moon*" is greater in scope, but still on the mundane level. To capture the higher meaning, one has to find the esoteric meaning "*of the Moon*". As such, one has to return to the actual name written, "*Lune*", which is the French spelling of the name for the goddess "*Luna*", also known as "*Selene*". The meaning of this Greek name is said to be "light," as "*the Moon*" acts as a night light. Thus, in astrology "*the Moon*" is described as a luminary, due to it casting light, albeit reflected light. This is then the esoteric meaning for "*to the Moon*", as understanding of the words of Nostradamus comes from reflection. However, there is another very important higher-level meaning "*of the Moon*".

On a religious level, "*the Moon*" is a reference to Islam. I described this connection with the name "*Venus*" also. Both "*the Moon*" and "*Venus*" are depicted in many flags of Islamic nations, as the "*Crescent Moon*" with a star at its point. The star is "*Venus*". For Nostradamus to write, "*to the Moon will have place*", he is telling of a time when Muslim nations will again have strength. This is a major theme in *The Prophecies*, addressed in both letters, many times.

Nostradamus ended this line with the word "*lieu*", and this most commonly translates as "*place*". However, "*lieu*" also translates as "*calling*" (as one would "*call*" a bluff in cards, or "*call*" in a debt), "*credit, esteem, reckoning, account,* or *dwelling place*". As such, "*the Moon will have reckoning*" is in line with the theme of Muslims rising to power. This is then a statement of retribution, where a long history of Crusades has pitted Christians against Muslims. The creation of the State of Israel was due to a weakness in the Muslim world; such that they could not protect Arab land against the strength afforded Israel by the Christian West. This statement of "*the Moon will have reckoning*", or "*account*", or "*dwelling place*", is already part of our current world events. The Muslims "*have place*" due to the power of oil.

All of this meaning comes from one separated line, which translates to state, "*for beneath all the concavity to the Moon will have place*". At this point, the ampersand emphasizes this line even more, raising the level of the first word ("*par*" in French) to an equivalence of capitalization. With the first word being a preposition, capitalizing acts to show the importance of direction, either "*by, for, through,* or *by reason of*". Since we have seen the higher importance Latin brings to Nostradamus' work, one find that "*par*" is derived from the Latin word "*per*". This Latin word typically translates to English as "*through*". That then makes a good first choice to examine, to find the extra value meaning capitalization brings to this line.

On a higher level, one can get the sense that something flows when this translation is used. As living human beings, life flows "*Through*" one's body as impulses of energy generated "*by*" both conscious and subconscious thoughts. In that sense, the body operates "*Through*" the control of the brain, where only about 5% of our brain's capacity can consciously be used at one time. This limitation keeps one from "*understanding*" all of "*the concavity*" of meaning, but only on that conscious level. Just as God connects "*Through*" our bodies to give us life, God runs "*Through*" our minds to give us knowledge. Thus, understanding The Prophecies is only consciously "*perceived*" after God allows one to see. The ability to understand is "*Through*" God.

This means God is "*beneath the whole*" of The Prophecies, as I have been stating all along. "*Through*" God entering us individually, one can come "*under*" God's power, becoming able to understand "*all*" that is involved in "*the concavity*" of meaning. "*Under*" God's assistance, one can feel the presence of God "*there*" (translation of "*la*" as "*là*"), with one "*there*" with God, as in "*the concavity*" of God's all-seeing eye. At that center of focus, "*all*" becomes clear.

Thus, "*For*" one to reach "*beneath*" the surface meaning, to "*see all*" the truth that can be told, one has to rise above the trappings of earthly existence. One has to transcend to "*there*", which is connecting to "*the concavity*" of God's light. One has to reflect on "*the whole*" of the "*Round*" (alternative translation of "*Luné*") surrounding the words of God. One has "*to*" reach "*the Moon*", which symbolizes the emotional center of one's self. Astrologically, "*the Moon*" represents the light within, which nurtures and feels. It is our emotional core, and thus it represents the heart. This means "*the Moon*" is where our hearts are, not our minds, such that one does not think God, one feels God.

When one is connected with God, one receives a "*calling*" to understand Nostradamus. This is not so much a line of work, but each individual will be made "*accountable*" for his or her own souls. The message of Nostradamus is about the strong "*Emotions*" ("*Moon*") many people "*will have for*" possessions. In the physical realm, which is "*beneath the concavity*" of Heaven, "*all*" is "*there for*" the taking. In that case, the "*place*" is a "*reckoning*", an "*accounting*" for "*all*" actions, relative to which "*dwelling place*" one seeks more. The message of The Prophecies is to connect with God and "*have*" a "*place*" in Heaven, or suffer the consequences.

When this series is fully understood, the ampersand that separates it then rejoins it with the previous series, to make a statement that (for length considerations) can be abbreviated to yield, "*long perceptions, AND reckoning*". This can be seen as the judgment that is believed to come at the end of one's life. For as "*long*" as humanity has wondered about what happens at death, the many "*perceptions*" that have resulted are "*through*" imagining the body returns to the earth "*under*" our feet, while the soul seeks the "*concavity*" of Heaven. It is "*Through*" the religions of the world that we maintain these "*perceptions*", and have for so "*long*". The difficulty is making the commitment to being accountable, before the time of "*reckoning*". The comma then acts to show the separation that makes it so hard to perceive the heavenly from an earthly existence, filling many with guilt because they cannot keep from falling prey to the trappings of earthly delights. The guilt comes from knowing, somehow, that all debts will eventually be due.

Following this line comes the second ampersand, which acts to separate that which follows as its own important paragraph. Without a comma to show sequence, what follows is directly related to the "*reckoning*", or "*place*". What follows is one word, in French written as "*intelligence*", but in English, that word has multiple translation possibilities. It can mean, "*Understanding, apprehension, capacity, conceit, sense, discretion,* and *judgment*", with "*intelligence*" also applying.[200] In other words, "*intelligence*" leans more toward how one applies knowledge, more than how one amasses knowledge.

intelligence
understanding
apprehension
capacity
conceit
sense
discretion
judgment
intelligence
8
8

For a translation that copies the original, "*intelligence*" is an important statement of timing. It generally states when the focus of *The Prophecies* begins, which is the Age of Reason, or Enlightenment (18th century). Humanity suddenly became smarter then, although that enlightenment led several revolutions. It then becomes important to recall that the fall from grace of Adam and Eve was due to them having eaten from the fruit of the Tree of Knowledge, of good and evil.

The second half of the 20th century is when "*intelligence*" hit unbelievable records in advancements. Many of the technological advances over the past sixty years have come from secret military projects, which is another form of "*intelligence*". All one has to do today to see the effect "*intelligence*" has, if not a complete control over, is to look around. A computer, an I-pod, a cell phone, a GPS in the car, a card to make purchases with, it all is "*intelligence*"; and while some may be good, there will be an "*account*" of the cost for all this "*intelligence*".

---

200   Randal Cotgrave's 1611 French-English Dictionary, http://www.pbm.com/~lindahl/cotgrave/search/5541.html

An alternate translation of *"intelligence"* is *"apprehension"*. I prefer this translation because this is also a translation of *"entension"* (*"entendre"*), which we saw ending the first string of words in this series of the Preface. As such, we find in one word the element of *"understanding"* (also found in *"entendre"*), while also finding the definition, "Fearful and uneasy anticipation of the future, dread."[201]

Consider also the Latin root for *"intelligence"* (*"intellegere"*), which means, "to understand, literally: to choose between."[202] This essence is caught in the contrasting definitions for *"apprehension"*. *"Understanding"* both the pros and cons does not mean the intelligent person makes the wise choice.

This multiplicity of meaning aptly follows the different ways to read, *"par soubz toute la concavité du Lune aura lieu,"* as either *"will have place"* in Heaven or Hell. Still, with *"lieu"* seen as *"reckoning"*, having the ampersand act to emphasize *"intelligence"* through implied capitalization, makes *"Judgment"* a perfect one-word choice. This becomes elevated to the level of God, and the return of Jesus. The capitalization of *"Intelligence"* is then the *"Knowledge"* of God, which was demonstrated after Adam and Eve had the *"intelligence"* suddenly to know they were naked, and had done wrong. The *"Intelligence"* of God knew their wrong and their *"place"*, yet asked, "Where are you?"

When combined with *"lieu"*, to form (using other alternate translations) *"for beneath all the concavity to the Moon will have degree"* (alternate translation of *"lieu"*) *"and capacity"* (alternate translation of *"intelligence"*), this is stating the changing nature of one's abilities. It means to amount of *"understanding"* one has of Nostradamus, the levels one has *"learned"* to be in touch with one's feelings towards others, and the limits one has set on personal lusts for individual gains. The *"degree"* can allude to one's astrological chart, and the *"place"* of *"the Moon"* (a *"degree"*), *"and"* one's *"capacity"* in these areas of feelings and intuitions.

When only the immediate words surrounding the ampersand are seen as making the elevated connection, *"calling AND apprehension"*, this is like a statement about how one connects with God. Often we make wishes, which usually do not come true, often to our own benefit that they do not. However, when Jesus is *"calling"* someone out, to see if someone is truly committed to him, one has to have fear, relative only for the consequences of not answering the call. Jesus presented Nostradamus with a *"calling AND"* Nostradamus was filled with *"understanding"* (*"apprehension"*). The *"apprehension"* (*"understanding"*) came from him receiving of the Holy Spirit. This combination is the *"calling AND apprehension"*, and is no different than when Jesus breathed upon the disciples saying, "Receive the spirit." Once the Spirit is within one, the *"intelligence"* is not one's own.

A colon and an ampersand then follow this one word statement of Nostradamus. This means that there is a separation, denoted by the ampersand, allowing the next line to become its own new paragraph.

---

201   The Free Dictionary by Farlex, http://www.thefreedictionary.com/apprehension
202   The Free Dictionary by Farlex, <u>Collins Essential English Dictionary</u> 2nd Edition, 2006, http://www.thefreedictionary.com/intelligence

However, the colon then denotes that this new paragraph will be for the specific purpose of clarifying the statement, *"intelligence"*. The next series states, *"ce entendant universellement par toute la terre les causes,"* where *"entendant"* is another state of the word *"entendre"*, the root word of *"entensions"*. These words translate to state, *"this meaning universally by the whole of the earth the causes"*.

The pronoun, *"this"*, is directly referencing *"intelligence"*, such that this line is following the colon as an explanation that will clarify the *"meaning"* of that important one-word statement. The *"intelligence"* is then explained to be the *"meaning"*, particularly the level of *"understanding"* one has for the true *"meaning"*. We must see how *"this"* refers to the *"capacity"* for *"understanding"*, the *"sense"* for *"apprehending"*, and the *"judgment"* for *"recognizing"* (all combinations from the matrices). We must then see how *"this"* is up to one's *"discretion"* as to whether or not one allows a *"dawning"* to come upon one.

ce	entendant	universellement	par	toute	la	terre	les	causes
this	understanding	universally	by	all	the	land	the (pl)	causes
that	conceiving	generally	through	the whole	there	earth	them	reasons
it	apprehending	wholly	for by reason	everything		ground		cases
these those	perceiving judging learning recognizing dawning	altogether	of of on	total		soil		matters
5	8	4	6	4	2	4	2	4
5	40	160	960	3,840	7,680	30,720	61,440	245,760

What *"understanding"* brings is awareness of the truth. While the "little-T truth" is all the facts and orders that make a quatrain solidly seen as telling of only one specific series of events, the "Big-T Truth" is much greater. This "truth" is defined as, "That which is considered to be the supreme reality and to have the ultimate meaning and value of existence."[203] It is a *"universally"* held truth.

The *"meaning"* of The Prophecies is the ultimate fate brought on by a world having turned away from God. This is commonly known, *"universally"*, as the End Times, with the word *"universally"* meaning all cultures and religions that share this belief. Thus, *"this universal meaning"* is to be known *"by all"*, as it is *"for all"* to know, *"through the whole of the earth"*. That *"understanding"* is then representative of the previous interpretations, where the capitalized form of *"Judgment"* came into play. Whether one

203   The Free Dictionary by Farlex, http://www.thefreedictionary.com/truth

believed in "*Judgment*" Day or not, "*all*" have a good "*understanding*" of what that means.

Finally, this line ends by stating, "*the causes,*" which are the events *The Prophecies* tell of, which lead up to the End Times. The same two words in French, "*les causes*", can be read to state, "*them*", who will be the "*reasons*" the world will be destroyed by "*them*". Nostradamus explained in the Preface the flip-flopping that will take place, where kings will be ousted, with common people ruling nations in their stead. The influences of religions will be reduced to such minimal importance that lusts for power and wealth will "*cause*" men to sell their souls. These "*matters*", as weaved in individual examples of each of these "*cases*", will make the time of the end. It must be understood that "*the causes*" for the end are the warning of *The Prophecies*, but God makes prophecies available to act as "*the causes*" to change those God loves from going the wrong way, to the go the right way. Whichever way humanity heads, "*the causes*" will be the responsibility of mankind, as God will not be the cause the end.

The ampersand acting to capitalize "*This*", shows the importance once again of "*Judgment*". It represents a time when "*reckoning*" will take "*place*". The capitalized importance does not focus simply on the anguish, terror, persecution, and death that make up the majority of the tales told by the quatrains; it focuses on the exchange of souls. It also forwards that emphasis to "*Understanding*", which means the "*Judgment*" will not be a shock to anyone. "*The whole of the*" people facing this "*calling AND accounting*" will be connected to the Godhead, "*Understanding*" everything ever done, towards that end. "*This*" then leads one to realize that "*the causes*" for the "*Judgment*" are the failures to connect to God, and willingly let oneself be led by His quite, inner voice. As such, anyone caught thinking the End Times would not come until "*the year 3797*", will be "*Apprehending*" their lack of faith in this lifetime as "*the cause*" for many to lose their souls.

Throughout the Preface, Nostradamus made addresses like the final line in this series, "*mon filz.*" There is typically only one translation for each word; thus, "*my son*" is the only meaning. Still, by repeating this statement throughout the Preface, people have mistakenly seen it as a letter to Nostradamus' son, Caesar, rather than the introductory explanation of the book that follows it. Since one has to see that Nostradamus is not the true author of *The Prophecies*, an address in the Preface to "*my son*" is to someone other than Caesar.

The Spirit of Jesus Christ is the true author. This makes the statement, "*my son*", be like a Father (priest) to a son (male parishioner), or as the Good Shepherd to his willing servant, in this case Nostradamus. Thus, Nostradamus tells "*the causes*" of the return of Christ, God's "*son*". By connecting to God, and "*understanding*" what Jesus calls one to do, and by seeing the "*meaning*" of Nostradamus' words, and "*seeing*" the parallels to The Revelation of John, one can also see one's self as God's child.

Let me make this additional thought be known, in reference to the reason I stated "*mon filz*" typically would only have one translation. This is based on the fact that Old French used certain letters that have been replaced with other letters in modern French. For instance, Old French wrote the word "*je*" ("I") as "*ie*", with no "*j*" in the 1611 Old French – English Dictionary. Further, the letter "*y*" was used instead of an "*i*", as has been demonstrated in the word for "*king*", written in Old French as "*roy*" (modern is "*roi*"). As such, another Old French letter that was used more frequently, than is used in modern French, is "*z*". This letter was frequently interchangeable with the letter "*s*". In that sense, "*filz*" is seen as "*fils*."

The problem is Old French wrote the word for "*son*", in the singular, the same way it is written in modern French, "*fils*." The alteration to a "*z*" ending is then the plural version, as "*sons*." This means all of Nostradamus' references to "*mon filz*" are statements to all of mankind, where the author of the words in the letter is not Nostradamus, on the highest sense of inspiration. On the mundane level, Nostradamus appears to address his "*son*", as a caring father. Likewise, but on the heavenly level of the source, Jesus Christ, the inspiration of Nostradamus' hand, is the sire of a bloodline to the kings of France. The letter is addressed to the "*sons*" of Jesus, and all Christians. This is how one overlooks an oddity, making an assumption based on what the mind wants to think is the necessary correction to make, based on syntax.

With all of this breaking down of words, translations and definitions, and the seeming repetitiveness created by the ampersands, it becomes difficult to see the forest for the trees. I hope that the "*understanding*" I have left at this point is one of Nostradamus making a complete statement (one "sentence" of six lines) on the topic of the misunderstandings relative to *The Prophecies*, particularly if one attempts to understand without God's assistance. The ampersands then can act like bullet points, where the details of this topic unfold. Knowing what I know from the word-by-word, mark-by-mark analysis, I can now summarize this segment of the Preface as saying:

- **&** What we see as lengthy predictions are "*perceptions*" based on what we allow ourselves to believe we see.
- **&** What we allow ourselves to believe in will be what we each will be "*judged*" on in the end.
- **&** What "*judgment*" we bring from God will be "*judgment*" known, because everyone is the "*cause*" of one's own choices.

The topic statement (the first series) began with, "*That possible will* **cause**", and ended (fifth series) stating, "*this knowing universally by all the earth the* **causes**". A "*cause*" means a consequence has been created (the effect). Thus, this "sentence" is stating the importance of *The Prophecies* as the source of prophetic wisdom to have the effect of saving one's soul, by "*seeing*" the "*causes*" of the End Times and acting responsibly. This "*seeing*" of that "*beneath the whole*" only comes from connecting to God, through Jesus Christ, and being led to "*understanding*". God guides us through "*perceptions*" ("*entension*"), "*intelligence*", and "*meaning*" ("*entendant*"), coming from the "*Heart*" ("*Lune*").

With such depth of explanation just completed, there is only one reason to include an example from the letter to Henry II. That reason is the letter to Henry II is even more of a puzzle. What appears to be a series of lines, broken into strings of words by the marks, just like the Preface, is not trustworthy, as is the Preface, because the Henry letter is out of order (like are the quatrains). One cannot select a complete "sentence" (capitalized first word to ending period) from the letter to Henry to analyze, until after everything has been broken into pieces, and then reconstructed in the right order. Therefore, the selection discussed from the Henry letter will be only those words that appear after an ampersand, up to the following mark.

Because I chose the shortest "sentence" in the Preface, I have chosen one of the shortest ampersand-led lines in the letter sent to Nostradamus' king. It is three words, with the lines preceding it and following it in no way connected to it. It is one line from a "sentence" that is almost a full page long, with over 200 words, 13 commas, and 12 ampersands. Due to such length, the only way to comprehend what Nostradamus said is by taking each string of words (between punctuation marks) as a separate statement (a "line", in poetic format). Once the individual line is understood, those separate statements can be matched with the appropriate connecting statements, which may come from other places within the letter. Matching means a main topic will be found stated, with the first word capitalized, and all subsequent lines connecting to that topic will be found to be addressing that topic, logically ordered.

Prior to this line I will use as an example, Nostradamus wrote many lines that mentioned specific dates (day and month), specific planets in specific signs, and specific alignment between planets and the nodes of the Moon (which are points that mark the intersection of the Moon's orbit around the Earth with the ecliptic and are illusory[204]). Following this line, Nostradamus wrote about persecution, in particular that which relates to the Christian church, Africans, ancient Rome, and the Byzantines. All of that specificity makes this line stand out as being a statement of generality.

The example line, led by an ampersand, states *"non du tout,"* which can translate to state, *"not of the whole sum"*. The preposition-article can change the direction of focus, with the other words also being alternated to make this to state, *"not from the total"*, *"no to the everything"*, or *"not with them any"*. This is then a statement about someone or something that is isolated or alone, against the majority. Because this is introduced by an ampersand, it is an important stand-alone statement of loneliness. Because it ends with a comma, this important statement is designated to be followed by a statement related to this isolation, as a subsequent element. Because it begins with an ampersand, it follows a statement that combines with this value of wholeness.

Simply because the objective here now is only to focus on the ampersand use, this statement's true power of relevance is suspended until the other pieces are understood, and shown to connect to it. This means that all that can be known from those three French words is what I stated prior. The true value of this example is how it separates from *"the whole"*. This example demonstrates how an ampersand acts to

204   Astrology – Numerology.com, article The Lunar Nodes, Michael McClain, http://www.astrology-numerology.com/nodes.html

divide the letter to Henry into pieces.

Ampersands with Punctuation

Perhaps some have noticed the odd placement of a comma before an ampersand. This is not a normal use of those marks, as together they become repetitive, with both stating a symbolic "and". The example I presented from the letter to Henry II is led by a ", &" and it ends with a ", &". Thus, it reads, ", & *non du tout, &*". In the "sentence" where this series is found, there are three other such combinations (", &") separating strings of words, with another line (in addition to the example) begun and ended with two of them. That line states, "*puissance levera ses aysles si treshault ne distant gueres aux forces de l'antique Rome,*" which translates as (one possibility), "*powerful will raise its wings so very-high not different but little ones in the strengths of the ancient Rome*".

This is also an important statement of loneliness, in the sense that a "*powerful*" nation has become empirical, "*not different*" than the empirical "*strengths*" shown in the past, "*of Rome*". If one places that information with the information from the three-word series I used in the first example from the letter to Henry, one could see how those words would play with the others. As such, if the two series were combined, in need of a common topic to detail, one could see how the "*powerful*" will have flown "*so very-high*", it is "*no*" (alternate translation of "*non*") longer "*with them*" (alternate translation of "*du*"), the rest that makes up the "*whole sum*" ("*tout*") of an empire. This means a fit could be found in these two "loose pieces" of the puzzle, as neither of them matches the topics relative to the strings of words attaching to them in the letter. Still, while new-forming statement can be seen as related to topic statement series (with a capitalized first word), "*not of the whole sum*", requires more to cement that idea.

The significance of this exercise is to see how the "edges" of the "puzzle pieces" are marked by the ", &" combination. This is a sign that says "cut here" in the letter. While all ampersands say "indent here", the inclusion of a comma prior to an ampersand is a purposeful direction that says, "This is the border of a puzzle piece." As such, all ", &" must be seen as signs to splice what had been a continuous flow of words and punctuation.

This is relevant to the quatrains and the Preface as a signal to splice to deeper meaning. Deeper meaning would be a separate thought on a matter, where understanding everything about the line following the ", &" is explained to a greater extent than would seem necessary. This means going deeper, even if that includes looking up history that is entirely irrelevant to the topic theme. Such thought has a way of adding to the overall meaning. However, this splice away to other thoughts does not remove the spliced line from the order found in the poems or the Preface, and the relationship each line has to the topic statement, or main theme.

This order and relationship to a topic is missing in the letter to Henry. The order must be restored, just as the quatrains need to be reordered. The quatrains are already separated into pieces, which are out of order. The Preface is the one document that is not in need of reordering. Thus, the letter to Henry, by being itself out of order, is an unwritten explanation that order must be restored to the verses. The letter must be cut into pieces and reordered. However, this cutting has to follow the direction of Nostradamus, through his oddly placed marks.

A capitalized first word marks the varied topic statements, and the period marks the end of a "sentence" of lines relating to a main topic or theme. The comma-ampersand combination is then the signal to splice and set a line aside, into an imaginary puzzle box. Once the whole letter is divided into pieces, they are all sorted to match other pieces of like topic. Once sorted, the reconstruction can begin. This whole process depends on recognizing the ", &" combination as a signal that the piece that follows it is "*not of the whole sum*" of this particular "sentence".

This element of the ampersand is venturing into that area that is outside the umbrella of pure ampersand use. This is why I have decided to include elements like the comma-ampersand combination as under the system of symbols, where it is not purely a mark of punctuation, covered under that system. The comma is then representing a need to separate the preceding line, while signaling an anticipated joining with a following line, just as it does under the system of punctuation. By combining with the ampersand immediately following the comma, the ampersand is emphasizing this comma break, as an important separation.

Whereas a normal ampersand falls between two words, as we saw where Nostradamus wrote "*lieu & intelligence*" in the Preface example, the separation is to recognize the importance of each word (*calling AND apprehension*), and each whole line surrounding the ampersand. This is typical of most of Nostradamus' ampersand usage, which makes a plain ampersand simply act to indent to a new paragraph that is related to the last paragraph. However, the fact that not all ampersands are this simple, those combining with punctuation stand out. With Nostradamus, anything standing out has purpose.

In Preface example of ampersand usage I presented, Nostradamus wrote, "*si longue entension, & par soubz toute*", where the ", &" combination is found there as well. There are combinations like this in the quatrains, which can easily been seen when looking for them. All such uses mean the same as I demonstrated in the example from the letter to Henry; but instead of linking two words together, the ampersand connects the punctuation to the first word of the line that follows. However, because the "sentence" in the Preface is in the correct order, the only splice a ", &" indicates is one to mark a jump to the third function the ampersand has, which is to conjoin two thoughts.

An uninterrupted ampersand joins the two words that surround it, which means "&" acts to create one thought as "<u>the word preceding</u> AND <u>the word following</u>". This is impossible when the ampersand is interrupted. Because of the presence of a mark before the ampersand, the ampersand calls for the union of an instruction relating one line to another line (the punctuation mark) to the instruction an ampersand serves to emphasize the line following it. Thus, the ", &" signals a need to find the key words from two lines that surround the ampersand, rather than focus on the immediate ampersand surroundings.

One has to realize this is not limited to only a comma and an ampersand combination. In the Preface example there is written, "*intelligence: & ce entendant*", where a colon-ampersand combination is shown. This is another combination, which says that the whole line prior to the ampersand must be understood, because following the ampersand an example or clarification will be emphasized. Both marks call for separation, leading to a deeper inspection of two. Then, this can allow two key words to join the two lines as one thought; but because both of these combinations are in an ordered letter, there is no need to splice as a piece to be put into a box for further comparison with other pieces. The point here is that any combination of punctuation and an ampersand found in the letter to Henry II are signals to splice a puzzle piece. Once spliced, only the ampersand attaches to the following line, while the punctuation remains with the preceding line.

As one can see, an ampersand is a vital symbol to understand. Still, other marks need to be addressed. The most important of these are accent marks.

Accent Marks

Accent marks are not widely used in English. Accent marks are mostly seen in foreign words that have become so commonly used in English they have been adopted, along with the accents (ex: passé, café, and résumé). Accent marks are also known as stress marks, with French employing three basic types of marks (diacritics) which indicate where one should stress the vowel over which they occur. These are acute accent (*é*), grave accent (*è, à, ù*), and an accent circumflex (*ê, â, û, î*). An umlaut is also used (*ë, ï*), but this is more of a signal for pronunciation than stress, as is the mark called a cedilla. The cedilla is only found under the consonant "C" (Ç, or ç), which changes the "c" sound to an "s", rather than accenting a syllable.

In my interpretations, I have noted where a word that Nostradamus wrote primarily has one translation, yet when seen differently, as an accented version of the same word, a viable alternate translation becomes possible. I last used "*Lune*" as such an example, where "*Lune*" translates as "*Moon*", but as "*Luné*" it bore the meaning of "*Round*", or "*Half-moon*". I also gave reason for seeing the word "*la*" (feminine form of "*the*") as potentially holding the meaning of "*là*" ("*there*"). As Nostradamus did not write accent marks in those words, it is just to question my decision to consider those variations. One could argue that I was promoting an argument that Nostradamus misspelled words, which I have already stated is impossible.

A "misspelled" word often is intended to be close enough to a correctly spelled word to get the reader to assume that is the meaning, only a misspelled word. For example, Nostradamus wrote "*Dannube*", which is correctly spelled *Danube*. By overlooking the extra "*n*", one misses the potential of a simple anagram making the "*n*" a contracted prefix, as "*n'Danube*", which makes a significant difference to the meaning. This is how one must realize there are no mistakes in *The Prophecies*. However, there is a disclaimer in support of Nostradamus' inconsistent use of accent marks.

The French did not consistently require the use accent marks during the 16th century, when Nostradamus lived. French words had been accented irregularly since the 14th century, but by 1555, there still were no standard rules to follow. The 17th century was when consistency began to take hold. Provençal French was often spelled differently, having its own stresses and accents; and this language was prominent where Nostradamus lived and published *The Prophecies*. This means such inconsistency allows *Lune* to be quite viable as *Luné*, because the accent mark was not officially part of the spelling then. It was more of an aide for written French, as a Frenchman would pronounce the accent if it was required. Still, there is more to this issue than a simple lack of standardization of the written French language.

Nostradamus wrote words that were partially accented, primarily focusing stress only on the last syllable. This is often how a noun and a past participle verb (or adjective) were distinguished from one another. There are many words where accentuation had already become standard, as found in the 1611 dictionary, but Nostradamus was not standard in his placement of accents on those words.

We see this in the printer-publisher result. For instance, the 1568 Lyon edition shows Nostradamus writing, "*l'année 3797*" in the Preface. The same edition then has him writing, "*l'annee 1585*", and "*l'annee 1606*", in the letter to Henry. The word for "year", as duration of time, was "*année*", with the accent, as evidenced in Randal Cotgrave's 1611 French-English Dictionary.

To spell an accented word with the proper accents only shows recognition of the proper pronunciation of a word. To spell an accented word without the accents only shows recognition of the proper spelling of a word. Both ways are correct. However, to omit an accent mark that would limit the meaning of a word's intent means this limitation is not to be in place at this time. The actual placement of accent marks then acts to restrict the possibilities of translation, because some translations will not serve to assist one's understanding. The placement of accents eliminates that confusion.

As was typical of Nostradamus' writing, as a way of indicating he knew the importance of accent marks, he would properly apply accents marks to one word, several times, in several quatrains, then in several more write the same word (spelled the same) without the accent marks. He did this with "*là*", writing it with the accent mark at times when "*there*" was his only focus. Still, in other places, where "*là*" was the only choice for understanding to come (alone, without a noun, or preceding a masculine noun), he wrote "*la*".

The same can be said of his use of "*a*", which in the unaccented form bears the meaning of the second person singular, present tense of the verb "*avoir.*" In nearly all cases one finds an unaccented "*a*", the proper way to read it is as "*à*". In many places, one sees an accented "*à*" written.

In reference to his use of "*annee*", most French words (if not all) that end with "*ee*", the first "*e*" is accented, such that seeing "*annee*" one would read, "*année*" Many times Nostradamus would simply show "*ee*", while some times he would show "*ée*". There are so many examples of this lack of accent marks, throughout the letters and quatrains, it is commonplace, and thus develops the rule. By his not placing the accent, one is allowed to do so. By his placing an accent, one is restricted from taking it away.

Numerals: Arabic and Roman

The second most important non-punctuation symbol used by Nostradamus was his use of number symbols in his work. By this, I mean numerals, as we saw in the example where "*the year 3797*" was important. This use, by itself, is odd because Nostradamus did not regularly use numerals to denote a numerical year. He normally spelled those out in the quatrains. For example, the 1568 Lyon edition shows Nostradamus spelling out the year 1558, as "*Mil cinq cens cinquantehuit*", when he closed his letter to Henry II. While this is the only edition I have found to show this spelling out of the year, the 1568 edition does so after having shown "*1555*" written, as the ending date of the Preface.

The spelling out of dates, particularly those identified as "*l'an*", is common in the quatrains. The same cannot be said for numerical depictions. This means the appearance of the numerals 3, 7, and 9 (followed by another 7) is not his normal way of presenting specific dates. With Nostradamus, something seeming specific and clear is usually anything but. This means something other than "*the year 3797*" was the intent of having written, "*the year 3797*".

At the end of the Preface (all editions observed), Nostradamus used numerals to write the date when the letter was finished. There he simply followed "*Mars*" (the month of *March*) with "*1555.*" He wrote those numerals, while he wrote out, "*ce premier de Mars*",[205] meaning "*this first of March*". He did not write out "*l'année*" at the end of the letter, as he did in the middle of the letter, as his lead into "*3797*". Thus, Nostradamus saw no need to indicate "*the year*" "*1555*". Simply by writing the year in numbers, it was understood to be that, without explanation.

Now in the letter to Henry II, Nostradamus wrote a series of lines where 4-digit numbers appear. They appear rather soon in the letter, such that the 1568 Lyon edition shows them on page three, with twenty-one pages representing that editions total for that letter. On page three, one sees that Nostradamus wrote, "<u>*mesmes de l'annee 1585. & de l'annee 1606. … , … de Mars 1557. & …*</u>", which translates to state,

[205] Editions vary on how this is written. For example, the 1557 Utrecht edition lists, "*ce premier jour de Mars,*" the 1568 Lyon edition states, "*ce premier de Mars,*" the 1566 Lyon edition says, "*ce I. de Mars*", and the 1555 Bonhomme edition shows, "*ce j. de Mars*".

"*same of the year 1585. & to the year 1606. ... , ... from March 1557. & ...*". The early placement of this numeral information in the Henry letter is no assurance that it needs to be discussed before the bulk of the other information, due to the letter being out of order. For these 4-digit numerals to be seen as specific references to the years they appear to be referencing, some context is necessary first.

The letter is printed in a new edition of "*Les Propheties de M Michel Nostradamus*", as the preface to the new additions found in the 1566-1568 editions (and later), *Centuries* eight through ten. The first edition was published in 1555 (with only four *Centuries*), with the Preface having the 4-digit numeral, *1555*, appearing at its end. The only other 4-digit numeral to appear in any part of the new "second edition", where the first edition is complete with seven *Centuries,* is the "*3797*" listing found in the Preface. No other numeric representations appear until the letter to Henry unleashes its barrage of three in quick 4-digit numerals in succession.

As stated, the 1568 Benoist Rigaud Lyon edition shows the ending to the letter to Henry as if Nostradamus wrote out the year, "*Mil cinq cens cinquantehuit*". This indicates in words, "*1558*". While all other editions show the numeral version ("*1558*"), following "*ce 27. de Juin*" ("*this 27th of June*"), this date turns out to be more than a year after his reference to "*quartozisme de Mars 1557*" ("*fourteenth of March 1557*") in the letter. This would indicate that the letter was constructed over a considerable length of time, where "*1557*" is a numeral indicating a specific year, relative to the year when the letter was completed. Due to their following in subsequent lines, connected by ampersands, thus not splices of separation,[206] "*1585*" and "*1606*" are indicating years as well.

This means that Nostradamus wrote the word "*l'annee*" preceding a 4-digit number once in the Preface ("*the year 3797*") and twice in the letter to Henry II ("*the year 1585*", and "*the year 1606*"). He is shown to have ended the Preface by simply writing "*1555*", and indicating "*1557*" and (in most editions) "*1558*" in the letter to Henry, without identifying either as "*the year*". With both letters being explanations of what can be found in *The Prophecies*, there are no examples of 4-digit numerals in any quatrain. However, there are multiple examples of what appear to be years and dates spelled out in words.

In the Preface, for instance, the only Arabic numerals used are the "*3797*" mentioned, and the "*1555*" at the very end. Various editions show the date of the month at the end differently, as either spelled out ("*premier*" – "*first*") or written in Roman numerals (upper case *I*, or lower case *j*). Still, these are not the only references to number, as all editions researched show Nostradamus writing, "*... au septiesme nombre de mille ... , ... du huictiesme ... de la huictiesme ...*", which states, "*... in the seventh number of the thousand ... , ... of the eighth ... to the eighth ...*". It also is not the only reference to time, as all

---

206 The French use a period mark in dates, with the only function being to designate "I have stopped writing numbers, and will now return to writing words." By seeing a combination mark, ".&" (period-ampersand), the same rule applies for separation and indent, with each year representing the end of a thought. Still, the letter to Henry II begins in the same way the preface does, and soon after begins to be completely disjointed. This means all of the years are part of the same series of segments, acting together.

editions researched show Nostradamus writing, *"que de present que ceci j'escriptz avant cent septante sept ans trios mois unze jours"*,[207] which says, *"that to the present this I writings before hundred seventy seven years three months eleven days"*. Due to this presence of reference to number, the numerical substitutions stand out.

Further along this line of thought, there is only one instance of Arabic numerals being written in all of the verses. This appears in the ninety-sixth quatrain of *Centurie Third*, and this particular style of numeral is only seen in the 1566 and 1568 Lyon editions. In those two editions researched, line four of that quatrain reads as, *"Saturne en Leo 13. Fevrier."* The other editions researched do not show Arabic numerals, instead showing Roman numerals, either in the upper case (*XIII.*) or in the lower case (*xiij*).[208] This brings to the forefront the use of Arabic numerals, verses Roman numerals.

In the editions that I have researched, only the 1555 Bonhomme versions show each individual quatrain as numbered by Arabic numerals. Thus, the above example is shown as number *"96"* in that earliest edition All subsequent editions of *The Prophecies* consistently show Roman numerals as the "serial number" listing each quatrain, within the *Centurie* each is found. All of these representations in Roman numerals are in the upper case. Additionally, due to a lack of standardization in Roman numerals in the 16th century, the numeral 4 is represented as *"IIII"*, rather than IV. Thus, the quatrain of the example, showing *"13. Fevrier"*, is listed in *Centurie Third* as quatrain number *"XCVI"*.

Due to the 1555 Bonhomme edition listing the quatrain containing the above reference from *"Centurie Tierce"*, with the Arabic numeral *"96"*, it is interesting that line four shows, *"XIII. Fevrier"*. This is the opposite of the presentation of numerals in the 1566 and 1568 Lyon editions, where the quatrain is numbered *"XCVI"*, with line four stating *"13. Fevrier"*. Both sets present both Arabic and Roman numerals. A similar duality exists in the 1557 Budapest and Utrecht editions, which list the quatrain in upper case Roman numerals, but list a lower case *"xiij"* as the numeral in line four.

This lower case representation of Roman numerals is not unique. The one edition that displays the most numeral presentation in the quatrains is the 1555 Bonhomme edition. There, three quatrains show Roman numerals (no Arabic numerals), with the seventh quatrain in *Centurie First* showing on its third line, *"xiiij"*, or the equivalent of fourteen. This representation is duplicated in the lower case in most editions researched, with only two exceptions.

One exception is found in the 1566 Lyon edition, where the upper case is used. This edition is one that adopted the standard now accepted for Roman numeral use, where a "four number" was represented in the listing of the quatrains as IV. This edition then shows *"XIV"* on line three, instead of XIII. The other

---

207 The 1555 Bonhomme edition shows an ampersand between *cent* and *septante*.
208 The 1555 Bonhomme edition, 1650 Pierre Riguad Lyon edition, and the 1698 Lyon edition all show upper case Roman numerals (*XIII.*). The 1557 Utrecht edition, and the 1557 Budapest edition both show lower case Roman numerals (*xiij*).

exception is in the 1557 Budapest edition, where an extra "*j*" is added, showing "*xiiijj*".

This would appear to be a misprint, as this quatrain is numbered in Roman numerals as "*VII*" in *Century First*, showing that a *V* was understood to represent the numeral five. It could be a misprint based on the 1557 Utrecht edition, which shows "*.xiiij.*" on line three in this quatrain. The normal placement of period marks after a numeral (Arabic or Roman) was not observed there, since that edition shows period marks both before and after the actual numeral. If the Budapest edition was copied from Utrecht edition, a "*j*" could have been inserted in the typeset instead of a period.

The 1555 Bonhomme edition shows Roman numerals in three quatrains, but all other editions researched show no more than two numeral uses. Those two uses are either the "*13.*" / "*XIII.*", or the "*xiiij*" / "*XIV*" discussed. The Bonhomme edition shows the eleventh quatrain in *Centurie Fourth* as containing "*XII*" in line three. However, all other editions show the word "*douze*" written, which is the equivalent number for the numeral twelve. What is interesting in these three numeral representations is they are sequential, as twelve, thirteen, and fourteen.

For the limited use of numerals in the Preface (two to three, depending on the edition) and the 948 quatrains (two to three, depending on the edition), the letter to Henry II goes well beyond this amount. Following the three years found early in the letter ("*1585*", "*1606*", and "*1557*"), which appear in all editions, some editions state that Nostradamus wrote, "*du 7. millenaire*", which means, "*to the 7th millennium*".[209] A few pages later in the published text, all editions researched show Nostradamus writing, "*50. & 52. degrez de hauteur*", followed not long afterwards with, "*de 48. degrez d'hauteur*", then about a half-page later repeating, "*48. degrez*". These numbers represent "*degrees of height*", which is referring to degrees of latitude.

Interestingly, Nostradamus wrote in the main theme line of the ninety-eighth quatrain of *Centurie Fifth*, "*A quarante huict degré climaterique,*" which states, "*At forty eight degree climacterically*". This has nothing to do with latitude, because "*degree climacterical*" is an astrological statement, but this quatrain can be found translated as if the number written is representative of the number *48*, with an appearance made as "*48 degrees*".

Further, Nostradamus wrote in the main theme line of the ninety-seventh quatrain found in *Centurie Sixth*, "*Cinq & quarante degrez ciel bruslera,*" which begins a rather popularized quatrain. It actually translates to state, "*Five & forty degrees sky will burn,*" but most people will ignore the presence of an ampersand and transform this main theme to be about something "*burning*" in the "*sky*" at 45 "*degrees*". The point to grasp from these two examples of "*degree*" in the quatrains is they were both spelled out, and not represented by numerals.

---

209   The 1568 Lyon edition has Nostradamus spelling the number out, as "*du septiesme millenaire*".

After Nostradamus went through this *"degree"* portion of the letter to Henri, about six pages later he wrote in dates of the months, referencing planetary movements. After beginning a section by spelling out numbers, writing, "*... à sept du mois d'Avril, jusques au quinze d'Avril*", or "*...in seven of the month of April, until to the fifteenth of April*", Nostradamus began using numerals. He then wrote, "*à 14. de Juin jusques 7. Octobre Mars depuis le 17. d'Avril, jusques au 22. Juin, Venus depuis 9. d'Avril jusques au 22. de May, Mercure depuis le 3. Fevrier, jusques au 27. dudit. En après du premier de Juin jusques au 24. dudit, & du 25. de Septembre jusques au 16. de Octobre*". This translates to state, "*with 14 of June until 7 October Mars since the 17th of April, until to the 22nd June, Venus since 9th of April until to the 22nd of May, Mercury since the 3rd February, until to the 27th, due said. In after to the first of June until to the 24th due said, & 25th of September until to the 16th of October*". From all of this specific timing, which is again relative to astrological phenomena, there are few examples of 2-digit Arabic numerals anywhere else in *The Prophecies*, certainly nothing like the number found in the letter to Henry II.

The 1568 Lyon edition lists the numeral "*xj.*" in the letter to Henry (on the 18th page of a 21-page document), where all other editions observed spell out the word, "*onze*". This edition also lists the Arabic numeral, "*25.*" in the same letter (on the 19th page of a 21-page document), when all other editions show this spelled out as well, "*vingt-cinq*". Both of these uses of numerals were in reference to the word "*ans*" (*years*), which followed each. It is once again interesting that another Roman numeral is used, but not in agreement with the other editions.

The use of "*xi.*" is also found to be present in the thirtieth quatrain in *Century Fourth*, in the lower-case, in the 1555 Albi edition. It appears in the upper case in the Bonhomme edition ("*XI*"), only to be spelled out in all subsequent editions ("*unze*"). From this difference, a pattern arises. When all uses of Roman numerals are found in the earliest editions of the quatrains (1555), they are consecutive in number (*XI., XII., XIII.*, and *xiiij*. [Bonhomme], or *xi., XII., XIII.*, and *.xiiij*. [Albi]). A consecutive string is represented (11 thru 14), with both lower case and upper case numerals presented.

It is also interesting that the 1568 Lyon edition ended the letter to Henri by dating it, "*De Salon ce xxvij. Juing. Mil cinq cens cinquantehuit,*" where the date of the month took more typeset than did the "*25. ans*" listed prior. He also spelled out the year, which was in line with the year verbiage of the quatrains. However, other editions consistently show Nostradamus dating the letter of explanation as, "*De Salon, ce 27. de Juin, 1558*".

At this point, the differences found displayed throughout the various surviving editions of *The Prophecies* make it seem that Nostradamus' manuscript was turned over into the hands of the printers, with free rein to do what they wanted, as far as numbers were concerned. This wide variety of presentations makes it difficult to determine which way was actually intended by the author. While I have my preferences as far as the various editions are concerned, and my feeling that some are more true to Nostradamus' instructions, in reference to duplicating the manuscript precisely as written, feelings cannot be proven.

Therefore, all possibilities have to be seen as being possible, and for a reason. Rather than eliminating any possibilities, all must be considered purposefully intended, even when shown different ways.

One element that should have been noticed in this discussion about numerals is the presence of period marks, or the transforming of a Roman numeral "*i*" into a "*j*". The period symbols follow the rules where the mark acts as a sign for abbreviation for ordinal number (i.e.: *27.* means *27th*). This symbol is also a sign for a full stop, as a separator between numeral and word. The "*j*" is probably a printers way of denoting the last figure in a lower-case set of Roman numerals. With multiple "*i's*" used, the ending placement of "*j*" acts like a comma, with the following period mark designating the end of the number. The combination, such as in "*xxvij.*" expresses an ending separation through the use of "*j*" as "*i,*" (as a number in date is separated by comma in English, as in "*May 21, 2010*"), while the period is the sign of abbreviation for an ordinal number.

In French, it is common to see period marks and commas used with numerals, which are opposite to those applied to numerals in English. For instance, numerals are separated into thousands by periods, rather than commas (12.345, rather than 12,345), and fractions are denoted by commas, rather than periods (9,45 Euros, versus 9.45 Dollars). These marks must be seen as signs that only attach to numerals.

The numerals are then marks that need to be seen as mathematical tools, more than a quicker way to symbolize numbers. As such tools they represent the math of time ("*the year*" and date of a month), distance ("*degré*", "*degrez*"), and ordinal number ("*xiiij*", "*XII.*"). This becomes obvious because of the examples of numbers found spelled out, representing years, distance, and ordinal number, in both letters and the quatrains. The math of these numerical elements can then be seen as drawing attention to the math of astrology-astronomy.

In the letter to Henry II, Nostradamus wrote, "*toutesfois esperant de laisser par escript le ans,*" which states, "*nevertheless trusting of to set aside by writing the years*". This is a statement that says the intent of The Prophecies was not to identify the years by specifically writing them, in number or numeral, so that they are plain to see and understand as such. Still, it is also a statement that Nostradamus had "*written the years*", as being identified specifically, which he did in his publications of yearly predictions. Each year was identified in the title, such as, "*PROGNOSTICATION, NOVVELLE, POUR L'AN, Mil cinq cens cinquante & huict.*" This states, "*PROGNOSTICATION, NEW, FOR THE YEAR, One thousand five hundred fifty & eight.*" Thus, years specifically written as "*1585*", "*1606*", and "*1557*", are relative to the almanacs, not The Prophecies.

Nostradamus followed his writing of "*1606*", in the letter to Henry, with the specific statement of "*depuis le temps present, qui est le 14. de Mars 1557*", stating, "*since the times present, which is the 14th of March 1557*". The PROGNOSTICATION listed above was dated in the first paragraph of the introduction as having been written, "*De Salon ce premier jour de May 1557,*" stating, "*From Salon this first day of*

May 1557". This means that a publication for any specific year, such as were the predictions for 1558, had to be completed more than six months in advance. Thus, to write predictions based on astrology, an astrologer would have to work year round figuring the movements of planets for the following year, just to be that specific and meet publishing deadlines.

Nostradamus, writing his letter to the king in 1557-58, would die in 1566. Thus, his statement, *"mesme de l'annee 1585"*, meant that the *"same to the year 1585"* would be a set pattern for royal astrologers to follow, in their producing yearly almanacs. This statement of sameness is then followed by Nostradamus writing, *"de l'annee 1606. accommençant depuis le temps present,"* which translates to say, *"from the year 1606 commencing since the times present"*. This is saying that *"the times present"* in The Prophecies will not begin, or commence, until *"the year 1606"*.

This does not mean anything in the poems is relative to that specific year. It means nothing of pertinence will be found in the verses until after then. Interestingly, *1606* is the year that a charter was established by the King of England (James I), for the establishment of settlements in Jamestown. That would be the beginning of what would become the United States of America; but the USA would not be worthy of prophetic poetry for quite some time.

When one sees how these explanations of years, found in the letter to Henry II, are referencing the explanation of the Preface, where Nostradamus explained The Prophecies was very different than the almanacs, one can see how *3797* was also a numerical breakdown of an astrologer's year of almanac preparations. In the Preface, leading up to his writing, *"the year 3797,"* Nostradamus was explaining his astrological-astronomical calculations, which were his prognostication almanacs. He wrote, *"j'ay composé livres de propheties, contenant chacun cent quatrains astronomiques de propheties,"* which says, *"I have composed books of prophecies, containing each one hundred quatrains astronomical to prophecies"*.

The plural of *"books"*, where *"livres"* can also translate as, *"works in writing, compositions, or dialogues,"* is referencing multiple past publications, not the multiple 'chapters' that are the Centuries. The word *"each"* then means all combined within *"each"*, for a total of *"one hundred quatrains"* having been produced prior to The Prophecies. These *"prophecies"* were known to have been a direct result of Nostradamus' skills as an astrologer. When this is then combined with the process of meeting the needs of publishers, the numbers *3*, *7*, and *9* become important.

One needs to realize that the months of *"each"* year were numbered according to the name of the month (i.e.: **Sept**ember was the seventh month, **Oct**ober was the eighth month, **Nov**ember was the ninth month, and **Dec**ember was the tenth month). March was the first month of the year, making May the third month. This was the date Nostradamus stated he finished the 1558 almanac, in *"1557"*. September is then the seventh month, which would be the deadline for amending his work, and having it in the hands of the publisher. Then, November would be the ninth month, which would be when the printing process would begin, so that enough issues could be produced to meet the demands when placed on sale, in December, prior to the January official beginning of the year. The final seven would then represent the number of years Nostradamus had produced almanacs, which would mean his first would have been for the year 1551. With seven being the number of years, the "*one hundred quatrains*" would have averaged around 14 per year, allowing for bonus material.

This is my theory on Nostradamus' use of numerals. The fact that the numeral "*3797*" was written means it has to have some functional meaning, particularly one where the function is mathematical. I offer my opinion based on my past work with *The Prophecies*, but this does not mean other meanings are impossible. What I hope to have accomplished is pointing out how nothing is insignificant in this document of Nostradamus. There is deeper meaning to everything written.

We are not finished addressing numbers, in particular dates and degrees, but we are finished with the use of numeral symbols. It must be understood that the mysterious elements of the quatrains is what is prefaced and explained in the two letters. The presences of numerals in those instructions are only relevant to the verses, if the verses mirror what the letters say. If the poems do not reflect those numerals, in particular the years, dates of planetary movement, and degrees, they represent extraneous information. We saw how the biblical timeline was extraneous to the actual stories of the quatrains, but the information was still pertinent to understanding that the stories were in need of reordering.

Greek Alphabet Letters and Glyphs

I include this section primarily because of the 1555 Bonhomme edition, most evidently in the 1555 Albi copy. In those two editions, in the eighty-first quatrain found in *Centurie First*, the first three words not only are Greek alphabet letters spelled out, the first letter of each word is actually the Greek letter the word spells. Whereas all other editions simply spell out, "*Kappa, Thita, Lambda*", those two editions show, "Καπ. Θhita λambda", with the word *Kappa* abbreviated, while written in all Greek letters. The Greek letter for *Lambda* is set in the lower case (along with "alpha pi"), with the *Kappa* and *Thita* letters in the upper case. Other than the period mark denoting the abbreviation, there is no punctuation between these three words.

Another place where the 1555 Bonhomme and Albi editions show a Greek alphabet letter is in the sixty-fourth quatrain found in *Centurie Third*. In the main theme line, the last word is presented in all capital letters, as "*OLXAΔES*," where the "XAΔ" are the Greek letters (Chi, Alpha, Delta) for "*ChAD*". This is why all other editions show, "*Olchade*" as what was written (without the ending "s", or the all-caps). This is reference to the *Olcades* region of southeastern Spain, between Valencia and the source for the Tagus River.

A third example is once again only found in the 1555 editions, where the thirty-second quatrain found in *Centurie Fourth* shows, "παντα χοινα φιλωμ". This is then commonly misspelled in most other editions as, "*Panta chiona philon*", where "*Panta*" is incorrectly capitalized, and where "*chiona*" incorrectly replaces the "*i*" with the one in "*chi*" (more properly "*chioina*"). This is a phonetic spelling of "*panta koina filon*, which is commonly accepted to be Greek for, "*All things common between friends*",[210] but literally translates to state, "*Always commonly friends*".

Since this is more than a sampling of Greek alphabet lettering, where whole Greek words are spelled out as Greeks would read them, the element of being Greek has to stand out as important. When one sees the other examples of Greek alphabet use, where capitalization adds to the importance, including the traditional spelling of "*Panta*" that way, one sees how the Greek language becomes an elevation to the text. Such an elevation would come from Greek being the language of the New Testament, thus immediately representing Christianity through symbols. This would apply in each of these three example quatrains, even in the cases where the Latin-based alphabet were later substituted for the Greek alphabet letters.

This use is worth mentioning because it is doubtful French publishers had boxes full of Greek letters at their disposal. One could assume some effort was made to produce these Greek words in Greek type, as the 1555 editions show. It should not be assumed the publishers were prepared to print books in all languages, in all their native alphabets. The time it most probably took, to obtain the proper letters for typeset, could be why later editions changed to simply spelling the words in the translated forms. It is my opinion that Nostradamus did include Greek alphabet letters in his original manuscript, and then later granted permission for them to be commonly substituted.

The same can be said for the appearance of glyphs, which appear in only one quatrain, the same quatrain that the Roman numeral "*XI.*" appears in. The thirtieth quatrain in *Centurie Fourth*, in the 1555 Bonhomme edition only, shows the main theme to be stated as, "*Plus XI. fois ☽.☉. ne voudra*". This shows in all post-1555 editions as, "*Plus onze fois Luna Sol ne vouldra*".[211] This translates to state, "*More eleven times Moon Sun not will want*".

The issue surrounding the lack of consistency in editions presenting glyphs would be just like that for Greek alphabet letters. A French publishing company in the 16th century would not be expected to have boxes of astrological glyph type around, with which to set for printing. The main theme is

---

210   Quote from A Treatise of Human Nature, Book III: Of Morals, from "Sect. II - Of the origin of justice and property", Hume, David, retrieved from McMaster University Archive, modified for presentation by the University of Idaho and Carl Mikelsen. http://www.class.uidaho.edu/mickelsen/texts/Hume%20Treatise/hume%20treatise3.htm#PART%20II

211   The 1555 Albi copy of the Mace Bonhomme (Lyon) edition shows the Roman numerals in the lower case, as "*xi.*", with a bold **R. Q.** instead of the glyphs for *Moon* and *Sun*. Some later editions have removed the *l* from *vouldra*, making it *voudra*, which is the modern representation of the third-person future tense form of the verb *vouloir*.

primarily making an astrological statement, thus the use of astrological symbols is an aid in making this determination quickly. However, that value is not necessary, when it became obvious (the Albi, Utrecht, and Vienna 1555 editions) that publishers would struggle trying to adhere to the manuscript, especially when unusual symbols were used. Nostradamus probably saw that substituting the written words for the symbols as a worthy replacement.

All of this conjecture about both symbolic uses, numerals and glyphs, is based on the 1555 Bonhomme edition being an accurate depiction of Nostradamus' original manuscript. The four 1555 Bonhomme editions researched (Lyon, Albi, Vienna, and Utrecht) all end after presenting 53 quatrains in *Centurie Fourth*.[212] This is very different from the seven chapters attributed to Nostradamus' first edition, which first appear in the 1557 editions I researched. Those editions, with seven *Centuries*, differ in many instances from the 1555 editions, in text, as well as lacking most of this use of numerals and glyphs. Therefore, the question does remain, "Did Nostradamus' original manuscript contain quatrains with numerals and glyphs?"

---

[212] All are basically duplicates of the Ches. Macè Bonhomme Lyon edition.

Chapter 26

The System of Symmetry

For this system, the definition of "symmetry" has to be understood as, "A relationship of characteristic correspondence, equivalence, or identity among constituents of an entity or between different entities."[213] It is also is well defined as, "beauty resulting from a balanced arrangement of parts", from the Greek word "*summetria*", meaning, "proportion".[214] This is because the system of symmetry is another thread that beautifully connects the poetic whole of a quatrain, allowing more to be realized than has already been discussed in the other systems.

Each quatrain is symmetrical in the sense that there is a rhyme scheme, where the last words in the first two lines are reflected by words with similar sounds in the second two lines. This type of symmetry is simply an element of poetry, and beyond being a way of informing the reader that each line is a separate element of a poetic verse, that symmetry in itself adds nothing more to the understanding of a specific quatrain. All quatrains contain this generic form of symmetry. The system of symmetry focuses on the elements within the individual quatrains that allow for greater understanding, where the specific symmetry of each quatrain is different and unique.

One important aspect of this system is found in the use of an ampersand, as we have already discussed. The symmetry is clearly seen in the third use of an ampersand, where two lines are joined, but in particular where two words are joined by a symbolic "*and*". The caveat in this element of symmetry is that another mark of punctuation appearing next to the ampersand acts to discount this. Thus, all use of ampersand, alone between two words, will show a symmetrical relationship of correspondence, either expressing similarities or differences in the surrounding words. Knowing this is helpful in determining the translations of the words surrounding an ampersand.

For example, in the quatrain used previously to demonstrate ampersand usage, the twenty-fourth found in *Centurie Fifth*, line one contains "*regne & loy*" and line three contains "*loy & regne*". These two words were translated with "*regne*" being "*reign*", and "*loy*" being "*law*". The system of symmetry might not be as pronounced with these two translations, although one can readily see that "*reign and law*" have to

---

213   The Free Dictionary by Farlex, http://www.thefreedictionary.com/symmetry
214   <u>Collins Essential English Dictionary</u> 2nd Edition 2006 © HarperCollins Publishers 2004, 2006, http://www.thefreedictionary.com/symmetry

go hand-in-hand for either to have any lasting strength. Then, if *"regne"* is translated to be *"rule"*, we can quite easily see that *"rule and law"*, or *"law and rule"* are similarities, such that rules are laws and laws are rules. However, there is more that can be seen when one recognizes an unobstructed ampersand calls for examining the relationship further.

Due to these words being found at the beginning of lines one (main theme line) and three (supporting details to the main theme), with a capitalized article linking to the first word of the pair, creating the essence of *"Reign & law"* and *"Law & reign"* one can see symmetrical differences. The capitalized *"Reign"* is more in line with the translations *"Kingdom"* and *"Realm"*, where a land or nation is the focus. The lower case *"law"* that is joined with that *"Rule"* is then the *"law"* of man, and mutable, changing, and adjusting to societal norms. Then, when *"Law"* is seen as God's *"Law"*, as the fixed and permanent Commandments, forever written in stone, this becomes the totality of the world recognizing the importance of this *"Law"*, regardless of national boundaries. Therefore, when paired as *"Law and reign"*, this is the inner *"rule"* one has over oneself, based on a higher power.

With line one being an "A" line, and line three also being an "A" line, symmetry is showing the similarities of *"rule and law"* being the theme of this specific quatrain. The similarity addresses the issue that everyone has to live according to these limitations and restrictions, or face the consequences of breaking the *"rules"*, as stated by the *"law"*. Still, it is stating the differences that each individual must deal with, as far as the separation between religion and government. These are opposing principles when they are not allowed to mix, as found in the United States of America, where freedom of religion also means a separation between Church and State. However, in Islamic lands, and even Communist nations, the *"Reign AND Law"* shows similar principles (atheistic or theocratic).

This element of symmetry, as applied to uninterrupted ampersand use, is present throughout the quatrains and letters. In cases of interrupted ampersands, such as *", &"*, one needs to look to the whole of the two lines surrounding the ampersand. For an example of this, I recommend a review of my interpretation of the segment from the letter to Henry II, where three ampersands were found. Look for the symmetry relative to the union of statements, as *"in seeing as extended perceptions, and for under all the concavity of the Moon will be reckoning"*. The symmetry is deeper, but finds similarity and difference in the possible translations of *"entension & lieu"*, where both represent a state of being. As either *"perceptions and reckoning"*, *"apprehensions and place"*, or *"understanding and calling"*, both words reflect a combination of external (empiricism) and internal (innatism) states of awareness.

The ampersand is only one element where symmetry is found. It is also found in the presentation of proper names, and the repeated use of the same words in one quatrain. Each quatrain, again, has its own symmetrical signature, but a typical example of a quatrain with multiple uses of symmetry can be found in the sixty-eighth verse of *Centurie Fifth*. The example shown is indicative of the one from the 1557 Utrecht edition, with line three's use of capitalization (or lack of use), and line four's lack of capitalization differing in some other publications.

Dans le Dannube & du Rin viendra boire,	*Within it Danube & from the Rhine will come to drink,*
Le grand Chameau ne s'en repentira:	*The great Camel not themselves upon will repent:*
Trembler du Rosne & plus fort ceulx de loire:	*To tremble to the Rhone & more strong those with loire:*
Et pres des Alpes coq le ruïnera.	*And nearby from the Alps cock he will ruin.*

Obviously, this quatrain also has two ampersands, with each on the "A" lines, one and three. The first ampersand is surrounded by capitalized names, "*le Dannube & du Rin*", which are the names of two major European rivers, "*the Danube and to the Rhine*". This similarity is also compounded by the fact that both rivers flow through Germany. At one point, the two rivers flow in opposite directions, less than fifteen miles apart, with the "*Danube*" in Germany and the "*Rhine*" in Switzerland. The two rivers together once represented most of the northern inland frontier of the Roman Empire.[215]

There is a difference in the fact that the "*Danube*" is sourced in Germany, while the "*Rhine*" is sourced in the Swiss Alps. The "*Rhine*" flows north, to the North Sea (bordering Switzerland and Germany, then bordering France and Germany), through Germany before flowing through the lowlands of The Netherlands. The "*Danube*", on the other hand, flows east, taking it through or bordering on ten eastern European countries, before emptying into the Black Sea. Thus, the "*Danube*" is mostly an Eastern European river, with the "*Rhine*" one of Western Europe.

The other ampersand then is surrounded by "*du Rosne*" and "*plus*", which specifically names another European river, "*of the Rhone*", and then implies "*more*" rivers. This is obviously symmetry of opposing principles, where the general balances the specific. However, at the end of the line begun by the ampersand is the word "*loire*", which is believed to be the name of the river "*Loire*", with some editions capitalizing it to be such.[216] The lower case adds to the symmetry of opposition, where the personification of a word is balanced by the generality of a word, with all names originating from words. However, the specificity of the "*Loire*" means a symmetry of similarity exists between lines one and three, where ampersands separate two rivers in one nation (both in Germany, both in France).

Both the "*Rhone and Loire*" are in France, with both flowing in opposite directions, less than 40 miles apart. This is similar to the closeness of the "*Danube*" and the "*Rhine*". The "*Loire*" flows north, before bending to the west and emptying into the Atlantic Ocean. The "*Rhone*" flows south from Switzerland (its source) and empties in the Mediterranean Sea. The "*Loire*" is the longest river in France, with the

---

215   Wikipedia the free encyclopedia, http://en.wikipedia.org/wiki/Rhine
216   Some editions have *rosne* and *loire* in the lower case (1557 Budapest edition), with some having *rhône* and *Loire* (1698 Lyon), and some having *Rosne* and *Loire* (1566 Lyon).

"*Rhone*" considered one of Europe's major rivers.

The symmetry created by this double grouping of European rivers, particularly rivers of Germany and France, is significant in determining the full meaning of this quatrain. All of the meaning that comes from these similarities and differences plays into that overall meaning. Still, there are other symmetrical elements of this quatrain.

The two "B" lines (two and four) each have a proper name listed, where capitalization signifies this. Those two reflective names are "*Chameau*" in line two and "*Alpes*" in line four, where "*Camel*" is relating to "*Alps*". This obviously is a dislike, but it brings to mind Hannibal's use of elephants when he crossed the "*Alps*" to invade Rome. The use of "*Camel*" is then symbolic of an indigenous creature of North Africa and the Middle East. While this symmetrical connection can very easily be missed, there is one more recognizable, where animals are similarly compared.

This symmetry compares the "*Camel*" of line two to the "*cock*" of line four. Some editions capitalize the word "*cock*", further showing how importance was recognized by this usage.[217] In this use of symmetry, the "*cock*" has to be recognized as one of the national symbols of France. The history of this symbol is rooted in the similarity in both the Latin word for "*cock*" and the Roman name for the inhabitants of Gaul (France), which were "*Gallus*" (Gaul) and "*gallicus*" (*cock*). This history dates to when Gaul was part of the Roman Empire.[218] This makes its use supportive of the uses of "*Rhone*" and "*more*", which would be "*those of loire*". This would then indicate that the "*Camel*" is likewise a symbol of a nation.

There is no nation whose symbol is the "*Camel*", although there is history that the Persians used the animals militarily in the sixth century B.C., when Cyrus II the Great used them to overtake the Asia Minor region of Lydia.[219] The greatest numbers of the world's population of "*Camels*" are found in Somalia, and the Somali region of Ethiopia, where half of the world's 14-million dromedaries are in Somalia alone.[220] One nation, Eritrea, lists the "*Camel*" as its national symbol, with that nation being located on the Red Sea, north of Ethiopia, east of Sudan (another nation with significant "*Camel*" population). Another nation, Kuwait, lists the "*Camel*" as its national animal. Neither of these nations depicts this creature on its flags.

This becomes evidence of a generalization applying to the specific, where the capitalized "*Camel*" is indicative of multiple nations in Africa and the Middle East. This is contrary to the strong evidence that the "*cock*" is symbolic only of France. The symmetry created then shows many versus one, which is vital information that assists understanding this quatrain. This is particularly true when the symmetry of the

---

217   The 1566 Lyon and 1698 Lyon editions both capitalized *Cock*.
218   French National Symbols: The Cockerel (UK cock, US rooster), http://www.languedoc-france. info/06141212_cockerel.htm
219   Wikipedia the free encyclopedia, http://en.wikipedia.org/wiki/Camel
220   Ibid.

verbs is considered.

Line one ends with the verb "*boire*", which means, "*to drink, to swallow up*", or even "*an ill savor*", which is an indication of the rivers of Europe being water sources for the people, with the potential of something polluting those sources. Line two presents a symmetrical line-ending verb, "*repentira*", which means, "*to repent, to grieve*, or *to be sorry for*". These verbs show a present situation that will lead to a future situation, one for which blame or responsibility is placed, where a lack of "*repentance*" shows the purpose of punishment, where "*sorrow*" is evident. This is symmetry of cause and effect, which is a symmetrical difference.

Symmetry of similarity then exists in the last two verbs of this quatrain. Line three begins with the capitalized first word, "*Trembler*" (meaning "*To tremble*", or "*To shake*"), and line four ends with the word "*ruinera*" (meaning "*will ruin, will subvert, will overthrow*, or *will destroy*"). The two together would represent the damage an earthquake would cause, where a present situation leads to a future situation, making this symmetrical to the cause an effect of the first verb pair. However, both verbs are similar in the element of physical abuse and forced control. This brings to mind the French (*cock*) involvement in Africa and the Middle East (*Camel*), as an empirical colonizer, or mandated controller, which could be the source of longstanding resentments that lead to retribution, due to a lack of "*repentance*".

One last element of symmetry, one that is a common element throughout the quatrains and the "sentences" of the letters, is the repeating directional preposition "*de*". This is found in line one, as "*du*" (*de* + *le*), in line three as "*du*" and "*de*", and to a lesser degree in line four, where the plural form, "*des*" (*de* + *les*), is found. The rule of symmetry is such that if one word has multiple translations possible, each representation of a repeated word bears a different translation. While each can have all possible translations used, each specific use eliminates that choice of translations for the repeated uses. Thus, this quatrain says, "...*from* the Rhine ... *to* the Rhone ... *with* sediment (root meaning of the word, from Latin "*Liger*", and Gaulish "*liga*")[221] ... *of the Alps*", while equally saying, "...*of the Rhine* ... *with* the Rhone ...*from* silt (alternate translation) ... *to the Alps*".

This same application of symmetry can apply to the three appearances of the repeated article "*le*". This can translate as "*the, him, a, an, it,* or *them*", causing a translation of, "**the** Danube ... **Them** great ... **him** will ruin." Likewise, it could state, "**it** Danube ... **Him** great ...**them** will ruin." This element of repeated words finding multiple translations is not only applicable to articles and prepositions, although they most frequently repeat. Any word that repeats has to be searched for alternate translation capabilities, so that added depth of the meaning can be gained.

By realizing there is a system of symmetry built into the language used, this becomes a valuable tool when coming upon "manufactured" words. Due to some words having greater difficulty involved in

---

221   Wikipedia the free encyclopedia, http://en.wikipedia.org/wiki/Loire_River

solving them, it is often a good move to leave them as they are, and move on to the other words of the quatrain. Each word position will have symmetrical positions in the other lines, again, dependent on the internal symmetry of each quatrain. Many times, I have seen where a known word is the symmetrical balance to the unknown word. This becomes helpful in looking again at the difficult word, in an effort to find meaning, which becomes a perfect fit to the other words with which it relates.

Chapter 27

The System of Figurative Language

So far in the systems, I have stressed the importance of sticking strictly with literal translations, in order to maintain the correct flow of words, and thus the correct flow of thought. In translating Nostradamus literally, one looks for literal applications for the multiple translation possibilities. However, this does not mean that every translation possibility is read literally.

Much of what Nostradamus wrote in *The Prophecies*, including the letters of instruction and explanation, has to be seen as figures of speech. A "figure of speech" can be defined as, "An expression that uses language in a nonliteral way".[222] These can be expressed as metaphors (a reference to something that symbolizes something else), similes (two unlike things compared), prosopopeia (the use of an absent or imaginary person as if real), and many other types of representation defined as being a figure of speech (synecdoche, anaphora, trope, etc.).

This use of figurative language can be sorted into three basic categories: Places, People, and Things (where "things" is anything other than places or specific people). Each basic category is then subdivided, such that the places are specific nations, cities, and geographic regions stated in the writings (*France, Paris, l'Europe*), either present or ancient (*France-Gaule, Ongrie-Pannons*). The category of people is one where all representatives are from classical literature, split into subsets of real and imaginary. The real people are then biblical (*Joel, Messie* [Messiah], *Ismaël*) or historical (*Agrippé, Plutarque* [Plutarch], *Plancus*), while the imaginary people are mythological (Greek, Roman, Celtic), and either gods (*Vulcan, Hermes, Latona*),[223] demigods (*Hercules, Phaëton, Achiles*), or humans (*Belleforon* [Bellerophon], *Mirmidon* [Myrmidon], *Castor*). The category of things I break down into animals (*Aigle, Coq, Loup*), colors (*blanc, azur, aerain*), and titles (*King, Prelate, Empereur*). All of these places, people, and things are examples of figurative language.

While all of these uses are figurative, the ones least apt to be figurative are the place names. In the preface, Nostradamus warned us to be careful about seeing too much in *"the places"* that are listed in the quatrains. He repeated *"lieux"* twice in a four series segment, found on page eight in the 1557 Utrecht

---
222   The Free Dictionary by Farlex, http://www.thefreedictionary.com/figure+of+speech
223   In this category, I have removed all which are Roman names for the known planets and orbs of astrology. That is a separate systemic category.

edition. The key string states, "*limitant les particulatité des lieux,*" which translates to say, "*limiting the particularity of the places*," where "*particularity*" means the special relationship of a name, to a place, is limited.

In other words, if Nostradamus wrote, "*Paris*", but the quatrain says nothing to indicate France is the "*place*", then it is okay to see what he wrote as "*Pari-s*". The word "*pari*" comes from the verb "*parier*", meaning, "to bet, wager, make a guess about the outcome of an event". Further, the plural form meaning, "*bets, wagers*" is "*paris.*" This means if "*Paris*" is limited, so it cannot be Paris, France, it means important ones (capitalization) who are making "*Wagers*" about some outcome. Thus, the word "*Paris*" is figuratively representing the true meaning intended with the word.

That example is not necessarily one that will be found in *The Prophecies*, but it is how one has to approach what first appears to be a proper name. To some degree, "*Paris*" will mean "*Paris*" the city, a place; but more often the placement of a place (city or region) in a quatrain is meant to be seen as the personification of the word(s) that are at the root of the city's name. This means the etymology of places plays a big role in seeing a name as the word the name came from. In reference to Paris, its name comes from the name of the people who first inhabited that place, the Parisii. They called themselves that because they were "working people", or "craftsmen", which comes from the Celtic Gallic word, "*parisio.*"[224] This could be seen as a form of reverse metonymy, where the meaning of the name is substituted for the name.

To use an example from a quatrain, Nostradamus wrote of "*Luxembourg*", which is the name of a specific place, but the root of the name for the place is "small castle" (from the word *Lucilinburhuc*). It can also be seen rooted in Latin, where "*Luxem bourg*" can be read as "*World*" (from "*Lux*" or "*Lucis*") "*castle*" (from "*burgus*"), or "*Dawn breaking*" (from "*Luxit*") "*fortress*" (from "*burgus*"). It can then be seen as wholly French, as "*Luxe*" (meaning "*Excess*") "*m*" (abbreviated "*me*") "*bourg*" (meaning "*a great town*"). In other words, the word "*Luxembourg*" can mean several other things that are more pertinent to the interpretation of a quatrain, than would be the specific small nation between Germany, France, and Belgium, or the city that bears the same name as the country.

Let me add one bit of advice about cities being seen as something other than the city of reference. Capitalization and correct spelling are very important. There are many places in the quatrains where Nostradamus specifically mentioned several cities, which act to specify that quatrain's event to one geographic area. In those cases, the cities will be near one another, or related to one another in some way that is part of the theme of the quatrain. However, each named city must be studied, to find its true measure in the quatrain's meaning.

One very famous (or infamous) case of Nostradamus lore is the belief that he named (a misspelling) Napoleon in the first quatrain of *Centurie Eighth*. The main theme line in that quatrain states, "*PAU, NAY,*

---

224 This is what some theorize as to the origin, as stated in the Wikopedia article on Paris, in the "etymology" section.

LORON plus feu qu'a sang fera". Some have seen this all-caps use, which correctly spells the names of three towns in southwestern France, as an anagram spelling out NAPOLUAN ROY. Supposedly, this somehow translates to be NAPOLEON KING (the translation of ROI). Unfortunately, the system of punctuation spoils this idea. The presence of two commas does not allow such foolishness to take place, let alone the butchering of Napoleon's name.

This main theme line states, *"PAU, NAY, OLORON more fire that with blood will be"*. *PAU*, *NAY*, and *OLORON* are all towns in the Pyrénées-Atlantiques Department of France, with each no more than 15 miles apart from the others. This region of France, along the Pyrenees Mountains, from Mediterranean Sea to Atlantic Ocean, is referenced by multiple quatrains that specifically list groups of cities in the same region of France, as this quatrain does. In that sense, the specificity of places, like cities, groups quatrains together.

The all-caps use is obvious in the 1566 and 1568 Lyon editions, although later editions simply show three proper noun names. The missing *"O"* from *OLORON* means *LORON* could become *L'OR-ON*, or *THE GOLD ONE*, or something from a Latin root, such as *"Lorum"* (meaning, "whip, scourge, leather strap"). However, it is fairly obvious that the intention is to see *"LORON"* as *"OLORON"*, at least on a secondary level, to match the other two places.

Due to the all-caps, higher importance can be found, for a relatively small town, by having it represent a broader area. With the river named *Oloron*, the towns named *Oloron*-Ste.-Marie, and Arros-de-*Oloron*, *"OLORON"* becomes greater than one town. When one finds west of *NAY* to be Arros-de-*Nay* (where *arros* refers to water), one can see how *"LORON"* is referencing both cities named *"NAY"* and *"OLORON"*, because the river of *"NAY"* and Arros-de-*Nay* is the *"PAU"* River.

For these three all-cap words, once one has found them to be places in close proximity of one another, one has to realize that three names, in all-caps, are beginning the main theme statement for this quatrain. The main theme has to make good sense, as, *"PAU, NAY, OLORON more fire that with blood will be"*. The presence of commas, making *"PAU"* a stand-alone statement, *"NAY"* another stand-alone statement, which has to lead one to understand, *"LORON plus feu qu'a sang fera"* as the third of three segments to create a strong theme. Looking at these three names this way should make one check the etymology before going further.

When this is done, one find *"pau"* is clean Old French, meaning, *"stake"*. The letters that spell *"NAY"*, due to the interchangeability of *"i"* and *"y"*, could actually state, *"nai"*, which is Old French for, "ship". Further, since the absence of an apostrophe does not mean one cannot be added, the letters *"NAY"* could be written as, *"n'ai"*. That contracted combination means, *"not have"*. Reviewing how *"LORON"* is short an *"O"*, it might make more sense as *"LOR-ON"*, as a manufactured word from Latin (due to all-caps meaning associating with Latin meaning), as, *"ONE WHIP"*. The line begins to take form as a more meaningful statement, stating, "*STAKE, NOT HAVE, ONE STRAP more fire that with blood will cause*". Something like this would become the primary focus, with the location of southwest France being where this will be happening.

This should make it clear how something appearing like a proper name can become something else, less limited, thus more meaningful. Still, not all cities are figures of speech. Some cities are necessary to be stated, so one knows what area of the world a quatrain focuses on. The system of figurative language applies most frequently to lines where the majority of the information presented appears to be little more than a list of cities. The presentation of names of "cities", missing the proper capitalization, (personification) is a hint to look behind the meaning of the name, not to change the text to capitalize, thus limit the meaning of what was written.

For example, in the ninetieth quatrain in *Centurie Fifth*, the first two lines (the main theme and the secondary theme) state, "*Dans les cyclades, en perinthe & larisse, / Dedans Sparte tout le Pelloponnesse*". This translates to say, "*In the cyclades, in perinthus & larissa, / Within Sparta all the Peloponnesse*". Every edition I researched shows the places listed in the main theme in the lower case, while all editions show *Sparte* in the upper case, with most showing *Pelloponnesse* in the upper case (although one spells it *Peloponnesse*, with only one "*l*").

The lack of capitalization in the main theme forces one to look at the Greek root to those recognized names of places: "*cyclades*" means "*around*"; "*perinthe*" has the Greek root word "*peri*", which means "*of, towards*"; and "*larissa*" is ancient Greek for "*stronghold*". Simply by seeing these meanings, one can get a feel for some of the ancient history of the islands "*around*" Greece, in particular the island of Samos (believed to be the origin of the *Perinthus*), and its resistance to Philippe of Macedon. Samos also played a role in the *Peloponnesian* War, siding with Athens against *Spartan* dominion. The *Spartan* power had grown after Persian invasion attempts had been thwarted in the islands. All of this can be seen presented in these two theme statements, when the place names are read as figures of speech.

This history, of course, has nothing to do with the storyline of *The Prophecies*. This quatrain is not telling about ancient history. It is telling about another example of how history tends to mimic itself, through similar events separated by spans of time. The main theme is better stated as, "*Inwardly them around, on towards & stronghold*". This main theme is deeper than one seen as being a statement about a series of places originally established by Greeks, which means little.

A group of islands that are part of Greece (the Cyclades), and a place known as *Heraclea Perinthus* in antiquity (although now known as Marmara Ereğli, in modern Turkey), makes a complete statement about nothing but those places. The ampersand then acts to emphasize the place known since antiquity as Larissa, which still exists, and is the capital of Thessaly, in Greece. Still, those places, while being the essence of ancient Greece, offer nothing that can act as the theme around which a quatrain can be solved.

The place of this activity, relative to the main theme, is then identified in the secondary theme, as, "*Within Sparta all them the Peloponnesse*". Notice that "*Pelloponnesse*" has been recognized as a simple anagram, where the extra "*l*" has been relocated to the front, creating a contracted combination, "*l'Peloponnesse*". With this inserted immediately after the word "*le*", to remove the redundancy ("the the"), the word "*le*" is translated as "*them*", to reflect the multiples of people in "*the Peloponnesse*" and the plural that "*all*" encompasses.

The place known as "*Sparta*" was a city on the southwestern mainland peninsula known as "*the Peloponnesse*". This peninsula represents the southernmost part of the mainland of the nation Greece, bordering on the Ionian Sea, the Mediterranean Sea, the Aegean Sea, and the Sea of Crete, while surrounded by numerous gulfs. The city named Larissa on the northern mainland, in the periphery known as Thessaly. The Cyclades are the southern Greek islands, in the Aegean Sea, between "*the Peloponnesse*" and Turkey, north of Crete. If "*perinthus*" is to be seen as part of the European isthmus of modern Turkey, one gets a feel for how far it is from the other locations, although in the proximity of Greece. The secondary theme is clearly one of Greece, but the main theme is about something taking a strong hold "*within*" and "*around*" southern Greece, as something that would spread.

The two supporting lines to the two themes then state, "*Si grand famine, peste, par faux connisse, / Neuf moys tiendra & tout le cherrouesse.*" This translates to say, "So great famine, plague, for false to put forth itself, / Nine months will hold & all it very costly breaking all of the joints of the wheels itself."[225] The word *connisse* is seen to be Latin, as "*conisus-se*" (the prefix *con-* can be written *conn-*), with the word "*cherrousse*" being French, as *cher-roues-se*, although Old French had a word, "*rouësse*", which was, "the name of a certain great pear."

These translations recognize that "*connisse*" is not a form of the word "*connaistre*", "*connoistrte*", or "*cognoistre*", thus having nothing to do with a French word for "knowledge". These translations also recognize that "*cherrouesse*" is not a misspelling of "*chersonese*", the Greek word for "peninsula." It is recognized that the intention would be to mislead, with the above possibilities playing roles as secondary translations that assist the overall interpretation, but they are not the primary focus. Thus, "*cherrouesse*" and "*connisse*" are manufactured words; and all manufactured words can only find Latin or French solutions.[226]

The key words of line three, "*famine*" and "*plague*", cannot act as being supportive of a theme of places, like the Cyclades, Perinthus, and Larissa, other than to indicate events happening there. They

---

[225] The manufactured words *connisse* and *cherrouesse* are Latin and French respectively. *Connisse* becomes *connis-se*, which is Latin meaning "*to put forth –itself*. *Cherrouesse* becomes *cher-roues-se*, which is French for *very costly-breaking all of the joints of the wheels-itself*. Two manufactured words in a quatrain are another example of the system of symmetry.

[226] From the System of Language (p. 166).

become supportive of a theme that is developed, where something comes upon people (with those places becoming themselves secondarily supportive as where the people are), "*inwardly, around,* and *towards*", and growing in considerable strength ("*& stronghold*").

The key words of the fourth line are first "*Nine*", where "*Neuf*" can also translate as "*New*" or "*Strange*", second "*months*", and third the central portion of "*cherrouesse*", "*roue*", which is French for "*wheel*". The "*wheel*" relates well with the circular meaning found in the main theme ("*around*"), and the disease element of line three ("*plague*"), and the Greek element of line two ("*Sparta*", and "*the Peloponnesse*"), as the Greek Medicine *Wheel*.

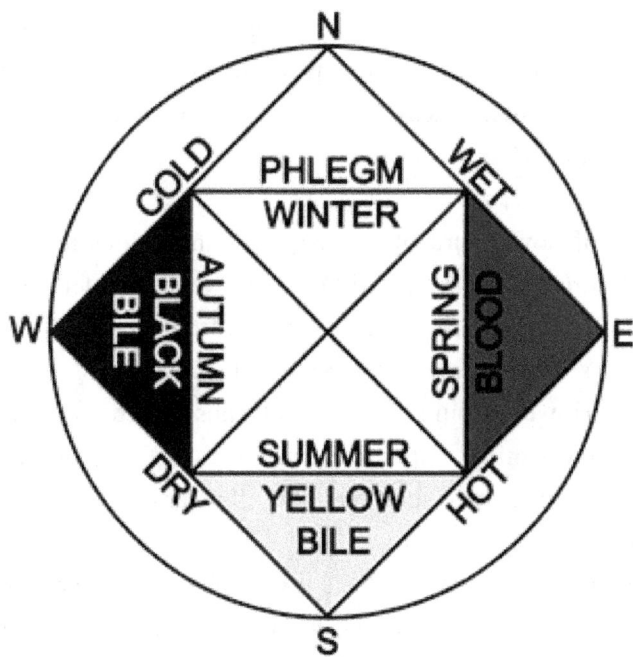

The Greek Medicine Wheel [227]

The Greek Medicine Wheel was a standard in the practice of medicine for centuries (up to 6,000 years[228]). It represented the view that health was always changing, with the functions of the body being relative to the "four humours" – Sanguine, Choleric, Phlegmatic, and Melancholic. Due to this representation as a wheel, which turns, the "*breaking of the wheel*" would become an indication of something upsetting this balance of natural health, through unnatural means.

Recognition of this use of figurative language means one can begin to read this quatrain as one telling of the advent of a powerful "*New strain*" (alternate translation of Latin "*connisus sum*") of toxin, which

---

227   David K. Osborne, copyright 2008, Greek Medicine.net, http://www.greekmedicine.net/b_p/The_greek_medicine_wheel.html
228   "The Four Humours", Kheper, http://www.kheper.net/topics/typology/four_humours.html

affects plants, and in turn ("*around*") humans, breaking down the food "*cycle*" (from "*cyclades*" and-or "*roue*"). This creates a "*New cycle*" that leads to "*famine*" and "*pestilence*" (alternate translation of "*peste*"), which would "*break the joints of the wheel*" over an important "*Nine months*" period. The use of the future tense verb, "*will hold*", in line four, is then reflective of how "*larisse*" translates as "*stronghold*", in the main theme. However, at this point it becomes necessary to see how "*larisse*" is misspelled, as "*Larissa*" ends with "*a*", not an "*e*".

One can then see "*larisse*" breaking down into "*l'aris-se*", where "*ari*" is Old French for, "Dried up; withered; without sap or humor; whose natural moisture is consumed." That translation turns the main theme into, "*Inwardly them around, on towards & the dried up ones themselves*". This further relates to the Greek Medicine *Wheel*, which acts as possibly timing the event, as beginning during the Summer-Autumn point on the "*wheel*". "*Nine month*" after would indicate a period that would last through the point of the following Spring-Summer. A season's worth of food would be lost, with "*famine*" already in place and intensified, along with "*plague*".

This is simply an example of how figure of speech plays in the quatrains. There is no doubt that Nostradamus knew "*les cyclades, perinthe*", and "*larisse*" were intended to have meaning relative to those places in the Aegean Sea region. As manufactured words, "*larisse, connisse*", and "*cherruesse*" (even "*Pelloponnesse*" is not spelled correctly) all represent some words that are similar to the spellings presented by Nostradamus. However, simply to give all those words only one meaning, one specific to those three places and three similarly spelled words, means the quatrain becomes too general to understand fully. The system of figurative speech allows all meaning to show.

Nostradamus went well beyond this example of his use of places as figures of speech. One particular form of allegorical figure of speech is the use of mythological figures, in particular those of Greek name. Nostradamus used 24 basic names (spelled various different ways), which are Greek, Latin-Roman, and Celtic names of gods, goddesses and heroes of ancient mythology. Many of these names can be found in the books of Virgil's *Aeneid*, or in Homer's *Iliad* and *Odyssey*. As books that Nostradamus would have been familiar with, from his university studies, he would be familiar with their characters. Those three books are excellent sources for understanding some of the details of *The Prophecies*, as we can see a future mimicking those past tales.

I have previously presented one example, where Nostradamus wrote of "*Castor & Pollux*" (he also wrote "*Castor Pollux*", without the ampersand, in another quatrain), who were twins (offspring of a god and a human), and nautical characters in Homer's *Odyssey*. There can be no doubt that Nostradamus was not prophesying about these two twins of Greek mythology, as far as actually having a role in our future. Their mention is a call for one to examine their mythological tales, so one can understand what moral qualities and/or abstractions can be taken from them and applied to some real person, who will be prepared to act as they did, in our future.

One such name was written nine times in the letter to Henry, and eight times in the quatrains, in one of two versions. The main version is "*Aquilon*", which is the Latin name of the "*North Wind*", but Nostradamus also referred to the "*Aquilonaire*", which becomes "*one of the North Wind*". Thus, "*Aquilon*" represents a nation or territory located at a northern latitude, and an "*Aquilonaire*" is an important leader from that nation or territory.

It then becomes easy to understand why Nostradamus did not mention "*Aquilon*" or "*Aquilonaire*" in the Preface, because the Preface is speaking in the general sense. The quatrains are the specifics, and the letter to Henry II is addressing the specifics, in general explanation. Thus, one reads the letter of explanation state, "*que tout iceluy Orient tremblera de la frayeur d'iceux freres, non freres Aquilonaires*", which translates to say, "*that all the same East will tremble from there fear of these brothers, not brothers of the North.*" Then, one reads the forty-ninth quatrain found in *Centurie First* stating in lines two and four, "*Ceux d'Orient par la vertu lunaire : / Subjugant presques le coing Aquilonaire.*" This translates to state, "*Those East through there virtue lunar: / Subjecting almost ones them wedge Northerners.*"

Two separate lines of text, both in the letter and in this one quatrain, contain the capitalized mid-line words "*Orient*" and "*Aquilonaire*".[229] In addition, words such as "*tremblera*" ("*will tremble*"), "*frayeur*" ("*terror*"), and "*subjugant*" ("*subjecting*") are found used, which are relative to a theme of persecution. When the letter is seen as explaining this quatrain, the quatrain has further support in holding meaning of "*Middle East Muslims*" (alternate substitution for "*d'Orient lunaire*") persecuting other Arabs ("*brothers*") who support "*Aquilon*" ("*the North*"). Since the "*Middle East*" is not a region "*of the North Wind*" (i.e.: a cold climate), "*Aquilonaire*", in this case can stand for anyone representing the interests of "*Aquilon*" in the Muslim world. As such, this represents the willingness of Muslims to kill other Muslims ("*brothers*"), in order to rid a land of foreign influence and cease those who would offer foreigners support.

This is just one meaning that can come from this example, as when "*Orient*" is left to stand along, it has meanings of alliance, with the "*Asia*" that borders the "*Middle East*", as well as the "*Far East.*" The "*East*" also has ramifications as "*Eastern* Europe", in particular due to their domination by the one true "*Aquilon*", Russia, a.k.a. the Soviet Union. As such, one word bears a wealth of possibilities, with all adding to the overall truth, even though one will take the primary lead role.

This example shows how some of Nostradamus' mythological references are duplicated in the Henry letter; but not all such usage finds equal presence in the letters of explanation. While Nostradamus frequently used "*Aquilon*" in the quatrains and the letter to Henry, he used "*Hercules*" seven times (including "*Hercles*" once), along with four uses of "*Ogmion*" (the Celtic version of *Hercules*), for a total of eleven uses in the verses, with only one mention of "*ogmium*" found in the Henry letter.

---

229   The 1566 Lyon edition.

Nostradamus also wrote in the quatrains about "*Diane*", "*Phebe*", "*Latona*", "*Artimide*", and "*Selin*", in various spellings, totaling 22 uses. All are related to the same (one or two) Greek mythological figures, relative to personifications of the Moon. None of these names are found duplicated in either letter. However, both letters and many other quatrains are found referencing "*Lune*" and "*Lunaires*". This multiplicity of naming, related to one central focus, is an example of the use of figurative language.

The point of Nostradamus using imaginary people is they are symbolic of the character flaws humans hold. All humans have an "Achilles heel", a place of vulnerability, which the gods know all too well. For every hero there is a fall (the story of "*Belleforon*"), and for everyone dedicated to his God there is salvation (the similar stories of "*Deucalion*" and "*Noë*"). This is how one has to come to know the individual characters used by Nostradamus. They all come with a history, which is symbolically relative to the story told in *The Prophecies*.

In the letter to Henry II, Nostradamus mentioned the real person "*Plutarque*", and then mentioned a character of one of his works, "*Lycurgus*". At that point in the letter, one is called upon to understand fully the legend of "*Lycurgus*", as told by "*Plutarch*", because of the traits "*Lycurgus*" stood for (rule of law, austerity, and citizen equality). Without understanding this tale from Plutarch's work, *The Life of Lycurgus*, we cannot understand the blocks of lines that follow in the letter. Nostradamus is repeating that story, as it is an important lesson that will need to be known, when the future of Nostradamus comes into focus. This is not found specifically in the verses, although everything in the verses is relative to that story, symbolically.

In my book, *The Letters of Nostradamus*, I wrote how Nostradamus meant more when he wrote, "*comme raconte le gravissime aucteur Plutarque en la vie Lycurgue, que voyant les offers & presens qu'on faisoit par sacrifices aux temples des dieux immortelz d'iceluy temps*". This literally translates to say, "*like told the gravest author Plutarch in the life Lycurgus, that seeing the offers & presents that one made by the sacrifices at the temples the two immortals of his times*". The systems tell us this means more than what first appears to be stated. The "more" here is the story told by "*Plutarch*", which unfolds when it is read thusly, in the voice of Nostradamus (the bold type denotes the literal translation of words written by Nostradamus):

> "**… it is like in the days of ancient Sparta. I know this because the story was told long ago, by the gravest or most serious author of Greek antiquity, Plutarch. I am reminded in the passages of the story Plutarch recounted, of the life of Lycurgus**. In **that** story, he wrote of Lycurgus' return to Sparta, after a period abroad, when two kings were fighting for control of the same land. No one was **seeing** a solution for this conflict, so they came to Lycurgus making him **the offers** for gaining the power to lead a unification of Sparta. Those offers led him to see a need to change the commonwealth. So, Lycurgus **presents** a plan **that** would make Sparta **one** nation, with two leaders.

To ensure that the graces of the gods would protect Sparta's unification, he **made** this secured **by** making holy **sacrifices, at** one of **the temples** of Apollo. That was the temple that housed the Oracle of Delphi, who was known to tell only the truth to those who questioned the priestess. The oracle confirmed that Sparta would indeed be best with **the two** kings, along with a Senate of 28 landowners, and with all sharing equal power. This arrangement was favored by **the immortals** then, just as Christ smiles at your willingness to share rule with the Church now; but, it is also important to know how Lycurgus' intent, based on the knowledge bestowed upon him by the deities **of his times**, was not understood by everyone."[230]

This is an example of how two real people, "*Plutarch*" and "*Lycurgus*" of Sparta, neither of which appears in any quatrain, are used to state figuratively how issues of debate can be settled. Their names were not chosen haphazardly. Their history must be known for understanding their references, as well as the symbolic meaning their references bring. Nostradamus wrote as if everyone fully understood the meaning behind his references of real and imaginary beings, such that by stating one name a figurative statement is made, for all that name means. One must then be prepared to investigate the details surrounding all such references, because even if one recognizes the name, confusion comes from pretending to know that detail.

The use of animals as a category of figurative language brings to mind the element of fable, and the name most related with fables, Aesop. The primary definition of the word, "*fable*", says it is, "A usually short narrative making an edifying or cautionary point and often employing as characters animals that speak and act like humans." This definition can then be used to explain the use of animals in heraldry, where each virtue of a people is depicted in the shields, crests, mottos, and supporters, such that animals were chosen to represent some quality found in those peoples.

The two animals most often found in European coats of arms are the lion and the eagle;[231] and Nostradamus frequently uses those two animals in the quatrains. His most used animal was the "*Aigle*", which he wrote 17 times into the quatrains. The "*Aigle*" represents the United States, by process of elimination. Although France has also been known to use the "*Eagle*" as its national symbol, Nostradamus used the older symbol, the "*Cock*", when he referenced France. He wrote "*Coq*" in the verses 16 times. His third most used animal symbol is "*Lyon*" (not counting the times he referred to Lyon, France), representing the "*Lion*" of England, which he wrote eight times in the quatrains and once in the letter to Henry.

While there are other animals Nostradamus wrote of, which strongly identify with a nation's coat of arms ("*Wolf*" – Italy, "*Leopard*" – Somalia, "*Bear*" – Russia, "*Camel*" – Eritrea), there are many other animals mentioned that do not have a national connection. Still, some animals are known through fables and other lore, to have strengths that are symbolized in those animals. For instance, a "*Fox*" ("*Renard*") is

---

230   Tippett, Robert, 2006, Katrina Pearls, Ridgeland, MS, p. 177.
231   Wikipedia the free encyclopedia, http://en.wikipedia.org/wiki/Heraldry

known to be sly, and a *"Horse"* (*"Cheval"*) is known for its military use, as the cavalry unit. Each time Nostradamus wrote an animal into his quatrains, it has some role to play in the figurative sense, even if the literal can be meant as well (*"flies"* [*"mouchez"*], *"wasps"* [*"guespes"*], *"cats"* [*"chats"*], and *"dogs"* [*"chiens"*]).

Since the use of animals has been shown to have a heraldic connection, the element of color can also fall under this heading somewhat. Heraldry has rules by which a coat of arms follows, one of which is called "tincture". This typically means "color", but in heraldry, it encompasses metals and furs as well. I include Nostradamus nine uses of *"or"* (*"gold"*), his eight uses of *"argent"* (*"silver"*), and his four uses of *"aerain"* *"bronze-brass-copper"*) as examples of his use of color, in the metallic realm. Metals are known for their values, in the sense they represent that which has traditionally backed currency. However, Nostradamus' two most used words of color were *"red"* (*"rouge"*) and *"black"* (*"noir"*), which he wrote in various ways 34 and 27 times, respectively. These colors have a different kind of value.

The colors *"red"* and *"black"* have significant connotations that they carry in the quatrains, which are not limited to simply one nation's symbolic color. The first impression one could get, from finding either of these words used in the text, is of excitement or darkness. Combined, the two would yield a sense of fear. However, this would be from taking a more literal approach to color symbolism; and that approach is incorrect.

One key for understanding Nostradamus' use of colors, comes from the tenth quatrain found in *Centurie Sixth*. The entire quatrain states:

Vn peu de temps les temples des couleurs	One scarce from times the temples to the colors
De blanc & noir des deux entre meslee :	Of white & black with the two together mingled:
Rouges & jaunes leur embleront les leurs,	Red ones & yellow ones theirs will be stealing away them their ones,
Sang, terre, peste, faim, feu, d'eau affollee.	Blood, earth, pestilence, famine, fire, to water spoiled.

This quatrain states in the main theme (line one) that *"colors"* are relative to religions, which is an indication from the use of the word *"temples"*. Further, the line is stating that the theme of *"colors"* relative to *"religions"* will have moved beyond the *"times"* when this *"color"* alignment was pure. At this point, the secondary theme explains the time will be when *"two"* of the *"colors"*, relating to two separate *"religions"*, will be no longer be such a pure way of seeing *"white and black"*. The two regions will be *"mixed together"*, but while the ampersand keeps the two separate, there is a graying of where one can then call the land of *"white"* *"and"* the land of *"black"*.

Throughout the quatrains, *"blanc"* (or *"white"*) is a reference to the people of Judeo-Christian religious values. While this may have some connection to the skin color of these worshippers, such a clear-cut division will no longer be the case. Thus, the *"noir"* worshippers (or *"blacks"*), have to be seen as those of Islam. This makes it clear that the colors do not represent race, instead being relative to the *"temples"* each holds dear. While *"temple"* is a word that has specific definitions aligned with Judaism, it is primarily defined in the most general, as "A building dedicated to religious ceremonies or worship."[232] Thus, *"temples to the colors"* means the figurative tinctures of the *"religions"* of the *"temples"*.

In reality, *"white and black"* are not truly *"colors"*, but instead the presence of light (*"white"*) and the absence of light (*"black"*), or the absence of *"color"* (*"white"*) and the presence of all *"color"* (*"black"*). It is in understanding this connection, stated in this quatrain, that one can see the connection to the Sun (light) and the Moon (reflected light), to the Sun's relationship with Christianity and the Moon's relationship with Islam. In heraldic rules, the metal tinctures, *"or"* (*"gold"*) and *"argent"* (*"silver"*), are related to the Sun and Moon, respectively, with gold's *"color"* being *"yellow"* and silver's being *"white"*.[233] This means the *"colors"* of this quatrain (VI – 10) are not references to heraldry, per se as *"colors"* of arms, but are *"colors of religions"*.

The secondary theme is then making the statement that *"the two together mingled"*, which is reference to both being from the same root, as children of Abraham. The *"two mingled"* during the *"times"* that Israel thrived, but had ceased to exist *"together"*, as nations worshipping different *"religions"*. This had caused the Middle East to be seen as Muslim land, whereas Europe and America became known as Christian lands. However, this quatrain deals with the *"times scarce from"* those past *"times"*, where Israel had returned to *"mingle"* on Arab soil.

The third line is then supporting the main theme of the *"times"* when *"temples"* will offer *"scarce"* comparison to its past hold over its people. Here, the *"colors"* *"Reds and yellows"* come into play, as supporting elements to the main theme (while symmetrical to the secondary theme *"Of white and black"*). This becomes where the focus of *"One scarce of the times"* is an indication of when *"the temples"* were important to people is stated.

These *"colors"* stated in line three then represent the philosophies that have weakened the *"religions"* of Christianity/Judaism and Islam, being Communism (*"Reds"*) and Buddhism (*"yellows"*). These two philosophies are "religious" in their concepts, which hold atheism (no God) and panentheism (God in the material plane) to their cores. They are thus challenges to those believing in one God as Creator, with separate views on a Messiah from God. Growth in these two *"religions"* will signal the *"times"* of The Prophecies, as it will be a story of the future when all four *"colors mingle together"*.

The series of words in line four, *"Blood, earth, pestilence, famine, fire, to water spoiled"*, becomes an

---

232   The Free Dictionary by Farlex, http://www.thefreedictionary.com/Temple
233   Wikipedia the free encyclopedia, http://en.wikipedia.org/wiki/Tincture_(heraldry)

indication of infirmity, in reference to the *"times"*, when the *"earth"* has become ill. This draws one's attention back to the Greek Medicine Wheel, where the four colors of health were *"white"*, *"black"*, *"red"*, and *"yellow"*. These *"colors"* are said to be representative of the four "humors", or the main bodily fluids that tell of a body's emotional wellbeing. Those *colors* relate to phlegm (*"white"*), melancholy blues, as *"black"* bile (*"black"*), blood (*"red"*), and *yellow* bile (*"yellow"*).

These four types of bodily fluids were thought to be found in excess when apathy and indifference were present (*"white"* phlegm), when cheerful optimism was low (dark blood), when anger and irritation took over (gall, or *"yellow"* bile), or when despondency and sadness ruled (*"black"* outlook).[234] This element of the *"colors"* must be seen in line four, as an indication of the illnesses brought upon the world through *"religions"* being weakened through *"mingling"*. In essence, when these four *"colors"* are separately maintained, the health of the *"earth"* is stable, as each plays a role in the natural course of change.

This quatrain is the only place Nostradamus used the word *"jaunes"* (*"yellow ones"*). He wrote some form of *"blanc"* (*"white"*) 16 other times. This goes along with the many references to *"black"* and *"red"*. The symbolism that must be seen is one of religious connections, but the *"religions"* have become incapable of acting as healthy bodies. This then allows one to see the military aspects of other colors, such as *"azure"*, the main color of the flag of the United Nations, and the color of the military forces serving under that flag. Nostradamus also wrote of the colors *"brode"* (*"black"*), *"gris"* (*"gray"*), and *"bureau"* (*"brown"*), which are earth tones that are commonly used in military camouflage schemes. All of these *"colors"* then become personified as referencing people of these *"colors"*.

Nostradamus used the color *"green"* (*"vert"*, *"verte"*) as an indication of growth, primarily by using *"verdure"* (*"greenness"*) and *"verdoiant"* (*"flourishing, full of greenness"*), where finding such new growth will become a major issue in the later times of *The Prophecies*. In this sense, his use of *"green"* is not much different from our modern use as a symbol for renewed ecological concerns ("going green"). However, with the advent of paper money (something not first issued in Europe until after Nostradamus' death), and the coloring of paper money *"green"*, one cannot help but wonder if Nostradamus did not know this modern association, particularly in the United States. That becomes the element of figurative language known as a "double entendre."

One can see how all possibilities come into play, particularly when Nostradamus mixed his color uses together. One finds *"green"* used in the same quatrain, along with two of the three repeated colors mentioned in the previous quatrain example, twice. We find it the last word of line four, in the thirtieth quatrain found in *Centurie Tenth*, where Nostradamus wrote, "En rouge & noir convertiront leur vert." This translates to say, "In red & black transforming their green." One can then also see a similar combination in the fourth line of the fourteenth quatrain in *Centurie Seventh*. There, Nostradamus wrote, "Pour blanches, noires, & pour antique verts." This translates to say, "For white ones, black ones, & in

---

[234] Color Academy 2005, 2006 Micro Academy, Symbolism, article by Ray Osborne (copyright 1998), http://www.coloracademy.co.uk/ColorAcademy%202006/subjects/symbolism/symbolism.htm

respect of ancient green ones."

In ancient times, prior to the advent of Christianity, *"green"* had an association with fertility, and thus an association with pagan idols. One in particular is known to have been the *"Green"* Man, with early artwork depicting a face with foliage. There is evidence this history goes back to Middle Eastern pagan worship. Due to this association with pagan idols, the color *"green"* was somewhat subdued in Christian color symbolism. However, the first example can mean the storing of grain (*"converting their green"*), while the second example seems to be pointing out the possibility of more fertility in the geographic regions known as the Fertile Crescent (*"ancient green ones"*).

The *"colors"* representing the metals, *"gold"*, *"silver"*, and *"bronze"* (the same word could also mean *"copper, brass"*), are the primary symbols of money and material value. This does not prevent another color also bearing this meaning, such as *"green"*, particularly since there no longer is a metallic standard backing money. Metal colors are based on what was valuable in the 16th century. This means land had value that truly represented wealth, with food (*"green"*) then an asset, certainly foreseen as remaining a valuable commodity. Nostradamus also wrote about *"oil"*, which can be figurative language for Middle Eastern wealth, as well as being a literal statement of the value of cooking and anointing. However, the twenty-fifth quatrain found in *Centurie Seventh* states what will occur in the economics of the future found in *The Prophecies*.

Par guerre longue tout l'exercité expuise,	By war continual all the trained infantry chased out by force,
Que pour soldats ne trouueront pecune :	That for soldiers not will be finding money:
Lieu d'or, d'argent, cuir on viendra cuser,	Place from gold, to silver, leather one will come this to use,
Gaulois aerain, signe croissant de Lune.	French copper, token (or note) crescent of Moon.

This quatrain is rather easy to understand, particularly when lines three and four show a progressive lessening of metal value. Payment in *"tokens"* that can be exchanged for food, such that a double entendre can be seen in *"cuir on viendra cuser"*, where *"cuir"* means *"leather"*, or *"skin"*, but *"cuire"* is the French verb meaning, "to cook". This quatrain makes the metal colors show how little value they will have in the future, meaning not allowing this future to happen is the best way to retain wealth.

Certainly, if left up to the common people to decide whether or not an End Times war should be fought, which will make food more valuable than *"gold"*, the decision should be fairly easy. Nostradamus paints a picture that is reminiscent of biblical prophecy. The Revelation 6:6 states, "And I heard a voice in the midst of the four beasts say, A measure of wheat for a penny, and three measures of barley for a penny; and see thou hurt not the oil and the wine."[235] However, when a penny represented a day's wages and a

---

[235] King James Version

measure the equivalent of a loaf of bread, those who still have pennies to spend might choose differently than the commoners.

This is where the use of titles becomes figurative language, and not literal representations of true royalty. For someone to be called "King", this simply is a designation of that person being related to a title, a position that existed before the person, which will exist well beyond the life of that person. The same person would have been born with a lower title bestowed upon it, having later risen into the position of "King". Thus, being called "King" is no different than being called the "Most Lionhearted", or the "Most Christian". It is a figure of speech used to identify the title held by a specific person. Thus, Henry was the person heading France during the times Nostradamus wrote *The Prophecies*, such that Henry was literally a "King". However, when one seen the figurative nature of "*King*", one can see how Henry was identified by name, with the true "*King*" the one who Henry owed his birthright to.

I have already explained the significant differences between Nostradamus capitalizing a title or not. There is a definite significance based on the system of capitalization. The word "*King*" was written by Nostradamus 106 times in the quatrains, and another nineteen times (singular and plural) in the letter to Henry II. What has to be realized from reading the letter to Henry (the explanation of *The Prophecies*) is that his references to "*King*" equally applied to true royalty of nations, to the "royalty" of the Church, to the common rulers of nations in the future, and to Jesus Christ. The context determines the primary use of this title, as a figure of speech.

The use of titles are then found in the quatrains to be specific titles given to men and women of national leadership ("*King*", "*Prince*", "*Dame*", "*Duke*", "*Queen*", "*Marquis*", and "*Ambassador*"), as well as to those leaders of the Roman Catholic Church ("*King*", "*Prelate*", "*Pontiff*", "*Pope*", "*Cardinal*", "*Emperor*", and "*Vicar*") and Judaism ("*Rabbi*"). While the British Royal family allows for several of these titles to retain modern significance, the element of capitalization is all-important in determining when Nostradamus' use of royal titles applies to that family. Since the Roman Catholic Church is still an active branch of royalty (with Vatican City recognized as sovereign city-state, with the *Pope* its ruler), all uses by Nostradamus in these title areas are capitalized. Thus, the British and the Church are identified as playing roles in the story of the future shown to Nostradamus.

In the letter to Henry II, Nostradamus referred to "*des Roys temporelz*", and "*un des horribles Roys temporelz,*" where he clearly stated the future would hold multiple "*temporary Kings*". It must be understood that all "*Kings*" are "*temporary*", with limited time to serve as "*King*", but his need to modify "*King*", as "*Kings temporary ones*", means he is capitalizing the title as an indication of a ruler of significant power over a nation, who will be elected to a limited numbers of years in office. Therefore, not all capitalization of royal titles need apply to the British royal family. The President of the United States, for example, could be identified as "*King*" in the letter, while later be referenced as "*king*", in the quatrains, as an indication of lesser right to rule.

This system of figurative language, in particular to the elements that apply to heraldry, where the elite are identified by crests, shields, and coats of arms, as well as by colors, animals, and titles, makes them appear to have godlike powers and qualities. The story told by Nostradamus begins with the first steps to remove the power from "*Kings*", both royal and ecclesiastic, to place the crowns on the heads of common men. It is therefore fitting that Nostradamus went to such lengths using figurative language to identify these descendants of commonality, who will rule "*horribly*" at the expense of the people. Those "*horrible ones … Kings … temporary ones …*" refer to both the leaders of nations and the leaders of religions.

Chapter 28

The System of Astrology

I have given considerable thought about how best to present the system of astrology. Because Nostradamus was known as a gifted astrologer, his use of astrology must be expected to be part of his terminology in *The Prophecies*. Because the presentation of astrological information in the quatrains and letters cannot seen by the average reader, making it automatically appear unintelligible, astrology needs some explanation.

Astrology was not commonly understood in 1555, and it is less commonly understood today. Despite that lack of understanding though through the years, many astrological terms have been generally identifiable. This means the typical reader has always been able to recognize where the author has given astrological clues, but due to a lack of understanding of astrology, the average reader has seen words they recognize that are instantly cloaked in meaning. The assumption has always been one that only astrologers could ever make sense of those astrological words. This makes partial understanding of *The Prophecies* require an astrologer's explanation.

That common perception is another example of how an obvious use of something found in *The Prophecies* is misleading. Anything obvious is never as it appears to be. Nostradamus used astrological clues in many ways, some that require no deep knowledge of astrology; and the proof comes from no astrologers having ever correctly interpreted an astrological quatrain, making it testable for its prophetic properties, through the use of astrology. In this system, one will come to realize the depth of meaning that comes from astrological terms, much of which becomes easily understandable without any knowledge of astrology required. However, simply because astrological terminology is found in the texts, some knowledge of astrology is necessary.

For that reason, I have concluded that it would make no sense to present a system astrology without a basic course in astrology accompanying it. Even though the majority of that basic information will play only a small role towards furthering knowledge of *The Prophecies*, I feel it is better to be over-informed, rather than to present the astrology of Nostradamus as if it was clearly understood by all. That leaves all of Nostradamus' astrology to be seen as whatever meaning the reader would like to apply, usually incorrectly.

The System of Astrology

There is nothing arbitrary about how astrology works. It operates under a consistent set of rules, symbolic connections, and combination formulae, so patterned that a computer program can be written to make basic astrological analyses. This procedural knowledge assists one in discerning the astrological clues of Nostradamus, but few possess any relevant knowledge of how astrology works. By making all of this known here, removing the assumption that all readers understand astrology correctly, it also removes any advantages an astrologer may possibly hold over one who has never had astrology accurately explained to them. Therefore, I have decided to make a rather lengthy presentation on the basic principles and mechanics of astrology.

With this basic understanding, one can best grasp what has been largely avoided, and conceive the importance that understanding astrology plays, towards finding powerful meaning in *The Prophecies*. For a student of astrology, or one who has considerable practice with the art, much of this chapter will be seen as little more than a refresher course, and find it more difficult to read than would a complete novice. However, the skilled astrologer will see that the astrology of *The Prophecies* does not require any more than general knowledge of astrology.

On the contrary, astrology is a topic that is best learned when sought to be learned. The purpose of this section is not to teach astrology, but to make some facets of the mechanics of astrology known by the novice. There is absolutely nothing evil associated with astrology, as it is a tool of divination, which means it was "invented" by God for human use. Some people are uncomfortable with divination because the Holy Bible warns against false prophets who use tools of divination. That warning is like saying, "Be wary of people who know how to make nooses out of rope." It does not make rope evil. It makes the people who misuse rope evil. Therefore, I can understand if some novices would prefer to skip this chapter entirely.

In that regard, let me make this immediately known. Nostradamus' use of astrological terms are not going to lock down and seal up some specific date that someone can go running to the presses to make an announcement, "Nostradamus says the end will be on this date!" The astrological usage is so esoteric that the primary meaning is not the specificity of planetary positioning, such that astronomical timing is the main point. While astronomical timing can be found to seal a deal, and confirm an event in hindsight, our eyes will be blinded to such attempts towards understanding specific future times. General times may be revealed as possible, but the esoteric values (stated astrologically) surrounding those times are of greater value to understand. Therefore, this section can be largely avoided, without missing much more than a lesson in "How not to fear astrology."

With that explanation, this chapter will seem more as an aside in many places than an explanation of a system for understanding Nostradamus. Still, let me begin by making the shocking assertion that astrology is not causal. This is a statement that should fly in the face of most believers and all non-believers, because astrologers commonly make statements that indicate situations like, "Venus will make one feel …", "Mercury made you say …," or "That was Mars causing anger …." Such talk is so commonplace that it gives the opinion that there is a cause-effect relationship between human life and the planets. There is none.

It is this faulty opinion that has caused so many to reject astrology, seeing it as possibly containing any pertinent information worthy of knowing, based on the assumption that it is unlikely the movement of an object in outer space will have any effect on the movement of something on earth. Astrologers perpetrate this faulty opinion by using terms of speech that states planets and stars exert some form of control over the lives of human beings. There is no cause-effect mechanics associated with astrology, but some will some evidence that makes the appearance of causation the answer. For instance, the sun's rays do effect growth of plants on earth, and the moon's gravitational pull does effect the earth's bodies of waters. The problem comes from thinking that such cause-effect mechanics has anything to do with astrology.

Because the two most apparent orbs in the earth's skies do have overt influence on the face of the earth, it is just a matter of jumping to a conclusion that less obvious influences are likewise being exerted. Studies in the areas of quantum-physics do show how all within the whole are connected, which may become an accepted explanation of the mechanics of astrology at some point in the future. After all, if an energy source the size of a cell phone can exert influence on a person receiving a cell phone call many thousands of miles away, why would not a "cell phone" the size of Pluto be within the realm of possibility to "phone home" to someone on earth?

Still, this approach to explaining astrology cannot be proved, at this time. The focus of explaining *The Prophecies* cannot be shifted to proving astrology. It is more important to realize astrology is has reason for being, which is not dependent on a belief in the concept of causation. There is a better explanation.

To grasp this concept, consider the cause-effect relationship that a map has to one reading a map. Certainly, when one needs to get from point A to point B, a map can be seen as causing this result. The places shown on a map have some relative association to that which is known, such that a city, town, river, highway, or mountain range is known to exist in proximity to one another, but no one believes a map is the actual place where those places will be found.

A map is then a tool designed to reflect that which is real, in a manageable size, based on one's depth of need (i.e.: one looks at a world map to see where a continent is located, while one looks as a city map to know how to get around the city). From one having known needs, one can determine what type of map will best help one reach a destination, such that a map can cause one to plot a course of travel. However, because one specific map caused one specific person to plot one specific path, after one specific viewing, it would be foolish to assume the map had some mystical properties that would expect the same results, time after time.

In this analogy, the real that is mapped by astrology is the movements of the solar system, of which the earth is a real part. In this sense, astrology is no different from astronomy, as the original focus that begets astronomy. It is at this juncture that one realizes astrology is not a tool by which to plot a course through outer space. This is where the symbolism of astrology comes into play. The axiom that most basically defines astrology is, "As above, so below." The metaphor one then applies to the earth's solar system is that of a mirror. It is reflective of one specific time, relative to one specific person using the mirror for one specific purpose.

To surround this concept with the imagery of an allegory, suppose the scenario of one person going to a mirror for the purpose of seeing if one's face was clean. Once one looks closely into the mirror, seeing the reflection of oneself in the mirror, one can make that personal judgment. Still, while examining the reflection for cleanliness of facial skin, one may find that one's hair needs brushing. At that time, one would seek a brush, and brush one's hair in an acceptable fashion. This could be seen as a reflection being a cause that effected an action.

Unfortunately, this cannot be seen as a cause-effect relationship. The reason is as simple as being the fact that what caused one to brush one's hair would not necessarily guarantee that the same result for another. This would certainly be the case if the other person were bald, having no hair at all to brush. Further, if the first person had a history of using the same mirror for a long period of time, one would expect the same result every time, if cause and effect were the reasoning. However, the reflection cast into a mirror at age ten would probably not elicit the same result at it would at age 21, based on different needs relative to different times.

All of this means that astrology is nothing more than a tool, just like a map, which is specific to one's needs, at a particular time. When one knows how to use a tool properly, the tools takes on valuable properties; but if one does not know how to use a tool, having one at one's disposal does one no good. When someone has a need to know something that requires the use of a tool to ascertain desirable knowledge, if one does not know how to use the tool, one employs one who does know how to use the tool. This is why astrologers are contacted, when someone has a particular need to know something, specific to him or her, but cannot ascertain that reflection of self in the planets, due to a lack of understanding that tool.

When agreement has been reached, accepting that astrology is nothing more than a tool that requires the practice of an art form to understand, one has to look Nostradamus' statements about how astrology becomes a tool with a high accuracy rate, one so high it exceeds any possible argument that chance plays a role in prediction. The statements made by Nostradamus, in both of his letters of explanation, make it clear that astrology is a creation of God, a gift for mankind, as a tool by which humanity can be led to live life properly. Accuracy is then dependent on an astrologer's ability to use the tool of astrology to make contact with God, and in turn willing to be led to see how astrology reflects the life of one in need of advice. Thus, all must be in agreement that normal errors, created by possibilities of chance, are impossible to be considered in *The Prophecies*.

One can either believe or disbelieve astrology's validity, just as one can either believe or disbelieve in God, but neither can be proven as believable or unbelievable. Nostradamus claimed that his successes with astrological predictions were due to divine assistance, which elevated him to a higher level of astrological interpretation, one that normal astrologers could never achieve simply through the memorized mechanics of a tool requiring much practice, before one ever begins to show competency with astrological interpretation. Without this connection to God being made, astrology is no longer a divine tool; and just like any tool, it can be misused by unskilled workers, with lackluster results.

Astrology has to be understood as a tool designed by God, as a way for one to monitor one's earthly image being reflected in the planetary movements in the heavens, just as one sees one's mundane image reflected in a standard mirror. The axiom of astrology is, "as above, so below", which states this level of reflection. It is the principal that sees comparisons between microcosms and macrocosms, where one does not cause the other. There are similarities between all, such that by understanding patterns repeating countless times, when one sees one repeating again, one can find reason to believe a similar result will be. It is from this perspective that human characteristics can be applied to lifeless heavenly bodies.

The art of astrology is not something mastered quickly. Nostradamus was a master astrologer, and while he was not the originator of the words found in the quatrains of *The Prophecies*, he understood certain words as having meanings, beyond the physical, astronomical meaning of planets in space. There is certainly the physical meaning that needs to be understood, but astrology takes one well beyond the physical, entering into the psychological and astrological, which are the symbolic meanings attached to each astrological reference. This is the aspect of *The Prophecies* that is most easily missed by those lacking knowledge of astrology.

Over the next several pages, I will present a basic overview of some of the major elements that make up basic astrology. The astrology of Nostradamus does not require more than a basic overview to make one capable of gaining deeper insight. The purpose of the next few sections is not to teach astrology, nor to promote astrology as some form of religion, or even to ask one to believe in astrology. The purpose is to give an overview that can remove some fears of the subject, while making one capable of grasping the astrology presented by Nostradamus.

Each element of astrology has its own definitions and meanings, such that each element must be understood before two elements can be combined for one overall meaning. We have discussed this as being the method necessary to understand the quatrains and letters. Therefore, I will give some information that has little to do with *The Prophecies*, so that one can exit these woods with some ability to discern for oneself what truly defines astrology. However, if one is too fearful of looking at something one is afraid of, I recommend skipping forward to the synthesis sections at the end of each subsection, where the astrology of Nostradamus will return.

Planets

In the system of figurative language, I mentioned that Nostradamus wrote the names of mythological beings, from Greek, Roman, and Celtic mythology. One major branch of that figurative usage has to be separated into its own systemic category, simply because the names of the planets and signs have come from Roman-Latin mythological names. In these cases, a reference in a quatrain, for example to Venus – the goddess of love and beauty, literally stands for the physical entity that is that planet. While there certainly is other meaning behind that planet being named (Venus' association with Islam for example), the astrological applications require special focus. Therefore, a separate category is necessary to define that special focus.

Nostradamus referred to each of the visible planets – "*Mercure*," "*Venus*," "*Mars*," "*Jupiter*," and "*Saturne*," by their Latin names, with the Greek god "*Hermes*" shown to be the only Greek equivalent to these five mentioned. There are two references to "*Hermes*", where the purpose is apparently to focus on the characteristic of the mythological god, rather than to the planet *Mercury*. Nostradamus also used names for the *Sun* ("*Sol*," "*Soleil*," and "*solaire*") and *Moon* (variations of "*Phebés*", variations of "*Selin*", "*Diane*", "*Lune*", "*Lunage*", and "*lunaire*") in a combination of Latin and Greek forms. The multiplicity of the lunar references seems to be representative of the changing phases of the *Moon*. However, the Greek references do seem to apply best as figurative speech, as particular people in the storyline told by Nostradamus, rather than to the earth's lone satellite.

One note of interest, from this Latin usage for the planets, is the references Nostradamus made to "*Neptune*". He wrote that name in six quatrains, also identifying that name with the god's scepter, the "*trident*". The name is now commonly associated with the planet, but "*Neptune*" would not officially be known as a planet until well after Nostradamus' death (discovered in 1846, 280 years beyond Nostradamus).

Nostradamus also referred to "*l'Océan*" in some verses, which is the French name of the Titan, *Oceanus*. While the Greeks saw *Oceanus* as the god of all salt water, as a belt of water around the Earth, there is a difference from *Neptune*. The Roman god *Neptune* is the equivalent of the Greek god *Poseidon*, whereas *Oceanus* was the son of the Titan known in Roman mythology as *Uranus*. The implication of a mythological god comes from the personification Nostradamus gave "*l'Océan*", where the capitalization acts in this way; and a connection can be made to *Neptune* simply from both being gods of "*the Ocean*". Nostradamus also wrote in the lower case, "*l'océan*", but this use is more to identify the Atlantic "*Ocean*", meaning the planet *Neptune*, as an astrological clue, is non-existent in *The Prophecies*.

Nostradamus did made references in the quatrains that can be seen as allusions to the planet Uranus, however, although he did not use that name specifically. The French name for the Greek god *Ouranus*, who was the Roman equivalent of Uranus, is "*le Ciel*", with all three names meaning, "*the Sky*". Nostradamus used this French personification in the quatrains, as well as writing the word "*ciel*", in the lower case, including several times as the second word in a line, following a capitalized first word article (preposition-article combination). This acts to represent, "*With the sky*", or "*From the sky*", as "*with*" or "*from*" "*the Sky*", where modern astrological characteristics of Uranus perfectly fit this context, with the implication being "lightening."

This is known to be more than mere coincidence, because one finds evidence of knowledge of the planet Uranus in the Preface. There, Nostradamus wrote, "*nous approchant huictiesme, ou est le firmament de la huictiesme sphere, qui est en dimension latitudinaire, ou le grand Dieu eternel viendra parachever la revolution: ou les images celestes retourneront à se mouvoir*". This translates to say, "*we approaching eighth, where is the firmament of the eighth sphere, which is in dimension latitudinal, where the great God eternal will come to accomplish the revolution: where the images celestial will be returning to themselves to allure*". This is describing the discovery of Uranus, but not the initial discovery by Herschel in 1781.

This verbiage details the discovery of unique features on the planet Uranus, found by the *Voyager 2* space probe. Information sent back to NASA determined that Uranus has a 97.77-degree axial tilt.[236] The Earth's axial tilt, by comparison, is around 23 degrees, a difference of nearly 75 degrees. At 23 degrees, the Earth's rotational axis longitudinal (north-south), but Uranus, with its central axis at 97.8 degrees, is "*latitudinal*".

This means the equator of Uranus is roughly where the polar axis would be on Earth, and vice versa. When *Voyage 2* flew past Uranus in 1986, the south pole of the planet was reported to have been pointed directly at the Sun.[237] This means that Uranus is "*dimension latitudinal*", whereas the Earth is "*dimension longitudinal*". With longitude recognized as the polar lines dividing a sphere, those lines appear as Earth's latitude lines on Uranus. The space program, NASA, knew of this discovery because of "*the images celestial ... returning to themselves*", to be made available to the public, "*to allure*" more interest in space exploration.

With only seven known orbs in the "*celestial*" during Nostradamus' times, the "*eighth sphere*" would be the seventh planet from the Sun, thus Uranus.[238] The French word "*firmament*" can also translate as "*the sky*", such that by Nostradamus stating, "*where is the sky*", he is stating "*the eighth sphere*", rather than reference by name, *Ouranus*, the Greek god, "*the Sky*". The Roman equivalent personification of "*the Sky*" god would have been *Caelus*.

---

236   Wikipedia the free encyclopedia, http://en.wikipedia.org/wiki/Uranus
237   Wikipedia the free encyclopedia, http://en.wikipedia.org/wiki/Uranus
238   The Sun is counted as the first orb, with the Earth counted as the fourth. Astronomically, moons of planets are not considered orbs associated with the Sun. However, astrologically the Moon replaces the Earth, due to a geocentric view of the celestial.

There is other supporting evidence to Nostradamus having been shown the planet Uranus. This can be found in the second quatrain found in *Century Third*. In the two theme statements (lines one and two), he wrote, *"Le divin verbe donnra à la substance / Comprins ciel terre, or occult au fait mystique"*. When the use of *"ciel"* is translated as *"the firmament"*, this states two themes as being, *"The divine word will give to there matter"* (a biblical statement of Creation), and *"Contained the firmament land, now hidden from them made sacred"* (a statement about the solar system larger than the one known by Nostradamus). Additionally, one can see how reference can be made to the polar axis of the *"the world"* (alternate translation of *"terre"*) that will be known as Uranus. That *"land"* was *"now hidden"*, during the 16th century, *"but occult"* (alternate translation *"or occult"*) once detection added it to the astrology focus. Again, the use of *"ciel"*, as *"Le ciel"*, can be an indication of the god Uranus, while being one of the large outer planets *"concealed"* in bands of clouds.

This quatrain certainly allows Uranus to have been foreseen as a planet before its discovery, but *Neptune* is not so defined in *The Prophecies*. We know now that *Neptune* is part of the Earth's *"firmament"* (*"ciel"*), but due to the telescope having not been created (first known telescope came in 1608),[239] this means *Neptune* was *"hidden"* (*"occulte"*), along with Uranus, at the time that Uranus would become uncovered.

Still, Nostradamus referred to these undiscovered planets symbolically, where *"Neptune"* stood for the deep waters of the ocean, and *"the Sky"* meant the Earth's atmosphere. He did not directly refer to unknown and thus unnamed planets as such. However, by modern discoveries making it reasonable to believe that Nostradamus was aware of the existence of other planets, beyond those visible to the naked eye, makes it possible to grasp some additional occult meaning from these references.

These additional inferences come from realizing the astrological meanings associated with each of the planets and signs. Esoteric meaning is attached to each of those elements, along with the angular relationships formed (the aspects). This is at the core of the principles of astrology. Since most people have absolutely no understanding of the symbolisms of astrology, it makes it very difficult, without this knowledge, to grasp some very important nuances in the quatrains.

An appendix is provided that lists some of the basic key words for some symbolic meanings associated with the planets, but astrological symbolism is separate from the symbolism assigned to each god, whose name has been given to the orbs. Astrologically, the Sun individually represents the self, the soul, or the ego. As the only star of significance in astrology, it represents the only source of light, thus a life-giving energy. As the one true light, it stands for the truth, which was a known trait of the god Apollo. That sun god oversaw the temples constructed in his honor, the most famous being the Oracle of Delphi. That place was known for providing querents with truthful answers. Because the Sun is always emitting light, and always forward in apparent motion (as seen from the earth), it has a masculine quality to it, which

---

239 Wikipedia the free encyclopedia, http://en.wikipedia.org/wiki/History_of_the_telescope

means it is penetrating, rather than receptive.

The Moon is the orb that is the apparent equal to the Sun, in size and ability to provide light, albeit reflected from the Sun. As a source of reflected light, the Moon represents the individual's inner feelings and understanding. This is the inner light that whispers guidance to us, as our conscience and intuitions. As the receiver of the Sun's rays, the Moon is seen as the mother principle, where nurturing is at the core being. The Moon represents the heart, where caring, sympathy, and love all find deeper meaning.

Mercury is the fastest planet, in time taken to circle the Sun. This relates to the quickness of the god Mercury, the winged messenger. Mercury is always never more than 30 degrees from the Sun, as viewed from a geocentric perspective. This closeness to the ego of the Sun makes Mercury a perfect partner as the mind and basic intellect. As the messenger, Mercury is closely associated with all forms of communication, particularly talking and writing. Because of the winged shoes and helmet, Mercury also is closely identified with travels, of the short variety, and other forms of movement within the local area one lives.

The goddess Venus is known as the goddess of love and beauty, which no mortal could resist. The planet Venus is then symbolic astrologically as love, beauty, and aesthetics. It is therefore associated with art, fashion, and that which brings such finery into one's life, where value is placed on things, in particular things representative of money. Venus stands for a strong feminine energy, like the Moon, but on a much less mature level. Venus symbolizes youthful feminine traits, which are what one finds attractive in life, whether male or female. Venus symbolizes where one seeks comforts, more than difficulty; and thus shuns work, preferring to rest and be waited upon. In astrology, Venus is known as the lesser benefic, because it makes the hardest aspects seem rather mild, compared to other planets, because of a disdain for inharmonious focus.

Mars is the exact opposite of Venus, thus the saying, "opposites attract." Mars was the Roman god of war, so it stands for fighting, blood (as well as the color red), individual sports, and the energy core within the individual that makes things start. Mars is so energetic that he often tires before finishing what he has started. As such, Mars also symbolizes the strategy of war and action. Venus is attracted to such male energy, and Mars reciprocates this attraction. It thus symbolizes the youthful male drive for sex, and the games of love. The planet Mars is known in astrology to be the lesser malefic, because it symbolizes the energy to get through its hardest aspects, no matter how painful they may be.

The largest planet in the solar system is Jupiter, and thus it has been given the name of the greatest Roman god, also known as Jove, the Greek equivalent of Zeus. Due to its size, the planet Jupiter is associated with growth, expansion, and increased prominence. Jupiter stands for judgment, as the king who sits at the gate to judge the people fairly. Jupiter, as king, also represents a higher wisdom than that of the basic mind, which makes judgment just. The planet is also known as the greater benefic, due to the wealth and abundance with which its aspects are associated, where, like Venus, the most difficult aspects have a tendency to be dulled significantly.

The last planet visible to the naked eye from Earth is Saturn. The Roman god named Saturn was known by the Greeks as the Titan, Cronus, or Father Time. Saturn was the father of Jupiter, thus Saturn stands for the father principle, where discipline, training, and distance are necessary skills to pass onto children, so the children will be able to grow up with the skills necessary for survival and success. As this requires time for children to mature, Saturn symbolizes time and maturity. Saturn was the god of the harvest (thus the association of Father Time with the scythe, as the Reaper), such that good yields mean patience and hard work, and endurance pays off at the end. When one has not paid those prices, the result is difficult times, such that Saturn represents cold and hard punishments for breaking rules. While Jupiter judges, Saturn administers justice with a blind eye and an unfeeling heart. Due to all of the hardship associated with Saturn, this planet is known in astrology to be the greater malefic.

Since there is evidence of Nostradamus being aware of the outer planets Uranus (eighth sphere)[240] and Neptune (ninth sphere),[241] it is good to be aware of their symbolic key words as well. Due to their late discoveries, astrologers had to observe what world happenings occurred around the times of their discoveries, then see if there was a repeat of the basic energies surrounding those events, which would correlate with the aspects of those planets. The results have produced some accurate associations of symbolism for both planets.

The planet Uranus was discovered in 1781, with the American Revolution (1776) and the French Revolution (1789) surrounding its discovery. Only six years after the French had removed their royal rulers, they invaded the Dutch Republic in 1795 and ended that nation's string of sovereigns, which had steadily ruled for 214 years. Thus, the planet Uranus became symbolic of revolution and independence. Because the issues of those times were focused on individual rights and freedoms, those have become two other trademarks for Uranus (individualism and freedom). In addition to those lightening quick changes that occurred (lightening and change are key words for Uranus), Uranus symbolized the Age of Enlightenment's rapid advancements through invention and unique ideas (invention and unique are key words for Uranus).

The planet Neptune was discovered in 1846. In one way, the times of Neptune's discovery, the Victorian Era (1837 – 1901), are like the esoteric values that have been bestowed upon the planet. While wars were fought during this period, the reign of Queen Victoria was one mostly known for being peaceful. While peace is not specifically a key term for Neptune, the motivation for the peace then can be seen through the various royal bloodline connections. Due to Victoria's relatives marrying into the royal lines all across Europe, diplomatic relationships existed between Great Britain and several key European nations. This period was thus ruled by the circulatory system of Europe, where individual health is often the result of a

---

240 This number included the Sun and Moon, where both are spherical.
241 Ibid.

balanced flow through the hidden fluids of one's body. These unseen fluids are associated with this planet named for the god of the deeps.

Two of the wars England fought during this period were called the Opium Wars, fought against China (1839 – 1842 and 1856-1860). These wars were fought because of the drug trade that was profitable for the East India Trade Company. That major British import-export company had greatly profited from the introduction of, and sweeping acceptance of the Chinese product, opium. The Victorian Era was a time when many people were paying customers in English opium dens. The popularity of this drug use spread around the world; and drug induced states, of any kind, are symbolized by the planet Neptune.

Religion is another closely associated area of life associated with Neptune, particularly the word spirituality. While the 18th century sought freedom of religion, the 19th century found new religions, through the creation of many new branches of religions. This period when Neptune became part of the world's consciousness is also called the Second Great Awakening (1790 – 1840). One religion, in particular, faced uncertain times after the death of its founder, Joseph Smith, Jr. in 1844. The Church of Christ (the original name for the Church of Jesus Christ of Latter Day Saints) then fell into what has become known as that sect's "crisis of authority." This is consistent with the association of Neptune to confusion and nebulosity, which is an offshoot of an altered state of mind.

Finally, the Irish potato famine was a major event that took place (1845 – 1849), where blight on an underground staple was unforeseen and unstoppable. This dire condition of hopelessness and inability to control a situation was mirrored on an economic level as well. This was felt in the United States due to the Panic of 1837, where failing banks led to a depression that lasted until 1845. Depression is a symptom associated with Neptune, which can come on one through waves of misfortune, which may appear as if from a higher power.

There are some very powerful statements made by Nostradamus that indicate specific events, which could not have possibly occurred before the discovery of the planet Pluto, in 1930.[242] The verbiage refers to the splitting of atoms, and the sickness of radiation, which was largely unexplained before research (x-rays, uranium radioactivity, and the discovery of radium) that began in the 1890s. The discovery of plutonium (1934) was through the continuation of this scientific process in determining new elements, and was the one element most associated with the development of weapons utilizing the unleashing of tremendous power through nuclear chain reactions. Still, Nostradamus did not name the Roman character Pluto, god of the underworld, as an indication that Pluto would become the planet astrologers would associate with massive power and control.

The point of this section is to make it clear that Nostradamus used both overt and hidden ways to list planets. From his perspective, in 1555, a planet was a reference to an astrological association with a

---

242   Pluto has since been downsized to a planetoid.

mythological figure, while also being a statement of a specific orb, only visible at certain times, in the night sky. It is important to think less of these planets as balls of circulating rock in the space surrounding our sun's gravitational pull (astronomical-astrological), and more as symbolic meaning associated with the names of planets.

I hope that this brief explanation of the symbolic associations astrology sees in the planets has been helpful. It should be easy to see how placing human characteristics on lifeless, distant spheres of rock and gas can come off as illogical and insane. Many astrologers have a tendency to speak in terms as if a planet were a god, and thus the cause of earthly happening, just as the gods were seen by the Greeks and Romans to be figuratively pulling the strings of human puppets. This is not the case.

Signs

Astrology entails five basic elements: the planets, the signs, the aspects, the imaginary points surrounding those three, and then all of this combined through the art of delineation and synthesis. The imaginary will be discussed later, but the areas of the signs and aspects also deal with the imaginary divisions of the earth's sky and the imagined relationships between orbs. One system of dividing the sky is based on the fact that all planets orbit the Sun's equator, plus or minus a few degrees. The breadth of this path (between 16-18 degrees) is then considered an imaginary belt around the Sun, called the zodiac.

The zodiac belt is actually a relationship between the Earth and the Sun, where something fixed has to become the reference point, to determine precisely what this relationship is. That fixed part is the backdrop of stars, which have been groups by human imagination into constellations. Those constellations along the belt of planetary movements then name the signs of the zodiac.

The signs are each allotted 30 degrees of arc, although some star constellations do not spread that wide, and others exceed this span. Some even believe the constellation Ophiuchus (the Serpent Bearer) is the thirteenth sign of the zodiac. This constellation is between Scorpio and Sagittarius, and the Sun moves through this space between November 30 and December 17 each year, although the Sun is said to be in the sign of Sagittarius during that time. It must be remembered that the signs are distant stars of the galaxy, which merely provide a backdrop for the movements within Earth's solar system. As backdrop configurations (basically, 2-dimensional interpretations), they are not part of the solar system. Therefore, the 30-degree divisions for "signs" actually have nothing to do with the backdrop, other than being named for the closest constellation of fixed stars along the belt of the Milky Way centered at the Sun's equator, and as viewed from Earth (geocentric). The astrological zodiac is a division of the 360-degree orbit into twelve zones, regardless of the presence of thirteen constellations in those zones.

The signs are thus nothing more than reference points, where any one point along the ecliptic can be said to be a starting point. This is the concept behind one's birthday being marked by the position of the planets at the time of one's birth. All births mark a starting point, with all orbs frozen in one specific position at the precise time of birth, such that this frozen picture marks each planet's orbit cycle, where all begin and end at that points held at one's birth. However, since everyone has a different birth (date, place, and time), the starting point for a zodiac cycle has to be whole earth related.

Since the majority of the earth's livable land mass is north of the equator, along with the vast majority of human life, astrology is northern hemisphere based.[243] As such, the beginning point for the first day of spring in the northern hemisphere is when the Sun is exactly at the equator (called at the Vernal Equinox), headed north to it apex point (the Summer Solstice), at the imaginary line called the Tropic of Cancer. This makes the starting point for the zodiac become Aries, the sign of the ram.

While the Sun crossing the Vernal Equinox for the northern hemisphere means the beginning of spring to most, it means the beginning of fall to those who live in the southern hemisphere. This, like the thirteenth sign in the zodiac, is meaningless as far as the earth's relationship with the Sun goes. Since most of the earth's seasonal arable landmasses are being reborn, due to the Sun's return to warm this majority, the choice of Aries as the beginning point is correct as a symbol of rebirth and renewal of the earth. Thus, Aries marks the starting point of the zodiac

In *The Prophecies*, Nostradamus named each of the known planets and luminary by name. His naming of the signs was not so standardized. Nostradamus used descriptive terms to allude to some of the signs. Since each of the signs is the name of a constellation, where the Latin names mean the ram, the bull, the twins, the crab, and so on, the names of the signs are themselves descriptive terms. Thus, Nostradamus made some references that are clearly implying an astrological sign, although not the official name of a constellation.

Nostradamus wrote *Aries*, *Taurus*, *Cancer*, *Leo*, *Libra*, *Scorpion*, *Sagitaire* [*Sagittaire*], *Capricorne*, and *pisces* in their Latin form (French versions), although *pisces* was never capitalized. Nostradamus referred to all of the signs, even if not via the Latinized names. Some of the signs he referred to in multiple ways, with Latin and French versions stated. Some others were only mentioned through lower case descriptive words, referencing the meaning of the Latin name.

For instance, Nostradamus clearly wrote *Taurus* in three quatrains: the twenty-eighth quatrain in *Century First*, the thirty-fifth quatrain found in *Century Fifth*, and the eighty-third quatrain of *Century Ninth*. In the forty-ninth quatrain in *Century Eighth*, it is clear he is making astrological sign references, using the word *boeuf*. There Nostradamus wrote in the main theme line, "*Satur, au boeuf jove en l'eau, Mars en fleiche,*" meaning, "*Saturn, with the bull played in the water, Mars in arrow*". That word is French for "ox, steer, or beef", particularly along with other astrological descriptive terms, becomes a bovine

---

[243] Only 29.2% of the earth's surface is land (not underwater). The land north of the equator totals 67.29%, and supports 88-90% of the human population. The remaining total in the southern hemisphere (32.71%) includes unlivable land in Antarctica (the 5th largest continent).

substitute for *taurus*, which in Latin means, "a bull".

Gemini is not directly stated by Nostradamus, nor is the French version, *Gémeaux*. Instead, he referred to the star constellation known in Greek as the *Dioscuri*, by the two brightest stars found in that constellation. Those are the references made to "*Castor, Pollux*" (the Gemini Twins). Nostradamus wrote those two names that specific way in the fifteenth quatrain found in *Century Second*, where he wrote, "*Castor, Pollux en nef, astre crinite*". This states, "*Castor, Pollux in ship, star hairy*" which gives the impression of the constellation where a comet will be spotted. That constellation would be Gemini. Nostradamus' one other mention of the twins has him separating the two names with an ampersand, as *Castro & Pollux*. This line four statement also gives overtures of being constellation related, in a secondary meaning sense.

Nostradamus did not write the Latin form of *Virgin*, or Virgo. Instead, he described this maiden quality as *Nonnay* (*Nun*), which is due to the vows of chastity a nun takes. The reference is clearly astrological, as Nostradamus wrote, "*Mars en Nonnay*". Still, he also made mention of *la Vierge* (the French form for Virgo, as *the Virgin*) in the thirty-fifth quatrain of *Century Sixth*, writing, "*Leo la Vierge*". His references to *la vierge*, *les vierges*, and *vierge(s)*, which are not personified with capitalization, are less identified with this astrological association.

Nostradamus referred to the sign *Libra* in the twenty-eighth quatrain of *Century First* (writing, "*Taurus & Libra*" to begin line four), the eighty-first quatrain found in *Century Second* (writing, "*Apres que Libra lairra son Phaëton*"), and the fiftieth verse in *Century Fourth* (writing, "*Libra verra regner les Hesperies*"). However, he also referred to this astrological sign as *la Balance* (in both upper and lower case versions), in three other quatrains (IV – 96, V – 42, and V – 70). His use in the main theme line of quatrain V-70 makes it clear he was referring to one of Libra ascendancy, when he wrote, "*Des regions subjectes à la Balance*". This use of *la Balance* is stating the French name for *Libra*, where *Libra* means *the Scales*, or *the Balance*, in Latin.

Sagittarius, which is Latin meaning "archer" or "of an arrow", is thus represented by Nostradamus as "*l'Arq*" (quatrains II – 35, II – 48, and II – 65), "*l'arche*" (quatrain III – 13), and "*en fleiche*" (quatrain VIII – 49). His uses of *l'Arq* are the most clear in making astrological statements. He presented the secondary theme in quatrain II – 48, stating, "*Saturne en l'Arq tournant du poisson Mars*". Then he wrote, "*Sol, l'Arq, & Caper*", to begin line four of quatrain II – 35; and then made the fourth line statement, "*Mercure en l'Arq Saturne fenera*", in quatrain II - 65. All of these names bear the same Latin meanings, in French. The French word *arquer* means, "to arch; to bend or bow like an arch", and the word *archer* means, "archer or bowman". The word *fleiche* (or *fleche*) means, "arrow". Nostradamus used these lower case descriptors primarily for other purposes, although they retain astrological meaning in the secondary sense.

Nostradamus wrote *Capricorne* in the fifteenth quatrain found in *Century Sixth*. That is the French name for *Capricorn*, which in Latin means, "*goat horn*". That statement from line three, "*L'Espaignol Roy en Capricorne mince,*" says (partially), "*King in Capricorn*". This can mean a leader of *Capricornian* nature, or infer that the Sun will be in that sign, at the winter solstice.

Nostradamus twice referred to *Caper* (quatrains II – 35 and X – 67*)*, which in Latin means "*he-goat*". Both his *Century Second* reference ("*Sol, l'Arq, & Caper*") and his *Century Tenth* statement ("*Saturne, Caper. Jupiter, Mercure au bœuf*") are clearly astrological. It is also possible that his use of the abbreviation "*Cap.*" carries a secondary association with the sign *Capricorn*. The context makes it doubtful that this is the primary focus, but the abbreviation certainly allows the characteristics of *Capricorn* to be read into the meaning of the three quatrains that make that presentation.

The sign Aquarius is known to be "the water-carrier" or "water-bearer," which is the meaning of that Latin word, although in context it can also mean, "belonging to water". This sign is frequently symbolized as a god-like figure on a cloud, pouring water from an urn to the earth below, thus pouring rain. Astrology considers this to be an Air Sign (not a Water Sign), such that it represents the clouds in the sky, which consist of water molecules.

While human water-bearers historically have been women, the water-carrier in the constellation Aquarius is an elderly man. This is due to Aquarius being associated with having masculine traits,[244] in part due to its association with the planet Saturn (the father principle). Thus, when Nostradamus wrote in the quatrains in reference to, "*l'urne*" (quatrains II – 81 and X – 50) and "*hurne*" (quatrains IX – 73 and X – 50), he was making a representation of *the urn* known both as Aquarius the god of the constellation and Aquarius the astrological sign.

The French name for Aquarius is *Le Verseau* (as the water-carrier, *le Vers-eau*), and while that name is not used in *The Prophecies*, per se, it is found somewhat nicknamed as "*versie*". In the ninety-first quatrain of *Century Fifth*, Nostradamus wrote (partially), "*Mars, Leo, Sat. vn versien*", where the implication of "*versien*" is "*spilt one,*" or the actions of a water-carrier.

Finally, the sign *Pisces* is Latin for the plural form of *Fish*. In French, this zodiac sign is named *les Poissons*. Nostradamus refers to the sign in the singular (*du poisson*), as a direct reference to this astrological sign in the quatrain found forty-eighth in *Century Second*. As the secondary theme of that quatrain, Nostradamus wrote, "*Saturne en l'Arq tournant du poisson Mars,*" which says, "*Saturn in Aquarius turning to the fish Mars*". Because Aquarius and Pisces are adjacent signs, with typical "forward" planetary movement

---

244   In astrology, all signs are either masculine or feminine, in alternating order. This distinction has noting to do with male or female, but with penetrating or receptive energy, of which males and females generally fit one or the other. Another way of stating this duality (masculine/feminine) is to say, "positive or negative." That, as one can see, brings up another discussion topic, as to how can such values are determined? Again, there is no value in the positive and negative poles of a battery. Positive and negative ions circulate equally in the core of the battery, with the poles being basically neutral charged, although each contains a slight residue of measurable charge.

naturally taking one from Aquarius to Pisces, this statement is telling one where two planets will be in the heavens. As I will discuss later, this is a significant statement to understand.

The lack of capitalization also has significance, in the case of Pisces. Due to the sign of Pisces being the one least concerned about self, being known as a completely self-sacrificing sign, Nostradamus could be making a statement about there being no need to apply personification to the words that symbolize it. A double entendre can be the point, particularly in a couple of other singular references to "*poisson*".

For example, in the twenty-first quatrain found in *Century Third*, Nostradamus wrote, "*un horride poisson*", which says, "*one horrible fish*". The primary focus of this use of "*fish*" is symbolic of an aquatic "*monster*", which would be the way someone from the 16th century would describe a submarine. When Nostradamus referred to "*poissons*" (plural form) in the verses, the focus readily appears to be literally to *fishes*, as a source of food, with the connection to Pisces being its esoteric meaning, adding secondary meaning only.

Since Nostradamus made so many references to the twelve astrological signs, it is important that one recognize the symbolic associations they carry. When a planetary alignment is stated in a quatrain, such as "*Saturn in Aquarius turning to the fish Mars*", the meaning of *Aquarius* and Pisces is primarily the astronomical. However, there is symbolic meaning associated with *Saturn in Aquarius*, and *Mars* in Pisces, which must be understood. This value will be greater than simply determining when those two planets will be, or have been, in those specific signs.

To help provide the serious learner with some basic information that will forego the need to purchase a "basic astrology" book, I will go through the signs as I went through the planets. In that way I will be presenting a synopsis of the symbolic meaning each sign brings to understanding *The Prophecies*. As an astrologer, Nostradamus would know these basic symbolic meanings, when told what to write by Christ. Depth of meaning comes from understanding all aspects an astrological term bears.

As an astrologer, I see the verbiage that is less visible as astrological, because it is now archaic. Still, being able to see it does not mean all meaning will readily be seen and comprehended. This is obvious from reading observations made about *The Prophecies* by others, who have called themselves astrologers in the past. They interpreted in times when archaic was standard, but that did not allow them to solve anything. Therefore, for novices I will present some observations that are designed to help one grasp some of the subtle meanings one word or name can express.

The ram symbolizes the starting point of the zodiac, as the sign Aries. Think of that imagery when Aries is read in the text. Then think of the mental images one typically gets when one sees a ram. There should be the image of two rams charging and butting horns. From that, the battering ram was designed, which was used to burst through barriers. There is a ramrod, the name given to a rod used to force a charge into a musket-style rifle, and the saying, "ram home," which means to "drive home a point or an argument."[245] All of this has some impact on the meaning of Aries.

As the first sign of the zodiac, when winter ends and spring begins, there is a rush forward after a time of hibernation. Animals mate in the spring, which is why rams butt heads. They are trying to attract the ewes by coming in first in individual battle. When a ram mates, the cycle of life is renewed through the birth of new lambs. Thus, Aries symbolizes that which bursts forth, full of energy, bowling over that which has held one back.

This energy symbolizes the self's burst from the womb as an infant. Aries must be first, with self the only focus. This is not only the needs of a newborn; it is the need for everyone, to some degree. Everyone has to place his or her self forward, to meet the challenge of battle, and to be born anew, repeatedly. Without the self, no one would be.

It might be noticeable that the drive of Aries is associated with the action seen in the planet Mars, such that similar symbolisms relate the two. This is a good comparison, because astrology sees Mars as the planet that "rules" the sign of Aries. By rulership, I mean that the planet Mars is most free to express its traits in a sign that provides it the opportunity to do so naturally, and with encouragement. Aries is considered to be a positive (or masculine) sign, which means it is an outgoing sign. Contrarily, Aries is too fast to be reflective; as it acts first and lets others do the reflecting on that action. Mars symbolize outgoing energy, where restlessness leads to activity. This is how it becomes associated with Aries.

The second sign of the zodiac is Taurus, which is symbolized by the bull. In French, the word *boeuf* is more closely translated as "ox," which is a castrated bull. Thus, an ox has been representative of a beast of burden. This makes strength a trait of Taurus, although the strength of Taurus is through endurance, unlike the constant strength of drive found in Aries. Taurus is more inclined to work hard for the comforts of life. Work is then translated into a set of values, where the things of the material world become symbolic of the hard work and the stamina required bringing about the things that display such efforts. This makes the stock market moniker of a "bull market" a perfect fit for the Taurean. This is when a prolonged (stamina) period of financial investments (hard work) yields increased value in stocks, which in return brings one a financial windfall (value), enough to buy symbolic things that are nice to have around (comfort).

The planet Venus is said to rule the sign of Taurus. Since Venus is the planet of beauty and aesthetics, it should come at no surprise that things of beauty generally cost more. Their costs are relative to the effort required to produce them. Things of aesthetic values are considered comforting, and of good tastes. While Venus is not a goddess that would be seen in the fields holding the reins of an ox, plowing, she was one that delighted in things of value, comforts, and wealth. This means Venus is the ultimate motivation

---

245   The Free Dictionary by Farlex, http://www.thefreedictionary.com/ram+home

for Taurus. Hard work is directed towards making enough to keep in reserve, so that hard work becomes a thing of the past. The axiom, "work smarter, not harder," can then be applied to Taurus, often to the extent that laziness becomes a negative trait of the sign. However, this negative (or feminine) sign, meaning internal values drive outer actions, is always focused on establishing security, as a natural next step to the establishment of self (Aries).

The third sign of the zodiac is Gemini. The twins symbolize this sign, thus immediately one has moved beyond the singular to the plural. Multiplicity is a key term for Gemini, which follows the natural progression from self-stability to realizing others are a necessity. Gemini then models the phrase, "no man is an island," thus symbolizing those one is raised by, learns from, and relates with as a social creature within a family. This then becomes siblings, the extended family (aunts, uncles, and cousins), neighbors, and early educators and caretakers. The symbolism of Gemini is the need to relate with others, such that communication and movement become necessary learned skills. Gemini is then associated with language, relatives, local travel, and basic intellect.

The planet Mercury is then said to be the ruler of the sign Gemini. This relates to the quickness of learning at an early age, where our brains rapidly absorb what we are presented. This aspect of Mercury is the positive (or masculine) expression, meaning Gemini is a sign of outward mobility and communication with external stimuli, which is a required stage of development so the mind can grow. Through spending time with many people, one learns how to adapt to socialization.

This adaptation is symbolic of the god Mercury, who is the messenger. Learning is symbolic of memorization, acclimation, and mimicry, rather than of deep understanding. In this sense, gossip and small talk become ways of practicing one's communication skills. Thinking can be sharp, in the form of quick wit, but mentality symbolized by Mercury and Gemini is shallow and reactive, particularly when compared to the advanced learning that is required for true wisdom to be achieved.

The fourth astrological sign is Cancer. The symbolic creature associated with Cancer is the crab. Simply by knowing the basic features of a crab, one can see why it is associated with this sign. A crab is typically a creature that walks the floor of large bodies of water, known for its thick exoskeleton and pinchers. This relates to the sign of Cancer because some of the traits associated with the sign are protective, where a hard outer shell is mostly presented towards strangers. Defensive posturing is expressed through the aggressive use of the claws. Just as crab legs are seen as a delicacy, with work required to break the shell in order to get to the sweet crabmeat inside, Cancer is known for having a soft core, under a hard exterior. Cancer is also symbolic of the seasonal molting of the shells, such that for brief periods the defense is lowered and vulnerability is allowed.

The Moon thus rules Cancer, where cycles of emotional change ebb and flow, representative of a crab's change from hard shell (new moon) to no shell (full moon). The Moon is the orb that represents womanhood, through the change to maturity that comes by the experience of childbirth. Thus, the Moon represents the mother principle, and the nurturing instinct required to raise a newborn. With its symbolic orb being the Moon, Cancer is a feminine (or negative) sign, meaning it is receptive more than penetrating. Just as a child grows inside the mother's womb, once born the mother attempts to maintain this outer covering relationship. The crab symbolizes the internal need to wrap around the infant like a protective shell, aggressively defending the child from predators. This is a necessary step for the growth and development of the child, but once the child gets older this excessive attention can feel smothering.

This internal drive to nurture, defend, and protect is due to close feelings held dear for one allowed to know the inner core of the crab. Thus, the Moon represents the feelings, emotions, and intuitive connections that naturally exist between mother and child (particularly when the child is in the womb). While these traits are most symbolic of the Moon, the sign Cancer absorbs them.

The fifth sign of the zodiac is Leo, and the lion symbolizes that sign. When one thinks of a lion, the king of the jungle image comes up. That meaning, as king, says there is none greater in power than the lion. In that sense, the lion is placed at the center of focus in the animal kingdom. This is a characteristic of Leo, where there is a need for adoration and recognition. Loyal subjects are then showered with the bounty of royalty, because like the fable of the lion and the mouse, in which the mouse pulled the thorn from the lion's paw, the lion never forgets a favor. On the other hand, a Leo never forgets when disloyalty occurs, or when one has failed to give the king his due. Just as a family of lions is called a pride, pride is a trait of Leo. It symbolizes one's drive to please self, while making that self find as much joy as possible. For this reason, Leo is associated with the ego of self, with vanity becoming the weakness of pride.

Leo is thus said to be ruled by the Sun, which can be seen as the king of our solar system, where all planets revolve around that central entity. The Sun is the only star that matters in astrology; such that is becomes the focal point for stardom. The Sun shines a light and radiates warmth that cannot be ignored. All attention is drawn to the Sun's rise and set. Leo is a sign that basks in the spotlight of the public eye. Light allows one to see, and Leo loves to be seen in the best light.

On an individual level, each person is the center of their own solar system, as one can only view those that revolve around one. Each human being has his or her own inner Sun, which is one's own soul, and the reason one's Sun sign bears more importance. The Sun, as all orbs, is in all signs over time, such that where the Sun was at one's birth illuminates the qualities of that sign within the individual. The Sun's rulership of Leo simply means that the ego of the self is best projected, through the positive (or masculine), outgoing nature symbolized by this sign.

Virgo is the sixth sign of the zodiac, and similar to Gemini it is symbolized by a human entity – the virgin. The virgin states the femininity (or negative) charge associated with this sign, meaning it is receptive, more than outgoing. The essence of a virgin is sacrifice, which can be seen in Nostradamus' references to this sign as *the Nun*. A nun has sacrificed the promises of carnal knowledge, as a symbolic gesture of saving one's self for the Lord. Therefore, the sign Virgo symbolizes the times when fertility (thus maturity) has arrived, but preparations must be made first, before one can embark upon the path of adulthood. The self must be sacrificed in order to share the world with others. This becomes an inner establishment of order and routine, so that plans can come to fruition.

The planet that is designated the ruler of Virgo is the same planet that is designated rulership over Gemini – Mercury. However, this is not the swift, winged messenger god Mercury, but instead the Mercury who was gifted the caduceus (a staff entwined with two snakes – the traditional symbol of medicine), while being the signaler of fertility to humans. Thus, the difference is this side of Mercury is focused on the internal awareness of function and purpose, as opposed to the external stimulus of learning and communicating. The Mercury of Virgo is the mind's ability to store, organize, process, and recall what has been learned. It is the part of the mind that automatically runs the body's inner functions, while also subconsciously modeling a favored style from which one has learned. This level of mind is still narrowly focused, such that the ways found proven to produce the best results become the only ways allowed and accepted. When a Virgo begins to encounter people who do things differently, criticism can become a negative trait of Virgo.

The seventh sign of astrology is Libra. Libra is symbolized by the only non-living entity in the zodiac – the scales. The imagery of a scale is to balance two sides with equal weigh. This is then a perfect symbol, because Libra is the first sign of the second half of the zodiac, with its cusp at the Autumnal Equinox, opposite the sign of Aries, whose cusp is on the Vernal Equinox. Aries is about self, whereas Libra is about how one's self is altered through compromise, in order to relate with others as a social creature. Compromise is reached through understanding more than one view on matters, as opposed to forcing one particular view on others. This willingness to understand and compromise is generally due to a dislike of confrontation. However, when caught in the middle between two opposing views, Libra's willingness to understand all views makes it difficult to be decisive about any side's stance.

The planet Venus, which is the planet of love, beauty, and aesthetics, rules Libra, just as it rules Taurus. The difference is Taurus focus on inner beauty, while Libra projects beauty outwardly. Venus is the opposite principle of Mars, the ruler of Aries, which makes Libra become a compliment of Aries. The symbolism of Venus makes Libra a sign associated with the arts, of all varieties. Venus symbolizes the willingness to avoid a physical fight, preferring to win its battles through a civilized crossing of wits and charms. Venus makes Libra represent a sign where fairness is always the desired path.

While Mars and Venus have a reputation for being male and female, boy and girl, both Aries and Libra are positive (or masculine) signs. This means that the attraction of Venus' association with Libra is not hidden within. It is projected, thus penetrating outward, as a means of returning that which the attraction is designed to capture. The inward values of Venus are then found in the sign Taurus, as one's personal, inner needs for comfort and security. The Venus of Libra is related to those values, as a means of projecting one's level of refinement in order to attract one who can appreciate those tastes.

The eighth sign of the zodiac is Scorpio, which is symbolized by the scorpion, the only insect (arthropod) representative. The scorpion is characteristically similar to the crab, in the sense that both have an exoskeleton, which periodically goes through molting, with pinchers. The difference is the scorpion is not a food source, it is smaller and thus more difficult to detect, and it has a venomous sting that is painful, if not deadly. The scorpion's habitat is usually under rocks and in holes, keeping out of sight during the day to avoid predators. It is most active at night, itself an opportunistic hunter of prey. This symbolism means that Scorpio is the most feared sign of the zodiac, primarily due to its inability to been seen clearly, and the lore that precedes its sting.

Scorpio is symbolically related to sexual activity, where the injection of venom is a metaphor for intercourse. As such, Scorpio is a negative (or feminine) sign, meaning it relates with the inner motivations, and biological processes of reproduction. Sex for the purposes of procreation requires another of the opposite sex, thus Scorpio is opposite the sign of Taurus. The personal values related with Taurus are then paired with Scorpio's sharing of the most personal of one's values, the body. This then translates to the level of familial relationships, where personal values of wealth are shared between couples and between relatives. This means Scorpio is associated with the issues surrounding inheritance, and thus issues surrounding death and transition.

The planet associated with rulership of Scorpio is traditionally Mars, although the modern discovery of the planet Pluto has caused some to allow this newly reclassified planetoid to be considered the Scorpion ruler. Nostradamus was a traditional astrologer, and there was no inkling made of Pluto the god (Hades in Greek) in *The Prophecies*. This makes Mars the planet best seen as the energy symbolized in Scorpio. This is another match between Mars and Venus, as was seen in the Libra-Aries opposition. The Venetian internal desires to value lineage then attracts and is attracted by the seductive inner lures of Martian lust. Thus, the result of sexual actions (Mars) brings those things that are personally comforting (babies), while becoming the inner motivations for attracting the financial means to support a family.

The ninth sign of the zodiac is Sagittarius, the archer, often symbolized by the constellation's depiction of a Centaur drawing an arrow on a bow. The primary association the archer has is to hunting, although the military applications also apply. This means the element of sport is present, as well as the athletic abilities required to make the chase. The arrow symbolizes the ability to live free, with a weapon capable of providing both defense and sustenance. Sagittarius thus symbolizes this freedom, as the realization that one is only free when allowed to go and follow the prey. This relates to the centaur, where this half man – half horse icon means societal needs cannot corral the movement required by a cavalry spirit. Sagittarius represents a constant drive to know more, through travel to distant places, the exploration of foreign languages and philosophies, and the seeking of the higher meanings of life, through advanced education and religious dogmas.

The planet seen to rule Sagittarius is Jupiter, where that planet's symbolism of growth and expansion fits the limitless boundaries that freedom represents to Sagittarius. Jupiter, as the god Zeus, represents the highest authority over mankind. This association of Jupiter to judgment gives Sagittarius the distinction of being associated with the legal system, where people are held to higher standards, but free to operate within the boundaries of the law. Jupiter is then seen as a higher level of mind, opposite that of Mercury; and as such, Sagittarius is a higher level of education, one provided by the world, more advanced than the basic education provided by the local environment that Gemini entail.

Sagittarius is a positive (or masculine) sign, as is its opposite Gemini. This means that learning of any kind comes from external stimuli. The primary focus of Sagittarius is to experience as much as possible; in an outreach that extends as far as one can shoot an arrow, and as fast as one can run on four legs, rather than as far as one can physically reach, or run on two feet. The internal processing of these stimuli is not a major concern, as life comes at one in the moment, regardless of how well one has studied to prepare for life. Thus, Sagittarius delights in the new, but becomes bored with the old.

The tenth sign of the zodiac is Capricorn, which is symbolized by the goat, although the constellation depicts a creature half-goat and half-fish (a sea-goat). The goat is similar to the ram (a sheep), with the goat known to prefer woody shrubs to grass. The symbol of the sea-goat is to depict the heights a Capricorn can climb (the mountain goat), as well as the depths one can achieve (the fish). These become key terms for the sign Capricorn, as the sign symbolizes the willingness to work hard to climb over obstacles, in order to achieve a goal. Mountain goats symbolize the abilities Capricorn represents, to travel narrow and difficult paths, where the most meager footing is surmounted by stamina, persistence, and endurance.

The planet that is seen as the ruler of Capricorn is Saturn, which is closely related with patience and hard work leading to success. The sign Capricorn is more closely identified with this success, as it is the one sign most willing to sacrifice short-term rewards for a long-term objective. Capricorn is therefore the sign that symbolizes responsibility, maturity, and reputation. Capricorn is goal driven, having learned from the master teacher (Saturn) what goals are most productive.

Capricorn is therefore a negative (or feminine) sign, meaning the character necessary for mature achievement comes from inner drives and determinations. This makes it opposite the sign of Cancer, which is ruled by the inner emotions of the Moon. This axis is the parental axis, where the Moon symbolizes the mother principle, and Saturn symbolizes the father principle. While the Moon rules over home, Saturn rules over career and the public spotlight of professional recognition. In this sense, both Cancer and Capricorn are outgoing, due to inner drives, related to the need to provide stability to the lives of their offspring. Capricorn is then the fortitude to do that which is necessary for the benefit of others, foregoing the freedom of doing what one would prefer for self alone. With Saturn as its ruler, Capricorn is prepared to follow the established rules set forth as the limits and boundaries to the ultimate goal of success.

The eleventh sign of the zodiac is Aquarius, and it is symbolized by the water-carrier. This image is a compliment to the image of a sea-goat of Capricorn, where fish and mammal are on two levels of activity (above water level and below). Likewise, the Aquarian god in the clouds is pouring water that is symbolic on two planes, the spiritual and the earthly. Aquarius is then associated with godsends, which come in the form of ideas that dawn on one, friends who appear at times of need, and the rewards that come to those who share. Because the constellation shows a male image pouring out the water that fills the constellations around Aquarius, this male has been seen in ancient mythology as the source of the Great Flood, or God. An Aquarian knows there is more to what is observable, and thus seeks to know as much as possible about how the material world works, trusting insight, even if not completely sure that God is the source. Knowledge is all-important to an Aquarian, as is sharing that knowledge with those of like mind.

The planet that has ruled Aquarius traditionally is Saturn, although the discovery of the planet Uranus has caused some to believe it should dethrone Saturn. This notion of Uranus should be disregarded, as the symbolism of Uranus is too sudden and erratic to fit the rational flow of knowledge, which comes from inspiration. Even when ideas come as bolts of lightening from the sky, they never come as complete thoughts, which have been tried and tested for validity and reliability. Aquarian knowledge depends on such tests, which means Saturn is the symbolic planet that best associates with Aquarius.

Aquarius is opposite the sign of Leo, such that Saturn is the counterpart for the Sun. The Sun represents the innocence and light of a child, while the imaginations and games of childhood are turned into tangible practices and conceptions through the application of mature wisdom, the light of an adult. Thus, Aquarius represents the ability to experiment and test new ideas. Both signs are also positive (or masculine), meaning the fun and enjoyment of the imaginary world is found in the outward expression of games physically being played, theories being tested in reality, and problems of limitation being solved through practical invention. Whereas the Saturn – Moon axis (Capricorn – Cancer) was the parental axis (father – mother), the Saturn – Sun axis (Aquarius – Leo) is the play axis (with adult friends – with children). However, due to the seriousness of Saturn, Aquarians are associated with a level of detachment, where the child must be allowed to make mistakes without intervention, so the child will grow up more self-sufficient.

The final sign of the zodiac is Pisces, which is symbolized by the fishes. Having come from the god symbol in Aquarius, which is above human existence, the fishes of Pisces come from the world beneath land, the depths of the lakes, seas, and oceans. While God gives breath to human through the atmosphere, fish find life from the oxygen content of water. Still, the complete symbol of Pisces is two fish strung together on a line, as fish caught for food. Pisces is then like a fish out of water, struggling to breathe in a land environment, soon to become sacrificed as food for others. These are all symbolic traits of the sign Pisces.

The planet Jupiter traditionally rules the sign Pisces, although the modern discovery of the planet Neptune has caused some to believe it should displace Jupiter as the ruler. Since Nostradamus did not consciously know of this modern planet, and even though the associations of the symbolisms of Neptune are consistent with those associated with Pisces, the planet Jupiter is best seen as the ruler of Pisces. From having already discussed Jupiter as the planet of growth and expansion, those traits fit the element of water, the fish's habitat, such that water expands until it finds the limits of its container. Pisces symbolizes limitless expansion, with Jupiter symbolizing the aspects of higher mind. This combination becomes the unbound expanse of the unknown, particularly that which delves deep into the psyche, as the subconscious. This is the deep world of dreams and fantasy, and it is the world where one can escape reality. Therefore, Pisces is the sign that symbolizes the spiritual and the psychic, films, dreams, and drugs that put one into an altered state. Due to Pisces being the most self-sacrificing sign, it is associated with the faith that is at the core of all religions, where faith is in that which is unseen, but deeply felt.

With this tour through the esoteric meanings behind the astrological signs, I hope I have given the reader a greater depth of understanding of astrology's basics. The signs are not related to the stars that are arbitrarily arranged to depict animals, gods, and things, as those depictions are nothing more than a projection of the qualities and characteristics of human beings. These stars have no causal relationship with humanity. Everything is symbolic of the various basic traits of life on earth. Thus, the zodiac reflects what we ourselves cause on earth, just as a mirror reflects the image we project into smooth reflective glass.

One can stand in front of a mirror as a child, and see a true image staring back. Then, the same one can stand in front of the same mirror as an adult, and still see a true image, but one that is nothing like the true image projected long before. Just as we go through life changes, so too do the planets keep on moving, not causing life on earth, but reflecting it. To understand how this works, one has to understand that it is the mechanics of God.

Synthesis of Planets in Signs

As to some synthesis of Nostradamus having written of planets in signs, I will present his use of astrology in the fifty-first quatrain of *Century First*. In the main theme line, Nostradamus wrote, "*Chef d'Aries, Jupiter, & Saturne,*" which means, "*Head of Aries, Jupiter, & Saturn*". The "*Head of Aries*" means the "*Ruler of Aries*", in one possible interpretation. We have found that "*Ruler*" is the planet Mars.

When that translation is recognized as an astrological statement of rulership, one is able to read this main theme as more than just the names of planets and the sign *Aries*. One can see a symbolic pattern of action, established by the series of commas (system of punctuation), and based on the symbolic meaning the planets present through astrology. This is especially important to understand, because the theme of *The Prophecies* is to tell of the coming of a Holy War in the future; and Mars (The Roman equivalent of *Aries*) is the god of war.

The sign *Aries* is seen to be the starter, the first, or the initiator. When the word "*Chef*" is used it can translate as "*chief, general, or principal commander*", while typically meaning, "*head*". [246] Such military titles are "*of Aries*", in that they were given sole charge of when to attack, if at all. In the area of the human body, various parts are assigned to sign and planet alignments, and it is said that *Aries* rules the head. This is due to it being a matter of "self", which is centered in a body's head; and likewise a military body (one-self) is led by its "*Head*". Such a leader is usually rather bold and ready to charge. By reading Mars as the "*Ruler of Aries*", it is easier to see a sudden burst into war is possible to interpret, due to a "*Head of Aries*" being led by thoughts of war and action.

The use of *Aries* is followed by a comma, which means that the word *Jupiter* comes after the war has begun. This planet, as we have now learned, represents judgment, as a way of seeking justice. With the capitalization of *Jupiter* the importance is maintained into the word used to symbolize *Jupiter*, showing the major level of *Judgment* that will be the next step relative to a "*Ruler of Aries*". In terms of War, particularly Holy War, this can then be seen as a statement of *Judgment* Day, of biblical proportions. As representing *Justice*, this indicates the side winning the war will see God as having favored them. A long time of oppression will have been made balanced, as *Justice* will prevail. The planet *Jupiter* symbolizes a period following major war, where growth and expansion occurs from war. In that sense, the "*Head of Aries*" will expand into foreign lands.

Following the word "*Jupiter*" there is a comma, followed by an ampersand. The comma separates "*Jupiter*" from the next word, with the ampersand placing emphasis on that word, "*Saturn*", which ends line one. The ampersand indicates that *Saturn* has a level of importance, which makes it stand alone, before it can connect to the preceding segments. By itself, as a capitalized word, one is able to understand *Saturn* as being the planet known as the Greater Malefic. This moniker was placed on *Saturn* because it had historically been associated with periods of pain, which befell those who were deserving of punishment. In any sense, "*Saturn*" stated by itself means a focus must be on patience, discipline, and austerity.

That separate meaning is then woven into the other meaning of the previous segments. Depending on whose view of *Justice* has been served ("*Jupiter*"), through the growth and expansion of war and battle ("*Aries*"), "*Saturn*" can represent an occupation. In this sense *Saturn*, acts as the following disciplinarian of *Jupiter's* justice. The sweeping expansion of "*Jupiter*" needs to establish fixed parameters of control,

[246]   Randle Cotgrave's 1611 French-English Dictionary, http://www.pbm.com/~lindahl/cotgrave/search/1891.html

which is the essence of "*Saturn*".

This means limits are set, as well as meaning the disciplinarian arm of Law is brought into action, to quell any uprisings that would come after the initial waves of war. This means punishment, which can mean persecution. When one understands the parallel to Nostradamus' prophecy as (among others) *The Revelation*, punishment can be expected to be quite severe. Together, "*Jupiter, & Saturn*" mean trial by law (even holy law), before significant repercussions are enforced. When the "*Head of Aries*" is the primary influence to everything, this main theme statement is telling of a system of military tribunal, as the "*Rule of War*".

This main theme becomes more vital to understand than does the an astronomical configuration that would be a triple conjunction of Mars ("*Ruler of Aries*"), "*Jupiter*", and "*Saturn*". Such a configuration is rather limited, as the slowest moving planet (*Saturn*) will not be conjunct with the second slowest moving planet (*Jupiter*) frequently, with occurrences being separated in decades apart in time. As infrequent as these conjunctions are, each time they occur a general historical trend can help identify how the combination of "symbolic energies" plays out in international affairs.

For instance, the last time *Jupiter* and *Saturn* were conjunct in the same sign was the year 2000, when bother were in the sign Taurus together, and exactly conjunct in late May. Between late March, and early May, Mars was also in the sign of Taurus, meaning it is possible the year 2000 was a significant time. The time before, when *Jupiter* and *Saturn* were in the same sign was 1981 (in Libra), but Mars did not enter Libra until after *Jupiter* moved into Scorpio. The next time all three planets will be in the same sign together will be the year 2020, with *Jupiter* and *Saturn* moving together in both Capricorn and Aquarius (both signs ruled by *Saturn*) over 2020 and 2021. This future combination can be compared to the conjunction between *Jupiter* and *Saturn* in Capricorn and Aquarius that occurred in 1960 and 1961, with both in Aquarius into early 1962. Mars joined the two (separately – conjunct with *Saturn* first, then *Jupiter*) in Aquarius, in February 1962.

This was the volatile early years of the Kennedy Administration, when international tensions feared an outbreak of nuclear war. At that time one can see how the "*Head of Aries*" came down to a showdown between two headstrong rams, the United States and the Soviet Union. They were prepared to ram home a point over Cuba, which was the American "*Justice*" of the Monroe Doctrine, and America's protection of the Western Hemisphere, versus a Soviet "*Expansion*" into that protected zone, as a "*Trial*" of America's will and resolve to live up to that "*Ideal*". America established "*Limits*", through a naval blockade, and used "*Patience*" and "*Determination*" to force the Soviets to back down, with the threat of the ultimate "*Punishment*" being the stakes the whole world held its breath over.

To lock this timeframe down to the meaning of quatrain I-51 would be incorrect, as the rest of the verbiage indicates a kind of prayer to God about the repetitiveness of such times when the "*Head of Aries*" rules.

While it may be possible to see a specific time that one could look to, to test if this is the ultimate purpose of this prophecy, one would be missing the true purpose, which is to understand how we must be ruled by the heart, towards love and acceptance. In this way, the esoteric is demonstrated to yield more impact than the literal, although the literal can be seen as supporting the timing of the esoteric.

Another good example of Nostradamus' presentation of astrology, where literal and symbolic meaning comes from the same words, is the thirty-fifth quatrain found in *Century Sixth*. In that quatrain the secondary theme line (line two) and the main theme supporting line (line three) are predominately astrological references. Nostradamus wrote, "*Aries, Taurus, Cancer, Leo, la Vierge: / Mars, Jupiter, le Sol, ardera grand plaine,*" which states, "*Aries, Taurus, Cancer, Leo, the Virgin: / Mars, Jupiter, the Sun, will burn great plain*".[247]

The secondary theme can be seen simply as a six-month period, between spring and fall, with the summer signs fully noted. This simplicity misses the significance of Gemini, since this sign is not overtly listed, but inclusive between *Taurus* and *Cancer*. If one reads the secondary theme as symbolic meanings associated with the signs, one can see the secondary theme becoming, "*Bold initiations, Values, Protectiveness, Loyalties, the Planning*". In this case, the meaning of Gemini is excluded.

This series of signs, and alternately statements of characteristics, flows in order of importance, then ends with a colon. The colon directly points to the next line as where to find an example or clarification of what was stated in the secondary theme, and in particular the essence of *Virgo*, or *the Planning*. Instead of three orbs immediately read as the meaning, the esoteric values "*Mars, Jupiter, le Sol*" carry, as "*War, Judgment, Christianity*". These lead to the final segment statement, which says, "*will burn (the) great flat*". This means the elements of symbolism in reference to the signs are designed to bring a *War* of *Judgment* against those representing *Christianity*, who are those deemed the *great*. The purpose of *the Planning* is to *burn* the West, by knocking them *flat*.

It is important to offer one alternative to this translation, as "*Sol*" is Latin for "*Sun*". While "*le Sol*" can mean, "*the Sun*", the usual French usage would be "*le Soleil*". The typical use of "*Sol*" means, "Soil, Ground, Land, Foundation, Bottom of a place." In this case, there is a connection made to the burning of a "*great plain*". When it is understood that the word "*great*" is not a superlative, but an indication of one of the superpowers of the world, "*great plain*" could be an indication of the part of the United States known as the "Great Plains." As a double entendre, allowing for the summer months associated with the secondary theme, "*the Sun*" does become hot in the Midwest, such that "*the Land*" of focus will be dried in "*the Sun*", making it easy to "*burn*".

This example, along with the prior, should demonstrate how understanding the esoteric values of planets and signs, along with the systems of capitalization, ampersands, and punctuation, brings great depth

---

247   The 1557 Utrecht edition does not have as many commas present, particularly on line three.

of meaning to just a few words. This depth does not even consider the additional information that is conveyed by understanding more about the system of astrology. To understand more, I must first resume my brief course on astrology.

Aspects

The aspects of astrology relate to the angular separation between two planets or luminaries (Sun or Moon). This is expressed in degrees of arc, and can never be greater than 180 degrees. By this, I mean that the angular separation is always the lesser arc, such that if one planet is found to be (for example) 72 degrees away from another orb, it is also found to be 288 degrees when the wide arc is considered. The widest arc of separation found in astrology is 180 degrees; and a 180-degree aspect is called an "opposition".

Conversely, the smallest degree of separation would be 0 degrees, which would mean two planets are in the same location in space, as viewed from earth, within the elliptical path of the zodiac belt. This aspect is called a "conjunction". All other aspects fall between the conjunction and the opposition, with the degrees of separation being determined by the divisible number of the 360-degree circle, by whole numbers one through twelve. Thus 1/360 would be a separation of 360 degrees, with the lesser arc equaling 0 degrees (i.e.: conjunction). The next whole number results in a 2/360 division, which results in a separation of 180 degrees (i.e.: the opposition).

The other aspects can be calculated similarly. The aspect for the division 3/360 is called a "trine" (120 degrees of separation). An aspect generated by dividing 4/360 is called a "square" (90 degrees of separation). When one divides 5/360, it creates two minor aspects of the quintile variety, in multiples of 72 degrees. A quintile is 72 degrees, with two such aspects being less than 180 degrees, such that the 144 degrees counterpart becomes known as a biquintile. The 6/360 division generates what is called a sextile, or 60 degrees of separation. Multiples of this division are the major aspects known as trine (120 degrees) and opposition (180 degrees); but when a sextile is not begun at the 0-degree angle, instead the 90-degree one, an aspect related to the sextile appears, a 150-degree (being 90 + 60) aspect known as a quincunx.

A quincunx (also known as an inconjunct) is actually a relative of the semi-sextile, which is a 12/360 aspect of 30 degrees. It is half of a sextile, which is 60 degrees. The word-name, quincunx, comes from Latin (*quinque + uncia*), meaning "five twelfths".[248] In the past, many astrologers saw the quincunx as a minor aspect, as they see the semi-sextile. However, most modern astrologers find the quincunx almost as important as a major aspect, only less obvious. It therefore falls into the category of a sextile, as an important minor aspect, thus the relationship is less to the semi-sextile, and more to a sextile stemming from the difficulties of a square aspect.

---

248   Wikipedia the free encyclopedia, http://en.wikipedia.org/wiki/Quincunx

The remainder of the divisions (7/360 = 51.4 degrees, 8/360 = 45 degrees, 9/360 = 40 degrees, 10/360 = 36 degrees, 11/360 = 32.7 degrees, and 12/360 = 30 degrees) create aspects that are all considered to be minor. By minor, the implication is that as natal (birth chart) aspects they do not reflect major strengths or weaknesses of character, or major life altering events to prepare for (transit charts compared to natal chart).

The divisions by one, two, three, and four are considered the major aspects, which again are the conjunction (0), opposition (180), square (90), and trine (120). The divisions by five (72 degrees), six (60 degrees), and twelve (30 degrees), with the quincunx (150 degrees) a factor of twelve, are seen as most important "minor aspects". Planets and luminaries in these minor aspectual relationships usually indicate characteristics that shape and color how the major aspects can be reflected.

Nostradamus did not go beyond this scope in detailing aspects in *The Prophecies*. There is some evidence of each of these major aspects, and some minor aspects being factored into the quatrains. Some are named indirectly, as were some of the astrological signs and planets. The ones of greatest significance that are found in the verses are the conjunction and the opposition. Nostradamus also wrote in abbreviations (in all-caps and capitalized first letter) words that certainly could be read as *SEXTILE* ("*SEX.*" in quatrain IV – 27) and *Sextile* ("*Sext.*" in quatrain V – 57).

All of the aspects have symbolic meanings, which are applied to the symbolic meanings of the planets and signs. While nouns, adjectives, and adverbs symbolically identify planets and signs, the aspects are the verbs. This means that a sentence can be constructed when two planets are in aspect to one another. Therefore, it is important to understand the symbolic meanings for the aspects.

A conjunction symbolizes when two or more join, or meet at the same location. Marriage is such a union between two people, but the same union can be expected when one joins a group. While each individual is unique and different, each individual is usually compromised in some way, in order to meet the needs of another or others. If one looked at this as if individuals were unique colored lights, like red and blue, for both to join together the result is neither red nor blue, but purple. Thus, a conjunction represents a blending of symbolisms, which are unique to each planet. It represents a melding, and a tempering of outward expression.

For instance, if Mars and Jupiter are conjunct, the energy, action, and fight of Mars are blended with the growth, expansion, and judgment of Jupiter. The result could be seen as a strong opportunity to exhibit an expansive drive towards some goal, or growing desires to act. Since a conjunction usually means two planets in the same sign, the expansive drive, or growing desire, would be highlighted by the symbolisms associated with the sign in which the two were joined. For instance, if Mars and Jupiter were conjunct in the sign of Libra, there could be an additional attempt to act gracefully, use artistic flare, or attempt to bring balance to a situation.

It must be noted that only in the ideal world are exact conjunctions found. Psychologists have done studies on the level of "personal space" surrounding individuals, and how close one will allow others to come into that space before one feels a blend with someone else, thus a need to react to this closeness. The act of sex is symbolic of an exact conjunction of 0 degrees of separation; but most of the time people in conjunction are only relatively close to each other. Likewise, the planets are considered to be in aspect with one another when two or more are in an angular relationship, within what is called an "acceptable degree of orb."

In determining what is acceptable for an accurate reading, the degree of separation may change from astrologer to astrologer. The reasoning should be based on the known characteristics of an individual, determined through consulting an astrologer. Without such a relationship established, the safest rule of thumb for separation allowance to establish a major aspect is five degrees. For an aspect between a natal orb position (these are fixed at the time of birth and do not move) and a transiting one would plus or minus five degrees, from the exact degree of aspect to the natal position. This means a span of ten degrees for a major aspect to a natal planet or luminary. Sometimes it may be appropriate to expand this orb allowance for a major aspect between natal orbs, in particular when one or both of the luminaries (Sun or Moon) are involved, up to ten degrees.[249] Determining what works best is like tuning a musical instrument by ear.

For example, two orbs are said to be in trine aspect when they are separated by 120 degrees. With a separation allowance, if the two are either 115 degrees or 125 degrees apart they are still considered to be in trine aspect. This allowance of a spread means that two planets can be conjunct one another, while one is in the beginning degrees of one sign, and the other in the ending degrees of the adjacent sign, within the 5-degree allowance. Considering the symbolisms of two signs in a conjunction adds to the complexity of reading that aspect.

The mechanics of a conjunction are still in effect, but in a slightly different manner. Instead of a blending in one place, each orb's symbolic properties become filtered through each orb's ability to express its natural qualities within the sign it appears. Planets and luminaries are either at odds or in concert with the symbolisms relative to the twelve signs. This can change how one orb blends with another, which is in another sign.

A sextile aspect (60 degrees) symbolically represents some form of opportunity is possible, involving two orbs that are certainly in two separate signs. Like a conjunction aspect, which is typically in the same sign, a sextile is when two orbs are two signs apart. The signs alternate between being compatible and being incompatible, or at ease and stressful with one another. Thus, two signs apart are usually compatible. However, with the separation allowance, two orbs can be three signs apart, turning what should be a comfortably opportunistic relationship into one that is more troubling.

---

249 A minor aspect has a narrower orb allowance, such that a good rule of thumb is 4-5 degrees of overall span is considered, or between 2-2.5 degrees of separation. Thus, a sextile aspect would be separation from between 57-58 degrees to 62 degrees, generally.

Opportunity is something that requires some effort. The saying goes, "when opportunity knocks, open the door", and this is the guide for this aspect. Because a sextile is considered an aspect that is passive, rather than aggressive, opportunities can often be left unrealized. This can be the case when the two orbs are in signs that limit a planet or luminary's symbolic quality. It can also be the case when two orbs are three signs apart.

Using the same two planets in sextile aspect, as we used in the conjunction, if Mars was found to be at 12 degrees of Gemini, and Jupiter was at 14 degrees of Leo, they would be 62 degrees apart, thus within the orb allowance for a sextile aspect. Mars in Gemini constructs the symbolic key words for those two (planet and sign) as Action-Communication, Mobile-Sports, or Multiple-Energies, among many other possibilities. Jupiter in Leo combines pairs like Expanding-Center of Attention, Benefit-Loyalty, or Big-Shows, again only to name a few scenarios. When the verb between these possibilities is centered on opportunity, this aspect could generate statements of possibility like, "Communication activity creates an opportunity for drawing expanded attention", "Auto racing provides a chance for one to make a big showing," and so forth.

A square aspect (90 degrees) is a very dynamic aspect. It is the most aggressive of the aspects, thus signaling an aspect of constant conflict, confrontation, and challenge. The aspect occurs when two planets are at right angles to one another. Right angles are important in building, thus a builder's tool for measuring right angles is called a square. Just as a builder's square is used to test for true stability, planets in a square aspect also test one another. In this way, a square represents a direct challenge, or an unavoidable confrontation. While such tests require strength to pass, tests of this nature represent the times of our lives when significant successes or failures can occur. Whatever the outcome, the results mean valuable lessons we learned.

Again using Mars and Jupiter, if Jupiter was at 22 degrees of Capricorn, and Mars was at 21 degrees of Aries, they would be square (89 degrees of separation). Jupiter in Capricorn combines the symbolisms of Growth, Benefit, and Greatness with Reputation, Dedication, and Hardness, which can be combined to represent (among many possibilities) Growing Reputation, Dedicated Benefits, and Great Hardness. Mars in Aries (Mars rules Aries, and thus is freer to express when in Aries) combines Energy, Action, and Drive with Selfishness, Boldness, and Fast Starts. These combinations can result in traits recognized as Selfish Energies, Bold Actions, and being Fast Driven. The test or challenge of these combinations, from being in square aspect to one another, means their expressions can result in statements like, "His Growing Reputation is confronted by his Selfish Energies," "Some Bold Actions threatened the sincerity of the company's Dedicated Benefits", and so on.

A trine aspect (120 degrees) represents one-third of the strongest structure possible – the triangle. When combined with a square base, four triangular sides become a pyramid, which is a symbol of great lasting strength, simply because the angled sides of a triangle rest on each other, without exerting any energy to resist outside opposing forces. In this way, a trine becomes an aspect that symbolizes strengths through ease, or natural abilities that do not require excess work to achieve. This aspect can signal where laziness can become a danger, simply because one is not forced to work hard for rewards.

An example, using different planets, Venus and Saturn, could be if Venus was at six degrees of Sagittarius, and Saturn was at 10 degrees of Aries. A separation of 124 degrees means the two would be in trine aspect. The combinations of symbolism for Venus are Love, Beauty, and Aesthetics, in the sign of Sagittarius, which represents Athletics, Free-Spirited, and Freedom. That placement of Venus could result in tendencies such as Uncommitted Love, Athletic Beauty, and Free-Spirited Aesthetics. The planet Saturn brings the key terms Patience, Restriction, and Testing into combination with the symbolisms of Aries: Self, Initiation, and Bold. This can result in characteristics like Self Control, Slow Starting, and Boldly Testing. When the trine verb, ease, is added to these combinations a statement can arise like, "A natural ability for Self-Control made her body an Athletic Beauty", "Typically a Cautious Starter in matters of the heart, he made it clear his interests was to be Friends with Benefits", and so on.

A quincunx aspect (150 degrees) is one that symbolizes a need for adjustment. While the sextile (60 degrees) shows a time of opportunity, the semi-sextile (30 degrees) represents hope that opportunity will come from observing the surroundings. Surroundings are often not of one's own choosing, and thus not something easily mastered, but through learning how to make the best of an unfamiliar situation, one hopes one will be better suited in the future to adjust quickly. As a semi-sextile is a 30-degree arc from the 180-degree opposition line, a quincunx is also the same arc, but to the opposite end. In that sense, the quincunx exposes where one's hopes are somewhat dashed, causing one to feel uneasy and lost. A quincunx represents the opportunity (sextile – 60 degrees) that waits beyond the successful defeat of a direct confrontation (a square aspect – 90 degrees), but without the battle being forced upon one. This represents when there is reluctance, from fear of the unknown, where the fears are in one's head. Still, it represents those times when one awkwardly attempts to deal with that which is well over one's head.

An example, using the planet Mercury and the Moon as the symbolic energies involved could be when Mercury is at seventeen degrees of Scorpio, with the Moon at sixteen degrees of Gemini (a separation of 151 degrees). The Mercury – Scorpio key words are Thought, Basic Education, and Communication combined with Sensuality, Depth, and Observation. This could result in symbolic traits of Sensual Thoughts, Observed Learning, and Deep Conversations. The Moon – Gemini combinations are symbolized as Emotions, Intuitions, and Nurturing with Multiplicity, Learning, and Changeability. This can result in characteristics like Quickly Changing Emotional States, Instinctive Learning, and a Shared Caregiver. When the verb of the quincunx is added, where adjusting or worry is seen as the catalyst, a statement can result like, "He did not know how to stop having Sensual Thoughts about his School Teacher", "Her Depth of Conversation was often a wild ride because of her Quick Emotional Shifts", and so on.

Finally, an opposition aspect (180 degrees) can be seen as the opposite of a conjunction, where instead of blending, two planets represent opposing points of view. While an opposition can represent a challenge, it differs from a square. A square is more of a blindsided conflict, where one is forced to react to an immediate situation. On the other hand, an opposition represents when two are face-to-face over differences. Conflict is not a foregone conclusion with an opposition, as both sides of an issue are clear to see. Therefore, an opposition calls for balance and compromise, more than trying to force one's way on another.

An example of an opposition, using the Sun and Mars key words, would be when the Sun is at 29 degrees of Aquarius, while Mars is at one degree of Virgo (178 degrees of separation). The Sun – Aquarius combination brings the symbolisms of Ego, Expression, and Basic Nature, with Friendly, Knowledgeable, and Detached, such that the result is Friendly Basic Nature, Knowledgeable Expression, and Detached Ego. Then there is the combination of Mars – Virgo, which has the key terms Energy, Action, and Drive, along with Planning, Order, and Detailed, which yields Actively Planning, Energetic Ordering, and Drive for Detail. When these are connected by the action of conflict resolution, a statement can result like, "His Friendly Basic Nature is checked by having to Energetically demand Order", "Her ability to Express Knowledge is compromised by a strong Drive for Detail", and so on.

These examples demonstrate that the systems of the art of astrology are not much different from the overall systems of Nostradamus, where each element must be understood before it can be connected to another related element. The synthesis of key words, based on the esoteric meaning associated with the planets in the signs, then according to their angular relationships, is like the synthesis of nouns, adjectives, and adverbs, connected by verbs, directed by punctuations, and relative to the order of the lines. The point is not to fine-tune the meaning to only one specific element. Instead, it is to expand the scope to see the breadth that limited input allows.

In the forty-eighth quatrain found in *Century Second*, Nostradamus wrote as the secondary theme, "*Saturne en l'Arq tournant du poisson Mars*", which says, "*Saturn in Sagittarius (the Bow) exchanging to the fish Mars*". The verb here is *tournant* (the present participle of *tourner*, meaning, "to turn, convert, alter, change"), such that this wording is stating a square aspect between *Saturn in Sagittarius* and *Mars* in Pisces ("*the fish*"). The meaning of this theme is then gained through the same processes as demonstrated above.

The symbolisms represented by *Saturn in Sagittarius* are Patience, Restriction, and Testing, combined with Hunting, Free Spirited, and Dogmatic. Some potential results could be Patient Hunting, Free Spirited Restrictions, and Dogmatic Testing. The elements of *Mars* in Pisces then represent Action, War, and Slashing, along with Sacrificial, Feelings, and Psychic Sense. These combinations can result in pairs like Sacrificial War, Cutting Feelings, and a Psychic Sense to Act. These are then placed into action as "*exchanging*", where there is no way to avoid forced conversion. The statements then found as possible in line two can be like, "Patient Hunting is converted into Sacrificial War", "Testing Dogma is turned into Feelings of Bleeding", and/or "Restrictions on one's desire to be Free Spirited are released when God's Voice commands one to Act".

Nostradamus only indicated astrological aspectual relationships between two planets, by their astrological aspect names, when he wrote of conjunctions. For instance, he wrote in the second quatrain appearing in *Century Eighth*, "*Sol, Mars conjoint au Lyon,*" meaning "*Sun (then) Mars conjunct in the Lion*", or *Leo*. He wrote of all other aspects in less obvious ways.

To state a lunar eclipse between the Sun and the Moon (an aspectual opposition), he wrote in the thirtieth quatrain listed in *Century Fourth* (main theme line), "*Luna Sol ne vouldra,*" meaning, "*Moon Sun not will want*". In the sixty-seventh quatrain of *Century Tenth*, Nostradamus indicated a trine aspect (120 degrees) when he stated in the secondary theme (line two), "*Saturn, Capricorn, Jupiter, Mercury in the bull*". The signs *Capricorn* and Taurus ("*the bull*") are four signs apart (4 signs x 30 degrees per sign = 120 degrees of separation), thus aspectual relationships between *Saturn* and *Jupiter* to *Mercury* could only be one within the orb allowance for a trine aspect. This is why one has to understand the possibilities of verb meanings associated with the aspects.

Houses

The aspects between the planets in the signs do not take place in a vacuum. These actions need an area of life through which to manifest. The basic areas of life are also symbolically displayed through astrology, indicated by the imaginary elements of astrology I mentioned. The imaginary element of astrology is rather large, but it is where the typical person misses when a possible astrological reference by Nostradamus was made.

I call them imaginary because there is nothing physical that can be seen to detect them. The imaginary element that provides an astrologer with the areas of life is the division of the twelve 30-degree signs into twelve "houses" of unequal arc. Each house represents a particular area of life, which all human beings experience one way or another. Still, other imaginary elements of astrology are the way it categorizes the twelve signs into four "elements", three "qualities", and two dualities (masculine and feminine), plus the importance of "hemispheres." The Moon is an important orb, but astrology places value on its projected path as it circles the Earth, noting which degree of the 360-degree elliptic represents where the Moon will cross from the equator into the Northern Hemisphere. Further, due to astrology being the geocentric relationship between the Earth and its solar system mates, the illusion of backwards planetary motions (retrogradation) is an imaginary element of importance. Nostradamus referred to some of each of these imaginary categories in his letters and quatrains.

As to the imaginary areas of life divisions, there are twelve houses, the same number of signs in the zodiac. While the geocentric position gives the illusion of the signs and planets constantly moving, the houses become fixed positions, based on the exact time of birth. There are several "house systems" to choose from, all of which are used to calculate six houses above the 180-degree east-west horizon. The six houses below the horizon then have the same corresponding degrees, so each is represented as a 180-degree line, to its opposite sign. The houses are imaginary divisions that become symbolically associated with areas of life, and are in fixed positions, numbered one through twelve, with the first house always being the one beginning with the eastern horizon, extending below that point. On an astrological chart, the eastern horizon is show as the furthest left point on the 360-degree circle, with the numbered houses progressing counter-clockwise, such that the last degree of the twelfth house is again the point of the eastern horizon.

Still, with the presence of twelve houses, each of the signs is considered to be "at home" in one of the particular houses. Since Aries is considered the first sign of the zodiac, it is naturally associated in the first house. Taurus, as the second sign, is then at home in the second house. This continues all the way through the signs and houses, such that the twelfth sign, Pisces, is aligned with the twelfth house. This, again, is a natural house-to-sign relationship, but a typical birth chart will not reflect this arrangement.

The houses are fixed in their relationship to the curvature of the earth, but these fixed houses are different for each individual. This is based on the constantly changing backdrop of the signs, such that an individual's houses are marked by the degrees of the signs that were "snapped" at the time of a native's birth. Each sign spans thirty degrees of arc (12/360 = 30), and so too does a theoretical house; but in reality, a house can be greater or lesser than thirty degrees, as long as any six consecutive houses equal 180 degrees. Thus, the cusps (degree boundaries) of one house are the same cusps of the house opposite it.

This means that if the third house of a native spans from 12 degrees of Aries to 16 degrees of Taurus (34 degree span), the corresponding ninth house will begin at 12 degrees of Libra (the opposite sign of Aries), and end at 16 degrees of Scorpio (the opposite sign of Taurus). Some houses can span 40 degrees, or so, completely absorbing a whole sign, such that no degree of that "intercepted" sign is on a cusp of a house. To compensate, the opposing sign is also "intercepted"; and for all signs over 30-degrees, there will be signs spanning less than 30-degrees, to maintain 180 degrees between all opposing house cusps.

Each house has its own symbolic representation, with each said to represent one of twelve basic areas of life. These areas of life are symbolic of the stages all human beings must encounter, in some form or another, from birth to death. The first house, as representing the first appearance into a world with life, symbolizes the physical body, crying, and breathing, full of life. This house is then symbolic of the image projected to the world, as well as the characteristics of the physical body.

The second house is then representative of the growth of a newborn into an awareness of that which makes it feel comfortable. A security blanket and huggie bear are representations of the possessions of a small child, which the child values deeply, on a personal level. Thus, the symbolisms of the second house relate to personal values, which always translate on some level to money, but are focused more on comfort, pleasure, and styles that reflect one's level of security.

The third house is representative of the child's growth to a level of awareness of others in his or her world, beyond the mother and father. This becomes the awareness of the routine, which is symbolized by formal and informal education (teachers in school, church, and at home), local travels of a regular nature, relatives (siblings, cousins, aunts & uncles, and grandparents), and neighbors. The third house stands for those areas of life where one learns to relate outwardly.

The fourth house represents primarily that which is most familiar to the native, outside of the self. Familiarity allows one to rest one's mind, and feel safe. It therefore is primarily associated with the home, as a place that becomes more than a house. The home is where one can relax and reenergize. It can also be representative of the idiom, "Home is where the heart is." The fourth house stands for that for which one cares, which is beyond one's control to choose. It then encompasses one's roots and traditions, including nationality, heritage, lineage, and related history, which one was born into and that by which one has become comfortably nurtured. This awareness comes when the child grows to realize the importance of having a larger identity with which to become one.

The fifth house represents that time of life when the child is most free to express him or herself, without any burden of responsibility limiting that expression. It is then called the house of play, or the playground. However, beyond the skills one develops through lighthearted competition, this house symbolizes creativity of all kinds. Natural talent abilities are often reflected in the fifth house; but it is also known as the house of children, reflecting how the child within becomes a parent to his or her own children. The fifth house is symbolic of how one views sex as a recreational activity, without thought about the consequences. Thus, the fifth represents the area of life where dating and courtship are reflected.

After the child has grown to the brink of adulthood, it begins to learn that life cannot be continued without paying the price of life. This means the sixth house represents the area of life where one learns the responsibility of work time, as a counter to play time, beginning with simple chores. This background of understanding becomes later the steps into the field of employment, as a paid worker. Beyond working for a living, the sixth house symbolizes the service of the needs of others, where one's own personal preferences are reflective of how one wishes to be served. When work becomes laborious, rather than fun, the body becomes more likely to break down and ache. Therefore, the sixth house is reflective of the health issues one regularly faces in a lifetime. From time to time, one is bound to run into others who seem to go out of their way creating unfair work, excessive demands, and health strains for the native. These can be for any number of reasons. When enemies are created, the sixth house symbolizes the manner in which one can see one's own character flaws being projected onto others.

The benefits of working (monetary savings and position advancement) lead one to remember the idiom, "Misery loves company." Instead of seeking someone to be miserable with, one begins to seek someone to make one forget one's miseries, and vice versa. While the sixth house represents a variety of work associates to commiserate with, the seventh house represents the need of the individual to find a special one-to-one relationship. Typically, this represents where one is strongly attracted to one of the opposite sex, for the awakening of the heart to love, such that the seventh house is known as the house of marriage. However, important bonding with another can also be reflected in special friendships, and even close business partnerships. The seventh house is paired with the first house, as the first set of opposing areas of life. This becomes representative of the "self" axis, where one pole is the self, alone, and the other is the self, with another self.

Once two are connected as one pair, the distinction of each individual is shed, adopting one identity as a couple. The eighth house is on the "value" axis, opposite the second house's personal values. Thus, the eighth house reflects shared resources, where the Shakespearian quote, "What's mine is yours, and what is yours is mine" is foremost. When love is the catalyst for this union, the body becomes the most important shared resource. Thus, the eighth house is symbolic of sex, with the caveat being for mutual satisfaction, more than simple pleasure. The yearnings of two almost always mean one desires offspring through relationship, which is another value system expression. This makes the sexual expression of married intercourse be heavily slanted towards procreation, and the renewal of the species. As the continuation of a lineage, by new births, is found reflected the eighth house, one also finds the first experiences of death. These can be relatives or old friends of the family, where witnessing funerals has an impact on one's maturity level. A resource that can then be shared through relatives is inheritance, or a shared legacy. Such an award then brings out the IRS as a partner of shared resources, which seeks taxation as a sign of one's national commitment. The second-eighth house axis is thus known as the "money axis."

The ninth house is reflective of the axis of "learning", where the routine and basic on one end (the 3rd) is then expanded on the other, as advanced awareness (the 9th). This is then symbolic of higher education, and although colleges and universities do align with this house, a higher education is not always gained from such a formal education. The horizons are more distant than the local environment, such that foreign travel is symbolized. Travel educates, as a form of learning the ways of foreign lands, including those languages to which one is unaccustomed. One of the highest forms of awareness is the boundary within which one must operate, such that the legal system is reflected in the area of life covered by the ninth house. This element of law is then elevated to recognition of the highest realm, which is worship to a higher power and deity. This makes the dogma of religion and philosophy another concern related to the ninth house.

Once one is properly educated, one can be held fully responsible for one's actions. The tenth house is then representative of the inner understanding that one has to use knowledge as a motivator for success. As the opposite house to the home (the fourth house), the tenth house is symbolic of the career, where one's inner drive and motivations are focused on the need to provide for others, either those at home, or those in the work family. Whereas the sixth house is the house of work and service, the tenth house symbolizes the area of life where one assumes leadership roles. Thus, it reflects where one faces the public spotlight. The tenth house, as how one accepts responsibility for others, is then associated with one's reputation among peers. As the house opposite to the home (4th house), the tenth house is the home to the work family, wherever that place may be.

The eleventh house is representative of that which becomes the result of a lifetime of diligence and effort for and with others. This is the area of life where all the knowledge, work, and sacrifice of a life find their just rewards. More than simply reaping things of material value, one finds a wealth of friends, associates, and acquaintances, all who played roles in bringing one his or her successes. This house then reflects how one values others, through retained friendships and networking contacts. On the financial end, the planning for the future (a tenth house sacrifice) pays off in the enjoyments of retirement. As such, this house is opposite the childhood house of play (the fifth house), and symbolizes the fun and games of adulthood, best shared with those who have remained important in one's life.

Finally, the twelfth house represents the end of one's life. This is not a focus on death, but the phases of life when one is not focused on the importance of self, or the worldly things that once took one's attention off the inner whispers and dreams. The twelfth house is where one finds more importance in the spiritual realm. This house is then symbolic of being in touch with one's inner being, where intuition is honed to the point of psychic awareness. It represents the realm of secrets, where personal, subconscious motivations lay hidden in ones psyche; and where secrets are exposed through sudden flashes of revelation. The twelfth house represents dreams, and that which is illusory and nebulous, difficult to grasp and put into words. This house is reflective of an awareness of a higher being, which prompts faith through spirituality. Since this house reflects the hidden, it is also representative of where those forces lie that seek to unravel one's being. Therefore, it is known to be the house of hidden enemies. As the house opposite the sixth house of drive to work and serve self, the twelfth house is where service is to others.

As stated before, each house is divided by imaginary lines called "cusps," which represent the beginning degree of the house. Signs also have cusps, where there is in reality no 0-degree or 30-degree points exist. While planets "on the cusp" of a sign can raise some debate issues, the degrees of a house are fixed, which become clear boundary markers. Of these house cusps, some are more important than the others, at least in the fact that they have been given specific names. These houses reflect the self (1st), the home (4th), relationships (7th), and career (10th).

The relationship of the Sun, Moon, and planets to the Earth makes all appear to move in a counterclockwise motion; but the Earth's rotation makes the movement of the signs on the houses move clockwise. This movement is rapid, compared to the movement of the celestial orbs. Because the Earth does one full rotation in a 24-hour period, each sign will spend on average two hours on each of the twelve house positions.[250] All of the house positions are relative to a frozen moment in time, which childbirth (first breath) marks.

The name for the cusp of the first house is the Ascendant. It is given this name because it represents the eastern horizon in a native's surroundings, at the precise time of birth. This fixed line, the east-west axis, represents of the rising and setting point for the visible sky overhead, based on the apparent movement of the Solar system. That movement rises in the east (Ascendant) and sets in the west. Thus, the seventh house is representative of where the sky sets, warranting the name Descendant. The cusp of the tenth house is called the Midheaven or the Medium Coeli in Latin, thus abbreviated astrologically as "M.C." This is representative of the place directly overhead, where the arc of the sky is at its height, before bending downward to the setting horizon. Opposite this is the Nadir, also known as the Imum Coeli, abbreviated astrologically as "I.C." This represents the point directly below one's feet, overhead on the opposite side of the Earth. All of these cusps are parts of the houses they represent, but additional importance is given to these angular imaginary points, in particular the Ascendant.

The Ascendant is a fixed point in all natal (birth) charts cast for an individual, representing a snapshot of where the eastern horizon was at the time of birth. Since the ascendant at the time of birth is marked within one of the twelve signs, at one specific degree of that sign, the sign of the ascendant is called the "rising sign." This rising sign is the true focus of the question, "What's your sign?" This is because the Ascendant is the important cusp that marks the area of life concerning the physical self.

Nostradamus addressed this imaginary astrological point in the quatrains in the fiftieth quatrain found in *Century Sixth*, where he wrote, "*Et aura Mars ascendant pour son astre.*" This states, "*And will have Mars rising for his star.*" In this usage, the planet *Mars* can be said to be in the first house, within the allowable orb for being in conjunction with the degree of the Ascendant. It could also mean the rising sign is one ruled by *Mars* (either Aries or Scorpio). While this quatrain is the only one where Nostradamus directly referred to the Ascendant by name, he did make statements that assumed the reader understood this element of astrology.

I have already made one reference to Nostradamus referring to the United States of America as the nation of "*the balance*". The astrological sign symbolized by *the balance*, or the scales, is Libra. In the fiftieth quatrain of *Century Fourth*, Nostradamus began the main theme line with this distinction, when he wrote, "*Libra verra regner les Hesperies*". This states, "*Libra will see to rule the Western lands*", and one cannot expect the literal to be true, where a star constellation rules over earth. This use of *Libra* is astrological metaphor, as a statement of a nation that projects the essence of the sign *Libra*. The United States of America has a birthday in the sign of Cancer, but a noon "incorporation" time would cause *Libra*

---

250 For a native born near the equator the houses will be closer to equal distance, thus the 2-hour timeframe is more applicable. As the birth place move north or south of the equator the houses are less equal in span, which means the time a sign is located in a house varies.

to be the rising sign. Since the rising sign symbolizes the way one projects to the world, one becomes identified by the Ascendant, more than the Sun sign.

This is an example of how Nostradamus used subtle ways to introduce astrological clues. While the other house cusps are not mentioned in the letters or quatrains, the descriptive terminology of his writings makes it possible to see what areas of life would be affected. In an overall theme of Holy War, where religions do battle for world supremacy, the ninth house is certainly one house that comes into to play often. By knowing the basic symbolisms of the houses, some words can make more sense.

Elements

The four elements of astrology are fire, earth, air, and water. This grouping is referred to as the Triplicities, because there are three signs in each elementary category. Each of the signs within one elemental group is 120 degrees from the other, forming a triangular shape. As such, the whole of each sign is in trine aspect to the others of its element. The fire signs are Aries, Leo, and Sagittarius. The earth signs are Taurus, Virgo, and Capricorn. The air signs are Gemini, Libra, and Aquarius. The water signs are Cancer, Scorpio, and Pisces. Each of these elements then has some key words that sum up the basic essence of the signs contained within the separate groups.

The fire signs are all active, in need of movement, where Aries bursts into the world selfishly, Leo projects within the world as dominant, and Sagittarius searches the outer edges of the world for excitement. This activity is related to the essence of fire, which goes from spark, to flame, to embers, consuming matter to the point of transforming it to a higher state. Thus, the fire signs are those aspiring to make something happen, through a constant need to avoid inertia.

The earth signs are all grounded and resistant to change, and enjoy inertia. Taurus develops values that are fixed as its own, Virgo has set plans and methods so that hard work is not needlessly repeated, and Capricorn remains stationary through inner goals for accomplishment, based on tried and true procedures. This activity is related to the essence of earth, where a solid foundation is required for stability, strength, and endurance. One has to know what one values first, in order to plan to reach those goals, and then remain focused to achieve the rewards that allow for the material things the world offers. Thus, the earth signs are where the world takes form and shape, so that a mold is cast, to which all can attach.

The air signs are all elevated and seeking new experiences, thus willing to change. In this way, Gemini is learning the differences of the surrounding terrain in order to adapt as a local, Libra is attracted to another who expresses intimate views, as well as new perspectives, and Aquarius is concerned with knowing how best to reward others through invention. This activity is related to the essence of oxygen in the air, which is breathed in so it may revitalize the blood before being exhaled in a changed state (carbon dioxide). This, in turn, benefits plants life, which then regenerates oxygen in a cyclic activity. Thus, the air signs are where the world is inspired by ideas, which are constantly in a state of flux, while yielding tangible things that benefit the world.

Finally, the water signs are all fluid, while taking states that are reflective of the outside temperature – frozen, liquid, or gas – representing the depth that is beyond the exterior appearance. Thus, the sign Cancer reflects the hard shell and defensive nature of protecting a softness inside, Scorpio projects the danger of penetration, where knowing what is inside of others is the best defense, and Pisces absorbs all blows as it senses the best defense is to not be offensive. This activity is reflective of the essence of water, which is always spreading to take the shape of its holder, be it the continental landmasses holding back the oceans, the rolling hills forming the rivers, or the mountains holding the glaciers. Thus, the water signs are where one finds fulfillment, particularly through emotional attachment to something of meaning.

In French, these elements are *feu*, *terre*, *air*, and *eau*. Nostradamus mentioned each of these elements so often that the astrological symbolism is often not recognized. For example, he wrote in the seventy-first quatrain in *Century Tenth*, as the main theme, "*La terre, l'air geleront si grand eau,*" which says, "*There earth, the air will be freezing so great water*". This statement can have the meaning of founding principles (*earth*) leading to (comma) the concept (*l'air*) of cold (*freezing*) emotions (*water*) in a place like the United States (*great*). While such a main theme would depend on the supporting lines of this quatrain, this meaning can certainly apply. Understanding the astrological meaning behind these words is helpful in gaining a deeper understanding of a quatrain.

Qualities

The three qualities of astrology are cardinal, fixed, and mutable. These designations are applied to signs, and because there are four signs to each quality, the group is called the Quadruplicities. Cardinal signs are in line with action principles, where a tendency is to keep moving and always seek to begin anew, or start something. The Cardinal signs are Aries, Cancer, Libra, and Capricorn (one sign of each element of the triplicities). These are the signs on the "angular" cusps, the Ascendant, Nadir, Descendant, and Midheaven. The Fixed signs are Taurus, Leo, Scorpio, and Aquarius (again, one of each element). These are the signs that represent the least changeable of each element. The Mutable signs are Gemini, Virgo,

Sagittarius, and Pisces (one of each element). Mutable is in line with the principle of adjustment, where the path of least resistance is sought. Nostradamus referred to each of these principles.

The houses are closely aligned to the signs that naturally rule them. As such, the houses relate to the quadruplicies, but go by a different classification name - the Quadrants. Whereas the signs are classified as Cardinal, Fixed, and Mutable, the Quadrants are divided into Angular, Succedent, and Cadent. The Cardinal signs are naturally at home in Angular houses. The Angular houses are the first (physical self), fourth (home), seventh (relationships), and tenth (career). The Fixed signs relate to the Succedent houses, which are the second (personal values), fifth (play), eighth (shared resources), and eleventh (friends). Finally, the Mutable signs relate to the Cadent houses, which are the third (basic education), sixth (work), ninth (higher education), and twelfth (inner being).

Just as the houses never change, such that the first house is always the house rising to the eastern horizon, the Quadrants likewise remain fixed. That means the first house is always an Angular house, along with the fourth, seventh, and tenth houses. However, just as the signs constantly move with the rotation of the earth, a sign like Scorpio (a Fixed sign) can be the sign of an Angular position, when it rotates into the position filled by those house positions. The same principle applies as well to the Succedent and Cadent houses, such that each Quadrant will rotate through all of the Quadruplicities.

Nostradamus wrote in the forty-sixth quatrain found in *Century Third*, the secondary theme, "*Par clairs insignes & par estoiles fixes,*" which states, "*By lights renowned ones & by stars fixed ones*". This is making a statement about the constellations (*stars*) and the planets (*lights renowned*), but by adding "*fixes*", Nostradamus is making it possible to further limit the constellations associating with *fixed* signs (Taurus, Leo, Scorpio, and Aquarius). In this way, he expressed an astrological statement disguised as an astronomical one.

Nostradamus also specifically stated the word *Cardinal*, which is generally understood to be a reference to a position held by a member of the Roman Catholic Church. However, by Nostradamus stating, "*Le Cardinal de France apparoîtra,*" meaning, "*The Cardinal of France will appear*", this could have a secondary meaning that is astrological. Since there is no syntax in the quatrains, *Cardinal* bears all meanings, including astrological meanings. As such, *The Cardinal of France* can mean the outgoing nature of *France*, to be the initiator, or the starter, rather than the follower. When the *Cardinal* is more specifically seen as a reference to the Ascendant, the Point of the projection of self, on the cusp of the Angular first house, a *Cardinal* sign becomes (Aries, Cancer, Libra, or Capricorn) the *appearance* of France. Thus, "*The Cardinal of France*" could mean the projection of a French persona to the world. It may then be that a Catholic *Cardinal* is assigned to carry out that projection.

As for the Mutable aspect in *The Prophecies*, one of the most frequent words found in the verses is "*change*", in some form or another. The future that Nostradamus was shown by Christ is all about change.

However, the willingness of the Mutable signs to seek change will not be the primary focus. Nostradamus wrote of forced change, where those least adaptable will struggle mightily. A trait of mutability is to adapt to those whose willpower is stronger, thus making change happen by willing support, without resistance.

It must be understood that Pisces on the twelfth house cusp represents the most changeable combination (Mutable Cadent), thus Pisces is the natural ruler of the twelfth house. The twelfth house is the area of life where one sacrifices in the material plane, from faith that a higher reward waits in a higher plane. Pisces is the sign of self-sacrifice, such that personal wishes change to meet the wishes of others. This makes Pisces perfect as a Mutable sign, the natural ruler of the Cadent twelfth house.

This combination can then be seen as symbolizing the essence of Jesus Christ. His sermons teaching others to "turn the other cheek" and "love your neighbor as yourself" are totally about a willingness to adapt to circumstances in the physical realm, rather than to force one's will on another. Through willing sacrificial change, without regrets and hidden angers, one paves a smoother road to a future of peace. This willingness to adapt and change is the lesson brought to the reader of *The Prophecies*, in that change is how one averts the future prophesied. That solution, however, is not painted into the scenario of the story lines Nostradamus told, nor is it in the story lines of The Revelation of John. One has to see the scenario as it will be if no change occurs, for one's heart to change. From there it is only a matter of the heart leading the head, which is the essence of Pisces.

Hemispheres

The hemispheric divisions of the houses act in two main ways. First, the zodiac is divided along the ascendant-descendant (x) axis, creating a northern and southern hemisphere. The Northern Hemisphere is related to the principles of the first six signs (Aries through Virgo), and thus the first six houses.[251] This hemisphere is considered to be the "personal hemisphere", where self, values, education, home, play, and work are on a level that is singular in nature (as me, versus we). The Southern Hemisphere is related to the principles of the second six signs (Libra through Pisces), and thus the second six houses. This hemisphere is considered the "popular hemisphere", where relationships, shared resources, higher education, career, friends, and inner being are dependent on the nature of plurality (as we, versus me).

The second way the zodiac is divided into hemispheres is along the Medium Coeli-Imum Coeli (y) axis, commonly called the Midheaven-Nadir division. This creates an eastern and western hemisphere, where the Eastern Hemisphere is related to the last three signs and the first three signs (Capricorn through Pisces, and Aries through Gemini), and thus the tenth, eleventh, and twelfth houses, along with the first, second, and third houses. This hemisphere is considered the "private hemisphere", where career motivations, associates, inner voice, self projection, personal values, and basic education are the least exposed aspects

---

251   Since the east (Ascendant) is depicted in a birth chart as the furthest most point to the left, the "Northern Hemisphere" is the bottom half of the chart, with the "Southern Hemisphere" the top half.

of one's core nature, shared with only those close to one's development. The Western Hemisphere is then related to the fourth through the ninth signs (Cancer through Sagittarius), and thus the fourth through the ninth houses. This hemisphere is considered the "public hemisphere", where one's home, types of games played, places of work, one-to-one relationships, shared resources, and higher education become the most exposed aspects of one's developing nature, shared with a variety of people, beyond one's ability to specifically choose by one's self.

When these two sets of hemispheres are overlapped, four quadrants emerge. The fist quadrant, representing Aries, Taurus, and Gemini, while also the first three houses, becomes the "personal-private quadrant". The nature of one's self, personal values, and basic education is up the individual to choose, given the circumstances into which one is born.

The second quadrant, representing the signs Cancer, Leo, and Virgo, and also the fourth, fifth, and sixth houses, is the "personal-public quadrant". Here, the nature of one's home, enjoyments, and service to others is personally driven, but based on close contacts with the outside world.

The third quadrant involves the signs Libra, Scorpio, and Sagittarius, as well as representing the seventh, eighth, and ninth houses. It represents the "popular-public quadrant." This area of life is where one must learn to compromise on the "personal-private" self (first quadrant), in order to better adapt to the world, as a social creature. One's basic nature for close relationships, sharing of values, and higher learning is completely dependent on one's ability to learn from the perspectives of others.

Finally, the fourth quadrant covers the signs Capricorn, Aquarius, and Pisces, as traditional rulers of the tenth, eleventh, and twelfth houses. This is the "popular-private quadrant." In this area, one has seen the deeper issues of life, where loyalty, dependency, and trust are foremost. This is where one learns that the public spotlight, lasting friendships, and inner tranquility come from releasing from a selfish mentality and becoming one with those one loves.

Nostradamus wrote of the Northern (*Aquilonaire* and *Septentrionale*), the South (*Midy*), the Eastern (*Oriental*, *Orient*, and *Orientaux*), and the West (*Occident*, *Hesperiques*, and *Hesperie*). Each reference bears some inference to hemispheric relationships. To see these four directions as simply being standard views of the world's divisions, from a European perspective, is to ignore the fact that Nostradamus was a first class astrologer. Additional meaning can be gained from seeing these descriptions in an astrological light.

For instance, in the thirty-fifth quatrain of *Century Third*, Nostradamus wrote a main theme line, along with a secondary theme supporting line (line four) that references two opposing hemispheres. There he wrote, "*Du plus profond de l'Occident d'Europe,*" (line one) and "*Sont bruit au regne d'Orient plus croistra*" (line four). These are stating, "*From the most deep of the West of Europe*" and "*Are rumor with *the reign of East more will grow.*" This means that the most eastern reaches of *Europe* (*the most deep of the West*), the former Soviet Bloc nations of Eastern *Europe*, will find a time when they will become more inclined toward the Middle *East* political view. The reason for this inclination will be because *West Europe*, and the *West* in general, will have neglected them for too long.

By understanding the astrological meaning of hemispheres, this change of support from *Europe* to the *East* gains more reason. The *Western* hemisphere is centered on reacting with the public, albeit a public one best identifies with. Due to the nations of *Eastern Europe* having been hidden or kept *secret* (an alternate translation of *profound*) by the Germans and Soviets for roughly fifty years, the *West* will not publicly warm to those strange relatives once they are freed by the collapse of communism. Instead, it will prefer to be publicly seen with the other wealthy nations of the *West*. This is an element of *Western* (Hemisphere) symbolism that generally prefers to boast and meddle, rather than take the time to truly understand and care. The *East* will then be able to coax those *Western* nations into an alliance, because their relationship will be privately supportive of one another.

Moon's Nodes

The projected path of the Moon, particularly where it is projected to cross the equator (the ecliptic), entering into the Northern Hemisphere, is called the "North Node". Opposite this point is the South Node, conversely where the Moon is projected to cross the equator headed into the Southern Hemisphere. This line of opposition creates the imaginary division of the individual's natal chart as the "nodal axis".

This axis is said to symbolize a karmic thread through one's life. As such, the nodes are an indication of reincarnation, where the South Node represents what baggage one brought into his or her present life. By "baggage", I mean that which one has known in the past and is most naturally accustomed to, thereby comforted by, in this life. Although this comfort is no longer the focus of one's present incarnation, one tends to be drawn to that which once represented security. Conversely, the North Node represents the direction one needs to go in the present life, learning to find comfort in new ways that will serve in future life developments.

This direction feels cold and unknown, making one act to avoid choosing to explore that way; but life circumstances confront one to move in this new direction. The Moon's nodes create this compass arrow because the Moon, in general, represents the memories that affect one. The deep subconscious includes instinctual knowledge, as well as personal past life experience, which has a subconscious pull to one's behavior. The nodal axis reflects this unexplained behavior.

In older times, the North Node was referred to as *Caput Draconis*, which is Latin meaning the Head of the Dragon. Contrarily, the opposite point was named *Caudus Draconis*, the Tail of the Dragon. Another symbolism would be the snake that eats its tail, creating a continuous circle of being the same soul in different bodies. Nostradamus referred to the "*teste du dragon*" (*head of the dragon*) twice in his letter to Henri, writing for example, "*la teste du Dragon sera avec une conjonction du Soleil à Jupiter*". This says, "*there head of the Dragon will be with one conjunction of the Sun with Jupiter*". This is an indication of a cold unknown direction, of karmic nature, creating a strong appeal through the rule (*Jupiter*) of Christianity (*Sun*), or generically ever spreading (*Jupiter*) ego (*Sun*).

The element of reincarnation and past-future lives is consistent with the laws of physics, where nothing new has been created, and nothing has been lost from the Universe that God made at the Creation. The matter God created has only changed states throughout all the eons since that beginning. This concept would include souls, such that a soul changing from a physical body to a spiritual body and then back again is a representation of the *Dragon* eating its tail. As long as this cycle continues, there will be no end to concern oneself with, as a failed life will only result in another life. The nodal axis tells what has been mastered, but also what has not. A story like that told in *The Prophecies* suggests an end to this opportunity to return another time. That would be an indication of when the concept of Hell truly begins. Therefore, it is good to know what references to the "*head of the Dragon*" mean.

Retrograde Motion

One last element of basic astrology is the imaginary backwards movements of planets. It is imaginary because all planets move in one constant direction in a relatively circular motion around the Sun (clockwise). However, due to the geocentric (earth-centered) view of the heavens, the orbit of the earth, combined with the orbits of the other planets, makes the other planets occasionally appear to reverse their ground, or retrace the "steps" of their zodiac path. This motion is retrogradation.

One note of interest is that neither the Sun, nor the Moon, makes this apparent retrograde motion. Only the planets will appear to move forward, then slow to a stop, before appearing to move backward. The period of time a planet appears to be in reverse mode depends on the planet. Mercury goes retrograde for three weeks at a time, every four months, or three times a year. Venus and Mars go retrograde less frequently than the other planets, due to their orbits being closest to the Earth's path. Due to this proximity, they are less able to reach points that make them appear to stop and travel backwards. Venus goes backwards once every eighteen months, while Mars takes roughly twenty-six months between its apparent regressions. Jupiter spends about four months of each year going in reverse. Saturn spends between four and a half to five months retracing its steps each year. The outer planets (those not visible to the naked eye), Uranus, Neptune, and Pluto, have increasing lengths of time in retrograde, such that the net forward motion through the zodiac becomes less and less. The elliptical orbits of the planets plays a role in this timing factor.

The symbolism of retrograde motion is significant, particularly for natives born at a time when one or more of the planets were in a retrograde moment. The direct, or forward, movement represents a natural outgoing expression of the characteristics of a planet, in the hue of a sign, portrayed in the area of life represented by a house. The retrograde movement then symbolizes a preference to do inward processing of that that has been learned. This is a necessity of life, such that one has to spend some time reflecting on what one has done, in order to understand the consequences of one's actions, and contemplate on whether one wants to repeat that action in the future. Thus, retrograde motion represents a time for pondering and deep thought.

While the Sun and Moon do not go in apparent backwards motions, they themselves represent the constant roles of outer projection and the inner awareness. As such, the Sun represents the direct motion of outward expression, while the Moon is symbolic of retrograde time for pondering inner feelings. Likewise, when a native is born (for instance) while there is an apparent retrograde Mercury, the symbolism is a general tendency to reflect on one's intellectual learning, rather than be an active communicator of what has been learned. In such a case, it reflects one who will tend to be static, more than mobile, preferring to plan movements. It is then those times when Mercury returns to its cycles of retrograde when such natives with Mercury retrograde feel a sense of security to express outwardly, perhaps through a release of pent-up communications and a need to travel.

In the main theme line of the ninety-seventh quatrain found in *Century Fourth*, Nostradamus wrote, "*L'an que Mercure, Mars, Venus, retrograde,*" which states, "*The year that Mercury, Mars, Venus, retrograde*". Besides knowing that *Mercury* goes *retrograde* four times a year, and that *Mars* and *Venus* are the planets that go in reverse the least frequently, the meaning implied is that the direct motion of these planets allowed their symbolic natures to express outwardly, before one at a time they would slow, stop, and the go into a reflective mode. This means that open talks cease, in order to contemplate what decisions to make (*Mercury*). It means that actions of aggression have reached a momentary truce, where two sides collect their dead and decide what new actions are called for (*Mars*). It then means that the need to make outward expressions of attractions, where calls to those who agree with one's values have been made, with a period then required for each party to mull over how those values indeed mirror their own. This then becomes a main theme like when one reaches a point of no return. Only fools rush in where angels fear to tread, causing the most valiant to pause and make sure of what lies ahead.

Certainly, this main theme is also stating a specific timing of events, where the rarity of a "*Mars retrograde*" occurring the same "*year*" as a "*Venus retrograde*" is the central timing theme. Such a precise order will occur in the year 2018, which would mean the information portrayed in the rest of the quatrains would be nonsensical to analyze for such a distant time. I welcome the reader to search history for other such occurrences in the past; but I have found none. Due to this distance in the future, the essence of the symbolic meaning is the greatest assistance in understanding that a time will come where reflection will be necessary.

Synthesis of Nostradamus through Delineation

THE SYSTEM OF ASTROLOGY

With these basic elements of astrology grasped, one can begin to approach a quatrain or letter section that talks astrologically with some reasonable idea of part of the meaning. The astrology in the quatrains does not require a deep understanding of the art of synthesis, or even require one to believe in astrology. One need only be aware of the mechanics behind the concept. From there it becomes a connect-the-dots formula.

A level of "cookbook astrology" is possible when I provide an appendix of key words, pertinent to what I have just explained. It then becomes a simple matter of plugging those key words into a matrix of word meanings. As such, the "speak" of astrology is not significantly different from the non-syntactical "speak" of *The Prophecies*. While it can be rattled off quickly, as if speaking in full sentences, the true meaning can only come from understanding all of the possibilities of each element of a statement.

For example, in the fourth line of the seventy-third quatrain of *Century Ninth*, Nostradamus wrote, "*Sol, Mars, Mercure prez la hurne.*"[252] This translates to state, "*Sun, Mars, Mercury near there the urn*", if *hurne* is seen as *l'urne*. Otherwise, it states, "*near the urn*"; but besides this literal translation, it is now known that *l'urne* is a symbolic way of stating the astrological sign of *Aquarius* (the water-carrier). Without the list of planets preceding it, "*la hurne*" would have to bear primarily the literal translation, "*the urn*" or "*there the urn*".

The separation of the orbs by commas means time is a factor in this line's statement. Once the sign of *Aquarius* is identified, it is only a matter of realizing that the *Sun* will enter the sign of *Aquarius* first. The *Sun* does this every year between the 20th and 21st of January, and stays in the sign until the 19th or 20th of February. This means that over about 29 days *Mars* and *Mercury* also entered *Aquarius*, such that all three will be "*near*", in proximity to one another. The word "*prez*" (or "*prés*") is translated by Randle Cotgrave as meaning, "*near, by, near by, fast by, hard by, near upon, well-nigh, or as it were touching.*"[253] This means a closeness that implies a conjunction aspect.

From consulting the Appendix A listing of key words, one finds that a conjunction is a blending of symbolic meanings. The key words for the *Sun, Mars,* and *Mercury* can then be "melded" together in combinations that become either: *Ego, Action, Thought*; *Expression, Sports, Basic Mind*; *Basic Nature, Blood, Movement*; or three other combinations of the same words. This is symbolic of energy that is driven by war mentality; and when placed in the sign of *Aquarius* (such that all are "*near*" in that sign) all becomes blended through that filter of *detached knowledge* (key words for *Aquarius*). From understanding this, one can get the feel from line four of a *detached war mind*. This would then be proven in the context of the whole quatrain, where line four acts to support both main and secondary

---

252 This comes from both the 1566 Lyon and 1568 Lyon editions. However, later editions (1650 and 1658) have added "*ensemble*" before *prez*, with the 1650 edition changing *prez* to "*après*", where *ensemble* means, "together". That would indicate a "conjunction" aspect.

253 Randle Cotgrave's 1611 French-English Dictionary, http://www.pbm.com/~lindahl/cotgrave/search/758r.html

themes, while expanding on the other support statement in line three.

This view of "*Sun, Mars, Mercury*" is astrological, but that is not the only way "*Sol, Mars, Mercure*" can be read. In French, those same words can equally mean, "*Soil, March, Quick-Silver*", or even "*Foundation, Iron, Mercury*", where the month of *March*, and/or alchemical elements (Fe = *Iron*, Hg = *Mercury*) are points of focus. In chemistry, *Mercury* reacts with almost all metals, where the substance created through conjunction is called an amalgam. However, *Iron* is a noted exception to this reactivity, such that *Iron* is used to containerize *Mercury*.[254]

Additionally, when the natures of the Roman gods are considered, where "*Sol, Mars, Mercury*" were each individual gods worshipped by Romans, other meaning comes forth that are at the symbolic core of each god. It must be understood that *Sol* is different from the god Apollo, whereas *Sol* is identified with *Janus* and *Sol Invictus*, or the *Unconquered Sun*. *Mars* is known as the god of war; and *Mercury* is known as the winged god, or the messenger of the gods, while also having been given the gift of healing from Apollo. *Mercury* was known as the god of trade, in particular that of grain. The French word *mars* also bears the meaning of "grain." When these three are together, thus *near*, there is an attitude present of invincibility, through warlike methods, where speed is of the essence.

All of these meanings come forth through the system of astrology, because this system recognizes the additional depth of meaning that comes from astrological symbolism. Still, beyond the aspectual meanings, the mythological meanings, the literal (French) meanings, and the symbolic meaning (such as the *Sun* symbolizing Christianity and the *Moon* symbolizing Islam, and so on), there is another vital meaning that can be found. This is based on the literal astrological, such that this is like the astronomical, being the physical placement of the planets in our solar system. This is important as a timing mechanism.

Astronomical Astrology

The reason the literal astrological is like the astronomical, but not literally astronomical, is that the astrological focuses on symbolism, while the astronomical focuses on placement. Nostradamus spoke in the literal astrological, such that a reference to a planet in a sign (as is "*Mercury near to the urn*") means the astrological placement of an orb in front of a constellation. Due to the condition known as precession, based on the Earth's wobble, the astronomical zodiac is different from the astrological zodiac, by about 30 degrees. This means a planet in the astrological sign of Aries is astronomically seen from earth as in the 'foreground' of the constellation Pisces. However, since astrology has not been adjusted to meet the newfound realities of constellation position changes, as time was adjusted with the Gregorian calendar, from the Julian calendar, two sets of records must now be maintained (astrological and astronomical).

The reasoning for the astrological not to change, or be adjusted, is the Earth is not in a relationship with the star constellations. While being an extended outpost of the Milky Way galaxy, that relationship is too

---

[254] Wikipedia the free encyclopedia, http://en.wikipedia.org/wiki/Mercury_(element)

distant to bear any meaning. The Milky Way is made up of stars, of which the signs are fabrications of an earthly imagination; but the Earth is not a star. The star of importance is the Sun, and the Earth is only in a relationship with that single star, as part of a solar system.

Thus, when the Sun crosses the equator significant changes occur on Earth. This marks the times of Spring and Fall from a Northern Hemisphere perspective, or one of Fall and Spring from a Southern Hemisphere view. This means the symbolism of Spring, which is the newness of rebirth, is aligned with the Sun, with the properties of Aries associated with that seasonal change. The stars that once existed as the backdrop for that equatorial crossing (visual perception) were named Aries, and the dots of stars were marked to show a ram's horns and head. The reality of the seasonal changes on Earth, due to the Sun's relationship with it, have nothing to do with the symbolism that was named Pisces; and the Milky Way stars that once graced the sky as markers for the end of Winter have nothing to do with any causal event on Earth. The Milky Way is only a background of reference to where the Sun, Moon, and planets of our solar system can be found, in relationship to the Earth. Therefore, no reason exists to alter the astrological zodiac.

At one time, a long time ago, the astrological zodiac was based on the astronomical positions of "fixed stars." Because those "fixed stars" were not truly fixed, but moved ever so slightly, astrology and astronomy has become separate entities. Astronomy is based on sidereal (star) positions, while astrology is a fixed relationship between the Sun and the Earth. These relationships are calculated by what is known as "tropical" positioning. Simply by knowing the convertibility of this difference, modern astrological ephemerides are able to list all of the planetary positions, for decades in advance, with precise accuracy, because the planets and luminaries move at relatively fixed rates of motion.

This rate of motion is dependent on the orbit of a planet around the Sun, along with various factors such as gravitational pulls from other planets, and the elliptical nature of orbits. Since all of these factors are known, the calculus can determine where a planet should be (astrological and astronomically), for an indefinite number of years into the future, as well as where the planets have been, for an indefinite number of years into the past. The planets and luminaries will be in the same place, regardless of what the backdrop is. The backdrop is the zodiac belt, which is the plane all planets move within as they circle the Sun. The backdrop makes it a point of reference for tracking planetary positions.

As part of this consistency in planetary rates of motion, each planet has its own time for making one orbit around the Sun. The Earth's cycle is one year, or 365.25 days. The planets outside the Earth's orbit take significantly longer to make one orbit, such that Mars takes roughly 1.88 earth years, Jupiter roughly 11.86 earth years, and Saturn roughly 29.66 earth years. This is significant when one realizes that the placement of one of these outer planets in a particular sign, along with another planet, is more limited in scope, as to how often this can physically happen. While all planets repeatedly visit all signs, with the Moon moving through the zodiac every 28.5 days (geocentric positioning), and the Sun, Mercury, and

Venus in each sign for up to thirty days, every year, a planet like Jupiter or Saturn makes these repeating possibilities limited in possibility to decades and generations of time.

In the example quatrain, where a triple conjunction is indicated by stating, "*Sun, Mars, Mercury near there Aquarius*", an ephemeris is where one needs to look for all three orbs in that sign. This is not as difficult as it may sound (assuming one has an ephemeris for the 20th century and another for the 21st century), because one simply needs to look for when the slowest moving planet was, is, or will be, in the sign of *Aquarius*. Of those three, *Mars*, is the slowest moving, as viewed from earth, when its rate of motion (about half a degree on average) is compared to that of the *Sun* (about 1 degree on average) and *Mercury* (slightly more than 1 degree on average).[255] Once one is looking for when *Mars* is in *Aquarius*, one need only look during the months of January and February, when the *Sun* is in *Aquarius* each year. When years are found with these two together, *Sun* first, then *Mars*, one needs to then look for *Mercury* entering *Aquarius*, and all three being no more than a total of ten degrees separating the trio.

From looking at the whole context of the seventy-third quatrain in *Century Ninth*, it is not easily recognizable as a past event, due to the verbiage. The full quatrain states in Old French: "*Dans Fois entrez ceiulée Turban, / Et regnera moins euolu Saturne, / Roy Turban blanc & Bisance coeur ban, / Sol, Mars, Mercure près la hurne.*" This translates as: "W*ithin Time enters this scorned Turban, / And will govern least evolved Saturn, / King Uproar-one white & Byzantium heart edict, / Sun, Mars, Mercury near there the urn.*"

This quatrain is one that can best be determined by working backwards, due to the manufactured word in line one, the repeating of "*Turban*" requiring a Latin meaning to balance the French meaning in line one. Backwards also helps understand the use of *Saturn* in line two, because of seeing how "*Sun, Mars, Mercury*" adds meaning to that reference, in line four. Once the timing is determined, the rest of this quatrain becomes crystal clear.

With the greatest number of unsolved quatrains dealing with the future, that is a good place to begin a search. Using my copy of *The American Ephemeris for the 21st Century: 2000 to 2050*, I searched and found nothing that perfectly fits the astrological placements, exactly as Nostradamus wrote them. I found that an exact occurrence took place during January and February 2009, with the *Sun* entering *Aquarius* on January 20, followed by *Mars* on February 4, then *Mercury* on February 15. These were not in a conjunction aspect, but all three orbs were in the same sign together. In February 2011, all three orbs will be in conjunction (less than 10 total degrees of separation), but the order of arrival into *Aquarius* is incorrect. The rest of the Twenty-first century (until 2050) is not a match either.

---

255   Mercury has a roughly 88-day orbit around the Sun, but due to its orbit being inferior to the Earth's, is always appears to be moving around the zodiac with the Sun, never more than 45 degrees in front, and never more than 45 degrees behind. Mercury spends about 19 days in one sign, when not retrograde, which is roughly 1.5 degrees of motion per day. However, it goes retrograde four times a year, for about three weeks each time. This apparent backwards motion is what reduces the average to 1 degree per day.

THE SYSTEM OF ASTROLOGY

The Twentieth Century is where one finds the exact timing of line four's statement. Roughly six times during that 100-year period (1900 – 1999) some similar alignments did occur, but only one time did it happen in the precise order. All were *near* one another in late January 1979, with all three orbs in Aquarius together until the middle of February. This period is significant as a series of events took place that had lasting international impact, which still affects the world's climate today. That period's events are very much a part of the theme Nostradamus wrote of in *The Prophecies*.

The period of conjunction begins on January 21, 1979. Both the *Sun* and *Mars* enter into *Aquarius* the same day, but the *Sun* enters first, at 7:45 PM Iran Time, with *Mars* entering at 9:00 PM IT. Both had been in conjunction since January 1, but in the sign of Capricorn (Sun at 9:58, Mars at 14:42). The Shah of Iran left his country, abdicating the throne on January 16, 1979. *Mercury* entered the sign of *Aquarius* on January 29. By January 31, only six and one half degrees separated all three orbs (*Sun* – 10.5, *Mars* – 8.0, *Mercury* – 4.0, all in *Aquarius*), putting all within an allowable orb for a conjunction. The Ayatollah Khomeini made his return to Iran, from his exile in France, on February 1, 1979. He established the Islamic Revolution on February 6, and then seized power over Iran on February 11. *Mercury* then left *Aquarius* on February 15, 1979, breaking that combination of orbs.

If you read the English part of the quatrain, the Shah is the *King* of *Uproar*, who made the edict that was called the "*White* Revolution". It was called that because he wanted to Westernize Iran. Westernization means Christianize, such that *white* equates (once again) to Christianity. The meaning of *Byzantium* is that it was where Constantinople was located (now Istanbul, Turkey), which meant the seat of the Byzantine Empire. It represented a *Time* when Christian theology ruled in the Arab-Muslim world. That was the model for the Shah's *White* Revolution.

The *King* in a *Turban* is the linen headdress clad Khomeini, as an Islamic Ayatollah. The rule of Khomeini has become known as a hard regime, not that the Shah's was any easier. For Nostradamus to state, "*will govern least evolved Saturn*", one can see how this reflects that Khomeini did not personally do the *ruling* over Iran. He let others run the government, through a President who was subservient to Khomeini's input. Khomeini became the moral judge for the people of Iran, under the astrological principles of *Saturn*. As far as law is concerned, Jupiter is the most evolved in that area, with *Saturn* being in line with the result of law. Thus, as the *least evolved*, Khomeini stressed Islamic law, with *Saturn* associated with the father principle, as the one who does not spare the rod of punishment.

This example shows how the astrology of Nostradamus is not only symbolic meaning that allows one to understand, but it also offers a specific timing capability. This is but one of many examples that can be found to offer such specificity of timing. Although the astronomical groupings are never unique to one time, as everything is always repeating over time, the uniqueness comes from narrowing the point of focus to one general period, such as the Twentieth and Twenty-first centuries.

Chapter 29

The System of Years and Degrees

After spending time seeing how specific planetary alignments can yield quite specific time frames, we come to the system of dates. Dates have often been recognized in the verses and letters, many of which have been seen as clearer presentations of time because they deal in numbers. We have already examined how Nostradamus wrote the numerals "*3797*", which has been taken as another representation of clarity, through numerals. However, if anything has been learned to this point, it is that nothing is ever so clear in *The Prophecies*.

In this system of dates and degrees, we do not address numerals, but instead look at Nostradamus' use of words of number. In particular, I will present several of those quatrains that have been popularized, due to the appearance of relativity to a specific time or a specific place, spelled out in numbers. These instances of time will often be identified by the introduction of "*L'an*", which in French states, "*The year*". Such references are clear in the fact that one 365-day period is the focus of those words. Still, other numbers will be followed by the word "*ans*", which says "*years*", indicating more than one year of time.

Another area of focus, more so in the letter to Henri II, but also of significance in the quatrains, will be the use of numbers with the word translated as "*degrees*". These numbers imply an importance related particularly to earthly latitude, but longitude is also a consideration. Since these imaginary lines circle the globe, all places that fall within the span of one degree (plus and minus 30 minutes) would qualify as residing at that place (without another coordinate to limit it), other clues within those quatrains have to act as the limiting factors.

Finally, while I did present some evidence of planetary positions being an excellent indication of specific times, there is still more to expound on in this area. At several places, Nostradamus wrote in the quatrains, "*En l'an que*", which translates to state, "*in the year that*". This repeated introduction then leads to specific ordering of planets in signs. This is an indication of one specific *year that* is rare. I will address some of these timing aspects as well.

This system takes one back to the discussion about the different presentations of years written in the Preface, where some editions display a numeral year, while others have the year spelled out in words. This becomes relevant again, because there is an obvious difference found between a numeral representation of a year and a year written out in words of number. When *The Prophecies* are the issue, differences are never insignificant.

The edition that is generally accepted to be the first print publication of *The Prophecies* is the 1555 Chés Macé Bonhomme version, out of Lyon, France. In this edition, the Preface ends with the numeral *1555*. So too does the Preface end with a numeral in every edition and imprint I have examined (1555s, 1557 Utrecht, 1566 Lyon, 1568 Lyon, 1650, and 1698). This consistency begins to change somewhat, after Nostradamus completed the three additional *Centuries*, such that the 1566 Lyon edition shows the numeral 1558 at the end of the Henri letter, while the 1568 Lyon edition spells out, "*Mil cinq cens cinquantehuit*" instead. Interestingly, the 1650 and the 1698 imprints of the Chez Pierre Rigaud 1558 addition to the 1555-57 originals (Lyon), both show the letter to Henri ending with the numeral, *1558*.

This is good evidence that a specific year was written in numerals, rather than spelled out. In our prior discussion, I presented evidence from the letters where numeral years were indicated, and could be accepted as (for instance) a reference to "*1557*", the year Nostradamus was writing the letter of explanation to his king. This does not mean that years were not spelled out, as there is substantial evidence in sixteenth century literature where that was a common practice. Nostradamus, however, is not to be seen as a common practitioner of writing; the writings of *The Prophecies* do not follow common rules. Nevertheless, there is still some valuable information that comes from the 1566 Lyon edition's closing with spelled out numbers.

Given that the other editions all show *1558*, the 1566 Lyon edition can be written off as printer (or typesetter) error, preferring to stray from the manuscript and write with the style of the day. That style was then exposed to have "*cinquantehuit*" written as one word. In French today, a hyphen is inserted, showing it as *cinquante-huit*, which still represents the numeral "58" in word number, the same as the English write, "fifty-eight." This is an important element to recognize, as there is a lack of this linking of two numbers as one in the letters and quatrains.

Previously, in the system of symbols, specific to numerals, I mentioned how the French word *année* means *year*, relative to a duration of time. The French word *an* also translates as *year*, but is mainly used to indicate an amount of time. However, one of the exceptions for the use of *an*, as representative of duration, is when a date is stated, with numbers following "*l'an*" (ex: *l'an six cent* = the date, the year 600). Further, *an* is pluralized when accompanying more than one year, with the number placed before it, showing it presents a duration of time (ex: *pour cinq ans* = the length of time, for five years).

One finds an example of this in the letter to Henri II, in both sections where Nostradamus is listing the times between the Biblical patriarchs. In one typical statement of this use of *ans* as duration, Nostradamus wrote, "*Adam fut devant Noé environ mille deux cens quarante deux ans*," which says, "*Adam was in *front of Noah around one thousand two hundred forty two years"*. In this case, a consecutive string of words representing cardinal numbers are all connected as one, due to them ending with the word *ans*.

The same can be said for the one example coming from the Preface stating a length of years. In that example, Nostradamus wrote, *"avant cent septante sept ans trios moys unze jours,"* which states, *"before one hundred seventy seven years three months eleven days"*. This again shows cardinal numbers leading to one word that connects the three separate words prior to it, such that it can be read as meaning, "177 *years, three months*, and *eleven days"*.

The same cannot be said for the reverse, as far as Nostradamus is concerned, when *l'an* precedes a string of cardinal numbers. The exception to the French rule for usage of *an* as more than an amount of time, such that *l'an six cent* is understood to mean *the year of history 600*, requires syntax. Since Nostradamus did not employ syntax, a series of numbers following the word denoting *"the year"* does not necessarily have to be connected, beyond the first cardinal number following *"l'an"*.

For example, in the letter to Henri, Nostradamus began to combine (somewhat) segments using *année*, with one stating *l'an*. Taken alone, without the context preceding it, it appears that Nostradamus is writing of a duration of time that is one specific year. He wrote, *"à l'an mil sept cens nonante deux que lon cuydera être une renovation de siecle"*. This translates to say, *"to the year one thousand seven hundred ninety two that the one will think to be one renovation of time"*. For the reverse to be true for Nostradamus, he would have to be seen as saying the year 1792 was so phenomenal that it seemed time would begin anew. While that argument has some merit (which the multiplicity of meaning in the words of Nostradamus allows for), it is not the primary focus.

This section of the letter to Henri is where cuts are made, as seen in the combination of commas followed by ampersands, such that the two references to *année* are separate from the segments containing the statement above. One reference followed astrological information, connecting to that data, so that it logically led to the statement, *"l'année sera pacifique sans eclypse,"* meaning, *"the year will be peaceable without eclypse"*. After two quick cuts separate that statement from connection, Nostradamus then wrote, *"commençant icelle année sera faicte plus grand persecution à l'Eglise Chrêtienne"*. This states, *"beginning her year will be made more great persecution to the Church Christian"*. In both disconnected uses of *année*, a duration of time is understood to be one twelve-month period.

The statement that appeared to be about the year 1792 is then preceded by Nostradamus writing, *"durera ceste icy jusques,"* which says, *"will endure this here until"*. Following a comma, indicating a separation in time, this endurance (presumably in France – *here* to Nostradamus) will then connect to the statement, *"to the year one thousand seven hundred ninety two that the one will think to be one renovation of time"*. This ends in a colon, which means the following statement clarifies this *year* and the *renovation of time*, which can also be a *renewal of century* (alternate translation of *siecle*). The statement of clarification says, "*après commencera le people Romain de se redresser,*" which states, "*after will commence the people Roman of itself to reform*". While the year 1792 was a year of adjustment for the Roman Catholic Church, due to the continuing effects of the French Revolution, there was no thinking it was the end of the way things would be done at the Vatican.

This is where it becomes important to discuss how French words for several cardinal numbers are the same word for something completely different. For example, the word *neuf* translates as either "nine" or "new". The word *sept* mainly translates as "*seven*", but can also be used to denote the month "September", even when written in the lower case. The word *deux* is primarily used to state the number "two," but it can indicate "both," as needed. Further, correct French uses "*quatre-vingts*" as "eighty", and "*quatre-vingts-dix*" as "ninety," but Belgian and Swiss uses "*octante*" and "*nonante*", with these becoming standard applications in French. Nostradamus used each of these multiple forms in his writings.

We can see how these carry the meaning of "eighty" and "ninety" in the statements made in the letter to Henri II. In fact, Nostradamus used both "*octante*" and "*huictante*" (Swiss) as representing the number "eighty". In the second section of the letter to Henri, telling of the patriarch times, Nostradamus wrote, "*Salomon au quariéme an de son regne, passerent quatre cens octante ou quatre vingt ans.*" This states, "*Solomon in the fourth year of his reign, passing four hundred eighty or four twenty years.*" This means that *octante* is the same as *quatre-vingts*, as *four* times *twenty*. In the first section of the same letter, Nostradamus wrote, "*de l'universel deluge, vint Abraham environ mille huictante ans,*" which says, "*from the universal flood, came Abraham around one thousand eighty years*".

Again, in the section where the timing of the Biblical patriarchs is broken down, Nostradamus wrote, "*Et depuis le fin du deluge jusques à la nativité de Abraham passa le nombre des ans de deux cens nonante cinq.*" This complete "sentence" states, "*And since the end of the flood until to the birth of Abraham will pass the number of the years to two hundred ninety five.*" When one does the arithmetic that is present in the Book of Genesis, this is an accurate statement, representing 295 years after the Great Flood ended, meaning *nonante* does represent *ninety* in this case. However, due to this not being Latin or pure French, it is not limited to this single translation, if French or Latin offers an alternative.

Another direction to look is the mutation between the word *cent* (meaning *hundred*) and *cens*. This is accepted to be the plural form of *cents*, which still means *hundred*, when read as "*deux cens*",[256] such that it is understood to mean "two hundred." However, Old French held the word *cens* to mean a form of rent, particularly "quick rent," which is defined as, "A rent paid by a freeman in lieu of the services required by feudal custom."[257]

The word *cens* was also an acceptable form of the word *cense*, meaning, "a general and public valuation of

---
256 The quote from the Letter to Henri show prior is from the 1568 Lyon edition, which shows "*cens*". The 1566 Lyon edition shows, "*passa le nombre des ans de deux cent nonante cinq.*"
257 The Free Dictionary by Farlex, http://www.thefreedictionary.com/quitrent

(a freeman's) goods and possessions."[258] Further, the word *cens* in Latin means (among several options) "estimate", as a form of the word *censeo*. Therefore, as far as Nostradamus' uses of words goes, these possibilities of translation and meaning cannot be ignored. Anything found to be inconsistently used by Nostradamus (he used *cent* in obvious plural places also) must have one asking oneself, "Why?"

Continuing the line of thought that French words of number have other translations, where "*neuf*" means, "nine" and "new", the word *nonante* can then be seen as capable of being broken down into *non-ante*, which in Latin says, "*not-before*". While the statement in the segment clearly listing the years of the Biblical patriarchs calls for *nonante* to mean *ninety*, as it ends with the word *ans*, another look at *nonante* when it follows the introduction of *l'an* is now necessary.

As one should recall, the statement that appeared to contain the year 1792 was questionable, since the words surrounding that *year* did not match the history of that period. In that example I presented earlier, Nostradamus wrote, "*à l'an mil sept cens nonante deux que lon cuydera être une renovation de siecle*", which I said translated to say, "*to the year one thousand seven hundred ninety two that the one will think to be one renovation of time* (or *century*)". However, look at the transformation when the same words are not translated as cardinal numbers.

It becomes, "*to the year one thousand September estimate not before two that the one will think to be one renewal of century*". While I did not mention this previously, this statement uses the word *mil*, instead of the word it is based from, *mille*, although both words are acceptable French meaning, "*one thousand*". When that number is preceded by the French word of amount of time, which is allowed to represent a duration of time when a cardinal number follows *l'an*, the combination *l'an mil* essentially means, "*the year of the millennium*".

This statement can then be seen to state that the true renewal of the next millennium (from Nostradamus' perspective) would be before the year 2002, in the month of *September*. This means *the year of the millennium* would be *the year 2001*. Since a *century* begins at *the year one*, and not *the year* zero, a collection of one hundred years ends in a year of double zeros (1600, 1700, 2000, etc.). Therefore, this statement is about *September* 2001, when an event would occur that would make *one think that* was the beginning of a new view of time. This would certainly be the beginning of a new set of one thousand years; but more importantly, it would indicate a time of *renovation* from the old. This would then indicate the true beginning of the time of *The Prophecies*, the end times.

One of the most popularized quatrains over the past few decades has been the prediction that was known to say, "In the year 1999, seventh month, from the sky will come the King of Terror." This was known soon after Nostradamus published it, but it became much more important as the year 1999 began to come near. This knowledge was based on the main theme line of the seventy-second quatrain in *Century*

[258]   Randal Cotgrave's 1611 French-English Dictionary, http://www.pbm.com/~lindahl/cotgrave/search/1691.html

Tenth, which states, "*L'an mil neuf cens nonante neuf sept mois*". This appears to translate as, "*The year one thousand nine hundred ninety nine seven month*," but now knowing how words can have multiple meanings, this can turn into, "*They year millennium nine estimate not before nine September month*".

To best understand this as a statement about *September 2001*, one has to realize the reason the *month September* is named that. It dates to an old Roman calendar system, where *September* was the seventh *month* in the calendar *year*. This stems from the Latin word *septem* meaning *seven*, with *octo* meaning eight, *novem* being nine, and *decem* the word for ten.[259] Thus, March was the first month of the official year prior to Julius creating a new calendar in 45 B.C., with *September* the seventh month.

The Julian calendar of Julius Caesar recognized January as the beginning of the year, but he did not change the names of the months. Later, Romans named July after Julius Caesar, and August after Augustus.[260] Nostradamus was playing off this name of *September* being from the root *seven*, although it was then *month* number *nine*. Further, the *estimate* of the date within this *new* (alternate translation of *neuf*) *month* number is *not before nine September*. Thus, the *renovation* of the first *century* of the *new millennium* (the letter to Henri explains the quatrains) would *not* begin *before September 9, 2001*.

There are several quatrains that have lines that state, "*L'an mil*", with all announcing, "*The year one thousand* (or *millennium*)". These differ on which line of the four they appear, as well as in what particular number word follows that introduction. Only one other quatrain places this in the main theme line, although it does not begin with a capital letter. That main theme is found in the ninety-first quatrain of *Century Tenth*, stating, "*Clergé Romain l'an mil six cens & neuf,*" which can say, "*Clergy Roman the year millennium six estimate & new*". This could be making a statement about the year 2006, or *six* years after the *millennium*, 2007. Alternatively, it can be about the *year 2001*, in the sixth month. This quatrain is not about anything that might have occurred in the year 1609.

Relative to this quatrain are two others. The secondary theme line of the seventy-first quatrain of *Century Eighth* states, "*L'an mil six cens & sept par sacrées glomes,*" which says, "*The year millennium six estimate & September through sacred ones collected ones*". Then, the fourth line of the fifty-fourth quatrain in *Century Sixth* offers this, "*L'an mil six cens & sept de Liturgie.*" This states, "*The year millennium six estimate & September of Liturgy.*" It becomes clear how these three quatrains could link, with nothing being relative to the years 1607.

Two other quatrains have lines that state, "*L'an mil sept*", or "*The year millennium September*". The seventy-seventh quatrain found in *Century Third* states as the secondary theme (line two), "*L'an mil sept cens vingt & sept en Octobre,*" which says, "*The year millennium September estimate twenty & seven*

---

259   Regents of the University of Minnesota, Media History Project, http://www.mediahistory.umn.edu/archive/month.html

260   Wikipedia the free encyclopedia, http://en.wikipedia.org/wiki/Julian_calendar#From_Julian_to_Gregorian

in *October*." This line includes the word *sept* twice, which means if multiple meanings are possible, each word bears a different meaning. Thus, *sept en Octobre* would make little sense translated to state, "September in October". The ampersand acts to show the separation and importance of *seven*, which is a number related to an event in *October*.

The forty-ninth quatrain in *Century First* states in the third line, the line supporting the main theme, "*Lan mil sept cent feront grand emmenées*". This states, "*The year millennium September one hundred will be making great lead unto ones* (or *captured ones*)". This statement, its quatrain, and the other matching statement ("*L'an mil sept*"), along with the other quatrain (III – 77), are referencing the same event, as central to other events happening in the world.

The central event is September 11, 2001. In the statement of the quatrain from *Century Third*, the estimated *twenty* is relative to the number of highjackers on four planes. Following the ampersand, which separates and indicates importance, the response of the United States and Great Britain was the first attack against the Taliban, in Afghanistan, on 7 October. The statement from *Century First* places the focus on the *great*, where this word is an indication of the U.S.A. and/or *Great* Britain. While the number *one hundred* could mean a specific number of people related to the attacks, it could also indicate a *century* had begun that *captured* the *great*. Comparatively, *one hundred* is but a few to those *great*.

As several of these examples make statements that many have translated as four-digit years, while surrounding an ampersand, such that "*mil six cens & sept*" has been translated as "1607", it is important to address numbers and ampersands. I remember my fourth grade teacher correcting those in my class who would pronounce a year with the word "and" included. She told us, "It is not nineteen hundred AND sixty-three. It is nineteen hundred sixty-three. The only time you use AND is when you are stating a decimal point." This means that ampersands act to separate all numbers surrounding one, making them represent only those numbers first. However, when combined to act as a number AND a number, the first number is whole, while the second number is a fraction.

Before I address numbers surrounding an ampersand, it is important to see that Nostradamus knew the correct way to present double-digit numbers in word form. One example is in the fortieth quatrain found in *Century Seventh*. There, some editions (1557 Utrecht and 1650 Lyon) clearly show the word "*vingtun*", meaning "*twenty-one*"; and although other editions (1566 and 1698 Lyon) show it clearly as "*vingt un*", the translation remains the same. Another example is in the fifty-ninth quatrain of *Century Tenth*, where some editions (1568 and 1650 Lyon) clearly show Nostradamus writing, "*vingtcinq*", whereas other editions (1566 and 1698 Lyon) hyphenate it, as "*vingt-cinq*", with both translated as "*twenty-five*".

This is also demonstrated in Nostradamus' use of teen numbers that are a combined form with the base word *dix* (*ten*). There are only three such teen numbers (seventeen, eighteen, and nineteen), and while modern French hyphenates these (i.e.: *dix-sept*), Old French spelled them as one-word, the way we do in English. Nostradamus wrote the number seventeen in three different quatrains (V – 71, V – 92, and VI – 59), with the 1557 Utrecht edition showing all three as, "*dixsept*".[261] In addition, both the 1566 and 1568 Lyon editions show Nostradamus writing the word nineteen in the thirty-ninth quatrain of *Century Tenth*, differing only in one being "*dixhuict*" (1568) and one being "*dix-huict*" (1566).

All of this shows that Nostradamus knew the proper way to present a double-digit number, such that an example like the one found in the seventy-seventh quatrain in *Century Eight* needs to be examined for its presentation in the secondary theme, "*Vingt & sept*", to see why this has commonly been translated as, "Twenty-seven".

In this case, the whole quatrain should be observed, because the secondary theme is not necessarily directly connected to the main theme, although all secondary lines and themes are related to the main theme. Thus, the secondary theme will best be viewed by observing the supporting statement to the secondary theme, which is in line four.

L'Antechrist trois bientost annichilez,	The Antechrist three quite quickly annihilated ones,
Vingt & sept ans sang durera sa guerre,	Twenty & seven years lineage will continue her war,
Les heretiques morts, captifs, exilez,	Them heretics dead ones, captive ones, exiled ones,
Sang corps humain eau rougie gresler terre.	Blood deaths human water blushed to hail land.

Without attempting to interpret this quatrain, which is one that has received some significant discussion over the years, it is easy to see that the main theme identifies multiple peoples that will be *annihilated*. The thought has been that it will be the Antichrist who will be destroyed; but this capitalized name is best seen as the significant one preceding Christ, as *ante-* is a French prefix meaning *pre-*, from the Latin, which translates as, "before". The number *three* is relative to this important person, such that there could be *three* branches related to the one. This entity will be removing people, as line three states. However, the *quite quickly* reference leads to *Twenty*, which indicates there will be *Twenty* important people *annihilated*. This will then begin *seven years* of *war*, which is detailed in line four.

This is evidence that Nostradamus did not write multi-digit numbers by inserting an ampersand. There is no example of numbers surrounding an ampersand that have the primary function of stating a number like, "the year one thousand six hundred and seven". While this becomes somewhat possible when the ampersand's function acts to combine two segments as one, this is nothing more than additional detail to solidify the primary interpretation, where the numbers are separate. Additionally, all examples have

---

261 The 1566 edition hyphenates the V-92 and VI-59 quatrains, as "*dix-sept*", while the 1568 shows those two like the 1557 Utrecht edition. However, both the 1566 and 1568 editions show quatrain V-71 as two separate words, as "*dix sept*".

been easy to mislead, because they have followed a normal pattern, where a larger number precedes the ampersand, followed by a single-digit number.

There is one important example of a single-digit number preceding an ampersand, with a double-digit number following it. This is where an ampersand can play a role in combining the two, but only as my old fourth grade teacher said – as an indicator of a decimal point. This example takes our focus away from numbers representing amounts of time, and takes us to degrees of measurement.

I have already presented the famous quatrain that appeared to predict the King of Terror coming from the sky in the ninth month of the year 1999. Naysayers have argued that the prediction was wrong, because Nostradamus got the year wrong. I have shown how those who read 1999 got the year wrong. Realizing how to read Nostradamus shows how he got the year perfectly right. Well, another famous quatrain tells of the sky burning in the new city, which is uncannily portraying the events of September 11, 2001, but naysayers point out Nostradamus got the degree coordinates wrong. This makes it worthwhile to present the whole quatrain for examination.

Cinq & quarante degrés ciel bruslera,	*Five & forty degrees sky will burn,*
Feu approcher de la grand cité neufue,	*Fire to approach to there great city new,*
Instant grand flamme esparse saultera,	*Instant mighty blaze dispersed to leap,*
Quand on voudra des Normans faire preuve.	*When one will want from the Normans to make proof.*

The first line of this quatrain has regularly been translated to state that the *"sky will burn"* at forty-five degrees. The latitude of the *new city*, or *New* York *City* (Manhattan), is 40 *degrees*, 46 minutes. This has been reason for people to say that Nostradamus got the coordinate (*degree*) wrong; but, as one can see, Nostradamus did not write "forty-five degrees". Following the ampersand, it is clear that Nostradamus wrote, *"forty degrees sky will burn"*. Nostradamus also never gave any evidence of writing double-digit numbers with the lower number before the higher number, such that he acted as if it was common to state "forty-five" as "five forty", or "five-forty", or "fiveforty". Therefore, this main theme is accurate to the *degrees* of Manhattan's latitude coordinate.

This means that the one word preceding the ampersand, the capitalized *"Five"*, is by itself a stand-alone statement of importance, where the number *Five* is significant. At this point, it is important to note that the main theme line does not refer to the *city new*. It only states, *"sky will burn"*. Thus, the number *Five* becomes important as the number of hijacked planes that were planned to *burn* in the *sky*. Four hijackings successfully took place once the planes were in the *sky*, but one crew was unable to make it to their appointed rendezvous. There were *Five* targets planned.

When *Five* is understood to be the number of planned hijacking crews, with *Five* men on each team, planned for *Five* targets, and then *forty degrees* is realized to be the specific targets that were the Twin Towers in Manhattan, the two statements surrounding the ampersand have made perfect sense. This is when the ampersand acts to join the two numbers as one, such that it states, "*Five AND forty degrees*". As my fourth grade teacher taught me, that means, "*Five POINT forty degrees*", which is represented by numerals as either, 5:40 (*Five degrees AND forty* minutes), or 5.40 (*Five POINT four zero degrees*).

When one realizes that planes took off from Boston, Massachusetts (42 degrees, 21 minutes, 30 seconds), Manhattan, and Washington, D.C. (the Pentagon is at 38:52:15), that represents a span of three *POINT forty*-two *degrees* of latitude. If Nostradamus was wrong about anything, it was in allowing a two extra degrees of "orb", one degree above Boston, and one degree below Washington, D.C., to reach the full *Five POINT forty degrees*, between which the *sky* would *burn*. That would be a span equivalent to that between Concord, (northern) Massachusetts and Newport News, (southern) Virginia, such that 5.48 *degrees* separate those two towns. In other words, Nostradamus picked a span that includes the states that include Boston and border Washington, D.C. (with Virginia being on the southern side of the Potomac River from Washington).

As for the question about why Nostradamus would state that the, "*sky will burn,*" rather than state the obvious, which would be buildings set on fire, against the backdrop of sky, that becomes too limiting. A Frenchman from the sixteenth century would have witnessed fire lighting up the sky before, and therefore would have been capable of knowing the difference, enough to write that specifically. However, Nostradamus saw the burning that would take place before the impact, which would be the engines of the jets, which were to be used as flaming projectiles.

While Leonardo da Vinci's life overlapped that of Nostradamus', with da Vinci dying when Nostradamus was between his fifteenth and sixteenth birthdays, it could be possible that Nostradamus had seen pictures of da Vinci's drawings of flying apparatuses. Still, not even da Vinci foresaw flight from flaming engines; and such ideas of military potential could have been seen as the equivalent of flying balls of burning pitch and naphtha, which would be catapulted through the air in the attack of a city. In such cases where a city was attacked, that could be described, as the *sky will burn* before the city will.

This example of Nostradamus stating *degrees* is then contrasted by the ninety-eighth quatrain in *Century Fifth*. In that case, Nostradamus wrote as the main theme line, "*A quarante huict degré climaterique,*" which says, "*At forty eight degree climacteric*". This statement precedes the singular use of *degree*, where the French word *degré* was typically used to denote, "a stair, step; rank, degree, place of honor, an occasion, means, or way to do something."[262] In other words, this statement focuses on one specific

[262] Randal Cotgrave's 1611 French-English Dictionary, http://www.pbm.com/~lindahl/cotgrave/search/278r.html

degree, relative to the number *forty-eight* and the *climacteric*. The word *climacteric* is defined as, "A critical stage, period, or year",[263] but in Old French it was specifically defined as, "the years of a man's life which corresponded with multiples of seven or nine, when critical periods would be faced".[264] Still, the word can be also used to state, "*climatic*," which is relative to where climate changes occur.

Since the word *degré* follows the separated numbers, *quarante huict*, they can be expected to act as *quarante-huict*, as we saw Nostradamus demonstrate with his listing of years (*ans*) in the letter to Henri, relative to the biblical timeline he created. When one then looks for a major city located on the 48th *degree* of latitude, there are none that stand out, although Seattle, Washington is close (47 degrees, 36 minutes), but not close enough. This is different when the 48th *degree* of longitude is examined. Kuwait City, Kuwait is at 47 degrees, 58 minutes, and 42 seconds of east longitude, which means the 48th degree of longitude runs through the eastern half of Kuwait City. To the north, also at 47 degrees, 58 minutes, is Iraq's only deep-water port, Khawr Umm Qasr. Both of these cities are on the shores of the Persian Gulf.

This area of the earth has to be seen as a primary focus as the main theme. Still, a secondary meaning can come from the fact that the two numbers are not joined together as one word, or hyphenated. This comes when the secondary theme is read, which states, "*A fin de Cancer si grande seicheresse*". This translates to say, "*At end of Cancer so great drought*", and with the introduction of the astrological sign *Cancer*, the words *degré climacterique* bring out an astrological meaning, as reference to a *critical degree*.

A *critical degree* is based on the Moon's movement through the zodiac, such that the 360 degrees are divided by the Moon's cycle through all the signs, which is roughly 28 days. Thus, every 12.9 degrees (360/28) marks one day of the Moon's imaginary movement, and beginning at the cusp of Aries (the first sign), at 0 degrees, 13 degrees are marked off through all of the signs. This means Aries has three *critical degrees*, one at 0 *degree*, a second at 13 *degree*, and a third at 26 *degree*. When 13 degrees is added to the 26 *degrees*, and with only 30 *degrees* in a sign, the next critical *degree* comes at 9 *degree* Taurus, then at 21 *degree* Taurus. Adding 13 to 21, then subtracting 30 (34-30), yields the next to be 4 *degree* Gemini, with another 13 producing 17 *degree* Gemini. At this point, another 13 brings one back to 0 *degree*, and this cycle continues. The result is all Cardinal signs (Aries, Cancer, Libra, and Capricorn) have three *critical degrees*: 0, 13, and 26.

This means the secondary theme mentioning, "*At end of Cancer*", is focusing on the time when the Sun is reaching the *critical degree* of 26 *Cancer*. This usually occurs somewhere between the 18th and 19th of July. When one then goes back to the main theme line, and sees it as stating *eight degree critical* (meaning of *climacteric*), the eighth *critical degree* of a astrological year occurs when the Sun enters *Cancer*. This event usually occurs between the 21st and 22nd of June, which means the timing of the main theme line is such that it occurs about 26 days before the secondary theme. In this way, the main theme <u>is stating where</u> and when an event will occur, when the secondary theme is factored in, and the numbers

263   The Free Dictionary by Farlex, http://www.thefreedictionary.com/climacteric
264   MEDIADICO, http://www.mediadico.com/dictionnaire/definition/climaterique/1

have extra flexibility due to not being connected as one (thus limited) word.

In this example, one can see how numbered degrees can represent a period of time, when they are associated with the movement of the Sun. The Sun moves one degree per day, never appearing to go backwards, such that it acts as the timing mechanism for one calendar year. As such, a particular year becomes identified by the other planetary phenomena that accompany that period marked by the Sun.

This is how one has to approach the astrological quatrains that begin with Nostradamus writing, "*In the year that*", or "*The year that*", or (in one example) "*The year following*". In several of the quatrains, lines are begun with these words, followed at some point by the names of three celestial bodies being listed, which identifies the year. It is this list that acts as ordinal numbers (rather than cardinal numbers), where one orb is named first, followed by the second one named, and then the third. In other quatrains, the year is identified by only one planet, or two planets separated by an ampersand, where the planet is identified by some astrological essence that is unique.

For example, two quatrains found in *Century Fourth* include Mars and Venus in their list of three. The eighty-fourth quatrain states, in its fourth line, "*En l'an que Mars, Venus, & Sol mis en esté.*" This translates to say, "*In the year that Mars, Venus, & Sun set in summer.*" Since the *summer* ends every year when the *Sun* is in the sign of Virgo, the ampersand acts to emphasize that timing. Then, the planets *Mars* and *Venus* will enter into Virgo, ahead of the *Sun*, with *Mars* first, followed by *Venus*, so that when the *Sun* enters Virgo the three will soon form a conjunction. This is unique, not typical, such that *the year that* this occurs will determine the timing of the quatrain, with a possible year being 2017.

In the ninety-seventh quatrain of that group of one hundred, Nostradamus wrote the main theme in a similar fashion. There, he wrote, "*L'an que Mercure, Mars, Venus retrograde,*" which translates to, "*The year that Mercury, Mars, Venus retrograde*". This states that these three planets will all appear to go into retrograde motion, in that specific order. That specificity, combined with the fact that *Venus* is the planet that goes *retrograde* the least frequently, yields a very unique timing element. An excellent example of *The year that* this will next occur is *the year* 2018.

This type of identification of a specific year is also found in the fifty-fifth quatrain of *Century Ninth*; only with the secondary theme beginning with, "*The year following*", and the supporting line (line four) listing three planets. Those two related lines state, (2) "*L'an ensuiuant viendra la pestilence,*" and (4) "*Sang, feu, Mercure, Mars, Jupiter en France.*" This says, (2) "*The year following will come there pestilence,*" and (4) "*Blood, fire, Mercury, Mars, Jupiter in France.*" This means that *The year following* will be found identified by a series (first, second, third) of events symbolized by the placements of *Mercury, Mars* and *Jupiter* in the same sign, although not at the same time.[265]

---

265   Due to the fastest moving planet (*Mercury*) being listed first, and the slowest moving planet (*Jupiter*) being listed third, the three cannot be conjunct in that specific order, unless retrograde is part of the mix.

One good example of this series is the period when the three will spend time in the sign of Libra. *Mercury* will enter the sign of Libra on August 27, 2015, while both *Mars* and *Jupiter* will be in the sign Virgo. Due to *Mercury* going retrograde before it exits Libra, it will not leave the sign until November 2, 2015. Then, on November 12, 2015 *Mars* will enter the sign of Libra, while *Jupiter* is left behind in Virgo. *Mars* will remain in Libra until January 3, 2016. *Jupiter* will shortly after go retrograde in Virgo, causing it to wait until September 9, 2016 to enter Libra. The planet *Mercury* will at that time be in the sign Virgo, but retrograde, keeping it from returning to the sign Libra until October 7, 2016. This means in *The year following Mercury*, from October 7, 2015 until October 7, 2016, three planets would symbolize the balancing qualities of Libra, where words (*Mercury*) are followed by actions (*Mars*), with the actions leading to justice (*Jupiter*).

In the sense that the esoteric value of a planet will come to identify a specific year, Nostradamus wrote three quatrains that identify a year with the planet Saturn. This requires one to understand that Saturn was known in Nostradamus' time as the Great Malefic, from which comes the element of time (an element of Cronus, relative of Saturn) known as the Grim Reaper. As such, each of these three quatrains addresses the timing of Saturn transitions, from one sign to another.

The first of these is found as the eighty-seventh quatrain in *Century Fifth*. There, Nostradamus wrote as the main theme, "*L'an que Saturne sera hors de servage*," which says, "*The year that Saturn will be out of servitude*". While the sixth house is known as the area of life that symbolizes "work, service, and health", I do not see this as a reference to the natural sign of the sixth house, Virgo. This is a reference to the sign Pisces, where selflessness leads to a life of slavery to the needs of others. Therefore, this main theme is stating when *Saturn* will move *out of* Pisces, into Aries.[266] This last occurred on April 7, 1996, and will next occur on May 25, 2025.

The second example of a "*Saturn year*" is found in the eighty-sixth quatrain in *Century Fourth*. There, Nostradamus wrote as the main theme, "*L'an que Saturne en eau sera conjoinct*," which says, "*The year that Saturn in water will be joined*". This, of course, means the main theme is stating a specific *year* when *Saturn* will begin a two-plus year period in one of the three *water* signs: Cancer, Scorpio, or Pisces. The planet *Saturn* last entered a *water* sign when it went into Cancer on June 4, 2003, leaving it on July 16, 2005. It will next enter the sign of Scorpio on October 12, 2012; but the last example implied Pisces, which is also a *water* sign. *Saturn* will enter Pisces next on March 7, 2023.

The last of these examples involving a *year* of *Saturn* also involves a *year* of *Mars*, such that each planet is individualized around an ampersand. Only after those planets are seen separately do they form a conjunction, as *Saturn AND Mars*. This information is offered in the main theme line of the sixty-seventh quatrain found in *Century Fourth*. In that line, Nostradamus wrote, "*L'an que Saturne & Mars esgaulx combust*," which states, "*The year that Saturn & Mars equals combust*". While the novice might read

---

266 If the sign of Virgo is to be considered, *Saturn* will next move *out of* Virgo on October 29, 2009.

combust as meaning, "fiery", or "an outburst", thinking this means a fire sign, this is not the only meaning.

The reality is the word, *combust*, is a traditional astrology term, which places a planet in a closeness with the Sun, regardless of which sign the Sun is in. The use must primarily be seen as defining the symbolic expressions of *Saturn* and *Mars*, during *The year*, with that *year* targeted by the slower moving *Saturn*, and the timing of its placement in a fire sign.

A planet is said to be in *combust* when it is within a range that spreads 8.5 degrees on either side of the Sun's placement, but is not behind the Sun. A planet has to be at least 17 minutes away from the Sun, not to be behind it. Traditional astrologers believed that planets were weakened by the Sun's aura, with *Mars* thought to be the exception. Nicholas DeVore wrote in his definition of the term that, "in the case of *Mars* (its strength is) intensified", such that he followed with the statement, "*Mars combust* is always the man who fights for what he wants".[267] According to this logic, the strength of *Saturn* (patience, durability, and teaching) is debilitated, causing it to become symbolized through outward expressions like impatience and unjust punishment.

Saturn will next be in the same fire sign as the Sun, to be followed by *Mars*, such that a condition of *combust* exists between *Saturn AND Mars*, with *Saturn AND Mars* also conjunct, between March 20 and April 28, 2026. *Saturn* will have moved into the fire sign Aries on February 14, 2026, becoming *combust* when the Sun will enter Aries on March 20, with little more than 4 degrees separating the two. *Mars* will enter Aries on April 9, 2026, conjunct with *Saturn*, only a little more than six degrees away and they will remain in conjunction until April 28. *Mars* will have had a *combust* period during the last week of January, until the middle of February, while both the Sun and *Mars* will have been in Aquarius (an air sign) together. During that time when *Mars* will be *combust*, *Saturn* will enter the fire sign Aries. Thus, each will *equally* be *combust*, while later being *equally fiery* in Aries, conjoined as one.

As one can see, the order of the movements is important for finding times that meet those specific requirements. In essence, the planets represent numbers, which are related to their length of orbit around the Sun, and thus rate of motion. Still, because of the repeatability of planets in signs, and in relationship to one another, a number of possibilities exist. However, it is the combinations of words that follow the timing elements in the main themes, which make unrecognizable events the results of those *years* of *Saturn*. This leads one to conclude these are events still to come, which will be more understandable once that actual time draws near.

---

[267] *Encyclopedia of Astrology*, The Philosophical Library, June 1947, p.44.

Chapter 30

Summing Everything Up

There is truth in the saying, "A picture is worth a thousand words." Every day with eyesight becomes a stream of pictures processed by our minds. Many are ordinary, standard, routine, and typical, but many are extraordinary and worthy of turning into a picture for someone else to view. Sometimes the ordinary has a beauty that is overlooked, because our lives seem to move so fast. Paint and cameras are tools that capture pictures for times when we can slow down and see what it is we often miss, or forget.

Another adage says, "Every picture tells a story." Pictures stimulate our thoughts of remembrance, and memories are best shared aloud with someone who cares. When two people share the same memory, a picture can spark just one word, or something simple like, "Remember Paris?" Two people's minds are then flowing with memories, such that one picture can lead to many stories worth telling.

The art of storytelling is ancient, coming from times when the pace of the world was slower, and people had plenty of time to listen. The art of writing stems from storytelling, as a way to preserve the stories and tales long told. Writing took time to complete, much longer that it would take to tell a story, as the writer often saw need to describe the settings, tones, and moods of the storyteller, which were as much a part of the story as the words, only seen and not spoken. Likewise, reading takes more time than simply listening to a story being told, because reading allows one time to pause and reflect on what has been read. This means both writing and reading are best done when one is not rushed.

Storytellers and writers learn their crafts well. It is important to choose the right words, such that one word is understood to mean several defining words unsaid. Some words have purposeful double meanings, which can become humorous puns, or serious depth to consider. The right words create vivid images in the listener-reader's mind. They paint a picture in words, which means they are laid out just as an artist plans a painting. Broad strokes and underlying color bases are placed on the canvass first, just as a writer introduces broad themes and general concepts before adding the details. The only problem with the comparison of painting with writing comes when the picture must be seen clearly. Often, a thousand words are not enough to make everything in one painting be clearly reproduced.

In my efforts to describe how one can get meaning from the words of Nostradamus, I have compared it to seeing the true purpose of a Magic Eye stereogram. In those pictures, everything at first appears to be without purpose. One could go into great length telling every detail of the picture, but all of that would be surface information, with the true purpose hidden underneath. The negative image underlying every Magic Eye stereogram can be picked up by the mind, making the picture become three-dimensional, with amazing purpose; but the eyes have to view the picture differently than the way one normally looks at pictures.

Imagine all the words that could be written about one Magic Eye picture, when one first described all the surface clutter, and then described how it all changed and became something quite remarkable. The only problems are two. First, the natural reaction is to start looking at the 3-D picture the way one normally uses the eyes. The mind thinks it can see more detail if it focuses. Unfortunately, that makes the amazing part disappear. Focusing leaves one with the meaningless surface picture again. One has to spend time letting the eyes lose focus once more, if one wants to see the true purpose return. Second, because it is difficult to put into words what is seen through unfocused eyes, and because the true purpose is designed for everyone to see it personally, a Magic Eye is best not explained in depth. It needs to be given to someone to be seen, with just a little instruction to help someone do just that. Afterwards, two people can share what they each saw, with less words said, if words are necessary.

The quatrains are all like individual Magic Eye pictures, waiting for someone to read them the right way. This means to not read them the way one normally reads. This book is all about how to read abnormally, so my words act as the instructions for reading Nostradamus correctly. By now, it is clear that I have spent well over one thousand words describing the "picture" that is *The Prophecies*. I have tried my best to make a list of elements that must be understood, in order to learn a new syntax; but there are no guarantees that I have not missed something "in the corner", out of my direct line of re-focused sight.

The meaning of the quatrains and letters of *The Prophecies* is something best determined by the reader, after one has digested the instructions that allow that meaning to be seen in the first place. I have opinions about what I see coming from the meaning of the words, and their order of placement, along with the direction signs written, but I cannot see all aspects of every piece and put it all to words. If I tried that (and I have before), my words would become confusing, even more than the basic instructions may seem. The more I try to expand on the meaning that just a few of the words written by Nostradamus can have, when connected together, is becomes more than a casual reader can bear. We are no longer in simple times, when patience allowed for a longwinded story.

Just as how something may be absolutely clear to me, but completely confusing to you, if you are able to see for yourself the right way, you can see things astounding, things which I never thought to see. The source of the meaning is certainly not Robert Tippett. It is not Nostradamus either. The source is God, and God can put so much meaning in only a few words that human beings will always be blind to much of God's meaning, without help and instructions to see. This means it is good for everyone to work together towards discerning all of the possibilities, realizing all meanings that must be discerned, so nothing is overlooked. You may be the one God enlightens on one key element written, which others cannot see. The purpose of *The Prophecies* is for everyone to see the meaning personally, rather than just wait to be told what someone else sees.

For me to be able to understand Nostradamus, and to be able to see the systems that become the new syntax for a new language, such that I can write this book, it must be understood that my words are not led by my own powers of intellectual acumen. I had no abilities to understand Nostradamus, to any degree more than what some book or television program told me to understand. My sudden abilities to begin to comprehend, and to continue to have my eyes opened to more and more, have been completely due to divine inspiration. What I know I have been allowed to know, and because I have been allowed to know for the purpose of letting others also know, I write books such as this book.

By understanding that I am not the sole author of my words, just as Nostradamus was not the sole author of his words, it next becomes important to realize you will not be able to understand my words, nor the words of Nostradamus, if you try to use your sole powers of intellect. Nostradamus has been misunderstood for over 450 years, with intelligent men and women trying to unravel his mysteries. The reason is God planned it that way, and as Jesus said, "It is not for you to know the times or dates the Father has set by his own authority."[268] Now is the time for understanding to be possible; but that understanding requires one be assisted by God. You will not be able to do anything more than glimpse pieces of my meaning, tiny fragments that will do more to confuse than to bring clarity, if you do not truly believe *The Prophecies* is a divine prophecy.

Because Nostradamus wrote words that tell of the influence of Jesus Christ being the direct source to him, as the Savior sent by God, understanding also requires belief in Christ. As such, prayer is a requirement that opens one up to receiving deeper awareness of the meanings of the letters and quatrains. It is not enough to want to know the meaning. One must open one's heart to the realization of a prophecy sent to humanity by God, through His Son, for the purpose of saving souls.

Over the last month, which has been months since I completed the first draft of this book, and while the final editing steps were taking place, I have come to understand yet another aspect of how one comes to understand *The Prophecies*. It is clear that Nostradamus wrote of his encounter with "the divine." His use of Biblical quotes attributed to Jesus, along with direct mentions of alternate names, like "Savior" and "Redeemer", lead one to draw a clear logical connection to Jesus Christ as the source. This is paired with his explaining how astrology can only be accurate into the future for short periods, and only if led by the whispers of "good angels," says that *The Prophecies* is a work guided by celestial influence. However, until recently I had never directly tied this assistance as being filled with the Holy Spirit, although I could envision the spirit of Christ "possessing" the body of Nostradamus.

---

268   Acts 1:7, New International Version.

SUMMARY

When one understands how the disciples were filled with the Holy Spirit on the day of Pentecost, one can begin to see how Nostradamus was likewise filled with an ability that was beyond his human limitations. The Holy Spirit gives one powers that are otherwise impossible to ordinary mortals. There was absolutely no conscious planning on the part of Nostradamus to write *The Prophecies*, because no talent known to man (astrology, psychology, flimflam magik, etc.) could produce the results that can be seen. The reason *The Prophecies* is not understood now (by everyone but myself, so far), and the reason it has not been understood since its creation, is that it is not in normal language. What I have taken this long to write, calling it the "Systems of Nostradamus", is really an explanation in how to understand what Nostradamus wrote, while he was filled with the Holy Spirit, such that he spoke in tongues (through writing).

On the day of Pentecost that chapter two of *The Acts of the Apostles* tells, the disciples began to speak in foreign languages (listed in verses 9, 10, and 11), which shocked those who fluently spoke those languages. They were shocked because they recognized it was Galileans speaking languages, meaning local Jews had no reason to know how to speak the languages of foreign lands. Those shocking abilities got the attention of the pilgrims to Jerusalem, so they stopped to inquire about this talent, and listen to their explanations.

We find that while a fluency in foreign tongues was a power the disciples possessed, which was clearly beyond their natural abilities, speaking fluently in known foreign languages is not the full scope of "speaking in tongues." Peter is given credit for being filled with the ability to speak in tongues, such that three thousand Jews had their hearts opened and their minds awakened to understanding the "other language" of David (Psalm 16:8-11). All who were listening knew those verses recited by Peter, but none had ever realized the words of David's song were prophecy, telling of the coming of Jesus Christ. All dedicated Jews had known the words; but they had been misunderstood for many centuries, because they were written through divine inspiration. David wrote his song as a prophecy, from an ecstatic state, filled with an ability to write in the "other language" of the Lord. The impact of Peter's explanation of that prophecy was so powerful that three thousand Jews became believers in Jesus as the Christ, on that day of Pentecost.

To understand divine prophecy requires as much assistance from the divine, as does uttering prophecy. As such, Peter and the other disciples were able to explain how Jesus was indeed the messiah, through the words of the prophets of Israel. This means that when David, or Isaiah, or Daniel, or Joel, or any of the prophets of Israel and Judah spoke words (known through the written record), none of them was able to explain that the imagery their words created were about a specific man to come, named Jesus. The prophesied about the coming of God's promised one, who would come many years later.

The prophecies of all the prophets were locked inside understandable words (common language), which immediately made some sense, but would not be fully understood until history had proven prophecy (uncommon language) to be the true purpose of the words. Only the divine could know the eventual meaning of the words written, such that only the divine could explain their meaning after the prophecies had come true. This is how the spirit of Jesus Christ walked in unrecognizable form with two close followers (Cleopas was one) on the road to Emmaus, explaining one prophetic meaning after another, all coming from the known verses of Moses, the prophets, and all of the Scriptures. The divine leads one to understanding the true meaning, when one does as the resurrected Jesus suggested to his disciples, to "receive the spirit" of understanding.

This is the meaning of the disciples being able to "speak in other languages" on the day of Pentecost, after what seemed to be "tongues of fire" separating from one source, landing within each of them, enabling each to speak with the authority of the Advocate Jesus promised to send them. That one source was God, from which the Holy Spirit emanates. God speaks through human beings via the Holy Spirit, in "other languages." The word of God can be understood as a language common to all, as that is one aspect of prophetic words. Through this common language, misunderstanding can occur; as much of the text seems repetitive and important only on a historical level, implying the text is more the word of authors, and not of God. However, for the deeper meaning to be seen, God's approval is required.

Often, Christians have come to the realization that the Holy Bible is a living document, meaning it comes alive with meaning applicable to current events. Passages that had little personal meaning at times before can suddenly spring to newfound meaning. Once times have changed and the reader is in need of seeing new meaning come from what had been ordinarily received before, the words of the Holy Bible come to assist the faithful through new insight.

This new awareness comes through the assistance of God. That which had little or no meaning becomes clear in a new context, as a hidden prophecy, sent by God many millennia before, designed to be understood later. This is how God's word is not to be read in one limited language, but in other languages that allow multiple meanings to be possible. This multiplicity requires one to receive the spirit of faith, so answers can come from being filled with the Holy Spirit, which allows one to speak in tongues.

Reading the words of Nostradamus has the same effect, when one has faith that *The Prophecies* is indeed from a divine source. The "Book of Nostradamus" could be added to the list of holy documents that have been canonized, if the verses could be reordered properly, so it told a story in poetic style. It would be much like the Book of Isaiah in that sense of verse style, but its random presentation leaves each quatrain to stand as an individual prophecy, out of context. One needs to be in touch with God to find this context.

The letters of Nostradamus provide the framework through which *The Prophecies* must be ordered, such that everything fits snugly together. In that sense, the whole of Nostradamus' work is like a Rubik's Cube, which is originally produced in the proper order, but it becomes a brainteaser when placed in a random order of colors. The challenge is to return it to the proper order, so the proper meaning can be seen. The letter to Henry II is scrambled like the quatrains, and everything requires solving the "other language" in which the words are written, to be able to solve the overall puzzle. Once one knows there is a purpose, and a method through which that purpose can become clearly visible, the whole becomes a test of one's dedication to solve the riddles of Jesus Christ, as written by his servant Nostradamus.

The message of *The Prophecies* is clearly one of predicted doom. The same message is found in *The Revelation of John*. The source is the same, the spirit of Jesus Christ. The message of Christ, through John, is known to be a prediction of doom, but the metaphor and allegory is so thick it cannot be seen clearly how war, disease, famine, and death (the Four Horsemen) will play out, through beasts, scorpions, and dragons. As a canonized book of the Holy Bible, there are many who believe *The Revelation of John* is a true prophecy of the divine, such that many have tried to attach meaning to the metaphor, through each subsequent generation since the book was first publicized. That same level of belief, as being from divine inspiration, is not attached to *The Prophecies* of Nostradamus.

The message of Nostradamus, while never properly understood, it has been kept alive by those who attach belief in human abilities to foresee the future. This has led to the popularization of a minimal amount of what Nostradamus wrote, as the wild imaginations that make words seem to fit various scenarios, when taken entirely out of context. The vast majority of the words of Nostradamus have remained senseless babble, such that those are largely ignored. The focus having been put on only a few verses has maintained interest in Nostradamus for over 450 years. That is an uncommon achievement, one that in itself is a sign of divine intervention. A hidden holy message has not been lost to time, so that it has continued to be within our reach.

The Apostle Paul wrote in his first letter to the people of Corinth that words spoken in tongues attract only the non-believers. Nostradamus has attracted such non-believers. This attraction is because "other tongues" can be interpreted to mean anything that one wants to see in their apparent vagueness. The result of such interpretation is doubt; and doubt lessens one's faith in an announced "prophecy", making one see it as nothing more than chance accuracy. The word "prophecy" becomes defined as nothing more than "a calculated prediction." Prediction does not bring faith, as much as it brings onlookers who want to see if a prediction will come true. Predictions that come true mean that anyone can foresee the future through probability, if one learns the tricks of prediction. Faith is not in God, but in mathematics and science, and the people who master those arts. Thus, Paul was prophesying that Nostradamus' tongues of mystery would only attract the believers of Man.

On the contrary, words spoken as accepted true prophecy attract believers, meaning those who believe in God and Christ. Prophecy is elevated above mere prediction, as visions of the future are impossible to be known by mortals, through any of the arts of Man. Prophecy is only explained through faith, such that only believers of God are attracted to prophecy, even though prophecy appears first as "other tongues." Simply because Nostradamus named his work, *The Prophecies*, does not prove it to be a divine prophecy, because it is cloaked in "tongues." It must be shown as a true prophecy so that believers can be attracted to a divine message.

Paul also wrote that he would rather state five words of intelligible instruction, than to recite ten thousand words of tongues. The meaning is that once one has been allowed to see the marvel of true prophecy, from the words of other tongues, or the other languages of the divine, it is more important to tell others how they can see for themselves how to "speak in other tongues." Without understandable instructions, by which others can be guided to their own personal awareness, few will see the truth that has been intended for many.

The New Testament parable of the talents (found in Matthew 25:14-30), and the similar parable of the minas (Luke 19:12-28), are guides for how the ones receiving special gifts from God and Christ, through the Holy Spirit, should act. While the master is away, it is up to the servants to grow the wealth bestowed upon them, something given to them without their expressing a desire for such gifts. The servants given the most wealth were the ones who reported to their returning master they had increased that value two-fold. Thus, one servant given ten minas had grown it by another ten. The servant given five talents had likewise doubled it by adding another five. These servants were then praised by the master and given his blessings, through increased responsibility. This means the good servants acted upon their gifts, and in turn gave the gifts to others, who also gave the gift to others. Christ, the master, is away; but in his absence he has left us the talent of understanding prophecy, which we cannot keep to ourselves. We must instruct others to understand, so when the master returns the good servants can report that the talents of the Holy Spirit have not been wasted.

I have been given the talent of understanding the prophecy of *The Prophecies*, and I cannot keep this understanding to myself. This book is an effort to instruct others, so others can read Nostradamus as a prophecy, and not as a trick of prediction. I have written other books that have attempted to explain the "other tongues" of Nostradamus in ordinary language, but this exercise seems to be what Paul meant by reciting ten thousand words of tongues. I am explaining what I see in my mind's eye, which is difficult for someone else to comprehend. It is better to explain in as few intelligible words as necessary, so someone else can make sense of those instructive words and see in their own mind's eye what I have seen.

Much of what Nostradamus has written in the quatrains paints a clear picture of horrible things that are to happen in the world. Much of what John wrote does the same; and much of the Old Testament tells of a vindictive God that used the same destructive elements that will be seen in the future (war, disease, famine, flood, etc.). Such "fire and brimstone" forecasts have caused some to question how an all-loving God can be so harsh and cold. Still, others of unquestioning faith prefer to ignore these questions that point out the seeming contradictions of the Holy Bible.

This is how the tongues of prophecy, found in every book of the Holy Bible, can seem to mean something other than the truth. It seems contradictory at times, while at other times it tells of events and people who can never be confirmed through archeological evidence. True belief in God requires unquestioned faith, but God does not want someone believing to be defenseless against those who question. Questioning and finding truth are how one truly becomes a believer in God; and finding truth always leads to more questions, as a true believer thirsts to learn the truth. This is why Jesus said, "Ask and you shall receive."

The truth comes not from one's intellect and abilities to solve problems. The truth comes when one is filled with the Holy Spirit's assistance towards understanding the answer to a question that is important in the development of one's faith. In the area of questioning that focuses on a cold and hard God, one needs to grasp the grand scope. This can only come from knowing the whole story. Such a perspective makes context valuable when discerning the truth. From a broader central theme, one can see the value of stories in the books of the Old Testament, of John, and of Nostradamus, such that all the pain and agony found in the words of God, through the authors and prophets, can only come from an all-loving God. To see the whole theme of the Holy Bible, just like being able to see the reordered story of *The Prophecies*, and know its central theme, requires being led to understanding by the Holy Spirit.

The truth comes to one in stages, or levels of understanding, just as one has to go through grades of schooling over years of life, before one is prepared to step into a world of knowledge. One cannot expect a seven-year-old child to understand college-level calculus immediately, simply because the child expressed a sincere desire to know the truth of that mathematic process. The truth is there for the child, but the child must process all of the basic components of mathematics first, before one is capable of understanding how those components lead one to understanding an advanced use of them. The child is able to advance in understanding as quickly as the child can learn to absorb each step internally, as a natural way of thought, hindered only in the child's access to advanced teaching so that all questions can be answered swiftly and correctly. Still, even the most adept mathematics students require a natural order of progressed learning before the whole truth can be known.

Public education is required by law (to a minimal degree of acquired knowledge), but religious education is voluntary. While religious education begins at a young age, with many parents entering their children in Sunday School, where they are taught "Bible Stories" and specific religious dogmas, adult Bible Studies is less stressed. Even those adults who wish to learn more about the "truth" that is found in the Holy Bible often find a deeper study of biblical books becomes the blind leading the blind, in group settings. This is because the Holy Bible is written in the other languages of God, and can only be taught by people who have been filled with understanding by the Holy Spirit. Likewise, it can only be understood by one being directly filled by the Holy Spirit.

Sadly, there are relatively few people who have truly filled by the Holy Spirit to understand the Holy Bible, well enough to teach its deepest meaning to others. There are many more among us who have used some form of brain-led intelligence, through college-level education, to come up with educated guesses and theories about biblical meaning. Much of this is becoming mainstream thought among

Christians seeking to understand the Holy Bible, but feel they are unable to discern the deeper meaning by themselves. The result is a world full of sheep that are easily misled by bad shepherds.

The "Systems of Nostradamus" acts as the "Tongues of Christ." In that sense, God speaks on a multi-dimensional level, such that no one earthly language can catch all of the intended meaning. Holy words are chosen for a specific purpose, rather than haphazardly chosen, or incorrectly applied. This purpose is to allow them to expand to meet more than one defining meaning, as long as context is maintained. Order is important, which makes the original language paramount. Translations often mutate this order, changing the meaning to fit a limited preconception. The application of punctuation (a modern addition to the written word) is intended to act as direction. Nothing is by chance, such as capitalization and number use, and symbolism being prevalent makes interpretation cover much more than the literal implies. The use of astrology, and astronomical placements, is explained in Nostradamus' preface as a tool invented by God, to guide men's lives. That particularly, as well as all mentioned, requires the source (the divine – Christ and God) to lead the reader to the truth in meaning.

I have found that practice in reading Nostradamus makes me more capable to find deeper meaning in biblical verses. On a brain level of conscious thought, I can look at punctuation as a guide to how to think next. I can see capitalization and the use of Latin as an indication that a higher meaning is behind those words. I can see how the order of planets leads me to look for that order in an ephemeris, which lists planetary positions. Likewise, I can see how a verse in a book of the Holy Bible uses punctuation, which if read like the use in *The Prophecies*, reveals a new insight to meaning that is completely overlooked by those reading the Bible ordinarily. I see the use of capitalized names in the books of the Old Testament (in particular) as an indication of higher meaning, which directs one to see the meaning behind the name. Deeper meaning comes from knowing that root information, which is not commonly seen, or sought to be known. I see how the uses of numbers in the books of the Holy Bible have esoteric meaning, relative to the study of numerology, an art practiced by the kabalistic priests of the Jewish Temple. The casual reader of the Bible does not commonly understand this meaning, but it is commonly accepted by Biblical scholars that this use of number is important for understanding.

Just as Nostradamus' work is a puzzle, with depth found through connecting the separate prophecies into a whole prophecy, I have also found that the four Gospels act likewise. They each are pieces of a greater puzzle, where each adds something the others do not. When one is overlaid with the others, they can be read as one, such that the four produce a detailed chronology that increases the understanding that each book holds separately. I have also found that the whole of the library of books that have been canonized tell one grand theme, which is of God's preparation for one religion that will act on God's behalf, to save the world from sin. All the preparation is leading to the introduction of Jesus as the Christ, who returns in spirit form (to John, his beloved disciple) to prophesy what problems the creation of sub-religions will bring.

That prophecy reflects all the woes that have happened in the world before, over ages of time, to repeat as one cataclysmic End Times. One can only be saved by rediscovering the true religion of God, who told of it by speaking through the prophets (all the writers of the books of the Holy Bible, Old and New Testament, as the other tongues of God), by modeling the ways of Jesus. The whole of the Holy Bible is instructing one to be saved by receiving the Holy Spirit; and that can only come through the sacrifice of the ego, allowing oneself to be led by the influence of Christ.

In this sense, all of the pain and suffering of life on earth is miniscule, when compared to eternity. All of the deaths of the past have been little more than like a coach calling a time out, and calling a player over to the sidelines to receive personal instruction on how to play the game right, before being put back in the game. In other words, the Holy Bible is telling of reincarnation of souls. In this way, God is showing His love for all who died, as those deaths were mere moments of time, flashes of inconvenience, because life on earth for mortals is a long series of tests, all designed to return the soul permanently to Heaven.

The problem comes when there is no longer an earth suitable for habitation by human beings, but souls remain who have forever disregarded the lessons of the Father. Rebirth beyond this End Time means an eternity of suffering, with no chance of death becoming a reward for another opportunity with a physical life. The Hell so many have speculated about is indeed on Earth; but Hell only exists in the future. The ultimate purpose of prophecy is to believe in God and act according to that belief, with faith. God has demonstrated an unending love by repeatedly giving humanity His gift, all teaching how to avoid this end.

Learning the Systems of Nostradamus can help one make that conscious realization that this is the last chance. We are living in the final age, because of degeneration through time that makes us less likely to act with belief now. The events of September 11, 2001 marked the beginning of the final countdown to all of the evils that Christ foretold through John and Nostradamus. The verbiage of Nostradamus is more recent, historically, such that what Nostradamus saw was described in 16th century terms, verses John's vision from a 1st century perspective. John had less technology to compare to those future happenings. This makes *The Prophecies* easier for modern human beings to interpret, when one is assisted by the whispers of "good angels."

This book is a guide for how to understand the words of *The Prophecies* of Nostradamus. It is my "five intelligible words to instruct" others in how to make sense of "ten thousand words in a tongue." The actual words of Nostradamus are mostly missing, although I have given some of those words as examples. I have sorted the quatrains into "buckets" of events, which are placed into an order of events that tells an epic story, in poetic style. I will make those quatrains available in an order that makes the story stand out, while also being consistent with the story order of a reconstructed letter to Henry II. I will make the letter to Henry II available as a separate book, demonstrating how to dissect it into pieces and paste it back into an intelligible order. I will also make the letter Nostradamus wrote as the preface to

The Prophecies available as a separate book, so one can see for oneself the instructions to use, to discern what the quatrains tell, and what their theme of story is. All of this will be intelligible words to instruct, but it will all seem like words in foreign tongues, without God's assistance.

Without the spirit of Christ sending the Advocate, the Holy Spirit he promised to send to those who ask for help with understanding, this book, and all others promised, will be only an exercise in futility to those who seek knowledge as power over others. For centuries, since the Roman Catholic Church put a ban on Nostradamus' writings, the rise of educational institutions has forsaken any opportunity to approach *The Prophecies* from a scholastic perspective. God did not want Nostradamus' work to be stigmatized by the doubts that modern universities have placed on the words of the Old and New Testaments. As such, nothing of Nostradamus has been discounted through logical argument. It has only been pushed aside as nonsense, without any deep study by unbiased observers.

One has to readjust one's way of seeing education, to see the dangers of acquired knowledge. The story of Adam and Eve is a story of becoming educated, as they had become fed by the fruit of the tree of knowledge, being able to distinguish between good and evil. No evil existed in the world of Adam and Eve, before they were made aware of it. They were immortals in Heaven before knowledge weighed them down to the earthly plane, making them mortal (although they still had longer than mere mortal lifespans). The point of this biblical story is that one is pure when God leads one; but one is far from Heaven when one thinks one is smart enough to run one's own life. Awareness, as administered by education, is the blindness that causes man to think the material plane is the reality, and all that is worth living to achieve. The true reality is Heaven, but that reality can only be achieved through a state of purity, where one is always honoring God, and not stroking one's ego as being able to think for ones self.

The point of this book, and all prior and subsequent books I write about understanding Nostradamus, is to instruct others to look in a certain direction when repeated characteristics are evident. I cannot instruct one in what one will see with one's own eyes. My instructions will merely suggest a possibility, but that suggestion should lead to an inner thought, or a whisper inside one's head, in one's own voice, making another suggestion as to where to look further, or how to grasp something, or what to do next. One has to accept that these whispers are coming from the Holy Spirit, sent by Christ. The spirit of Jesus Christ is not going to come and sit in a chair beside one, and tell one in plain terms what everything means. One has to prove one's merit by listening to the insights given, and acting on those insights, looking something up, or putting things together in new ways not ordinarily seen. One has to let go of one's ego, thinking one is in control of one's destiny, and give in to the influences of the good angels.

The reason this cannot be taught in educational institutions is the teacher is not a man or woman at the head of a classroom. The teacher is within; and one has to request this teacher to come forth and lead one to understanding. Such requests must be made with earnestness and sincerity. Such requests are made through prayer, at which point one confesses one's sins to God and Christ, asking emotionally for forgiveness. One must visualize the errors of one's ways, and see one's own faults on a personal level. One must be willing to understand that the meaning of *The Prophecies*, and the reason a dire future is before us is because of one's own actions, or inactions. One must see how one must accept responsibility for a dismal present and future, and beg God and Christ for understanding, so one can act as the whispers lead one to act.

Without that request being made, this book will be unworthy of its price. Little will make sense, and the examples given will seem to be wild stretches of imagination. The future Christ showed to Nostradamus is all about a world filled with non-believers, even though the non-believers will claim to be believers. The future known as Armageddon will be fought between core groups who call themselves believers; but their beliefs will have God secondary to leaders who claim to be in touch with God. Religions will be given such a bad name that, due to their being associated only to the results of their actions, they will formally cease to exist. The Western world is already leaning in this direction, as what once used to be a bastion of Christianity has become eroded from within by people who cling to doctrines that religions only bring pain to the world. Those of this persuasion will have little attraction to a book that claims to instruct one in how to understand holy prophecy.

This conclusion has been rewritten, months after I ended the body of work that fills this book. In that time, I have come to see my work in a new light, as I have explained here. During the time that has elapsed since the majority of work was completed, until these moments that I type now, a couple from church bought a copy of my book *The Letters of Nostradamus: Realizing a Prophecy of Jesus Christ*. After they had held the book for a couple of weeks, I saw the couple at church, and I asked if they had begun to read the book. The woman's reply was, "I started to read it, and then skipped to the conclusion. From reading that I decided the body was too frightening to read, so I will not read your book."

I see that conversation as a sign, now as I look at it in hindsight. This conclusion is thus designed to meet such reader's needs. The impatience of those who want to skip all the hard work, and go right to the summation, is a sign of the times in which we live. The fears of a message of doom are related to that impatience. The summation of this book now says that one does not need to read this book. Nothing can be gained from these words without one having the dedication required to believe in God, and have faith *The Prophecies* is indeed a prophecy.

In the end, all anyone needs is to be filled with the Holy Spirit, which comes quick, like a rush of wind, but only comes after one has been prepared to receive the spirit. Once filled with that Advocate, one can be led to live life on earth like Jesus did, even though that life will lead one to be persecuted by all those who will become envious of one's dedication to those principles. The story of *The Prophecies* will be understood through living in a world without faith, without any need to read those words.

This book, more than likely, will have had little effect on the number of souls who became aware of a holy warning to "get right with God and Christ" and saved themselves. There is nothing more I can do, as far as reaching an unseen audience is concerned. I will have more affect directly confronting people willing to listen. However, if this book has any positive affect towards one lost soul, to have that person feel the need to act on his or her faith, to be fearless in cutting ties to a cancerous world and taking a leap of faith that God will bless one's actions, then my work has not been for naught.

Appendix

Astrological Key Words

Planets

Sun	Ego, Expression, Basic Nature
Moon	Emotions, Intuitions, Nurturing
Mercury	Thought, Basic Mind, Movement
Venus	Love, Beauty, Aesthetics
Mars	Action, Sports, Blood
Jupiter	Growth, Expansion, Benefit
Saturn	Patience, Restriction, Testing
Uranus	Individuality, Sudden Change, Revolution
Neptune	Fluidity, Nebulosity, Spirituality

Signs

Aries	Self, Initiator, Bold
Taurus	Comfort, Security, Lazy
Gemini	Communicator, Mobile, Gossip
Cancer	Mothering, Caring, Worrier
Leo	Center of attention, Loyal, Vain
Virgo	Planning, Ordering, Critical
Libra	Compromise, Artistic, Indecisive
Scorpio	Sensual, Deep, Vindictive
Sagittarius	Athletic, Free Spirited, Uncommitted
Capricorn	Dedicated, Responsible, Cold
Aquarius	Friendly, Knowledgeable, Detached
Pisces	Psychic, Feeling, Sacrificial

Houses

First	Physical Body, Appearance, and Attractiveness
Second	Personal Values, Talents, and Money
Third	Early Education, Relatives, and Neighborhood
Fourth	Home, Ancestry, and Parents
Fifth	Pleasure, Creativity, and Children
Sixth	Work, Service, and Health
Seventh	Relationships, Partnerships, and Marriage
Eighth	Sex, Inheritance, and Death
Ninth	Higher Education, Travels, and Religion
Tenth	Career, Reputation, and Authority
Eleventh	Friends, Associations, and Goals
Twelfth	Subconscious Mind, Dreams, and Secrets

Aspects

Conjunction	0 Degrees	Blending, Melding, Tempering
Sextile	60 Degrees	Opportunity, Time to Act
Square	90 Degrees	Challenging, Forced to Act
Trine	120 Degrees	Ease, Dependency, Natural Acts
Quincunx	150 Degrees	Discomfort, Unprepared to Act
Opposition	180 Degrees	Confronting, Responding to Acts

Elements

Fire	Aspiring
Earth	Molding
Air	Intellectual
Water	Fulfilling

Qualities

Cardinal	Energizing
Fixed	Immovable
Mutable	Changing

Hemispheres

Eastern	Private
Western	Public
Northern	Personal
Southern	Popular

Nodes

North Node	Karmic Life Direction
South Node	Karmic Past Life

Retrograde

Respective
Reflective
Internalizing

Concluding Scripture

To these He also presented Himself alive after His suffering, by many convincing proofs, appearing to them over a period of forty days and speaking of the things concerning the kingdom of God. Gathering them together, He commanded them not to leave Jerusalem, but to wait for what the Father had promised, "Which," He said, "you heard of from Me; for John baptized with water, but you will be baptized with the Holy Spirit not many days from now." So when they had come together, they were asking Him, saying, "Lord, is it at this time You are restoring the kingdom to Israel?" He said to them, "It is not for you to know times or epochs which the Father has fixed by His own authority; but you will receive power when the Holy Spirit has come upon you; and you shall be My witnesses both in Jerusalem, and in all Judea and Samaria, and even to the remotest part of the earth." And after He had said these things, He was lifted up while they were looking on, and a cloud received Him out of their sight. And as they were gazing intently into the sky while He was going, behold, two men in white clothing stood beside them. They also said, "Men of Galilee, why do you stand looking into the sky? This Jesus, who has been taken up from you into heaven, will come in just the same way as you have watched Him go into heaven." When the day of Pentecost had come, they were all together in one place. And suddenly there came from heaven a noise like a violent rushing wind, and it filled the whole house where they were sitting. And there appeared to them tongues as of fire distributing themselves, and they rested on each one of them. And they were all filled with the Holy Spirit and began to speak with other tongues, as the Spirit was giving them utterance.

Acts 1:3-11; 2:1-4
New American Standard Bible Version

www.ingramcontent.com/pod-product-compliance
Lightning Source LLC
Chambersburg PA
CBHW051206290426
44109CB00021B/2365